Steve Benner,
David Bruni,
et al

TRICKS OF THE

DOOM

PROGRAMMING GURUS

™

201 West 103rd Street
Indianapolis, Indiana 46290

SAMS
PUBLISHING

TRADEMARKS

OVERVIEW

CONTENTS

EPISODE 4: THE TOOLS OF THE GODS

FOREWORD

Sams Publishing has worked to deliver a quality product—this book—with the help of a large number of people. Care was taken to insure that all people affected by this book were notified. Sams talked with the developers of each piece of software discussed within the book. Sams also put a large amount of time into contacting each person whose software is included on the accompanying CD-ROM. Each editor, utility, WAD file, or other file was included with permission of its developer.

id Software has been gracious in allowing people to manipulate their WAD files. Their request is that people who do this do so with registered versions of their software. If you use this book, you should do so with a registered copy of the DOOM, DOOM II, or Heretic. id Software has allowed the world within their games to be modified, with the request that the modifier use a legal, registered version.

The editors discussed in this book were designed to only work with registered versions of the software. All of the discussed software products work with DOOM. Most of them also work with DOOM II. A few, such as DeeP, work with Heretic. (DeeP's sister editor for Heretic is called HeeP.)

ACKNOWLEDGMENTS

Sams Publishing would like to acknowledge the DOOM gurus who helped to make this book possible. They are: David Bruni, Steve Benner, Steve McCrea, Justin Fisher, Raphaël Quinet, Jeff Rabenhorst, Geoff Allen, Matthew Ayers, Matt Tagliaferri, Ben Morris, Greg Lewis, Jens Hykkelbjerg, Frank Palazzolo, Bill Neisius, Mike LaFavers, Olivier Montanuy, Grant Willison, Nick Sabinske, Chris Badger, and Piotr Kapiszewski. Without their time, assistance, guidance, wisdom, and patience this book would not have been feasible. Only those truly devoted to their craft can and will take the time to create software as you'll find described in this book.

Finally, Sams Publishing would like to thank all the people who contributed editors, utilities, and levels for the CD-ROM. They are: Vincenzo Alcamo, John W. Anderson, James Atchison, Piet Barber, Nicholas Barnard, Dusty Bedford, Nicholas Bell, Cimarron Benjamin, David Biggs, Mark Billingham, Robert Bingham, Mal Blackwell, Vance Andrew Blevins, Daniel Bondurant, Doug Branch, Lawrence Britt, Gerry Browne, Antony Burden, Peter Captijn, Matthew S. Carauddo, Scott Coleman, Scott F. Crank, Garth Cumming, Colin John Dickens, Scott Dougherty, Jason Dyer, Doug Dziedzic, Edgar Easterly IV, Andrew Elliott, Andrea Farnocchia, Barry Ferg, Glenn Fisher, Kenneth S. Forte, Tom Frial, Jean-Serge Gagnon, Corrado Giustozzi, Mark K. Gresbach, Jr., Daniel Griffiths, Magne Roar Groenhuis, Stefan Gustavson, Charles R. Halderman, Terry Hamel, Ryan Hare, Timothy Harris, Mark Harrison, Noah Haskell, Bjorn Hermans, David J. Hill, Jan Hladik, Pavel Hodek, Shawn Holmstead, Lawrence Hosken, Drew Hurlstone, Danny Hyde, Jim Imes, John Jablonski, Jawed Karim, Gerhard Karnik, Robin Charles Kay, Matthew E. Keller, Christen David Klie, Jeffrey Kung, Ricardo Lafaurie, Jr., Sam Lantinga, Nelson Laviolette, Joe Lawrence, Joe Liccel, Phil Longueuil, Andre Lucas, John C. Lyons, Stefan Maes, Jon Mandigo, Michael Marsh, Dr. Leo Marvin, Brian Martin, Bill McClendon, David McGruther, Jason Michelsen, Olivier Montanuy, Larry Mulcahy, Gordon Mulcaster, Andrew Murphy, Dr. Roger MW Musson, Cameron Newham, Jens Nielsen, Rutger Nijlunsing, Pete Nilson, Denis Papp, Steven and Rand Phares, Joe Popp, Warren Racz, Eric C. Reuter, Steve Rice, Anthony Rocchio, Todd Rodowsky, C. Bradford Rose, Doug Ryerson, Dave Sawford, Andrew Scarvell, Klas Scholdstrom, Eric Severn, Lloyd Shelby, Ryan Shephard, Jimmy Sieben, Scott A. Smith, Craig and Brian Sparks, Glenn Storm, Phil Stracchino, Alfred Svoboda, Dave Swift, Erwen Tang, Sam Taylor, Robert Teegarden, James Thompson, Paul Turnbull, M. Van der Heide, Jack Vermeulen, Michael Videki, John Wakelin, Russ Walsh, Larry Wangemann, Richard Ward, Phillip Wayne, Daniel Weed, Chris White, Keith Wilkins, Matt Williams, Myles Williams, Ron Williams, Timothy Willits, Don Wood, and Russell Wronski.

Sams Publishing would also like to acknowledge and thank id Software, which is responsible for bringing DOOM to the world. Without DOOM, this book would not be possible.

INTRODUCTION

DOOM, from id Software, is a remarkable computer game that has been played by countless people all over the world. It has monopolized hundreds of millions of hours of computer time in businesses, schools, and homes. DOOM's sequels—DOOM II and Heretic—have extended the legacy. DOOM is now the yardstick by which other computer games are measured, even if those games are not intended to compete with DOOM directly.

There are many things that set DOOM apart, and a particular feature that is virtually unique to DOOM created the need for this book. The makers of DOOM gave the public permission to not only play their game in a full-featured shareware version, but also to change the registered version and to share the results with other players. The original developers of DOOM have not prevented people from tampering with the support (WAD) file that contains the details of how the game looks and sounds. However, they state a couple of pre-conditions: First, if you're going to make changes, if you're going to create your own new graphics or sounds, or if you're going to create an entire new world, you have to use a registered version of the game. (After all, fair's fair, and this enables you to purchase a game engine, enjoy DOOM, then set about to drive others crazy with your own levels.) The other major request is that you do not distribute any WAD files that contained a majority of the original DOOM worlds.

From the beginning, people not only made changes to the files, but they did even more. Many people created utilities and editors, making the changes easier. These people become experts—or gurus—on how to program the supplemental (WAD) file that drives the DOOM engine. Instead of simply programming or changing the WAD files, they created the tools necessary to make it easy for anyone to change the files. These programming gurus started the avalanche of new variations that can be experienced within the DOOM game.

In this book, the gurus talk. You will quickly find that this is not a book about playing DOOM, nor is it a book about playing DOOM WAD files. Nor is it documentation for a particular WAD file or editor. This is a book that will not only teach you the ins and outs of creating DOOM's WAD files, but it also will teach you to develop your own worlds. First, you will learn how the WAD file that contains the DOOM information is set up and what type of information it contains. Then you will learn how to create your *own* world, as the gurus lead you in the step-by-step process.

You will also be presented with some of the best WADs that are currently available, WADS that take the original DOOM environment and populate it with colorful monsters, inventive artifacts, offbeat sound effects, and striking locales. Technical information on the development of these WADs will help you in developing your own worlds.

This book also includes a multitude of editors and other tools for you to use. You will learn about many of these tools from the people who actually created them.

Because no book or CD could ever contain all the files that can be found or used, the final episode of the book contains information on where you can go online to obtain more DOOM files. There is also information on how and where you can distribute your WAD files. (If you are interested in DOOM, there are definitely a lot of places to go and people to see.)

A CD-ROM is provided to help supplement what you will find in the book. Unlike every other DOOM-related CD currently available, this CD was created by asking each of the actual developers of DOOM tools or WAD files to include their products. On this one CD you will find everything you need to create your own worlds in DOOM, DOOM II, and Heretic. Not only will you find tools, but you also will find a number of WAD files that you can play to see what other people have done.

The programming information in this book is based on information for developing applications for Windows 95 made public by Microsoft as of 9/9/94. Since this information was made public before the final release of the product, there may have been changes to some of the programming interfaces by the time the product is finally released. We encourage you to check the updated development information that should be part of your development system for resolving issues that might arise.

The end-user information in this book is based on information on Windows 95 made public by Microsoft as of 9/9/94. Since this information was made public before the release of the product, we encourage you to visit your local bookstore at that time for updated books on Windows 95.

If you have a modem or access to the Internet, you can always get up-to-the-minute information on Windows 95 direct from Microsoft on WinNews:

On CompuServe: `GO WINNEWS`

On the Internet:
`ftp://ftp.microsoft.com/PerOpSys/Win_News/Chicago`
`http://www.microsoft.com`

On AOL: keyword `WINNEWS`

On Prodigy: jumpword `WINNEWS`

On GEnie: `WINNEWS` file area on Windows RTC

You also can subscribe to Microsoft's WinNews electronic newsletter by sending Internet e-mail to `news@microsoft.nwnet.com` and putting the words `SUBSCRIBE WINNEWS` in the text of the e-mail.

KNEE DEEP IN DOOM

MISSION 1: INTRODUCTION TO DOOM

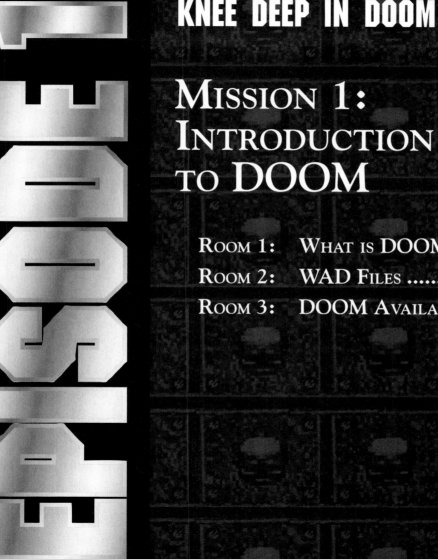

EPISODE 1

ROOM 1

By David Bruni

WHAT IS DOOM?

DOOM. Who would have thought this one word would become *the* standard by which all other games would be judged? What is DOOM? DOOM is a phenomenon. DOOM is also a fast-paced, virtual reality, 3-D type game created by id Software. In DOOM, you use quick reflexes and wits to maneuver through a myriad of mazes, monsters, and acid pits. The capacity to involve other players—whether in cooperation or Deathmatch mode—creates additional complications. The object of the game is simple: survival. But making it through DOOM alive is not as easy as it may seem—even with weapons ranging from a shotgun to a rocket launcher. (Some of the DOOM monsters can take a lot of hits before dying.)

DOOM and DOOM II are state-of-the-art computer games. They are tremendously popular and great fun to play. This book, however, is not a player's manual. This book is for designers and developers who want to create their own levels for DOOM and DOOM II. Many features of these games will be discussed, and all of the current editors and utilities will be examined in detail. Every effort will be made in this book to present proven techniques for what you can do with DOOM and DOOM II—from how to create your own levels to changing the music and building Deathmatch-only levels. This book is an in-depth study of DOOM and DOOM II and is technical in its scope. This book will guide you through the complex world of DOOM and take a little of the mystery out of the game.

WOLFENSTEIN 3D

To understand DOOM and its popularity, you have to take a look at its predecessor, Wolfenstein 3D. DOOM has its roots in Wolfenstein 3D, but DOOM is like Wolfenstein 3D on steroids. Wolfenstein 3D revolutionized the gaming world. DOOM, on the other hand, turned the gaming world on its head.

Wolfenstein 3D was an instant hit when it was released and won many awards for its originality, its game characteristics, and—above all—its realistic rendering of characters and locales. DOOM improved all these aspects of Wolfenstein 3D and added some new ones. Table 1.1 presents a quick overview of features that have been added to DOOM above and beyond what was available in Wolfenstein 3D.

Table 1.1. DOOM characteristics as improvements over Wolfenstein 3D.

Wolfenstein 3D	DOOM
1. Walls only 90° to each other.	1. Walls any angle to each other.
2. Floors and ceilings fixed at 64 units.	2. Floors and ceilings can be 0 to 512 units high.

Wolfenstein 3D	DOOM
3. No useable stairs or elevators.	3. Useable stairs and elevators possible.
4. No transporters.	4. Transporters are allowed.
5. Lights are limited in functionality and are only for decoration.	5. Lights are limited in functionality, but can be made to seem like they work through sector specials.
6. Floors and ceilings can't be changed.	6. Floor and ceiling textures are added and are changeable.
	7. "Crushing" ceilings.
	8. Tripwires.
	9. Wall and floor textures that change automatically to make it appear they are animated.
	10. Switches that work for lights, elevators, doors, and so forth.
	11. Windows.
	12. Exploding barrels.
	13. A host of new features, including Blur Artifacts, Light Amplification Visors, Computer Maps, Backpacks, Berserk Packs, Security Armor, Combat Armor, Health Potions, Spiritual Armor, Radiation Suits, Soul Spheres,

continues

DOOM PROGRAMMING GURUS

1 ROOM

1 MISSION

1 EPISODE

Table 1.1. continued

Wolfenstein 3D	DOOM
	Mega Spheres and Invulnerability Artifacts.
	14. More and tougher monsters.
	15. More and better guns.

In Wolfenstein 3D, the walls were always perpendicular (at 90° to each other). This was a programming limitation of the Wolfenstein 3D engine. The walls were actually four-sided blocks with the same wall design on all four sides. The way you made levels for Wolfenstein 3D was by placing these blocks on a fixed grid. The fixed grid was made up of a 64 x 64 square area similar to a chess board (only bigger). Each square on the grid represented an area approximately 8 feet square. This made all the rooms seem box-like and confining. Wolfenstein 3D also had fixed floor and ceiling heights that were always 64 units tall. In DOOM, floor and ceiling heights can vary, but normally no single room would be more than 512 units high.

PHYSICAL MEASUREMENTS

Wolfenstein 3D and DOOM use measurement systems that take a little getting used to. These measurement systems don't translate very easily. The blocks in Wolfenstein 3D were about 8 feet square, but DOOM is a little different. Everything in DOOM is in units, and the units are different horizontally and vertically. Sounds confusing? In DOOM, 16 horizontal units are equal to about one horizontal foot in real-world dimensions, and 10 vertical units are equal to about one vertical foot in real-world dimensions. These are approximations, and you may have to experiment to achieve the effect you're looking for. Trying to mimic an actual building or house may not work out in quite the way you expect.

THE DOOM ENGINE

The DOOM engine wasn't a redo of the Wolfenstein 3D engine. Instead, it was rewritten from the ground up and vastly improved. In DOOM, the walls can be any angle, relative to one another. The floor and ceiling heights can vary and even move. You can also designate vertices, then lines, and finally create sectors and assign various attributes to either the lines or the sectors. This enables the designers to make just about any shape they like.

1 EPISODE

1 MISSION

1 ROOM

DOOM PROGRAMMING GURUS

You'll have to become familiar with a few new terms when you begin to create DOOM levels. *Vertices* are the points where the lines converge or meet. Think of vertices as the corners of rooms. *Lines* are used to assign textures and floor/ceiling heights. *Sectors* are made up of vertices and lines. (A more complete description of these terms is provided in Episode 1, Mission 2, "Running DOOM.")

DOOM also introduced *line* and *sector specials,* which are fixed actions you can assign to lines or sectors. These line specials or attributes enable you to make many things happen. Line specials are used to make elevators, tripwires, transporters, crushing ceilings, lighting effects, and many other things. DOOM has more than 100 different line specials.

Whereas Wolfenstein 3D made limited use of lighting, DOOM takes full advantage of special lighting effects. You can vary from rooms with absolutely no light to rooms with very bright lights. You can make the lights blink, shimmer, or pulsate; you can set them up to turn off and on with a switch; and you can otherwise emulate real life in many ways. DOOM has even added the effect of light diminishing: Depending upon the light level you chose, the farther away you get from something, the darker it gets. DOOM has 34 levels of lighting, ranging from 0 to 255—levels incrementally increase by about 8 points each—although settings 100 and below are very dark and appear about the same.

Floor and ceiling textures were added to DOOM to make it more realistic than Wolfenstein 3D. Sky textures were added as well. The only limitation here is there are only three sky textures available—one for each episode. The sky textures were a welcome addition to DOOM. Outdoor areas are easy to make and add the illusion of vast areas. The ability to use floor and ceiling textures were also big improvements over Wolfenstein 3D. These heightened the realism of the game. There are also special floor and ceiling textures that make the floor or ceiling appear to pulsate. That's what you see when you look at the acid pits. DOOM handles the switching of textures automatically.

One interesting side note about sky textures is that they are nothing more than cleverly tiled ceiling patterns. All remaining floor and ceiling textures are oriented squares with a 64 x 64 grid. The sky textures don't have a fixed orientation. They tile differently and can cover large irregular areas and still look correct. If, however, you use a sky texture on a wall, it will tile like any other wall texture. You can use sky textures on the floor or ceiling. You can't use them on both the floor and ceiling in the same room.

TYPICAL GRID LAYOUT

Figure 1.1 shows a typical DOOM level with a standard 64 x 64 grid setting. You're looking at an *overhead* or *plan view* of the level. This is the normal viewing of DOOM levels within all the editors. Some of the editors have 3-D viewing capabilities, but you can't edit the levels in the 3-D views.

The small crosses are the actual grid. Notice the horizontal lines are lined up with the grid. In the lower right of the figure, you can see a 64 x 64 piece hanging below a long corridor. Notice that it is lined up square with the grid. This is to ensure that the floor and ceiling textures will not be cut off and display incorrectly. This is important when you're using the transporter patterns or any patterns that are designed as 64 squares. On the left of the figure, you can see the corridors going up at a 45° angle. Because the floor/ceiling patterns are always oriented square with the grid, the floor/ceiling patterns will be skewed in these corridors.

There are many more wall textures to choose from in DOOM than there were in Wolfenstein 3D.

Figure 1.1.
Typical 64 x 64 grid layout.

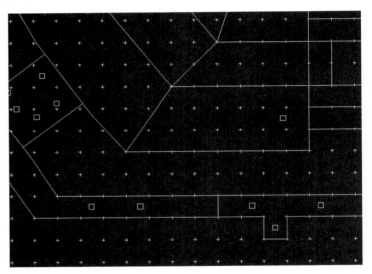

Some of the wall patterns are switches that change the way they look when thrown. DOOM handles this automatically. Some wall textures are see-through, walk-through, and shoot-through. Interesting effects can be achieved with these textures. You can make cages to confine monsters and still be able to shoot them—or be shot *by* them.

TYPICAL WALL, FLOOR, AND CEILING PATTERNS

Figure 1.2 shows a few of the typical textures that are in DOOM. The top left texture is one of the see-through textures. It can be used for making cages or windows. This texture is 128 x 128 units. You can, however, make it smaller without destroying its integrity. In other words, you can make it 128 units long by 64 units tall. Or, you could make it 128 units tall by 64 units wide. Either way, the basic shape is not lost by cutting the size down. There are other textures that are similar in nature.

The texture on the top right is a texture that wouldn't look right if the size were changed. It's also 128 x 128 units square. You could probably squeeze it a little in both directions, but not much without losing something. Textures such as this are best fitted to walls that exactly match their size. It's really not worth the effort to try to shrink them. Why make it harder than it has to be?

Figure 1.2.
Typical wall, floor, and ceiling textures.

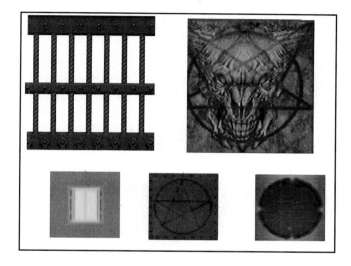

The three remaining textures shown in Figure 1.2 are floor and ceiling textures. They're interchangeable between the floor and ceiling. There's nothing stopping you from using them in either place. All three of these textures are set up to be aligned with the grid as described earlier. They are 64 x 64 units square, and if you don't align them, the design will be cut off and won't look right. When you're aligning your floor and ceiling textures, you have to be aware of the grid settings. Some editors, such as DoomED, have fixed grids that can't be adjusted. The grid is always set at 64 units. Other editors, such as the DOOM Edit Utility (DEU), have adjustable grid settings. Make sure you set the grid to 64 if you want the floor and ceiling patterns to line up correctly. Some floor and ceiling textures don't have any design to them and don't need to be aligned with the grid.

OTHER DOOM IMPROVEMENTS

One of the most popular improvements to DOOM is the variable floor and ceiling heights. Also, stairs are now possible along with elevators. Stairs can even rise out of a flat floor. Windows are now a reality, using the previously mentioned wall textures. In Wolfenstein 3D, the closest you could come to making a window was to place two blocks with a light or plant between them. Through clever designing techniques, you can make DOOM appear to be three-dimensional (which it is not. Rooms can't be stacked on top of each other and you can't create a bridge that can be walked over and underneath). There's nothing like shooting a monster up on a ledge and having it fall off the ledge down to the ground—that's realism!

Transporters are another new feature that DOOM introduced. They add a certain amount of flexibility to designing levels. You can design areas in a level that are not physically connected, but with transporters you can still access these areas. This is handy if you back yourself into a corner and need a quick fix for a way out of the room.

Not all of the decorations in DOOM are friendly. Wolfenstein 3D had barrels, but not exploding barrels. In DOOM, if you or one of the monsters shoots a barrel, it can blow up and damage or kill anything nearby. You can use this feature to your advantage when you're running low on ammo and need a way out of a sticky situation. Some of the artifacts in DOOM can really help you, too. The Blur Artifacts (invisibility spheres) are great for making monsters miss you when they shoot at you. It's at its best in a Deathmatch. There's nothing like walking right up to your opponents and fragging them. They won't know what hit them.

DEATHMATCH

What is a Deathmatch? It is the greatest feature that was added to DOOM. You can now play against a real opponent instead of just the game itself. DOOM supports play by modem, null-modem, or network. Up to four people can play at once on a network. This is the true test of your DOOM playing abilities. Whereas the monsters in DOOM aren't sneaky, most of your Deathmatch opponents probably will be. Anything goes in a Deathmatch. Shooting your opponent in the back is fair. Hiding by the exit and waiting for your opponents to try to exit the level and fragging them there is perfectly acceptable. Even jumping in an acid pit and committing suicide to keep your opponent from killing you is all right.

You haven't done DOOM until you've done a Deathmatch. It's a whole new ball game and makes the game even more enjoyable. You can even talk to your opponent directly during a Deathmatch. An additional multiplayer feature that creates a level playing field is the fact that the *cheat* or *hot keys* cannot be used. Figure 1.3 presents an image of what it's like to kill a human opponent in a DOOM Deathmatch.

1 EPISODE

1 MISSION

1 ROOM

DOOM
PROGRAMMING
GURUS

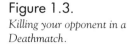
Figure 1.3.
Killing your opponent in a Deathmatch.

WEAPONS

The weapons in DOOM are better than those in Wolfenstein 3D. One of the new additions to your arsenal is a chainsaw. This is very good for use in tight spots or when you've run out of ammunition. It works much better than using your fists (which you lose after picking up the chainsaw, anyway). (Before you acquire a chainsaw, you can still use your fists, but that's not recommended, unless you pick up the Berserk Pack, which gives you temporary super-punching ability.) The pistol is about the same as the pistol in Wolfenstein. The shotgun is new and is a great all-around weapon; it can kill almost any monster that you're likely to come across. The chaingun is similar to the one in Wolfenstein 3D; it's only drawback is that it uses lots of ammo. For the tougher monsters, there's a rocket launcher or bazooka, which can have devastating effects. You have to be careful with it, though, because you can inadvertently kill yourself. The plasma gun is new, too; it can handle all the monsters that DOOM will throw at you. If the plasma gun can't handle it, then the BFG 9000 can. It doesn't shoot fast, but it can clear a room of monsters very fast. Even the Cyberdemon can be defeated rather quickly with the BFG. (For the uninitiated, BFG is also known as *Big F**king Gun*.)

MONSTERS

The monsters in DOOM are tough. They are much harder to kill than the adversaries in Wolfenstein 3D, and there are many additional types of them. The Former Humans and Former Human Sergeants (shown in figures 1.4 and 1.5, respectively) are comparable to the Guards and SS Troopers in

DOOM
PROGRAMMING
GURUS

1
ROOM

1
MISSION

1
EPISODE

Wolfenstein 3D. The Demons and Spectres are new and have no counterparts in Wolfenstein 3D. (See figures 1.6 and 1.7.) The good thing about these creatures is that they don't shoot at you. That doesn't make them any easier to kill, however. The Spectres are especially effective in dark rooms, when they become almost totally invisible. The Imps were thrown in just to be annoying. (See Figure 1.8.)

DOOM also has strange creatures called *Lost Souls*, which are flying skulls. (See Figure 1.9.) They are very effective in areas with limited space because they fly in the air. Cacodemons, or flying eye-balls, are new monsters and are difficult to kill. (See Figure 1.10.) They fly in the air and spit out fireballs of destruction. Don't try to tackle these monsters unless you have at least the shotgun. They are not very fast, but it takes a number of shotgun blasts to kill them. Finally, the last monsters are the Baron of Hell, the Spider Mastermind, and the Cyberdemon. (See figures 1.11, 1.12, and 1.13.) I will never forget the first time I came up against not one but *two* of them in the last episode of the shareware version of DOOM. It took forever to get good enough to kill them. Endless saves and reloads. When you go up against the Barons, it's a good idea to have the rocket launcher. Anything less and you'll be fighting them for hours. They are the toughest of all the monsters to kill.

Figure 1.4.
A Former Human getting ready to shoot.

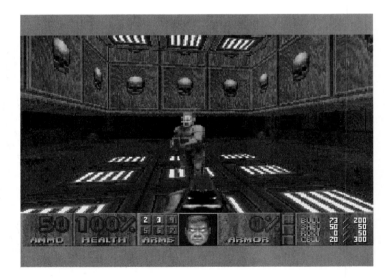

1
EPISODE

1
MISSION

1
ROOM

DOOM
PROGRAMMING
GURUS

Figure 1.5.

*A Former Human
Sergeant shooting away.*

Figure 1.6.

A Demon attacking.

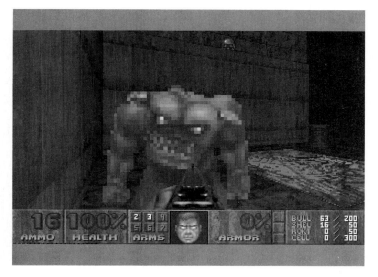

DOOM
PROGRAMMING
GURUS

1
ROOM

1
MISSION

1
EPISODE

Figure 1.7.
A Spectre attacking.

Figure 1.8.
*One of those annoying Imps
getting ready to strike.*

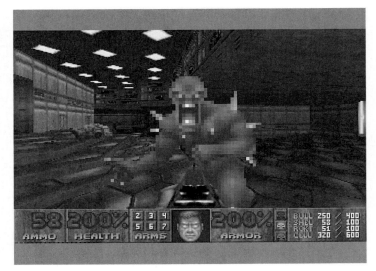

 EPISODE

 MISSION

 ROOM

**DOOM
PROGRAMMING
GURUS**

Figure 1.9.
A Lost Soul taking a bite out of you.

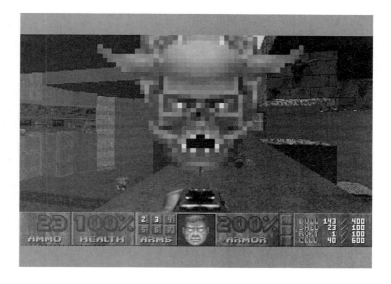

Figure 1.10.
A Cacodemon preparing to shoot a fireball.

Figure 1.11.
A Baron of Hell sizing you up.

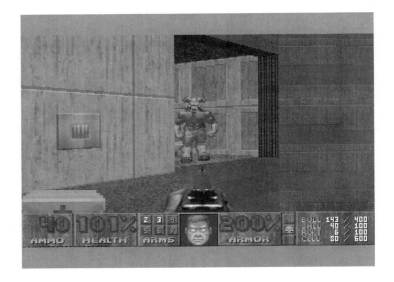

Figure 1.12.
Getting up close and personal with the Spider Mastermind.

Figure 1.13.
The final showdown with the Cyberdemon.

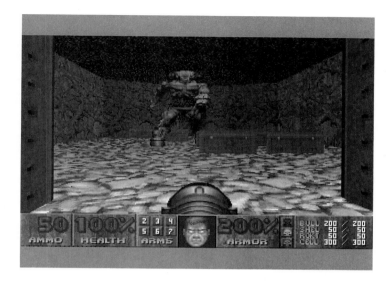

ID SOFTWARE HELPED OUT

The makers of DOOM decided to make it very easy for developers and designers to create and add their own levels to the game. id Software released information about the game that made it possible for aspiring programmers to create map editors and produce their own variations on DOOM. You are only limited by your imagination. This book will show you in detail how to choose your tools— and how to use them to make your own version of Hell. This book is geared to the DOOM developer.

DOOM II

The only game that could have followed DOOM is, of course, DOOM II. This is DOOM taken to its most extreme. The makers of DOOM II took a great game and made it even better. This was no small task. DOOM II includes 32 new levels of pure excitement. Here are some of the advantages DOOM II has over DOOM:

- New combat shotgun
- New sky textures
- New wall textures
- Two Wolfenstein 3D secret levels (This is not a misprint.)
- Seven new monsters

- A Mega Sphere
- More line specials
- Improved Deathmatch
- New music

Most of the original elements of DOOM were retained in DOOM II but were enhanced. A new gun, new wall, floor and ceiling textures, new artifacts, new music, new monsters, and new line specials were added. The new double-barreled combat shotgun can take out two or three monsters at once. Reloading is a little slow, but its firepower makes up for it. The rest of the weapons are the same as in DOOM.

DOOM II added many new and exciting wall textures. A few of the original textures were dropped. The new textures more than make up for this. For example, the sky textures were replaced with a superior pattern. One of the sky textures looks more like the skyline of a city and it looks quite good in a city-type layout.

DOOM II has its roots in Wolfenstein 3D, just like DOOM. So much so, there are two Wolfenstein 3D levels in DOOM II. You have to see them to believe them. The textures were redone, but they look like the originals. DOOM and DOOM II use wall patterns that are usually 128 x 128 units or multiples thereof, whereas Wolfenstein 3D only used wall textures that were fixed at 64 x 64. As a result, Wolfenstein 3D in DOOM II looks better than ever. Even the old SS guards are there. Figure 1.14 presents how Wolfenstein 3D looks with the DOOM II enhancements.

Figure 1.14.
A Wolfenstein 3D SS guard in one of two secret DOOM II levels.

DOOM II MONSTERS

Probably the most significant change in DOOM II is the lineup of new monsters. The Former Commandos carry chainguns that can chew you up in a hurry. (See Figure 1.15.) The Barons of Hell have little brothers called Hell Knights, who are almost as tough as their bigger siblings. (See Figure 1.16.) They're not the only relatives in DOOM II. The Spider Mastermind had a bunch of little spiders called Arachnotrons. (See Figure 1.17.) Don't let their size fool you—they carry plasma guns and can cook you quick. You had best have the plasma gun yourself before taking these guys on. There's a guy called Pain Elemental who spits out Lost Souls almost faster than you can shoot them. (See Figure 1.18.) When you kill him, he'll spit out three final Lost Souls just to spite you. The Revenant looks like a walking skeleton, but he's got two rocket launchers to back him up. (See Figure 1.19.) He is a tough monster to kill. When he's not shooting you with rockets, he's clobbering you with his fists. The Mancubus is a widebody who's got rocket launchers for hands and he can pummel you with fireballs. (See Figure 1.20.) Perhaps the toughest monster of all is the Arch-Vile. (See Figure 1.21.) When he blasts you, it knocks you up in the air and surrounds you with fire. If that wasn't bad enough, he can revive dead monsters that you worked so hard to kill in the first place.

Figure 1.15.
A Former Commando using his chaingun.

Figure 1.16.
A Hell Knight doing his thing.

Figure 1.17.
An Arachnotron getting ready to try out his plasma gun.

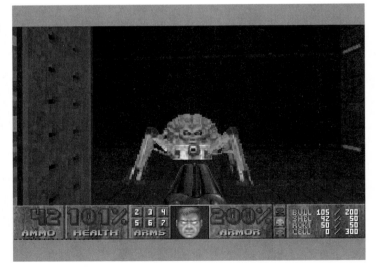

1
EPISODE

1
MISSION

1
ROOM

**DOOM
PROGRAMMING
GURUS**

Figure 1.18.
A Pain Elemental giving birth to Lost Souls.

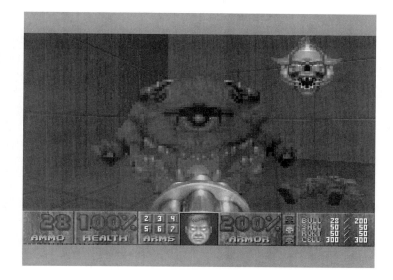

Figure 1.19.
A Revenant looking for someone to kill.

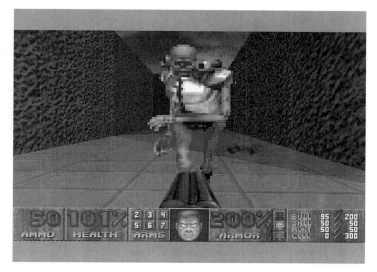

DOOM
PROGRAMMING
GURUS

1
ROOM

1
MISSION

1
EPISODE

Figure 1.20.
The Mancubus and his two rocket launching arms.

Figure 1.21.
The Arch-Vile conjuring up dead monsters.

ADDITIONAL FEATURES OF DOOM II

Deathmatch rules and options were changed slightly in DOOM II. There's now a parameter called -ALTDEATH that makes all the objects regenerate after about 30 seconds. The only objects that don't regenerate are the Blur Artifacts and the Invulnerability Artifacts. This is great for the designer of external PWADs. In a Deathmatch, all the ammo, health kits, armor, and so on are regenerated, and the players can keep playing a single level for hours without having to exit the level. There's also a new parameter called -TURBO that accepts a value from 0 to 250 and increases your speed accordingly. You can also make demo recordings of multiple player Deathmatches.

SUMMARY

The layout and number of monsters in DOOM II make it many times harder than DOOM. The levels in DOOM II are more complicated and make good use of puzzle-solving skills similar to those used in Wolfenstein 3D. There are more buttons, tricks, and brain teasers in DOOM II. Sometimes you'll have to jump from ledges to access other parts of the level. DOOM II added more line specials and sector specials, making the process of designing your own levels even more challenging. Some of the DOOM II levels may take more than a few tries to complete and many hours of work.

ROOM 2

By David Bruni

WAD FILES

WAD files or PWAD files are external levels created to be used with either the DOOM or DOOM II engine. There are various editors available for making your own levels. Some of the more popular ones are the DOOM Edit Utility (DEU), DoomED—The Real Thing, DoomCAD, DOOM Construction Kit (DCK), and EdMap. Most of them have built-in node builders. The majority of the time, however, you will be using an external node builder such as BSP 1.2 to build the nodes on your levels. All WAD files must have the nodes built before they are playable. We'll discuss nodes in a while.

WHAT EXACTLY ARE WAD FILES?

What exactly is a WAD file? In DOOM and DOOM II, there are two types of WAD files. The main DOOM.WAD file is called an *IWAD* or *internal WAD* file. It has to be present in order for DOOM to run. The other type is a *PWAD* or *patch WAD* file. When you create a PWAD file, you have to assign it an episode/mission number in DOOM and a map level in DOOM II. Then when you run the WAD file inside of DOOM or DOOM II, it will replace, in memory, the information in the main DOOM.WAD file with the information in the PWAD file. A PWAD file will not permanently overwrite any information in the main DOOM.WAD file. Most editors do have an option that will let you permanently input information into the main DOOM.WAD file, but this is inadvisable. For one thing, if you change the main DOOM.WAD file, you will be unable to play with other people by modem unless they have an exact copy of the modified DOOM.WAD file. This is a problem because id Software doesn't allow the distribution of the main DOOM.WAD file and it is more than 10MB in size. (The actual meaning of the extension .WAD has yet to be determined.)

There are many DOOM editors and utilities available that enable you to manipulate almost every aspect of WAD files. You not only can create you own levels, using DOOM itself as a resource, for such things as the monsters, the weapons, the music, and so on, but you can change the entire way DOOM looks and just about make a completely different game. Some of the utilities do specific things like change the graphics or music. Some can change the sprites or monsters, and others can change the weapons used in DOOM.

Some editors, such as DEU, enable you to combine multiple WAD files into one big WAD file. You can conceivably create your own complete 10-mission episode. With other utilities, such as DMGRAPH or DeuTEX, you can change the wall textures to those of your own choosing. There have been some very impressive WAD files created with utilities that this book will show you how to use.

WHAT TO CONSIDER WHEN BUILDING WAD FILES

There are many things to consider when designing DOOM or DOOM II WAD files. Fortunately, most of the very technical things are handled by the various utilities. This does not mean, however, that WAD files are easy to make. It still takes a lot of work and a more-than-passing interest in DOOM. There are thousands of WAD files available at different locations, but there's not that many truly great ones. The very best WAD files make good use of all the many add-on utilities and require planning and hundreds of hours of work. In addition, some of the utilities don't contain explicit-enough instructions on how to use them.

Care has to be taken not only in using the editors but also in the layout and planning of a level. Taking one big room and putting in hundreds of monsters is not what makes a good level. In the true spirit of DOOM, the level should be playable. In other words, you should not have to use cheat codes to successfully complete a level. Many people overlook this simple premise. A PWAD file should also be free of any defects, such as the Hall of Mirrors (HOM) effect. This is a strange video glitch that arises from different conditions such as missing textures where there should be a texture. Many of the editors have error checkers that help to minimize errors such as that. The best way to minimize all errors is to play-test a level thoroughly before releasing it.

Another important thing to remember is that DOOM and DOOM II are not truly three-dimensional. The designers of the original game did a good job of disguising this fact. You can, as well, but you have to at least be able to think three-dimensionally. This can be one of the hardest things to do when designing a DOOM level. A well-planned and executed level can immortalize you in the Designers' Hall of Fame. A poorly planned level with lots of errors will get you nowhere.

To become good at level designing takes practice, patience, and hard work. You have to become intimate with the terms DOOM uses to describe levels. Terms such as *vertices*, *linedefs*, *sidedefs*, *sectors*, *upper* and *lower textures* are a few of the things you have to know before you start.

TECHNICAL TERMS FOR WORKING WITH WAD FILES

VERTICES

By definition, *vertex* means the termination or intersection of lines or curves. This meaning holds true for DOOM. Vertices in DOOM are the points at which the lines converge. You can see them when you're building a level with the different editors. Some of the editors enable you to insert individual vertices, other editors, insert the vertices with the sectors. When you play DOOM, you can think of the vertices as the corners of walls. Lining up vertices is easy with most editors because they have a fixed grid that can be displayed.

Some grids are adjustable, which enables the placing of vertices in exact locations. This can be important when you're trying to fit a texture between two vertices without truncating the texture. Vertices are the basic building blocks of DOOM levels. All the editors enable you to move vertices around to just about any location. Sectors can share vertices between them. Different editors manipulate vertices in various ways. They're all similar in most respects. The maximum number of vertices you can use in a level will be limited more by the editor you use than by the DOOM engine itself.

Most editors can only handle WAD files of a certain size. Once you exceed this limit, the level might not save or the editor will start acting erratically. There does appear to be a limit to the maximum number of vertices that a single sector can contain. It's somewhere in the neighborhood of 25 to 30. It's best to break up areas with many vertices into two or more separate sectors. Errors such as these are hard to track down and fix. That's why play-testing your level after adding each sector will help you localize the problem and save you much grief later on.

LINES

Lines in DOOM are where you assign such things as textures for walls, line actions for things like doors, elevators, transporters, and so forth. Lines have much information associated with them. A thorough understanding of lines is essential to making quality PWADs.

Most editors use techniques that enable you to place vertices first and then add the lines between them. Some editors can insert sectors or groups of lines and vertices in one step. Some editors can do it either way. Under ideal conditions, you could insert sectors, connect them together, and everything is fine. If something goes wrong, then you will have to fix the level manually. This is where a good understanding of the structure of DOOM is necessary. Otherwise, you can waste hours and hours of time trying to debug a level and get everything right.

LINEDEFS AND SIDEDEFS

Lines are actually made up of two different parts, *linedefs* and *sidedefs*. Linedefs are the actual lines and define the limits of the level. All linedefs are numbered and have one required attribute assigned to them. They have to be either impassable or two-sided. All other attributes are optional. Table 2.1 lists some of the other line attributes. Most editors will set the impassable or two-sided attribute automatically. Removing one or the other of these two attributes can result in the Hall of

Mirrors (HOM) effect or crash the game when played. This is very important to keep in mind when you start changing things.

Table 2.1. Other linedef attributes.

Type of Attribute	Description
Monsters can't cross	This is good for keeping monsters confined to one area.
Upper texture unpegged	This is used on door jambs and on the textures around windows to make the textures of the adjacent walls line up with the textures above and below the window.
Lower texture unpegged	This is used around windows also.
Secret	This is used so a line will appear normal in map mode and not give away a secret room or area. It's not what determines the secret ratio at the end of the game. This is set through the sector attributes.
Block sounds	This means that sound will not cross the line.
Not on map	A line assigned this attribute is not shown in the map mode.
Already on map	The line will be visible in map mode when the game is started.

All linedefs also have to have a type. Some lines are designated as doors, some are switches, others perform line actions when the player walks across them or shoots them. DOOM has 100 line specials that can be assigned to linedefs. DOOM II increased this to 125. The line specials encompass all the special things that can be done in DOOM and DOOM II. Everything from doors to lighting to crushing ceilings are assigned to lines through the line attributes.

FIRST AND SECOND SIDEDEFS

Linedefs can have one or two sidedefs, depending on whether they are impassable or two-sided. Impassable lines only need to have a first sidedef, because you can't see the other side while you are playing the game. Two-sided lines will have two sidedefs: a first and a second. Sidedefs have been a source of great confusion. They are one of the harder things to understand about designing DOOM levels. A thorough understanding of them is also essential to making quality WAD files. If the sidedefs aren't set correctly, this will cause problems, most notably the HOM effect. Each sidedef is further broken down into three parts: the upper texture, the lower texture, and the normal texture. These designate which part of the line will be assigned a texture. This comes into play when you want to create a difference in surface heights, such as a stairstep or ceilings in adjacent sectors.

Most of the editors have a way of designating which sidedef is the first and which is the second. This is an important consideration when you start changing lines by hand. The majority of the editors have a small line perpendicular to the sidedef, which designates the first sidedef. When you look at a level in an editor, the picture you are seeing is an overhead view. The first sidedef will be on one side of the linedef and the second sidedef will be on the other side of the line. Picturing this in your mind is easier if you look at something such as a door in your house. One side of the door would be the first sidedef, and the other side of the door would be the second sidedef. The upper texture would be the part of the wall above the door, and the lower texture would be used only if there is a step that you have to step up onto, in order to cross through the door. The normal texture would be the actual door itself. Some editors will assign the correct texture for the parts of the sidedef; others won't. Failing to set a texture for one of the parts of a sidedef will result in the HOM effect.

An example of a situation that requires a good understanding of sidedefs and the different parts of the lines is creating an elevator. Most editors do not make elevators for you automatically. This means knowing which way the sidedefs are pointing and which part of the sidedef needs a texture is up to you. You have to assign a texture to the correct part of the line for the elevator in the up position and the down position, or else you'll again get the HOM effect. The better editors (including DEU 5.21 and DoomED 4.2) have error checkers that can usually tell you if you have a missing texture.

There are a few special situations that you need to be aware of when assigning textures to linedefs. If you assign a texture to the normal part of a sidedef, it has to be a see-through texture. Otherwise you will get the *Medusa effect*, which is another strange video glitch. Some of the see-through textures are easy to determine. Cage bars are one of the obvious see-through textures. There are, however, other not-so-obvious, see-through textures available. As long as a texture is made up of one patch, it can be used as a see-through texture. Most wall textures are made up of multiple patches and can't be used as see-through textures. To be able to walk through a see-through texture, you have to designate it as two-sided.

You can also manually adjust the location of the texture on the wall by changing the X/Y offset coordinates for the sidedef. The X is the horizontal movement the texture will take, and the Y is the vertical movement. A few editors (including DEU) have an auto-align tool that will automatically line up the textures horizontally for you. This will enable you to get very professional results.

Most of the editors also have a button or tool that enables you to swap ends on linedefs or rotate them 180 degrees. This can be very useful in certain situations.

SECTORS

The next thing you need to understand about WAD files is *sectors*. Depending on the editor you use, sectors will be set up in different ways. Some editors enable you to insert whole sectors, while in other editors you will have to make the sectors yourself.

Basically, a sector is a group of linedefs and vertices that work as a unit. Sectors are assigned numbers. Sectors can also have attributes assigned to them. You set things such as the lighting effects, health loss, secret designations that count at the end of the game, and a few other things. Sectors also contain the floor and ceiling height information and the textures that are assigned to the linedefs that make up the sector. Think of sectors as rooms, doors, acid pits, and so forth. All the structures in a WAD file are made up of sectors.

NODES

One thing that is good to know (although not essential to building WAD files) is the concept of nodes (and node builders). Sooner or later you may get an error message while building nodes that says "nodeline not found"; then the program crashes. This is usually caused by incorrectly connected sectors, a stray line not associated with a sector, or an unclosed sector.

You can't see nodes as you can see vertices or lines. Nodes are branches in a *Binary Space Partition* (BSP) that break up the level and are used by the DOOM engine to determine which walls are in front of others and can be viewed at one time from a particular viewpoint. When you run a node builder (which you have to do), it's basically a complicated algorithm or set of mathematical equations that turns the WAD file into a playable wad. Luckily, nodes and node builders are not something that you must be concerned with. The only thing you really need to know about node builders is that one must be run on a WAD file before you can play it.

REJECT RESOURCE

Another important utility is the *reject builder*, which will set the *reject resource*. This is used to speed up slow WAD files. The reject data is used by the DOOM engine to determine when monsters can see the player and what sectors can be seen from various locations. It can be used to speed up WAD files because it can save the DOOM engine from making unneeded calculations for line of sight while you are playing the game. If you have a WAD file with lots of lines in view at once and it runs slowly, then run a reject builder on it.

Building WAD files is not hard, but there are many little things that you have to consider. Don't expect your first WAD file to be your best. It may take building two or three WAD files to really get the hang of it. The important thing to remember is to play-test your level often to minimize the chance of error. Find out as much information about WAD files as you can, especially by reading the rest of this book. Play other people's WAD files to see how they apply particular techniques. Don't get discouraged if things don't work out exactly as you planned. The best WAD files require much hard work and many long hours.

1
EPISODE

1
MISSION

2
ROOM

DOOM
PROGRAMMING
GURUS

ROOM 3

By David Bruni

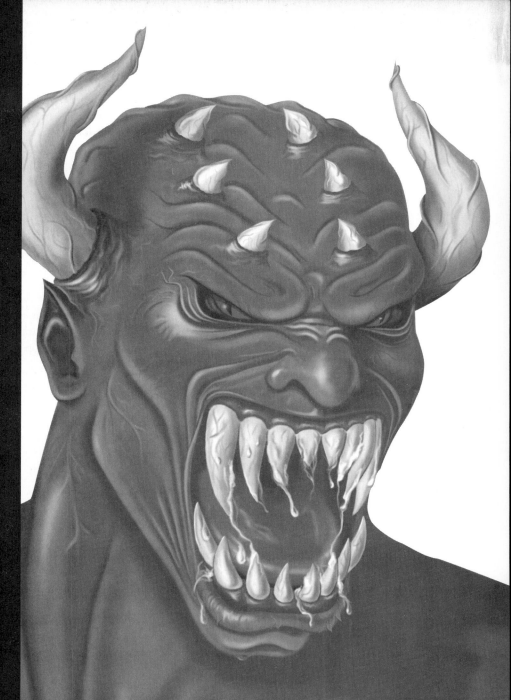

DOOM AVAILABILITY

At the time of this writing, DOOM was available for a couple different platforms, with more in the planning stages. Of course, the DOS version started everything. I just recently saw a MAC version of the shareware game. The Jaguar version for Atari appears to be available now. There is an OS/2 version in the works, although the DOS version will already run under OS/2.

WinDOOM was in beta testing at the time of this writing. It's a 32-bit application designed to run under Windows NT and Windows 95. It will run under Windows 3.x if you have Win32s installed on your machine. However, there a few bugs to be worked out before it will be available.

If you can't wait for WinDOOM, you can run DOOM under Windows 3.x if you make a few changes to your working environment. You should have at least 8MB of RAM before even trying it, and then it will still run slow and jerky. You probably won't see that much of a slowdown if your computer has a minimum of 16MB of RAM. If you have a sound card, you should turn it off. You'll also want to turn off any other running applications and make DOOM the only thing that you're running. The only real advantage to running the DOS version of DOOM under Windows would be for play-testing the levels you create with a Windows-based editor. This way you don't have to exit Windows over and over to test your levels. For normal game play, it's probably better to not run DOOM under Windows, because of the speed penalty.

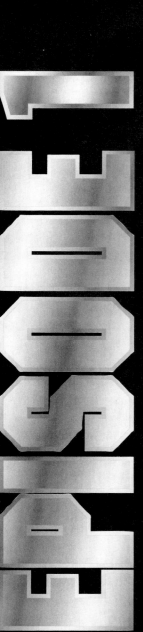

KNEE DEEP IN DOOM

MISSION 2:
RUNNING DOOM

ROOM 1

By David Bruni

USING THE SETUP
PROGRAM

The Setup menu enables you to choose and configure your sound card, select and configure your controller type, configure and run DOOM or DOOM II for multiplayer games, and run saved multiplayer games. The Setup menu is the same for DOOM 1.666 and DOOM II.

ACCESSING THE SETUP MENU

To access the Setup menu, change to your DOOM or DOOM II directory and type SETUP, then hit Enter. This brings up the Main Menu dialog box and the Current Configuration dialog box. Under Current Configuration, you'll see "Control Type=," which will tell you if DOOM is setup for the keyboard, mouse, or joystick (or a combination of keyboard and mouse or keyboard and joystick). "Music Card=" will be set to a particular type of music card, the PC Speaker, or none. "Sound FX=" is similar to "Music Card=." The Sound FX setting is for the sounds of the guns firing, doors opening, the sounds the monsters make, and so on.

THE MAIN MENU

Through the Main menu you can change and reset all the settings for your sound card and controller, and configure and run multiplayer games. At any time during the setup process, you can hit the Escape key to abort the setup program. When you hit Escape, it brings up a small dialog box that gives you a chance to save the settings or discard everything that you've changed. To make a change, you pick the thing you want to change and hit Enter. Figure 1.1 presents the Main menu.

Figure 1.1.
The Main menu in the Setup program.

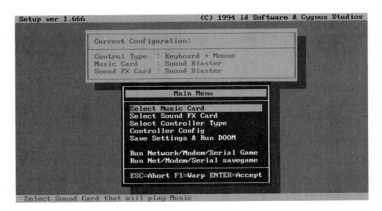

1 EPISODE   2 MISSION   1 ROOM   DOOM PROGRAMMING GURUS

SELECT MUSIC CARD

Let's look at each option one by one.

The Select Music Card option enables you to select from a list of available sound cards that DOOM and DOOM II supports, as shown in Figure 1.2. DOOM 1.666 and DOOM II each list eight different cards (and a choice for "none"). If your sound card is listed there, use the arrow keys on your keyboard to scroll down to your card, then hit Enter. This will bring up the Available PORTs dialog box. (See Figure 1.3.) The default is 220. You can accept the default or choose a different one if your sound card documentation lists a different one. If you're unsure about which one you need to pick, go with the default.

If you have a sound card that's not listed, you can try setting it up with the Sound Blaster settings. This may or may not work.

Figure 1.2.
The Select Music Playback Device dialog box.

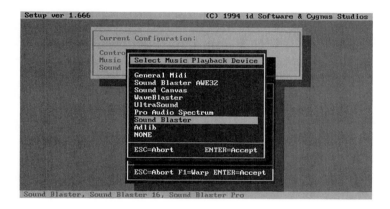

Figure 1.3.
The Available PORTs dialog box.

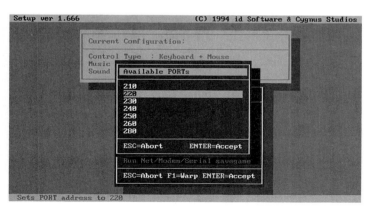

SELECT SOUND FX CARD

The Select Sound FX card option, shown in Figure 1.4, is similar to the Select Music Card option. There are three sound cards listed, as well as a PC Speaker option and a "none" option. Pick the one for your card and hit Enter. When you select a sound card, this brings up the Available PORTs dialog box again. (See Figure 1.3.) You can accept the default of 220 or choose a different one if your sound card documentation suggests one. Once you pick a PORT, another dialog box comes on screen that shows you the available IRQs (Interrupts) for your sound card. (See Figure 1.5.) After you pick an IRQ, you're presented with the Available DMA Channel dialog box. (See Figure 1.6.) You can accept the default of 1 or pick another one. After that, you're presented with the Number of Sound FX to mix dialog box. (See Figure 1.7.) You can accept the default of Three or choose a different one. (Note: Making selections other than the defaults could give you unpredictable results. Only select non-defaults if you're sure of what you're doing.)

Figure 1.4.
The Select Sound FX Device dialog box.

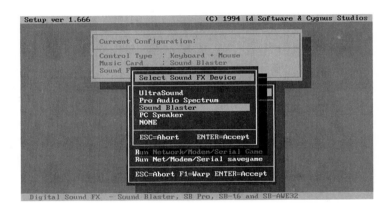

Figure 1.5.
The Available IRQs dialog box.

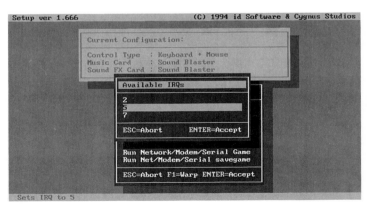

Figure 1.6.
The Available DMA Channels dialog box.

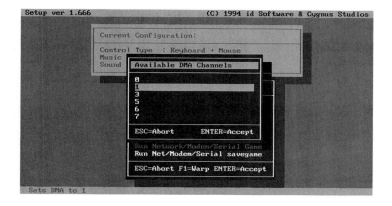

Figure 1.7.
The Number of Sound FX to mix dialog box.

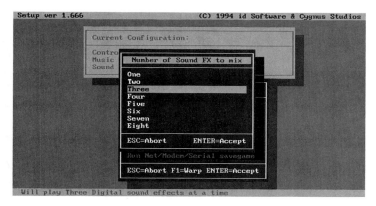

SELECT CONTROLLER TYPE

The next option is Select Controller Type. (See Figure 1.8.) This is a straightforward dialog box. You can pick keyboard only, keyboard and mouse, or keyboard and joystick. Pick one and hit Enter.

You then have the option of fine tuning your controller type through the Controller Configuration dialog boxes. (See figures 1.9, 1.10, 1.11, and 1.12.) These let you change which keys on the keyboard control the players' movement and which key opens doors, fires the guns, and controls the players' speed. You can also configure the mouse or a joystick through this dialog box.

Figure 1.8.
The Select Controller Type dialog box.

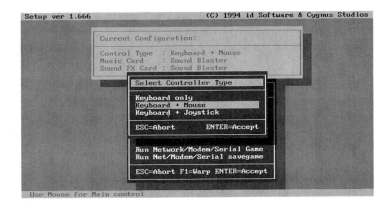

Figure 1.9.
The Controller Configuration dialog box.

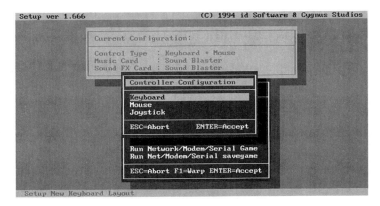

Figure 1.10.
The Keyboard Configuration dialog box.

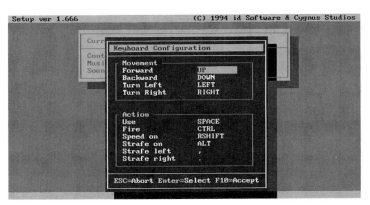

Figure 1.11.
The Mouse Config-
uration dialog box.

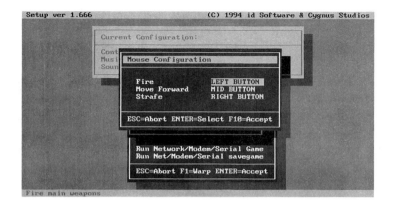

Figure 1.12.
The Joystick Config-
uration dialog box.

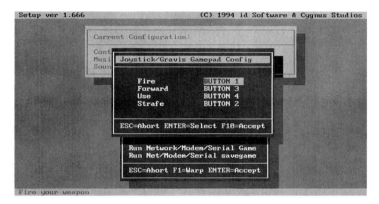

You can now either choose Save Settings and Run DOOM to play the game, or you can hit the Escape key and answer Yes to save the settings and exit the setup program.

RUNNING A NETWORK, MODEM, OR SERIAL GAME

The last two options in the Main menu are for running DOOM and DOOM II as a network game, a modem game, a serial game, or running a savegame for one of the three multiplayer options. To run DOOM and DOOM II on a network, you have to use IPX network drivers. Some networks are already IPX compatible. Other networks, such as Windows for Workgroups, are not IPX compatible, and with such networks you'll be required to install the IPX drivers before DOOM and DOOM II will run as a network game. The appropriate drivers can be found on many online services.

You can also run a network game or serial-link game by using either the IPXSETUP or SERSETUP programs that come with DOOM and DOOM II. You can include line parameters with these two programs as outlined in Episode 1, Mission 2, Room 2, "DOOM's Command Line."

RUNNING A NETWORK GAME

To run a network game, select Run Network/Modem/Serial Game from the Main Menu. This will bring up the Select Networking Device dialog box. (See Figure 1.13.) You can pick either IPX-compatible network, modem, or serial-link modes. If you pick IPX-compatible network, this brings up the Network Configuration dialog box. (See Figure 1.14.) You have the option of picking the number of players, the episode, the skill level, and a Cooperative or Deathmatch game. With DOOM 1.666 and DOOM II, you can press F1 to bring up the Warp dialog box. (See Figure 1.15.) This has selections for no monsters, respawn, and Deathmatch 2.0 rules. Use the arrow keys to scroll down and the spacebar to make a selection. You can then scroll down through all the episode/mission numbers and pick one. This starts the game. If you don't use the Warp, you can make your selections and hit F10 to start. Everyone who is going to play on the network has to do this. All the settings should be the same for each player.

Figure 1.13.
The Select Networking Device dialog box.

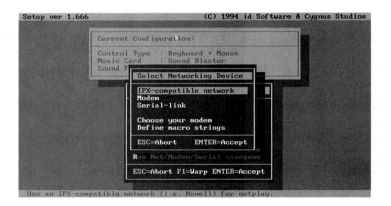

Figure 1.14.
*The Network Config-
uration dialog box.*

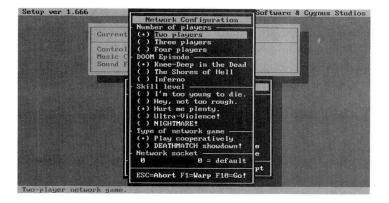

Figure 1.15.
The Level Warp dialog box.

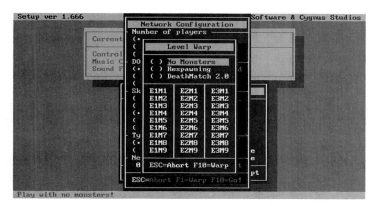

RUNNING A MODEM GAME

To run a modem game, select Run Network/Modem/Serial Game from the Main menu. This will bring up the Select Networking Device dialog box. (See Figure 1.13.) Go down to where it says Choose Your Modem. This will bring up a list of common modems. (See Figure 1.16.) If you don't see your modem in the list, pick one of the generic ones. The settings are saved in a file called MODEM.CFG in your DOOM/DOOM II directory. Also, DOOM and DOOM II will only work on modems with at least 9600 bps. Anything less will not work. Now pick Modem from the menu. This brings up the Modem Configuration dialog box. (See Figure 1.17.) It's similar to the Network Configuration dialog box. You have to pick an episode/mission, the skill level, and Cooperative or Deathmatch mode.

You also have to pick a COM port for your modem. You need to know which COM port that you're connected to before going through the modem setup. At the bottom of the dialog box you'll see the Connect Method. "Already Connected" is for changing episode/missions, skill levels, and so on, after you've made a connection. "Wait For Call" means just that: You're waiting for your opponent to call you. You can pick the Call option and enter a phone number of the person you want to play. You can also hit F2 in DOOM 1.666 and DOOM II to access a phone list with frequently called numbers. (See Figure 1.18.) This is saved in a text file called MODEM.NUM, and you can edit it with any text editor. DOOM 1.666 and DOOM II also uses F1 for the Warp dialog box. Make all your selections and hit F10 to start. There's an option to Define Macro Strings; this is for creating pre-defined things to say to your opponent while playing. (See Figure 1.19.) It's faster and safer than trying to type out a message while you're playing.

Figure 1.16.
The Select Modem dialog box.

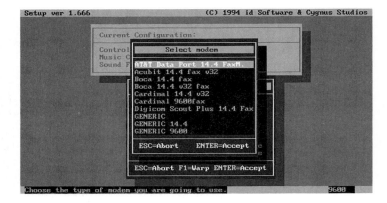

Figure 1.17.
The Modem Configuration dialog box.

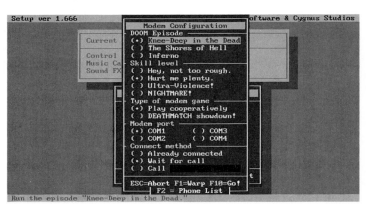

Figure 1.18.
The Select who to call dialog box.

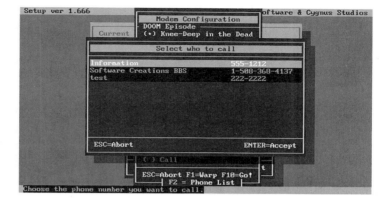

Figure 1.19.
The Macro Definition dialog box.

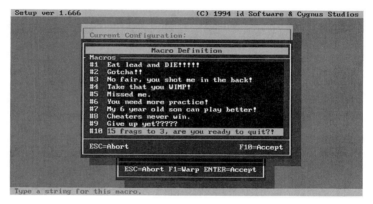

RUNNING A SERIAL GAME

To run a Serial-link game, select Run Network/Modem/Serial Game from the Main Menu. This will bring up the Select Networking Device dialog box. (See Figure 1.13, shown previously.) Pick Serial-link from the menu. This brings up the Serial Configuration dialog box. (See Figure 1.20.) It has basically the same options as the other two setups. Make your selections and hit F10 to start.

Figure 1.20.

The Serial Configuration dialog box.

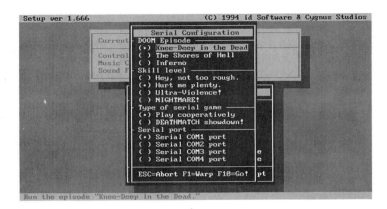

RUNNING A NETWORK, MODEM, OR SERIAL SAVEGAME

Finally, you have the option of loading a previously saved game. You have to make sure that you load a saved game from the original DOOM or DOOM II. If you try to load an external PWAD through the Setup menu, it won't work and you'll lock up your computer. You'll have to use a different front-end program to do this. There have been some great WAD files designed for Deathmatch-only play and you should try them if you get a chance.

So, in the Main menu, pick Run Net/Modem/Serial savegame. This brings up the Select Networking Device dialog box. (See Figure 1.21.) Pick one of the three network options. This will bring up one of three different dialog boxes. (See figures 1.22, 1.23, or 1.24.) Pick the game you'd like to load and the other available options, then press F10 to start.

Figure 1.21.

The Select Networking Device dialog box.

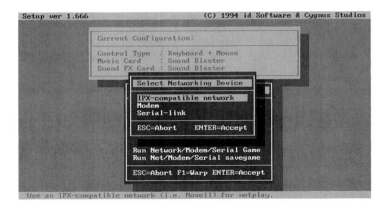

Figure 1.22.
The Network savegame options dialog box.

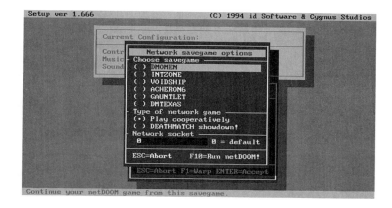

Figure 1.23.
The Modem savegame options dialog box.

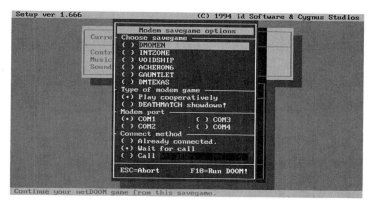

Figure 1.24.
The Serial savegame options dialog box.

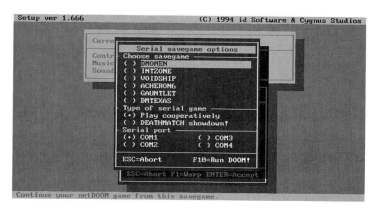

DOOM
PROGRAMMING
GURUS

1
ROOM

2
MISSION

1
EPISODE

OPTIONAL FRONT ENDS

There are many front end programs available for running modem games. Some of them are versatile and easy to use. Check your favorite BBS or other online service for availability. Look in Episode 4, Mission 6, "Entering the Abyss," for some of the more popular front-end programs.

ROOM 2

By David Bruni

DOOM'S COMMAND LINE

There are many parameters that you can pass to DOOM or DOOM II directly from the command line when you start the game. If you find yourself using one particular string of parameters quite often, you should turn the string into a batch file. For instance, as you develop a WAD file, you will be play-testing it over and over. Typing a 25-character string to start the game can get tiresome and you're prone to making typing mistakes. So it's much easier to save the string as a batch file and give it a one- or two-letter name. Thus you can reuse it and you don't have to worry about starting the game, loading your WAD file, and warping to a specific level. Also, when you're finished with your WAD file and are ready to upload it, you can include the batch file with the WAD file so the people who download your WAD file can use it to start the game. All DOOM players do not know the correct syntax to successfully load a WAD file. It saves everyone a lot of time and effort.

TYPICAL START-UP STRING

A typical start-up string to load a WAD file would look something like this:

For DOOM:

```
doom -devparm -file mywad.wad -warp 2 1 -skill 4
```

For DOOM II:

```
doom2 -file mywad.wad -warp 2 -skill 4
```

Let's look at each line, parameter-by-parameter. The first line for the DOOM example does as follows: `doom` starts the game, just as you would do normally. The next parameter, `-devparm`, puts you into developer's mode. You have to use this to be able to use the `-warp` parameter to warp straight to the level of your WAD file. The next parameter, `-file`, is how you load an external WAD file. `MYWAD.WAD` can be any valid WAD filename. You have to use the `.WAD` extension to make it work. The `-warp 2 1` parameter tells DOOM that you want to go to Episode 2, Mission 1. The first number can be 1-3, the second number can be 1-9. There does appear to be another parameter, called `-wart`, that does the same thing as the `-warp` parameter. Either one will send you directly to the episode/mission you tell it to. When you use the `-warp` parameter, it skips the usual start-up screen and sends you straight to the floor. The last parameter, `-skill`, is optional and sets the skill level for the WAD file. Valid numbers for it are 1-5, with 5 being Nightmare mode. If you don't specify a skill level, then the game defaults to skill-level 3.

The command line to start DOOM II does the following: The first parameter, `doom2`, starts the game as always. (Make sure you don't leave out the 2 that follows the word `doom`.) You don't need to use the `-devparm` parameter as in DOOM; the `-warp` parameter works without it. The `-file` parameter is the same as for DOOM. It accepts any valid WAD filename. Again, don't forget the `.WAD` file extension. The `-warp` command will send you straight to the level you want. Remember that the format of the levels changed for DOOM II—there's no more episode/mission numbers. So, valid numbers to use with the -warp parameter are 1-32. (30 is the last level of the game proper, and 31 and 32 are the two secret Wolfenstein 3D levels.) The -skill parameter is the same as for DOOM and accepts numbers 1-5.

UPGRADE TO DOOM 1.666

During the subsequent upgrading of DOOM from versions 1.1 to 1.666, some new parameters were added. If you are playing a version of DOOM that is earlier than v1.666, not all the parameters will work. I'd recommend upgrading to DOOM v1.666 regardless, because some minor bugs were also fixed. There are also new Deathmatch rules that make playing it more enjoyable.

AVAILABLE COMMAND-LINE PARAMETERS

Let's look at all the available command-line parameters, one-by-one. Some are only applicable to network or modem Deathmatch play. One additional option you have is to make a screen capture while you play. You have to use the -devparm parameter to do this. Once inside the game, you can press F1, and that will create a PCX file in your DOOM or DOOM II directory of whatever was on-screen when you pressed F1. Most of the command-line parameters used for DOOM require the -devparm parameter. DOOM II no longer requires the -devparm parameter. Some of these parameters are not listed in the README files for DOOM and DOOM II but work just the same. Also note, where a parameter is listed in brackets (<...>), you do not include these in the string.

The @<filename> parameter is for loading a Response file, which can contain up to 100 command-line arguments. The Response file is a text file that contains all the parameters you want to pass to DOOM or DOOM II. Each parameter has to be on its own line, with a carriage return at the end of the line. The parameters are typed just the same as if you were loading them from the command line. This works very similarly to a batch file.

The -altdeath parameter is for activating the Deathmatch v2.0 rules. This makes all the items such as health kits, ammo, and armor respawn after 30 seconds. The Invulnerability Artifacts and Blur Artifacts do not respawn. This makes it possible to play a single DOOM or DOOM II level for an infinite amount of time without running out of ammo or health. The new Deathmatch rules also make committing suicide illegal, and you will receive a negative frag for doing this. The old rules enabled you to commit suicide if you were low on health to keep your opponent from being able to kill you easily.

The -config <filename> parameter is for loading an alternate configuration file. This is mainly for playing DOOM or DOOM II on a network where the network stations don't have hard disks. You

DOOM PROGRAMMING GURUS   2 ROOM   2 MISSION   1 EPISODE

have to rename the DEFAULT.CFG file to something different, such as MYCONFIG.CFG, and provide a path to the new configuration file when you load the new configuration file.

The -deathmatch parameter can be used in single-player mode and in network and modem games. The reason you would use this in a single-player game would be to test the Deathmatch start locations. In network or modem games, if you don't specify this parameter, DOOM defaults to Cooperative mode. This parameter does not require the -devparm parameter for DOOM.

The -debugfile <parameter> dumps debugging information into a file called debug<parameter>.txt.

The -devparm parameter, as stated previously, puts you into the developer's mode and is used only for DOOM.

The -episode <# of the episode> parameter sets the episode number you wish to play. This is only valid for DOOM and does not require the -devparm parameter. Valid numbers you can pass to this parameter are 1-3.

The -fast parameter is used to make the monsters react like they do in Nightmare mode. They will shoot at you and move up to three times faster than normal. They do not respawn, however. The -fast parameter only works with the -warp parameter.

The -file <filename.wad> parameter is used to load external PWAD files.

The -left parameter is a bizarre parameter that can be used in a three-player network setup. It works in conjunction with the -right parameter.

The -loadgame <game number> parameter is for loading a saved game. Valid game numbers are 0-5. The numbers correspond to the Save Game slots. This does not require the -devparm parameter for DOOM. Also note that saved games made prior to DOOM v1.666 do not work with DOOM v1.666.

The -maxdemo <#> parameter is used to specify the size in kilobytes of a demo file that you record. This is used with the -record parameter. If you don't specify the -maxdemo parameter, then the demo will default to 128KB. To increase this size, you would pass the parameter as follows:

-record <filename> maxdemo 1024. This would allocate 1MB to the file size. Either way, as soon as the maximum size for the demo file is reached, the game ends for both players and you're returned to DOS. The demo file is saved as an LMP file. This parameter does not require the -devparm parameter for DOOM.

The -net <# of players> is for network games with 1-4 players.

The -nodes <# of players> parameter is for starting DOOM or DOOM II as a network game for 1-4 players. If no players are specified, then DOOM defaults to 2. This seems to do the same thing as the -net parameter.

The `-nojoy` parameter disables the joystick.

The `-nomonsters` parameter enables you to start a game without any monsters present. This is good for debugging single-player levels and for playing Deathmatches when you don't want to shoot any monsters. This is used with the `-warp` parameter.

The `-nomouse` parameter disables the mouse.

The `-nomusic` parameter turns off the music.

The `-nosfx` parameter turns off the special-effects sound (such as your gun firing) and all the sounds the monsters make.

The `-nosound` parameter turns off all sound.

The `-playdemo` `<filename>` parameter will run a previously recorded demo LMP file. You don't need to include the LMP extension in the filename. The parameter does not require the `-devparm` parameter for DOOM.

The `-port` `<# of port>` parameter is for setting the port for a network game. This enables more than one group of players to play on a network.

The `-record` `<filename>` parameter is for recording a demo file. You don't need to include the LMP extension in the filename. This parameter does not require the `-devparm` parameter for DOOM.

The `-recordfrom` `<0-5>` `<demo name>` parameter records a demo file from a saved game. This parameter does not require the `-devparm` parameter for DOOM.

The `-respawn` parameter is for making the monsters respawn without playing in Nightmare mode. It works with the `-warp` parameter and does not require the `-devparm` parameter for DOOM.

The `-right` parameter works with the `-left` parameter.

The `-skill` `<skill level>` parameter is for setting the skill level from 1-5. It works with the `-warp` parameter and does not require the `-devparm` parameter for DOOM.

The `-timedemo` `<filename>` parameter is for calculating the number of times the screen is redrawn when playing a demo. You don't need to include the LMP extension in the filename.

The `-timer` `<# of minutes>` parameter is used to make DOOM or DOOM II exit the current level you're playing after the specified time. This option is only useful in Deathmatch mode.

The `-turbo` `<#>` parameter is used to increase the speed at which the player moves while playing the game. Valid numbers are from 0-250.

DOOM
PROGRAMMING
GURUS

2
ROOM

2
MISSION

1
EPISODE

The `-warp` `<episode #>` `<mission #>` parameter for DOOM and the `-warp` `<map #>` parameter for DOOM II are used to warp directly to the specified floor.

The `-wart` `<episode #>` `<mission #>` parameter has the same effect as the `-warp` parameter.

As you can see, there are many command-line parameters available. That is why it's probably better to make batch files to run the different parameters, especially if you use the same parameters over and over to start a WAD file.

1
EPISODE

2
MISSION

2
ROOM

DOOM
PROGRAMMING
GURUS

ROOM 3

RECORDING YOUR LIVING HELL

By David Bruni

The creators of DOOM provided a means of recording your game play. You can make recordings of single-player games and multiplayer Deathmatches; both are done in a similar manner. All you have to do is pass the correct command-line parameters.

If you have access to CompuServe or a similar online service, then you've probably noticed some demo files that have been uploaded. There's everything from demos of people playing through a whole level using nothing but their fists to demos of Level 30 in DOOM II showing how to defeat the Final Boss. There are also multiplayer demo files available that help determine who's the better of two players and determines who owns the bragging rights.

TYPICAL RECORDING STRINGS

A typical recording string would be something like the following:

```
doom -record <filename>
```

This will make a recording with a size of 128KB, the DOOM default. If you want to make a larger recording that is longer in duration, then you can add the -maxdemo parameter to the end of the command line and give it a size in kilobytes. For example:

```
doom -record <filename> -maxdemo 1024
```

This will record a 1MB demo file that will be approximately one hour in duration. One thing to keep in mind is that if you're making a recording of a Deathmatch, both players have to use the same command-line parameters in order for the recording to work. The recording you make will be stored in a file with an .LMP extension. You can quit recording at any time by pressing **Q** or F10, and both players will exit to DOS. The game will also end if the recording reaches the maxdemo size.

You can use the -record parameter in conjunction with any other parameters that you want. You can put it at the end of the command line when you load external WAD files.

If you pass the record parameter to DOOM with the maxdemo added and DOOM crashes to DOS with a Z_MALLOC error, then you don't have enough memory for the size of the demo file you specified. You'll need to decrease the maxdemo size.

To play the demo back, you would type the following: doom -playdemo <filename>. If it is a recording of a Deathmatch, you can see the game through the other player's view by pressing the F12 key.

ROOM 4

By David Bruni

RUNNING A DEMO

After making a recording of your WAD-file game play as described in the previous room, you can take the LMP demo file and add it to the WAD file that you will eventually upload. It will take the place of the built-in demo that runs before you start playing DOOM. It's a good way to show off your WAD file before people play it. You can also reveal a few of the secrets for the level in the demo file if you like.

The best way to add a demo to a WAD file is by using a DOOM editor such as the DOOM Edit Utility that can group multiple WAD files together. You'll have to check the documentation that comes with your editor of choice to see if it can do this.

One thing that you need to be aware of when adding demos into WAD files is that the version numbers of DOOM have to be the same for the WAD file and the demo. You can't take a demo from DOOM 1.2 and incorporate it into a DOOM 1.666 WAD file.

1
EPISODE

2
MISSION

4
ROOM

DOOM
PROGRAMMING
GURUS

ROOM 5

By David Bruni

CHEATER'S GUIDE

Most diehard DOOM players consider using cheat codes to play the game unfair and not in the true spirit of DOOM. But in the development of WAD files, they can make debugging your level much easier.

WHY ARE CHEAT CODES EVEN HERE?

Cheat codes were originally put into DOOM to enable the developers at id Software to test different things in DOOM while they were developing it. Cheat codes can be very useful to the PWAD designer for the same reason. The cheat codes give you the freedom to move around your WAD in God mode, for instance, without getting killed. This makes play-testing your levels easier and faster.

ACTIVATING CHEAT CODES

To activate any of the cheat codes during the game, all you do is type the appropriate code while playing. You don't need to hit ENTER or anything else. To deactivate a cheat code, just type the code again. There are a few differences in the cheat codes between DOOM and DOOM II. These will be pointed out as we come to them.

ENSURING THE PLAYABILITY OF YOUR WAD FILE

To ensure the playability of your WAD file, you should play-test it without cheat codes every now and then to make sure that everything works as you intended. It's very easy to get into the habit of using cheat codes all the time. This can work against the PWAD designer to a certain extent. If you play your level in the God mode all the time, then it will be hard for you to determine the difficulty level of your WAD file. The God mode should be used only after you've played your level without it and decided that the number of monsters isn't too overwhelming for the average player.

THE GOD MODE

To activate the God mode, you type IDDQD any time during the game. The God mode is also known as *degreelessness* mode. There also is another way around your game other than using the God mode—and in certain situations it may be more desirable than the God mode. What you'll have to do is set up a batch file or type all the parameters to load your WAD file and use the parameter -NOMONSTERS. This way you can play test your level and not have to worry about using the God mode, shooting all the monsters, or trying to avoid them.

ALL WEAPONS, FULL HEALTH, AND ALL KEYS

The cheat code IDKFA can be used to get all the weapons, full health, and all the keys. In DOOM II, you can type IDFA to get full ammo without getting the keys. Being able to get the keys can make getting to remote parts of your WAD file easier than in Wolfenstein 3D. In Wolfenstein 3D you had to find the keys, because there was no cheat code that gave them to you. The IDFA code for DOOM II enables you to cheat to a certain extent without taking all the fun out of normal game play.

NO-CLIPPING MODE

The no-clipping cheat codes, IDSPISPOPD for DOOM and IDCLIP for DOOM II, make getting the keys with the previously described code unnecessary. With the no-clipping mode, you don't need the keys—you can walk right through doors and walls. This makes accessing those remote areas even easier. All you have to do is type the code, switch to map mode, and go where you need to go. One problem with using the no-clipping mode is that you won't be able to pick up anything such as health or ammo. You also won't be able to use the transporters. This mode can make some debugging tasks rather difficult and should only be used to get to remote parts of the level. You should never design a level that requires the use of the no-clipping mode.

SEEING THE ENTIRE MAP IN MAP MODE

Another handy cheat code that can be used in developing WAD files is IDDT. This only works when you toggle to map mode by pressing the Tab key. When you type this code, the entire map will be displayed. Typing it again will display all the monsters in the level. The monsters that have been activated can be seen moving around. If a monster hasn't been activated, it will appear as stationary.

WARPING TO DIFFERENT LEVELS

When testing a multiple-episode WAD file, you can type IDCLEV, followed by the mission and episode numbers, and warp straight to that level. For example, if you type IDCLEV23, that will warp you to Episode 2, Mission 3 in DOOM 1. In DOOM II, it would take you to Map (level) 23. DOOM II changed the way the levels were arranged. This way you can check out many different levels without having to complete a level or restart the game.

PICKING UP ADDITIONAL ITEMS

Some of the other items can be picked up by typing IDBEHOLD, followed by one of the following letters: S gives you the Berserk Pack; I gives you invisibility; V gives you invulnerability; A gives you the Computer Map; R gives you the Radiation Suit; and L gives you the Light Amplification Visor. These are all useful things that you may need at one time or another.

CHAINSAW ONLY

I'm not sure why this cheat code is a separate command. It gives you only the chainsaw. You access it by typing IDCHOPPERS.

YOUR POSITION IN HEX CODE

The final cheat code doesn't really have a practical purpose as far I can tell. It gives you your position in the map in hex notation. You type IDMYPOS to use it. It's possible in a Deathmatch to use this to let your opponent know your exact position in case you get stuck.

ROOM 6

PLAYING WITH OTHERS

By David Bruni

There are many different opinions about what constitutes a good Deathmatch or Cooperative-mode WAD file. However you configure your file, there are a few specific details that you need to pay attention to.

COOPERATIVE WAD FILES

When you play DOOM or DOOM II in Cooperative mode, you are working as a team with one or more people. The first thing that you need to keep in mind is where are your starting positions are going to be. It's a good idea to group co-op starts together. There are, however, two problems with this. First, if you have a big WAD file that occupies a lot of area, each player may die at a different time. This means that a lot of the time you have to play catch-up. In other words, you might die, but your partner won't. Then you have to restart and try to find your partner to resume play. Secondly, you could insert more than four co-op starts in large WAD files, but you'll have the same problem with players dying at different times and locations throughout the level. As a developer, there's really not much you can do to avoid this.

Another consideration for co-op WAD files is to make sure you put in enough ammunition and weapons for each player. Where you would normally put in one chaingun, for a co-op WAD you might try putting in two instead. That way the players don't look at each other and say, "You pick up the gun; I'll get the next one." Thus, when you're inserting objects for co-op WADs, try doubling up on the items.

Designing WADs for co-op play has to be approached differently than designing WADs made for Deathmatches. You probably want to avoid tight hallways that would require the players to move through them in single file. This will minimize the chances of the players accidentally shooting each other in the back. (There's nothing worse than killing your partner by mistake.)

You should make any elevators large enough for two people to fit on. That way the players won't have to wait on each other or have one of the players reach another area populated by lots of enemies and be overwhelmed.

DEATHMATCH WAD FILES

Deathmatches are probably more popular to play than co-op levels, and thus most of the levels you design will be Deathmatch levels. Some designers even make levels that are Deathmatch-only and not recommended for single-player mode. Other designers do Deathmatch levels with no monsters in them. It's probably preferable to put monsters in the level and let the players decide whether or not they want the monsters in there or not. Keeping the monsters from appearing can be accomplished by using the -nomonsters parameter in the command line.

When you design Deathmatch levels, you don't have to worry about the locations of the starts as much as in co-op levels. It's a good idea to put in lots of Deathmatch starts in different locations throughout the level. It tends to get boring playing a level where you restart in the same location every time. Eight or 12 starts should be adequate for a medium-to-large WAD.

It's also nice to provide a lot of ambush settings where the players can lie in wait for their opponent(s). Windows overlooking the locations of the bigger weapons are also fun for the players. That's the key to good Deathmatch WADs: making them fun. It's always a kick to watch your opponent retrieve a weapon and then run smack-dab into your ambush and get wasted.

Overly large WAD files should be avoided for Deathmatches. It's easy to lose track of your opponent in a big level. It's no fun to wander aimlessly around a level looking for something or someone to shoot. Smaller, well-constructed levels are more challenging and more fun.

Probably the most important thing to remember when creating Deathmatch levels is to not put starting positions behind one-way doors. This is the single most frustrating design flaw in a Deathmatch. Also avoid creating areas that can trap a player where the only way out is to be shot by the other player. This is really not a fair thing to do.

DON'T LOSE YOUR PERSPECTIVE

Sometimes when you're designing WAD files, it's easy to lose your perspective on the game play. Many beginners get carried away by all these grandiose ideas of how they can beat the other players and forget about providing an enjoyable experience for everyone involved. Real-world playability can be the difference between a ho-hum level that gets lukewarm response and a great level that everyone wants. (And of course, generating demand is the goal of every PWAD author.) Design a level that people talk about and enjoy playing.

ORIGINAL IDEAS

One difficulty in designing WAD files is coming up with original ideas. With thousands of WAD files already available, new ideas are hard to come by. If you play a WAD file and see something that you would like to use for yourself, you have two choices. One is to simply take whatever you want, with no regard for the person who came up with the idea. The better course of action is to write the person who came up with the original idea and ask them if they would mind if you used it. Nine times out of 10, it will be OK and flattering to them for you to use their idea. This is a matter of common courtesy.

TRY YOUR OWN LEVELS

There are as many opinions about what makes a good Deathmatch level as there are players. Try your level out in a Deathmatch and see how it plays for you. Remember, you can't cheat in a Deathmatch, and thus you can see for yourself if the level is fun or if it is just another one of those levels with a lot of monsters in it and little or no ammo. If it's not fun to play for you, then chances are it won't be fun for other people, either. You do not want to make your levels so hard that players quit in frustration.

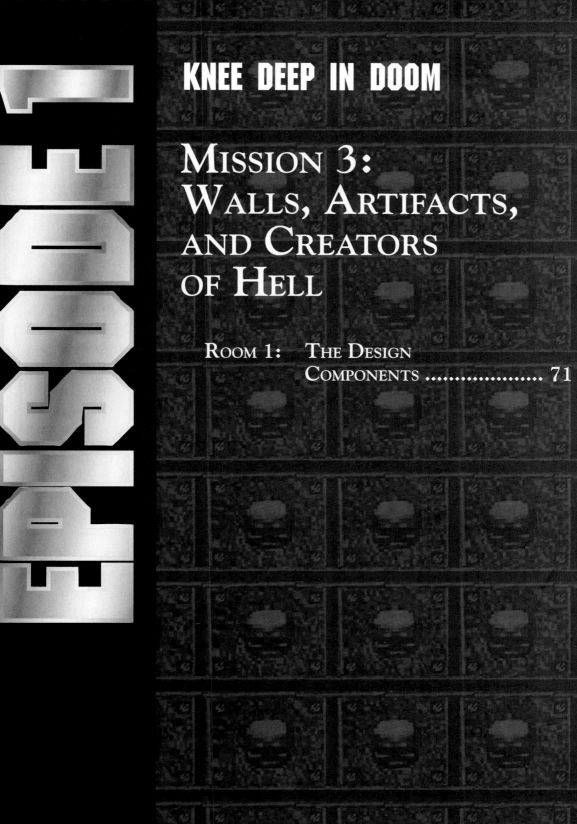

KNEE DEEP IN DOOM

MISSION 3: WALLS, ARTIFACTS, AND CREATORS OF HELL

ROOM 1

THE DESIGN COMPONENTS

By David Bruni

This room will discuss the various components that are in DOOM and DOOM II. These include all the monsters in the game, your arsenal of weapons, and all the items that you can pick up while playing DOOM and DOOM II. We'll also talk more about walls and doors and the sounds of DOOM and DOOM II.

DOOM ENEMIES

As stated in earlier missions, the monsters in DOOM are tougher than those found in Wolfenstein 3D. Some of the DOOM monsters are comparable to those in Wolfenstein 3D, but DOOM generally has many more.

Most editors permit you to assign any monster to a particular skill level. This can be useful when you're designing a WAD file. You should provide at least two different skill levels: a hard level with lots of monsters for the diehard DOOMer, and an easy level for the average player. You have to keep in mind that you're trying to make a WAD file that will appeal to a wide variety of players. Making at least two skill levels will help you reach a broader range of players. There have been some WAD files that overdid the number of monsters in a level. For most people, these are not enjoyable WAD files to play. Your level should always be made playable without the user resorting to cheat codes. Some people tend to ignore real-world playability, but it's an important consideration.

You also need to be careful when placing monsters. If you get them too close together or too close to a wall, they won't move. What happens is the monsters can be placed partly in the wall itself, and they become stuck. There isn't a hard boundary defined by the editors to prevent this. Some editors actually display the monsters as circles, along with their approximate size. This is handy for placing monsters and still maintaining a reasonable distance between them.

You may have noticed that the monsters will fight each other. They'll do that as long as they are of different types. For example, the Troopers will fight the Imps, but the Imps won't fight each other. This can lead to all sorts of interesting scenarios. You can find out really fast which are the tougher monsters. You can also fool the unsuspecting player into thinking that an area is harder than it looks. Sometimes the only way to make it through a WAD file is by getting the monsters to fight and kill each other.

Another thing to consider before placing monsters is: Will they fit in the area where you want to put them? You have to provide enough clearance in your rooms so the monsters don't end up stuck in a wall or ceiling. Table 10.1 presents a list of height and width clearances for each of the characters. Remember, these are minimum clearances. It's probably a good idea to increase the height and width clearances a little to insure that there will be no problems.

Table 10.1. Minimum clearances in units for various DOOM characters.

Character	Minimum Vertical Clearance	Minimum Horizontal Clearance
Player	56 units	33 units
Troopers	56 units	44 units
Sergeants	56 units	44 units
Imps	56 units	44 units
Demons	56 units	64 units
Spectres	56 units	64 units
Cacodemons	56 units	64 units
Lost Souls	56 units	56 units
Barons of Hell	64 units	64 units
Cyberdemons	110 units	110 units
Spider Masterminds	100 units	256 units

You also need to consider the width of the monsters and players. A monster is less likely to cross through a door that is near or at the minimum width clearance. The player is able to squeeze through doorways that the monsters can't. You can use this information to your advantage in certain situations.

Determining if a monster will walk up or down steps is mostly done by trial and error. There doesn't appear to be any firm guidelines, such as there are for height and side clearances. Monsters are limited to a maximum height they can step up, just as the player is: 24 units. The problem, though, is that a monster may or may not step up or down that high depending on the depth of the step. If one or more of your monsters won't go up or down stairs, try adjusting the height of the step first, then adjust the depth of the step. Monsters also seem to be afraid to step off a ledge that they can't step up onto. In other words, if you have a ledge over 25 units in height, the monsters won't step off it. This way, you don't have to assign the line attribute "nothing can cross" or "monsters can't cross." This is also good because if you shoot monsters on a ledge such as this and hit them just right, they fall off the ledge. This adds to the realism of the game. (This doesn't apply to the floating or flying monsters.)

Monsters also seem reluctant to step out onto a narrow walkway that drops down on both sides. You can use this technique to limit the monsters' mobility. If a walkway has less than the minimum side clearance, the monsters probably won't go out on that walkway.

DOOM PROGRAMMING GURUS   1 ROOM   3 MISSION   1 EPISODE

One final thing you need to be aware of when adding monsters to a WAD file is not to use so many monsters as to overload the DOOM engine. The engine can only display so many things at once. When you overload the engine with too many monsters and other objects, things can get unpredictable. Objects can disappear or you may get the Hall-Of-Mirrors effect. So try not to overdo it.

The Former Humans are the easiest monsters to kill and aren't too much of a threat to you as a player. They are fairly slow and usually only take one or two shots to kill. These guys are useful to scatter throughout your WAD file, especially at the beginning. You can use them as a warm-up for things to come. They're also good to use in ambushes in which the player crosses a line and secret doors open to release these guys from hidden rooms. They're very versatile, and four or five can give the player a good fight. These monsters are also known as Troopers. When a player kills one of these monsters, the monster will drop a clip of ammo. Keep this in mind when you start to place weapons and ammo.

The Former Human Sergeants are similar in appearance and actions as the Former Human Troopers. They are a little bit tougher to kill, but not much. They can usually be stopped with a shotgun blast, or one or two well-placed pistol shots. Placing these monsters in a WAD file is similar to placing Former Humans. Three to four Sergeants are a good challenge for the player. The Sergeants do move a little faster than the Troopers do. When a player kills a Sergeant, the Sergeant drops a shotgun that the player can pick up. These monsters are like a cross between the two kinds of guards in Wolfenstein 3D: the regular guards and the SS guards. They don't have machine guns—as do the SS guards—but they are a little harder to kill than regular guards.

The Imps are a new type of monster, and they are not comparable to any monster from Wolfenstein 3D. Imps don't have guns but instead shoot fireballs out of their mouths. These fireballs can hurt a player considerably. Imps are good to put on ledges, because they can shoot a long way and are hard to kill from far away. At close quarters, Imps can physically attack the player and make him lose health just as quickly as they can by hitting him with fireballs. When designing WAD files, you probably won't want to use more than three of these in one area against the player. With more than that, the player can be overwhelmed, unless he's heavily armed. One shotgun blast can usually take care of an Imp, whereas it takes about three or four pistol shots to kill one. As you add monsters, you need to be cognizant of the number of shots required to kill them, so that your WAD file is challenging but not unfair. No one wants to be accused of making a WAD file that is too hard to play.

The large, pink Demons aren't equipped with weapons, but that doesn't make them any easier for the player to kill. These guys are very good to place in close quarters, because they are hard to kill. It usually takes one well-placed shotgun blast, or two to three wounding shotgun blasts, to take a Demon down. Demons move slowly, so if you put them in a fairly open area, it's easy for the player to out-run or out-maneuver them. They're much more effective in small, enclosed areas. The shotgun or the chainsaw is the best weapon to use against these monsters. If you arm the player with only the pistol, remember that it takes about five or six shots from it to kill the Demons. Don't put five or six Demons in one room and give the player only the pistol to deal with them. Your WAD file has to be playable. If you get the reputation of making unplayable WAD files, people will be reluctant to download them.

The Spectres behave just like the pink Demons, only they're harder to see. Spectres can be used anywhere that you would use a Demon. They can be very effective in dark rooms, because they're hard to see in the dark—the darker the room, the more dangerous they are. In certain situations, they can be almost invisible to the player and are great for surprise attacks.

Lost Souls are one of the two flying monsters in DOOM. They're nothing more than flying skulls, but used correctly, they can be quite challenging to the player. They work well in small, confining rooms but seem to be better suited to large rooms with high ceilings. That way, they're free to move and fly around. Running into a nest of five or six Lost Souls is always a good way to keep the player on his toes. It will usually only take one well-placed shotgun blast to kill them.

Cacodemons are the first of the really tough monsters. They're big, they're bad, they fly, and they take about four shotgun blasts to kill. Their main weakness is that they can't move very fast. They're most effective in large open areas. They can also squeeze into small openings and walkways but are fairly easy to kill at close range. All the player has to do is get in their face and keep shooting, and they'll die pretty much without a fight. But a surprise attack or ambush at close range by the Cacodemons can be deadly. If you plan on using a lot of these monsters in one room, be sure to arm the player with at least the shotgun or chaingun and enough ammo so he can put up a good fight. Otherwise, a couple of fireballs from the Cacos will kill the player quickly.

Barons of Hell are tough. It takes 15 shotgun blasts or 100 bullets from the chaingun to kill one. Barons should be used sparingly toward the middle or end of a WAD. Barons don't move very fast, and their fireballs can be side-stepped with a little practice. No more than two or three should be used in one area, and you must make sure that the player has the right weapons to fight them. It's totally unfair to put the player up against a Baron of Hell with only the pistol to defend himself. If the player has the shotgun, then use one Baron. If you've made it possible for the player to get the chaingun, then you can use two Barons. Remember, though, that it takes 100 shots to kill one, so supply enough ammo to accomplish this. If you've given the player the rocket launcher, then you can use three or four Barons. It takes about five rockets to kill a Baron. The plasma gun uses about 50 cells to kill a Baron. It might be a bit of overkill to give a player a plasma gun unless there's a room full of Barons.

The Spider Mastermind and the Cyberdemon are the hardest monsters to kill and should only be used in special situations under the right circumstances. They have not been particularly popular with players. A lot of people don't like to see them in WAD files because they're so hard to kill without cheating. There are ways around this, though. You can always put an invulnerability sphere

DOOM
PROGRAMMING
GURUS

1
ROOM

3
MISSION

1
EPISODE

close by, so the player has a chance. The minimum gun that the player needs to have a chance against them is the rocket launcher. Anything less and there's not much hope for the player. It still takes about 15 to 20 rockets to kill either one of these monsters. The plasma gun is better for both of them, and the BFG 9000 can usually take them out with no problem. So if you have to use one of these two monsters, make it so the player can kill them without too much trouble.

The DeHackEd program does enable you to change all the monsters in DOOM into something else. There are patches available that change the monsters into all sorts of weird creatures. Some are nothing more than a curiosity, such as Barney DOOM, in which DOOM creatures are replaced by everyone's not-so-favorite, purple-and-green singing dinosaur. Other patches, such as *Alien* DOOM (based on the popular sci-fi movie trilogy), have taken the game to new heights of sophistication. This particular WAD file has to rank as one of the best available. It takes a lot of work to make a WAD file as good as *Alien* DOOM, and such an undertaking is not for the novice. Changing the monsters in DOOM takes a lot of thought and planning to be successful.

DOOM II ENEMIES

With the release of DOOM II, id Software pulled out all the stops. They improved everything about DOOM. One of the most obvious improvements is in the new monsters in DOOM II. There are eight new ones to contend with, and they're all bad news for the unsuspecting player.

One of the first monsters you're likely to run into is the Former Human Commando. They're a lot like the Former Sergeants, only these guys are packing chainguns. The good thing about Commandoes is that when you kill one, you can pick up his chaingun. This makes locating chainguns in your levels almost unnecessary. You'll probably be using quite a few of these in your DOOM II levels. Try not to go overboard with them, though, because their extra firepower is more than enough to destroy an average player. If you've planned ahead and provided the player with a chaingun of his own, as well as the double-barreled shotgun, then three or four Former Human Commandoes would be a good start in most areas of your WAD file. You could increase this number if you've given the player an opportunity to get the rocket launcher or the plasma gun.

DOOM II in "Ultra-Violence" mode is very difficult to complete without resorting to cheat codes. If you plan on using as many of the new monsters as were used in the original release of DOOM II, be sure and make at least two different skill settings. Otherwise, you may get more than a few e-mail messages about your level being too hard. I realize that it's *supposed* to be hard, but DOOM II does provide an easier skill-level setting. It may be hard to resist making a really tough level with all the new available monsters, but try not to use so many monsters that your level becomes impossible to play without cheating. Most of the new monsters in DOOM II are much harder to kill than the monsters in DOOM. Keep that in mind when you start adding them to your WAD file.

The Hell Knights look and act very similar to the Barons of Hell from DOOM. The main difference is that they are a little easier to kill. You should use them just about anywhere that you would normally use a Baron of Hell. With them being easier to kill, you can almost use them at a two-to-one ratio as compared to the Barons. The Hell Knights fit in very well as an intermediate-type monster. They're not as tough as a Baron, but they're tougher than the lesser monsters such as pink Demons. If you plan on using some of these in your level, make sure that you give the player at least the assault shotgun or the chaingun to deal with them. There's just no way to kill any of the new monsters with only the pistol. The player will die long before he can fire enough pistol shots to kill them. Even with the shotgun, it takes anywhere from five to 10 hits to kill the new monsters. This has been a point of contention since the very first WAD files began to appear. Some of the designers thought that a hard level was one that had 10 Barons of Hell, and then those same designers failed to provide the player with adequate weapons to deal with them. Such WAD files soon faded away when nobody wanted to play them. To make it into the WAD Hall of Fame, your level has to be many things—but being impossible to beat isn't one of them. Making it unbeatable will get your WAD file deleted quicker than any other thing you can do.

The Mancubus is another difficult monster to contend with. There's really not a monster in DOOM to compare him with. Both of his arms are guns that shoot out fireballs, and he'll shoot six fireballs at a time at the player. You'll probably want to use him in large open areas because of his firepower. The good thing for the player is that the Mancubus isn't very fast and can be avoided without too much trouble. He's also good to use as a long-range shooter. His fireballs can carry a long distance. If the player is equipped with only the shotgun, then two or three of these monsters would be about all they could handle. It takes about nine shots from the shotgun—or four rockets—to kill a Mancubus. The plasma gun seems to be the best weapon to use against him. It only takes a couple of blasts from the plasma gun to kill him. So plan on giving the player a decent weapon against these guys.

The Revenant is a rocket-launching, walking skeleton that packs some heavy firepower. His rockets will take out a player without much problem. Up close, he'll also pound the player with his fists. A Revenant is good to use in small rooms or large areas. He's a little easier to kill than the Mancubus— it only takes about four shotgun blasts or two rockets. You could use a Revenant in place of a Baron of Hell or a Hell Knight. Three or four Revenants will give the player a good fight. He also is good as a long-range shooter, because his rockets carry a long way. He can be extremely tough in small areas, because the player won't be able to use the rocket launcher and will either have to use the shotgun or plasma gun. The Revenant's punching ability can be very annoying to the player, too.

The Pain Elemental is another very nasty monster to deal with. He's similar to a Cacodemon in that he can fly through the air and isn't confined to the ground. His power is that he spits out Lost Souls almost as fast as the player can shoot them. Not only does the player have to try to kill the Pain Elemental, but he also has to kill all the accompanying Lost Souls. It doesn't take long for a room to fill up with the Lost Souls that the Pain Elemental can spit at you. The best weapon to use against one of these is probably the plasma gun. It also seems to be the best gun to kill the Lost Souls with. Large, open areas with high ceilings are the place to put these monsters. The Pain Elemental himself doesn't move very fast, but the Lost Souls can fly pretty fast and are hard to hit in large rooms. When the player does finally kill the Pain Elemental, it'll spit out three last Lost Souls—just for spite.

The Arachnotrons look like little Spider Masterminds, but instead of having chainguns to shoot, they have plasma guns. They're very hard to kill because they can shoot long distances, and it's hard to get up close to them without being killed. Luckily, they're nowhere near as hard to kill as Spider Masterminds. Therefore, using them in your level shouldn't be received with too much objection— that is, unless you use too many of them in one area. If you do that, make sure you give the player the plasma gun so he can be on even terms with them. You'll probably want to use these monsters in wide open places with plenty of room for the player to move around and try to avoid the plasma gun that these guys have. Small, closed rooms may be a little too much for handling the Arachnotrons and probably should be avoided. A whole nest of Arachnotrons could prove to be interesting.

The Arch-Vile has to be one of the hardest monsters to contend with. Not only is he hard to kill, but he'll also bring the dead monsters back to life. All sorts of devious uses come to mind for the Arch-Vile. The fact that he can bring other monsters back from the dead makes him very hard to contend with. You'll normally only want to use one of these monsters in your level, but two of them could be interesting because they could bring *each other* back from the dead, too. Another possibility is to put one of these monsters in a room that opens with a tripwire that the player crosses. This room could be behind the player so that all of the monsters the player has already killed are brought back and are waiting for him if he had to backtrack. The important thing to ensure when using the Arch-Vile is that the level doesn't become too difficult to complete.

I don't know if the Final Boss on level 30 can be considered a real monster or not. And I can't say for sure if it would be a good idea to use this in your WAD file. After all, level 30 is the toughest level, and the way that it's designed forces the player to shoot as the column is coming up. You'll have to decide for yourself if you think this is a good idea to use in a WAD file or not.

As a final note, remember that DOOM II added two Wolfenstein 3D levels, which include the SS guards. They look the same as they always did, complete with their machine guns and everything. If you want to add some variety to your WAD file, try adding a few of these guys to it. They even sound the same as they used to.

WEAPONS AND AMMUNITION

The DeHackEd program will enable you to change all the guns into either rapid-fire weapons of death or just about anything you want. If you do plan on using this program, be sure to let the player know through a text file that the DeHackEd program will change the DOOM.EXE file permanently. Warn the players that they need to make a backup of the DOOM.EXE file before running the DeHackEd program. This way they can restore DOOM to it's original setup.

The weapons in DOOM are a lot better and more fun than what was available in Wolfenstein 3D. Of course, this is only logical because the monsters are tougher.

When a WAD file first starts, by default the player has the pistol. The pistol is only useful against the lesser monsters, and you should give the player the chance to pick up the shotgun (at least) some- time soon after the game starts. The shotgun and two boxes of bullets should be adequate to start a WAD file. Bear in mind that at skill level 1 (the easiest level), the number of bullets you get when you pick up a box of bullets is greater. The shotgun is probably the best all-around weapon in DOOM. It can handle all the monsters up to the Barons of Hell. However, the shotgun is not very useful against the Cyberdemon or Spider Mastermind. You should put a couple of shotguns in your WAD file.

One way to make it appear that a level has less ammo than it really does is to put two boxes of ammo next to each other. That way the player has to be careful when picking it up. He can waste a lot of needless ammo if he picked up ammo when he didn't really require it. For example, if the player already has 48 shotgun shells, and then picks up a box of 20 shotgun shells, he would, in effect, waste 18 shells. This is because DOOM and DOOM II limit the player to no more than 50 shotgun shells without first picking up the backpack.

In most circumstances, you don't want to force the player to run out of ammo and use his fists. You can, however, use the Berserk Pack in your WAD, which will give the player super-punching ability plus full health. If you do want to make it hard for the player, at least give him the chainsaw. It's useful against most of the monsters, with the exception of the Barons and higher. The chainsaw can be really fun in Deathmatches. So make sure you scatter a couple of them around your WAD file.

The chaingun is useful against just about all the monsters except the last two big monsters. It's big- gest drawback is that it uses up ammunition very quickly. It is good for clearing a room full of lesser monsters. For example, if you want to pack 20 or so Imps and Sergeants in a room, then the chaingun would be perfect for the player. Just make sure to throw in a few boxes of ammo somewhere.

You should always plan to put the chaingun somewhere in your level. You'll usually want to put it towards the middle of your level, unless you plan on using a lot of monsters at the beginning. You also must decide whether you want to make getting the chaingun easy or hard. You can put it in the middle of a room, where the player only has to grab it, or you can make it tough and put it behind something so that the player has to push a remote button. It's probably a good idea not to tease the player with weapons (or anything else for that matter) that they can't retrieve. This will tend to make a player angry or frustrated.

A good but not devious trick is to put the chaingun in a sector by itself so you can transform all the lines around into tripwires. This way, when the player crosses any of the lines to get the chaingun, you can make the tripwires open secret doors with some surprise monsters behind them.

The rocket launcher is your next available gun. It's a great weapon. It can take care of just about any of the monsters in DOOM. It's also one of the best weapons you can use in a Deathmatch. One shot from the rocket launcher and your opponent is toast. Some of the best Deathmatches I've played have been fought over the rocket launcher. You should always include it when you design Deathmatch WADs. You might even want to put two rocket launchers in a Deathmatch WAD.

Most of the DOOM editors will permit you to restrict any weapon or other object to appear only in Deathmatch mode. This is convenient because you'll normally want more weapons in a Deathmatch than in a single-player WAD. You can also do this for ammo, health, and monsters. Some people like to have no monsters at all in their Deathmatches. You can either leave the monsters out or include the monsters and leave it up to the players to use the `-nomonsters` parameter when starting the WAD. This way you can please more people with your WAD file.

The plasma rifle is another good gun to have in a Deathmatch. It gives one player a big edge and can lead to fierce fighting to acquire it. A very good scenario is to have the plasma gun in the middle of a room surrounded by a lot of hiding places for ambushes. This can lead to some very tense situations in which one player is waiting on the other to grab the gun. You'll open the door and see the gun, but in the back of your mind you know the other guy is in there waiting for you.

You can defeat most of the monsters with the plasma rifle rather easily—with the possible exception of the Cyberdemon. With this in mind, you should design your levels around an appropriate hierarchy of available weapons. Putting the plasma rifle at the beginning of your WAD to use against Troopers and Imps probably isn't a good idea. When you place the plasma rifle, make sure you use appropriate monsters with it. That way, the monsters and the difficulty level compliment each other. Remember, you are trying for a good balance when you design WAD files.

The BFG 9000 is the last gun available in DOOM. It can make quick work of all the monsters in DOOM, including the Cyberdemon. It's also good for clearing a room full of lesser monsters. It's not the best weapon for all-around use, because it shoots slowly and uses a lot of ammo. Normally you'll want the player to work hard for the BFG. Make them have to think about how to get it. Don't just put it in easy reach. It's the most powerful gun, and the player needs to earn it. The only time you would want to give it to the player easily is if you have a room full of monsters guarding the exit. You then could give the player only enough ammo to kill some of the monsters. You don't want to make it too easy to beat your level. The BFG can give the player the feeling of total power—that is, until he runs out of ammunition.

DOOM II only added one new gun that wasn't available in DOOM. That's the doubled-barreled combat shotgun. It's a great gun and can take out two or three lesser monsters at the same time. Its only drawback is that it doesn't reload very quickly. Its extra punch does seem to make up for this, though. You'll want to use one of these in all your levels. Players expect to be able to use it, and it's a good idea to give the players what they want.

ARTIFACTS AND POWERUPS

Now let's consider the various objects that the player can pick up as he plays through your WAD file. There are lots of different artifacts that you can include, and you need to know when and where to use them.

First of all, keys are important to your WAD file. If you make key doors in your WAD file, you need to include the correct color key to open the doors. There are three different colored keys and two different types of keys. There are the keys that look like cards, and there are the ones that look like skulls. Both types are interchangeable. It doesn't matter which type you use—it's mostly personal preference. Just make sure you match the line attribute for the key door to the same color of key you use. And make sure you don't accidentally put the key behind the door that it's supposed to open. (I know that sounds a little elementary, but it's an easy mistake to make.) Make the player work for the keys—but not too hard. Remember that it's easy for the player to get frustrated looking for the keys and end up typing the cheat code to get it. You can use as many key doors as you like, and it's always good to require the player to find all three to exit.

As you design a level, you need to stock it with ammunition. Deciding how much ammo to put into a level is where play-testing comes into the picture. You may have to play your level numerous times before you feel comfortable with the amount of ammo you've included. Keep in mind that you're making the WAD file for other people, and their skill levels vary. The last thing anybody wants to do is run out of ammo. That leaves the player feeling helpless. This is one of the hardest things to judge when you design a WAD file. It is helpful to have a friend or relative play-test your level as you design it. Make sure they don't know where all the secrets and enemies are, so you can get a natural reaction. This will help you decide where your WAD file needs work.

Be sure to include the correct ammo for the weapons in your WAD file. You don't want to use a box of rockets when the player will need shotgun shells. You can scatter ammunition in various places or make a hidden cache with lots of ammo.

Ammunition comes in various shapes, sizes, and quantities. When you kill a Former Human, he drops an ammo clip with five bullets in it. Likewise, when you kill a Sergeant, he drops a shotgun with four shells in it. This may or may not help you design your level. It's good to know, but don't rely on it. The clips that the Former Humans drop are the same as the regular bullet clips. The big green boxes of ammo hold 50 rounds. It will take four boxes to fill up the chaingun. The bullets for the chaingun and the pistol are the same. When you pick up the chaingun, it will only have 20 rounds in it. That's not too many. Throw a couple boxes of bullets next to the chaingun when you include it. That way the player can use the chaingun to kill more than three or four monsters. It can get very frustrating having a good gun and no ammo to go along with it. The whole idea is to make a WAD file that's fun to play, one that is both challenging but fair. If your only intention in making a WAD file is to trick and confound the player, he'll tire of this and quit playing your WAD file to go on to the next one. There are thousands of WAD files available, and it's very easy for someone to begin another one.

There are four ways to reload the shotgun. First is the way I mentioned before: kill the Sergeant and pick up his four dropped shotgun shells. The second is to pick up a pack of four shells. The third way is to pick up a whole box of shells—which holds 20 rounds in the "Ultra-Violence" level. (Remember, the amount of ammo the player gets is more for skill level 1.) The last way to reload the shotgun is by picking up the shotgun itself in the level. It holds eight shots.

It's easier to use a box of shotgun shells than to use five separate clips of shells. Also keep in mind that until the player picks up the backpack, he'll only be able to carry 50 shots for the shotgun. So two boxes will almost fill them up. That's a good way to start a level. Put the shotgun within easy reach, along with two boxes of shells. That gets the player ready to start the level with a good feeling.

Loading up the rocket launcher is not so easy. When you pick up the rocket launcher itself, you only get two rockets with it. Boxes of rockets aren't very generous, either; you only get five rockets per box. Remember playing the Tower of Babel, E2M8 of DOOM? This is a killer level for Deathmatch-mode because once all the boxes of rockets are gone, you can only get two rockets at a time when you pick up the rocket launcher. At two shots per clip, it takes forever to kill the Cyberdemon in that level. You can also use singles of rockets. Those are good for placing in rooms, and you can practically use them as decorations. The rocket launcher is a good all-around gun, and you should use it in all your WAD files. Players like to use it. Sometimes you can check to see if the player is paying attention by using the rocket launcher in a small room and then attacking the player with monsters. If the player isn't fast enough and doesn't change guns, he'll blow himself up. This is a fair way to test the player's skill level without being too blatant.

The plasma gun comes with 40 cells when it's picked up. But again, as far as ammunition goes, this isn't very much. The ammo for the plasma gun comes in two sizes. The cell pack holds 20 cells. The energy charge or bulk cell holds 100 cells. Six of the larger cell packs will fill up the plasma gun after the player has picked up the backpack. The cell packs also work with the BFG 9000.

Remember: Throw some ammunition around your level, play it, then decide if the amount of ammunition is adequate for the amount of monsters.

The exploding barrels can't technically be considered ammo, but you can use them to kill monsters. It's good to use barrels to even the odds by placing them in rooms that have lots of monsters. They're also good to use in these situations because the monsters can blow up the barrels just as the player can. Strategic placing of barrels will help enhance your WAD file. It's also quite fun to frag your opponent in a Deathmatch by blowing up a barrel! Therefore, place the barrels so they can be used as well as looked at.

You must also be sure that your level has enough health paraphernalia for the player to make it through. Players like to win when they play, so you need to provide enough health factors that the player can survive long enough to beat the level. Again, your level doesn't have to be easy, but it should be beatable.

The blue bottles are Health Potions. Each bottle only increases the player's health by 1 percent, but they do enable him to boost his health past the normal 100 percent. It takes a lot of these blue bottles to really provide any benefit, so they're mostly cosmetic. The players have become accustomed to seeing them in DOOM levels, so you might throw in a few for looks. The Stimpacks, which are little medical kits, will give the player a 10 percent boost in health. It's a good idea to scatter a few of these around your level. The Medikits are even better; they will give the player a 25 percent increase in health. It's best to use these in areas with heavy concentrations of monsters. Just like deciding how much ammo your level needs, the same principles apply to the amount of health you put in your level. The only way to determine this is by play-testing your level a few times. You should use enough health paraphernalia to enable the player to move from one area to the next without running so low on health paraphernalia that a few shots will kill him.

You may not know this, but the Berserk Pack not only gives the player super punching ability but also increases his health to 100 percent. This enables you to provide fewer Medikits and Stimpacks in your level. Limiting the total number of objects is not as critical as it was with DOOM 1.2, because version 1.4 increased the savegame buffer. What this means is you can use more things in your level and not have to worry that the game will abort with an error message because of too many artifacts in the level.

Armor comes in three types. Each piece of Spiritual Armor, which is a fancy term for the helmets, will give the player a protection-factor increase of 1 percent. The Spiritual Armor does, however, let the player go up over the 200 percent level. It's good to scatter some of this armor throughout your level. The green Security Armor will give the player a 100 percent armor bonus. You'll usually use only one of these in your level, preferably near the beginning. The armor bonuses are a gimme, and you would normally not make the player have to work hard to acquire these. The blue Combat Armor is the heavy-duty armor and will give the player an armor bonus of 200 percent. Again, you'll probably want to use only one set of blue armor in your level, unless you plan on making a large level with lots of monsters.

One of the others things that you'll want to use in almost all your levels is the backpack. This will let the player pick up more ammo. It also gives the player extra ammo when he picks it up. This is an important thing to use when designing levels, especially if you plan on using lots of monsters.

Radiation suits should be used anywhere you have acid pits that the player has to cross. This is particularly true if you're using the −20 percent sector attribute for the acid pits. It won't take long for the player to die crossing acid pits of this type. If your design is such that the player will have to cross through the acid pit more than once, you may need to put two or more radiation suits in the area. Also keep in mind that the radiation suits are time based. So if your acid pit is a large area, you'll need to adjust the number of suits accordingly.

The Light Amplification Visors should be used anywhere that you've made your WAD file very dark. They're of temporary value and will brighten things up for about a minute. Use these at your own discretion.

The Computer Map, when picked up, will show the player the entire layout of the level. The areas where he hasn't gone are shown in grey. This artifact is made nearly obsolete by the cheat code IDDT. The only difference is that the map provided by the cheat code doesn't highlight the unvisited areas in grey.

The last couple of artifacts are some of the best. The Soul Sphere (the blue happy-face looking thing) will give the player a health increase of 100 percent. These are usually reserved as a prize after a very hard-fought battle to not only boost the player's health but his morale as well. You could instead insert one before the big battle room to boost the player's health to the maximum for the ensuing fight.

The Blur Artifact, or invisibility sphere, makes the player invisible for a short period of time. These are good to use in large rooms that have a lot of monsters in them. Thus the player can move freely without being pulverized by all the creatures. You'll probably only use one of these in your level. (You may want to use two and mark one as Deathmatch-only. That way, both players have a chance to acquire one during a Deathmatch.)

Invulnerability Artifacts should be used in levels where there is either the Cyberdemon or the Spider Mastermind. This gives the player a reasonable chance of defeating them. Using it in other situations isn't really sporting or in the true spirit of DOOM.

DOOM II also added only one new artifact: the Mega Sphere. It combines the power of the blue Combat Armor and a Soul Sphere. These should be used in about the same situations as a regular Soul Sphere. They were probably added to DOOM II to give the player a little extra boost because of all the new and tougher monsters.

WALLS AND DOORS

DOOM has spawned a flood of utilities that enable the enterprising person to modify almost every aspect of the game. Some utilities, such as DMGraph and DeuTex, enable you to modify the standard wall textures in DOOM into different designs, designs that are only limited by your imagination. The *Aliens* WAD and Trinity WAD are very good examples of how you can modify DOOM to resemble just about anything you like.

Most of the walls in DOOM are based on a measure of 128 x 128 units square or multiples thereof. Some wall patterns are 64 units high and others are 256 units long. There are a few wall patterns that are 72 units high. As you design your level, you should try to keep your floor/ceiling heights in multiples of 64 units. This will help you to keep the textures aligned vertically and make your WAD file look more professional. Aligning the textures horizontally is a bit more involved. Sometimes it's not possible to make the textures the exact length that they are normally. If you're lucky enough to be using an editor with an auto aligning tool, this will make it a little easier. Otherwise, you'll have to do a bit of arithmetic to get the textures to line up correctly.

There are ways to work around this, though. You can always break the wall textures with a generic-looking texture such as the METAL texture. I've found it to be a very useful texture in certain situations. Sometimes you will have to adjust the length of the lines to be exactly or nearly exactly the actual length of the texture. This is especially true for walls that have pictures or faces on them. It's also important for doors to make the lines of the doors the same length as the textures. You can, however, shorten the ceiling heights of doors without sacrificing the look of the doors. You should experiment in this area to achieve the look you want.

To find out how to change the wall graphics, you should read Episode 4, Mission 4, "Mutations in DOOMspace." It will explain in detail how to change the walls from the standard DOOM wall textures.

Along with all the new monsters, the new wall textures in DOOM II added a new dimension to the game. Not only did id Software add new wall textures, but the designers changed all the sky patterns too. There are so many new wall textures that I can't list them all. You now have the ability to create some very striking levels. It almost makes using a texture-changing utility such as DMGraph no longer necessary. Plus, the two Wolfenstein 3D levels bring back a little of the old days. Not all of the original textures from Wolfenstein 3D are included, but enough of them are included so you can make a level that looks almost like the original.

There are approximately 37 new line specials used in DOOM II. These will also work with DOOM 1.666 if the editor you're using supports them. They weren't used in DOOM 1.666, but you can use them for it. Most of these are for the fast-opening doors. There are two monster-only teleporter line specials. There are also about four new fast-elevator line specials, and a few other miscellaneous line specials.

SOUNDS

The sounds in DOOM are one of the more enjoyable things about the game. If you don't have a sound card yet, you should seriously consider buying one—you're missing out on a lot of the game. Without a sound card, you're not able to hear the different music that each episode has. The rest of the sounds are also much better with a sound card. You can hear the monsters breathing and grunting before you can even see them. The weapons sound more realistic, too.

There are utilities that allow you change or replace all the sounds in DOOM. You can compose your own music and add it to your level. Before you replace the music with anything well known, you should check the copyright to make sure you're not in violation of any laws. If you like, you can replace the sounds of the weapons or the sounds that the monsters make.

The sounds in DOOM II are similar to those in DOOM. The music has all changed and the sounds for the new monsters are different. Other than that, it's the same.

CREATING YOUR OWN DOOM

MISSION 1:
A HELL OF YOUR
VERY OWN

ROOM 1

By Steve Benner

PRELIMINARY RECONNAISSANCE

By now, you should know what DOOM is capable of, and you are probably itching to start building your own hair-raising scenario. In this mission, you will learn how to do just that. This mission's primary objective is to introduce you, through each of its various rooms, to the main aspects of WAD development. This mission starts with the simple laying out of the lines of the map and progresses through each of the essential features of WADs in turn. Throughout, you will be led on a series of Sorties which are designed not only to enable you to try out for yourself the features presented in the briefings, but also to produce a complete, fully featured WAD of your own.

In this first room, you will find a checklist of the equipment you are going to need. You will be shown how to prepare your tools and will receive some elementary training in their use. You will also be led on a quick reconnaissance Sortie into the domain of the WAD-builder.

BEFORE YOU START: CHECKING YOUR KIT

There are four important things you must have before you can start building your own WADs:

- A copy of DOOM
- The appropriate software editing tools
- A design idea
- A lot of patience

Each of these essentials will be examined in turn.

DOOM ITSELF

Before you can venture forth on a WAD-building expedition, you will, of course, need a copy of id Software's DOOM program—the full registered version. The shareware versions are not adequate for PWAD development: they are incomplete; editors will work with them and versions later than v1.4 cannot use PWADs in any case. You can use any of the major releases of the registered version, though. (DOOM v1.2 lacks some of the features added to later revisions and runs up against its limits more quickly than other versions, but many WAD designers still prefer to work with it, believing it to have fewer bugs than later releases.) Not surprisingly, id Software recommends the use of the latest version of the game, currently 1.9. The so-called "commercial" version of the game DOOM II provides some extra baddies and new weapons, and some of the scenic elements have been changed from the original DOOM. There are no significant differences between the various revisions of DOOM II.

2	1		1		DOOM
EPISODE	MISSION		ROOM		PROGRAMMING GURUS

The example WADs that are developed during the course of this mission assume that you are using at least v1.2 of DOOM. The additional features provided by the later revisions of the game are covered in the text but are not included in the examples—although particular instances where the newer features could be employed are mentioned in passing.

If you are using DOOM v1.4 or later, you may want to utilize the new features where you see fit, as you work through the example WADs.

For the benefit of readers with DOOM II, a parallel series of example WAD files is supplied on the accompanying CD-ROM. The specific details of how these WADs differ from the ones described in the text are given in DOOM II note boxes like this one in the appropriate WAD Sortie sections.

Making WADs for the DOOM-Alikes

Some of the new third-party adaptations of the DOOM engine, such as Raven Software's Heretic, use the DOOM PWAD file structure for their data files. Many of the DOOM WAD editors will produce useable add-on files for these adaptations. However, lack of space precludes any consideration of these new developments here. This mission concerns itself solely with the development of WAD files for use with the original DOOM and DOOM II versions of the game.

EDITING TOOLS

In addition to a copy of the game engine itself, you will need access to some WAD-editing tools. First and foremost, you will need a map editor (also known as a WAD editor or mission editor). This will enable you to lay out your map and to populate it with goodies and baddies. In addition, you may also need a *nodes builder*. Before you can submit a map to DOOM, it will need to contain a structure known as the *binary space partition* or *nodes tree*. This fearsome-sounding structure holds the results of some essential pre-game calculations: it lightens DOOM's math-loading and enables the graphical engine to function better in real time. Some editors are capable of performing the nodes calculations themselves, while others need a separate nodes-building utility. You will need to check the details of your chosen editor to see if a separate nodes builder is necessary or whether the editor performs this function as an integral part of its operation.

A variety of other tools are available to allow full customization of your DOOM WADs, but for now you should proceed without them. The use of these more advanced tools is covered in Episode 4, "The Tools of the Gods," of this book. All of the sample WADs developed in the current mission can be produced using any of the map editors on the accompanying CD-ROM, together with any external nodes builder that the editor may require. No other utilities are needed at this stage.

THE DESIGN

With the right tools at hand, building a DOOM WAD can be a fairly simple task. Finding an effective blend of design elements and producing a *good* DOOM WAD can be much more tricky!

You probably already have some ideas about what you'd like in your WADs and are just dying to try them out. Before you get too carried away, however, you need to be aware that while the number of features available in DOOM is very large, it is by no means limitless. There are, in fact, a large number of design restrictions within which you must work—restrictions imposed by limitations in the game engine, as well as by the structure of the WAD files themselves. To produce good, playable missions, you will not only need to be fully aware of these restrictions but also learn how to work around them.

I suggest that you hold off trying to produce your own killer design right away and that you start instead by following the Sorties quite closely. The final WAD that you will produce this way is relatively simple and straightforward in its design, but I hope you will find that it is still fairly exciting and challenging to play. By building the WAD according to the game plan prescribed here, you will encounter all of the major design elements of DOOM WADs in an ordered and structured sequence. The potential pitfalls for would-be WAD designers are many and various. By staying close to the plan throughout this mission, you will learn to recognize them and thus to avoid them when you do set off alone.

PATIENCE IS A VIRTUE

The final essential in WAD-making is patience—and you may need a lot of it! Like many computer-related tasks, WAD-building can be simple to perform but complex to master. You can expect to spend many hours switching to and fro between your editor and the game engine, as you lay out, test, and refine your creation, until you produce something that you feel can be released to the world. Expect to make mistakes, and be prepared to spend long hours tracking them down and rectifying them.

Remember that most of the available WAD-editing utilities are produced not by large and successful software houses but by keen individuals working largely in their spare time. This is not to say that these programs are of poor quality; many are produced to high professional standards. But do bear in mind that the resources available to these eager young programmers may not have permitted rigorous testing of all of the component parts; programs may have been released hurriedly, perhaps so that people could start to make use of them quickly, and they may be a little less than complete. You may find, for example, that a user interface is not as polished as you would like; or documentation may be lacking, requiring you to indulge in some trial-and-error guesswork before you can benefit fully from some of the utilities. You may even find that some programs crash more often than you would want. But you should not be put off by these cautionary words; most of the programs supplied on the CD-ROM are very powerful and easy to use, once you have mastered a few basics. And if you protect your work with frequent backups, you should be just fine.

Bear in mind, too, that WAD-editing is very much a pioneering activity and requires you to have something of a pioneering spirit to get the most from it. Many of the "rules" of WAD structure and design have been formulated by amateurs working long hours, discovering things by experimentation. The nuances of WAD design are far from settled, and there is still much to discover. You should feel free to explore and experiment with the capabilities of the DOOM engine yourself. But be prepared for a certain amount of frustration and confusion if you venture too far into uncharted territory alone. Your WAD-building adventure will begin, though, in the relative safety of the well-charted areas of WAD production.

PREPARATION FOR THE SORTIES

Before you can set out on even the first reconnaisance Sortie, you will need to gather some tools and prepare them for use. Let's do that now.

COLLECT THE GOODIES FROM THE CD-ROM

The CD-ROM that accompanies this book contains a large number of WAD-building utilities. You will find details of what is offered in Episode 5, Mission 2, Room 1, "The DOOMed CD." For now, concentrate on finding a suitable map editor. Your choice may well be determined by the capabilities of your computer and by the operating environment you prefer to use.

| DOOM PROGRAMMING GURUS | | 1 ROOM | | 1 MISSION | 2 EPISODE |

Throughout this mission, I shall be describing WAD-production using Matthew Ayres' WADED program. I have chosen to use this editor simply because it suits my particular style of working. It provides a good selection of features without overwhelming the user and, most importantly as far as I am concerned, it has a virtually faultless (and fully automatic) nodes builder, making the generation of useable WADs a simple matter. It is also a DOS-based editor and, beyond the need for a mouse, it does not require anything more than a PC that is capable of running DOOM.

You do not need to use this particular editor for your WADs if you don't want to (although the early WAD Sorties will be easier to follow if you do). One of the beauties of WAD-editing is that with the structure of the files being standardized and editors so readily available, it is possible to try out a range of editors, or even routinely employ several, using each for whatever features you particularly like. So feel free to chop and change; or pick one that looks good from its description and stay with it, just as you fancy. The choice is yours.

INSTALLING THE EDITOR

Once you have picked your editor (or editors), follow the instructions given on the CD install page and install the necessary software to the hard disk of your computer. If, like me, you are working from DOS, you may wish to write yourself a couple of simple batch files to make switching between editor and DOOM a little easier. I use a number of simple ones such as this:

```
EDITWAD.BAT

@echo off
cd \doom\waded
waded %1.wad %2 %3
cd ..


TRYWAD.BAT

doom -file waded\%1.wad %2 %3 %4 %5 %6 %7 %8 %9


EDITWAD2.BAT

@echo off
cd \doom\waded
waded %1.wad -2 %2 %3
cd ..


TRYWAD2.BAT

@echo off
f:
cd \doom2cd
doom -cdrom -file e:\doom\waded\%1.wad %2 %3 %4 %5 %6 %7 %8 %9
e:
```

2	1		1	DOOM
EPISODE	MISSION		ROOM	PROGRAMMING GURUS

These ensure that my WADs are always kept in a convenient directory (the same as my editor), and they also minimize the amount of typing I need to do to move between the editor and the game engine.

If you have decided to follow my example and use WADED, now would be a good time to start the program. The first thing that it will do is display an opening configuration screen, which requires you to supply the location of your main DOOM.WAD file.

> Even though you may not intend to change the main id-supplied maps, most editors need to read information from these files and will not operate unless they can find them.

WADED can work with DOOM and/or DOOM II WADs (Heretic files, too!), but you must have copies of each game that you want it to work with, and WADED will need to know where you keep them. Leave a blank entry for games you do not have. WADED only needs to be told this information once, storing it in its configuration file.

> If you ever want to change the information in WADED's configuration file—maybe, for instance, you have acquired an additional WADED-compatible game—you can force WADED to present the screen for alteration by invoking WADED with a -c command-line switch. Alternatively, you can edit the file (WADED.CFG) with any standard text editor.

Once you have entered the location of your main files, WADED will go through an initialization sequence and is then ready for you to use on a WAD.

WAD SORTIE 1: A QUICK FIRST WAD

With the editor sitting there ready for you to use, I expect you will want to try it out immediately. I will, therefore, lead you straightaway on a quick and dirty WAD-editing Sortie. At this stage, I will not weigh you down with too much theory, explanations, or design issues. For now, treat this as a reconnaissance trip. You can worry more about where you are heading (and where you've been) later.

THE OPENING VIEW

After WADED has gone through its opening initialization sequence, you will be presented with its main editing screen. If you didn't specify a WAD to work on, WADED will present the opening map of the main game: DOOM's E1M1, or MAP01 if you're working with DOOM II. Figure 1.1 shows how this looks.

Figure 1.1.
WADED's main editing screen, as seen at startup.

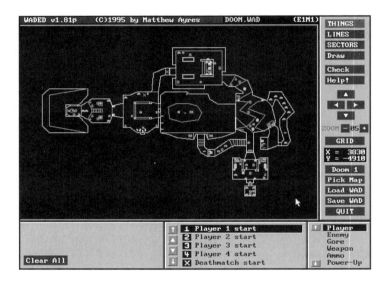

Readers using DOOM II rather than DOOM will have a different map displayed, but everything else should be more or less the same.

Most of the display is taken up by the main map, but to its right, down the side of the screen, are a number of buttons (all but the top one of which are blue). Also in this right-hand button bar is an X,Y indicator box, showing the location of the mouse pointer whenever it is positioned over the map window.

At this stage, do not bother yourself with what all of the buttons do—I'll cover that in due course. For now, just follow the instructions and don't worry too much if you do not understand what the steps are actually achieving—again, all will be revealed shortly.

CLEARING THE CURRENT MAP

Throughout these instructions, the term *clicking* means clicking with the left mouse button, unless otherwise indicated.

Start by clicking the fourth button from the top, at the right of the screen—the one labeled Draw. As you click this button, the map display changes somewhat and a new button bar appears along the bottom of the screen, beneath the map display. Of these, the one labeled Lines, in the left-most Draw column, should be red, with all of the others blue. Click the Scratch button to remove the E1M1 (or MAP01) map from the screen—don't worry, you won't affect your DOOM.WAD here—and confirm, when asked, that you want to start from scratch. You should now have a completely empty map area. The Lines button should still show red. WADED is now ready to accept your new map.

A FEW PRACTICE LINES

You may find WADED's drawing technique is just a little different from that used by other drawing packages. This is because it is geared to WAD production and is often making assumptions about what you are going to draw. It is probably worth taking a little time now to become familiar with its behavior.

Start your drawing by clicking once with the left mouse button somewhere in the map area (it does not matter where). You should notice that a small magenta square appears beneath the mouse pointer. If you now move the mouse pointer, the square turns red and is left behind, while another red square follows the pointer. Between these two squares stretches a magenta line, with a small tick mark at its center. As you move the pointer, the X,Y indicator at the right-hand side of the screen updates as usual, and another indicator box in the lower portion of the screen displays two other values: the length of the line that you currently have attached to your pointer and the angle at which that line is running.

If you now click the left mouse button some distance away from the location of the first click, you will find that the red block under the pointer turns magenta while, at the same time, the line be-tween the two blocks turns from magenta to a pulsating red. As soon as you move the mouse away from this new point, however, the block turns red again while the line turns magenta, loses its cen-tral tick mark, and no longer follows the pointer. Instead, a new tick-marked line appears, stretched between a new red square at the mouse pointer and the location of your last click. WADED will continue to add squares and lines to your map each time you click the left mouse button, until you click back on one of your existing red blocks or at some point on one of your lines (which will turn red before you click, to let you know that you are about to make contact with it).

The normal way of ending a drawing in WADED is to close out a shape (by contacting with existing blocks or lines) but you can also terminate the drawing process by clicking (anywhere) with the right mouse button. This will erase the current line-in-progress, but it will leave everything intact up to your last left-button click.

At this point, you might like to practice drawing some lines and shapes in the map-editing area for a little while.

ZOOMING AROUND

When you have a few squiggles and assorted shapes on your map, you might also like to try out WADED's map-scrolling buttons (they are together in a cluster in the center of the right-hand button bar) as well as the Zoom –, and + buttons just beneath them. The cursor keys on the keyboard also will scroll the map display. The Home key is also worth trying out; it will re-center your drawing in the map display, which is useful if you've done a lot of scrolling off to one side.

Notice, incidentally, that you can still access and use the scroll and zoom buttons while you are drawing lines. WADED may stretch the current line disconcertingly off the screen to follow the pointer, but you will not confuse it by using these buttons at the same time.

For now, do not concern yourself with how to move or erase lines that you have placed.

STARTING FOR REAL

When you are comfortable with the process of drawing and viewing your lines in WADED, click the Scratch button again, and confirm the deletion of your recent doodles. Check that the Zoom level is set to 05 and that the (Draw) Lines button is still red. (Just click it if it isn't.) You are now ready to make a start on your first WAD.

This first WAD will be very rudimentary—nothing more than the bare essentials. It will consist of a simple hexagonal room with a pillar in it.

Figure 1.2 shows how your first map should look when you've finished; the next section will lead you through the drawing process.

Figure 1.2.
The map you are aiming for.

Start here

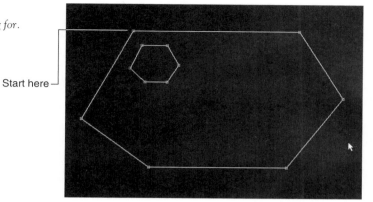

DRAWING YOUR FIRST MAP

Do not be tempted to speed up the production of your first WAD by skipping any stage of the instructions that follow. They are all essential.

Begin your drawing by clicking with the left mouse button at the point indicated in Figure 1.2. The exact location of your first click does not matter, but you should allow space for drawing to the right of (and also a little to the left of) and below your starting position. You can, of course, scroll the display later if you find that you need more space, but life may be a little easier if you plan not to have to!

Having placed the first point of your map, move the mouse to the right and draw a horizontal line (Angle: 90) that is 900 units or so long. (Do not worry if WADED won't let you have a line of exactly 900 units. This is normal.) This is line 1. Now add successive lines of the lengths and angles given in Table 1.1. Again, don't worry about getting the values precisely as specified.

Table 1.1. Four more lines for the first hexagon.

Line	Angle	Length
2	147	450
3	218	500
4	270	750
5	307	460

Finish this part of the drawing by connecting back to the first point you placed. You should now have a magenta hexagon in your map display area.

Now add another, much smaller, hexagon to the map, as follows. Start by positioning the mouse about 50 units east and 60 units south of the first point you placed. Make sure that none of your current lines show red (if any do, you are too close—move a little further away) before clicking. Then draw the new lines detailed in Table 1.2.

As you draw, take care not to get so close to any of the lines of the larger, outer hexagon that WADED tries to connect any of your new lines to it. You will need to start over if such a connection happens.

Table 1.2. Lines for the second hexagon.

Line	Angle	Length
7	90	136
8	150	130
9	214	115
10	270	120
11	315	113

Line 11 should end in such a position that the line needed to close out the hexagon will be more-or-less parallel to the adjacent line of the larger hexagon (line 6). Complete the new hexagon by connecting line 12 to the start of line 7. Again, take care that you connect to the starting point of the inner hexagon, not to any point of the outer one.

You should now have two magenta hexagons. At this point, you should select the Make Sector button, located in the center of the lower screen section. This button will turn red, as the (Draw) Lines button turns blue. Position the mouse pointer anywhere within the larger hexagon but outside the smaller one, and then click once with the left mouse button. Both hexagons will turn to a pulsating red color. Notice that when you move the mouse away from both hexagons now, they turn white. Take care not to click anywhere else on the map while the Make Sector button is red.

COMPLETING THE MAP

Next, click the THINGS button, located in the top-right corner of the screen. The lower portion of the screen changes to a largely blank area on the left, with two scrolling lists to the right of this area. The right-most scrolling list should have the entry "Player" highlighted, while the central list has "Player 1 start" highlighted as in Figure 1.3.

Figure 1.3.
WADED's "Things"
selection boxes, with
"Player 1 start" selected.

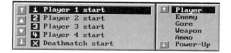

Position the mouse pointer somewhere inside the larger hexagon, about 40 units in from one of its southwestern corners. Click once with the *right* mouse button. A small number "1" should appear on your map, enclosed in a green rectangle. Various details (which you can ignore for now) should also appear in the lower-left information box.

SAVING THE WAD

You now have enough of a map to try out in DOOM, so click the Save WAD button (located towards the bottom of the right button bar) to make a popup box appear in the center of the screen, as shown in Figure 1.4.

Figure 1.4.
WADED's Save
WAD popup.

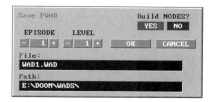

Click the File: entry box in this popup and type a name for your WAD (perhaps WAD1.WAD) and press the Return key. Check that the path is okay and change it if necessary (if you do this, you will need to press Return again after typing the new path). Notice which level your WAD will play as—the default is E1M1 (MAP01 in DOOM II). I suggest you leave this set as it is for now. Make sure that the Build Nodes: YES button is red.

When you are happy with the settings in the Save WAD popup, click the OK button. WADED will rapidly display a sequence of messages (mostly too quickly for you to read) and then save your WAD. You can now leave the editor (click the Quit button) and start DOOM to try out your handiwork.

TRYING YOUR NEW WAD

Don't forget to start DOOM with an appropriate `-file` command-line switch. (Or use the batch file I recommended earlier.) On startup, DOOM will advise you that the game has been modified (by the addition of your new WAD) and that you are now on your own as far as help from id Software is concerned.

You can then try out your new map by starting a new game of the appropriate episode. You should find yourself located in one corner of a hexagonal room, with a pillar somewhere to your left.

If DOOM starts up with a standard map, rather than your own, check that you did indeed start DOOM with the `-file` switch, that you typed the appropriate path to your WAD file, and that you typed its name correctly. Check also that you are starting the same episode and mission (or level, in DOOM II) as you specified when you saved your WAD. If all else fails, go back to WADED and follow through the instructions again—but more carefully this time!

With luck, your WAD loaded and started without trouble and you can now take a walk around your first DOOM scenario. (See Figure 1.5.) Not bad for a few minutes of work, eh? Future WAD Sorties will build on this first, simple, one-room WAD.

Figure 1.5.
A view of your first WAD.

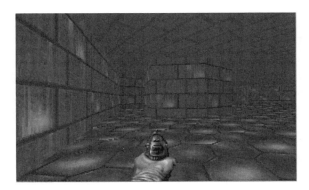

TECHNIQUES FOR EDITING AND TESTING WADS

Now that you have seen just how easy it is to produce a working WAD, you are probably keener than ever to dive in and make a real start. Before you do, however, we should review some of the practicalities of WAD development, starting with the mechanics of moving between editor and game engine.

MOVING BETWEEN EDITOR AND DOOM

By now, you will hopefully have a feel for what is involved in putting together and testing a WAD file, and you have already experienced something you will probably spend a lot of time doing from now on: moving to and fro between the editor and the game engine. Because it can be such a large part of DOOM WAD development, it is worth learning how to make this process as simple and painless as possible.

If your PC has sufficient memory and can run DOOM under Microsoft Windows, you may like to take advantage of the task-switching capabilities of that environment. Many designers like to cut down on the time spent waiting for programs to load by starting up their favorite editor in one Window and running DOOM in another, and then simply switching between the two with a couple of key-presses. For many, this is the ideal way to work. To do this, you would need plenty of memory— enough to run Windows, DOOM, and your editor simultaneously. Thus you would probably need 16MB as a good working minimum.

On the other hand, it is perfectly feasible (and some would say decidedly safer) to stay entirely within the confines of DOS. However, you would then need to resign yourself to a lot of waiting as your various programs load. You can make life somewhat easier by using some carefully constructed batch files, such as those listed earlier, but you will still spend a lot of time waiting for programs to start. You may therefore wish to adopt a couple of working habits that make switching back and forth less tiresome. Some of these practices are briefly discussed in the following sections.

OPTIMIZING THE EDIT-SAVE-TEST CYCLE

However you decide to operate your editor, you should resist the temptation to draw up too much of your map at one time. Learn to gauge the amount of detail that you can add to your map before you will need to test it. This can make a big difference in the speed at which you work. If you draw too little, you will spend a disproportionate amount of your working time waiting for programs to switch.

If you draw too much, you run the risk of having so much to test that you miss some of the problems, or of finding a mistake that requires a lot of undoing, thereby wasting a lot of your previous edit. If you can find the right frequency, switching between the two tasks may also help to keep your mind fresher for longer.

As you follow through the examples in this book, you should develop a feel for just how much you can add to a map before you need to test what you have done. You will also learn which things need (and take) the most testing.

Along with developing an edit-save-play strategy that optimizes the switching between editor and engine, remember that you can utilize the time spent waiting for programs to load by taking stock of just where you are in the current stage of development of your WAD and planning your next step.

KEEPING NOTES

Throughout the WAD-development process, you will find it useful to keep a notebook handy. Along with sketching out your WAD before you start, you should keep a list of the things you add during each edit, so that you will know exactly what you need to test during the next play session. As you wait for the game engine to start, decide on a logical strategy for working through everything that needs to be tested in this session. Make sure that you test all of your new additions before going back to the editor to fix any errors you spotted or put in any changes you thought of as you played your WAD. And of course, write down the problems you encounter and ideas you have while testing, so that you will have a list to work from when you return to the editor. Yes, you are right—it is just like programming.

USING AN APPROPRIATE MAP NUMBER

For convenience in starting your new WAD in DOOM, you are advised always to save your WADs as startup games, at least during the developmental stages. This means saving them as E1M1, E2M1, or E3M1 in DOOM, or as MAP01 in DOOM II. That way, you can go straight to your WAD to test it out when you begin DOOM. Even if you are working on a multi-map WAD, you should develop each map in a separate WAD file initially and, when they are all complete, use a utility such as WADCAT to assemble your multi-map WAD for final testing and distribution. This will keep your WAD files small and quicker to load (and also reduce the damage that can occur if you have an accident with the editor).

2	1		1		DOOM
EPISODE	**MISSION**		**ROOM**		**PROGRAMMING GURUS**

DECIDING WHEN TO ADD MONSTERS

Opinions differ as to what stage of WAD development to start adding monsters and such-like, largely because of the added effort of checking a WAD populated with enemies. Many developers will leave the adding of the bad guys until almost the very end. I prefer to add some creatures to my WADs quite early on, usually so that I can check whether the various geographic components work well together as a combat arena. I find the easiest way of checking sightlines and firing lines is to put some monsters around the place and see how they behave. When WAD-building, it is easy to be seduced into producing clever scenery that *looks* very pretty but that turns out to be virtually useless when it comes to *fighting* in it. It is especially tempting when working with a map editor to build rooms and corridors that map out some grand design when viewed *as a map*, but which turn out to be boring to play. I find that adding creatures to the map as I go along keeps me concentrating on the real business at hand: providing the player with a survival challenge.

Once you start populating your WAD with hazards, be it with monsters or harmful scenery elements, the business of moving through it, testing out its general playability, and looking for faults becomes more difficult and time consuming. At this stage, you will find that the task of testing your work will be made easier if you learn the proper use of the developmental aids that id Software has provided: the command-line switches and the so-called cheat codes. (Other players may use these codes to cheat during play—you, of course, will only use them as they were intended: as aids to play-testing. Quite a different matter!)

USING SWITCHES AND CHEATS

Full details of the various command-line switches and cheat codes available in DOOM were presented in Episode 1, Mission 2, Room 5, "Cheater's Guide," of this book. Those that are particularly useful during play-testing are worth recapping here.

The -nomonsters switch is useful for walk-through testing when you simply want to look around and inspect your scenery, layout, and so on. Having to battle monsters as you move through your WAD will just distract you from the real task at hand, and it will quickly become more of a chore than a pleasure.

The drawback of the -nomonsters switch is that you will need to quit DOOM and reload it in order to switch the monsters back on. An alternative is to make all the test monster-placings applicable only to the higher difficulty settings; you can then play-test without monsters simply by restarting the game at a lower difficulty setting. You will learn how to do this later.

A useful cheat code for checking out monster behavioral patterns is IDDTIDDT. Watch the map and use this code to check that monsters move around your layout and hunt the player as you intended. Of course, if you spend a lot of time simply observing the monsters from locations where they can see you, you will probably need to use IDDQD to stay alive long enough to see how they behave. IDKFA is useful for the later stages of your design, when you are trying to decide how much of what kind of weaponry and ammunition to make available, and also for moving quickly through areas that have keyed doors.

You may be tempted to use IDSPISPOPD (IDCLIP in DOOM II) to take shortcuts through your map to areas that you are working on that are far from the start. I do not recommend the use of this cheat in this way. You will find that the game plays very differently with this cheat active. You will not get a proper feel for your geography while you are using it. In my view, it is much better (and usually simpler) to relocate the player's start position on your map so that you are already positioned at a convenient point when the WAD starts. This no-clipping cheat is useful for occasional quick trips through a WAD to check small fixes to the scenery, though.

Other codes can be usefully employed at various times during the play-testing process, but the ones mentioned here are generally the most useful. You should always bear in mind just what is available, though, and be sure to use whatever will speed up your play-testing the most.

THE IMPORTANCE OF PROPER FILE MANAGEMENT

The final point to make about the WAD-production process is really just a matter of common sense: don't forget to take regular backups of your work in progress. Even the best of editors can occasionally get into something of a tangle. Often the only way of dealing with these tangles is to give up, load an earlier version of the WAD file, and rebuild your work from there. If you follow the strategy outlined here—of only working in fairly small and manageable chunks, and saving each major edit to a new file—then even when the worst does happen, you should never end up losing too much work.

EXIT: MOPPING UP AND MOVING ON

This concludes the preliminaries. It is now time to take stock and move on.

From this room, you should have outfitted yourself for the WAD-building adventure ahead. You have had a chance to build and play a simple WAD and have been given some hints on the most painless ways to proceed.

In the next room, you will find an explanation of the steps you have just taken, an introduction to the basic elements of WADs, and more details about the use of WADED.

ROOM 2

By Steve Benner

RECONNAISSANCE DEBRIEFING

In your first room of this mission, you experienced the thrill of producing your own WAD. In this room we will examine precisely what it was you did. We will introduce you to some of the fundamental constructs of all WAD files, showing you what the various map components are and how they interact.

You will be led on two further WAD Sorties, where you will learn more about using WADED to edit both the lines of your maps and the things located within it.

SECURING THE SECTOR

In the preceding room, we produced a simple one-room WAD without too much effort. The WAD was built without much explanation, either. It is time now to review the actions we took in that first session and explain why we took them and what we achieved by them. You may find it helpful to restart WADED with that first WAD (you can do this by typing `EDITWAD WAD1` if you implemented my suggested batch file) before reading on.

DIVIDING SPACE INTO SECTORS AND VOID

Believe it or not, probably the single most important step you took in building your first WAD was making the mouse click in the middle of your "room," right after selecting the `Make Sector` button. It was this one action that brought all of your other actions together and created the single room of this simple WAD. What you really created with that mouse-click was a special division of DOOM-space known as a *sector*. The extent of a sector is determined by the lines that bound it; when you made that mouse-click, WADED used the 12 lines that bound the space in which you clicked to mark out this WAD's single sector.

WHAT EXACTLY IS A SECTOR?

The game engine regards the sector as the fundamental building block of DOOM WADs. Sectors enable the engine to distinguish game-space from *void* space—that is, space within the map area which is not utilized during the game. In essence, they provide the engine's point of access to all of the information about any particular location on the map. Any point on the map that is not assigned to a sector is regarded by the game engine as belonging to the void.

In your first WAD, you created a single sector, consisting of a hexagonal annular space. This was seen and displayed by the game engine as a single room. As far as DOOM was concerned, there was nothing outside the sector's enclosing walls or even within the hexagonal pillar. It is a WAD-building rule that any area of the map into which a player can ever see must be assigned to a sector; otherwise an error results.

You can think of a sector as simply a designer-defined area of the DOOM map. That area is of a specific extent, defined by a series of lines. In order to mark off such an area without ambiguity, a sector's bounding lines must completely enclose the space. There can be no gaps in the lines. Figure 2.1 illustrates this.

Figure 2.1.
Closed and unclosed shapes.

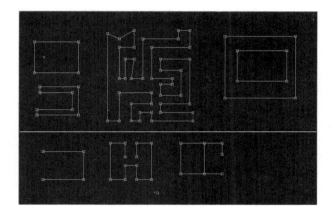

The upper four shapes are all valid closed shapes—they could all form sectors (the right-most shape could form one or two sectors). The lower three sets of lines form unclosed shapes—these shapes cannot form sectors, and they will crash both WADED and DOOM if you try to use them.

LOOKING AT THE DIVISION OF SPACE

If you have WADED loaded and your WAD1 map on the screen in front of you, you can readily observe this division of the map into sectors and void.

Click the Draw button and then on the Make Sector button. Now, taking care not to click the mouse button on the map while you do so, move the pointer around over the area of the map. Whenever the pointer is over space that belongs to a sector, the bounding lines of that sector will show up as pulsating red lines. You should find that the only time any lines are highlighted in your WAD is when the pointer is over the annular space of your single room, at which time all the lines are highlighted. Whenever the mouse pointer is outside your large hexagon, or inside the small one, it is in the void, and all lines will show as white.

ATTRIBUTES OF SECTORS

Each sector has a specific set of attributes, which tell the DOOM engine how that space looks and behaves during play. It is important to remember that a sector's attributes are applied across its entire extent. A sector's main attributes consist of the following:

- Floor details
- Ceiling details
- A brightness level
- A special characteristic

You will learn all about these attributes later; they are considered here only briefly. Note that there is no information here about your WAD's walls. You'll find out more about them later, too.

Viewing Sector Attributes in WADED

In WADED, you can view a sector's attributes by clicking the SECTORS button in the right-hand button bar. (You can safely click the map again now.) The settings of the currently selected sector appear in the bottom section of the screen, as shown in Figure 2.2.

Figure 2.2.
WADED's sector-attribute box.

FLOOR AND CEILING

The *floor* of a sector is the horizontal plane that forms the lower boundary of the sector in space. It is the surface upon which the player (and most monsters) will walk while they are in that area of the map. The *ceiling* is the horizontal surface forming the sector's upper boundary.

These surfaces are truly horizontal and cannot slope. You will learn more about this and other limitations of DOOM-space later.

A sector's floor and ceiling each possesses two definable properties:

- A height
- A texture

The *height* value specifies the surface's absolute vertical placement in the range -32768 to +32767. Naturally, the ceiling is normally placed higher than the floor, and the difference between the two heights provides the apparent height of this area of the map, as seen by the player.

The *texture* value consists of an eight-character name that tells the game engine which pattern to render on the screen when showing this particular surface.

SECTOR BRIGHTNESS

A sector's *brightness level*, expressed as a number between 0 and 255, determines how brightly anything occupying that sector (including the floor and ceiling textures) will be displayed on the screen.

SPECIAL CHARACTERISTIC

The *special characteristic* of a sector determines whether the game engine will do anything special with it. Examples might be making the lights flicker or doing damage to a player in the sector. The majority of sectors will have no special-characteristic set.

Room 7, "Activating Sectors," of this mission looks at the special-characteristic property of sectors. The next WAD Sortie will take a closer look at sector settings within your own embryonic WAD.

The following WAD Sortie builds on the WAD produced in the last Sortie of the previous room. If you did not accompany me on that Sortie but would like to come along on this one, you should use WAD1.WAD (DOOM) or D2WAD1.WAD (DOOM II) from the CD-ROM as your starting point.

WAD SORTIE 2: CHANGING SECTOR ATTRIBUTES

You are probably wondering how your WAD managed to acquire ceiling, floor, and brightness settings without you having to specify any values for these attributes. The answer is that WADED, like many editors, will generally supply sensible defaults for all values that you do not specify. Of course, WADED also provides the facility for you to specify all of these settings for yourself. You may want to change some of them now.

Assuming you are running WADED, with WAD1.WAD loaded, click the SECTORS button in the right-hand button bar. Click anywhere inside your only sector, and you will see its attributes displayed at the bottom of the screen. The sector identification number is shown at the far left of the Attributes bar, with the current value of the special characteristic next to it. You can ignore these values for the time being. Next to the Special value is displayed the sector's brightness level (called Lighting by WADED) and, to the right of that, the current ceiling and floor heights, as well as the names of the textures in use by those surfaces.

CHANGING SETTINGS

To change any of the numerical settings, you can either use the + or - buttons alongside the particular value, or you can click the value itself and directly type in a new value, ending with a press of the Return key. Try reducing the sector's lighting level to 144, say, and bring the ceiling down a little, to 120.

You might also fancy a change of floor texture. In the bottom right-hand corner of the screen, to the right of the attributes area, you will see a list of eight-character names, arranged in alphabetical order. These are the available floor and ceiling textures. The arrows to the left of the names enable you to scroll this list up and down.

Use the right mouse button on the arrows for rapid scrolling.

The **J** button enables you to jump to a particular part of the list—you click the button and then enter an initial letter—while the **P** button brings up a larger pick list from which you can select a texture.

WADED provides a number of ways to view the textures. You can use the **V** button to see the texture that is currently highlighted; you can right mouse click a texture name in the list; or you can preview textures using the appropriate button within the pick list. When previewing a texture using any of these techniques, WADED removes the map-editing screen and displays a single "tile" of the chosen texture in the middle of the screen, as shown in Figure 2.3.

Here, you can use the cursor-left and -right arrow keys to view other textures, or press the **Q** (or the Escape) key to return to the editor. The texture you last viewed will be highlighted in the Textures list box.

You can change the current floor texture as follows. With the main map-editing screen visible, scroll through the list of texture names until, say, MFLR8_1 becomes visible. Click the entry to select it. Now click your sector's floor-texture field, located in the Sector Attributes bar (where it currently says FLOOR4_8). With this mouse-click, the sector's floor-texture name field changes to the new name.

Save this WAD as WAD2.WAD and try it out. The differences are slight, so you may not notice them immediately, but you have now changed the way your room looks.

Figure 2.3.
WADED's preview of floor/ceiling texture MFLR8_1.

DRAWING THE BATTLE LINES

While the sector may be regarded as the DOOM engine's starting point in its interpretation of your WAD, you began your drawing with something rather more fundamental: a series of lines. In fact, your map lines consist of even smaller units: the vertices between which the lines themselves are stretched.

LINES AND VERTICES

Lines and *vertices* are very simple elements to understand. Each vertex is nothing more than an X and a Y coordinate, representing a point location on the DOOM map. Lines are marks on the map running between two of these vertices. Lines cannot exist without a vertex at each end.

Linked Creation of Lines and Vertices in WADED

With WADED, you don't need to worry about the creation of vertices, because this is handled automatically each time you draw a line. WADED shows vertices as small squares on your map. You have already seen that each line you draw has such a square at each of its ends.

THE HANDEDNESS OF LINES

It is important to realize that lines in DOOM WADs are regarded by the game engine as vectors. In other words, they are deemed to run in a particular direction *from* one vertex (the starting vertex) *to* another (the finishing vertex). Most editors (WADED included) watch the way you draw your lines and will take the vectoring information from your actions.

This vectoring of the lines can also be regarded as a handedness; lines are said to have *right* sides and *left* sides. WADED (along with most other editors) shows a line's right side by means of a small tick mark. To appreciate what this signifies, imagine yourself standing on a line's starting vertex (as made by the mouse-click that started the line), looking towards the line's finishing vertex. This line's right side lies to your right. Simple really—but confusing sometimes; hence the tick.

LINEDEFS AND SIDEDEFS

It so happens that lines in DOOM WADs are actually composite structures consisting of more than just start and end points. Each line has its own particular attributes (you will learn more about these in due course), which are held in a data structure called a linedef (short for 'line definition'). In addition, each linedef has information attached to each of its sides, in a pair of additional structures known as sidedefs (short for "side definitions"). A line may have both a right sidedef and a left sidedef to tell the DOOM engine how it appears to the player when viewed from either side.

To economize on space in the WAD, if a line can only possibly be seen from one of its sides (like all of the lines in your first WAD), then only one sidedef is needed, and the second can be omitted. By convention, single-sided lines have only a right sidedef. Lines that can be viewed from either side must have a right and a left sidedef, or an error will occur.

WADED's Treatment of Lines

For simplicity, WADED does not distinguish between linedefs and their attached sidedefs, calling the composite structure a line. This is a great convenience; WADED is usually smart enough to know exactly how many sidedefs each of your linedefs needs and handles the generation of all of the appropriate information automatically. It is often helpful, however (especially when trying to track down map faults), to bear in mind that all map lines are really tripartite structures, consisting of a linedef and (potentially) two sidedefs.

You will encounter more about the roles of these structures in Room 4, "At the Sector's Edge," of this mission.

Line Handedness in WADED

Although WADED is aware of the direction in which you drew your lines, it is also smart enough to know that a single-sided line's only sidedef should be on its right side. As you build sectors, WADED may flip single-sided lines around to ensure that their right sides are always used. Don't be concerned, therefore, if you find that lines in your WAD do not always appear to run in the direction you remember drawing them. WADED is just trying to make life easier for you.

CONTROLLING THE THINGS

In addition to the lines of the map—whose principal role is to mark out the sectors, remember—WADs can contain a number of items that are not part of the geography but that represent the various objects which the player will encounter when the WAD is played. These map items are termed *Things*. These are placed on the map by the designer to indicate where they will be when the WAD is started. Some Things may subsequently move with the progression of the game.

THINGS

You probably have a fair idea already what the family of DOOM Things include. Monsters are Things, as are all weapons, bonuses, and ammunition supplies. There are also a number of other items that you may not immediately think of as Things—their main categories are:

- Player start positions
- Enemies
- Gore (pools of blood, dead monsters, and so on)
- Weapons
- Ammunition
- Power-ups (health and armor bonuses, and so forth)
- Keycards
- Obstacles (barrels, pillars, and so on)
- Miscellaneous (currently just the teleport destination)

You will learn more about the use of Things as you progress through this mission. A full list of all Things available in DOOM and DOOM II is given in Appendix A, "Essential DOOM Thing Information."

The only essential Thing that every map of every WAD must have is a single Player 1 Start Position. Without one of these, the WAD will crash DOOM when you attempt to start a new game.

ATTRIBUTES OF THINGS

Each WAD Thing can possess a number of attributes which the designer can set. These are as follows:

- A facing angle
- Skill-level options
- A deaf guard option
- A multiplayer option

Not all categories of Thing can utilize all of these attributes, even though they possess them.

FACING ANGLE

The *facing angle* attribute determines the direction in which the Thing will be facing at the start of the mission. Only player starts, monsters, and teleport destinations make use of this attribute. All other categories of Thing look the same from all directions. (Have you noticed how corpses turn around as you walk around them?) The default facing angle is East.

SKILL-LEVEL OPTIONS

The *skill-level options* determine at which difficulty level settings of the game the Thing will appear. There may be fewer difficulty levels than you might expect. They are as follows:

- Level 0 ("I'm too young to die" and "Hey, not too rough")
- Level 1 ("Hurt me plenty")
- Level 2 ("Ultra-Violence" and "Nightmare")

Note the joining together of the "I'm too young to die" and "Not too rough" skill levels, as well as the "Ultra-Violence" and "Nightmare" levels. The differences within each of these groupings are achieved by mechanisms other than Thing availability. All Things may be set to appear (or not) at any of the three difficulty levels independently.

DEAF GUARD OPTION

The normal behavior of enemies is to remain asleep at their posts until they either see a player or hear a sound made by a player. The *deaf guard option* enables you to set particular monsters to awaken only upon seeing the player (or being hit by a shot). This attribute has no meaning for any other category of Thing.

You will learn more about the way sound propagates in Room 12, "Populating Your DOOM World," of this mission.

MULTIPLAYER OPTION

The *multiplayer option* enables the use of Things that will only appear in Cooperative or Deathmatch multiplayer games. This is useful for the addition of obstacles to prevent player access to items such as teleports and for creating a different distribution of weapon and ammunition supplies for multiplayer games.

HIDDEN EXTRAS

For the sake of completeness, it should be said that there are a number of other essential resources that every WAD needs in order to operate. Principally, these are as follows:

- The blockmap
- The BSP (or nodes tree)
- The reject table

These resources will be considered here briefly.

BLOCKMAP

In order to speed up the collision-detection process during play, DOOM requires the map to be divided up into a series of blocks. These blocks provide the game engine with a list of lines for their particular area of the map. Without this *blockmap*, all lines would become completely walk-through and DOOM would become a very strange game indeed. The "no-clipping" cheat code operates, in fact, by telling DOOM to stop consulting the blockmap. Editors should build a blockmap automatically without you needing to worry about it.

BSP (NODES TREE)

The *binary space partition* has already been mentioned as an essential WAD resource. It is needed to enable the game engine to display all of the WAD scenery in real time. This structure is calculated from the lines you draw. Some editors include the generation of the nodes as an integral part of their operation; others require a separate nodes builder to be used before the WAD can be used.

> The symptoms of a faulty nodes tree vary greatly. Sometimes the WAD simply refuses to play, with DOOM crashing to DOS (or worse). Usually, however, you find that the WAD simply displays oddly, with some walls missing, or with transparent stripes or flickering patterns. This is discussed in Room 14, "The Anomalies," of this mission.

THE REJECT TABLE

The *reject table* (or *map*) provides DOOM with some shortcuts for working out whether monsters can see the player(s) as they all move around. The purpose of this structure is to save the DOOM engine from some math calculations during operation of the game, thus speeding up play. Most editors will produce an empty reject table. This enables the WAD to operate, but not optimally. Unless your WAD contains a lot of monsters and many sectors, however, this will not be a problem for you. A special utility, known as a Reject Builder, is needed to produce a fully optimized reject table. (Details of this utility are given in Episode 4, Mission 3, Room 1, "RMB.")

Blockmap, Nodes, and Reject Generation in WADED

When WADED reads a WAD file, it discards the blockmap, generating a new one when you save the edited file to disk. It will only need to rebuild the nodes, though, if you have entered Draw mode at all.

Also, because node generation can be a lengthy process on a large WAD, WADED makes this step optional at the point of saving. The value of the Build Nodes? option that appears in the SAVE WAD pop-up is set to NO as you load a WAD and changes to YES if you add or move any lines on the map. The option can usually be trusted to be in the most appropriate setting automatically, but if in doubt, set it to YES.

If you suspect your WAD of having a faulty nodes tree, load it into WADED, press B to force an immediate build of the nodes, and then resave the WAD.

WADs produced or edited with WADED will have an empty reject table.

WAD SORTIE 3: MOVING THINGS AROUND

This Sortie builds on the WAD produced in the previous one. If you did not produce that WAD, you should use WAD2.WAD (DOOM) or D2WAD2.WAD (DOOM II) from the CD-ROM as your starting point here.

So far, you have seen how to add new lines to a map but not how to move lines or how to reshape your layout. If you would care to start up WADED again, I shall now show you how to do this, along with a few other useful things.

SPEAKING OF THINGS...

As WADED always starts up in Things mode, it is worth having a quick look here at Thing placement in more detail. You have already seen how to place a Thing into a WAD; you did this when you set your Player 1 Start Position just before saving your first WAD.

WADED's Thing placement process is very simple: Click the THINGS button at the top of the right-hand button bar. (If you've just started WADED, this step is unnecessary.) Then scroll the right-most list box at the bottom of the screen until the desired category of Thing is visible, using the left mouse button to select it. Do this now to select the Obstacle category.

The scroll box to the left of the Thing-category list shows a list of Things which belong to the currently selected category. The box displays a descriptive name of the Thing and also shows the icon that WADED will use to indicate this Thing's position on the map. Scroll this list box's highlight down quite a way, to the entry labeled Tall, Techno Column. Now, to place a tall techno-column in your room, move the mouse pointer to the location that you would like the column to occupy (the middle of the large hexagon, perhaps?), and click once with the right mouse button. Note that a copy of the gray, spherical icon used to represent the techno-column's position appears on your map, surrounded by a green rectangle. WADED uses this green rectangle to indicate which of the things on the map is currently selected. A Thing becomes selected as it is placed, or subsequently by clicking with the left mouse button on its icon. A selected Thing's details appear in the details box at lower left. Figure 2.4 shows how the WADED screen should look after placing your new techno-column.

Figure 2.4.
The WADED edit screen with Tall, Techno Column selected.

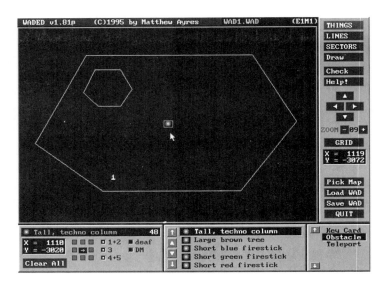

CHANGING A THING'S ATTRIBUTES

Details of a selected Thing's attributes appear in the Thing's details box in the lower left of the screen. On/Off check boxes enable you to alter the various options of the currently selected Thing. The Thing's facing angle is shown by means of a white arrow, which is surrounded by a number of gray blocks. Click an appropriate gray block to change the angle at which the selected Thing faces.

There is no point changing the way the techno-column faces, as this will have no effect on it. You may want to select your current Player 1 Start Position, though, and change the way your player faces at the start of the game.

Although the only essential thing that your WAD must have before you can play it is a Player 1 Start, if your WAD is ever to be used in multiplayer mode, it must also have the requisite number of additional Cooperative and Deathmatch Player Starts. Even if you have not designed the WAD with multiplayer use in mind, you should make sure that such positions are provided so that your WAD is at least useable in multiplayer mode. It is easy to forget to add such starting positions later, so I suggest you add them now. Place start positions for each of the other Cooperative players alongside Player 1. Also place four Deathmatch start positions around your central techno-column and make sure they start up with their backs to each other, won't you?

MOVING THINGS AROUND

You can move a Thing around on the map simply by using the left mouse button to drag it to where you would like it. Try placing a Cyber-boss (of the Enemy category) somewhere in your WAD. (Cyber-boss is WADED's name for the Cyberdemon.) Drag it around a bit and try to decide where you would like it to be when you start the WAD. You can put a few items of gore about the place, for practice, if you must.

If you don't like the names that WADED uses for the Things in the scrolling list boxes, you can change them. You will find a text file called WADED.T in your WADED directory. Edit this to change the names. Don't change any of the other information about the Things, though, or your WADs will not work properly and could crash DOOM.

It is perfectly possible to place or drag Things into void space, but doing so is singularly pointless. The player can never see into the void, so decorations placed there are wasted. The player can never enter the void, so bonuses placed there can never be collected. Monsters there will awaken at the player's first shot, but as they can never enter any sector space, they can never be encountered (although the player will hear them wandering around the void trying to get in!) and so will never be killed. DOOM won't mind about this waste, but it will notice that the player has not encountered the items left suspended in the void and will report the score appropriately at the conclusion of the level.

Void space, remember, is space that is not assigned to a sector.

DELETING UNWANTED THINGS

Have you found a good spot for that Cyberdemon yet? No, you're right, it is maybe not a good idea to have one here. Click your map's Cyber-boss icon with the right mouse button. Poof! (Don't you wish it was that easy to be rid of them during play?)

Table 2.1 summarizes the mouse operations used for editing a Thing's placement in WADED.

Table 2.1. WADED's mouse operations for Thing-placement editing.

Button	Operation	Effect
Right	Click in open space	Adds a new Thing of selected type
Right	Click Thing icon	Deletes a Thing
Left	Click Thing icon	Selects a Thing
Left	Drag Thing icon	Moves a Thing

MOVING LINES AND VERTICES AROUND

WADED's map-editing operations can rarely be undone. You may want to save your WAD before going on, in case you make a mess of it experimenting with the following operations.

To move map elements other than Things around, you need to click first on the Draw button in the right-hand button bar. The three buttons that then appear in the Move/Del column of the lower button bar should be self-explanatory by now. If you click this column's Vertices button, WADED will enable you to select and move vertices (they are the square blocks at the ends of your lines, remember) around the map by dragging with the left mouse button. You might want to try this out, refining the shapes of your hexagons a little.

Do not move any vertex so far that a nearby line turns red. If you do this by accident, move it away again *before* releasing the mouse button. If you do release the mouse button while a line is red, the vertex you are moving will become connected to the red line. This action cannot be undone.

If you move a vertex too close to another vertex and release the mouse button, WADED will ask whether you want to merge the two vertices. Ordinarily, this enables you to connect otherwise-disconnected lines and can be useful. Not here though. It also cannot be undone.

Selecting the (Move) Lines button enables you to select and move lines around as you just moved vertices. Notice that when moving lines, WADED preserves the angle and length of the line being moved, but it resizes and reorients any that are connected to the vertices at its ends.

As you've probably guessed, the (Move) Sector button permits the movement of entire sectors around. Having only one sector in this WAD, it doesn't achieve a great deal here, of course.

DELETING MAP ELEMENTS

If you have not already done so and you want to keep the changes you just made, make sure you save your WAD *now*. Your next experimentation is likely to destroy essential information in your WAD. Use the name WAD3.WAD to keep your WAD names synchronized with mine.

To delete unwanted lines or vertices in WADED, you need to have the appropriate Move/Del column button selected, just as if you were going to move the element. Then, a single click with the right mouse button on the offending element is all that is needed to delete it.

Use this feature with extreme caution at all times. Deleting map elements can have far-reaching effects. Remember that deleting a vertex will affect its connected lines; at least one line will always be removed as well. Deletion of a line may leave a sector open (and therefore in error). You will need to redefine sectors that are damaged in this way, which may result in extra work.

Plan all modifications to your map for minimal removal of existing lines. Try to reuse lines rather than deleting them. Later WAD workshops will show you how.

You may want to experiment with the line- and vertex-deletion capabilities of WADED for a while now, just to see how this operates. Don't attempt to put any lines back afterwards, however. Just Quit the program *without* saving the WAD when you have finished. Load DOOM and try out the last WAD you saved. This should be your reshaped room with a tall techno-column at its center and whatever other items you scattered around. (You did remember to remove that Cyberdemon, didn't you?)

EXIT: MOPPING UP AND MOVING ON

This room showed you how lines are used to divide DOOM-space into sectors within the void. You also learned that lines have a handedness and that they really consist of linedefs with a vertex at each end and sidedefs attached to their sides. You saw that sectors are responsible for supplying floor, ceiling, and lighting information to DOOM. In addition, you were given a fleeting glimpse of some of the more esoteric wonders that lie at the heart of WAD files, and you learned a little about some of the objects that populate DOOM levels. You also had further lessons in the operation of WADED and have made some cosmetic changes to your embryonic WAD. (See Figure 2.5.)

In the next room you will find more about the way DOOM-space is measured and organized.

Figure 2.5.
Oops! You should have taken it out while you could!

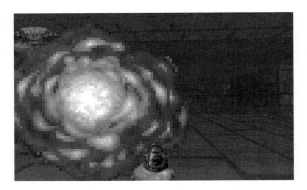

ROOM 3

MEASURING AND MAPPING DOOM

By Steve Benner

From the previous room, you know that DOOM's map area is divided into sectors and void space. This room's briefing will discuss sectors in more detail, explaining their true role, showing you why they are needed and how you should use them. It provides some useful rules for the layout of your maps.

Continuing previous WAD Sorties, you will also begin a tentative expansion of your embryonic WAD by adding a new passageway as well as another room. You will also discover that there are pitfalls along the way.

The briefing starts with an exploration of the nature of DOOM-space itself, showing you just what is and is not possible within it. Take note that vital information is contained here about the limitations that the DOOM engine imposes on your design. Ignore it at your peril!

UNDERSTANDING DOOM-SPACE

The lines of your first WAD were laid out in a fairly arbitrary manner in the blank space of WADED's map-editing window. You drew them with little regard for position. The lengths you used were largely arbitrary, too. Before you can decide how to draw any of your own lines, you need to know how DOOM-space is measured and how big it is. And you need to know something of its limitations.

DOOM METRICS

The basic unit of measurement in DOOM is essentially the pixel. Understand that this is not a screen pixel, but the smallest picture element of a DOOM engine graphic. The sizes of all DOOM elements are expressed in terms of the number of such pixels, or blocks of color, that it will take to paint them. This measurement system is used throughout the entire WAD world. Map coordinates follow exactly this scheme, so a wall that is, say, 128 units long will have exactly 128 blocks of color along its length.

Figure 3.1 shows a close-up view of some features of the DOOM world. The individual blocks of color that compose them can be quite large—look in particular at the closest area of the door and at the nearby Trooper.

Deciding how pixel measurements convert to real-world units is a little tricky. It seems that the folks at id Software have distorted their game world somewhat, making exact comparisons with the real world difficult. The best rule of thumb seems to be that each horizontal unit in the game approximates to 2 centimeters in the real world, with the vertical unit being nearer to 3 cm, in keeping with the PC screen-pixel's 3:2 aspect ratio. Vertical scaling is generally more difficult to judge, though, as it seems to vary with the distance of objects from the viewer and is distorted by the different zoom levels that the player can select. Although you will need to have some idea of DOOM's scaling if you are trying to reproduce some real-world setting in your WAD, you will find that, in practice, you rarely need to know the equivalent real-world sizes of DOOM objects. As you progress, you will quickly learn to start gauging DOOM-space for yourself. (There will be more to say about the implementation of real-world settings shortly.)

All Things in DOOM (including the player) have specific heights and widths (expressed as a diameter). This limits the space into which they can fit. The full details of these limitations and the consequences of ignoring them are the subject of Room 6, "Putting Sectors to Work," of this mission.

Figure 3.1.
A close-up view of some DOOM pixels.

THE EXTENT OF DOOM-SPACE

Map coordinates can range from -32768 to +32767. Therefore, in theory at least, DOOM maps could be quite large—this range gives the gaming space a theoretical maximum area equivalent to something in excess of 1 kilometer square. In practice, however, other engine limits will be encountered long before this space is filled. This should give you some idea, though, of the space available for you to build in.

Don't get too carried away with the vastness of DOOM-space and start building huge open areas. They are not only boring to play, they also have a tendency to be rendered poorly on- screen, owing to limitations in the game engine and current display technologies. As a rough guide, aim to keep walls shorter than a couple of thousand units long and rooms less than 500 units high (preferably even smaller if you are using DOOM v1.2)—Room 14, "The Anomalies," of this mission will show you why!

2-D OR 3-D?

A common misconception amongst DOOM players is that their gaming world is fully three-dimensional. As a designer, it is essential that you understand the fallacy of this notion. DOOM-space is what is normally termed pseudo-three-dimensional (sometimes termed 2 1/2-D). The map consists of a series of items (lines, vertices, and Things) placed into a two-dimensional playing grid. Particular areas within that grid are then notified to the engine as being at specific elevations.

You have already seen how lines are arranged to create special divisions of DOOM-space called sectors. These line and sector structures hold the information about the division of the playing grid and the various elevations of its parts. This is why areas not defined as sectors are deemed void by the game engine—there is simply no information whatsoever about them in the WAD.

PRACTICAL CONSEQUENCES

The main consequence of this pseudo-3-D nature of DOOM-space is its inability to permit any location on the map to possess more than one vertical elevation. What this means for the designer is that no sector (or part thereof) can ever overlap any other sector. This imposes a severe limitation on permitted designs. Rooms atop one another are not possible, for example. Corridors or passageways that cross at different levels are out. So too are archways through which players can pass while enemies lurk over their heads.

This particular spatial restriction is often the one that is hardest for designers to come to terms with when planning their WADs. It can be difficult to limit one's imagined geography in this way. And of course, many real-world environments are immediately prohibited. Gone is any chance of implementing your favorite office or school block, for instance.

Fortunately, there are some simple rules of layout which, provided you follow them, should keep you out of trouble. It is worth looking at these rules in some detail.

CORRECT LINE LAYOUTS

Perhaps the single most important key to trouble-free DOOM maps is the correct laying out of lines. This really boils down to a full understanding of the role of sectors and hence to the correct employment of them in your design. Spelling out the guiding rules for line layout first, however, should make the whole issue of the correct use of sectors more obvious.

NEVER CROSS LINES

The first guiding principle in laying out your maps is that no lines must ever cross. If they meet, all lines must be connected by means of a vertex. This rule ensures that all division of space on the map occurs unambiguously and that unique floor and ceiling heights can be assigned to each location through the use of appropriate sectors.

Following are some examples to illustrate this rule. Figure 3.2 shows some line layouts that are not permitted. The errors are all caused by illegal line crossings. These attempted line crossings are sure-fire indicators of the designer trying to overlap sectors at differing heights.

Figure 3.2.
Illegal DOOM line layouts.

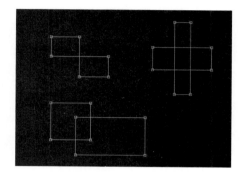

Figure 3.3 shows the correct way to lay out these areas. Note that the connections break up the space in a way that discourages you from thinking of areas that physically overlap. Areas that previously might have been thought of as two sectors are now clearly seen to be three or even five.

Figure 3.3.
The correct way to lay out lines.

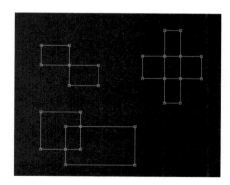

THINK OF WALLS AS VOIDS

The second guiding rule for correct line layout requires you to remember the simple fact that the lines of your maps have no thickness. This means that a line is *not* a wall. It can be the *surface* of a wall, but never the wall itself. The wall is never really part of the map; what the player may perceive as a wall is formed by the void behind the lines. It often helps to think of lines as paint, or as wall-paper, hung to hide the void beyond.

Figure 3.4 shows how this rule is applied to create two adjacent rooms off a single corridor. Notice how all of the walls have had to be drawn explicitly using two lines, not just one.

Figure 3.4.
A line layout that produces a pair of adjacent rooms with a wall between them.

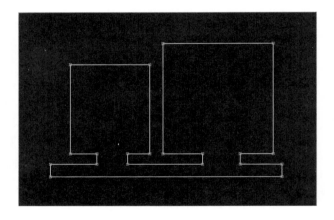

AVOID UNCONNECTED LINES

The final guideline for trouble-free maps is to avoid lines that are not connected at both ends to other lines. Although such lines are not illegal in DOOM, they are rarely used, and until you fully understand their use, you should avoid them. This will remove any risk of your sectors failing to close and will also help to reinforce the previous guideline.

ROOMS VERSUS SECTORS

You may feel that I have been using the word "room" interchangeably with the term "sector," and consequently you may be wondering how these two ideas relate to each other. You may even be equating them with each other in your mind.

So far, I have used the word "room" rather loosely. This is because a room (as I use it in this book) is a perceptual construct within a WAD design. It is important to appreciate that a room really only exists in the mind of the players who are guiding their game-world alter egos through the virtual environment of a WAD (and hopefully, in the mind of the designer who planned it!). It has no matching data construct in the hard, numerical world of the DOOM WAD-file.

The sector, on the other hand, is a rigidly defined data structure, designed to inform the DOOM engine about the disposition of virtual floors and ceilings within its map space.

In planning and designing your DOOM battleground, you are free to think in terms of rooms, corridors, stairways, caves, ledges and whatever other spatial entities are appropriate to the environment you are modeling. When it comes to implementing the WAD that holds your design, you must break your map up into sectors for the purpose of informing DOOM how your world should be arranged. You will need a new sector each time you need to change any of the following: ceiling height or texture, floor height or texture, brightness level, or special sector characteristics. The proper use of sectors to provide playing spaces will become more apparent as you progress deeper into this mission.

The following WAD Sortie builds on the WAD produced in the last Sortie of the previous room. If you did not come along on that Sortie but would like to accompany me on this one, you should use WAD3.WAD (DOOM) or D2WAD3.WAD (DOOM II) from the CD-ROM as your starting point.

WAD SORTIE 4: BREAKING THROUGH THE WALLS

With the lessons of this briefing in mind, you can now begin the expansion of your embryonic WAD. To demonstrate the need for walls to have thickness, I will lead you through the addition of some territory beyond the confines of your initial hexagonal room, starting with a short passageway. The opening into the passageway will be narrower than the passageway itself, so as to create some apparent walls to the hexagonal room.

You should load up WADED with WAD3.WAD as a starting point.

SYNCHRONIZING WADS

Before you start, you will need to check that the shape of your room is a close approximation to mine. Look at Figure 3.5 and compare it with your own map. The important feature to have the same is the line that marks the southeast wall of the hexagonal room. Mine is about 500 units long and runs at an angle of 230. It doesn't matter too much if yours is a little different; if it looks similar on your screen to the one in the figure, you should be okay. Use your knowledge from earlier Sorties to adjust the vertex positions if you need to change the layout of your lines to match mine.

Figure 3.5.
The suggested starting shape.
(This is my WAD3.WAD.)

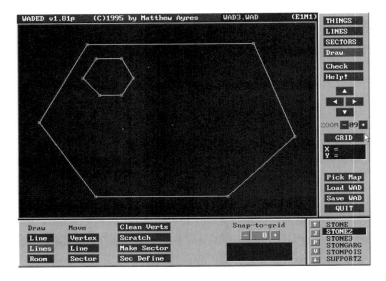

Before you start drawing the new section, you may find it helpful to adjust the Zoom factor to 08, and scroll the view of your map so that the line of that crucial southeastern wall of the main hexagon is toward the left of the screen, leaving yourself some space in which to work to the right. Make sure you have the Draw button clicked along with (Draw) Lines.

DRAWING THE NEW PASSAGE

To begin the new part of the map, move your mouse pointer to the center of the southeastern line of your main hexagon. This is where the new passage will join the main room. When the mouse pointer is properly in contact with the existing line, the line will change to the familiar pulsating red. When this happens, click once with the left mouse button to create a new vertex, connected to the existing line and splitting it into two halves. When you move the mouse, you will find you are in the process of drawing a third line from this new vertex.

Add the lines listed in Table 3.1 to your map—once again, measurements and angles are approximate but note that the first line should be perpendicular to the one you have just split and the second one should be parallel to it.

Table 3.1. Some new lines for your map.

Line	Angle	Length
1	140	50
2	50	74
3	140	110
4	90	448
5	180	192
6	270	672
7	320	96
8	50	96

These additions should leave you with just one line to draw to complete the new shape, shown in Figure 3.6.

Figure 3.6.
The new addition to the southeast corner of the map.

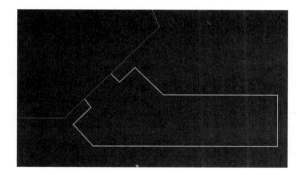

The final new line needs to connect back with the original southeastern wall of the hexagon. Aim to do this about halfway along the line that runs southwest from the new shape's starting point. Your final line must connect with the original hexagon wall, so make sure that the appropriate line shows red before you click it. If your connection is successful, WADED will terminate the drawing process, as it recognizes that you have produced a closed shape.

If the drawing process does not terminate with your last click, it is because you failed to connect your last vertex to the original line. You can salvage this situation quite easily. Click (anywhere) with the right mouse button to terminate the drawing process. This should leave everything intact up to your final vertex. Now click the (Move) Vertices button, and then drag your errant final vertex onto the line to which it should have connected. As this line turns red, release the mouse button and the desired connection will be made.

You may also wish to confirm that the vertex with which you began this new section connects properly. With (Move) Vertices selected, try moving it a little and check that all three lines move with it. If they don't, simply drag the vertex to the point on the original line where you would like it connected and release the mouse button as the line turns red.

The original southeast line of your hexagon is now split into three sections by the addition of the two new vertices. You may find, in fact, that this line is now no longer the nice straight line it once was. Use the appropriate buttons in the Move/Del column and reposition any of your new area's lines or vertices if they are not to your liking.

You can make diagonal lines easier to place in WADED by reducing the Snap-to-Grid setting while drawing. Generally, though, this is best left set at 8.

You may discover that diagonal lines are tricky to get just right in most editors. If you have areas where you need lines to run parallel or perpendicular to each other, or which need to be of particular lengths, it is often best if you can arrange for these lines to run east-west or north-south on the map. Drawing them will be easier this way, and you may find that it causes fewer problems for the nodes builder and the game engine, too—more good reasons for planning out your WAD on paper first.

MAKING A NEW SECTOR

Notice that all of your new lines are still magenta. WADED uses this color to warn you that these lines are not yet part of any sector—they therefore will mean nothing to the game engine and will cause an error if you try to play this WAD. So, when you are happy with the layout of your lines, click the Make Sector button and follow this with a single click somewhere within your new shape.

All of the enclosing lines of your new shape should turn red as WADED incorporates them into a new sector.

Click the SECTORS button (in the right-hand button bar). Now click in each of your two sectors in turn. Observe that WADED has transferred the attributes from your original sector to your new one. The only item that changes in the lower region of the screen as you select each sector is the Sector identification number shown at the extreme left.

ADMIRING YOUR NEW WALLS

Press the Home key to center your map in the map-editing area, and then save the WAD as WAD4.WAD. (Make sure that WADED knows it has to build the nodes before you OK the Save WAD pop-up.) Then you can Quit from WADED and load DOOM to try out your extended WAD. Take the player over toward your new passage and look carefully at the entrance to it. Admire those nice, thick stone walls. (See Figure 3.7.)

Figure 3.7.
A view of your new walls.

ADDING ANOTHER ROOM

Now that you have seen how simple it is to extend your map by adding new sectors, you are no doubt eager to add some more. You should be confident enough to add another room without too much help from me, so start up WADED again with WAD4.WAD as your starting point.

Figure 3.8 shows the basic shape of a new room, this time connected to the original hexagon's southwest wall. You may find a Zoom factor of 08 useful before you start. As before, begin your new drawing at one of the points of connection with the existing hexagon, working around the shape to the other point of connection. I won't give you specific details of the new room, except to say that its long, southern wall should be made about 1,100 units long. You can copy the rest of the shape from the figure.

Figure 3.8.
The new shape for the
southwest corner of the map.

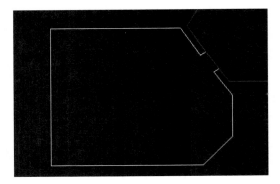

Once the shape is complete, use Make Sector in the usual way to create a new sector out of it. To add a little variety, make this new room a bit brighter than the first. Click the SECTORS button in the right-hand button bar and then click anywhere in the new sector. Increase the Lighting level to 224. Raise the ceiling height to 160, as well, and change its texture to CEIL3_6. Then save the WAD as WAD4A.WAD and take a look at it.

EXAMINING THE NEW ROOM

Take the player into the new room and have a good look around. Everything may seem OK at first, but if you look closely you may see that, in fact, we didn't do too well this time.

First of all, take a close look at the ceiling. I deliberately chose a pattern that has lights in it to explain the increased light level in this room. It doesn't look too good where it meets a diagonal wall, does it? (Yours may not be as bad as mine; it depends on the exact location of your walls. Look at Figure 3.9 if you can't see what I'm complaining about.)

And what about the opening between the two rooms? That hasn't worked very well this time, has it? The floor appears fine, but the ceiling is definitely odd. Do you remember that we set the ceiling of the new room higher than the old? There seems to be some visual confusion over this in the opening, doesn't there?

Finally, take a close look at the walls as you move through the opening. Notice how the mortar lines of one room don't meet up properly with those from the other. (Again, Figure 3.9 shows the problem.) What on earth can have gone wrong?

Figure 3.9.
A messy junction of rooms.

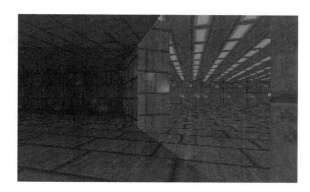

EXIT: MOPPING UP AND MOVING ON

It looks like there is some real mopping up to do here. You have learned some salutary lessons about the limitations of DOOM-space, learned a lot about the laying out of lines, and seen how easy it is to extend a WAD by adding new sectors. You have also seen how easy it is to make a mess of things.

Take heart, though, for the next room will lead you some way toward a solution to the present problem. It will reveal more about lines and shine some light on the mystery of how walls are painted.

DOOM
PROGRAMMING
GURUS

3
ROOM

1
MISSION

2
EPISODE

ROOM 4

By Steve Benner

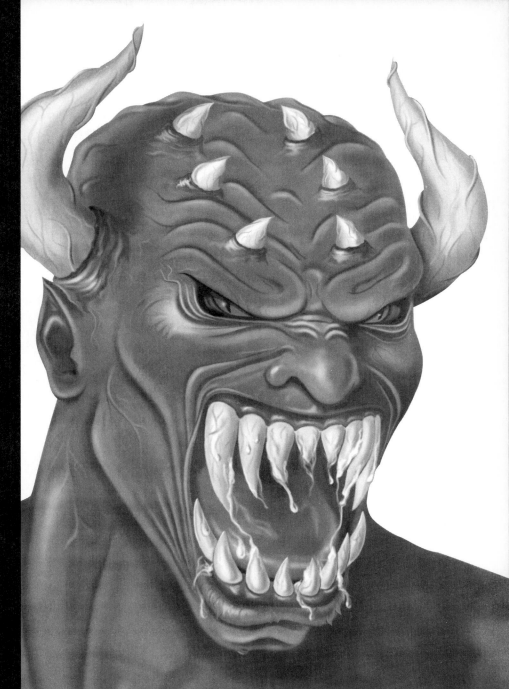

AT THE SECTOR'S EDGE

In your last editing Sortie, you successfully broke out of the single room of your first WAD (although you did so without any real explanation of how it was achieved or of exactly where your old wall went). The mission was not a complete success, however, in its attempt to add another room to your growing WAD. You discovered that DOOM's walls don't automatically look right on their own.

This room will provide you with some more explanations of what you have been doing with your editor and how much it has been doing by itself. A further Sortie will attempt to correct some of the problems which earlier Sorties of this mission introduced to your developing WAD.

The briefing starts with a look at how lines really work.

A CLOSER LOOK AT LINES

So far, you have had no detailed information about what lines do in DOOM WADs. You have been told that they always run between vertices, that they consist of a linedef with a couple of sidedefs attached, and that they define the extent of sectors. You have not been given any real details of what these structures are, what they do, or how they do it. It may have been apparent to you that your current lines are providing DOOM with the walls of your rooms. Yet you have been told that your lines are not the walls themselves. And you broke out of the walls of your first room without deleting (or even apparently changing) any of your original lines. You are probably wondering, therefore, how all of this fits together.

Start up WADED with your latest WAD, and I'll show you.

WHAT LINES *REALLY* DO

The principal role of the lines in DOOM WADs is really very simple. It is to tell the game engine about the *edge* of a sector. Remember that the sector is DOOM's basic division of space. You have seen how, in essence, each sector has a floor, a ceiling, and a light level. At the edge of each sector, something must happen to those three items. Lines tell DOOM precisely what that is.

THE LINEDEF STRUCTURE

You know already that a linedef runs between two vertices. This determines both where the line lies on the map and also its handedness. In addition, each linedef provides a set of attributes that tell the game engine how the line should be treated during play.

Viewing Linedef Attributes in WADED

In WADED, you can view all of a line's attributes (remember that linedefs and sidedefs are treated as one entity in WADED) by clicking the LINES button located towards the top of the right-hand button bar. When you select this button, the Line Attributes bar is displayed in the lower portion of the screen below the main map-editing area. (See Figure 4.1.) Click any of your lines to select it and view its attributes.

Many of a line's attributes are under automatic control in WADED. For now, look but don't change anything!

Figure 4.1.
*WADED's Line
Atributes bar.*

LINEDEF ATTRIBUTES

Most *linedef attributes* are single-bit (on/off) flags that determine a line's main characteristics. These on/off characteristics are as follows:

- 2-sided/see-through/shoot-through
- Impassable
- Secret on map
- Blocks sound
- Not on map
- On map from start
- Blocks monsters
- Upper unpegged
- Lower unpegged

WADED uses slightly different terms, but the correspondence should be obvious.

THE LINEDEF SPECIAL ACTION CHARACTERISTIC

In addition to the above simple attributes, each linedef also possesses a *special action* characteristic, which enables it to trigger particular actions during play. This characteristic will be the subject of several later rooms, but you can ignore it for now.

LINE FLAGS

The simple attributes of linedefs (which I shall term *line flags* from now on) warrant further inspection.

2-SIDED / SEE-THROUGH / SHOOT-THROUGH

The *2-sided/see-through/shoot-through flag* (or just *2-sided flag*, as it is more conveniently termed) serves a large number of purposes, as you can tell from its name. It is used principally to inform the game engine whether or not there are sectors on both sides of a line (although it does not need to reflect the true state of affairs here). This information is used by the graphic engine to decide whether there is anything more to draw beyond this line. It is also used to ascertain whether monsters can see through the line, and to determine the fate of bullets and shotgun pellets (but *not* rockets or plasma) that reach the line.

There are other ramifications for lines flagged as 2-sided, as you will see shortly. For now, you should leave the manipulation of this particular flag strictly to your editor.

IMPASSABLE

A line's *impassable flag* determines whether players or monsters can cross it: they will never be able to cross a line that has this flag set. If there is no sector beyond a line, this flag is redundant and DOOM will ignore it, whatever its setting. Note that this flag has no effect on the passage of bullets or projectiles.

2
EPISODE

1
MISSION

4
ROOM

DOOM
PROGRAMMING
GURUS

> ## WADED's Automated Flag Waving
>
> WADED automatically adjusts all of the lines' 2-sided and impassable flags as needed, provided that you build your sectors with the Make Sector button. (You will see another way of making sectors later.) A quick inspection of the lines of your map should show you that virtually all of your current lines have their impassable flags set; however, you should also be able to spot two that haven't.

SECRET ON MAP

Lines with the *Secret on Map* flag set appear as standard red lines on the DOOM auto-map during play. This is used to hide secret doors and such-like from the players prior to their discovery. Secret areas are the subject of Room 11, "Let's Get the Hell Out of Here!" of this mission.

BLOCKS SOUND

Setting a line's *Blocks Sounds* flag limits the transmission of sound from sector to sector, thus preventing any non-deaf monsters from waking and hunting the player as soon as the first shot is fired. Such lines do not stop sound dead, though—you will learn more about sound propagation in Room 12, "Populating Your DOOM World," of this mission.

NOT ON MAP

Lines with their *Not on Map* flag set do not appear on DOOM's auto-map at all, even if the player acquires the computer-map power-up. This flag enables you to hide any lines from the player that you feel may cause confusion. It also permits the hiding of special action lines, so that no clues to their presence can be gleaned from the map.

ON MAP FROM START

Lines with their *On Map from Start* flag set will appear on DOOM's auto-map as soon as the level starts, even though they may not yet have been "seen" by the player. You can use this flag to give the player clues about secret locations by hinting at additional map areas. It should rarely be needed in a well-designed WAD.

BLOCKS MONSTERS

The *Blocks Monsters* flag enables a line to block the movements of monsters without impeding the player. You will have occasion to use this flag in later rooms.

UPPER/LOWER UNPEGGED

A line's two *unpegged* flags contribute to the way in which patterns are painted on the vertical plane that the line represents. The purpose and use of these two flags is covered in detail in Episode 2, Mission 1, Room 5, "The Low-Down on Textures." Before you learn the use of these flags, though, you need to know how the walls get painted in the first place.

PAINTING THE WALLS

You have now seen how linedefs tell the DOOM engine how each line contributes to the operation of the game. On its own though, a linedef says little about the way lines look. For that, DOOM needs to consult the sidedef.

THE ROLE OF THE SIDEDEF

To understand fully the role of sidedefs, you have to appreciate that each sidedef belongs to a sector as well as to a linedef. Lines will therefore need as many sidedefs as they have sectors bordering them. It is the sidedef that truly connects each sector to its surrounding linedefs and which is responsible for informing the game engine about the view of that line from its particular sector. The graphical engine consults the appropriate sidedef whenever it needs to render a sector's boundary on the screen; the connection of the sidedefs through their linedefs then provides the links out to adjacent sectors and the data required to render fully all of the surfaces in the player's field of view at any moment.

This interconnection and mutual ownership of data structures may sound complex, but it provides the DOOM engine with a quick and convenient way of obtaining the information it needs in order to display its world.

THE SIDEDEF STRUCTURE

Sidedefs provide details of the view of their particular sector edge by supplying texture names to the DOOM engine, in a similar manner to the way that the sector structure supplies texture names for its floor and ceiling. Because of the added complication brought about by the potential vertical displacement of adjacent sectors, sidedefs need to provide a little more information than just a single texture name. Each sidedef may be called upon to supply up to three texture names, depending upon the precise disposition of the floors and ceilings of adjacent sectors. Each sidedef therefore consists of three texture *slots*, each of which holds one texture name.

A sidedef's three textures are as follows:

- The normal (or main) texture
- The upper texture
- The lower texture

Additionally, each sidedef supplies a horizontal (X) and vertical (Y) displacement value that allows for the precise alignment of the specified textures at the time of painting. (Our discussion of the intricate details of texture alignment is deferred until the next room.)

Viewing Sidedef Information in WADED

As has already been noted (as seen in Figure 4.1, shown previously), by selecting WADED's LINES button to view the linedef attributes, you are also presented with any sidedef data in the same information bar. The sidedef information for the currently selected line appears in two columns, just to the right of the full column of linedef flags. Each sidedef column consists of three text field boxes, with two blue numerical value buttons beneath them. The leftmost of these two columns displays data from the line's left sidedef, if one exists (these fields will be empty if the line is single-sided), while the rightmost column displays the information from the line's right sidedef.

A SIDEDEF'S THREE TEXTURES

Between them, a sidedef's three textures can supply all of the information that is ever needed to render successfully any DOOM wall surface. This is illustrated in Figure 4.2, which shows all possible vertical arrangements of two adjacent sectors.

In all cases, a dashed line shows the two-sided line lying on the boundary between the two sectors. Letters indicate which texture slot provides the appropriate pattern for all visible wall surfaces. Remember that each sidedef supplies the engine with the details of what is seen when viewed from within its particular sector.

Figure 4.2.

Locations of textures on lines between sectors.

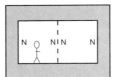

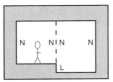

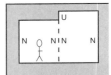

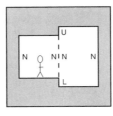

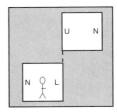

THE NORMAL (OR MAIN) TEXTURE

A single-sided line can have nothing beyond it. DOOM knows, therefore, that when rendering any visible portion of such a line, it will need to apply paint between the current sector's ceiling and its floor in order to completely block off any further view. It obtains the name of the pattern to use as this paint from the line's normal-texture slot.

The outer walls of the sectors in Figure 4.2 (with letter Ns adjacent to them) consist of lines of this type.

A line with a sector on each side of it needs to have the relative heights of the floors and ceilings of these sectors taken into consideration before anything can be painted. In these cases, the normal texture is only applied to the gap between the *lower* of the two ceilings and the *higher* of the two floors. Again, Figure 4.2 shows these areas with a letter N, this time on the dashed lines between the sectors. Note that one such letter occurs on each side of these lines. Each provides the view of that space from its own particular side.

> DOOM does not permit all wall textures to be applied to a two-sided line's normal texture. You should be able to tell from Figure 4.2, though, that you are unlikely to want any texture there in most situations. (The application of textures to two-sided lines is discussed in detail in later rooms.)

After dealing with the normal texture, there may still be other portions of the wall to be painted, as will happen when a sector's floor is lower, or its ceiling higher, than its neighbor's. The other two texture slots are used to provide the paint for these additional areas.

UPPER TEXTURE

The *upper texture* is used to paint the wall area between a sector's ceiling and any lower adjacent ceiling. Figure 4.2 marks these areas with the letter U.

LOWER TEXTURE

The *lower texture* is used to paint the wall area between a sector's floor and any higher adjacent floor. Figure 4.2 marks these areas with the letter L.

> DOOM's decision about whether a line has anything beyond it or not is based only the setting of the line's two-sided flag. It does not count the line's sidedefs. An incorrect setting of this flag will therefore drastically affect the way the line displays.

MISSING OUT THE PAINT

In some cases, you will want a line to be completely transparent—as with most of the normal textures on the two-sided lines shown in Figure 4.2. Most lines between adjacent sectors are like this, in fact, to enable a player to see from one sector to the next. DOOM uses a *null* or *transparent* texture setting to achieve this. This special value is designated by means of a dash character (–) in the appropriate texture slot.

This special texture (which is really a lack of texture, of course) causes the engine to paint whatever is in view *beyond* the line, rather than painting some pattern in the line's vertical plane. It may therefore only be used in a location where there is another sector to be seen through it; otherwise you are inviting a view of the void—an action you will always regret. An inspection of Figure 4.2 should indicate which locations these are.

More Automatic Line Changing by WADED

When you build sectors up against each other, as you did in the previous WAD Sortie, WADED will automatically make all the changes to your lines that it deems appropriate. Usually this means making any lines that are common to the two sectors passable, two-sided, and transparent. "But," you may ask, "what if I wanted an impassable wall between my two adjacent rooms?" In such a case, don't build the wall out of a single line. Use two single-sided lines with a void between them, just as I showed you in the previous room.

PUTTING PAINT IN THE RIGHT PLACES

As you can undoubtedly appreciate, with a WAD's potential for complex geometric arrangements, it is vital that the graphical engine be supplied with correct and complete information if it is to perform its task of rendering the DOOM world correctly on the screen. It is important that you learn to recognize the areas where texture information is crucial, if you are to avoid problems with the way your WADs appear.

ESSENTIAL TEXTURES

The biggest cause of serious problems in the on-screen rendering of DOOM WADs is the omission of essential textures. By this, I mean the use of the *transparent* texture in an area of wall that has nothing to see beyond it. You should regard the following as places where a texture is essential:

- The main texture of any single-sided line
- Any upper texture where the current sector's ceiling is higher than its neighbor's
- Any lower texture where the current sector's floor is lower than its neighbor's

Again, look back to Figure 4.2 if you can't immediately see why trying to look through these areas is not a good idea.

Discussion of the full consequences of omitting essential textures is deferred until the next room. For now, just note where the presence of a texture is crucial and try to ensure that you don't omit textures from these locations.

Essential Texture Notification in WADED

WADED alerts you to essential textures by marking such slots in the Line Attributes bar with a red background (instead of the usual black). It only marks slots in this way that are essential by virtue of the relative elevations of adjacent sectors; it assumes you will take care of the main texture of single-sided lines yourself. WADED always assigns a main texture to a line as you draw it—it is not unreasonable, therefore, for WADED to assume that you know what you are doing if you subsequently remove it.

The following WAD Sortie builds on the WAD produced in the previous room's Sortie. If you did not accompany me on that Sortie but would like to come along on this one, you should use WAD4A.WAD (DOOM) or D2WAD4A.WAD (DOOM II) from the CD-ROM as your starting point.

WAD SORTIE 5: FIXING THE MESS

Now that you understand something of the way in which lines work, you should take a more detailed look at your WAD to see how WADED has handled line settings so far (that is, when left to its own devices). The causes of the problems might even become apparent.

LOOKING AT THE LINES

With WAD4A.WAD loaded and the LINES button selected, try clicking a few of your lines in turn. Notice how just about all of your lines are flagged as impassable, have no left sidedef (shown by the left-textures column being entirely empty), and have STONE2 as the right main-texture, with the transparent texture (–) in the right upper- and lower-texture slots. In other words, all of your lines represent impassable surfaces, painted with the STONE2 texture from ceiling to floor. I hope this sounds reasonable!

If you inspect the line that separates the main hexagon from the passage in the southeast corner, however, you will see that this is different from most of your other lines. This line is flagged as two-sided, having right and left sidedefs, with the transparent (–) texture assigned to all slots. This is, therefore, a line through which the player can both see and walk—it is an opening in the "wall" of impassable lines around it. This is the line that WADED changed when you used Make Sector to add the southeastern passage to the family of sectors in your WAD. WADED made this hole in the wall for you by switching two flags (impassable and two-sided) and removing the paint from the right normal.

You may have already noticed that WADED gave you a visual clue to the action it took—look carefully at this particular line on your map and you will see that it is displayed less prominently than your other lines. WADED always uses this dimmer color and thinner linestroke to distinguish two-sided lines from single-sided ones on your map, so that you can always tell at a glance which is which.

THE OFFENDING LINE

Turn your attention to the equivalent line in the southwest wall of your hexagon—the one that connects the hexagon to the new room off to the southwest. You can spot now, I hope, that this is two-sided, even before you click it. When you do click it, observe that its settings are identical to its counterpart in the southeast wall. But notice that here WADED marks the left upper-texture-slot with a *red* background. This is a warning that there is a texture missing from this line.

Remember that you made the ceiling of the new room quite a bit higher than the ceiling of the hexagonal room? When viewed from inside the new room, there will be a step down along this line from the level of its ceiling to the level of the adjacent ceiling. DOOM will need to be told what to paint on the vertical surface of this downward step. (It will, of course, have no such requirement when viewing the southwest room from within the hexagonal room. From there, the step up on the other side of the line is hidden by the hexagonal room's lower ceiling. Hence the need for two sidedefs in these situations. Again, look back to Figure 4.2 if you're having difficulty visualizing this.)

It would be sensible, I suppose, to fill this missing texture with the same texture as used for the neighboring walls. I'm getting tired of STONE2, however, as I'm sure you are, so I suggest you look for an alternative. It would be nice to use a new texture for the whole of the new room, wouldn't it? Let's see what we can find.

CHOOSING A WALL TEXTURE

While viewing lines in WADED, a list of available wall textures is displayed in the extreme bottom-right corner of the screen. This list box operates in exactly the same way as the Floor/Ceiling Texture list box that appears when you are viewing sectors. Notice how STONE2 is the currently selected texture. Using the right mouse button, click an entry in the list box to preview it on the screen, just as you did with the floor textures. The preview of a wall texture (Figure 4.3 shows the familiar STONE2) is similar to that of a floor tile, but the graphic is generally bigger and there is a little more information displayed. The next room will examine wall textures in more detail, so I won't dwell on the subject here.

Take a look at the texture called STONE3. This would seem like a good texture to introduce into the new room—it is related to the texture of its neighbor's walls but different.

Figure 4.3.
*WADED's preview of the
wall texture, STONE2.*

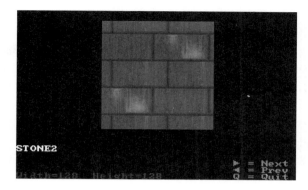

Don't get carried away introducing new textures at random through your WADs. This will
make them look amateurish. Think through your use of textures. Make changes gradually
and with reason. Texture changes that the player hardly notices usually work out best.

CHANGING LINES EN-MASSE

Now that you have a new texture for the new room, it needs to be applied to all of the lines that
make up this southwestern sector. Selecting all of these lines in turn and changing the entry in all
of their right normal texture-slots sounds rather tedious, though, doesn't it? Fortunately, WADED
provides a shortcut, in the form of its MULTI button. I will show you how to use it.

Click the MULTI button. It will turn red. In addition, any line you had selected reverts to its normal color, and all of the information in the Line Attributes bar changes to Xs (or green dots in the
case of the flags). Click a line now and notice that even though you have selected it in the usual way
(it has turned red), none of its attributes are displayed. If you click more lines, you will see that each
new line becomes selected in addition to earlier selections. Click a line that is already selected and
it becomes deselected. In this mode, you can now select each of the lines you want to change. Click
all nine lines that you added to form the new room in the southwest corner of your map. Do not
include the two-sided line linking this room with your hexagon. Make sure that no other lines are
included in your selection before going on; click any that are, to deselect them.

DOOM
PROGRAMMING
GURUS

4
ROOM

1
MISSION

2
EPISODE

When you have all nine lines selected, make sure that STONE3 is the highlighted texture in the Wall Textures list box and then click once using the left mouse button on the middle texture-field of the right-hand column of line textures. The X that was there should be replaced by the name STONE3. WADED gives you the chance to change your mind about multi-line operations such as this and will not affect the change until you click the APPLY button.

> If you decide you don't want to make any multi-line changes, you can click MULTI again to return to single-line selection without applying any.

When you are sure that you have the correct nine lines selected and STONE3 in the appropriate texture field, click APPLY, and WADED will make the changes you have requested and then re-turn to its normal single line-selection mode. The line you had selected immediately prior to click-ing the MULTI button will be the current line.

FIXING THE PROBLEMS (MAYBE)

Now select the line that runs across the entrance to your newly painted room. Apply STONE3 to the missing essential texture field. Right, that's one problem solved.

One of my other complaints about this room is the poor ceiling texture. I didn't like the way the lights disappeared into the walls. You can rectify this by applying a new ceiling texture. Click SECTORS to access sector attributes; click in the southwest sector to access its attributes; scroll the Textures list down to TLITE6_6 and apply this texture to the ceiling.

When you've done that, save the file as WAD5.WAD (there should be no need to build the nodes) and try the WAD out. Is that opening into the new room any better now? (See Figure 4.4.)

Figure 4.4.
Better—but still not right!

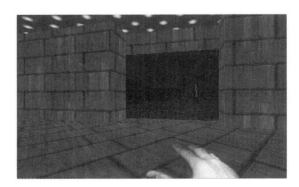

Never mind. Soldier on. Let's look at the problem more closely.

RE-EXAMINING THE PROBLEM

What is it that looks odd about your gap through the wall now? Well, there is still a problem with the matching of the mortar-lines. There remains a discontinuity where the lines on the hexagonal room's walls meet those coming through the gap. You didn't expect these to change with the latest modification, though, did you? The vertical step down from the higher level of the southwest room's ceiling to that of its neighbor does appear in the view now. (Figure 4.4 shows this.) The mortar lines on this wall section (as it now appears) don't align too well with its neighbors', however. And it looks to be in a rather odd place—wouldn't you expect that step down to occur in a plane flush with the *inner* surface of the southwestern room's walls? Maybe it is time to return briefly to the drawing board and rethink this area of the WAD.

First, ask yourself what it is that makes this opening different from the opening at the other side of the hexagonal room. You experienced no difficulties there, so why are there problems here? The answer, of course, lies in the change of ceiling height across the opening. The southeastern opening uses the same floor and ceiling heights as the main room. In fact, it uses the same floor and ceiling textures as well as the same lighting level. There was no necessity to create a new sector there at all—you could have merely extended the hexagonal room sector around the new shape.

Don't worry, though. It was expedient to develop the WAD the way you did, and there is nothing much wasted as a result. You could recombine the lines into one sector, but there is little to be gained by so doing. As it is, it is always possible to change either one independently of the other should you ever want to. I'd leave it as it is.

So, having identified the problem as the change in ceiling height, let's examine the solution afresh.

RETHINKING THE SOLUTION

Consider what is really wanted here: a hexagonal room connecting to another room, through an opening in the wall. Now, how many sectors is this? The WAD currently implements this in two sectors. Would it not be better as three? Consider the following:

- Hexagon room
- The southwest room
- The hole in the wall

DOOM
PROGRAMMING
GURUS

4
ROOM

1
MISSION

2
EPISODE

This way, each area can have its own ceiling height, with the interconnecting hole handled independently of the two rooms.

Your WAD is suffering from a case of insufficient sectors! This is quite a common fault in the WADs of beginners. It generally demonstrates that the novice has yet to grasp fully the correct use of sectors.

Now return to your WAD, wiser than you were. You need to change the way the two rooms interconnect.

REBUILDING THE INTERCONNECTION

Reload WADED with WAD5.WAD. Enter Draw mode and amend the interconnecting gap between the hexagonal room and its southwestern neighbor. This gap currently has a single line between the two rooms, marking the line of the hexagonal room's southwest wall. There are two vertices that, if connected to each other by a line, would provide another line, parallel to the first, and fulfill a similar role in completing the line of the southwestern room's northeast wall. Add this missing line.

You now need to create a new sector out of the small rectangle you have just completed and that represents the interconnecting area through the wall between the two rooms. Use Make Sector to do this. This will "steal" this area away from the sector that currently owns it (the old southwestern room) and create a new sector out of it. After you have done this, move the mouse pointer away into the void somewhere and notice that WADED is now displaying your new line in the brighter color that signifies a single-sided line. If you now move the mouse into the remaining area of the southwestern room, you will see that the southwest sector is no longer closed—the new line has not automatically been incorporated into it. Click somewhere in the southwest room to make WADED correct this error. You should see that doing this turns your new line two-sided.

You should now select SECTORS (in the right-hand button bar) and inspect the new interconnecting sector. Notice that it has inherited the settings from the adjacent hexagonal room, even though this area originally belonged to the sector to the southwest—the reason for this odd behavior is explained in a later Sortie. Click LINES and inspect the textures of the new line. Notice how this time WADED has supplied something for the essential upper texture. It may not be particularly appropriate, but at least it has tried. Change it to STONE3 to match its neighboring lines, then save the WAD as WAD5A.WAD and try it out.

Examine the "improved" doorway. It does look a little better when viewed from the southwest, doesn't it? The lintel is now flush with the walls, which improves its appearance somewhat, but the mortar lines still don't match up. If you look closely and compare the current WAD's view through the gap with the earlier view, you will see that the mortar alignment problem through the gap has changed but not noticeably for the better.

MODIFYING THE INTERCONNECTION

Try one more modification. Reload WAD5A.WAD, click SECTORS, and select the small inter-connecting sector you just made. Reduce the ceiling height to 104. Doing this will create another essential texture—can you work out where it is?

To see the missing essential, take a look at the boundary between the interconnecting sector and the hexagonal room. The left upper-texture is still set for STONE3. This is marked as unnecessary now (its field has a black background), and you can delete it if you wish (although it does no harm if you leave it). Simply click it with the right mouse button. Note that the right upper-texture is now marked as essential by WADED (although it hasn't bothered to supply it!). You should be able to work out for yourself why this texture is essential. (The fact that WADED doesn't supply one can be ascribed to a bug.)

Apply STONE2 to this slot. Save as WAD5B.WAD—no node-building should be necessary. Quit, then try the WAD.

You should find that this has produced an opening that looks (structurally) better from both sides— although it has now completely messed up all of the mortar-line alignments around the opening!

It would seem that there are still some things to learn here.

EXIT: MOPPING UP AND MOVING ON

In this room, you learned a lot about the way lines work in DOOM. You learned how they can be made to produce both walls and the openings in them. You found out how and where paint can be applied, and you have learned to recognize where it is needed. You saw how to access some more features of WADED, and you have moved away from the ubiquitous gray stone of your first WAD.

Your latest Sortie made some progress towards correcting the faults around your WAD's doorway. What you need now is the low-down on how textures are applied to the walls, so that we can mount a full-scale rescue attempt on this area of your WAD. You will find everything you need in the next room.

ROOMS

By Steve Benner

THE LOW-DOWN ON TEXTURES

So far in this episode you have used a number of floor, ceiling, and wall textures to paint the "hard surfaces" of your WAD. You have seen that while it may be easy to specify their use, making them look right is not always so simple.

This room provides you with the full low-down on DOOM textures. You will see and use textures that act as more than mere paint. You will also be shown something of the full richness of the texture palette that has been provided by the designers at id Software.

In addition, the rules for applying textures will be discussed in full, along with the consequences of transgressing those rules. By the time you complete this room, you will know how to apply textures to any of your WAD's surfaces and have them look just right.

This room also leads you on three WAD Sorties, building on the WADs produced in previous rooms. During these sorties, you will see something of DOOM's great outdoors, with the addition of a court-yard to your WAD. At long last, you will also be shown how to cure the problems of texture alignment which have been plaguing your WAD throughout the last few Sorties.

CEILING AND FLOOR TEXTURES

Your first introduction to textures in this mission was as tiles for ceilings and floors. These ceiling and floor textures make a good topic with which to begin a full survey of DOOM textures.

FLATS

Figure 5.1 shows a sample view of a DOOM floor or ceiling texture. The graphic itself is a 64 x 64 block of pixels. All floor and ceiling textures use graphics of this size.

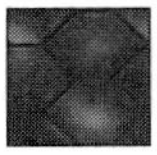

Figure 5.1.
A single occurrence of the FLOOR5_1 floor texture.

These simple, square, graphical textures are often termed floor and ceiling *flats* or *tiles* to distinguish them from the more complex wall textures that you will encounter later in this room. The DOOM game engine will allow flats to be applied interchangeably to floors or ceilings. You may find, however, that not all textures will look equally good on both surfaces—and some may look downright odd if used inappropriately.

As they are all of a standard size, DOOM's graphical engine applies flats in a standard way to floor and ceiling surfaces. A flat's exact position is determined from the map's X,Y coordinate grid: Flats are always placed starting at a coordinate that is a multiple of 64.

As well as being positioned firmly on this grid, tiles are always oriented the same way, along a north-south axis. The flat's first pixel (the pixel from its top left corner when viewed as in Figure 5.1) is copied to the appropriate surface at the starting coordinate. Subsequent pixels are transferred to adjacent locations to the east (working across the graphic) and south (working down the graphic). If the same texture is applied to both the floor and ceiling of a sector, these two surfaces will appear as mirror images of each other. Each pixel on the ceiling will be the same color as the pixel on the floor directly below it.

Because they are locked to the coordinate system in the manner just described, floors and ceilings have their patterns rendered with no reference to walls or other map elements (except that these textures are clipped by their sector boundaries, of course). This methodology ensures that adjacent sectors having the same floor or ceiling heights can have their textures connected smoothly across the boundary between them, whatever the shape or orientation of that boundary. It also means that if the designer is not careful, walls may cut blithely across features in the ceiling or floor textures, making them look odd. Remember the abortive attempt to use the CEIL3_6 texture in the south-western room of your WAD, back in WAD Sortie 4?

Note that the only way of changing the way that floor and ceiling textures line up with your sector boundaries is to reposition your map-lines to make them clip the flats differently. The flats themselves cannot be moved or rotated.

Assistance with Flat Alignment in WADED

To assist in the placement of lines for the best alignment of flats, WADED supplies you with an optional *grid overlay*, which shows where flats will be placed in your map. This overlay is activated and deactivated by means of the GRID button, located in the right button bar. Use this grid to position your lines along the joins of the flats to ensure the best painting of floors and ceilings.

SEEING THE SKY

The previous room taught you that walls can be assigned a transparent texture (or have texture omitted, depending upon how you care to think of it) to allow sectors beyond them to be visible through them. You are possibly wondering whether there is an equivalent transparent texture for ceilings, one that will enable the player to see out to the sky and the rest of the outside world. After all, you have seen something like this in DOOM, haven't you?

The answers are "Yes" and "What outside world?" DOOM is capable of displaying the sky and distant mountains and such-like, but don't think that such "outside" elements exist anywhere on your map (or anywhere else, for that matter).

When you want your players to see sky, the ceiling texture to use goes by the name of F_SKY1. As its name suggests, this texture provides you with something rather more special than transparent paint—it provides you with sky (mountains too, in version 1 of DOOM). This shouldn't surprise you. After all, what use would transparent paint be on the ceiling? There is nothing beyond the ceiling to see, only void. And, as you will find out shortly, that is not a pretty sight.

If you try to preview F_SKY1, however, you may be a little surprised by what you see. (See Figure 5.2.)

Figure 5.2.
The surprise preview of
F_SKY1.

"Where is the sky?" you may ask. "And how could they get it all into a 64×64 tile anyway? It surely wouldn't work! Are you *sure* about this?" I can see that I'm going to have to convince you.

> The following WAD Sortie builds on the WAD produced in the last Sortie of the previous room. If you did not accompany me on that Sortie but would like to come along on this one, you should use WAD5B.WAD (DOOM) or D2WAD5B.WAD (DOOM II) from the CD-ROM as your starting point.

WAD SORTIE 6: ADDING AN OUTDOOR SECTOR

This WAD Sortie will extend your existing WAD by leading you through the steps needed for the addition of an outdoor courtyard area.

BREAKING OUT

Start by adding just three new lines to the south wall of the southwest room, as shown in Figure 5.3. These will eventually form the exit from the southwest room to the new courtyard.

The short ends of the rectangle are about 56 units long. The long dimension isn't critical, but don't make it too long; 360 units is fine.

Figure 5.3.
Three new lines for the WAD.

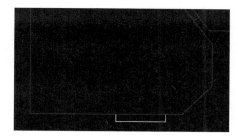

DEFINING THE COURTYARD

After adding these three lines, with WADED in (Draw) Lines mode, find and select the texture called BROWN1 in the scrolling texture list in the bottom right corner of the screen. (Yes, you've guessed it. This will change the wall texture that WADED uses for your next lines to something new. I think it's time for a bit of a change, don't you?) Now draw the additional lines shown in Figure 5.4. These lines will form the courtyard's enclosing walls.

Figure 5.4.
More new lines for the WAD.

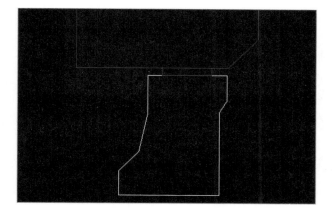

Don't worry about the precise size or shape of this area (but don't encroach too far to the West: I have other things planned for there), just make it match the basic form shown in Figure 5.4.

When you've added all of the new lines and are happy that everything connects properly, click Make Sector. Click next in the new, small rectangle to break out of the southwest room; and then in the larger shape, to add the courtyard area to the list of sectors. Click SECTORS (at upper right) and then somewhere in the new area that is to be the courtyard. This should be Sector 5.

If you always build your sectors sequentially in this way, working out from existing sectors, WADED has something to build from (a neighboring sector) and will assign more useful values to the various attributes by copying them from the adjacent sector.

TAKING THE ROOF OFF

Now, using the *right* mouse button, click once in the ceiling-texture field of the courtyard sector. This is WADED's shortcut for applying F_SKY1. The floor texture MFLR8_1, inherited from the inner rooms, is rather inappropriate for a courtyard, so I suggest you change it while you're here. I think you'll find that FLAT1_1 fits the bill nicely. And because it's a bright sunny day in the land of DOOM, why not take the lighting level up to 255? Then save the file as WAD6.WAD (you may find that the nodes are taking a little longer to build by now) and try it out.

Now do you believe me? I know the transition between sky and building doesn't look right yet (see Figure 5.5), but you will have a chance to fix that in a moment. For now, I just wanted you to see the sky.

Figure 5.5.
Behold! The sky!

FAKING THE GREAT OUTDOORS

Now that you have seen the reality of F_SKY1, you need to know how to use it. There are a number of aspects of this particular texture that can be confusing, so I'll set you straight on these first.

SOURCES OF CONFUSION WITH DOOM SKIES

You have already observed the principal confusing aspect: the absence of the flat itself from the list of ceiling textures. The reason that there is no ceiling flat for this texture is the obvious one: A realistic and believable rendering of the sky could not be obtained by tiling a 64×64 graphic. Not surprisingly, therefore, DOOM doesn't use one. (Quite what it is that you see when previewing F_SKY1 remains something of a mystery—probably a dummy entry in the flats table to keep the graphics engine happy.)

To add to the confusion, the sky textures (for, as you will see, there are more than one) can be found lurking amongst the wall textures. Preview the wall texture called SKY1 and you will see the sky graphic used in your last WAD. Wall textures SKY2 and SKY3 should look familiar, too.

Remember, you will need to be in LINES mode to preview wall textures in WADED.

> The names used for the sky textures in DOOM II are the same as those used in DOOM, but the textures look different.

This leads me to the final point of confusion: the fact that there are *three* separate graphics for portraying the sky, but only one ceiling-texture name for obtaining them.

All of this confusion can be cleared up by realizing that F_SKY1 is not a texture at all. It is a special name, used to trigger a different ceiling-painting technique. To utilize it properly, you need to understand how it works.

HOW IT ALL WORKS

This is how the process operates. When the game engine comes to paint a ceiling marked as F_SKY1, it checks first to see what the current episode is (or level, in DOOM II). From this information, the engine decides which sky texture to use. SKY1 is used for Episode 1, SKY2 for Episode 2, and SKY3 for Episode 3. (DOOM II spreads the three sky textures out over its 30-odd levels in a similar manner.) You, therefore, can only choose which of the three sky textures you want to appear in your WAD by choosing the episode (or level) that your map appears in.

Having located the appropriate texture (stored amongst the wall textures), the graphical engine pastes this into the ceiling space of the appropriate sector. Rather than performing the graphical transformations necessary to create the normal ceiling perspective, however, the texture is pasted onto the screen area, pixel for pixel, starting at the top of the screen and working down (clipped, of course, by any other textured surfaces in view at the time). The player's viewing direction is used to determine the horizontal screen displacement of the graphic so that the sky (and any associated distant vista) appears to rotate correctly as the player turns. No other scaling is ever performed on this graphic, thus giving it the appearance of being at an infinite distance from the player at all times.

USING THE SKY TEXTURE EFFECTIVELY

Once this process is properly understood, use of the F_SKY1 texture becomes a fairly simple and straightforward matter. Look back at your sample outdoor area. (See Figure 5.5.) If you ignore the details of the sky graphic and imagine ceiling tiles placed over the area that it occupies, you should be able to see quite easily that the sky does indeed act as a replacement for the ceiling, in that it occupies precisely the same area as tiles would. Notice how the plane of the "outdoor ceiling" runs continuously into the ceiling of the adjacent "indoor" area. It does so because the ceiling heights are the same in all three of the sectors in view.

To create an illusion that the "building" the player has just left has height beyond its ceiling, as a real building would have, the *outdoor* sector must have its ceiling raised. Why? To make the sky higher. This will create an upper texture in the step down from this higher sky to the ceiling of the adjacent indoor sector. By using a pattern appropriate to the outside surface of the building as the texture for this step down, you can create the upper facade of the building. Used with care, this can produce reasonably realistic-looking buildings. It does need care, however, because this facade is just like those of a Western movie-set: flat, with nothing of substance behind it. Allow the player too close to its edges and it will be seen around, giving the trick away.

Another useful characteristic of the F_SKY1 painting technique is that the sky texture used is always rendered at a constant brightness, regardless of the brightness level specified for the sector. This allows the use of variations in lighting level in outdoor sectors to simulate areas of shade without making the sky look odd as a consequence. However, the inability to apply sloping shadow areas to walls can limit the usefulness of this, as you will see shortly.

USING THE SKY TEXTURE IN OTHER PLACES

F_SKY1 can be applied to the floor, but, not surprisingly, it produces an odd effect there. Remember that the display position of a texture applied as F_SKY1 is always reckoned from the top of the *screen*. Being 128 pixels high, it will need to repeat before it reaches the space set aside for it on the floor. The result is generally somewhat less than attractive and never realistic—the effect does bear experimentation, however.

2	1		5		DOOM
EPISODE	MISSION		ROOM		PROGRAMMING GURUS

Similarly, any of the SKY textures can be applied to walls, where they will look and act like any other wall texture. They will not behave as if they had been painted as sky; they will simply look like a picture of the sky painted on the walls—which, of course, is what they will be.

WAD SORTIE 7: IMPROVING THE OUTDOOR SECTOR

This Sortie builds on the WAD produced in the previous one. If you did not produce that WAD, you should use WAD6.WAD (DOOM) or D2WAD6.WAD (DOOM II) from the CD-ROM as your starting point here.

If you would like to start up WADED again, I will show you how to improve the appearance of the outer courtyard by applying some of these techniques.

You have learned that to create the appearance of a building adjoining the courtyard, the ceiling of the outdoor sector needs to be raised. If the ceiling of the entire courtyard area were to be raised, however, it would also have the effect of raising all of the enclosing walls, as they are formed by the bounding lines of this sector. I would like these walls to stay the height they currently are: any higher and this space will start to feel cramped and the walls would look artificially high. To achieve the desired effect, the current single courtyard sector needs to be divided up into various new sectors, each responsible for different sections of the outer walls. This will enable the heights of these wall sections to be varied independently of each other.

PRESERVING THE EXISTING WALL HEIGHTS

The walls along the western and southern boundaries are fine as they are: to prevent them from being changed when the main sector's ceiling is raised, they need to be placed in a sector of their own. To achieve that, you will need to add some more lines to your map.

Start at the vertex in the northwestern corner of the courtyard. Draw a line from this vertex at an angle of about 135 until you are a little way, 80 units or so, from the western wall. Add lines sufficient to mark off an area of the courtyard sector that contains all of its western and southern walls. The exact shape is unimportant, but aim to keep the new area fairly thin so as to consume as little of the main courtyard sector as possible. End the drawing at the vertex in the southeastern corner of the courtyard. Leave enough room at this southeastern vertex for additional lines to be added to permit similar treatment of the eastern walls later.

BUILDING THE FACADE

When the addition of these lines is complete, click Make Sector, then click first in the larger central area of the courtyard, before clicking in the thinner western strip.

This order of clicks will cause WADED to redefine the larger area as a new sector first and then, with your second click, reconsolidate what remains of the original Sector 5 (together with the appropriate sides of your new lines) into the outer strip. This ensures that the settings for Sector 5 (the original courtyard) are preserved for the area close to the western and southern walls—unfortunately, the new main courtyard area will obtain its settings from the interconnection to its north. You will therefore need to select SECTORS mode and change the settings of this main courtyard area.

If you are confused by Make Sector's seemingly arbitrary creation of sectors, please be patient. The next room, "Putting Sectors to Work," will provide a full explanation of its operation.

The ceiling and floor textures will need to be changed to F_SKY1 and FLAT1_1, respectively, while the lighting level should be adjusted to 255. Take the ceiling up to 216.

Thinking about this particular sector, it is probably worth lowering the floor a touch, in order to make the change in floor pattern between the indoor and outdoor areas more natural. Therefore, take the floor down to -16. This, of course, changes the sector's elevation relative to the other outdoor sector to its west and south, so you will need to reduce that sector's floor to match. In turn, this modification will alter the apparent wall heights that these changes were designed to preserve, so be sure to bring the outer sector's ceiling down by 16 units, as well, to 144.

Yes, all of this sector juggling can be tedious and time consuming—another good reason for you to plan your maps out on paper first!

Finally, to complete the facade of the building, apply BROWN1 to both essential textures of the line shared by the courtyard and the gap through the wall.

UPPER TEXTURES BETWEEN F___SKY1 SECTORS

You may be worrying about some other texture locations that you know to be essential and to which you have, as yet, applied no texture: the upper textures of the eastern side of the lines dividing your two courtyard sectors. You may be wondering just how these areas can be dealt with. After all, you don't want to see any textures here—they would seem to be hanging in thin air, wouldn't they? And yet, you have been taught that such textures are essential. If you inspect these lines now, you will see that WADED thinks so, too—it has marked them in red. But what can be put there that won't look odd?

The answer is that it doesn't matter what you put there—DOOM won't use it anyway! Another change in the painting technique invoked by the use of the F_SKY1 texture is that upper textures between adjacent sectors with F_SKY1 specified for their ceilings will not be painted. This enables the designer to vary the ceiling heights of outdoor sectors in order to alter the heights of surrounding walls and still have the sky effect work correctly.

MODIFYING THE EASTERN WALL

This might be a good point to save your WAD. Call it WAD7.WAD. Before trying it out, though, it is worth making a few more changes.

The modifications you have just made should have created a raised wall to the north of the outside courtyard, while keeping the western and southern walls as they were. The eastern wall has not been given its own sector, however, so this will now be at the same height as the "building" to the North. In my opinion, it would be better to have this wall closer in height to the other outer walls, so this eastern area needs to be split away from the main courtyard sector, too. You could introduce a little visual interest to the courtyard by varying the wall's texture as well; one of the vine textures would go well here. Vines tend to look a bit odd growing out of paving-stones, though, so while you're adding a sector to bring the walls down, why not put it to use by letting it create a border to the paving?

You may need to set the Zoom factor to 9 or above to complete the next set of modifications without making spurious connections to existing lines.

Separate the eastern wall from the main courtyard by making another new sector. Start at the extreme southeast vertex and draw a series of lines parallel to and about 32 units away from the lines that mark out the eastern wall of the courtyard. These should connect to the existing lines at the south and north ends of the eastern wall. The short lines that connect the new series of lines to the existing ones will need to run at an angle of about 45° to the others in order not to cross or connect to other lines. It is imperative that your new sector takes none but the eastern walls away from existing sectors, otherwise the desired height effects will be spoiled.

This time, apply Make Sector first to the new thin strip before clicking in the main courtyard area to redefine that sector's reduced area. (This sequence prevents you from having to change all the main courtyard sector's attributes yet again!) Set the floor height of the new thin sector to –20. (The vine border should be a little lower than the stone of the courtyard, don't you think?) A ceiling height of 108 will bring the walls down, as desired.

You will need to enter these values from the keyboard rather than by using the mouse.

Set the floor texture to FLAT10—this seems suited to the task of providing something for a vine to grow in—and the ceiling to F_SKY1. Reduce the lighting to 144. (This vine is going to be in the shade of the wall.)

Now that you have finished adjusting the sector attributes, switch to LINES mode and apply the BROVINE texture to the main texture slot of the courtyard's eastern wall sections.

Users of DOOM II will need to use BROVINE2 instead of BROVINE.

This just leaves the new western lines of the vine-border strip. If you inspect these lines, you will discover that WADED has done something odd here: It has given you some textures you do not want and left off a texture that is essential. You will need to work along all of your new lines in turn, removing everything from their western sides and changing the essential (eastern) lower textures to BROWN1 (I suggest). Think carefully about which side of the line is which when it comes to changing the textures.

Save the WAD as WAD7A.WAD before going on.

ADDING AN AREA OF SHADE

The\ final modification to make to this WAD before trying out your handiwork is to add an area of shade to the courtyard.

Readers using DOOM II may wish to omit the additional new sector added here. Shadow techniques do not work well in DOOM II. The generally gloomy and cloudy nature of the skies makes bright areas and shadows look silly. Instead, you may just wish to reduce the brightness level of the whole of the outer area to 196.

The eastern vine-border has already been set to a lower brightness level than the rest of the court-yard. Leaving the shade coincident with this border will create a somewhat artificial appearance, though, so it is worth adding another sector to extend the shade some way over the paving to make it more credible.

The new sector should start and finish at the same vertices as the previous one: the southern and northern ends of the eastern wall. Again, start drawing at the extreme southeast vertex. By setting the Zoom factor to a minimum of 11 and making sure that WADED does not show any of your existing lines in red until you are ready to connect to existing vertices, you can draw the connecting lines running as close to the northern and southern boundaries of the courtyard as possible without having them connect. The rest of the lines should run parallel to the eastern wall, somewhere to the west of the western edge of the vine-border sector. Remember that you are drawing the shadow line that would be produced by the sun if it were due east and quite high in the sky. Figure 5.6 shows the final arrangement of lines you are aiming for.

Figure 5.6.

The lines needed to implement the courtyard fully.

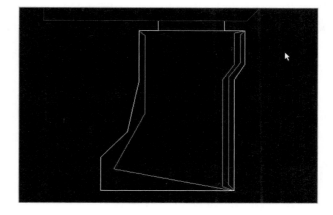

After successfully drawing the new lines, use Make Sector to create a sector out of the thin area of shade. You will then need to click in the (ever-shrinking) main courtyard area, to force it to acquire its share of the new lines. Change your new sector's floor to FLAT1_1 (the ceiling should already be F_SKY1) and its floor and ceiling heights to –16 and 216, respectively, to match the main courtyard sector. Leave its brightness at 144.

FIXING THE INTERCONNECTION

Finally, reduce the ceiling of the interconnection between indoors and out to a height of 128. This will create an essential texture inside the room. Apply STONE3 to that texture, to match its neighbors. You might also want to change the interconnection's ceiling texture, as lights will look a bit odd here. You should find that CEIL5_2 is OK. Finally, save the WAD as WAD7B.WAD and try it out.

REVIEWING YOUR HANDIWORK

Head straight out to inspect your courtyard. In passing, you may notice that, unlike your previous opening in a wall, the one out to the courtyard has ended up looking OK from inside the building. When viewed from the outside, though, texture alignment isn't too good around the opening. Apart from that, everything else should look fine. (See Figure 5.7.) (Well, maybe the shady area isn't perfect, but it's about as good as DOOM allows.)

Figure 5.7.
The new improved courtyard.

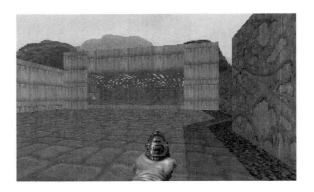

WALL TEXTURES REVISITED

Having seen how floors and ceilings are painted, the intricate details of how textures make it on to the walls will now be revealed.

THE DIFFERENCES BETWEEN WALL AND CEILING TEXTURES

You have seen that ceiling and floor flats are all the same size: 64 x 64 pixels. If you care to preview a few wall textures, however, you will quickly see that wall textures vary widely in size, both in their horizontal and their vertical dimensions. Figure 5.8 gives you an idea of the variety: the familiar STONE2 is 128 pixels square; STEP1 is just 32 wide by 8 pixels high; BROVINE is a comparatively massive 256 by 128 pixels, while LITE4 is 16 x 128.

Figure 5.8.
A collection of wall textures.

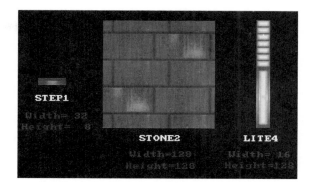

The differences between flats and wall textures go beyond variation in size, however. If you watch carefully as WADED's texture previewer draws the BROVINE texture, you will notice that rather than supplying the image in a smooth sweep from left to right (as it does when showing SKY1, for example), the image appears in a series of scattered patches that, once they are assembled, are finally overlaid with the image of a vine.

Readers using DOOM II will need to watch the BROWNPIP texture being previewed to observe a patchiness similar to BROVINE's.

DOOM II NOTE

This effect is brought about by the way in which wall textures are stored. To optimize the use of space in the main WAD file (where all of these textures are stored), wall textures are broken down

DOOM PROGRAMMING GURUS

5 ROOM

1 MISSION

2 EPISODE

into a series of common graphical *patches*. The textures themselves are then created as an assemblage of these smaller patches. In this way, a large number of different wall textures can be created by careful repetition, juxtaposition, and overlapping of a surprisingly small number of graphical elements.

The patches themselves can be virtually any size, although the final texture height must not exceed 128 pixels. Some wall textures are made up of just a single large patch (CEMENT1, for instance), while others, such as LITE3, are produced from many repetitions of the same small patch. This multi-patch characteristic of some wall textures can limit their use, as you will see shortly.

The final main difference between flats and wall textures is that it is possible for wall textures to have transparent areas within them. The previous room introduced you to the notion of the transparent texture, which provides completely see-through lines on your map. That, of course, is not any special texture but an absence of texture altogether. You will find, though, that there are wall textures that, in effect, use a transparent paint to produce holes through which a player can see. Preview the texture MIDGRATE to see an example of these see-through textures. (See Figure 5.9.)

Figure 5.9.
The MIDGRATE see-through texture.

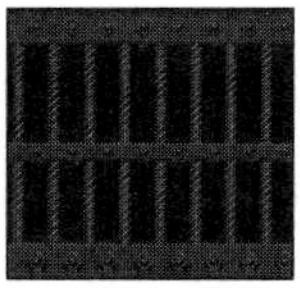

SUMMARY OF TYPES OF WALL TEXTURE

In summary, then, the textures that can be applied to a line's various texture slots may be:

- **The transparent texture (really no texture at all):** Nothing is rendered here, except the view beyond the line.
- **A solid texture:** The texture completely covers the specified area.
- **A see-through texture:** The texture has holes in it through which the view beyond the line is rendered.

There are a couple of other special effects of which wall textures are capable; you will learn more of these towards the end of this room.

THE CONSEQUENCES OF OMITTING ESSENTIAL TEXTURES

So far, you have been told that essential textures are so-named because they block a player's view of the void. You have been warned that to allow a player to view the void is to court mishap and disaster. It is time that you were told the true extent of the dangers inherent in viewing the void.

MISSING ESSENTIAL UPPERS/LOWERS

You have already seen the effect of omitting essential upper textures: DOOM fills the gap with *ceiling* texture from the adjacent sector. This will produce visual confusion, as you will remember from one of your early WADs. Other than that, though, the result is not serious—indeed, if you hunt around, you will find that id Software has missed quite a few from their own WADs.

The effect of a missing lower is similar: the adjacent sector's *floor* appears to be at the level of the current sector's—until the player reaches it, whereupon the step up comes as a surprise!

This description of what happens when essential upper and lower textures are omitted only applies to sector arrangements which result in a view containing a glimpse of the appropriate ceiling or floor texture beyond the line. If no such glimpse is afforded, the result is the same as if a main texture was omitted. This effect is described next.

MISSING ESSENTIAL MAIN TEXTURE

The effect of a transparent main texture on a single-sided line is much more disastrous—it results in what is known as the Hall of Mirrors (HOM) effect. Rather than leaving the line's space empty, the graphical engine fills it with copies of various other parts of the current view, producing a flickering display of seeming reflections, reminiscent of the fairground amusement from which the effect derives its name. It is extremely disturbing for the player to encounter the Hall of Mirrors effect in a WAD. It cannot be used to any constructive effect and most players will simply see it as a fault (which, of course, it is).

Avoid this effect by making sure you never omit any essential main textures.

HOM can result from other faults in the WAD; these will be covered in due course. If the effect always manifests itself on the *same* wall segment, wherever it is viewed from, you should always suspect a missing essential and check your texture assignments carefully.

SEE-THROUGH ESSENTIALS

See-through textures used as essentials produce another type of fault known as the *Tutti-Frutti* effect. The solid parts of the texture are shown correctly, but the gaps through which the player can normally see are filled with pixels of random color. This can sometimes be put to decorative use in a WAD, but mostly it just looks wrong. The effect is best avoided by ensuring that all essential textures are covered by completely solid coloring.

If you want to place a grating in a wall that appears to look into a pitch-black room, create a small sector behind the grating with a brightness level of 0. Set the grating-line's impassable flag to prevent the player from passing through it.

TEXTURE PLACEMENT

Now that you know more about the nature of wall textures and what happens if they are missed off your lines, the precise details of the process whereby the paint is applied to the walls can be considered.

The mechanism that the DOOM engine uses for the placement of wall textures is as follows. First, the main texture name is consulted and the appropriate set of component patches are assembled into the graphic to be used. What happens with that graphic depends on the setting of the line's two-sided flag. The single-sided line is the simpler case and will be examined first.

PAINTING SINGLE-SIDED LINES

Because a single-sided line lies at a single sector's boundary with only void beyond it, such lines can only ever possess a main texture. DOOM renders a single-sided line on-screen by pasting the graphic for its main texture into the upper left corner of its space, at the point where this space meets the ceiling. The pattern is repeatedly applied, like tiles, horizontally and vertically until the entire wall space, from left to right and ceiling to floor, is covered. Figure 5.10 illustrates this process schematically for the simple graphical pattern shown at the left of the figure.

Figure 5.10.

The process of painting a single-sided wall.

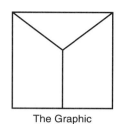

The Graphic

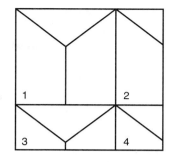

This process may sound straightforward but, in fact, it only works correctly with textures of the right size: the graphic must be either precisely 128 pixels tall, or tall enough to fill the space without vertical repetition. This is because the DOOM engine only gets its vertical repetitions correct if they occur at 128-pixel intervals. The use of graphics that need to be repeated at intervals other than 128 pixels leads to small gaps in the rendering. These fill with multi-colored graphical noise, producing the so-called *Pink Bug* effect. Like Tutti-Frutti, this can sometimes be used as a decorative effect but is generally to be avoided. To avoid Pink Bug, ensure that you use textures that are 128 pixels high on single-sided walls, or textures that are at least as tall as the wall space into which they will be painted.

> If its two-sided flag is clear, a line is treated by DOOM as single-sided, even if there is, in fact, a sector on the other side of it. It will therefore be painted over its full height using the above method, with complete disregard for adjacent ceiling and floor heights.

PAINTING TWO-SIDED LINES

The graphics engine handles two-sided lines in a different manner. The painting starts in the usual way with the main texture. If none is given, the space is left clear, as you have seen; otherwise, the specified graphic is applied, as a tile, in the top left-hand corner of the main texture space. Note that this will only be at the ceiling if no upper texture is required on this side of the line. The main texture pattern is repeated horizontally, just as with single-sided lines, but it is *not* repeated down the vertical dimension of the wall. This may leave a horizontal strip of the wall unpainted. This strip will be treated as transparent (which is perfectly okay on a two-sided main texture, remember).

After considering the main texture, DOOM then paints a two-sided line's other textures as necessary. The lower texture is painted in the same manner as the main texture of a single-sided line. The painting starts at the top left corner of the lower texture space and repeats horizontally and vertically until the space is filled.

The upper texture is painted in a similar manner, with the exception that here the pattern is painted first at the *bottom* left corner of the upper texture. The graphic is repeated horizontally to the right, as usual, and vertically upwards until the space is filled.

Figure 5.11 illustrates schematically DOOM's default method of painting a two-sided line's (potentially) three textures, using the same simple graphical pattern used in Figure 5.10.

Figure 5.11.
DOOM's default method of painting a two-sided line.

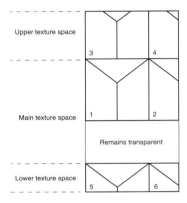

Once again, if vertical repetitions are needed to fill the space of the upper and lower textures, these will only occur correctly when the appropriate graphics are precisely 128 pixels tall.

> Although it is possible for a line with sectors on each side of it to have its 2-sided flag *clear*—such lines are treated as if there is nothing beyond them, remember—it is vital that lines which have their 2-sided flag *set* really do have two sidedefs. DOOM will crash if led to expect sectors which are not present!

SPECIAL TREATMENT OF TWO-SIDED LINE MAIN TEXTURES

You need to be aware that DOOM gives special consideration to the main texture of a two-sided line. Remember that these lines, by definition, connect adjacent sectors. They therefore represent an interconnection between one space and another; as such, one would ordinarily expect these main textures to be transparent. If they carry a texture at all, it is most likely to be one of the see-through textures of the grid and grating variety.

Because this space is not really part of a wall, any pattern which occupies this area is rendered on the screen not by the usual wall-painting part of the game engine, but by that part which is responsible for the handling of Things. Now, this area of the graphics engine knows nothing about vertical tiling (monsters don't normally stand on each other's shoulders!) It consequently won't produce any—although it will repeat the patterns horizontally as needed. This usually causes no problems, as the majority of grid and fencing textures would look strange if tiled vertically.

More significantly, however, because the graphics associated with Things are always single-patch pictures (called *sprites*), this part of the graphics engine cannot cope with wall textures that consist of complex, overlaid patches. It will handle single-patch wall textures (which is what all of the see-through textures are) and textures that, when assembled, have all of their patches placed side-by-side horizontally and without overlap. Other arrangements of patches cannot be used.

If you use a texture that is made up of overlapping patches, or patches that are arranged vertically, as the main texture of a two-sided line, a serious error will occur. Whenever it is asked to display such a texture, DOOM will pour weird streams of color down from the offending wall-space, often to the bottom of the screen. At the same time, the PC will slow to a crawl. This is known as the *Medusa* effect (so-named because the player sees snakes and is turned to stone!). Medusa makes the WAD unplayable while the offending space is in view. To eliminate it, you need to ensure that the main textures of your two-sided lines are all either transparent, or do not consist of vertically positioned or overlapping patches.

This restriction does not apply to upper or lower textures, because these are always handled by the wall-painting part of the engine.

USES FOR SOLID TEXTURES ON TWO-SIDED LINES

The treatment of two-sided lines described previously—the lack of vertical repetition of the main texture and the limitations on what those textures may be—is neither as strange nor as restrictive as it may at first appear. As already noted, the textures that are usually applied here—the grids and gratings—you would not normally want tiled.

The only times that you might want to employ a solid graphic as a two-sided main texture is in the creation of secret entrances or sniper ambush spots, as used in the hidden upper passage of id Software's E1M1. Such locations leave the player open to attack from monsters (or, in Deathmatch play, other players) who cannot be seen and whose presence is only given away when they open fire. These spots are made by placing a solid main texture on one side of a line while leaving the other

DOOM
PROGRAMMING
GURUS

5
ROOM

1
MISSION

2
EPISODE

transparent. The solid texture prevents a player from seeing through the side that carries it, but, from the other side, the line remains transparent. Remember also that the 2-sided flag is more properly termed the 2-sided/see-through/shoot-through flag. Setting it enables players and monsters to shoot through the line's main texture space without impediment. (Now you see why this creates an ambush spot!)

> Monsters are able to see both ways through all two-sided lines, regardless of texturing. It is therefore not possible using standard map-editing techniques to set up locations where the player can snipe at them unseen. The effect can be created using a reject map builder, however.

Remember that a line's impassability is also determined by a flag. Unless you set this flag, a two-sided line can be passed through—by player or enemies—regardless of the main texture. The "magic" or "secret" entrances that appear in various locations of the main DOOM.WAD—such as the curtains of fire through which a player can walk—are made in this way, too.

In summary: Remember that not all of the available textures can be used to create locations such as the ones just described. If you want a two-sided main texture to look solid, it must consist of either single or side-by-side, non-overlapping patches, and, because it will not be vertically tiled, it also needs to be tall enough to fill the space completely.

TEXTURE ALIGNMENT

As you have already observed in your own WADs, the game engine's default application of wall textures does not always result in the desired rendering of the walls. Having had the default mechanism described, you can, no doubt, see why. All is not lost, however, for DOOM provides the designer with a number of controls over the paint-application process, allowing surfaces to be rendered in ways other than by the default painting method.

To demonstrate how these controls work, I shall use two different wall textures: MARBLE2 and BRNSMAL1. Figure 5.12 shows these textures. MARBLE2 is a fairly standard 128 x 128 solid graphic. It is useful here because it has easily identifiable upper and lower edges. BRNSMAL1 is a 64 x 64 see-through texture.

2
EPISODE

1
MISSION

5
ROOM

DOOM
PROGRAMMING
GURUS

Figure 5.12.
*Wall textures MARBLE2
and BRNSMAL1.*

DEFAULT WALL TEXTURE ALIGNMENT

Consider the application of the MARBLE2 texture to a wall that is taller than 128 units. The texture will be applied from the ceiling down, repeated as necessary until the floor is reached. The texture is 128 pixels tall, so there will be no problem with Pink Bug. Above and below an opening in the wall, though, something different will happen. Figure 5.13 illustrates the result: The walls on either side of the central opening consist of straightforward single-sided lines. The central opening itself is a two-sided line, with a pitch-black sector beyond it. MARBLE2 is used above and below the opening; the line's main texture is set to BRNSMAL1. The figure shows DOOM's default rendering of this configuration.

Figure 5.13.
*DOOM's default painting
around an opening.*

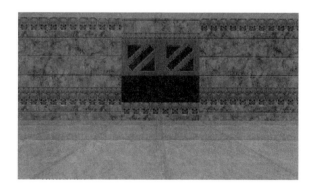

DOOM
PROGRAMMING
GURUS

5
ROOM

1
MISSION

2
EPISODE

You can see that where the wall is solid, the pattern has been applied from the ceiling down and repeated over the full height of the wall. The upper texture of the two-sided line, however, has been painted upwards from its meeting with the main texture. The main texture itself has been painted from its upper edge but without vertical repetition of the pattern. As a consequence, the grating appears to be suspended from the top of the opening. Beneath the opening, on the line's lower texture, the marble pattern is applied from the bottom of the main texture down.

Sometimes, this default method of applying the paint achieves the desired effect. Usually though, as here, it spoils the alignment of the upper and lower textures. You probably recognize this effect from your own WADs.

CHANGING DOOM'S PAINTING METHOD

DOOM provides two mechanisms for changing its wall-painting method. The first is termed *unpegging*, the second is *texture offsetting*. I will explain what these terms mean and how they are accessed, before considering how they can be employed.

UNPEGGING

By default, lines are said to have their textures *pegged* to their surfaces. In other words, the graphical patterns are painted on their surfaces starting from a particular location. These reference locations are the top of the main texture space for the main and upper texture patterns, and at the bottom of the main texture space for the lower. Naturally, this greatly affects the way in which textures align from one wall section to the next. You may recall from the previous room that there are two flags to control a line's pegging: the upper unpegged flag and the lower unpegged flag. Note that these are linedef attributes; they will therefore affect both sides of a line.

TEXTURE OFFSETTING

A *texture offset* is a displacement that can be applied to the horizontal and/or vertical position of a texture's starting point. Using such displacement, you may shift a texture any number of pixels in any direction on any wall. This mechanism provides you with fine control over the graphic's placement. Again, you may recall from the previous room that each of a line's two sidedefs supply X- and Y-offset values for texture displacement. These values enable textures to be aligned independently on each side of a line. Note, however, that the offset will be applied to all textures on that side of the line.

UNPEGGED TEXTURES ON TWO-SIDED LINES

You have seen that, by default, a two-sided line's upper texture is pegged to its lower edge. By setting the upper unpegged flag, you can unpeg this texture from the structure of the line and have the paint applied from the sector's ceiling instead. This forces the upper texture to be applied in the same way as it would be on any adjacent single-sided lines, causing their patterns to line up.

Setting a line's lower unpegged flag will cause the line's lower texture to lose its pegging to the bottom of the main texture. Again, the unpegged texture's placement is reckoned from the ceiling, bringing its pattern into alignment with any adjacent single-sided line.

Confusingly, setting the lower unpegged flag will also change the painting of a line's main texture. Remember that any graphic in this space is normally "hung" from its top and may have transparent space below it. Setting a line's lower unpegged flag causes this graphic to be placed at the bottom of the main texture space instead. It will still not repeat vertically, so there may now be a transparent area above it. Figure 5.14 shows how the earlier wall-opening is rendered when *both* upper and lower textures are unpegged.

Figure 5.14.
The effect of unpegging upper and lower textures.

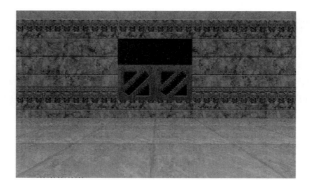

UNPEGGING SINGLE-SIDED LINES

It is possible to set the unpegged flags of single-sided lines, even though they have neither upper nor lower textures. The effect is precisely the same as happens to the main texture of a two-sided line when unpegging is used there. Setting the lower unpegged flag will cause the line's main (and only) texture to be applied from the floor up, rather than from the ceiling down. Changing the upper unpegged flag has no effect on the rendering of single-sided lines.

In Figure 5.15, the wall to the left of the corner has had its lower unpegged flag set, while the wall to the right uses the default painting method.

Figure 5.15.
The effect of lower unpegging on single-sided lines.

The unpegged flags will feature prominently in a later room.

Examining Other Combinations of Unpegging

If you would like to look at the effect of other combinations of unpegging around openings in walls, examine the example WAD called MWALLS.WAD (the DOOM II version is called D2MWALLS.WAD) on the CD-ROM that accompanies this book. It shows all of the possible combinations of the unpegged flags for the example opening described previously.

USING TEXTURE OFFSETS

There are occasions when simple unpegging will not achieve the precise alignment effect that a designer wants. Examples would be the small but deliberate misalignment of textures used to give hints of the presence of secret doors; or the adjustment of textures across, rather than up and down, a wall—centering a texture between two adjacent walls, for instance. In cases like these, total control over texture alignment is needed.

To provide this level of control, each sidedef allows the specification of individual X- or Y-offsets. These values may be positive or negative numbers in the range −128 to 127. The X-offset produces a shift of the texture to the left (negative values to the right), while the Y-offset produces a shift upwards (negative values, downward) of the texture, in each case by the specified number of pixels.

COMBINING UNPEGGING WITH TEXTURE OFFSETTING

The use of these two texture-alignment mechanisms is not mutually exclusive. The graphical engine applies any X- and Y-offset values specified in the sidedefs after all pegging information has been acted upon, so the offset values can always be used to effect small adjustments to the alignment of your textures.

WAD SORTIE 8: TIDYING UP THE WALLS

This Sortie builds on the WAD produced in the previous one. If you did not produce that WAD, you should use WAD7B.WAD (DOOM) or D2WAD7B.WAD (DOOM II) from the CD-ROM as your starting point here.

With all of the previous information at your fingertips, you should now be able to perform a simple walk-through of your WAD, noting the alignment problems that exist and deciding on a method for fixing them. Start DOOM and let's walk through the WAD together.

FIXING THE FIRST OPENING

The first problem area is around the southwest exit from the hexagonal room. You should now recognize the alignment fault over the opening as a pegging error. The upper textures need to be unpegged on both sides of this opening. Make a note to do this when you next return to the editor.

The second fault with this exit is the alignment of the mortar lines through the gap. Here you have a major problem. Simple realignment of the textures on the short through-wall sections cannot solve the fault, because, as a careful inspection will show you, the mortar lines of the hexagonal room do not line up with those of the southwest room. Now, you could just cheat at this point and apply some kind of neutral texture through the interconnection and hope that no one notices the alignment fault between the two rooms. You wouldn't learn much by doing that, though, so on this occasion at least, you ought to do things properly!

From the earlier description of the texture-application process, you know that textures are always applied to single-sided lines from the ceiling down. Look at the walls of these two rooms and you will see that this is indeed the case here. The misalignment of textures on each side of the opening is a result of an awkward difference in ceiling height. Now, you could realign all of one room's textures, but to do this would require the adjustment of the Y-offset of the textures on *all* of that room's walls. This would be tedious in the extreme. Fortunately, there is another way out here— why not just change a ceiling height?

The STONE2 and STONE3 textures have four courses of "bricks" up their 128-pixel height. (You can verify this for yourself using WADED's previewer, if you like; for now, just trust me.) A quick bit of math tells you, then, that the mortar lines of these graphics occur at 32-pixel intervals up each texture. Provided, therefore, you make sure that these two rooms' ceiling heights differ by an integral multiple of 32, these textures should align automatically.

The current difference is 40, so the problem can be fixed by changing one of the ceiling heights by 8 units. Now, the hexagonal room contains a techno-column that just fits between ceiling and floor and, in addition, has a further sector beyond it, which is fine the way it is. It would therefore make more sense to apply the change to the southwest room's ceiling, bringing it down 8 units to 152. Make a note of this for your next edit, too.

The same mathematics can be applied to the interconnecting sector, too, of course. Its walls are painted, like all of the rest, down from its ceiling. The current difference between this ceiling height and that of the hexagonal room is 16. That's 16 pixels short of the 32-unit interval needed to make the textures align properly. Bringing the interconnection's ceiling down by this amount may make the opening rather low, however. It would be better to apply these 16 units as a Y-offset on the two troublesome lines. Forcing the wall textures down 16 pixels will need a Y-offset of −16. Make another note, then proceed to the next opening, the one out to the courtyard.

FIXING THE SECOND OPENING

From inside, the next opening looks fine, doesn't it? Remember, though, that you have just made a note to bring this room's ceiling height down. This opening will no longer look right, after that fix, so make a note to unpeg this upper texture as well. I suggest that you don't bother realigning this opening's through-textures, though; STONE3 looks a bit odd here, anyway. I recommend that you replace both side-walls' main textures with BROWNHUG. (No, you're not cheating, just refining the design!)

Moving out into the courtyard now, take a look at the final problem area, the other side of the opening to the courtyard. The misalignment of the upper texture here can again be fixed by unpegging. The lower texture looks okay as it is, to me. It doesn't align with the textures on either side, but I think that makes it look more like a step, so I vote it stays the way it is.

So, is that everything that needs fixing? It depends on how great a perfectionist you are. The vine texture doesn't continue perfectly around the bend in the eastern wall, but this is barely noticeable

2 EPISODE   **1** MISSION   **5** ROOM   **DOOM PROGRAMMING GURUS**

and certainly not worth the effort involved in fixing it. Of course, if you'd like to calculate the X-offsets that need to be applied to two of the vine wall-sections to produce a seamless join, I'll not stop you. There is one other little change I would make, though, to something you have probably not seen. Press Tab and take a look at the auto-map. Notice how the lines marking off the western and southern walls of your outdoor area show up. I would be inclined to hide these lines by setting their Not on Map flag; that way, the map-watching player is not likely to waste time trying to determine their significance during play.

So, notebook at the ready, try loading WADED and making a new WAD8.WAD, with all of these problems fixed.

Applying Texture Offsets in WADED

To adjust the Y-offset of a texture in WADED, you need first to be in LINES mode. You can then bring up the texture-offsets pop-up box (shown in Figure 5.16) by clicking any of the four offset buttons (which appear below the lower texture slots). The pop-up shows the X- and Y-displacements of left and right sidedefs (in that order): each value can be changed by means of the + and - buttons beside them.

Figure 5.16.
WADED's texture displacement settings popup.

MOVING ON

When you have effected all of the changes, try out your new WAD8.WAD. Hopefully, with these latest revisions, all of the previous defects in your WAD will have been cleared up and you will be ready to move on and extend your design further. To complete this room, though, there are a few more details you need to know about textures.

ANIMATED TEXTURES

All of the textures you have seen so far have been flat and static, just like paint. But DOOM also provides a family of textures that are rather more exciting than ordinary paint—they are animated.

USING ANIMATED TEXTURES

After all you have just read about textures, you may be surprised to learn that the use of animated textures is simplicity itself. There are animated textures for walls as well as for floors and ceilings; their names appear in the lists of available textures along with the static ones you are familiar with. You can use them like any other texture. Apply them to the appropriate surface, and the DOOM engine will do the rest.

It is not possible to tell animated textures from static textures in most editors' texture lists.

DOOM performs the animation by cycling around a series of texture names. You specify the entire animation sequence by specifying any name within it. You don't have to choose a texture from any particular point of the sequence to obtain the complete animation. Note, however, that DOOM steps all animated textures on to their next "frame" at the same time. This means that areas that are given different textures from within the same animation will remain out of phase by the same amount throughout the game.

ANIMATED WALL TEXTURES

Table 5.1 lists all of the animated wall-texture sequences available in DOOM and DOOM II.

Table 5.1. DOOM's animated wall-texture sequences.

Sequence	DOOM	DOOM II	Description
BFALL1, BFALL2, BFALL3, BFALL4	–	X	Falling curtain of blood
BLODGR1, BLODGR2, BLODGR3, BLODGR4	X	–	Nukage slime dripping from ruptured pipework
BLODRIP1, BLODRIP2, BLODRIP3, BLODRIP4	X	X	Blood dripping from ruptured pipework
DBRAIN1, DBRAIN2, DBRAIN3, DBRAIN4	–	X	Dancing red and yellow blotches

Sequence	DOOM	DOOM II	Description
FIREBLU1, FIREBLU2	X	X	Pulsating red and blue flame
FIRELAVA, FIRELAV3	X	X	Dense curtain of flame
FIREMAG1, FIREMAG2, FIREMAG3	X	X	Dancing red and blue flames
FIREWALL, FIREWALA, FIREWALB	X	X	Wall of fire over embers
GSTFONT1, GSTFONT2, GSTFONT3	X	X	Stone gargoyle spouting blood
ROCKRED1, ROCKRED2, ROCKRED3	X	X	Glowing red-hot rock
SFALL1, SFALL2, SFALL3, SFALL4	–	X	Falling curtain of nukage slime
SLADRIP1, SLADRIP2, SLADRIP3	X	–	Nukage slime pouring from grating

The texture called FIRELAV2 is not part of the FIRELAVA sequence. It is a static texture.

Most of these textures are not designed to tile vertically and so will need to be used on walls of an appropriate height. Many will look odd if used on short walls using the default rendering operation. You will need to set the lower unpegged flag in most cases.

Be aware that FIREWALL (and the other "frames" in its sequence) is a short texture. It will manifest the Pink Bug effect if used on an essential texture space that is more than 112-units high.

Animated wall-textures can be used on any texture slot. If you have more than 40 areas using animated textures in any one map, however, DOOM will crash.

Versions of DOOM prior to v1.4 will not animate the main texture of a two-sided line.

ANIMATED FLOOR/CEILING TEXTURES

Table 5.2 lists all of the animated floor-texture sequences available in DOOM and DOOM II.

Table 5.2. DOOM's animated floor-texture sequences.

Sequence	DOOM	DOOM II	Description
BLOOD1, BLOOD2, BLOOD3	X	X	Blood, maybe?
FWATER1, FWATER2, FWATER3, FWATER4	X	X	Water
LAVA1, LAVA2, LAVA3, LAVA4	X	X	Lava
NUKAGE1, NUKAGE2, NUKAGE3	X	X	Nukage slime
RROCK05, RROCK06, RROCK07, RROCK08	–	X	Pulsating red cracks between rocks
SLIME01, SLIME02, SLIME03, SLIME04	–	X	Blotchy brown slime
SLIME05, SLIME06, SLIME07, SLIME08	–	X	More uniform brown slime
SLIME09, SLIME10, SLIME11, SLIME12	–	X	Fine-texture version of RROCK05 (Yes, really!)

Like all flats, the animated floor textures can be applied to ceilings, but they rarely look convincing—somehow, slime just doesn't look right up there.

Many of these textures are often associated with areas that damage players who linger in them. The damaging aspect of these areas is not a product of the textures themselves. You will learn more about this later.

SCROLLING TEXTURES

In addition to animated texture sequences, walls can be made to scroll the texture displayed on them horizontally. This is done by setting a line's special characteristic to a particular value and is thus exclusive to walls. This effect can be applied to any texture, animated or static, on single- or two-sided lines. The setting of a lines special characteristic is the subject of Room 7, "Activating Sectors."

EXTENDING THE TEXTURE PALETTE

Rich though the id Software-provided texture palette is, there are times when it just seems to lack the precise type of texture you'd like. Often you would like to customize the appearance of your walls, floors, and ceilings to match the scenario of your WAD better. Tools are available to enable you to do this. The techniques involved go beyond simple editing of the map, however, so this topic is deferred until Episode 3, "The Land of the Gods."

EXIT: MOPPING UP AND MOVING ON

In this extensive room, you learned more about DOOM's palette of textures for ceiling, floor, and wall surfaces. You learned how DOOM's sky works and saw how to add realistic outdoor areas to your map. You learned, too, how the DOOM engine goes about painting its world and precisely what happens if it isn't provided with all of the textures it needs in order to do it. You saw how to make the game engine paint the walls exactly as you want them by utilizing the alignment mechanisms that are provided. You had a taste of the use of those mechanisms as you fixed all of the remaining problems in your own WAD. Finally, you were told that DOOM's paint doesn't need to be static but can be animated.

In the next room, as well as trying out some animated textures, you will start to expand your map with new sectors as you learn the techniques for implementing many of the standard elements of the DOOM world.

You will also receive some of your final lessons in the use of WADED.

ROOM 6

By Steve Benner

PUTTING SECTORS TO WORK

By now, you should be familiar with the role of the sector in DOOM WADs and be comfortable with its use and structure. In this room, you will be shown how sectors are put together to form the common types of elements that make up the traditional DOOM world. The various Sorties from this room will lead you through the addition of several new areas to the WAD that has been developed in earlier rooms.

Remember, though, that WAD-building is more of an art than a science—there are no fixed ways of producing anything. Consequently, you will not be given rigid rules or instructions for the implementation of every scenery element you will ever want. This room is intended as a gallery of ideas. Use it as a starting point for planning your own maps.

AREA DESIGN

Part of the secret of successful WAD-building is learning to plan and construct your sectors. You have already seen that with WADED, for instance, the careless and haphazard addition of sectors within your WAD can cost you a lot of time in redefining line and sector settings. You will find that the same holds true with all other WAD editors. No matter which you use, you will find that before you start work with the editor, careful planning of your WAD (and its sector layout in particular) will pay dividends when you finally do begin.

PLANNING THE MAP

In planning your WADs, you should remember that no matter how beautiful (or ugly, if that's what you prefer) you make your WAD, it is unlikely to be much admired unless it plays well. Keep this thought uppermost in your mind at all stages of design.

In particular, you should question your motives for the introduction of every new area. Ask yourself "Why am I creating this area? What will it contribute to the game?" Keep a mental tally of how many times you reply "For decoration" or "To add atmosphere." Ornamentation is undoubtedly a significant aspect of any design, but if it becomes more important to you than creating a functional space to hide weapons or to ambush opponents, you are probably spending too much time using your editor and not enough time playing what you produce there!

Once you've answered the fundamental question of what your new map area is really for, you can turn to the more practical questions of how it should look, from the specifics of textures to the overall design scheme. How high will it be, how wide, how long? Will it be brightly lit or should it be dark? How high above other areas should it be? Will it have overlooks? Should it be hidden? Will it contain any tricks or traps?

In considering your approach to these design questions, you should be fully aware of all the features of the DOOM world that are available for exploitation. You also need to know about DOOM's inherent design restrictions.

APPEARANCE

The look and feel of your map will develop as you go along. You've seen some of this already. You know a little bit about textures and lighting levels, and you will see some more specific and atmospheric examples of these capabilities as this episode progresses. These aspects of your map's appearance can be used for more than simply adding atmosphere, however. DOOM's lighting levels can vary from very bright (a setting of 255) to pitch black (a setting of 0). Obviously, dimly lit areas can be used to make the players' task harder; it is easier for you to hide things in the dark—be they goodies, switches, traps, monsters, or the pathway itself. Try to use lighting levels realistically—take a close look at the way lighting levels are utilized throughout id Software's E1M1 for an excellent example of this. Also, try to vary the lighting levels through your WAD so that players don't get too accustomed to (or bored with) playing at a particular light level. Areas of darkness can be much harder to play when they follow immediately after well-lit areas.

Exercise careful thought in your use of textures, too. Aim for more than mere decoration. Beside lending atmosphere to your WAD, textures can create challenges of their own—some enemies are harder to spot against some surface colorings, for instance. Textures are also invaluable in providing clues to various aspects of your design, clues about such things as hazards, traps, and secret locations. Observant players will soon pick up on your textural pointers and will enjoy the game all the more. Of course, you can always throw the occasional false pointer into the mix to trip them up every now and then!

There are no hard-and-fast rules about the basic appearance of your map areas. If you've played many WADs, you will already know what particular design aspects you like. If you can't decide, perhaps you should play some more and give it additional thought.

LARGE AREAS OR SMALL?

The sizes of the various areas of your map will be influenced by the functions you see these areas fulfilling. Do you intend to give the player a large open space in which to charge around and battle many foes simultaneously? Will you force the player to take on a few monsters at a time by confining the action to a smaller space? Do you want to restrict the player's options for movement or escape?

Is this one of those twisty mazes that do their best to disorient and confuse the player? Will this area be built to contain a particularly unusual menace?

The effectiveness of many of the weapons in DOOM is related to the geography in which they are used. The geography also affects the way monsters behave, particularly in their tracking of the player. You should test out these aspects of your design fairly early in the design process, especially before you have too many lines and sectors to rearrange if you find that things are not working well.

To create map areas that *function* correctly, you will need to know something of the way DOOM's objects and its geography interact. You need to know what can fit where in the DOOM world. You also need to be aware of the movement constraints that DOOM applies to both players and enemies.

SIZE CONSIDERATIONS

If you want areas of your map to contain particular objects, you will need to make sure that the areas are large enough to hold whatever you place there. You need to know something, therefore, of how things are measured and the restrictions on where they fit.

THING METRICS

You will remember from Episode 2, Mission 1, Room 2, "Reconnaissance Debriefing," that all Things have both a diameter and a height. These two values determine an object's "extent"—how much map area it needs and what headroom it requires.

> The metric values for all of DOOM's Things are given in Appendix A, "Essential DOOM Thing Information."

The term "diameter" as it is applied to Things is misleading, for it implies that Things are circular, whereas, in fact, they are square. This square is always oriented with the map's coordinate system, irrespective of the direction in which the Thing faces. This needs to be taken into account when calculating where Things will fit, particularly for those Things that can move around, such as players and monsters.

THING COLLISION DETECTION

A Thing is deemed to be in contact with anything that touches or overlaps the square it occupies. The consequences of these contacts depend upon the type of Thing involved. Players who touch upon bonuses will obtain them; monsters reaching walls will change direction; players or monsters colliding with Things that are classed as obstacles will find their progress barred.

Things that move around (players and monsters) can only enter gaps that are wider than their diameter (allowing for the fact that it is really a square) and at least as tall as they are.

> DOOM has an inconsistency here. Height restrictions do not operate as tightly as width restrictions!

Note that for the purposes of inter-object collision detection, DOOM regards all Things of the obstacle category as being of infinite height. Players can never leap over a barrel, for example, no matter how far below them it is.

Figure 6.1.

Gaps may be smaller than they look.

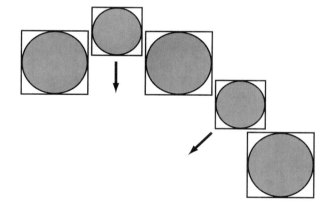

The fact that Things' extents are square and do not rotate complicates the WAD designer's job. You have to bear in mind that players and monsters are wider when moving at angles other than one of the cardinal directions. Thus, wider gaps will be needed between obstacles if the player is to pass between them at angles other than due north, south, east or west, as Figure 6.1 shows.

In this figure, the smaller circles represent players, who are moving in the directions shown by the arrows. The larger circles represent obstructions (such as barrels). Notice how the real (square) extents of these items interact very differently from the way their visible (circular) shapes would suggest. The player moving due south between the obstacles can pass freely through a gap that would seem to be much narrower than the one which the other player is about to find impassable.

OVERLAPPING THINGS—STUCK MONSTERS

Most editors will enable Things to be placed anywhere on the map, even if they are actually too large for the chosen spot. Any object larger than the space in which it is placed, however, will look unsightly. The entire object will be rendered on screen by the engine, even though it is visually too large for the space it is in. As you can imagine, this usually looks odd.

If your objects are purely decorative, such as pillars, lamps, firesticks, and so forth, then it is largely up to you how tight a fit you want to make them. Objects growing out of walls, ceilings, or floors are likely to be viewed as errors, but that should be the only consequence of carelessly placed decorations and bonuses. On the other hand, the consequences of placing player and monster start positions in tight spaces can be much more serious.

If you place monsters or players in spaces where they do not fit, you will find that they stick tight and are unable to participate in the game. Stuck monsters will not attack a player, but they can be injured and killed, either by a player or by other monsters if they get caught in a crossfire. This effect has been used intentionally in some WADs—usually to 'glue' several powerful monsters together. None of these monsters can attack the player, who will set about disposing of them and then suddenly discover, with the demise of the last of its colleagues, the final monster becomes free to attack—usually just as the player runs out of ammunition!

Stuck players are there for good—or until they think to use the no-clipping cheat code! This is not an effect that many players will view as worthwhile.

REACHING GOODIES

If you are placing bonus items around your map, you will normally need to make it possible for the player to get at them. You will therefore need to ensure that the player can either enter the area (eventually!) to collect the booty, or can reach in to grab it. Players are 56 units high and have a diameter of 32 units, so they can only enter areas that are at least 56 units high by 33 units wide. As you've seen, this width restriction may be imposed by walls, or by impassable Things.

It is possible for players to reach the distance of their *radius* (16 units on the coordinate system axis) into areas they cannot wholly enter, provided that the area's floor is not above their head—in other words, it must be less than 56 units above the floor on which they are standing.

RESTRICTIONS ON A PLAYER'S VERTICAL MOVEMENT

From playing DOOM, you will know that there is a restriction on the height that a player can step up from one sector to the next. This height restriction is 24 units—any greater and the engine will refuse to let the player continue onward. There is no limit on the downward distance that a player may fall without taking damage.

In the previous section, you were told that a sector must be 56 units high if a player is to enter. Whenever the player tries to step from one sector to another, DOOM checks that there is a gap of this size between the higher floor and lower ceiling of the two sectors. Therefore, if you are building stepped sector sequences, bear in mind that the player will be unable to pass up or down the steps if any floor-to-ceiling space between adjacent sectors is less than 56 units high.

MONSTER MOVEMENTS

Sector sizes are also important for determining monster behavior. Whenever they are awake, monsters will always tend to track players. Even when the player is not in their line of sight, awakened monsters remain aware of the direction of players and will generally head towards them, unless they are distracted—usually by being struck with weapons' fire from other monsters who can see the player—or are constrained in some way.

Like players, free-roaming monsters cannot enter spaces that are smaller than they are. They also demonstrate a reluctance to enter spaces that will be a tight fit for them; the smaller the gap, the more reluctant a monster will be to enter it. For completely unimpeded movement, a monster will need a sector to be at least twice as wide as the monster's own diameter.

Monsters can climb stairs just as a player can—all monsters with legs can step up 24 units but no higher. They are more careful than players about coming down, however (a topic that will be explored in more detail shortly).

MONSTERS' REACH

Again, like players, clawed monsters (such as Imps) can reach into sectors they cannot enter—not to collect goodies, of course, but to savage players! For a player to be safe from such a savaging, monsters must be constrained far enough away for their (square) extent not to touch the player's.

Monsters can inflict clawing damage from any distance below the player, so don't confine a player to a tall, narrow pillar in an Imp-infested pit unless you want survival to be impossible!

SIZING FOR BETTER TEXTURE ALIGNMENT

You have already seen the final sizing consideration: fixing sector sizes to ensure better texture alignment. In addition to the alignment problems you have experienced for yourself, some textures will look strange when replicated up or along walls. Often you will need to limit your sectors to certain absolute sizes (as well as grid locations) in order to use particular textures effectively or to minimize problems with their alignment.

Usually, however, the choice of textures, and the adjustment of the map to make them work properly, will be completely subordinate to the size and shape that the area needs to be to play well. If you have areas that already work well but you find that you cannot get the textures to look right with any of the available alignment mechanisms, it is usually best to look for another texture to use rather than to compromise your WAD's playability for the sake of its appearance.

DIVIDING ROOMS INTO SECTORS

Once you've answered the fundamental questions of what an area is for and how it needs to be arranged, you can start to think about how it may need to be divided into its component sectors. You already know a lot about this.

WHEN DO YOU NEED ANOTHER SECTOR?

Way back in Room 2 of this mission, you learned about the fundamental role of the sector in the WAD, and you learned to distinguish the WADster's sector from the DOOMster's "room." By now you should be comfortable with the use of sectors and know when you should need to create a new one. It is worth summarizing here, however, the occasions when an area of the map will need to be in a sector of its own:

- When it needs to have a different ceiling height from its neighbors
- When it needs to have a different ceiling texture from its neighbors
- When it needs to have a different floor height from its neighbors
- When it needs to have a different floor texture from its neighbors
- When it needs to have a different lighting level from its neighbors
- Any combination of these

These are the reasons you are already familiar with. There is another:

- When it needs to be able to do something special

The next room deals with these special activities of sectors. The current room is confined to considerations of the kinds of scenery components (such as alcoves, staircases, and so on) that will require only simple floor, ceiling, or lighting changes for their implementation.

Note that all of the areas covered in the rest of this room are no more than perceptual elements of a map. Within the WAD, they are implemented either as individual sectors or as particular arrangements of sectors, but there is nothing particularly special about them.

SIMPLE SECTORS

Many areas of the map require (or at least benefit from) additional sectors within or adjacent to them, acting as both decorative and structural features. These sectors are frequently very simple in form. They generally fall into a number of fairly loose categories.

PILLARS AND COLUMNS

Pillars and *columns* provide useful cover for players in otherwise open rooms. They can be added either by leaving void areas marked out within the room sectors (as you saw in our first WAD sortie), or by means of their own sectors, with suitably elevated floors. Which method is adopted depends largely on the appearance you want the pillars to have: if the pillar is to reach from floor to ceiling (as most do), the easier and more economical method in terms of space is to use the void.

ALCOVES, LEDGES, AND PLATFORMS

Alcoves are small areas generally set into the walls of larger rooms or passageways. *Ledges* are longer, thinner areas, usually running along the walls of rooms: they are frequently at a considerable height from the main room floor, and, if the player is to enter them, they will need to have some mechanism or provision for access. *Platforms* are usually raised areas within rooms.

All of these areas are common components of DOOM WADs and provide good spots for scattering bonuses, power-ups, and, of course, enemies. Trying to locate the access points to these locations (or even just spotting the locations themselves) can be a major element in playing rooms that contain them. As well as providing good ambush points, alcoves are suitable locations for secret switches and such like—which you will learn more about shortly.

You should already know enough about sectors to see how all of these areas can be implemented. Each is likely to need nothing more than an appropriate sector, set as necessary into or alongside a larger sector. You will see the building process in the next WAD Sortie.

DOOM PROGRAMMING GURUS

6 ROOM

1 MISSION

2 EPISODE

POOLS, PONDS, AND PITS

Pools are areas containing liquids through which a player may pass, with or without harm. *Ponds* are usually deeper, and their higher sides may trap the player, forcing a hunt for an exit—usually in the form of a single step or a lower side somewhere. *Pits* are deep areas from which players can expect to have major difficulties extracting themselves. Pits may need to have some special sort of escape provided if you don't want the player to be trapped in them forever.

Again, these types of areas should already be familiar to you. They are used as traps for the unwary, areas that wreak havoc if the player falls into them, or simply as obstacles that need to be skirted.

The techniques for building these areas should already be obvious to you. They are simply sectors with appropriately lowered floors. Pools and ponds will generally have animated textures on these floors. Often, these areas will cause harm to players who spend time in them. (You will see how to implement these harmful effects in the next room.)

STEPS

Steps are a common feature of DOOM WADs. You have one in your own WAD already. Additional sectors functioning as steps are needed to enable the player (and/or monsters) to move freely between sectors with a difference of floor height greater than 24 units. They provide changes in the vertical levels of your WAD, preventing the player from always having to fight on the flat, which thus makes for a more interesting game. You have already seen that they can affect monsters' behavior, too. Steps are also a convenient means of making floor texture changes look better.

> The WAD Sortie that follows builds on the WAD produced in the last Sortie of the previous room. If you did not accompany me on that Sortie, but would like to participate in this one, you should use WAD8.WAD (DOOM) or D2WAD8.WAD (DOOM II) from the CD-ROM as your starting point.

WAD SORTIE 9: ADDING ALCOVES, PLATFORMS, AND POOLS

Having described a number of basic map elements, I think it would be useful for you to add a few of them to your WAD. By doing this, you will get a better feel for the way sectors can work together and become more conversant with WADED's methodology for adding sectors to your map.

WADED'S TREATMENT OF SECTORS

So far, you have been using WADED's sector creation facilities strictly according to my dictates. I will now explain the way these operate so that in the future you will be able to work out the correct way to use them for yourself.

CREATING/FIXING SECTORS IN WADED

The operation of WADED's Make Sector facility can sometimes be very confusing, even to experienced users of the program. The confusion arises because it is not always obvious when the clicking action will make a *new* sector and when it will simply "fix" an existing sector by incorporating extra lines into it. The methodology behind Make Sector is actually quite straightforward—the key to its operation lies in the color of the lines surrounding the area of the mouse-click.

Make Sector recognizes three significant combinations of lines surrounding the mouse pointer:

- **At least one magenta line is present:** Under these circumstances, WADED knows that you have added at least one new line to the map. It assumes therefore that you wish to add a new sector, either in the void or by dividing up an existing sector.

- **All lines are white:** With Make Sector active, if an area with the mouse pointer in it is completely surrounded by white lines, that area must currently be void space. Consequently, WADED assumes that you want a new sector created out of this void space.

- **At least one red (but no magenta) line is present:** For there to be any red lines around the area, the mouse pointer must be in at least the remains of an existing sector; but because there are no magenta lines present, no new lines can have been drawn. Under these circumstances, WADED assumes that the existing sector is merely being rebuilt, and it will therefore not create a new sector but will ensure that the area's lines are incorporated into the same (existing) sector.

MAKE SECTOR'S AUTOMATIC SIDEDEF GENERATION

Make Sector always tries to generate appropriate sidedefs for all of the lines that make up the sector on which it operates. It does this by checking each of the lines composing the boundary of the sector as follows:

- **Line is magenta:** Magenta lines have no sidedefs. (That is why they are magenta.) WADED will therefore add a right sidedef to this line and then, if necessary, flip the line so that this side faces into the sector that has just been created. WADED also sets this line's `impassable` flag.

- **Line is white:** A white line will already have one sidedef. This will, however, be on the opposite side from the current sector. A new left sidedef is therefore added to the line; its `2-sided` flag is set and its `impassable` flag is cleared. If a new sector has just been created and this is the first white line encountered, Make Sector will take the settings from the existing sector on this line's right side as the default settings for the new sector.

- **Line is red:** A red line will already have a sidedef on its appropriate side. WADED merely makes sure that this sidedef belongs to the correct sector but makes no other change to the line.

Although it shouldn't make any difference, you will find that Make Sector usually works best if you draw lines in a way that will require the minimum number of them to have their directions changed. For best results, draw complete sectors in a clockwise manner for best results.

AUTOMATIC SECTOR SETTINGS

As mentioned previously, Make Sector generates settings automatically for new sectors. If a new sector is bounded by any line that is already a member of a sector on its other side, then Make Sector will create the new sector with its neighbor's attributes; otherwise a set of arbitrary values will be assigned.

Note also, that each time WADED adds a second sidedef to a line, it also sets the line's 2-sided flag. Unfortunately, it takes this rather too far: Contrary to DOOM's rules, the current version of WADED insists that a line's 2-sided flag always matches the true number of sidedefs. If the user switches off this flag on a two-sided line, the program will see this as a request to delete the left sidedef. This it will do, destroying the integrity of the sector that owned it. This fault is scheduled for correction in a future version of the program.

The correct order for drawing lines, using Make Sector, and setting sector attributes takes some getting used to; therefore, the next few WAD Sorties will continue to provide guidance on this function's use. Gradually this guidance will be withdrawn, but by then you should be fully conversant with this aspect of the program.

There is an additional sector-defining function in WADED: the Sec Define button, located below the Make Sector button. This feature can be awkward to use, but it is useful for

 2
EPISODE

1
MISSION

6
ROOM

DOOM
PROGRAMMING
GURUS

minor amendments to the WAD's sector information. Its use will be demonstrated in a later WAD Sortie in this room.

ADDING ALCOVES

The areas that are to be added in this Sortie are relatively straightforward. Start WADED with WAD8.WAD and begin with a simple alcove or two, as described in the following text.

Feel free to save your WAD at appropriate times during this Sortie. Use a series of names such as TEMP9A, TEMP9B, and so on.

At this stage, the alcoves you are adding may appear purely decorative in function. I have plans for them later, however, so don't let that worry you after all I've said about decorations!

ENTRANCE DOOR

The first addition is something which, in my opinion, no WAD should be without: an explanation of how the player got to the start position. I always feel that a player's materialization at some arbitrary point in the middle of a room detracts immediately from the realism of the situation. Therefore, this WAD will have an entrance door. The door will be firmly locked with no hope of escape through it, but at least the player will have some point of reference from the start of the WAD.

All that is needed for this entrance is a simple alcove of an appropriate size to hold the right textures. For this job, I consider the textures given in Table 6.1 to be the right ones.

Table 6.1. The textures for the entrance.

Surface	Texture
The locked door	DOOR3
Side walls	LITE3
Floor and ceiling	FLAT18

Preview these textures and note the following information: DOOR3 is 64 pixels wide and 72 pixels high. This texture needs to fill the alcove's back wall completely; its size therefore dictates the width and height of the alcove. LITE3 is 32 pixels wide; this provides the depth of the alcove. FLAT18 looks to be composed of two tiles, each 64 pixels wide by 32 deep. Either half of this flat will therefore fit conveniently on the floor and ceiling of the planned alcove, but you will need to ensure that the alcove is drawn squarely in either the northern or southern half of one of the map's grid squares. At this point, you might want to turn the grid on, and you may find that a Zoom factor of around 10 helps also.

The new alcove is to be added towards the western end of the south wall of the main hexagonal room. Start by adjusting the line that marks the southern wall so that it lies along one of the east-west grid lines (or precisely halfway between two, if that is easier). Then add the new lines for the alcove in a clockwise sequence, with each running along conveniently located grid lines. Remember that you want the new sector covering exactly one half of one of the grid squares; this will automatically make it 32 units deep and 64 units wide.

Apply Make Sector to the new alcove and then set the new sector's floor height to 8 and its ceiling at 80. (It needs to be 72 units high, remember).

The line on the northern edge of the alcove is not a new line and therefore was white when you used Make Sector. It consequently will be made two-sided and its new sidedef incorporated into the new sector, while its other side remains as it was. The sector on the other side of this line (the main hexagonal room) provides the settings for the new sector and is itself left untouched. It will therefore need no repair after using Make Sector on the new alcove.

The lighting level of the new sector can be left at 144. Apply the appropriate textures to the alcove's surfaces. There are a couple of essential textures that will need to be dealt with where the alcove meets the main room. STONE2 would seem appropriate for these. Unpeg the upper and lower textures here to ensure that the textures align correctly with the adjacent walls. Finally, put the player start positions close enough nearby to suggest that this is the door through which they've arrived.

PASSAGEWAY ALCOVES

The next additions to the WAD will be a pair of alcoves in the southeastern passageway. I'd like these to face each other in the section of the passage that runs SE-NW, just out of the hexagonal room. One of these alcoves is to have the SW1GARG texture on its back wall, the other is to have SW1LION. Both of these textures are 64 pixels wide, so each alcove needs to be this width. Their depth is not crucial—a value of 24 units or so will be fine.

You should be able to add the appropriate new lines and create these two new sectors without any further instructions from me. Getting the lines the right length here may prove tricky—just do your best. Reducing the Snap-to-Grid setting to 4 or so may make the job a little easier. The grid won't help you much—you may want to turn it off.

> The same remarks about the use of Make Sector apply to these alcoves as they did to the previous one.

I would like each alcove to be 72 units high; once you've made the new sectors, bring the ceiling height down appropriately. The rest of the sector settings can be left the same as those of the passageway. Use STONE2 for the side walls of the alcoves to match the passageway. You will need a Y-offset of -16 to keep the mortar lines continuous here. The upper essential should be STONE2 also, and, as you know by now, will need to be unpegged. Finally, apply the SW1GARG and SW1LION textures as required to the back walls of the alcoves. If you preview these textures and visualize how they will be rendered on a wall that is 72 pixels high, you will see that the default rendering will cause a problem. These textures have important details that need to be kept at the correct height from the floor. They will therefore need to have their lower unpegged flag set, so that they are rendered from the floor up.

This completes the addition of alcoves to the WAD. You can save it and try it out now, if you wish.

ADDING A PLATFORM

The next addition to the WAD is a platform inside the hexagonal room. Figure 6.2 shows its position and shape: another hexagon in the northeastern corner of the main room. The new hexagon should be drawn in a clockwise manner, keeping about the same distance from the outer walls of the main room as the pillar is in the other corner.

Figure 6.2.

Lines for a new platform in the hexagonal room.

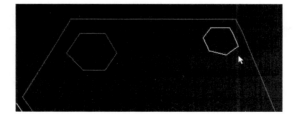

This time, all of the lines of the new area are magenta. Make Sector will need to be applied inside the new hexagon first, so that a new sector is created from the new lines. All of the new lines will be created single-sided, however, so Make Sector will need to be applied subsequently to the original hexagonal room to make that sector take over the second sides of the new lines. The settings for the new sector will be arbitrary.

Set this new sector's floor to BLOOD1 at height 32, the ceiling to TLITE6_5 at height 104, and the lighting level to 160. Put STONE on all essentials.

Notice that this new sector's floor is too high above the floor of the main room for the player to climb onto it directly. This platform is going to provide the player with the WAD's first puzzle—not a particularly difficult one, but a puzzle, nonetheless. It is going to house some security armor (100 percent armor). You can place that now, if you wish. Put it close to the southwestern edge of the new sector, but not so close that the player will be able to reach it from the floor of the main room. It will need to be about 40 units in from the edge.

Now, to enable the player to gain the armor, you will need to provide access to the platform. You should do this by adding a step, but don't make the presence of the step obvious: tuck it away in the extreme northeast corner of the hexagonal room, between the platform and the main wall. Players will only discover this step by walking round the platform. The careless player may miss it altogether.

To implement the step, you should add a new line connecting the northeastern corner of the platform to the nearby corner vertex of the room. Then add another new line some way to the south, connecting the platform to a point on the main room's northeast wall.

After using Make Sector on the new step sector, you will need to use it on the main room sector again, because this sector has acquired two new lines. You shouldn't need to use it on the platform sector again, though, because you haven't added any lines to that. Pass the mouse over it and watch the lines turn red to confirm this. By now, you should know what settings WADED will have given to your new sector.

Set the new step's floor to FLAT20 at height 16. This provides the necessary step up to the platform. This floor texture is fairly granular and won't require careful alignment. Now, it is often considered polite to provide clues to the solution of DOOM's problems, and even though this is a fairly simple problem, I suggest you do that here. Let this sector provide a hint of its existence by changing its ceiling (visible from the other side of the platform, unlike the step itself) and lighting level. Apply FLAT20 to the step sector's ceiling, and change its height to 112. Check that the lighting level is 160. Put STONE on the lower essentials and STONE2 on the uppers. The section of the original outer wall that this sector has acquired will now need a Y-offset applied to compensate for its new ceiling height. The texture will need to be moved up by the same amount as you brought the ceiling down; a Y-offset of 8 will achieve this.

This completes the first puzzle area in your WAD. Try it out, if you like.

ADDING A POND

The final addition to your WAD in this Sortie will be another little puzzle for the player, this time located out in the courtyard. Figure 6.3 shows the shapes to add here. Draw them now.

Figure 6.3.
Lines for the pond added to the courtyard.

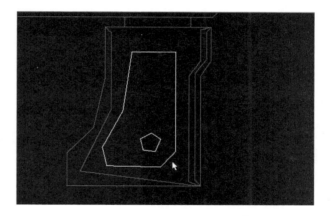

Use Make Sector on the larger of the two shapes before applying it to the smaller, inner shape. Don't forget to use it also on the main courtyard sector afterwards.

This new area is to be a pond. Its edges are going be made too high for the player to climb out. Unless the player is to be forced to perish here, there needs to be some form of escape mechanism.

It is not good design practice to set dead-end traps for players. It may seem tempting to set a pond's edge height to 25 units in the full expectation that players will not notice it until they find themselves trapped. Remember, though, that this will only catch players once—if you provide no escape mechanism from this trap, I would guess that a player would be unlikely to come back to discover what other neat ideas you've incorporated into your WAD!

The escape mechanism here will be a step, but not one that is simple for the player to use. It will take the form of a small island in the pond, carefully positioned so that it can be used as a step only when the player takes a run at it.

Use the settings shown in Table 6.2 for the two new sectors. Notice that the lighting level of the main pond sector is reduced just to make it look a little more threatening.

Table 6.2. Settings for the pond sectors.

Lighting	Ceiling		Floor		Essentials
160	216	F_SKY1	-48	FWATER1	BROWNHUG
255	216	F_SKY1	-24	FLAT1_1	BROWNHUG

You will now need to save and play test the WAD a few times to get the size and the position of your island just right. Start with it about 80 units from the eastern edge of the pond and adjust its position and size until it's tricky, but possible, to use it to escape from the water.

You may find the (Move) Sector facility useful here.

When you're happy with all of your latest additions, save your final WAD as WAD9.WAD.

USING STAIRS

In the previous room we discussed briefly the uses of steps. Often in DOOM WADs, steps are arranged in long runs, providing staircases between areas of widely differing floor elevations. These structures are required often enough, and are sufficiently interesting, to warrant a separate examination.

STAIRCASES

Staircases with twists and turns can provide limited visibility ahead and make for good constricted fighting areas. They also provide natural funnels to limit the attacks on a player, while providing no place to hide or run to. They are good for ambush spots, too.

Staircases generally require no special design considerations. The maximum step-up size of 24 units applies here as elsewhere. Note, though, that there is no minimum tread width: the player will climb steps with treads as narrow as one pixel (provided your editor will let you draw them)!

Don't get carried away with long stairways. DOOM has a limit on the number of surfaces it can render at any one time, and this limit is not very high: 128 in v1.2 and 256 in later versions. If you overload DOOM in this way, the engine renders only the first 128 (or 256) surfaces in view and then leaves the remainder unpainted—but filled with the Hall of Mirrors effect. It is not clear precisely how the surface count is reckoned. It would seem to be a count of the number of separate polygons of continuous texture. Intervening structures—such as pillars—cutting across the view of an otherwise continuous surface will divide its space into two, for example. No matter how this limit is actually reckoned, though, stairways can quickly cause DOOM to reach it. If you consider that each step has the potential to add a further five surfaces to the view, a 20-step stairway could provide DOOM v1.2 with most of its permitted surfaces.

ONE-WAY STAIRCASES

You already know that when a player moves from one sector to another, DOOM checks for a maximum step height of 24 units and a minimum gap of 56 units (the height of the player) between one sector's floor and the adjacent ceiling. Additionally, a player can only pass into a gap that is 33-units wide. There is an interesting flaw in the method by which DOOM checks on these conditions when climbing and descending, a flaw that allows the construction of a useful addition to the repertoire of scenery elements: the one-way staircase.

When moving *up* from one sector to another, DOOM does not consider the destination sector's depth (for instance, the direction the player is moving). All that can prevent the player from making the upwards step is the riser height and the size of the floor-ceiling gap. If the destination sector is not deep enough to take the player completely, it doesn't matter—the player will simply not move wholly into it but will "overhang" the previous sector a little.

Coming down, however, the DOOM engine will not enable a step to be taken unless the player can move wholly (in other words, a full 33 units) into the destination sector. The engine will therefore check that the ceiling height is no less than 56 units above the player's *current* floor for the *entire* 33-unit distance ahead. Treads narrower than 33 units can thus be used with carefully calculated ceiling heights to produce stairs that players can ascend without problem—only to find themselves unable to reverse the maneuver.

Staircases that enable descent but not ascent are even easier to produce: Simply include a step size that exceeds the 24-unit maximum.

As previously noted in the section on ponds, you should make sure that areas entered via one-way staircases have another means of exit. Generally, you should ensure that trap features such as this do not force players into positions from which there is no escape, particularly if they take no harm from being there—players who are forced to die of boredom will not return to play your WAD again. It is considered polite to add a warning of some sort too!

MONSTER BEHAVIOR ON STAIRCASES

When designing staircases, you should bear in mind that steps and stairs have an effect on the way monsters follow the player. As you have already seen, all monsters with legs share the same restriction as the player when it comes to climbing: 24 units is the maximum height they can manage. Monsters are much more reluctant than most players about descending steps, however. They will never step down more than 24 units and, in addition, they are fussy about steep stairs. Generally speaking, the greater the downward step-distance, the deeper each tread needs to be for monsters to be lured down them. Also, you may need to adjust the tread depth to suit the particular monsters you are using—the larger the monster, the more wary of steep steps they are.

Experimentation has shown that on stairs with the maximum 24-unit risers, the treads need to be at least 0.85 of a monster's diameter before the monster will venture down them. This figure is for steps aligned with the coordinate system; those at an angle will need correspondingly larger treads. Of course, you may wish to use this fact to produce stairs that monsters are *less* likely to descend, so that the player can fight them from the comparative safety of the bottom!

Floating monsters are, of course, completely oblivious to the presence of steps, up or down, when it comes to chasing the player.

WAD SORTIE 10: STAIRWAYS TO HELL

This Sortie builds on the WAD produced in the previous one. If you did not produce that WAD, you should use WAD9.WAD (DOOM) or D2WAD9.WAD (DOOM II) from the CD-ROM as your starting point here.

This Sortie will give you plenty of practice in the use of WADED's Make Sector facility. During the Sortie, you will add a couple of stairways to your WAD. In particular, it will demonstrate how much easier it is to extend a WAD out from existing sectors into the void than it is to build within existing sectors. Start with WAD9.WAD and feel free to save your WAD as often as necessary during the course of this Sortie, using a sequence of TEMP10A.WAD, TEMP10B.WAD, and so on, for the names.

EXTENDING THE SOUTHEAST PASSAGEWAY

For this addition, you will find it useful to have the Grid turned on and a Zoom factor set at about 10. Try to draw as much as possible in a clockwise manner. With (Draw) Lines selected, but before drawing anything, select MARBLE3 as the default texture for the new lines. Then scroll your map so that the eastern end of the southeast passageway lies toward the bottom of the screen. The first new staircase is to be a one-way staircase heading north from the eastern end of this passageway. Figure 6.4 shows how the map will look after the new additions. Follow the instructions given forthwith for the most efficient way of adding them. Delay using Make Sector until all the new lines are drawn. Again, the most efficient way is given forthwith.

Figure 6.4.
The new lines for the staircase.

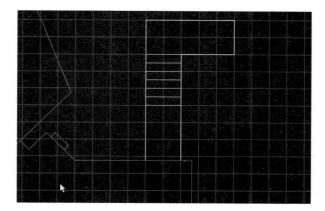

Start by adding a short corridor out through the north wall of the passageway. This corridor needs to be 128-units wide, so make sure that its western and eastern walls run along grid lines. Make it about 200-units long. The exact length is immaterial but, again, make sure its northern edge runs along a grid line. This sets you up for easier construction of the stairs.

Now, to catch players, one-way stairs need to be less than 33-units deep. Utilize the grid, therefore, to add four more rectangles to the map, maintaining the new corridor's width of 128 units but making each rectangle only 32-units (exactly half a grid square) deep from north to south. Change the default texture to MARBLE1, then add two more rectangles of the same size. You should now have (in magenta) the lines for six steps, as well as a corridor connecting the stairs to the original passageway.

Finally, add the lines for a new passageway running east from the northern end of the stairs. It should run a total of 320 units east from the western end and be 128 units north-south.

When you have all of the lines drawn, you can think about creating the sectors.

MAKING THE STAIR SECTORS

Apply Make Sector to the southern corridor area first. Then, before making any more sectors, change the new corridor's ceiling-height to 128 and apply DEM1_5 to both ceiling and floor. Put MARBLE3 on the essential over the new opening and unpeg it.

Now use Make Sector on the next rectangle—the bottom step—and then inspect that sector's settings. Put DEM1_6 on its floor, and increase its floor-height to 16. Now apply Make Sector to the second step. You should find that WADED has copied the first step's settings onto the second and all you need to do is to increase the new step's floor-height to 32. Note how you are using Make Sector to transfer sector settings in your favor.

Continue in this manner, successively using Make Sector and adjusting each new sector's settings, before moving on to the next. Table 6.3 shows the settings to use for the sectors you are adding.

Table 6.3. Floor and ceiling settings for the new sectors.

Area	Floor height	Ceiling height
Southern corridor	0	128
Bottom step	16	128
Second step	32	128
Third step	48	128
Fourth step	64	144
Fifth step	80	240
Sixth step	96	240
Top corridor	112	240

Notice how the floor heights form an orderly progression, each rising 16 units above the previous one. The ceilings don't follow the same progression, however—they start out 128 units above the floor at either end of the stairway, reducing to 80 units over the third and fourth steps.

With 16-unit risers, as here, a ceiling-floor height of 80 units will provide a 64-unit gap between the ceiling of one step and the floor of the next one up. Consequently, there will be no problem for a player climbing these stairs. Coming down will be a different matter, however.

The treads of these steps are only 32-units deep. In considering the downward movement, therefore, the engine will have to look *two* ceilings ahead of the player's sector to determine the ceiling-floor gap 33 units ahead. Over the third and fourth steps, this gap reduces to 48 units. So, once the player is over the third step, there will be no going back.

Of course, you could have built the entire staircase using a ceiling-floor height of 80 units. In such case, it would have been a one-way stair from top to bottom. I want to provide the player with a chance to notice what is happening here, though, so the configuration you have just been given has only two "non-return" steps.

FIXING THE TEXTURES

Now that all of the sectors are made, you can fix the missing textures. Start with the riser of the bottom step. Make it MARBLE1. Do the same with the next two steps' risers. The next step is the dangerous one—it cannot be reversed—so give a clue to the hazard by using MARBLE3 on both essentials. This places the clue on the step riser, so that it is visible on the approach to the stairs, and also on the wall face above the step, so that it will be at the players' eye level when they attempt to descend the stairs—rather too late for them to do anything about it, but it may make them notice the clue the next time they see it!

Preview the MARBLE3 texture to see how it provides a clue to the hazard ahead. Remember that only the top 16 pixels of the pattern will be displayed on these textures.

Use MARBLE3 on both essentials of the next riser, but revert to MARBLE1 for the remaining risers. Finally, put MARBFACE on the western wall of the top corridor, just to add a threatening touch there.

You can now save your WAD and try it out. Of course, having ascended your new staircase, you will need to press Escape and restart the game to do anything else! The exit from this particular trap will be added in a later WAD Sortie.

DOOM
PROGRAMMING
GURUS

6
ROOM

1
MISSION

2
EPISODE

Use of Traps

Be wary of adding traps such as this to your WADs. While they may work fine in single-player games—forcing the player to tackle particular areas of a WAD without hope of retreat or to find other routes through the WAD—they can cause complications during multi-player games by limiting players' movements. This is not to say that these are bad things, just that you may need to take some extra care with these features if you intend your WAD to be used in Deathmatch or Cooperative play.

COMBINING STAIRWAYS AND PLATFORMS

Stairways are often used to provide a player with access to a platform that is at some height above a surrounding area. This provides players with a good view around—and exposes them to attack from all sides! Let's build a platform like this in the large room to the north of the courtyard. Figure 6.5 shows the configuration of lines to add. Once again, you will be led through the additions.

Figure 6.5.
New lines to add inside the old southwest room.

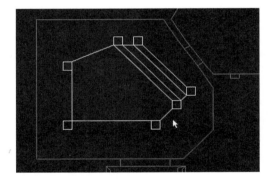

These lines represent seven pillars (the small squares) around a high platform reached by three steps from the floor of the main room. The seven pillars will not quite reach to the ceiling, and so they will need to be separate sectors rather than left as voids.

Start with these seven small square pillars; these should all be exactly 64 pixels square. Apply Make Sector to each of these as you draw them, but do not fix the original outer area just yet. Next, draw the lines that link the squares and make up the perimeter of the new area. Work round in a clockwise manner. This should leave just three of the new lines undrawn. Before adding these, use Make Sector on the large area you have just marked out in the middle of the room. Don't bother with this sector's settings, though, as later operations will destroy them anyway.

Now you should Make Sector what remains of the original southwest room sector. This room will need greater headroom because of the platform, so take its ceiling up to 184. (Note that this preserves the 32-pixel increment that was needed in this room to make the doorway texture alignments work.)

You can then draw the three additional lines marking the stairs climbing from the doorway out of the hexagonal room. You will need to add these lines with care—this area is becoming a little complex for Make Sector's liking. Start by drawing the two lines that mark out the first step down from the platform, and make this step's sector before using Make Sector to fix the large platform sector. (You have just added a new line to it, remember.) Finally, add the remaining line and make sectors out of the areas on each side of it.

Now work around all of the new sectors, correcting any settings that differ from the ones given in Table 6.4. You may find the MULTI function available in SECTORS mode to be of use here. (This function works in precisely the same way as the MULTI function available in LINES mode.)

Table 6.4. Sector settings for the new platform area.

Lighting	Ceiling		Floor	
	Main sectors, west - east			
144	256	CEIL5_1	88	FLAT5_2
144	256	CEIL5_1	72	FLAT5_2
144	256	CEIL5_1	48	FLAT5_2
144	256	CEIL5_1	24	FLAT5_2
	Pillar sectors from NE corner, clockwise			
192	256	CONS1_1	152	FLOOR4_8
192	256	CONS1_7	152	FLOOR4_8
144	256	CEIL5_1	152	FLOOR4_8
192	256	CONS1_5	152	FLOOR4_8
192	256	CONS1_7	152	FLOOR4_8
192	256	CONS1_7	152	FLOOR4_8
192	256	CONS1_1	152	FLOOR4_8

Finally, apply the textures given in Table 6.5 to the new lines, unpegging *all* of the upper textures. Again, MULTI may come in handy.

DOOM II does not have the ICKWALL6 texture—use ICKWALL5 in its place.

Table 6.5. Line textures needed for the new area.

Lowers	Uppers: North wall	East wall	South wall	West Wall
	Pillar essentials, from NE pillar working clockwise			
STONE3	ICKWALL6	ICKWALL5	–	ICKWALL2
STONE3	ICKWALL2	ICKWALL2	ICKWALL2	–
STONE3	–	ICKWALL6	ICKWALL5	–
STONE3	–	ICKWALL2	ICKWALL5	ICKWALL2
STONE3	GRAYBIG	GRAYBIG	GRAYBIG	GRAYBIG
STONE3	GRAYBIG	–	GRAYBIG	GRAYBIG
STONE3	ICKWALL4	ICKWALL2	–	ICKWALL7

Lowers	Uppers			
	Peripheral line essentials, from long NE boundary, clockwise			
WOOD5	ICKWALL3			
WOOD5	ICKWALL1			
WOOD5	ICKWALL7			
WOOD5	COMPSTA1			
WOOD5	COMPSTA2			
WOOD5	COMPSTA1			
WOOD5	ICKWALL7			

You may find it easier to work with the wall textures required for the pillar essentials if you scroll ICKWALL2 to the top of the scrolling list box by using the [and] keys.

Three additional lines need WOOD5 added to their lower essentials—these are the risers formed by the last three lines you added to the map.

Finally, fix a railing to one edge of this platform. Apply the texture BRNSMALC as the main texture of both sides of the line running between the northwestern pillar and the next pillar to the east. Save the WAD and inspect your handiwork. (This WAD is WAD10.WAD on the CD-ROM.)

INSPECTING THE PLATFORM

If all has gone well, there should be no major troubles with the appearance of your WAD. It is probably a bit ragged in places, with some less-than-perfect texture alignments, especially around the tops of the pillars. If there are any glaring omissions of textures, make a note of where they are and return to the editor to check that everything is as given in the tables above. Before doing that, though, take a good look at the grating texture you added. Not quite right, is it? Climb up onto the platform and try walking into the grating. You shouldn't be able to pass straight through it like that, should you?

To see how to fix that, we need to review see-through textures and the use of the two-sided line. So, if you have other problems with your WAD that need attention, return to WADED and try to fix those first. I'll meet you when you're ready to fix that railing.

SECTOR EDGES: THE TWO-SIDED LINE REVISITED

In this room, the nature of the two-sided line is reviewed, starting with its role in providing a link between sectors.

MOVEMENT THROUGH TWO-SIDED LINES

You already know that by definition a two-sided line (a line with sidedefs on each side) lies on the boundary between one sector and another. By now you are used to passing freely from one sector to another through these two-sided lines.

What is it about these lines that enables a player to pass through? Simply their two-sidedness: the fact that there is another sector on the other side to pass into. When determining whether a player can move through a line, DOOM will first look "through" the line to see whether there is anywhere for the player to go beyond it. If not, as happens at a single-sided line, progress comes to an abrupt halt. With two-sided lines, floor- and ceiling-height mismatches are required to prevent further progress—or, you may recall, the line's impassable flag needs to be set.

This explains why your players can pass freely through the railing texture and leap from your platform—the texture is placed on a two-sided line. To make this railing seem solid, you will need to mark the line as impassable.

UNPEGGING OF TWO-SIDED LINES

Before heading back to the editor to make this fix, examine the grating texture used around the platform and see if you can decide what mars its appearance. (See Figure 6.6.)

Figure 6.6.
The prototype grating installation.

If, like me, you left the default pegging on this line, your grating texture will be aligned with the top of the gap. It would really look better on the floor, wouldn't it? If you agree, make a note to unpeg this line's lower texture. The real problem though, to my eyes, is that the grating looks unrealistic just petering out at the pillars. Let's take a closer look at the grating texture in use here.

MULTIPART TEXTURES: THE BRNSMAL___ SERIES

Figure 6.7 shows the BRNSMALC texture that was used for the railing. Notice how the texture is open at both ends to enable it to be repeated as necessary to cover the entire length of a line. Also shown in the figure are two more textures in the BRNSMAL_ series: BRNSMALL and BRNSMALR. These two textures provide the left and right ends, respectively, of the open grating pattern. To use these grating patterns correctly, the main texture should have these end pieces attached.

Notice the size of the two end textures: each is 32-pixels wide. It is clear that these particular textures will not repeat correctly horizontally; they will each need to be on a line precisely 32-pixels long. Note also that they will only connect seamlessly to the center texture if they meet that texture at the appropriate point in the pattern—in this case, on an exact repeat of the 32-pixel wide main structure of the grating.

Let's make these modifications to your WAD now.

Figure 6.7.
*The BRNSMAL_ series of
grating textures.*

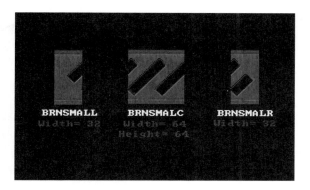

WAD SORTIE 11: PUTTING TEXTURES TO WORK ON TWO-SIDED LINES

This Sortie builds on the WAD produced in the previous one. If you did not produce that WAD, you should use WAD10.WAD (DOOM) or D2WAD10.WAD (DOOM II) from the CD-ROM as your starting point here.

You have seen that in order to create realistic railings along the edge of your platform using the BRNSMAL_ series of textures, you will need to reorganize the way the platform is structured. Let us look at the necessary restructuring in detail.

CHANGING THE LINE

To utilize the three textures that we have just examined, you will need to divide the line carrying the railing into three pieces of precise lengths. The two end sections need to be 32 pixels exactly, while the central section must be a whole multiple of 32 pixels. Look at the line involved here—it isn't going to be easy dividing it, is it? For a start, it is currently not of an appropriate length. The first task, then, will be to make it an integral multiple of 32 pixels long.

The easiest way to do this is to make the line run true from east to west and then use the grid to get the lengths just right. So, with the grid turned on, use Draw mode's Move functions to reshape this area to match that shown in Figure 6.8.

Figure 6.8.

The realigned platform area.

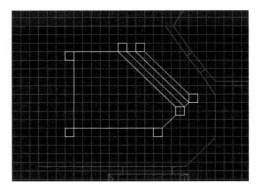

With this rearrangement, the majority of the pillar sectors now lie on the grid so that the interconnecting lines are generally multiples of 64 units. The line that is to carry the grating texture can now be split into three sections of the appropriate sizes. This is easily achieved. With the (Draw) Lines button activated, click the line at one of the desired split points, exactly 32 pixels in from one of its ends. This action splits the line, placing a vertex at the join. It also starts a new line, of course—in this case, a line you don't want. Click the right mouse button to abort it.

Repeat this operation 32 pixels in from the other end of the line and you've done it. You don't need to use Make Sector, because you haven't added any new lines—you just split some existing ones. All of the original line's settings—including sector ownership—will have transferred to the new smaller sections, so no fixes are required to any sectors.

FIXING GRATINGS AROUND THE PLATFORM

Now, while you're at it, apply the same treatment to the two lines that make up the western and southern boundaries of the platform and fence off more of the platform area. This will force the player to come and go via the stairs.

With these three platform edges split into the correctly sized pieces, you should now be able to set the appropriate flags and apply the necessary textures to make substantial railings around your platform. Think carefully about which textures need to be applied at what ends (and on what sides) of all these railings. At this point, you'll probably discover something you'd never noticed about these textures when you played DOOM—I'll tell you what it is in a moment.

When you think you've got the application of the gratings correct, save the WAD and try it out. Did you get it all right?

You should have realized (or discovered) that this series of textures only provides sufficient components to represent the view of the structure from one side. The railing will therefore have to be built looking the same from each side, which is not how it would appear in reality. But don't worry—it would take a very observant player to notice this anomaly.

FURTHER ADJUSTMENTS TO THE PLATFORM EDGE

You should also have found that this modification tidies up the messy textures over the pillars too. Maybe you hadn't noticed them. (Or maybe yours weren't messy in the first place.) The problems now are that the COMPSTA_ textures (on the upper slots above the gratings) don't look good when split into 32-pixel pieces at the line ends; and also, to my eyes, the western edge of the platform looks strange—it ought really to run between the pillar midlines, not the corners as it currently does.

Fixing the uppers is simple. They just need a change of texture. Altering the line of the western edge of the platform may at first glance seem tricky—it looks as if it needs major restructuring—but actually this is fairly simple, too.

MOVING THE PLATFORM EDGE

First consider the northern end of the western edge. Here it is a relatively simple matter to reform the edge's connection to the northwestern pillar. Start by splitting the line that marks the eastern face of this pillar. Start a new line from the mid-point of this face and then use the right mouse button to abort it. This gives you a square pillar with five vertices around its edges, instead of four.

Next, move the pillar's current southeastern vertex 32 pixels to the west, thus putting the connection between the pillar and the platform's western edge where you want it. You can now restore the original shape of the pillar by moving its new vertex south to become the southeast corner.

Having fixed the northern end of the platform's western edge, you can now turn your attention to its southern end. This area cannot be treated in the same way as was the previous one because both the western and southern edges of the platform currently connect to the southwest pillar at the same vertex. This will need to be changed.

Here, then, it is necessary to delete the short line that connects the western edge of the platform to the southwest pillar. Do this by selecting (Move/Del) Line and then clicking the line with the right mouse button. Use (Draw) Line to draw a new connecting line from the midpoint of the northern face of the southwest pillar to the southern end of the line marking the western edge of the platform. Make sure that the new line's right side faces towards the platform sector. Finally, straighten up the platform's edge by moving its central section to the west. Take care not to move the line north or south at all, because you need to keep the two end pieces 32-units long, remember.

DOOM
PROGRAMMING
GURUS

6
ROOM

1
MISSION

2
EPISODE

ASSIGNING THE NEW LINE TO APPROPRIATE SECTORS

After this modification, you will have a line that displays in magenta. This is the new line that you have added to your map and that currently belongs to no sector. You may be tempted to use Make Sector to bind this line into your existing sectors, but remember the way in which Make Sector works—if it encounters a magenta line, it will create a new sector. You don't want to do that here— all you want is to incorporate the new line into the existing sectors.

To achieve this, you will need to use the Sec Define button. This is a fully manual sector-defining facility. It requires you to ensure that all lines have the appropriate number of sides before you use it, though, so go into LINES mode and set the 2-sided flag of your new line. This makes WADED add a left sidedef to it. You can set the impassable and lower unpegged flags at the same time.

Now, return to Draw mode and select Sec Define. Using the *right* mouse button, click somewhere in the area of the platform sector. (This is just selecting an existing sector with which to work.) When you have the lines of the platform sector highlighted, left-click your new line. A small popup with four options will appear with the mouse pointer positioned beside it.

This pop-up enables you to add (or remove) any side of the chosen line to the currently selected sector. Note that this pop-up uses the terminology *front* and *back* (of line), rather than *right* and *left*. Click the Front button to add the new line's right side to the platform sector. Next, click the short eastern section of the northern face of the southwestern pillar and make sure that its back (its left side) is transferred to the platform sector, too.

To assign the other side of your new line to the outer southwest room sector, *right*-click somewhere in that sector to highlight it, and then left-click your new line and add its back to this sector. You should find that WADED has worked out what you're doing by now and just adds the line to the sector as you click (without bothering with the pop-up).

This completes the work that is needed with Sec Define. All that remains to do now is to apply some textures to your new line. And don't forget also that the upper textures for the railing end pieces were going to be changed; use GRAY1 instead of the COMPSTA_ textures they currently carry.

Save the WAD as WAD11.WAD and try it out. Hopefully all is well. If not (did you remember those lowers?), fix any problems. I'll see you back in WADED when you're ready to move on to the next addition to the WAD.

ADDING A SNIPER LOCATION

The last part of this Sortie will demonstrate the use of a solid texture on a two-sided normal texture to produce a sniper position. The sniper's lair will be located at the southern end of the courtyard area. For this, draw and create a new sector utilizing new lines running along the grid as indicated in Figure 6.9.

Figure 6.9.
Additional lines to add for a sniper's den.

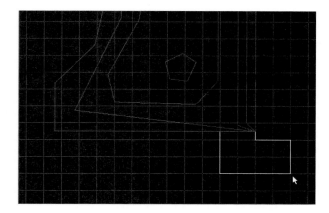

Having created this sector, you will now need some way to keep whatever you use as a sniper inside it. Any monster placed here will be able to walk straight out through the sector's northern end—and will do so as soon as it sees a player, thus spoiling the secret. In addition, as the sector is now constructed, a player could quite easily blunder through this wall—an action that could result from using the escape-route from the pond.

PREVENTING EARLY DISCOVERY OF THE DEN

Setting the line's blocks monsters flag would hold the sniper in place but would not prevent the player from finding the sniper's location by walking into it. Use of the impassable flag is not a practical option here—that would make the line impassable for all time, and I want to enable the player to enter this sector eventually. Rather than use the flags, I recommend the use of an appropriate difference of floor height between the sniper's den and the courtyard.

If the new sector's floor level is made 32 units higher than the paving-stones outside, the player will be unable to step up into it and the sniper will not step down out of it. All other sector settings can be left the same as the courtyard for now.

Now, the intention is to hide this sector from the player by using a solid texture on the courtyard side of its northern-most line, making it appear as part of the southern wall of the courtyard. Currently, the rest of this wall uses the BROWN1 texture. This cannot be used on a two-sided main texture, however, because it consists of tiled texture patches—recall that this would cause the Medusa effect if used here. BROWN96 can be used, as it is a similar texture but is not tiled. Apply this texture, therefore, to the main and essential lower texture-slots of the outer side of the line that separates the sniper's den from the courtyard.

Used on its own, this one panel of BROWN96 would quickly give away the location of the sniper's den, so change the whole of the southern wall of the courtyard to this texture. Note how the width of the new sector was chosen carefully so that this line could take a complete width of this texture without betraying its presence with a seam.

You ought to set the secret on map flag of this line also, so that the map doesn't give the game away here.

Finally, place a Former Human Sergeant in the new sector facing north, towards the courtyard. Set it to be present at difficulty levels 4 and 5 only, so that the sniper will only appear in Ultra-Violence and Nightmare settings. This will enable the WAD to be play tested at lower settings if you want to try it out without monsters in it. Save the WAD as WAD11A.WAD and start the game at Ultra-Violence level to test out the sniper's behavior.

OPENINGS IN WALLS: DOORWAYS AND WINDOWS

The final part of this examination of plain sectors considers the simple openings through walls that form doorways and windows.

DOORWAYS

You have already seen doorways formed from holes in the wall. They are generally short sectors with ceilings lower than the sectors on either side. Doorways containing real doors that open and close are the subject of the next room.

WINDOWS

Windows are a common feature of DOOM levels. They are really a variant on the simple doorway. They are made in the same way but have their floors brought up to a suitable level. Windows usually need both of their upper and lower textures unpegged to ensure that the walls above and below the opening line up correctly with the textures either side.

Plate glass windows can be simulated by setting the impassable flag on the lines composing them. (You can find an example of this in the large windows looking out of the very first room in id Software's E1M1 map.)

WAD SORTIE 12: COMPLETING THE PLATFORM ROOM

This Sortie builds on the WAD produced in the previous one. If you did not produce that WAD, you should use WAD11A.WAD (DOOM) or D2WAD11A.WAD (DOOM II) from the CD-ROM as your starting point here.

You can now complete the construction of the southwest room by adding some windows to it.

CHANGING THE OPENING TO THE COURTYARD

You can construct the first window from the existing opening into the courtyard. Just take this opening's floor level up to 56, changing the texture to CEIL5_2 at the same time. You have now created a new essential texture inside the room. Apply STONE3 to this set the appropriate unpegged flag for proper texture alignment.

ADDING A NEW WINDOW

Next, add two new sectors to the north of the southwest room to form a window looking out over another thin outdoor area. (See Figure 6.10.) Make the new window sector about 550-units wide and 32-units deep.

Use STARGR3 on the northern walls of the new outdoor area; put STONE3 on the southern walls and around the window, not forgetting to unpeg the textures above and below the opening. Set the window sector's floor level to 56 and the ceiling to 120—this makes life easier with through-wall texture alignment. Put CEIL5_2 on the floor and ceiling of the window sector.

Finally, make the northern sector open to the sky by applying F_SKY1, and set its floor to FLAT1_1. Adjust the brightness level to 255, the ceiling level to 216, and the floor to –64.

DOOM
PROGRAMMING
GURUS

6
ROOM

1
MISSION

2
EPISODE

Figure 6.10.
Two new sectors north of the southwest room.

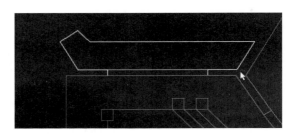

TESTING IT ALL

Now load up both courtyards with half a dozen Imps at skill levels 4 and 5, save as WAD12.WAD, and try out your platform.

Dreadful, isn't it? Hardly a sign of an Imp anywhere. But you know there's something in the southern courtyard, because, more often than not, they kill your sniper for you! (You will only notice this if you have the sound effects switched on, or by watching what is happening with IDDTIDDT in operation.)

This design needs a bit of refining, don't you think? Try playing around with the height of the platform and the northern outdoor area to see if you can improve things any. Don't try to kill off the Imps yourself during this experimentation—just set IDDQD and watch how they attack you as you move around the platform and the rest of the southwest room.

The next section has details of the final refinements I think are necessary here.

THE FINAL REFINEMENTS

Your experimentation may have shown you that with the northern sector's floor set at 16, Imps in that sector can see the player through the window as soon as the southwest room is entered. Setting the floor to 8, however, results in them being unable to shoot over the window's lower wall. Raising the floor level of the platform to encourage them to shoot higher doesn't help any, either.

One solution to this problem is to leave the outdoor sector's floor at the lower setting of 8 units, placing the Imps here initially, and then add another sector within the northern outdoor area. The new area should border the window and have a floor level of 32. The Imps will then only spot players who climb onto the platform, not those who stay at the level of the main room's floor. Once awake, however, the Imps will enter the new sector. From its greater height, they can fire unimpeded through the window, either at players on the platform or elsewhere in the room. They can also step unimpeded into the window sector as well. If you want to prevent this, set the blocks monsters flag on the outer edge of the window sector.

Improvement can also be gained by dragging each of the platform's northern pillars a complete grid square to the south. (Make room for the northwestern pillar to move by shortening the long section of the western edge of the platform by 64 units first). This reduces the size of the platform and flattens out the Imps' firing angle, making it harder for the player to avoid their fire. Figure 6.11 shows the final layout of lines I used for this area of my WAD. All other sector settings I left as given in the earlier tables.

Figure 6.11.

The final arrangement of lines: my WAD12A.WAD.

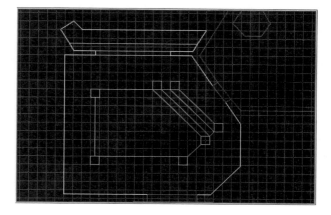

Finally, I reduced the number of Imps in the southern courtyard to two, placing one of them on the island in the pool. This way, one remains visible in the pool while the other comes close under the window wall—impossible for the player to dispose of, and a continuing danger when the player finally discovers how to enter the courtyard. With only two Imps in the courtyard, the sniper has less chance of hitting them accidentally and causing them to fire at him.

Other solutions might be to change the sniper to an Imp, or to remove the southern courtyard Imps altogether and increase the number of snipers. (I will leave further experimentation in this area to you.)

EXIT: MOPPING UP AND MOVING ON

In this room, you saw how sectors are used to build up the geography of your WAD. You were shown how sectors are commonly arranged to produce the static elements of WADs. You have extended your own WAD considerably with alcoves, platforms, staircases and windows; and by now you should be fully conversant with the use of WADED's main editing facilities.

In the next room you will see some real action: the introduction of special effects to your sectors and the first of the active sector types—the door.

ROOM 7

By Steve Benner

ACTIVATING SECTORS

So far, you have seen how sectors can be put to use in a multiplicity of ways simply by varying their basic size, elevation, lighting, and textural characteristics. Previous rooms have touched lightly upon the fact that sectors possess an additional attribute: their *special characteristics*. In this room, you will learn about that characteristic, and see how it can be used. You will also be introduced to the notion of sectors that change and move, and will learn about the simplest of the moving sectors, the door.

In the WAD Sorties from this room, the WAD which has been developing from room to room during this mission will be given some areas where a player should not linger, as well as some new spaces beyond a couple of doors.

SPECIAL SECTOR ACTIONS

A sector can be given special properties, or be made to act continuously in certain ways, by making use of its special characteristic—a numerical attribute of a sector that has been ignored so far in your own sector settings.

THE SPECIAL CHARACTERISTIC OF SECTORS

A sector's special characteristic determines the particular special action that that sector carries out. The actions themselves are hard-coded into the DOOM engine and cannot be changed. Setting the special characteristic merely invokes them. The setting itself consists of a code number telling DOOM which of the available effects to employ. The effect is applied across the entire extent of the sector. Note that sectors only possess one special characteristic; such effects, therefore, cannot be used in combination within a single sector. When creating a new sector, most editors set its special characteristic to 0, by default, thus producing an ordinary sector, with no special behavior.

SPECIAL SECTOR TYPES

For the purposes of describing them, the available special actions of sectors can be divided into four categories, as follows:

- Damaging effects
- Lighting effects
- Miscellaneous effects
- Combined effects

These will each be examined in turn.

DAMAGING EFFECTS

Damaging special effects do harm to a player who enters the sector. There are three levels of damaging effects—high, medium, and low—with the actual amount of harm done being dependent on the skill level at which the game is being played. Table 7.1 summarizes the effect of these three levels of damage.

Table 7.1. Harm done by the three classes of damaging sector.

Damage Class	I'm Too Young to Die	Higher skill levels
High Damage	–10 percent	–20 percent
Medium Damage	–5 percent	–10 percent
Low Damage	–2 percent	–5 percent

The harm a damaging sector does is applied once per second, for as long as the player is in contact with the sector's floor. The harm values quoted in the table are applied to a player's health score, unless armor is being worn, in which case the damage is divided equally between health and armor. Damaging sectors only affect players; monsters are completely immune to their effects.

LIGHTING EFFECTS

The special lighting effects consist of blinking, flickering, and oscillating light levels within the sector. All of these lighting changes are generated by reference to the brightness level of the sector and the brightness levels of immediately adjacent sectors. The value specified for the sector's own brightness level determines the upper limit of the fluctuation, while its lower limit is taken from the lowest light level amongst all immediately adjacent sectors. If there are no adjacent sectors with a lower lighting setting, then the sector's lighting will usually fluctuate between its specified setting and total darkness. The available lighting effects are as follows:

- **Blink off:** Lighting is at the specified level for most of the time, but drops to the lower level momentarily.
- **Blink on:** Lighting is at the lower level for most of the time, but takes on the specified setting momentarily.
- **Oscillate:** Lighting moves smoothly from the specified level to the lower level and back again. If there is no adjacent sector with a lower light setting, this effect does nothing.

Additionally, some lighting effects are synchronized, so that all of the participating sectors adjust their lights together. Unsynchronized sectors change their lighting levels independently of each other.

MISCELLANEOUS EFFECTS

The miscellaneous effects provide some very special effects indeed. They are as follows:

- Timed door close
- Timed door open
- Award secret credit
- Kill player and end level/game

These particular effects will be looked at in more detail in later rooms.

COMBINED EFFECTS

There is currently only one combined effect: it combines the blink-on lighting effect with high damage.

SUMMARY OF SPECIAL SECTOR TYPES

Table 7.2 gives a list of all of the effects that are currently available through a sector's special characteristic.

Table 7.2. Special sector types, ordered by code.

Code	Effect
0	Normal sector; no special effect
1	Blink off (random intervals)
2	Blink on (0.5 second intervals)
3	Blink on (1 second intervals)
4	High damage; blink on at 0.5 second intervals
5	Medium damage
6	NOT IMPLEMENTED
7	Low damage
8	Oscillate lighting
9	Award secret credit
10	Close sector 30 seconds into level
11	High damage and end level/game

Code	Effect
12	Synchronized blink on (1 second intervals)
13	Synchronized blink off (0.5 second intervals)
14	Open sector 5 minutes into level
15	NOT IMPLEMENTED
16	High damage
17	Flicker light on and off at random (DOOM v1.666 and later only)

Using any other special sector setting (or any of the unused codes) will cause DOOM to crash back to DOS as soon as a player enters the sector.

There is usually no need to remember all of the code numbers for the various effects—most editors will provide a more meaningful list for you to choose the effects from.

The next WAD Sortie builds on the WAD produced in Sortie 12 at the end of the previous room. If you did not complete that Sortie but would like to come along on this one, you should use WAD12A.WAD (DOOM) or D2WAD12A.WAD (DOOM II) from the CD-ROM as your starting point.

WAD SORTIE 13: ADDING SOME SPECIAL SECTORS

In this Sortie, you will get to try out some of these special effects by adding a few surprises for the player. As usual, you should build onto your latest WAD.

ADDING BITE

Obtaining that suit of armor is a little too easy, isn't it? Let's make it a touch harder—or at least a touch more painful! Click the SECTORS button, select the hexagonal room's platform sector, and set its special value to 5, either in the familiar way or by selecting the adjacent LIST button and selecting effect 5 from the pop-up list box that appears.

Add a surprise to the outdoor pond, too, by setting its special value to 7. Who says water has to be harmless?

FLASHING AND FLICKERING LIGHTS

To try out the special lighting effects, add a new area to your WAD out from the southwest corner of the old southwest room (now the platform room). Figure 7.1 shows the new lines needed to add a staircase and passageway descending from this room.

Figure 7.1.

Lines for a new staircase and passageway.

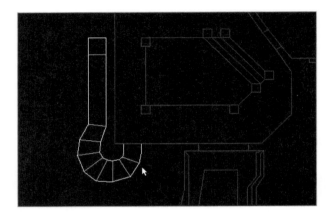

Draw the new lines using BROWN96 as the default texture. The precise shape of these new sectors is not important; you may wish to refine the shape after play-testing it. One wall has the texture LITE3 on it (see Table 7.2); you may want to make this wall the correct length to hold this texture. Also, the very end sector will need to sit precisely within the grid squares in order for its ceiling texture to be rendered correctly.

By now you should be confident enough in the use of Make Sector to construct these sectors without further help. Table 7.3 gives all of the settings for the new sectors, working out in order from the platform room. Note how the floors form a progression downwards by 16 units, with most other things staying the same. The wall textures given are for the left and right walls, as seen by a player progressing through the new sectors in the same sequence as given in the table.

Table 7.3. Sector settings for the new stairway and passage.

Lighting	Ceiling		Floor		Walls: Left	Right
144	120	FLOOR7_1	0	FLOOR7_1	BROWN96	BROWN96
176	120	FLOOR7_1	−16	FLOOR7_1	BROWN96	LITE3
144	120	FLOOR7_1	−32	FLOOR7_1	BROWN96	BROWN96

Lighting	Ceiling		Floor		Walls: Left	Right
128	120	FLOOR7_1	−48	FLOOR7_1	BROWN96	BROWN96
112	120	FLOOR7_1	−64	FLOOR7_1	BROWN96	BROWN96
112	120	FLOOR7_1	−80	FLOOR7_1	BROWN96	BROWN96
96	120	FLOOR7_1	−96	FLOOR7_1	BROWN96	BROWN96
80	120	FLOOR7_1	−112	FLOOR7_1	BROWNHUG	BROWNHUG
80	24	FLOOR7_1	−112	FLOOR7_1	BROWNHUG	BROWNHUG
128	0	TLITE6_5	−128	FLOOR4_1	PIPE2	PIPE2

The end of the corridor should have PIPE2 on it also. Use STEPTOP on the essential lowers of all steps and BROWNHUG on the essential uppers of the long section of the passageway. The essential upper over the new doorway should have STONE3 on it and will need to be unpegged.

The Use of Short Textures on Step Risers

The STEPTOP texture used on the risers of these stairs is one of several "short" textures provided for use in such places. These short textures are commonly only 16 or 24 pixels high. Remember that such textures will not tile properly if used in spaces that are too tall to take them. On stair risers, this will generally not cause any problems, because stairs must be kept below 24 units if the player is to climb them.

Be careful about the pegging of stair risers, however. Remember that if you unpeg the riser's lower texture, you are asking DOOM to recalculate this texture's placement from the sector's ceiling. Doing this with a texture that is other than 128 pixels high will produce the Pink Bug effect on the riser.

When you have the sector layout to your satisfaction, set the special characteristic of the sector that has the LITE3 texture on one of its walls to 1, and set the final sector's special characteristic to 4.

Finally, save the WAD as WAD13.WAD and inspect your latest modifications.

TRIGGERED ACTIONS

Earlier in this room, passing reference was made to an interesting pair of special sector types: the two time-triggered doors. It is worth looking in some detail at the way these operate. They provide a useful introduction to the operation of doors in general.

TIME-LOCKED DOORS

Special sector type 10 provides a timed lock-out of an area. It operates by reducing the sector's ceiling height to the level of its floor 30 seconds into the game, thus effectively closing the sector to access from players and monsters alike.

Special sector type 14 provides the opposite effect, a timed opening of an area. This action takes place five minutes after the level starts. At this time, this sector's ceiling will rise from its specified height (usually the same as the sector's floor) to a position just below the lowest adjacent ceiling, thus allowing the player to pass out through this sector (and allowing more monsters to pass in, of course!). Five seconds later, the sector will close again, this time for good.

As you can see, these two special sector actions are very simple in their operation, but very effective. In fact, this mechanism of moving a sector's ceiling from one height to another is used a great deal in DOOM to achieve a number of useful WAD elements. It is, for instance, the mechanism by which all doors operate. The only difference between these two rather esoteric types of door and the more common types is the activation mechanism that they employ. The time-triggered doors are activated automatically at the appointed moment, whereas normal door types are triggered by the players (or occasionally by monsters) taking particular steps (often quite literally).

Let us consider these triggering actions in more detail and compare them with the actions taking place in special sectors.

TRIGGERED EVENTS VERSUS CONTINUOUS EVENTS

The actions of the majority of the special sector types may be viewed as continuous: sectors employing lighting effects have lights that fluctuate throughout the game, damaging sectors cause harm for as long as the player remains upon their floor, and so on.

By comparison, the movements of doors triggered by players and monsters (and other events that will be examined in later rooms) are not continuous. They require particular actions to be carried out *at particular locations*.

Furthermore, the locations where these actions are performed may be at some distance from the sectors which they affect. You are no doubt familiar with DOOM's switches and know that they frequently operate well away from the doors that they open or the platforms they raise. For this reason, these triggered actions are not attached directly to sectors. Instead, they are attached to lines.

2
EPISODE

1
MISSION

7
ROOM

DOOM
PROGRAMMING
GURUS

LINES AS TRIGGERS

You are familiar with the role of DOOM's lines. You know that they provide the game engine with vital information about the disposition and appearances of the edges of sectors. They can play a secondary role, also: they can act as triggers. You may recall from Room 4 of this episode, "At the Sector's Edge," that in addition to its flags, each linedef carries a special-action attribute. This attribute determines the nature of the triggering action which the line may carry out. It is another code number, like the sector's special characteristic. Usually a line will have this value set to 0, meaning that it carries out no special activation. Lines with non-zero settings of this attribute are usually termed lines of *special type*.

Once again, the actions triggered by these special codes are determined by the game engine. You can only utilize what is provided, not add to or alter any of them. Just as sectors cannot possess more than one special characteristic, so lines cannot initiate more than one trigger action—although, as you will see, they may initiate that action in more than one location.

It is possible to use lines for their triggering action without having them contribute to the provision of sector-edge information. In this way, trigger lines can be laid out across sectors—as trip-wires, for example. The usual rules for placing lines still apply: they must run from vertex to vertex, and they cannot cross other lines. They do not need to form continuous or closed shapes, though, provided that the sector that contains them is itself properly closed. Lines used in this way will need to be two-sided, with both of their sidedefs assigned to the enclosing sector. The use of such lines will be demonstrated in later rooms.

Making Internal Triggers in WADED

To create trigger lines laid across sectors in WADED, you will need to add the lines after you have used Make Sector to create the sector itself. You will need to make the new line two-sided manually, and use Sec Define to add both of its sides to the appropriate sector.

INTRODUCING SPECIAL LINES

There is a very wide range of special line-types—sufficient, in fact, to fill a further four rooms of this book! They all operate from the same basic activation mechanisms, however.

TRIGGER TYPES

Each special line is triggered in a particular way, depending upon the value of its special attribute. There are four basic activation mechanisms used amongst the line-types:

- Permanently active
- Spacebar activated
- Walk-through activated
- Impact activated

Additionally, each special action may be either repeatable or not. Repeatable actions may be performed any number of times; non-repeatable actions may be carried out once only and then never again during the level. Some actions that are classed as repeatable may trigger events that can only be repeated provided that some other action subsequently returns things to an appropriate position first. (You will see an example of this in the next room.)

Some special line actions can be activated by monsters, but there aren't many of these.

ACTIVATION MECHANISMS

The action that is triggered by a line's special attribute is generally carried out on some associated sector. The process by which DOOM selects which sector to affect when a line is activated varies from action to action but falls into two basic categories:

- Local actions
- Remote actions

Local actions operate on the sector that owns the *left* sidedef of the active line. These actions all provide doors of some kind; their use will be examined shortly. Remote actions are more complicated. They will be the subject of later rooms.

THE ODD ONE OUT: HORIZONTALLY SCROLLING TEXTURES

There is one special line action that is completely different from all others. It requires no triggering and does not affect any sectors. In fact, it operates continuously and affects only its own line. It is special action 48—the horizontally scrolling texture. Any lines having this action will automatically scroll their textures horizontally while the game is in progress. Note that because horizontal scrolling is implemented through a line's special attribute, lines using it cannot act as any other type of trigger.

OPEN (AND CLOSE) SESAME!

The remainder of this room will concentrate on locally-activated special lines. In id Software's parlance, these are all classed as *manual door* lines. The basic DOOM door is activated through the first of these manual door lines: special line-type 1.

THE BASIC DOOR

Special line-type 1 provides a repeatable, space- and monster-activated, local-action effect. It operates as follows: whenever a player is standing by this line and presses the spacebar, the game engine will raise the ceiling of the sector on the line's left side to a position just below that sector's lowest *adjacent* ceiling, thus simulating the opening of a door. This action is accompanied by the sound of a door opening. The ceiling stays in this position for five seconds and then lowers to the sector's floor again, thus effectively closing the door.

This action can be retriggered any number of times; and the current motion or state of the door can be reversed with a further press of the spacebar. An enemy who simply approaches this line will also cause the door to open.

Figure 7.2 shows how the door action is provided by the movement of a single sector's ceiling. The upper view is of the cross-section of a WAD with the player positioned close to a sector that has its ceiling set to the same height as its floor. Beneath is another view showing how this sector's ceiling could rise to provide an open door. Alongside these views is a sample map that might be used to implement this area. The arrows indicate which lines carry the appropriate special attributes necessary to permit the door to be opened from both sides.

MAKING SURE A DOOR WORKS CORRECTLY

In order to operate correctly as a door, the participating sector needs to be set up properly, of course. Firstly, notice which way the door sector's activating lines face in Figure 7.2. A manual door line will always move the ceiling of the sector on its left side. If you have this line facing the wrong way, the ceiling of the sector in which the player is standing could be the one that is moved—usually with catastrophic effect! Make sure, then, that both of the lines that form the rising face of the door have their right sides facing out from the door sector itself.

Figure 7.2.
Implementation of a DOOM door.

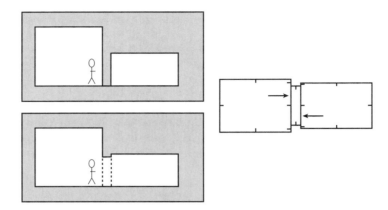

Secondly, the sector needs to have its ceiling level set at an appropriate height. DOOM will assume that the first activation of a manual door line is to open the door; it will therefore always take the ceiling up. You should make sure, then, that all of your door sectors are created with their ceilings at the lower positions—usually at the same level as their floors. It doesn't matter to DOOM if you don't set all of your doors like this at the start, though. Even if a door is not completely closed at the beginning, the game engine will still open it properly when it is activated, and all doors close completely to the floor afterwards, irrespective of their starting position.

Players usually expect to be able to pass through doors that they can open. Don't forget to allow for this, both in changes of floor height through your doors and in the final open height of doorways. The limit of the upward motion of a door sector's ceiling is determined by the height of the lowest ceiling adjacent to the door sector—the rising ceiling stops 4 pixels below this height.

For a player to be able to pass through the door after it has opened, you must allow for a minimum gap of 56 units between the door sector's floor height and the final resting height of its ceiling.

OTHER THINGS TO LOOK OUT FOR

The actual size and shape of the door sector is largely immaterial. The doors of most WADs tend to be a standard 64 or 128 pixels wide and 16 pixels deep, to take advantage of the standard door textures, but they do not need to be. Sectors of any shape will function as doors. All you need are appropriate lines accessible to the player with which to activate them.

Don't forget also that most doors will need to be capable of being opened from both sides. Sectors that make up doors will therefore need two manual door triggers, as you have seen in Figure 7.2. You can, of course, omit either of these triggering special attributes and make your doors capable of being opened from only the one side, if that is what you want.

APPLYING TEXTURES TO DOORS

The designers of DOOM have provided a large number of textures specifically for doors. The names of door textures generally start with DOOR or BIGDOOR. As already noted, the majority of these are 64 or 128 pixels wide by 128 pixels high. A few are somewhat shorter than the standard 128-pixel height, however, and will produce the Pink Bug effect if used in areas that are too large for them.

You should already have worked out that the door texture itself needs to be applied to the line's upper texture—the main texture will normally be left transparent, to provide the doorway once the sector opens. If you place a solid texture on the main texture slot of a door line, the door will seem to rise, but no opening will appear beneath it. The player will still be able to step through it, though. If you omit the texture from the door's upper slot, the result will usually be HOM.

In its closed position, of course, the line's main texture will occupy no space and therefore not appear.

USING DOOR RECESSES

Although most door textures will tile correctly vertically, doors generally look odd if allowed to repeat very far up a wall. Figure 7.3 shows the effect. This door has been implemented using the arrangement of sectors shown earlier in Figure 7.2. Notice how the door looks wrong, running right up to the ceiling like this.

Figure 7.3.

The effect of placing door sectors directly on the side of tall rooms.

To avoid this unsightly implementation, doors out of tall rooms usually require additional thin sectors, 16 units or so deep, separating them from the main room sector. Each thin sector should have a ceiling-height 128 units above their floor, to provide a recess in which the door then appears. Figure 7.4 shows the appropriate arrangement of sectors.

Figure 7.4.

Sector arrangement to provide a door in a recess.

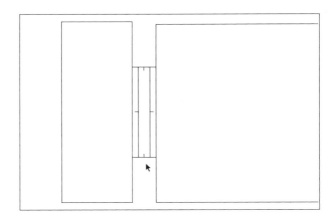

Figure 7.5 shows the improved appearance of the door brought about by this sector arrangement.

Figure 7.5.

An improved door, in a recess.

PEGGING CONSIDERATIONS

The changes in ceiling height that simulate a door opening do not occur instantaneously, of course. For the action to look like a door opening, the textures associated with the door sector will need to behave in an appropriate manner. It is the job of the texture pegs to ensure that this happens.

Consider first the face of the door, as viewed by a player opening it. Remember that the appearance of this face is provided by the line's upper texture. You will recall that the starting location for the painting of an upper texture is determined by the state of the line's upper unpegged flag. The pattern is either painted from the lower edge of the texture upwards (when pegged), or from the ceiling downwards (when unpegged).

2
EPISODE

1
MISSION

7
ROOM

DOOM
PROGRAMMING
GURUS

DOOM opens doors by moving a sector's ceiling upwards. A player viewing this action from a nearby sector will observe the shrinking of the upper texture (the face of the door) and the growth of the main texture (the opening) below it. In order for this action to look natural, the shrinking upper texture must have its pattern rise as if being pushed into the ceiling.

To achieve this, the upper texture of the door face needs to remain pegged to its lower edge. If the upper texture were to be unpegged, the effect would be to cause the door face to remain stationary, with its pattern anchored at the ceiling adjacent to the door. Rather than appearing to move up into the ceiling, the door itself would look as though it was being eaten away by a gap rising from the floor. This effect looks unnatural. Make sure, therefore, that you clear the upper unpegged flag of all lines that represent door faces.

FURTHER PEGGING CONSIDERATIONS AROUND DOORS

Finally in this examination of the construction of simple doors, consider the sides of the sector making up the door. These will usually be single-sided lines forming the "wall" through which the doorway passes. They will therefore need only main textures. As the door opens, the height of these texture spaces will increase.

You will recall from Episode 2, Mission 1, Room 5, "The Low-Down on Textures," that single-sided lines' main textures are usually painted from their sector's ceiling down. The implication for these side walls of the doorway, then, is that these textures will move with their sector's ceiling as the door opens. This would look unrealistic. The side walls should stay static as the door opens and closes. This can be achieved by setting their lower unpegged flag—you will recall that this will cause these textures to be painted from the (static) floor up.

SUMMARY OF STEPS INVOLVED IN MAKING A BASIC DOOR

In summary, then, these are the steps involved in producing a basic spacebar-operated door:

1. Create appropriate sectors. Any shape will do for the door, but it will need two adjacent sectors for the doorway to connect between. Unless you particularly want a tall door, make sure that the sectors adjoining the door have ceilings no more than about 128 units from their floors; use recess sectors as necessary.

2. Make sure that the lines bordering adjacent sectors have their right sides facing out from the door sector.

3. Set the sector's ceiling height to the same as its floor.

4. Put appropriate door textures on the *upper* texture slots of the lines representing the faces of the door; *clear* their upper unpegged flag.

5. Put appropriate textures on the side walls of the door sector; set their lower unpegged flag.

6. Set the special attribute of each door face that you want a player to be able to activate to 1.

The next Sortie lets you try this out for yourself.

WAD SORTIE 14: ADDING A DOOR

> This Sortie builds on the WAD produced in the previous one. If you did not produce that WAD, you should use WAD13.WAD (DOOM) or D2WAD13.WAD (DOOM II) from the CD-ROM as your starting point here.

OK—so much for the theory. Let's see how it is done in practice. Load up WADED with your latest WAD and I'll lead you through the addition of a basic spacebar-operated door.

> Many editors provide canned procedures for the automatic construction of doors. WADED is no exception—you have no doubt already noticed the Make Door button. Usually, though, such ready-made doors need just as much work to customize their appearance as they would have needed to build them from scratch! I recommend doing it manually.

ADDING A DOOR

The new door will be placed across the opening into the stairway that you added to the southwest corner of the platform room in the last Sortie.

Start by adding two new lines across the opening into the stairway. Place the first line 16 units south of the line currently dividing the platform room from the corridor. Add the second 16 units south of the first. The area between these two lines is to be the new door sector. Apply Make Sector as necessary, and then check that both of the new lines have their right sides facing out from the new door sector. If either of the lines has its tick mark pointing into the sector, select the offending line and press **F** to flip it over.

It is important that the node tree be rebuilt before playing a WAD that has had a line flipped in this way. WADED doesn't always notice this, so you will need to keep an eye out for it yourself. Remember this especially if you are loading a WAD into the editor just to fix a line that faces the wrong way. Make sure that the nodes are rebuilt as the WAD is saved.

The consequence of flipping a line without rebuilding the nodes is that the game engine becomes confused about which side of the line is in view. Visual turmoil results, with sectors being displayed at the wrong heights.

Table 7.4 shows the settings that are needed for the changed areas.

Table 7.4. Sector settings around the new door.

Sector	Lighting	Ceiling		Floor	
Room alcove	208	120	FLAT3	0	MFLR8_1
Door	192	0	FLAT3	0	FLOOR7_1
Top step landing	144	120	FLOOR7_1	0	FLOOR7_1

The alcove side-wall textures need to be changed to STONE3 to match the rest of the platform room. Remember that this texture has a 32-pixel vertical pattern repeat. The difference in ceiling height between the alcove and the main room is $184 - 120 = 64$ units, so no adjustment is needed to keep these textures aligned with their neighbors.

To create the door, use BIGDOOR6 as the texture facing into the room (on the upper texture, re-member) and BIGDOOR7 on the staircase side. Make sure that both of these textures are pegged. Set the special value to 1 for both of the lines with these textures, so that the door can be opened from either side.

WADED will show these locally activating door lines in cyan.

Put DOORTRAK on the side-walls of the door sector, with the lower unpegged flag set so that the textures don't move up and down with the door. Finally, save the WAD as WAD14.WAD and try it out.

Does it work properly? If not, check the way the door lines face, and that you have used the correct value for the lines' special attributes; and then try again.

VARIATIONS ON THE THEME OF DOORS

In addition to the standard spacebar- (and monster), activated door that you implemented in the last Sortie, there are a number of other active line-types that provide variations on this door, implemented through the same mechanism. These doors are constructed in exactly the same way as the basic door you have just seen—all that needs to be changed is the activating line's special attribute.

DOORS THAT STAY OPEN

Line-type 31 provides a door that works in the same way as a standard door but which, once activated, remains open. Such doors are useful, of course, for committing the player to dealing with whatever lies beyond them. Because the door will not close, whatever monsters the area beyond contains may now be awakened and will pursue the player.

Note that only players can open these doors.

DOORS THAT NEED KEYS

Table 7.5 gives the line-types that implement doors that require the player to have found and collected the appropriate key cards.

Table 7.5. Special attributes to provide key-coded doors.

Code	Action
26	Door requires blue key to open.
27	Door requires yellow key to open.
28	Door requires red key to open.

Note that there is no difference between the standard and the skull keys—there are only three key types, not six as it might appear from playing the game. Once the proper key is in the player's possession, these doors operate in exactly the same way as standard doors, except that monsters cannot activate them.

It is usual to provide some indication that a door requires a key before it will open, rather than simply relying on DOOM's text messages. The normal method is to apply an appropriate texture to reveal each side of the recess into which such doors are usually set.

> In architectural terminology, a *reveal* is that wall of an opening or recess at right angles to the face of the window or door which occupies the opening.

Figure 7.6 illustrates how such doors may appear during the game. Note, though, that it is not the presence of the warning lights at the side of the door that cause the door to require a key, but rather the use of the appropriate special line-type as the face of the door sector.

Figure 7.6.
A keyed door.

Table 7.6 gives the line-types that provide keyed doors that stay open once activated.

Table 7.6. Codes for latch-open key-coded doors.

Code	Action
32	Door requires blue key, stays open.
33	Door requires red key, stays open.
34	Door requires yellow key, stays open.

DOOM
PROGRAMMING
GURUS

7
ROOM

1
MISSION

2
EPISODE

Using Keyed Doors

The principal use of keyed doors is, of course, to force players to find and obtain an appropriate key before they can go on. The use of this feature in a WAD usually has an objective beyond the simple addition of another puzzle, however.

Keyed doors force an order to the players' progression though a map by locking them out of a new area until some other area has been played to completion. You should regard keys as rewards to the player for the completion of some specific task, or for finding the solution to some puzzle or other.

Use keyed doors as a way of keeping players concentrated on solving one puzzle before moving on to the next; or to ensure that particular weapons have been located before allowing them into more hazardous areas. Keyed doors should contribute to a player's structured completion of a mission, rather than be seen as impediments to progress through it.

TURBO DOORS

DOOM v1.4 introduced a new type of door, not used in id Software's WADs until DOOM II: the turbo (or blazing) door. These doors work in the same way as the standard doors, except that they open and close much faster (and with a different sound). Their line-types (which, naturally, are only available in v1.4 of DOOM and later) are given in Table 7.7.

Table 7.7. Line-types for turbo doors.

Code	Action
117	Turbo open/close door
118	Turbo door; stays open

There are turbo versions of the keyed doors, but these are *not* locally activated doors; they are therefore the subject of the next room.

SECRET DOORS

Secret doors do not require any special implementation in DOOM. They are simply disguised or hidden from the player by wearing standard wall textures as camouflage. Their presence may also be kept from the player by setting their Secret on Map flag.

> It is usually regarded as polite to give some hint of the presence of secret doors. This rewards the more observant players and removes the need for players to wander around trying all walls in the search for that elusive last secret location.

Secret locations are the subject of Episode 2, Mission 1, Room 11, "Let's Get the Hell Out of Here!"

SUMMARY OF LOCALLY-OPERATED DOORS

Table 7.8 is a summary of all of the line-types that provide locally-activated doors. This table's activation category column indicates whether each action is classed as manual repeatable (MR) or as manual non-repeatable (M1).

Table 7.8. Special line codes for locally-activated doors.

Action	Activation Category	Code
Open, pause, close	MR	1
Open, pause, close; blue key	MR	26
Open, pause, close; yellow key	MR	27
Open, pause, close; red key	MR	28
Open and stay	MR	31
Open and stay; blue key	M1	32
Open and stay; red key	M1	33
Open and stay; yellow key	M1	34
Open, pause, close (v1.4+)	MR	117
Open and stay (v1.4+)	M1	118

Only basic type 1 doors can be opened by enemies.

If any player or monster is standing in the door sector as it closes, the ceiling's motion will reverse (and the door re-open) as soon as it contacts the obstructing object.

Once again, there should be no need for you to remember the various code numbers responsible for providing each of these actions—most editors will provide a list of special line-types for you to choose from.

Line-Type Codes in WADED

In common with most editors, WADED provides lists of line-types grouped by action. These lists can be accessed by clicking the LIST button, located beneath a line's SPECIAL attribute field, which is displayed whenever you are in LINES mode.

Each category of line-types can be selected by means of the selection buttons in each pop-up list. Unfortunately, WADED's categorization of special line-types is far from perfect; its descriptions of their actions is often misleading and sometimes just plain wrong. (Many other editors share this affliction.) Always use the numbers given in this book, therefore, rather than selecting codes that would seem, from WADED's description, to be closer to the required action.

WAD SORTIE 15: ADDING KEYED AND SECRET DOORS

This Sortie builds on the WAD produced in the previous one. If you did not produce that WAD, you should use WAD14.WAD (DOOM) or D2WAD14.WAD (DOOM II) from the CD-ROM as your starting point here.

In the previous Sortie, you added a basic spacebar-operated door to separate the platform room from the stairway leading out of it. In this Sortie, you will add some other kinds of doors. First, a keyed door, leading into a new area of the WAD, south out of the original southeast passageway. This door will require the blue key to be found before it will open. It will give admission to another outdoor area of the WAD—this time with covered overhangs along its sides.

The second new door to be added to the WAD will be a secret door. It will be placed in the original outdoor courtyard, in the far southwestern corner, beyond the pond.

ADDING A KEYED DOOR

Start your addition of the keyed door by creating a recess in the south wall of the southeast passage-way 16 units deep by 256 units wide. Use DOORBLU on the short walls of this sector to act as an indicator of the fact that the blue key is needed before it will open. Create another sector of the same size, bordering this one to the south—this will be the door itself. Make sure that its lines face the correct way after you have used Make Sector on it. Place DOORTRAK on the short wall sections of this sector, setting each line's lower unpegged flag. Then draw the lines making up the sectors on the other side of the door, as shown in Figure 7.7. Use STARTAN3 as the default drawing texture for all of the lines beyond the door.

Figure 7.7.

The lines for sectors through the keyed door.

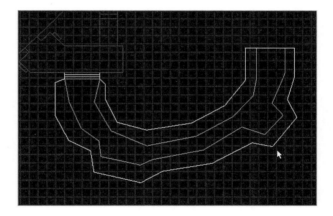

There are three major sectors beyond the door. Together they form a long curving outdoor space. The central sector is open to the sky, while the two sectors bordering it form covered areas. Table 7.9 gives the settings for all of the new sectors.

Table 7.9. Sector settings for the areas around the keyed door.

Sector	Lighting	Ceiling		Floor	
Inner recess	144	112	CEIL3_5	0	MFLR8_1
Door	144	0	CEIL3_5	0	MFLR8_1

continues

Table 7.9. continued

Sector	Lighting	Ceiling		Floor	
Outer recess	144	144	CEIL3_5	0	FLAT1_2
Outer area (center)	255	184	F_SKY1	0	FLAT1_2
Outer area (edges)	176	144	FLOOR7_1	0	FLAT1_2

Use BIGDOOR2 on both door faces, setting their special attributes to 26. (This value will be found in the pop-up list of specials in the DOORS-3 category.) STONE2 should be used on the upper (unpegged) texture over the inner recess and STARTAN3 on all essential textures in the large outer areas.

Don't concern yourself with the alignment of the textures in the outer area—there are some extensions to be carried out here later. You can tidy up then.

Finally, don't forget that if you want to be able to open and pass through this new door, you will either have to place a blue key somewhere in the WAD (right by the door would be a sensible place, for now) or play the WAD with the IDKFA cheat code.

Try this WAD out now. Is it okay?

> If you have a nasty case of HOM where your door should be, you have a missing essential texture. You did apply the BIGDOOR2 texture to the line's *upper* texture slot, didn't you?

ADDING A SECRET DOOR

Once you are happy with the keyed door, move on and add a secret door to the original courtyard.

For this area, you will need new sectors at the southwest corner of the original courtyard as shown in Figure 7.8.

In order, from the courtyard itself, these new sectors will form the following:

- **An outer recess:** A door will look odd opening into the sky. This recess provides a more realistic setting. You may think it makes the presence of the door too obvious, though.

- **The door itself:** The door will be hidden by the application of a standard wall texture to match the rest of the western wall of the courtyard. Once opened, it will stay open. Again, make sure this sector's lines face the correct way after you have used Make Sector to create it.

■ **The inner room:** The development of the room to which access is gained by opening the door will be carried out later. Don't worry too much about its appearance for now. Its ceiling is low, though, so a further recess on this side of the door is unnecessary.

Figure 7.8.

Lines for another secret area off the courtyard.

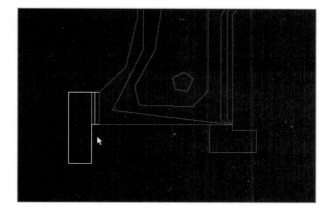

Table 7.10 has the settings for the new sectors.

Table 7.10. Settings for the new secret area off the courtyard.

Sector	Lighting	Ceiling			Floor
Outer recess	176	120	FLOOR4_1	−16	FLAT1_1
Door	176	−16	FLOOR4_1	−16	FLAT1_1
Inner room	144	120	FLOOR4_1	−16	FLAT1_1

Put BROWN1 on all of the new walls—including the uppers of the door sector itself and the upper essential over the outer recess—except the one that extends the southern wall of the courtyard into the outer recess (use BROWN96 here to match its neighboring wall section) and the sides of the new door sector (use DOORTRAK, lower unpegged, as usual).

Apply a Y-offset of 24 to the two walls in the alcove to realign these textures to the rest of the courtyard. Then apply a Y-offset of 24 to the face of the door for better alignment and also set this line's Secret on Map flag.

Complete the construction of the door by setting the special attribute of the line marking its outer face to 31. You don't need to worry about a trigger on the inner face of this door, because the player cannot reach it while the door is closed and, once opened, it will stay open.

Finally, don't forget to reduce the height of the window ledge in the north wall of the courtyard to 0 temporarily to allow access—or move the player 1 start position into the courtyard just to try out the new secret door. Save the WAD as WAD15.WAD and try out your latest additions.

EXIT: MOPPING UP AND MOVING ON

This room introduced you to the active sector. In it, you learned how to add bite to your WADs and you were shown the ins and outs of building locally activated (or manual) doors. You learned how to make doors function correctly and how to ensure that they look right while they are doing it. Your own WAD should be coming along nicely by now.

The exploration of DOOM's doors continues in the next room which contains an introduction to the remotely-operated doors and other effects. It will show you how to use the various types of switches available in DOOM—the kinds the player can see, as well as the ones that are hidden.

ROOM 8

By Steve Benner

REMOTE-CONTROL SECTORS

In the previous room, you had your first encounter with DOOM's active sectors. You learned about the sector's special characteristic, which imbues a sector with a particular behavior during play. You were also introduced to the ability of lines to initiate certain actions in sectors. In that room we concentrated on locally activated sectors: sectors which have their actions triggered from one of their own lines.

In this room we will turn our attention to remotely activated sectors. These sectors may have the triggers for their actions located at some distance from them. You have seen that the local, manually activated sector actions are, in fact, all doors of one kind or another. In this room you will discover more ways to make doors operate: you will be shown the use of wall-mounted switches and trip-wires.

The WAD that we have been developing from room to room in this mission will gain some additional doors during the forthcoming Sorties. We will also begin the development of a future area of maze with the introduction of some fairly complex light switching arrangements. We start our exploration of these remotely controlled sectors, though, by examining in detail the remote activation mechanism itself.

TRIGGERS AND TAGS

As you have already seen, a locally activated sector is connected to its initiating line through that line's left sidedef. It would be somewhat restrictive to force all activating lines to be connected to their target sectors in this way, though. DOOM therefore provides an additional way of connecting special lines to the sectors they affect. This mechanism is called *tagging*.

TAGGED ACTIONS

The tagging of lines and sectors is a simple process. As well as having a special attribute, each of a WAD's lines and sectors also carries a tag number. Ordinarily, this tag number will be set to zero—meaning that the tag is not in use. Actions that utilize the tagging mechanism—all of those provided by the remotely activating special line-types—operate by matching the tag of the activating line to that of a target sector, whenever the line is triggered. All sectors that are found with a matching tag are subjected to the action that the line initiates.

The tag number itself is nothing more than an arbitrary identification number. Most map editors assign tag numbers automatically as needed; you should never need to know their actual value. All you should need to do is set an appropriate special line-type defining both the action that will occur and the method by which it will be triggered, and also indicate a target sector where you want the action specified by the line-type to be carried out.

MULTI-ACTION TRIGGERS

DOOM does not insist that lines or sectors possess unique tag numbers. Indeed, you may not wish them to: a single line can thus initiate its specified action in several sectors simultaneously, just by having these sectors share the same tag number. Similarly, a sector (or a group of sectors with the same tag) can be made to undergo different actions by using more than one activation line with a common tag number. It is therefore possible, for example, to have a line that opens several doors simultaneously; or to have a door that can be opened from a number of different switch lines; or, indeed, to have a sector that can behave as a door, say, if one line is used but as a crushing ceiling if activated from another.

Because a line only has one special attribute, it is not possible to have a single activation line trigger *different* actions. You could not, for example, have a trip-wire that opened a door behind the player at the same time as it turned the lights out ahead. Furthermore, if you have sectors that share a common tag number, those sectors will remain linked for all actions applied to them through the tagging mechanism. It would not be possible, say, to have a line that caused a group of sectors to open as doors and to have a line elsewhere rigged to close just one of them.

The locally activating triggers explored in the last room remain unaware of such groupings, though, because they do not use the tagging system. It is possible, therefore, to have a number of doors, each of which could be opened as a basic door but which can also be operated as a group through the use of shared tag numbers.

THE ACTIVATION MECHANISM

Because it is possible to have more than one line trigger any particular sector, there exists the potential for activation conflicts. DOOM has a simple way of resolving conflicting requests made of the same sector. The rule, generally, is that if a sector is already involved in an activity, that action must be complete before the sector can participate in any other kind of activity. Trigger requests are not queued. If a particular target sector is not available to participate as a line is triggered, then that sector will be left out of the action.

Additionally, some actions lock out all further actions on a sector, while others can entrain additional, untagged sectors in their activity. Some actions require their participating sectors to be set up carefully for them to be effective. The linking together of sector actions to form complex arrangements of moving and changing sectors will be covered in more detail in Episode 2, Mission 1, Room 10, "Complex Moving Sectors."

MISSING TAG VALUES

Although the tagging of active lines to their target sectors is often made simple by map editors, it is always possible to make slips. The most common mistakes and their consequences include:

- **Not setting a tag number for a remotely-activated line-type:** The precise result of this depends upon the line-type involved. Some will simply not activate; others will locate all sectors with a tag value of zero (usually the majority of the sectors in the WAD) and apply the action to these. Needless to say, this can lead to some unexpected and often spectacular results when the line is activated. If you find that all of your ceiling and floor heights have suddenly changed, for example, as you move around your WAD, suspect the presence of a line with a special line-type and a tag value of zero.

- **No sector has a matching tag number:** The outcome of this error again depends on the particular line-type. The usual result, though, is a crash to DOS when the line is activated. This error can easily come about if you have a special line tagged to a sector and then subsequently alter the sector's tag number by tagging it to a different line.

Many editors will provide internal consistency checks to alert you to the presence of these errors.

TOO MANY ACTIVE SECTORS

Note that the number of sectors that DOOM can have in motion simultaneously is limited to 30, which should be ample for most WADs. If this number is exceeded, DOOM will crash back to DOS with the message P_AddActivePlat: no more plats!

> If you find that DOOM gives a no more plats! error message when you know there should be nothing like 30 sectors in motion, you have probably forgotten to tag a trigger to its target sector—DOOM is trying to move all untagged sectors in your WAD simultaneously!

TYPES OF SWITCHES

Table 8.1 gives the categories into which all special line-types are divided. The table also shows the standard two-letter identifying codes that are usually given to these categories.

Table 8.1. Categories of special line-types.

Category	Code	Mode of operation
Manual	M1/MR	Manual, local activated; action is triggered by the spacebar and may be one-off (M1) or repeatable (MR).
Trigger	W1	Walk-through activated; action does not repeat.
Retrigger	WR	Walk-through activated; action can be repeated any number of times.
Impact	G1/GR	Action is activated by being shot at; action may be one-off (G1) or may be repeatable (GR).
Switch	S1	Spacebar activated; action does not repeat.
Button	SR	Spacebar activated; action can be repeated any number of times.

MANUAL ACTIONS

The locally activated (or manual) sector actions were the subject of Room 7 of this mission, "Activating Sectors." They are listed again here for completeness.

TRIGGERS/RETRIGGERS

Walk-through triggers are activated as soon as the player steps over them. Consequently, they are only of use on two-sided lines. These lines can be either standard lines between sectors, or lines added within sectors. Note that players are deemed to have stepped over a line only when their center point makes a transition from one side of it to the other. This means that there will need to be a gap of at least a player's radius (16 units) on each side of any walk-through line for it ever to be activated.

Walk-through lines often act as invisible trip-wires used to spring surprises on the player. These lines can be activated from either side. The retrigger actions will occur on each crossing of the line, while the trigger class of actions will only happen the first time the player crosses the line.

GUN-ACTIVATED ACTIONS

Impact-activated lines require the player to fire a gun (or aim a punch) at them. (Note that rockets and plasma fired at these lines have no effect. The fist and chainsaw will work on them, though!) Suitably armed monsters firing at these lines will also activate them. There are not enough of these types of action to warrant separate names to distinguish the one-off from the repeatable actions.

SWITCHES AND BUTTONS

The final category of remotely activated lines requires the player to press the spacebar while adjacent to and facing the line. Note that players cannot activate a switch or button that is not in front of them. In addition, these special lines can only be activated from their *right*. If a player attempts to operate a switch-line from its left side, nothing happens.

A player does not need to be pressed close up against these lines to activate them. If a player's center point is within 31 units of a switch or button when the spacebar is pressed, the line will be activated, provided that there are no other intervening special lines (of *any* type). Note that this prohibits the stacking of several spacebar-activated lines close together in an attempt to have them all triggered at once when a player presses the spacebar in their proximity. In such cases, only the line closest to the player can be activated (and only then if the player is to its right). Similarly, any walk-through trigger placed to the right of a spacebar-activated trigger will need to be crossed before a player can operate the latter.

SWITCH-LINE TEXTURES

Some "solid" surface is often needed for a switch or button line, if only to constrain the player in the correct position to operate it. It is also usual to provide the player with some indication that there is a switch line waiting to be activated. This is normally achieved through the use of appropriate wall textures.

GENERAL TEXTURES

A number of textures are available to make switch-lines look like whatever they represent: a door face, a switch to be thrown, or a button to be pressed, for instance. Figure 8.1 shows some of them. Use these textures as necessary to encourage players to use the spacebar to perform whatever action is provided by the line.

Figure 8.1.

A selection of wall textures that will tempt the player to press the spacebar.

You have already used some of these textures in your own WADs—not only various door textures but also a couple of the switch textures. These latter textures are interesting because of their special properties and capabilities. Their use will be examined in some detail.

SPECIAL SWITCH TEXTURES

The designers at id Software have provided a number of special wall textures to simulate wall-mounted switches and buttons. The names of these textures all begin with SW1. If you look at a full list of the wall-texture names (you can do this in WADED by clicking the **P** button adjacent to the texture list, while in LINES mode), you will see that each SW1 texture has a matching SW2 partner. Together, each SW1/SW2 pair of textures provides the patterns for a switch or button in both untriggered (SW1) and triggered (SW2) states. Figure 8.2 shows one such pair of textures.

Figure 8.2.
The SWxBRN1 texture pair.

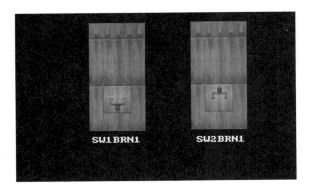

SW1 BRN1   SW2 BRN1

The two textures SW1LION and SW1GARG, which you have already used in your WAD, fall into the switch texture category. You may have discovered that when they are used on their own, these textures do not automatically provide you with any switching action. They do not change to their partner pattern, just by pressing the spacebar. Try playing your latest WAD again if you hadn't noticed this. Walk the player over to each of the alcoves and observe that these textures are quite static, whatever you do to them. (If you haven't been building this mission's WADs, WAD15.WAD on the accompanying CD-ROM—or D2WAD15.WAD if you have DOOM II—can be used here. The alcoves in question are in the passageway to the east of the player's starting position.)

Used in conjunction with appropriate special line-types, however, these lines will animate automatically. DOOM will change a SW1 texture to its matching SW2 counterpart whenever the player activates a switch or button line. DOOM also knows whether to change the texture permanently (for a switch action) or just temporarily (for a button action).

Do not be confused by the terminology into thinking that those textures that look like switches must be used on switch-type lines, while button-type lines require the push-button textures. Any SW1 texture will function correctly on either type of line.

Use of an SW1 texture on a special line also causes DOOM to emit the characteristic "clunk" as the line is activated. This sound is produced whenever additional sounds may be associated with the action.

USING THE SWITCH TEXTURES

The SW1/SW2 texture pairs may be used on any suitable upper, lower, or main texture slot, as dictated by the particular sector arrangements. Thought will need to be given to the alignment and pegging arrangements used, in order to keep the representation of the switch at the correct height—note that the precise switch position varies from texture to texture. You need to check this carefully when you use these textures.

Generally, lines that use these textures on the main slot will need to have their lower unpegged flag set to force the texture to take its alignment from the floor. If you cannot set a line's lower unpegged flag for some reason, you will need to apply appropriate Y-offsets. This can occur where the switch itself is required to take part in some movement or other—on a door-face, for instance—or is located adjacent to floors that move.

You may need to position the switch line in an alcove or other recess, in order to limit the number of vertical and horizontal repetitions of the pattern—multiple images of the same switch look weird and will confuse the player into thinking that more than one switch is present.

If you want a single switch to appear in the middle of a long wall without using an alcove then, provided that the sector ceiling is sufficiently low for the texture not to repeat vertically, you can break the long wall into more than one line. The length of the line acting as the switch should be made the same as the width of the switch texture. Most of the SW1/SW2 texture pairs provide switch images superimposed on the standard wall textures to enable you to do just this. Use the standard wall texture on the adjacent wall sections, and a matching SW1 texture on the section carrying the switch action.

The superimposition of the switch image on standard wall texture makes the majority of SW1/SW2 textures unsuited for use as two-sided main textures. If you use them in this way, the result will be the Medusa effect.

MORE DOORS

The previous section examined locally activated doors. This section looks at DOOM's door mechanisms further and presents the remaining special line-types provided for their implementation.

SETTING UP REMOTELY ACTIVATED DOORS

The procedure for setting up remotely activated doors is very similar to that employed for basic doors. Here are the essential steps:

1. Create appropriate sectors. For doors to look good, make the sectors adjoining the door have ceilings no more than about 128 units from their floors; use recess sectors if necessary.

2. Make sure that door lines bordering adjacent sectors have their left sides facing into the door sector. This step remains necessary even for remotely activated doors. Odd effects result from getting this wrong. You can find all of your ceilings (or even your floors) moving when you activate incorrectly made doors!

3. Set the door sector's ceiling height to the same as its floor so that the door starts in the closed position. Put appropriate door textures on the *upper* texture of the lines representing the faces of the door; check that the upper unpegged flag of each of these lines is clear. Use appropriate textures on the side walls of the door sector with the lower unpegged flag set.

4. Choose an appropriate activating line for the door and set its special attribute to the required value (given shortly).

5. Tag the activating line to the door sector.

The next WAD Sortie will lead you through this process in detail.

REMOTELY ACTIVATED DOORS

Table 8.2 gives a full list of the codes for remotely activated doors. Note that not all types of doors are available in all activation categories.

Table 8.2. Special line codes for remotely activated doors.

| Action | Activation Category | | | | |
	W1	WR	S1	SR	GR
Door: open, pause, close	4†	90	29	63	–
Door: open and stay	2	86	103	61	46
Door: close	3	75	50	42	–
Door: close for 30 seconds, open	16	76	–	–	–
Turbo Door: open, pause, close	108*	105*	111*	114*	–
Turbo Door: open and stay	109*	106*	112*	115*	–
Turbo Door: close	110*	107*	113*	116*	–
Blue-keyed turbo door	–	–	133*	99*	–
Red-keyed turbo door	–	–	135*	134*	–
Yellow-keyed turbo door	–	–	137*	136*	–

Only the trigger indicated † can be activated directly by monsters. Suitably armed enemies can open a gun-activated door, though, if their fire misses its target and hits the appropriate trigger line.

* Turbo doors are only available in DOOM v1.4 or later.

If any player or monster is standing in any of these door sectors as the door closes, the door will re-open as soon as it contacts the obstruction.

You are already familiar with the majority of these door types. All that differs in most cases from basic doors are the activation mechanisms. There is, though, an additional category of actions to note: those that specifically make doors *close*. These special line-types can be used either to close a door that has been opened by one of the open-and-stay actions, or to close a sector that was set open from the start. The target door will either close until re-opened by some *other* activating line, or it will close for a timed period of 30 seconds. These latter types are commonly used to trap players in a hostile area, forcing them to face whatever it contains and letting them out again only if they survive long enough.

The Door: close triggers generate the sound of a door closing, even if the door was already closed when the line is activated.

SHOOT-EM-UP DOORS

The only available impact-activated (or gun-activated) door does not close automatically, even though it is classed as a repeatable action (GR). If you want to have a door that the player must shoot at repeatedly in order to keep it open, you will have to tag an additional active line to this door to close it in some way between openings. A later Sortie shows you how this can be achieved.

Many editors show the impact-activated door as a manual (locally activating) action and claim that it is not necessary to tag lines using it to a sector. This is not the case—as you will quickly discover if you try it!

> The following WAD Sortie builds on the WAD produced in the last Sortie of the previous room. If you did not accompany me on that Sortie but would like to come along on this one, you should use WAD15.WAD (DOOM) or D2WAD15.WAD (DOOM II) from the CD-ROM as your starting point.

WAD SORTIE 16: ADDING SOME MORE DOORS

It is time now to enhance your WAD with additional doors. Let's start with a trip-wire activated door.

ADDING A TRIP-WIRE ACTIVATED DOOR

The dark and winding staircase leading out of the platform room would seem an ideal location for a trip-wire activated door. This area is calling out for a door that opens as the stairs are descended, disgorging monsters into the stairway behind the player.

Figure 8.3 shows the sectors to add to implement a secret door off the stairway, with another room behind it.

Figure 8.3.
Lines for a secret door and room off the dark stairway.

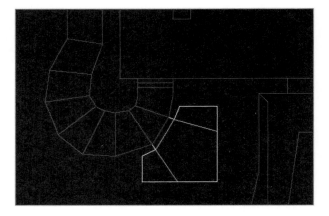

THE NEW AREA

Notice how the new area has been divided into four sectors:

- ■ **The door into the room:** This door is to be opened by the player descending the stairs in the corridor outside it.
- ■ **The central section of the room:** This section will have its lighting set so that it appears to be illuminated through the door by the lights in the section of corridor outside it.
- ■ **Two "wings" of the room:** Either side of the illuminated central section are two darker sections. These are in the shadows cast by the sides of the doorway. They will be useful hiding places later for various goodies.

FIXING THE LIGHTS FOR THE NEW ROOM

Add the lines for these new sectors, using BROWN96 as the default wall texture. Before you apply Make Sector, though, you have a decision to make.

At the moment, the stair sector that this new area will adjoin has a special characteristic in use: type 1. This blinks the lights off at random intervals. You need to decide what you want to do with this. Remember that the central sector of the new secret room is to appear as though it is illuminated by the lights in the wall facing its door. If you leave this blinking in effect, you will need to find a way to make the lights of the inner room and doorway flicker in synchronization with the corridor lights.

Special sector type 1 does not provide synchronized flickering. The lights blink randomly and independently in all sectors with the setting, so special sector type 1 cannot be used here—if it were, the result would look odd. Sector specials 12 and 13 each provide synchronized blinking of lights, but both of these effects are classed as blink-on, so if used, the sectors will be at the lower lighting level most of the time and will only blink to the higher level momentarily. You need to decide, then, which effect you would prefer—synchronized blink-on, with these areas in semi-darkness most of the time, or steady illumination.

When you have made up your mind, apply the appropriate code to the existing corridor sector's special characteristic, and then use Make Sector in each of your new areas in turn, starting with the door sector. You should find that the sector settings for the corridor are applied throughout all of your new sectors this way. Table 8.3 provides the remaining settings for the new sectors. Two sets of lighting figures are given in this table. The principal figure is for use in areas with the blink-on special setting in use; the figures in parentheses should be used if the area is set for static lighting.

DOOM PROGRAMMING GURUS   8 ROOM   1 MISSION   2 EPISODE

Table 8.3. Sector settings for the new secret areas off the stairway.

Area	Lighting		Ceiling		Floor	
Door	176	(144)	–16	FLOOR7_1	–16	FLOOR7_1
Room (center)	144	(144)	88	FLOOR7_1	–16	FLOOR7_1
Room (wings)	112	(96)	88	FLOOR7_1	–16	FLOOR7_1

Take special notice of the brightness levels used for these new sectors. The principal figures have been chosen carefully to keep the blink-on lighting effect working correctly throughout the new area. In this arrangement, the door and main room sectors both have neighbors with lower brightness settings. Had these been set to the same value, then the door sector would not have had a neighboring sector with a lower light level, and its light level would then drop to zero between blinks. This would look unnatural. When the values in the table are used, only the wings of the room have no neighbors with lower light levels, and it is acceptable for these areas to drop to total darkness.

Note also how the settings have been increased a little over the ideal static brightness settings to make allowance for the periods of illumination being short.

INSTALLING THE TRIP-WIRE

Now pick a suitable trip-line for the activation of this door; one of the stair risers around the corner from the door would seem to be a good choice. Enter LINES mode and click with the left mouse button to select your chosen trip-line. Set this line's special attribute to 2—to cause a door to be opened as soon as a player walks over this line. Tell WADED which sector is to be the door by right-clicking in the new door sector while your trigger line is selected. WADED will mark the chosen sector in green to show that it is now tagged to the selected line.

This tagging indication works the other way round, too. If you go into SECTORS mode and select the door sector, the trigger line will be shown in green. This feature saves you from having to remember which of your lines activate each of your sectors.

Once opened, this door will stay open for the rest of the game. In particular, it will enable whatever monsters you care to place in the room either to track the player (once they have been awakened) or to lie in wait against the player's return.

BUILDING THE DOOR

Check that both the lines that represent the faces of the new door have their right sides facing out from the door sector. You will probably have to flip one of these. (Select it and press **F**, remember.) Then apply BROWN96 to the appropriate upper textures. This is to be a secret door, so there should be no hint of its presence through texture changes. Set the `Secret on map` flag for the outer face, to prevent the map from giving the game away, too.

Now consider the texture alignment of the corridor-side door face. Because the player will discover the existence of this door soon enough, this face should contain no clue to the door's presence. You need to ensure, therefore, that its texture aligns precisely with its neighbors'. A casual consideration may lead you to think that no treatment is needed; it is easy to be misled into thinking that this wall section has not been changed substantially by the addition of the new sector. This would be wrong, though. The wall's texture is no longer provided by a *main* texture, but by an *upper*.

Remember that (pegged) upper textures are painted from their lower edge up (currently the floor, in this case), while the adjacent main textures are painted from the ceiling down. Consequently, these textures will only align with each other if the corridor is precisely the same height as (or a whole multiple of) the texture pattern: 128 pixels. It isn't. The door-face texture will therefore need alignment if it isn't to be obvious to the player.

Don't be tempted to just unpeg the upper texture. This would solve the texture alignment problem, but it would also spoil the effect of the door opening. You will need to use a Y-offset to adjust this texture alignment.

> To work out the correct Y-offset needed to realign a door's face with its neighboring walls, use the formula:
>
> Y-offset = height of door face − height of pattern + adjacent wall Y-offset

The door face is 136 units high here, BROWN96 is 128 pixels tall, and no Y-offset is in use on the adjacent walls. To keep its pattern in alignment with the walls, therefore, you will need to use a Y-offset on the outer face of the door of 136 − 128 + 0 = 8 units.

Finally, check that the short through-wall sides of the door sector have their lower unpegged flags set, to prevent them from moving with the door. (The BROWN96 texture can be left on them, in my opinion.) Your new area should then be ready for a tryout. Put a couple of monsters in the new room if you want to see how they react to the player tripping the door. I'll leave a full consideration of the populating of this room until a later Sortie.

REFINING THE DOOR ACTION

After trying this modification out, you may wish to use a different line for the trigger. To do this, you will first need to break the link between the current trigger and the door. Do that by selecting the trigger line in LINES mode and right-clicking in the door sector, just as you did to make the link. The green lines will disappear from the door sector to show you that the link has been broken. Don't forget to reset the line's special attribute back to 0; otherwise this line will continue to attempt to open a door—one that DOOM won't be able to find. You can then link another trigger to the door sector, just as you did your first.

When you're happy with this area, I'll show you how to add a differently triggered door.

ADDING BUTTON-ACTIVATED DOORS

As already observed, you have a couple of alcoves in your WAD with suitable SW1 textures on their walls, ready and waiting for the implementation of some switch-activated doors. Let's start by hiding the marble corridor, which leads to the one-way staircase, behind another secret door.

CUTTING OFF THE MARBLE CORRIDOR

Add a new line in the marble corridor some 16 units north of its junction with the southeast passageway. Use Make Sector on the new thin area you have just produced (the new door) and then in the corridor beyond it. The new sector's lighting level should be 144. Both the floor and ceiling should be at a height of 0 and have DEM1_5 on them.

BUILDING THE NEW DOOR

Flip any of the new door's face lines that are the wrong way around. (The new line is probably at fault here.) Then put MARBFAC3 on the new line's essential upper texture. Use STONE2 on the upper part of the passageway line, keeping this texture's mortar lines aligned with those of the adjacent walls by using an appropriate Y-offset. Applying the formula presented earlier, you should find that this needs to be $120 - 128 + 0 = -8$.

This face of the door used to be the wall over the doorway. You will therefore need to change the line's pegging to something more appropriate. There is also a redundant texture to remove. Set this line's Secret on map flag, too, to hide the new door on the auto-map.

Put DOORTRAK on the through-wall side-lines of the new sector, and set their lower unpegged flags. Now tag the rear wall of the northern of the two SW1 alcoves to the new door sector by selecting the alcove line and right-clicking in the door sector. Set the switch line's special setting to 63 (you will find it in the LIST of special attributes, in the DOORS-1 category) to provide a repeatable open-and-close door action from this line.

ADDING ANOTHER TRIGGER

You have now created a door that the player can open from the alcove switch any number of times. There is currently no way to open the door from the other side, however. Any player who makes it through this door before it closes will become trapped when it does close. (Using this door as a trap makes the one-way stair rather obsolete, doesn't it?)

You could set the special attribute of the inner face of this door to 1. That would allow the door to be opened from the marble-corridor side as a standard door. Rather than doing this, though, I suggest a different approach: put line-type 90 (WR Door: open and close) on the line forming the riser of the second step, tagging this to the door sector. In my opinion, this is a better solution than making a standard door, because a player may be tempted to try the door before proceeding up the stairs, just to see whether it can be opened from this side. A player who thinks that it can't—as my proposed method will make it appear—will be relieved to discover that the door does, in fact, open as the stairs are climbed. The relief may be short-lived, however, if they fail to notice the stair-trap!

If, on the other hand, the player climbs the stairs without trying the door, the trigger on the step should at least make them jump, causing them to think that another door is opening somewhere. Of course, very fast players will not notice a thing, because they will have crossed the trigger before the door has even closed. They, of course, will have other things to worry about!

Alternatively, you may prefer to move the retrigger action to a stair riser beyond the stair-trap. This would provide hope for the player that there is a way back down the stairs. I think this makes the stair-trap less effective, though, as it now forces the player to climb the stairs, making the warning on the fourth step somewhat pointless.

CLOSING OFF THE HEXAGONAL ROOM

Complete the addition of button-activated doors with a new door to lock the player in the hexagonal room at the start by closing off the gap into the platform room. All you need are two new lines across the doorway through the southwest wall of the hexagonal room as shown in Figure 8.4.

| DOOM PROGRAMMING GURUS | | 8 ROOM | | 1 MISSION | 2 EPISODE |

Figure 8.4.
The lines needed for a new door.

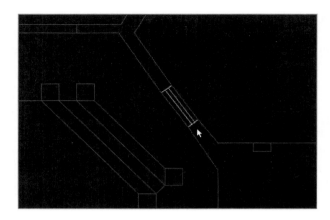

To add these lines, you will probably need to turn the Snap to Grid setting down to 4 or maybe lower. You also need to take extra special care to ensure that the new lines connect properly to the opening's side-lines. As you have probably noticed, WADED sometimes has difficulty detecting that the mouse is over lines that run at an angle.

Only when you are convinced that your new lines connect properly at both ends should you apply Make Sector. Work from the new door sector out. You may find that you have to click in the new sector (and the two adjacent recess sectors) a couple of times to make Make Sector handle them properly.

Table 8.4 has the settings for the three sectors that you have made out of the old opening through the wall.

Table 8.4. Settings for the three new sectors.

Area	Lighting		Ceiling		Floor	
Platform room recess	224	104	CEIL3_5	0	MFLR8_1	
Door	192	0	CEIL5_1	0	MFLR8_1	
Hexagonal room recess	144	104	CEIL3_5	0	MFLR8_1	

Change the side walls of the recess in the hexagonal room to STONE2 to match their neighbors, taking care to leave the offset that was applied several rooms ago. Put DOORTRAK on the side-lines of the door sector and set their lower unpegged flags.

BUILDING THE NEW DOOR

Make sure that the two-sided door lines have their right sides facing out of the door sector. Use BIGDOOR6 on the line facing into the platform room but put STONE2 on the side of the door facing the hexagonal room. You may need to apply an X-offset to both of these textures to center them, as the gap is unlikely to be of a convenient length. Additionally, to have the STONE2 texture align properly with its neighboring walls, it will need a Y-offset. Again, the formula presented earlier is used to calculate this: $104 - 128 + 16 = -8$ units.

This door will be opened from a switch—the one located on the rear wall of the second alcove in the southeast passageway. This is nicely out of sight of the door, and it may cause the player to wonder what it does. Put special line-type 63 (SR Door: open and close) on the back wall of the appropriate alcove and tag it to the new door sector. This door will only stay open for five seconds. You should find that the player will have to run across the hexagonal room to get through it before it closes.

> Readers with DOOM v1.4 or later may wish to use line-type 114 (SR Turbo door: open and close) instead.

From the other side, the new door is to be capable of opening as a standard door, so set the special attribute of this face of the door to 1 (MR Door: open and close). There is no need to tag the line to the sector, of course.

Finally, I don't see any need to hide the fact that this is a door by setting any lines' Secret on map flags. Having the player aware that there is a door but unable to find the switch is effective enough!

ADDING A SHOT-ACTIVATED DOOR

The final new door in this Sortie is to be an impact-activated door, located at the end of the passageway at the bottom of the stairs leading from the platform room—that should wake up those monsters lurking in the room behind the player! Figure 8.5 shows the extra lines that are needed to implement the new sectors. These will provide the door and a further room beyond it.

The settings for the new sectors are given in Table 8.5. Don't forget to check the special characteristic setting here, as these sectors are likely to inherit one from nearby.

Figure 8.5.

Lines for an impact-activated door and room beyond.

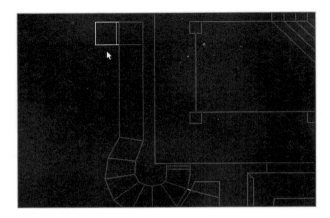

Table 8.5. Sector settings for the new door and room.

Area	Lighting	Ceiling		Floor	
Door	96	–112	FLOOR4_1	–112	FLOOR4_1
Inner room	128	24	TLITE6_1	–112	FLOOR4_1

Use PIPE2 on all of the new lines, but use PIPE4 on the face of the new door. It will be needed on both the upper and lower texture slots here, because the door sector's floor is at a different height from the floor of the end of the passage.

Change the texture on the end wall of the original corridor to PIPE4, too. This is a shot-up version of PIPE2 and is to be used in this area as a visual clue to the presence of the door and the nature of its activation mechanism. Using it on a wall alongside the real door makes the texture's presence more conspicuous but stops it from being immediately obvious which of the walls hides the door.

Don't bother aligning the texture on the door face here. There is absolutely no need to line up the bullet holes on the two wall sections, and the other adjacent wall has a different texture anyway. Put whatever you fancy on the inner face of this door, bearing in mind that only its lower four pixels are ever likely to be seen.

Hide the door on the auto-map by setting the Secret on map flag of the appropriate line. As usual, make sure that the faces of the door have their right sides facing out from the door sector. Then use special type 46 (GR Door: stays open) on the outer door-face, explicitly tagged to the door sector.

2
EPISODE

1
MISSION

8
ROOM

DOOM
PROGRAMMING
GURUS

The rear face of this door doesn't need any trigger mechanism, because the door will latch open. Don't forget, though, to set the lower unpegged flag of the door sector's side lines. Their textures can be left as PIPE2.

Finally, save your WAD (as WAD16.WAD to stay in step with my numbering) and try out your latest additions.

LIGHT SWITCHES

Having seen how the remotely triggered mechanism can be applied to an action with which you are familiar—the door—we can now move on and look at other types of triggered actions. The first of these is the simple alteration of sector lighting levels through the use of brightness-level switches.

BRIGHTNESS-LEVEL SWITCHES

DOOM does not provide many options for player-triggered light-level changes. Table 8.6 shows what is available. (Line-types marked * require DOOM v1.666 or later.)

Table 8.6. Special line-type codes for brightness-level switching.

Action	Activation Category		
	W1	WR	SR
Switch lights off (brightness level 0)	35	79	139*
Switch lights on full (brightness level 255)	13	81	138*
Switch light level to match lowest adjacent	104	78	–
Switch light level to match highest adjacent	12	80	–
Make light blink on every 1.0 seconds	17	–	–

The new settings brought about by these actions replace the specified sector-brightness values, which are lost forever. Once it is changed through these actions, there is no way to restore a sector's original brightness setting, except by having an adjacent sector to act as a copy of it (as will be demonstrated in the next WAD Sortie).

The actions of the brightness-level switches described here break the normal rule that sectors can only partake in one action at a time. Actions that affect the brightness level of a sector will always act immediately on their target sectors, regardless of any other action they are currently engaged in.

AUTOMATIC LIGHTING VARIATIONS

It is possible to build areas that have the lights switch on as players move into them and switch off again as they leave (or vice versa). All that is required is a careful arrangement of retriggering lines. Such features are also good for multiplayer games, because it is possible for players to turn the lights out on their opponents, in order to give themselves the advantage. The next WAD Sortie demonstrates part of the necessary arrangement of lines. You may wish to experiment further with it yourself after completing your next WAD.

WAD SORTIE 17: TRIPPING THE LIGHTS— FANTASTIC!

This Sortie builds on the WAD produced in the previous one. Even if you did not produce that WAD, however, you can still follow this Sortie using the WADs supplied on the accompanying CD-ROM.

This Sortie will explore just one possible arrangement of switched lights. The area in which this will be used will be developed in later Sorties into a confusing maze area. These areas generally take a lot of time (and patience) to develop correctly. They can be a severe test of both the designer and the WAD editor. My advice is that you work on these areas in stages, perfecting each aspect of them in turn. Let's start here by looking at the thinking behind the lighting design.

SWITCHED LIGHTS: THE THEORY

Figure 8.6 shows a schematic arrangement for the lighting "tricks" that are to be played in the principal maze sectors.

The maze comprises three main areas:

Figure 8.6.

Schematic arrangement of triggers for the maze's lighting effects.

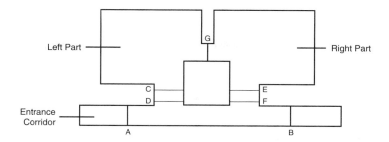

- An entrance corridor
- A left part
- A right part

The complexity of the maze shape has been omitted from Figure 8.6 so that you can better see and understand the scheme.

Each of these areas is rigged to have the lighting change as the player moves around. The effects are intended to operate as follows:

- The first time that the player enters the entrance corridor, the lights of this corridor will go out. Switch line A is the trigger for this. The lights will remain on in the rest of the maze. The lights to this corridor can only be turned back on by locating the appropriate switch (line B). Once the lights have been turned back on with this trigger, they will stay on.

- As the player enters the left part of the maze, its lights will go out. This is achieved by switch line C. Switch line D turns the lights back on when the player leaves this section of the maze. This happens each time the player passes over these lines. Notice how this arrangement has to differ from real light switches, because of the nature of DOOM's line actions. As each line can only perform one function, two lines are needed if the lights are to be turned both on and off. Furthermore, both lines are retrigger lines. Each will attempt to carry out its action every time the player crosses it, regardless of the current light settings. The arrangement of these lines is therefore critical. The lights in this part of the maze will always be in whatever state the last line-crossing left them in. When entering, the off-switch is the last triggered; when leaving, the on-switch has the final say.

- The right part of the maze is rigged in the same way as the left, through switch lines E and F. These operate in exactly the same way as C and D, respectively, but they act on the right part of the maze.

- The right and left parts of the maze are linked through another line G. This line is an ordinary, inactive line. To explore the right part of the maze with the benefit of the lights, then, the player should enter the left part first but pass into the right section through this line. Leaving the maze by reversing this route will turn the lights back on in the left part, allowing that side to be explored with the lights on after re-entering it through line G from the right. However, if this area is constructed carefully enough, it could be quite a while before this tactic presents itself to the player.

BUILDING IT IN PRACTICE

Figure 8.7 shows how the preceding idea has been implemented in my WAD17.WAD (D2WAD17.WAD is the DOOM II equivalent). The left part of the maze has been made a little more maze-like, and one or two details have been reworked slightly, but the three major divisions outlined in the preceding scheme should still be discernible. The locations of the seven lines that function as the lines A to G are marked.

Figure 8.7.
WAD17.WAD's implementation of the lighting effects.

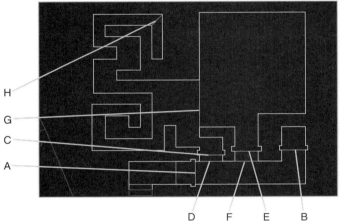

You may like to start DOOM with this example WAD and walk through this area, observing its main features as they are described forthwith.

THE ENTRANCE CORRIDOR

The new area has been added at the end of the marble corridor at the top of the one-way staircase. The corridor has been extended to the east, with the two "halves" of the maze area to the north of it.

The main east/west section of the extended corridor has a trigger line just before the entrance to the maze. This acts like trigger line A in the preceding: as the player passes it, it plunges the eastern end of the corridor into darkness. A special line of type 35 (W1 Lights: off), tagged to the eastern sector of the corridor, has been used to implement this.

At its eastern end, the corridor turns to the north to meet a short additional sector. The line bordering these two sectors has the trigger action 80 (WR Lights: match highest adjacent) on it to turn the corridor lights back on. This action takes the new light-level setting from the adjacent sector with the highest brightness setting. As the sectors at either end of this corridor have the same brightness level as the corridor originally had, the lights will always come back up to the starting level.

EXTRA WARNINGS

The walls of the corridor have MARBLE1 on them to match the corridor leading in from the staircase. Close to the lighting trigger lines, though, the corridor walls have been embellished a little, to signal the presence of these triggers to the player. Not that there is really very much that the player can do to avoid them—the warning is really to panic the player a little. Having discovered what the warnings mean by crossing the first trigger, a player may hesitate before crossing others. Similar warnings have been placed at each entrance to the main maze, too.

The warning itself is provided by small alcoves placed next to each end of the lighting trigger lines. These alcoves have conspicuous textures on the back walls. Next to triggers that turns lights off, LITERED is used (in D2WAD17.WAD, BFALL1 has had to be used instead), while by the line that restores the main corridor lights, LITEBLU4 (SFALL1 in D2WAD17.WAD) is in use. (I haven't bothered putting any notification against the lines that restore the inner maze lights—I thought players should discover these lines for themselves!)

All of the lines with these warning textures have the special attribute 48 (Effect: horizontal scroll) assigned to them to make them really noticeable. This should be enough to make most players wary of passing between them. The construction of the alcoves is completed by using BROWNHUG on their side walls.

Note that these small alcoves have not been made into sectors of their own, because they have no settings different from those used in the adjacent part of the corridor.

IN THE MAZE

The left and right parts of the maze have been drawn using the texture CRATE2. This is generally a good texture to use in maze areas, although it doesn't really matter what is used here at the

DOOM
PROGRAMMING
GURUS

8
ROOM

1
MISSION

2
EPISODE

moment, because the full development of the maze itself will, no doubt, result in much further modification of the textures used.

The trip-lines required to turn the main maze lights off and back on again are provided by two lines across the entrances to each part. The inner lines of each half of the maze (lines C and E) use special line-type 79 (WR Lights: off) to turn the lights off as each maze sector is entered. The outer lines, (D and F) use special line-type 80 (WR Lights: match highest adjacent) to turn the lights back up again as the player leaves the maze this way.

In my implementation, I have made each of the areas between these pairs of trip-lines into sectors of their own, and set their lighting levels to 144 in order to have them act as buffer zones between the outer corridor and the inner maze areas. This allows the retrigger that restores the lights to operate regardless of whether the outer corridor is in darkness or not, by providing an illuminated adjacent sector for each half of the maze.

You could add a little extra sting in the tail of this lighting arrangement by dispensing with the buffer sectors, so that the inner maze areas border directly on the corridor (or by tagging the triggers to the buffers as well as to their own half of the maze). Doing this would make the inner areas rather more complicated to explore until the player discovers how to turn the outer corridor's lights back on. (I'll leave you to work out why!)

FURTHER EMBELLISHMENTS

Just to be really mean, I added an extra internal line to the inner area of the left part of the maze (line H in Figure 8.7). This has a special attribute of 104 (W1 Lights: off) and is tagged to its own half of the maze. In my maze, even if players work out how to get this far with the lights on, they will still have to find their way out in the dark.

You might like to wander around a bit through the various parts of the maze to satisfy yourself that it does indeed operate as described.

COSMETIC CHANGES

I made a few cosmetic variations by altering some floor and ceiling heights, and a couple of textures. Table 8.7 gives the settings used for all of the sectors in this area in the example WAD17.WAD. (D2WAD17.WAD varies in the single regard already noted.)

Table 8.7. Sector settings for the entire maze area.

Area	Lighting	Ceiling		Floor	
Original marble corridor	144	240	DEM1_5	112	DEM1_6
Short sector to east	144	248	FLAT2	96	DEM1_6
Eastern corridor section	144	240	DEM1_5	96	DEM1_6
Northern end of corridor	144	224	FLAT2	112	DEM1_6
Entrance buffers	144	224	FLOOR6_2	96	DEM1_6
Inner maze areas	144	240	DEM1_5	112	DEM1_6

MARBLE1 is used on all upper essentials, with the upper unpegged flags set in all cases, while NUKE24 appears on all lower essentials. This latter texture is usually used on 24-pixel edges around nukage-slime pools, but it blends well here, too. The side walls of the entrance buffers use MARBLE1, with Y-offsets of 16 units to ensure correct alignment with the walls of the corridor. Finally, I placed a few floor lamps around the place for effect—and to provide something for the player to navigate by in the dark!

YOUR TURN

Once you have taken a look at this example WAD for yourself, you should examine the map in the editor, noting the main features of its construction. You may then like to experiment by building a similar area in your own WAD, with or without embellishments of your choice. Leave the maze areas fairly open for now—they will be developed later—and don't extend them out much further than the area they occupy in Figure 8.7.

A FINAL STAB IN THE BACK

Lastly, as a sort of coda to this room on remote-control sectors, you may care to add a further little development at the top of the one-way stairs, just to add to the players' misery in this area. I'm thinking of another room full of monsters to surprise them from behind. Figure 8.8 shows the arrangement.

Figure 8.8.

Lines for two new sectors at the top of the one-way stairs.

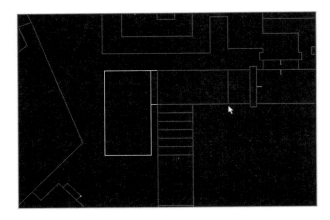

ADDING ANOTHER ROOM WITH A DOOR

Start by adding two sectors as shown in Figure 8.8. These represent a door sector (to be hidden, of course) behind the MARBFACE texture at the western end of the marble corridor; and a room beyond it. Use STONE2 as the texture for the new lines.

Table 8.8 gives the settings for these two new sectors.

Table 8.8. Sector settings for the secret door and room.

Area	Lighting	Ceiling		Floor	
Door	144	112	FLOOR6_2	112	DEM1_6
Room	96	208	DEM1_5	112	DEM1_6

The outer face of the door needs MARBFACE on its upper level, to preserve the original appearance of the corridor at this point, and this line should be flagged as Secret on map. The inner face of the door should use STONE2, along with the through-door walls (the latter with their lower unpegged flags set). As usual, make sure that the right sides of the appropriate lines of the door sector face the correct way.

TRIGGERING THE DOOR

The new door is to be triggered in several ways: first, there should be a single trigger line of type 4 (W1: Door: open and close) some way along the marble corridor to the east. My WAD uses the line to which the mouse arrow is pointing in Figure 8.8. Apply this special attribute to an appropriate line in your WAD and then tag it to the door sector. This line will act in a similar fashion to the trigger line on the darkened stairway out of the platform room, enabling monsters to ambush the player from behind. The door will open long enough for the monsters in it to see the player and awaken.

When this happens, the monsters in the room will move towards the player and should manage to leave the room before the door closes. By placing a standard line-type 1 trigger on the back face of this door, though, any who haven't emerged by the time the door closes but who are on the track of the player, will be able to open the door when they reach it. Therefore, set the rear face of the door to line-type 1.

Why not just set the corridor trigger to a type that leaves the door open? Well, hopefully, the player will be too busy dealing with the monsters emerging from the room to bother too much about the door itself, initially. By the time the bad guys have been dealt with, and the player wants to enter the room behind it in search of loot, the door will be firmly closed. The trigger line that opened it at first will not now reopen it—it's a single trigger action, remember—so the player must find another way to open this door.

Putting an impact trigger of type 46 on the face of this door will provide this. Do that now, tagging the outer face of the door to the door sector. Players can now re-open this door by firing at it. It may be a while before they think to try it, though. On the other hand, they may not need to think of it— stray shots from the fight that has just taken place will, in all likelihood, have caused the door to open anyway!

Another retrigger line, this time of special type 75 (WR Door: close) tagged to the door sector, and located somewhere in the corridor, will take care of this. With this modification, players who withdraw to fight from the eastern end of the marble corridor will close the door themselves when they do approach it. Again, it may be a while before they think to shoot at it to reopen it, as they will probably not realize that it was their shots that opened it before.

Finally, I added a further little surprise in the form of another line of type 75 to close the door as the inner room is entered. This may panic players a little—by now they probably won't immediately think of trying to open the door in the normal way. Of course, there will need to be some goodies placed here to lure players far enough into the room to trip this line, but I'll leave that for another Sortie.

The final arrangement of trigger lines for this new door is shown in Figure 8.9.

DOOM PROGRAMMING GURUS

8 ROOM

1 MISSION

2 EPISODE

Figure 8.9.

*Arrangement of triggers for
the secret door at the top of
the marble stairs.*

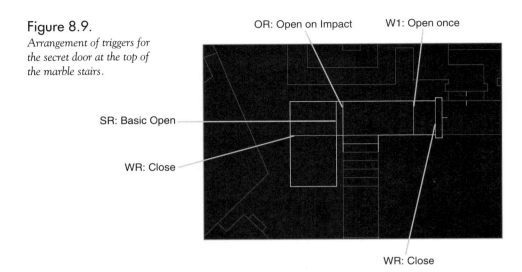

OR: Open on Impact   W1: Open once

SR: Basic Open

WR: Close

WR: Close

 The two lines to close the door (type 75) should both be added to existing sectors manually, using
Sec Define—don't forget to use LINES mode to flag them two-sided first—and then tagged to the
door sector.

When you're happy with the arrangement of triggers in this area, add a few monsters to the room
(just at difficulty levels 4 and 5, for now) and then save this WAD as WAD17A.WAD and see how
well it all works.

EXIT: MOPPING UP AND MOVING ON

This room introduced you to the idea of tags between lines and sectors, to provide sectors that can
be activated from afar. You have now seen more of DOOM's doors and seen some fancy tricks with
the lights.

The next room will continue this theme of activating sectors remotely and show you how surfaces
other than the floors of sectors can be moved.

2
EPISODE

1
MISSION

8
ROOM

**DOOM
PROGRAMMING
GURUS**

ROOM 9

By Steve Benner

SIMPLE MOVING
SECTORS

The previous room introduced you to the concept of the remotely activated sector. The exploration of the range of actions that these sectors can be made to undergo continues in this room. In particular, you will extend your repertory of effects that use moving ceilings and be introduced to those that involve moving floors.

The WAD Sorties from this room will have you adding some additional traps for the unsuspecting players of your growing WAD. There are also a few cautionary words against setting traps for yourself!

We begin, though, with one of the most useful moving floor effects: the lift (or "elevator" as some readers probably prefer to call it).

LIFTS AND MOVING PLATFORMS

In earlier rooms, you saw how DOOM produces the effect of a door by the simple expedient of moving a sector's ceiling from the level of its floor to some other higher setting. Lifts are produced by an equally simple process. They are obtained by moving a sector's *floor* from one level to another and back again. This creates a traveling platform that will carry whatever is standing on it along with it.

HOW LIFTS OPERATE

DOOM's lifts all operate on the same basic principle: When activated, the floor of the lift sector moves down from its starting elevation to the level of the lowest adjacent floor. There it pauses for five seconds before returning to its starting position. Appropriate sounds are produced as the lift starts to move and as it docks at each end of its travel.

Note that DOOM expects to start the motion of all lifts by moving them downwards. If a sector that has no lower floor adjacent to it is activated as a lift, it will not move. Furthermore, lift sectors always return to their starting elevation.

Lifts always move from the starting elevation to the lowest adjacent floor. They cannot be made to pause at the position of some intermediary floor. If you want to have a lift at the side of a tall room, say, operating between a high ledge and another ledge below it (but higher than the floor of the room), you will need to isolate the lift sector in some way from the main room to prevent it from continuing down past the intervening ledge to the floor of the room.

For a moving sector to function as a lift, players (and monsters) must be able to enter and leave the sector in both its upper and lower positions. Make sure that you allow appropriate headroom and maneuvering space in and around these sectors, if you want players and/or monsters to be able to use them. Don't forget you will have to allow for the full travel of the moving floor.

If a lift's floor is prevented from returning to its starting position because of the presence of a player or monster—either because there is insufficient headroom in the floor's uppermost position or because the object overhangs the sides of the lift sector and thus contacts with an adjacent ceiling—then the movement of the lift will immediately reverse and the floor will return to its lower position. The lift will, however, persevere in its attempts to return to the starting position until it succeeds.

TURBO LIFTS

DOOM v1.4 introduced a high-speed version of the lift, the turbo lift. Turbo lifts are the lift effect's equivalent of the turbo doors. Apart from their higher speed, they operate in exactly the same way as standard lifts.

TRIGGERS FOR LIFTS

Table 9.1 gives the line-type codes that activate lift movements. Like all remotely activated effects, all lines employing these special attributes must be tagged to an appropriate sector to provide the action.

Table 9.1. Special line types providing lift actions.

| Action | Activation Category | | | |
	W1	WR	S1	SR
Standard lift	10	88	21	62
Turbo lift	121*	120*	122*	123*
*Turbo lifts require DOOM v1.4 and above.				

The majority of lift actions can only be activated by players. Line-type 88 (WR Lift), however, will also trigger a lift movement if a monster walks over it.

In early versions of DOOM, line-type 88 could also be triggered by projectiles, such as rockets and Imp fireballs. This feature has been removed from v1.666 and later.

DECIDING TRIGGER POSITIONS

Often the hardest part of building a lift is deciding upon a suitable triggering arrangement. You will recall that spacebar activators can only be operated from their *right* sides. This has major implications in the building of lifts, particularly if you want the lift to be capable of being operated from above and from below. Figure 9.1 illustrates the problem.

Figure 9.1.

Typical lift trigger arrangements.

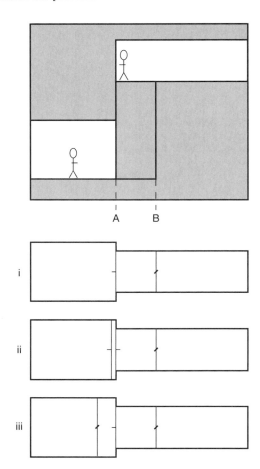

The upper part of this figure shows a common arrangement, with a lift providing a link between two areas, the lower of which has its ceiling below the level of the upper area's floor. In Figure 9.1, the lift is in its upper (resting) position. As you can see, both the upper and lower corridors end at the same line—the line marked A.

This line would be a natural place to have the spacebar activate the lift. This cannot be made to work from both above and below the lift, however, as this would require line A to be active from both sides. An alternative method must be found for triggering this lift. There are a number of possible solutions, all of which are commonly used.

THE SIMPLEST SOLUTION

The simplest way of arranging triggers for a lift is to orient its lower sector boundary (line A in Figure 9.1) with its right side facing away from the lift sector, and set this line to be a spacebar activator of the sector's movement. This enables a player to summon the lift from below, while standing against the sector edge. The lift is set to trigger from above by means of a walk-through trigger action placed on the lift sector's upper boundary (line B in Figure 9.1). This causes the lift to descend as soon as a player steps into it from the adjacent upper area.

Case *i* in Figure 9.1 shows the arrangement of trigger lines. A right-angle tick mark on a line shows a spacebar-activated line's right side; oblique ticks mark walk-through trigger lines.

This configuration of triggers requires the player to think of activating the lift from below, while providing automatic triggering from above. It can be used to build lifts that may not be obvious at their lower level, and thus are missed, or lifts that surprise the player who enters them from above with sudden, unexpected activation. (Readers familiar with the start of Level 5 of DOOM II may recognize this!) These lifts can also deliver monsters automatically from the higher to the lower level.

In building a lift in this way, remember that the walk-through line providing the upper trigger will operate whichever way it is walked through. Players traveling up in this lift will therefore send the lift back down as they step *from* the lift at the top. You may regard this action as undesirable; or you may wish to use it so that the lift is sent back down to collect whatever is tracking the player along the lower level!

FORCING MANUAL OPERATION FROM ABOVE AND BELOW

To implement a lift that the player must activate manually from above *and* below, an additional trigger line is needed. If this line is positioned 16 units or less from line A, the difference in floor heights that occurs at that line will prevent the player's center point from crossing the additional line. (Players are 32 units wide, remember.) By orienting these two lines with their right sides facing away from each other, and placing the same special attribute on each, the lift's lower boundary can be made to appear active from both sides. A player will be able to activate the lift from the "end" of either corridor. Case *ii* in Figure 9.1 illustrates this configuration of triggers.

It does not matter on which side of line A the new line is placed, provided that it is no further from it than 16 units and that the two lines have their right sides facing away from each other. If the lines are placed farther apart than a player's radius, it will be possible for the player to stand between the two lines and be on the left side of each—and thus not able to operate the lift!

A lift configured to use switches in this way cannot be activated by monsters.

FULLY AUTOMATIC LIFTS

A fully automatic lift is produced by using walk-over triggers on both the line of the upper boundary of the lift sector (as before) and on the approach to the lift from below. This also requires an additional line, of course. Note that here the activator used on the lower approach must be positioned more than 16 units from line A to provide the player with the space to cross it when the lift is in its raised position.

Provided the triggers are of the standard (non-turbo) variety, such a lift could be activated by monsters from either side. For effective use by monsters from below, however, the lower activator will need careful placement. It must be placed far enough from the lift to enable a monster to cross the activator and provide the lift with sufficient time to descend. The distance should not be so great, however, that the monster cannot reach the lift before it goes back up. If a monster cannot step straight onto the lift sector's floor when it gets to it, then it will turn and wander off in another direction. You may need to spend some time experimenting, using IDDTIDDT to watch the way monsters behave to get these lines just right.

TRIPLE TRIGGER OPERATION

In the previous arrangement of active lines, players who step off the lift at the lower level will need to move forward to cross the lower activator if they wish to summon the lift back. As the lower activator will not normally be visible, few players will think to do this, especially if, having seen what is at the lower level, they decide they need to beat a hasty retreat! It is common, therefore, to arrange for the line-A boundary of the lift to provide an additional spacebar activator for summoning the lift from below. This triple-triggering is probably the most useful arrangement of lift triggers. It is shown in Figure 9.1 as case *iii*.

Note that again it is vital that the lower walk-through activator be positioned more than 16 units from line A. If it is any closer, neither of the triggers for summoning the lift from below will work. The walk-through trigger fails because there is no space for the player to walk through it; the spacebar trigger fails because DOOM will not enable the player to access it through the walk-through trigger that lies between the player and the line of the lift.

| 2 | 1 | | 9 | | DOOM PROGRAMMING GURUS |
| EPISODE | MISSION | | ROOM | | |

UTILIZING DIRECTION CHANGES

Lifts are generally good places to have a corridor change direction. This has two advantages. First, it can force the player to turn rapidly as the lift operates in order to face the hazard on the other level. Second, it can make the placement of triggers simpler.

Figure 9.2 shows a plan view of two corridors at different levels running at 90° to each other. The corridors meet at a lift. Assuming the corridor from the south is the higher of the two, line U in Figure 9.2 could be used by players approaching from the upper level to operate the lift using the spacebar. Line L can then be utilized as the spacebar activator for players in the lower corridor.

Figure 9.2.

Suggested trigger lines for a lift joining corridors at a corner.

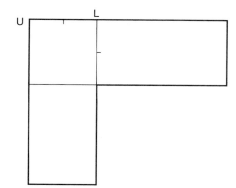

COMPLETELY REMOTE OPERATION

There is no reason, of course, for a lift's activating triggers to be positioned on or around the lift itself. They could be moved well away and placed on any standard trip or switch line. This can force players to hunt around for either the lift, the switch, or both. (They will usually need to make a run for it, too!)

ONE-WAY LIFTS

Similarly, there is no requirement for lifts to be capable of operating from above *and* below if you don't want them to. Remember that players can always jump from open-sided lifts.

TEXTURE CONSIDERATIONS AROUND LIFTS

As with all surfaces that the user is expected to activate with the spacebar, it makes sense to use lift-like textures on the visible faces of lifts in order to alert the player to their presence. PLAT1 is the usual lift-face texture, although some of the door textures are suitable, as indeed are many of the standard wall textures.

More important than the textures themselves, though, is their application to the appropriate texture slots. Note that line A has essential textures on both sides: an upper when viewed from the lift sector itself, and a lower when viewed from the bottom corridor. (See Figure 9.3.)

Figure 9.3.
The exposure of additional textures by the movement of a lift.

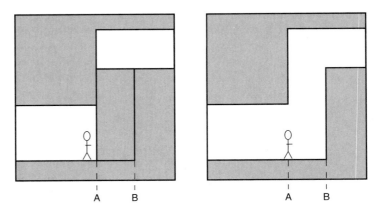

It is also easy to forget that moving floors expose additional surfaces. Figure 9.3 shows how a lift sector gains a completely new lower texture (along line B) when it moves to its lower position. Few editors will check the range of a lift's operation sufficiently to provide you with a warning of such so-called *latent essential* textures.

PEGGING CONSIDERATIONS FOR LIFTS

Pegging considerations around lifts are much easier than around doors. You usually want all textures to use the default arrangement. Ceiling relationships don't change with the operation of lifts, so the state of the upper unpegged flag is always immaterial. Lower textures are usually left in the pegged state so that any visible outer face of the lift moves up and down with its floor, while the inner faces of the lift (the walls of the lift shaft, as it were) remain pegged to the static floors outside the lift sector, and thus stay stationary themselves.

STEPS INVOLVED IN BUILDING A LIFT

The steps involved in building a lift are as follows:

1. Make a suitable arrangement of sectors. The floor of the lift sector should be set at the upper limit of its travel.

2. Check that textures are applied to all lower texture slots that will be exposed by the movement of the lift.

3. Check that the `lower unpegged` flags of all lines bordering the lift are clear.

4. Decide on suitable trigger lines. The disposition of these will depend upon the precise arrangement of the lift and adjacent sectors. Assign the appropriate special attributes to the trigger lines, and tag all of these lines to the lift sector. Make sure that any spacebar-activated lines have their right sides facing the direction from which the player will approach them.

The next WAD Sortie takes you through this process in your own WAD.

The following WAD Sortie builds on the WAD produced in the last Sortie of the previous room. If you did not accompany me on that Sortie but would like to take part in this one, you should use WAD17A.WAD (DOOM) or D2WAD17A.WAD (DOOM II) from the CD-ROM as your starting point.

WAD SORTIE 18: LIFTS AND MOVING PLATFORMS

The first step in adding a lift to your WAD is to construct the upper and lower areas that the lift is to connect. The lower level will be an entirely new area of your WAD, to the north of the platform room, while the upper area will be an extension of the corridor that leads out of the platform room.

PREPARING THE NEW AREAS

Figure 9.4 shows how the new areas fit into the existing map.

Begin by drawing a large open arena connected to the existing thin courtyard sector beyond the platform room's northern window. Make sure you draw this new area in a clockwise manner—don't worry about its exact size and shape—and connect it correctly to the existing sector. Use Make Sector on this large sector and lower its floor to –256 before continuing.

Next, set the default texture to GSTONE1—this will make life easier later—and draw and make the first of the sectors that lead out of the large sector's southwest edge. Set this new sector's ceiling to –128 and its floor and ceiling textures to DEM1_5 before drawing and making the subsequent sectors of this new lower area of the map. It doesn't really matter how many lines or sectors you use to come around the corner—just aim to meet up with the existing corridor behind the impact-activated door, noting from Figure 9.4 how this is to be extended.

The full development of this lower area will be left to later Sorties.

Figure 9.4.
New areas in preparation for the installation of a lift.

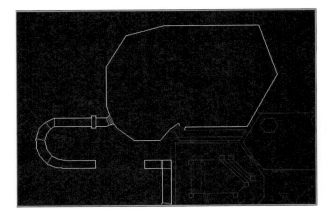

To draw the new area above the lift, change the default texture to PIPE2 and add new sectors as shown in Figure 9.5, working from the room beyond the impact-activated door. In order, these new areas will be the following:

- A second impact-activated door
- A short corridor beyond
- A third impact-activated door
- A further short corridor
- The lift

When fully drawn, the two new areas of the map should be left with a gap of about 24 units between them. Figure 9.5 has the mouse cursor pointing to this gap.

Table 9.2 gives the sector settings for the new areas above the lift. The lower areas can be left as they are, for now.

Figure 9.5.

New sectors as far as the lift.

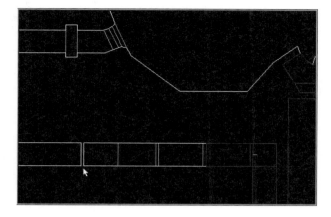

Table 9.2. Sector settings for the extension to the upper corridor.

Area	Lighting	Ceiling		Floor	
East Door	128	–112	FLOOR4_1	–112	FLOOR4_1
East Corridor	128	8	CEIL3_4	–112	FLOOR4_1
West Door	96	–112	FLOOR4_1	–112	FLOOR4_1
West Corridor	96	–8	CEIL3_3	–112	FLOOR4_1
Lift	96	–24	CEIL5_2	–104	FLOOR4_5

Finally, bridge the connection between the new areas of the map by adding the two missing lines and making the new sector. Set this sector's ceiling at –128 and its floor at –256.

MAKING THE LIFT

This lift is to be spacebar-operated from above—its presence is not going to be too obvious—but automatic from below. To make the lift, set the special attribute of the western line of the lift sector to 62 (SR Lift), making sure that this line's right side faces east, into the upper corridor. Tag the line to the lift sector. This will enable the player to activate the lift with the spacebar from the upper level.

To make the lift come automatically to a player approaching from the lower area to its west, set the special attribute of the line at the western edge of the thin interconnecting sector to 88 (WR: Lift) and tag this line to the lift sector too. Make sure that this line is more than 16 units from the lift; otherwise the player will not be able to cross it to activate it from the west when the lift is up.

Now deal with the textures for the lift. Use BROWN1 for the side walls, with BROWNPIP on the end wall of the upper corridor. Remember that this wall is formed from the upper texture of the lift sector's western bounding line. (If you put BROWNPIP on the main texture of this line, you can expect the Medusa effect when you activate the lift.) Set this texture's upper unpegged flag for better texture alignment (remember that this flag can be used with impunity around lifts) and give it a Y-offset of 72. This is to give a small visual clue to the presence of something below the floor. Put PIPE4 on the western face of the lift where it blocks the lower corridor (the lower texture on the other side of the same line as above, of course).

Next, apply textures to the essentials on the eastern edge of the lift. Use STEPTOP on the eastern lower essential. This essential is brought about by the fact that the lift's floor is set higher than its neighbor's to the east. As the lift's ceiling is lower, this line also has an upper essential. Use PIPE2 on that. Don't forget that the lower texture slot on the western side of this line will become an essential as the lift descends, so you will need to put texture there too—I'll leave the choice to you. This completes the construction of the lift.

FINISHING THE CORRIDOR TO THE LIFT

Before trying out your new addition, finish the approach to it by setting appropriate triggers and tags for the two new impact-activated doors. Use the PIPE4 texture on their uppers with some different X- and Y-offsets applied to move the bullet holes around a bit. You should also set the appropriate Secret on map flags for these doors. You can leave the PIPE2 texture on the through-door side walls.

Try a modification of the hazardous area of this corridor just outside the original impact-activated door, too, by putting the BLOOD1 texture on the corner sector's floor, as some warning of the harmful effect of standing in this sector. Next, add some explanation of the presence of blood here by splitting this sector's eastern wall so that it has a small section somewhere in it of 32 pixels length. Put BLODRIP1 on this small section of wall. This texture has a blood-splashed lower edge and will need its neighbors to be set to the matching PIPE1 if it is not to look odd.

This change creates a further problem, though. You now have a single blood-splashed wall that even in the lower lighting conditions of this sector will look a little odd if surrounded by clean walls. Some adjacent textures need to be changed to match. These currently carry a hint to the player on how to proceed further, though, through the presence of their bullet holes. It would be nice to be able to preserve this hint.

The wall that is really the impact-activated door presents no problem—it uses both upper and lower textures. Its lower texture can be changed to PIPE1, with a Y-offset of −16 to move the pattern's lower edge down to the floor of the blood pool. PIPE4 can be left on the upper, as these two textures will meet with a correct match. The lower texture between the corner sector and the corridor to the south can be changed in a similar manner.

That just leaves the northern wall. There is a problem here because DOOM does not provide a texture that has both a blood-splashed lower edge and bullet holes. It seems as though our visual clue may have to be sacrificed. Rather than do this, though, why not treat this wall in the same way as the western edge of the pool? If you turned the northern wall into a door, you could use its upper and lower textures to hold the two different patterns needed to satisfy the various visual requirements.

To do this, draw a new sector to the north of the corner as shown in Figure 9.6. Only a single sector is needed: it will act as both door and room. For now, just make the room—don't bother implementing the door trigger, that will be taken care of later.

Figure 9.6.
A new sector to the north of the "improved" blood pool.

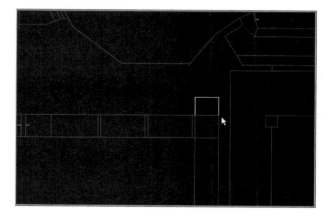

The new sector's floor and ceiling heights should be set at –96 (32 units above the floor of the blood pool). Set the lighting level to 96, and use FLOOR4_1 as the floor and ceiling texture. The walls can be whatever you fancy. Use PIPE1 on the essential lower texture beneath the face of the new door, applying an offset of –32 to compensate for the raised floor of the new door-room. Put PIPE4 back on this line's upper. Don't forget to remove the damaging special characteristic that the new sector will have inherited from its neighbor.

ANOTHER LIFT

Finally, before trying out the WAD, add another lift to make it easier to get back from the large open arena at the end of the new passageways. Mark off a small portion of the arena where it adjoins the thin sector to its south, as shown in Figure 9.7 (near the mouse cursor).

Figure 9.7.
Lines for another lift.

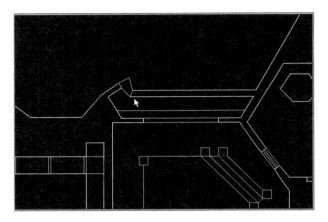

The new sector should be given the same settings as the area adjoining it to the south (so use Make Sector in the new sector, before applying it in the large open arena). Then flip one of its northern lines around so that its right side faces into the arena sector to the north. Give this line a special attribute of 62 (SR Lift) and tag it to the new small lift sector. Deal with all of its essentials.

Before saving as WAD18.WAD and trying it out, you might also like to make it a little easier to test this WAD by moving the Player 1 Start position nearer to the area of interest. You should find that you can do a circular trip out from the platform room, through all of your new sectors, and finally arrive back through the platform room's northern window. You may find you have some essential textures to fix along the way but everything should work fine.

OTHER MOVERS

Apart from doors and lifts, DOOM provides a number of additional triggers for the activation of simple floor and ceiling movements. These actions come into the general category of *movers*.

SIMPLE MOVERS

All movers operate between their current level and some target level. Most are designed to act in one direction only, either up or down, in an on-off movement. The movement itself will be accompanied by a grating sound that continues until the movement is completed. Players (or monsters) trapped by these movers in gaps too small for them will stall the movement while they remain in the sector. The sound of the action will continue, however, and the movement will go on to completion as soon as the cause of the obstruction leaves the sector.

The moving sector itself will not prevent players or monsters caught in it from moving, although its motion relative to adjacent sectors may, of course, make it impossible for them to leave. Trapping players in this way is not a good design feature: it requires the game to be aborted—never a popular move.

SIMPLE FLOOR MOVERS

Table 9.3 gives details of all of DOOM's simple floor-moving actions. Although there are a lot of different varieties, not all types are available in all activation categories and it can require some careful planning of your relative sector changes to make effective use of what is available. Unless otherwise indicated in the table, all floor movers operate at about half the speed of a lift.

Table 9.3. Simple floor movers.

Action	Activation Category				
	W1	WR	S1	SR	G1
Absolute Movers					
Raise floor by 24 units	58	92	–	–	–
Raise floor by 512 units (lift speed)	–	–	140*	–	–
Raise floor to match next higher floor	119*	128*	18	69	–
Turbo version of the preceding	130*	129*	131*	132*	–
Raise floor by shortest lower texture	30	96	–	–	–
Relative Movers					
Move floor up to lowest local ceiling	5	91	101	64	24
Move floor down to lowest adjacent floor	38	82	23	60	–
Move floor down to highest adjacent floor	19	83	102	45	–
Move floor down to 8 units above highest adjacent floor (turbo)	36	98	71	70	–

Actions marked * are available only in DOOM v1.666 and later.

ABSOLUTE MOVERS

Absolute movers will only move in one direction to the finishing height. Note that those that move up by a constant amount do so per activation and will move even if doing so takes the sector's floor above its own ceiling. It is probably wise to prevent this from happening, by limiting in some way the number of times that players can access the trigger.

The actions that move a floor to its next higher adjacent sector will act cumulatively. The floor will move up to successively higher levels on each activation until there are no more higher neighboring floors.

USE OF SHORTEST LOWER TEXTURE

The actions that raise floors by the amount of the shortest lower texture determine how far to move by inspecting the textures used on the sidedefs facing out from the active sector. DOOM looks at the height of the patterns in use on the lower texture slots of all of these sidedefs and moves the sector by the height of the smallest short texture it finds there. If there are no textures of less than 128-pixel height in use on these lower slots, then the sector moves 72 pixels instead. (No, I don't know why.)

> Remember that a short texture is any texture less than 128 pixels tall.

Note that the distance to move is determined from the height of the texture itself, not the space it is occupying, and is therefore independent of relative sector elevations. This action is designed to provide steps that rise out of the floor. The short lower texture usually provides the pattern for a riser. Bear in mind that raising the sector to a height where more than one vertical tiling of the short texture is required to render the space it occupies will cause the Pink Bug effect. A short texture could, however, be used on a face that will never be visible to act as a control of how far the sector will rise on each activation. Once again, this action can drive the floor above a sector's own ceiling if allowed to repeat too many times.

RELATIVE MOVERS

Relative movers take their target positions from adjacent sectors. These may be above or below the sector's current floor level. DOOM has specific expectations of the direction in which each particular action will move the floor. These are indicated in Table 9.3. If the target position lies in the direction opposite to that which is expected, the movement will still occur, but it will be instantaneous and (virtually) silent. If these actions occur out of the players' sight, this limitation may not matter to you.

MOVING CEILINGS

In comparison to moving floors, there are surprisingly few actions that create simple moving ceilings. Table 9.4 gives the list of what is available. These actions differ from doors in their speed (they are much slower) and their accompanying sound, which is the standard grating noise associated with movers.

Table 9.4. Simple ceiling movers.

Action	Activation Category			
	W1	WR	S1	SR
Move ceiling up to highest adjacent ceiling	40	85	–	–
Lower ceiling to floor	–	–	41	43
Lower ceiling to 8 above floor	44	72	49	–

The first of these actions (40) behaves as a relative mover. If the highest adjacent ceiling is below the target sector's ceiling, then the ceiling will come down instantly.

Again, as with simple floor movers, the presence of players or monsters in the active sector can prevent the action from completing until the sector is vacated. This does no harm to player or monsters.

The next room, "Complex Moving Sectors," examines moving ceilings and floors that *do* harm anything caught between them. Before that though, the next WAD Sortie leads you through the addition of some simple movers to your WAD.

WAD SORTIE 19: SOME SIMPLE MOVERS

This Sortie builds on the WAD produced in the previous one. If you did not produce that WAD, you should use WAD18.WAD (DOOM) or D2WAD18.WAD (DOOM II) from the CD-ROM as your starting point here.

In this Sortie, you will develop the area beyond the lift and add some simple movers. Before that though, there are a couple of movers to add to the platform room.

A WAY INTO THE SOUTHERN COURTYARD

So far, whenever you have wanted to examine additions to the southern courtyard, you have had to lower the floor of the window sector in the editor before playing the WAD. Let us create a switch to do this during play. This switch will be positioned in the secret room that was made a couple of Sorties ago off the southwest stairway, just outside the platform room.

The modifications needed to implement this change are straightforward. Start by putting a SW1BROWN texture on one wall of the secret room. (I suggest putting it somewhere on a short wall in one of the shadowy wings, where it may go unnoticed.) Take whatever steps are necessary to center a single instance of the switch texture horizontally on your chosen wall. Set the special attribute of the line carrying the switch texture to 102 (S1 Floor: move down to highest adjacent) and tag the line to the platform room's southern window sector.

Note that the secret room's height is somewhat small for this switch texture to look good here; the switch will be very low if the default alignment is used. Changing that alignment will spoil the match of the BROWN1 component of this texture, though, and will draw more attention to it. The best solution here is to reduce the floor level of this wing of the room—take it down to –32. Put a suitable texture on the essential lower texture that this produces and the changes in the secret room are complete.

Don't forget to check that the tagged window sector's floor is set at 56 units—otherwise this switch will have no work to do! You ought really to check that the lower texture of the wall under the window is pegged so that it appears to open correctly. However, because the player is unlikely to make it back in time to see this action occur, and because the lower texture is unpegged to provide better texture alignment, I suggest you leave it as it is.

MODIFYING THE NORTHERN WINDOW

Let us also modify the platform room's northern window, by making it start closed and arranging for the player to trigger the opening of it. It would be nice to have the ceiling rise from the window sector's floor position, but the only actions that achieve this are door actions—which would be inappropriate—and a ceiling mover that ends at the height of the highest adjacent ceiling.

This latter could be used, but it would be fiddly to implement. Because this mover takes the ceiling to the *highest* adjacent sector, using it would require the closed window sector to be isolated from both the outdoor sector and the room sector. This would necessitate the splitting of the existing window sector into three long, thin areas: a new window sector down the middle, with the remains of the original window sector on each side of it, cutting it off from the sectors with high ceilings and providing the desired target ceiling height. Furthermore the presence of the window would be suggested by the remaining recess visible from inside the room, and while this could be disguised with the use of suitable textures, it would still be less than satisfactory.

A simpler solution is to use a moving floor, starting at the current window sector's ceiling level. This solution will still require the splitting of the existing window sector to provide the final floor height, but it will only need to be split into two sectors, not three.

Using a fairly high Zoom factor, divide the current opening into the platform room down its long center line to turn it into two long thin sectors, as shown in Figure 9.8. Use Make Sector on the southern of the two new sectors first. Set its lighting level and ceiling and floor textures to match the original sector's. Set its floor and ceiling levels to match the outer window sector's ceiling height.

Figure 9.8.
Modification of the platform room's northern window.

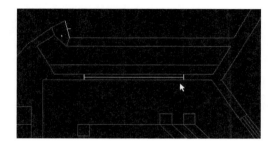

Put STONE3 on the appropriate lower texture of the new line. You may need some offsets applying to the through-wall textures to keep the bricks looking right here.

Finally, choose a line to act as a trigger to open the window. (I suggest the line of the second step up to the platform, so that the window opens as the player climbs the steps.) Tag the chosen line to the new sector, using a special attribute of 19 (W1 Floor: down to highest adjacent).

You may like to try out these modifications before continuing with the development beyond the lift.

DEVELOPING THE LOWER AREA OF THE WAD

Figure 9.9 shows how the corridor area beyond the lift can be developed. You may like to try implementing this area, working from the description that follows.

Figure 9.9.
Sectors beyond the lift.

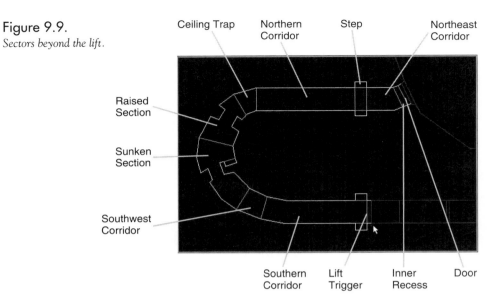

The area beyond the lift (the lift is indicated by the mouse cursor in Figure 9.9) has been broken up into a number of sectors to provide variations in floor and ceiling height, a puzzle (or two), and alcoves for switches.

Working around from the lift, the new areas are as follows:

- Lift trigger sector
- Long southern corridor (with switch alcoves)
- Southwest corner section
- A sunken section of corridor (with another switch alcove)
- A raised section of corridor
- Northwest corner section (ceiling trap)
- Long northern corridor
- A small step (with switch alcoves)
- Short northeastern corridor section
- Door recess
- Door

The location of these areas is marked in Figure 9.9. There is also another door recess between the door and the large outer arena, but that will be left as it is for now and will not be discussed further in this Sortie.

Before implementing any of these areas, it might be helpful for you to know something about the functions that they will perform.

THE CORRIDOR

Overall, the corridor provides a long, curving connection between the bottom of the lift and the outer arena, as you have already seen. The intention now is to develop that area into something more than simply a long tube from one place to another. Its curving form will be used to limit the distance that players can see ahead; and variations in floor height will be introduced to make the player unsure as to whether the area is leading them further down in level or back up. (This, combined with the curving nature of the corridor, is a good way of disorienting even those players with good spatial sense. And disorienting players is a good way of making them nervous!)

Sudden and erratic changes in corridor width, combined with the general shift in direction, will also be used. These things add to the disorienting nature of the corridor, but also provide nooks and crannies in which to hide various things and keep the players distracted.

THE PUZZLE

One section of the corridor—termed the *sunken* section throughout this description—will be set with its floor much lower than the next section. It will be set so low, in fact, that further progress will be barred until a way has been found to raise this floor. A floor mover will be used here, of course, activated from a suitable switch.

THE TRAP

The arena beyond this corridor area will contain a heavy concentration of enemies. It will start sealed off from the corridor by a door. After opening this door, and seeing what is beyond, players may wish to retreat back into the corridor for a time! The benefit to be gained from this maneuver will be limited here by two aspects of the current development. First, the door will be made to stay open, so any monsters spotting the player will be free to follow him down the corridor. Second, a ceiling trap will be sprung to close the corridor against retreat. The player will not be forced into springing this trap, though—merely encouraged. Two switches will be provided at the door end of the corridor: one will open the door, the other will spring the trap. The first time this area is played, it's a fairly safe bet that the ceiling will be lowered.

ADDITIONAL SWITCHES

This area will also be used to provide the switch that opens the additional room off the blood pool that was added in the previous Sortie. The implementation shown in Figure 9.9 also provides another switch alcove for later use.

IMPLEMENTING THE CHANGES

The development of this lower area requires the existing walls to be broken into quite a few new sections, and the long corridor divided up into appropriate sectors. The exact forms and shapes of these are not important, although there are a number of aspects of the development that will work better visually if certain sizes are used.

First, the various alcoves all use switch textures that are 64 pixels wide. These will sit best if the alcoves are made exactly 64 units wide. Secondly, the ceiling trap uses MARBFAC_ textures in various locations: on the outside wall of its sector, and on the face that closes off the long northern corridor after the trap has been sprung. These textures are 128 pixels wide and, again, will look best if used on correctly sized lines.

Additionally, the lighting level in this sector will be elevated relative to adjacent sectors. The wall section opposite the marble face will be made to look as though it is the source of illumination. To produce the right effect visually, this wall section should be quite short, and parallel to the wall opposite. Because of the textures used, it will also need to be split into three sections, in order to give a sensible border to the central (bright) texture—I'll give details of that later.

Table 9.5 gives the sector settings for each of the areas in this development, working along the corridor from the bottom of the lift, around towards the arena door. Also given in this table is a column of Y-offset values. These are the vertical texture alignment values that are required to maintain the correct alignment of lines facing into the sectors that use GSTONE1 (or a derivative) anywhere on them.

This texture is used almost exclusively on the walls of this area. All of the GSTONE_ textures need careful alignment (the vertical brick spacing is not constant up these textures) if the walls are not to look odd from sector to sector—especially with as many variations as this area contains. When you come to implement this area, you should check the table to see whether a Y-offset is specified. If it is, this offset should be applied everywhere that a GSTONE texture faces into the sector (which means most of the lines, I'm afraid).

Table 9.5. Sector settings in the corridor beyond the lift.

Area	Lighting	Ceiling	Floor	Y-Offset
Thin sector beyond lift	144	−216	−320	24
Long southern corridor	144	−216	−320	24
Alcoves off the above	128	−248	−320	0
Southwest corner section	144	−216	−336	24
Sunken corridor section	144	−192	−336	0
Alcove off sunken corridor	144	−224	−312	−32
Raised corridor section	144	−192	−288	0
Northwest corner (ceiling trap)	208	−160	−288	–
Northern corridor section	144	−160	−288	16
Step (by alcoves)	144	−160	−272	16
Alcoves off first step	112	−176	−272	0
Short northeast corridor	144	−128	−264	−16
Door recess	144	−128	−256	−16
Door	255	−256	−256	–

DEM1_5 is used on all floors and ceilings.

Additional implementation details of each of these sectors are given in the same order in the following section.

LONG SOUTH CORRIDOR, WITH SWITCH ALCOVES

Each of the switch alcoves just beyond the lift use SW1HOT as the texture for their rear walls, with the lower unpegged flags set. Their side walls also have this flag set. The one on the northern side of the corridor is tagged to the secret room adjacent to the blood pool above the lift, with a special attribute of 103 (S1 Door: open). The other alcove currently provides no switching action. The lines between the corridor and these alcoves should have GSTONE1 (unpegged) on their upper essentials, with the Y-offset appropriate for the sector into which they face. (See Table 9.5.)

SOUTHWEST CORNER SECTION

This sector has a lower essential where it borders with the previous corridor section to its east; NUKE24 is used here. GSTONE1 is used on the essential upper texture, with its upper unpegged flag set and an appropriate Y-offset.

SUNKEN CORRIDOR SECTION

Extra embellishments have been added to the sunken area of the corridor by adding protruding sections of wall. The faces of these narrow areas carry the GSTSATYR texture for variation. Don't make the corridor too narrow, here, will you?

GSTONE1 is used on the lower essential where this sector adjoins the next sector to its north, with the `lower` unpegged flag set. Tucked away in an alcove around the back of the protruding section of the eastern wall is the switch to move this sector and allow further progress down the corridor. The line separating this alcove from the sunken area has GSTONE1 on its upper and lower essentials, both unpegged. Figure 9.10 shows a view of this part of the corridor, showing the blockage caused by the sunken floor—the alcove switch is just visible at the right edge of the figure.

Figure 9.10.
A view from the sunken section of corridor.

ALCOVE OFF SUNKEN SECTOR

This alcove uses SW1GSTON on its rear wall, with its lower unpegged flag set. This line is tagged to the sunken sector with a special attribute of 18 (S1 Floor: up to next higher) to provide the switch action. The floor of the alcove sector itself provides the new level, 24 units up from the sunken sector's current setting—sufficient to allow the remaining step up to the next sector to become feasible. Only the side walls require the Y-offset from the table.

RAISED CORRIDOR SECTION

Wall protrusions have been added to the raised section of the corridor too. These use GSTLION on their faces. Again, don't make the gap between them so small that players cannot pass through.

CORNER SECTION (CEILING TRAP)

The corner sector is to act as the ceiling trap described earlier. Some warning of this trap is provided in the textures in use: the side wall on the outside of the bend uses MARBFAC3—as already noted, this line will need to be the right length to carry it. To produce the lighting effect described earlier, the wall that is opposite the marble face needs some special treatment. It should be divided into three, with the outer sections each about 12 units long and having SUPPORT3 on them. Between them, the middle section carries SKULWALL with an X-offset to keep the skulls central in the gap.

Readers using DOOM II will need to find a replacement for the SKULWALL texture. Something like SLOPPY2 would do.

MARBLE3 is used on the upper essential between this sector and its neighbor to the southwest: a Y-offset of 32 is used to make the skulls along the bottom of this texture visible.

The change that this sector will undergo as the ceiling trap is activated produces some latent essential textures and generates some pegging requirements. The eastern face of the sector should have MARBFACE on its outward facing upper, while the southwestern face uses GSTONE1. All the side wall lines of this sector have their lower unpegged flags set to prevent them from moving when the ceiling comes down.

REMAINING CORRIDOR SECTIONS

The sections of the corridor leading east from the ceiling trap corner have little of note in them. NUKE24 is used on all essential lower textures here, with GSTONE1 on any uppers. Upper textures are generally unpegged and need the Y-offset appropriate to their sector.

SWITCH ALCOVES

The pair of switch alcoves by the bottom step out of the long corridor use SW1GSTON on their rear walls. These textures have their lower unpegged flags set, as do all of the alcoves' side walls, which use the ubiquitous GSTONE1. The northern of these alcoves has its rear wall tagged to the corner section of the corridor, with a special attribute of 41 (S1 Ceiling: move down to floor)—it is here that the ceiling trap is activated. The MARBLE3 texture is used as the upper essential over this alcove, with its upper unpegged flag set, as a visual warning (not that many players will notice it!).

The southern alcove is tagged to the door sector at the eastern end of this corridor, with a special attribute of 103 (S1 Door: open). This opens the door, allowing the player into the arena—or allowing whatever is out there into the corridor!

THE DOOR TO THE ARENA

Finally, the door sector at the end of this corridor uses BIGDOOR7 on both faces, and DOORTRAK on its side walls, with the lower unpegged flag set, as is usual for doors.

TRYING THE MODIFICATIONS

That completes the modifications to the corridor beyond the lift. If you have implemented these changes, you may like to try the WAD out and see how well it works. (It is available on the CD-ROM as WAD19.WAD.) You may discover that, as it stands, the WAD contains a number of nasty traps for the player—some of which were not intended and which need rectification.

A WORD ABOUT TRAPS

No one doubts the need for traps in a WAD. They add a mental challenge to the game, making players keep an eye open for things other than the obvious and providing them with something more than an exercise in grabbing the goodies and shooting the monsters. However, it is easy to have traps backfire on you as a designer, and turn what seemed a nice idea at the time into a major irritation that detracts from play rather than contributes to it.

Consider, for example, the ceiling trap that has just been added to the WAD. Its main aim is to cut off the line of retreat down the corridor, forcing the player to face whatever is out in the arena once the next door is opened. In this sense, this trap works well. It has some unfortunate side effects, however.

2	1		9		DOOM
EPISODE	MISSION		ROOM		PROGRAMMING GURUS

First, it makes it necessary for the player to find another way out of the arena, this exit being closed. Now, you made another way out earlier: the lift up to the window of the platform room. This works fine—provided that the window was previously opened! If not, the player is trapped here for good.

Second, it is just possible for a fast player to make it back under the closing ceiling. Any players doing this gain nothing, however, for the ceiling will still close and will now deny them access to the arena (and whatever it contains). The game will need to be restarted before the arena can be entered—an annoyance, to say the least.

The important lesson to learn here is that traps need to be examined carefully for all possible ramifications. Remember that not everyone plays in the same way—what may seem to you a logical way of proceeding through a WAD may never occur to other players. As a designer, you need to foresee every action that your players may attempt and consider all possible sequences in which these actions will be carried out.

KEEPING TRAPS UNDER CONTROL

The key to the successful management of traps is to plan around the WAD as a whole, not around the traps you fancy using. Do not be seduced by neat traps and tricks. Consider rather what constraints you want to put on the players, and implement traps to bring these about.

Remember, too, that traps limit a player's options. You should use them only to force players into taking particular paths that you want them to go down. If you force them down too rigid a pathway, prescribing their play in too great a detail, you prevent players from finding their own solutions. The result is bored players.

In planning your areas for particular playing methodologies, always allow for others. Only use traps if you want to close off particular (easy) options. The traps that the WAD developed in the Sorties so far have been added with little regard for the playability of the WAD as a whole; they have largely been illustrative of the techniques. And this has made the WAD a bit of a mess.

EXAMINING THE PROBLEM HERE

Let us look at the details of the current predicament, starting with the window. The intention in having this area closed at the start of the game was to make the opening of the window a surprise for the player climbing towards the platform—just one more thing to worry about while busy dealing with whatever the platform room contains.

If the player decides to pass straight through the platform room and the subsequent corridors down to the arena below, though, that surprise is no longer needed. There is therefore nothing to be lost by enabling this window to be opened from its arena side if it is still closed when the player reaches it. You may wish to enable the player to do this manually—locating the switch could be a further puzzle here—or have it happen automatically by using suitably placed trips (on the approach to or exit from the arena lift, for example).

Second, look at the ceiling trap. As already noted, the purpose of this trap is to force the player who trips it to face whatever lies ahead. There is no good reason to have this prevent him from returning along this corridor later, once the arena has been cleared. You may wish to provide a switch somewhere in the arena to open this section of corridor again from there. (Something to bear in mind when that area comes to be developed.) More immediately useful, perhaps, would be the provision of some means of opening it from its other side, just in case a player makes it back there.

REPAIRING THE WAD

You should, therefore, make some minor repairs to your WAD, to correct the current glut of traps. Start by adding some mechanism to open the platform room's northern window from the arena side. Then, allow the lower corridor's corner section to be opened from its southwestern side in the event that a player returns here after the ceiling trap has been sprung. A standard manual door action on this section would allow any player back through this blockage, but would still have it close again in case the arena monsters hadn't been dealt with!

Save your final, corrected WAD as WAD19A.WAD to stay in step with my WAD numbering.

> I am aware that the maze section of the WAD still has no exit. This will be dealt with in future Sorties, have no fear.

CRUSHERS

The floor and ceiling movements that have been examined so far have all been delayed (or temporarily reversed) by players or monsters who become caught up in their actions. No harm is done to players or monsters when this happens. There are two categories of actions that work very differently: the crushing floors and the crushing ceilings.

CRUSHING FLOORS

DOOM's crushing floors operate by moving up to 8 units below their sector's ceiling, catching anything that is in the sector and crushing it. The crushing action does considerable harm to whatever is caught in the action and is usually fatal for players and smaller monsters. Barrels caught in the action will explode, adding their quota of damage to anything nearby.

A floor crusher's motion continues to completion even when things are caught in it; anything thus caught is quickly pinned to the ceiling. Monsters not killed are unable to move or fight. The floor travels at standard mover speed, so players will need to shift rapidly to escape the pinning action.

The F_SKY1 ceiling "texture" is as fatal as any other here!

Other sector actions can be applied after this action is complete, although a bug in the game engine prevents further floor or ceiling movements if anything remains trapped and alive in the crusher.

Table 9.6 gives the special line codes to implement crushing floors.

Table 9.6. Special line codes for the implementation of crushing floors.

Action	Activation Category			
	W1	WR	S1	SR
Crushing floor	56	94	55	65

CRUSHING CEILINGS

DOOM's crushing ceilings operate somewhat differently from the crushing floors. Whereas the floors move once, from their starting position to just below the ceiling, the crushing ceilings, once activated, continue to operate, cycling between their starting height and 8 units above their sector's floor. They become what are termed *perpetual movers*. The next section examines perpetual movers in detail.

PERPETUAL MOVERS

Most of the actions initiated by lines' special attributes operate for a finite time only. Once they terminate, the actions are deemed to be over and the affected sectors are free to participate in further actions. Perpetual mover actions do not function like this. Their actions never terminate.

PERPETUAL ACTIONS

It is important to realize that it is not the movement that these actions initiate, which is perpetual, but the action. This means that DOOM regards these actions as ongoing for the rest of the game, even if the movement has been stopped. Perpetual movers are therefore never free to participate in any other sector-changing action (except adjustments to the lighting levels, which always occur whether or not other activities are taking place).

The action is deemed never to finish because the motions that these special lines trigger are cyclic in nature and therefore without logical termination. Additional special line types are provided to stop the motions of perpetual movers, but they only *pause* the action. Any further triggering of this action will cause the mover to continue in its original cycle of movement, starting up again from where it was paused.

Perpetually moving platforms do, of course, consume processing power, and they contribute to the count of surfaces in motion. It is a sensible idea, therefore, to make sure that you include lines in your map to suspend their motion as the player moves away from them. If you want to give the player the impression that their motion is indeed continuous, you can always arrange multiple on/off trip-wire arrangements, as were used for the lights in the previous room.

PERPETUAL CRUSHERS

The crushing ceilings are all classed as perpetual crushers. They begin their cycle of movement by moving downwards from their starting height. This initial height is the uppermost limit of their travel. The lower limit of their travel is 8 units above their sector floor.

Crushing ceilings operate at two speeds: fast and slow. The fast crushers move at the same speed as standard lifts and doors, while the slow crushers move at the speed of a mover. With one exception, they all make the standard mover sound. The exception is the new crusher introduced in DOOM v1.666: the so-called silent crusher. This is a fast crusher, which is silent during its travel. It does makes a clunk sound as it starts to move, though, and at each end of its travel.

The fast crushers continue in their motion regardless of whether anything is caught in them or not; slow crushers, on the other hand, reduce their speed of descent drastically when something is caught in them, reverting to the normal speed as the motion reverses. As both types of crusher hold on to anything so caught, inflicting harm for as long as it takes them to move from the object's height to their lower limit of travel and back, slow crushers will do considerably more damage per crush than will fast crushers.

Table 9.7 gives the line-type codes for the crushing ceilings.

Table 9.7. Special line codes for the implementation of crushing ceilings.

Action	Activation Category	
	W1	WR
Start/resume slow crushing ceiling	25	73
Start/resume fast crushing ceiling	6	77
Start/resume slow, silent crushing ceiling	141*	–
Pause crushing ceiling	57	74
Actions marked * available only in DOOM v1.666 and above.		

As perpetual movers, sectors that are started as crushers never become free to participate in any subsequent action that might try to affect their floor or ceiling. All of the start/resume triggers will operate on these sectors, however, causing the crushing motion to resume, even if they are triggers for a different type of crushing action. The action that resumes is always of the original type.

PERPETUAL LIFTS

The other type of perpetual mover is the continuously operating lift. Once activated, this lift operates by moving its floor continuously up and down from one extreme of its travel to the other, moving at about half the speed of standard lifts. There is a three–second pause as the direction of travel reverses. These lifts make the same sound as ordinary lifts as they start, reverse, and stop their motions.

A perpetual lift obtains *both* extremes of its motion from adjacent sectors (or its own starting floor level, if this is beyond either of these extremes). The range over which the lift operates is calculated once, at the point when the perpetual motion is first initiated. From then on, the action operates over this range regardless of whether adjacent sectors' floors subsequently move.

The initial direction of travel is determined by the lift's starting location within its range of motion: The lift always starts by heading away from the closest extreme of travel. If initiated when positioned exactly in the middle, it starts by moving up. If positioned anywhere other than at the lower extreme, motion begins immediately after the action is initiated. If started while at its lower extreme, the lift will pause for three seconds (its usual turn–round period) before moving.

Like any perpetual mover, if the action is paused, any retrigger of the action will cause the lift to resume the motion that was under way when it was interrupted. This means the lift will operate over its full range, as before, irrespective of any changes that may have taken place around it.

Table 9.8 gives the line–type codes for perpetual lifts.

Table 9.8. Special line codes for the implementation of perpetual lifts.

Action	Activation Category	
	W1	WR
Perpetual lift start/resume	53	87
Perpetual lift pause	54	89

Like standard lifts, these lifts automatically reverse their travel if players or monsters become caught between their floors and its own or adjacent ceilings. This causes no harm to players or monsters.

WAD SORTIE 20: ADDING A CRUSHER

> This Sortie builds on the WAD produced in the previous one. If you did not produce that WAD, you should use WAD19A.WAD (DOOM) or D2WAD19A.WAD (DOOM II) from the CD-ROM as your starting point here.

This Sortie will concentrate on the addition of a single crusher.

A SETTING FOR THE CRUSHER

The new crusher is to be located in a new area south of the southern courtyard, in a corridor linking the secret room with the sniper's den.

New sectors making the connection between the two existing areas will provide:

- Another hidden door, shot-activated
- A short corridor
- A perpetual crushing ceiling
- A longer corridor
- A further door

In addition, a recess will be needed beyond the door just inside the sniper's den. Figure 9.11 shows how these new areas link in.

Figure 9.11.
New lines south of the courtyard.

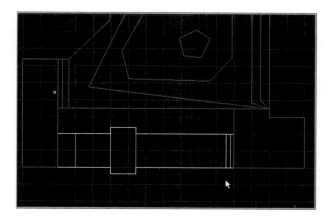

ADDING THE NEW AREA

The secret room and/or the sniper's den may need extending or reshaping a little to allow convenient connection of the new areas, which should be drawn using WOOD3 as the default wall texture.

Table 9.9 gives the settings for the new sectors.

Table 9.9. Settings for the sectors around the crusher.

Area	Lighting		Ceiling		Floor
West door	144	0	FLOOR4_1	0	FLAT5
West corridor	144	128	FLOOR4_1	0	FLAT5
Crusher	144	104	FLOOR4_1	0	FLAT5
East corridor	144	128	FLOOR4_1	0	FLAT5
East door	196	16	FLAT5	16	FLAT5
Recess	192	128	FLOOR4_1	16	FLAT1_1
Sniper's den	192	136	FLAT5_5	16	FLAT1_1

Table 9.10 gives the places where WOOD3 is not used.

Table 9.10. Texture settings for surfaces in the crusher corridor.

Surface	Texture Details
Outer face of western door	BROWN1, with Y-offset of –8
Inner face of western door	BIGDOOR7
Faces of crusher	WOOD4
Sides of crusher	DOORTRAK, with lower unpegged flag set
Crusher recess reveals	SUPPORT3, with lower unpegged flag set
Inner face of eastern door	WOOD4, with Y-offset of –48
Outer face of eastern door	BROWN1
Wall over door recess	BROWN1, with upper unpegged flag set
Inner sides of door recess	BROWN1, with Y-offset of 16
All walls of sniper's den	BROWN1

In addition, make sure that BROWN96 remains on the outer surface of the sniper's wall. It will now be needed on an additional texture slot here and have its upper and lower unpegged flags set to allow for the changes to the sector behind it.

Make the western door an impact-activated door, in the usual way. Make the eastern door capable of being opened from the corridor side only. Have it latch open, once activated.

BUILDING THE CRUSHER

To implement the crusher itself, use the inner surface of the new area's western door to start the motion: this line should be tagged to the crushing sector with a special attribute of 73 (WR Crusher: slow start/resume). Remember that you need to make sure that perpetual movers are turned off as players leave this area. Use line-type 74 (WR Crusher: pause) on suitable lines to achieve this. Remember also that you will need to cover both halves of the new area to allow for players leaving by either route. I suggest using the sniper's wall itself, and one of the lines in the southwestern courtyard recess. Any one of these lines that is not currently active will do, provided that it is not so close to a spacebar-activated trigger that it will stop that trigger from working.

Finally, save this WAD as WAD20.WAD and try out this latest area. Of course, you'll have to get in there first.

EXIT: MOPPING UP AND MOVING ON

In this room you encountered several more types of active sectors: lifts; simple moving floors and ceilings; and crushers. You have been shown how each of these operates and how to construct them in your own WADs.

The next room contains yet more active sectors and shows you how to manage complex active-sector arrangements.

DOOM
PROGRAMMING
GURUS

9
ROOM

1
MISSION

2
EPISODE

ROOM 10

By Steve Benner

COMPLEX MOVING SECTORS

In recent rooms, you have encountered the actions that single sectors can undergo when activated by the special lines. In this room, you will see how a group of active sectors will operate in concert. You will also be shown how sectors can be made to change their special characteristics, and you will see how some active sectors drag others along with them in their actions.

The WAD that has been developed in earlier WAD Sorties will be extended again with further Sorties from this room. First, the single crushing ceiling added at the end of the previous room will acquire some neighbors: together these will act as a chain of crushers through which players will need to time their dash carefully if they are to survive. Additional Sorties will add sectors that move and change to the WAD and finally some actions that entrain several sectors to provide some of DOOM's most complex multi-sector actions—the donut-eater and self-raising stairs.

ALL TOGETHER NOW

When you were first introduced to remotely-activated sectors several rooms ago, you were told that it is possible to tag more than one sector to a single trigger. So far, though, you have not seen how these grouped, active sectors behave.

GROUPING ACTIVE SECTORS

When more than one sector is tagged to a single trigger, there are three ways in which the resulting group of sectors may respond to an activation of the trigger:

- As a united group, with each member of the group changing to the same new setting
- As a loose assemblage of sectors, with each member largely doing its own thing, but with occasional actions in one sector affecting some of the other members of the group
- As a set of individual participants in an action, with each unaware of the actions of the others

Just which of these modes of behavior applies to the group, depends upon the specific action being triggered. For the vast majority of actions, the third type of grouping will apply.

ACTING IN UNISON

The only actions that cause groups of sectors to act in unison are those affecting the sectors' lighting levels. If there is more than one sector tagged to a lighting effect trigger, then all of the sectors within the grouping will have their lights brought to the same level. Those actions that refer to adjacent sectors for the new value will obtain that value from amongst the neighbors of only *one* member—

2 EPISODE   **1** MISSION   **10** ROOM   DOOM PROGRAMMING GURUS the lowest numbered—of the group. The neighbors of the other members of the group are *not* considered at all. If you are not careful, this can result in some undesired results, with the entire group refusing to change or changing to an unexpected level. Figure 10.1 illustrates how this could come about.

Figure 10.1.

An arrangement of dark and bright sectors.

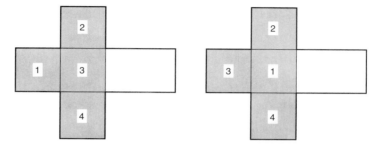

In Figure 10.1, the four shaded sectors are grouped to a single trigger somewhere of type 80 (WR Lights: match highest adjacent level). These sectors are all of the same brightness level, lower than the other sectors in the figure. Note that if these sectors had been created in the order indicated by the numbers in the left half of Figure 10.1, then the group's lowest numbered member (sector 1) has only one neighbor from which to take the new light level value, sector 3. As this sector is itself part of the group (and therefore already at that group's brightness level), no visible change will result.

It would require the sectors to be numbered as shown in the right half of Figure 10.1 for any change to occur when the trigger was activated. Only with this ordering of sectors does the lowest numbered member of the group have a neighbor that is outside of the group itself. Note that few editors enable you to control the numbering of your sectors. You usually need to have drawn the sectors in the correct order when laying out the WAD. Bear this in mind, then, when planning areas that will use lighting effects involving grouped sectors.

LOOSE ASSEMBLAGES OF SECTORS

Loose assemblages occur when multiple sectors are in motion as slow crushers. Ordinarily, crushers move independently of each other, moving at a constant speed between each extreme of their travel. Slow crushers, you will recall, slow their motion further when something becomes caught in their downward travel. When several slow crushers are in motion together, the slowing of one can affect the motion of others. DOOM may pass the slowing of the action on to any other crusher that is also moving downwards while the crush occurs. Whether the slowing effect is transmitted or not is determined randomly for each separate crush and is completely outside the WAD designer's control.

The term "randomly" is used here to mean "unpredictably." DOOM's game engine does not generate or use random events—it merely seems to.

INDEPENDENT ACTIONS

With the exception of the two categories of action just described, tagging more than one sector to a single trigger will not create any significant grouping of participant sectors. Most of the time, what you achieve with such multi-tagged lines is to use a single line to initiate the same action in more than one location simultaneously, with each sector responding to the action independently of all others. If any member of the group is not available to participate for some reason, then that particular sector will simply not be activated. This non-participant will not prevent any other sector from joining in the action. Similarly, any sector that has its action cut short for any reason will not affect any concurrent activity going on elsewhere.

END POINTS OF INDEPENDENT ACTIONS

It is important to appreciate that the end points of normal independent sector movements are calculated from the conditions pertaining at the point of initiation and without regard for any other changes that may be in progress at the time. By way of illustration, consider three sectors side-by-side, in a line from west to east, as shown in Figure 10.2.

Imagine first of all (case *i* in Figure 10.2) that the floor heights in these three sectors, in order from west to east, are 64, 24, and 0 units and that the western and central sectors are both tagged to a single trigger somewhere of type 82. This trigger brings its target sectors' floors down to their lowest adjacent floor level.

Consider what happens when this line is triggered. At the point of activation, the western sector's lowest adjacent floor is to its east, at 24 units, while the central sector's lowest adjacent floor is also to its east, at 0 units. These are the heights to which these floors will move on the first triggering of this action. You should be able to see that a subsequent triggering of this action will bring the western sector's floor down to 0 with no movement from the central sector. After that, further activation of the line will have no effect.

Now imagine the same arrangement of sectors and triggers but with different starting heights for the floors of 64, 64, and 0. (Case *ii* in Figure 10.2.) On the trigger's first activation, the central sector will descend to the level of its eastern neighbor, as before. The western sector will not move, however, because at the point of activation it has no neighbor at a different height. A second activation of the trigger is needed to make this sector's floor move down to join the neighboring floor at its new level.

Figure 10.2.

Various configurations of grouped moving floors.

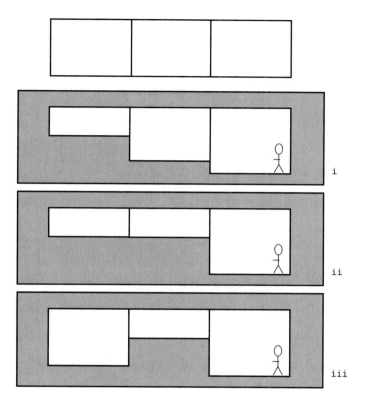

i

ii

iii

Note this well: it is a common mistake to group sectors like this in the hope that the tagged pair will move in unison to the lower level. They will not. DOOM considers the movement of each member of the group individually.

Finally, consider what happens if the floors start out at heights of 24, 64, and 0, as shown in case *iii*. The first time the line is triggered here, the western sector will move *up* to 64 units—the height of its lowest neighbor at the time of activation. This movement will occur instantaneously. (If you don't remember why, you may wish to review the previous room's discussion of movers.) The central sector will move down, at the normal speed, to level 0. Once again, the western sector will move its floor to 0 in the normal manner on the second triggering of the action.

DOOM
PROGRAMMING
GURUS

10
ROOM

1
MISSION

2
EPISODE

COORDINATING AND SYNCHRONIZING MULTI-SECTOR ACTIONS

It is common to want several sectors to operate together as a single coordinated or synchronized unit—usually in chains of crushers and other perpetual movers. As you have already seen, though, when moving freely, each participating sector in a multi-sector action will take as much or as little time as it needs to complete its own action, without regard for the movement of any other sector. The only way to achieve synchronization, therefore, is to use the same travel distance for each component.

Bear in mind, too, that slow crushers and perpetual lifts can be delayed in their action as a result of players and monsters becoming caught up in them. When this occurs to single members of a chain of such movers, it will wreak havoc with any synchronization of motion that you had set up.

If you want perpetual movers to remain in phase with each other, you will need to ensure that the range of travel of each participant is the same. With crushers, though, it is often better to make the range of travel different for each component, so that they drift in and out of phase with each other, making it harder for players to time their dash through the entire chain. The next WAD Sortie lets you try a crusher chain out for yourself.

> The following WAD Sortie builds on the WAD produced in WAD Sortie 20 of the previous room. If you did not accompany me on that Sortie but would like to come along on this one, you should use WAD20.WAD (DOOM) or D2WAD20.WAD (DOOM II) from the CD-ROM as your starting point.

WAD SORTIE 21: BUILDING A CRUSHER CHAIN

In this Sortie, you will add two more crushers alongside your existing one to complete the secret area located to the south of the southern courtyard.

AMENDING THE CURRENT CRUSHER ROOM

Figure 10.3 shows the arrangement you are aiming for in the modified crusher corridor.

The new areas are easy to add. You need to split each of the long eastern corridor walls, putting four new vertices where each end of a crusher will appear. By repositioning the inner pair of these vertices, you can reshape the sides of the corridor to provide the required recess. Repeat the operation for each new crusher recess and finally add the new cross-corridor lines that make the faces of the crusher. You should not need to create any further vertices to add these extra lines.

Figure 10.3.
Lines for the complete crusher chain.

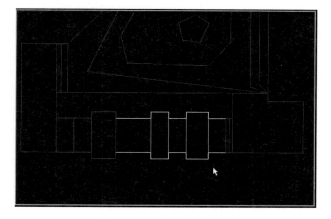

When you have made the rearrangements and drawn the new lines, you can create all of the necessary new sectors, matching everything to the existing settings and textures. To connect the two new crushers to the same triggers as the original, in order to have them operate as a group, select one of the existing crusher activation lines. With this line selected, right click each of the two new crusher sectors in turn. This assigns the same tag number to all three of these sectors, so that they will be affected by all of the same lines.

Finally decide on suitable settings for each of the crushing sectors. As well as their heights, you may like to experiment with the overall size of each crusher, as well as the spacing between them. Save and play a few variants to find the best result. Observe how the slow crushers behave as a group when you become caught in one of them. (You will use IDDQD first, won't you?)

You could try out the room with faster crushers, too. When you are happy with the arrangement, tidy up the texture alignment and name your final WAD WAD21.WAD.

Readers with DOOM v1.666 or later should remember that they have the so-called silent crusher at their disposal, too.

Figure 10.4 gives a view of the completed crusher room.

Figure 10.4.
The completed crushers.

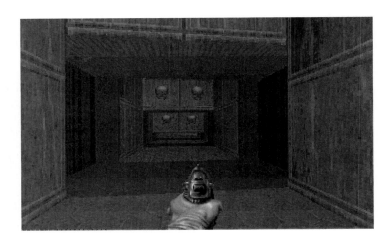

RINGING THE CHANGES

The next group of sector actions to consider are the *changers*: sectors that change their appearance and behavior as they move.

THE MOVEMENT OF CHANGERS

All movements associated with changer actions affect only the target sectors' floors. In this aspect of their operation, changers behave just like movers. Where they differ is in the alterations that their sectors undergo while moving.

THE CHANGES

As well as moving their floors to new locations, changer actions affect their target sectors in two further ways:

- **The sector's floor texture changes:** This provides sectors that can sink into other areas and vanish, or rise up out of a large area of one floor texture and acquire a new texture to differentiate them from their surroundings.

- **The sector's special characteristic alters:** All changers alter the special characteristic of the sector they affect. Some reset it to 0, cancelling out any special effect that the sector was using. This can turn a sector from a damaging area into a harmless one. Other changers can be made to copy a special characteristic from elsewhere, so that sectors can be turned into harmful ones.

THE ROLE MODEL

The changes that are wrought by these actions are determined partly by the code of the action and partly through the involvement of an additional sector, known as a *role model*. The function of the role model is to provide DOOM with a source for the new settings that the changing sector is to acquire.

The game engine employs two different methods to determine which sector will act in this capacity, depending upon which special line-type initiates the action:

- **The trigger method:** Trigger-method changers take the sector on the right side of their action's *trigger line* as the role model for the changing sector.

- **The first-neighbor (or numeric) method:** Changers in this category use a more complicated method of locating a sector to act as a role model. They examine the changing sector itself to find its lowest numbered two-sided linedef, taking the sector on the other side of this—the changing sector's first neighbor—as the role model.

A sector's first neighbor is usually the one it gained earliest in the creation of the WAD.

When triggered, a changer action will use whichever role-model method is appropriate to its own operation to locate the role-model sector. This sector's floor texture and, if applicable, its special characteristic are then copied to the tagged target sector as that sector moves.

Figure 10.5 shows these two types of changer in action on the same sector (S). At the top is shown the layout of sectors and floor patterns prior to activation of any changers. The numbers on the lines of the tagged sector show the order in which these lines were drawn (in the WAD as a whole). The lower parts of the figure show the following:

- i. The effect of a trigger-method changer, activated from line T. Notice how the floor texture from the sector on the right side of line T has been transferred to the active sector.

- ii. The effect of a first-neighbor changer, activated from the same line as the preceding. Notice how the new floor texture for the active sector has been acquired from its first neighbor.

Different results could be achieved here, of course, by drawing the lines of the tagged sector in a different order.

These actions may appear complicated to use, particularly those involving first-neighbor method changers. Fortunately, in practice, they are rarely so. Areas that are to utilize such changers do need to be planned carefully in advance, however.

Figure 10.5.
The effects of the different role-model methods.

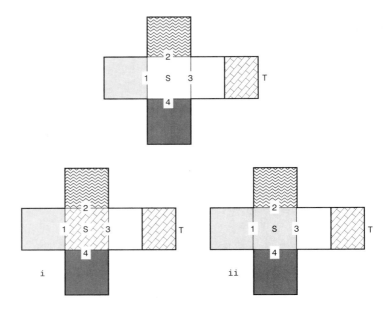

CHANGES TO THE SPECIAL CHARACTERISTIC

Not all values of a sector's special characteristic can be transferred to a changing sector. Table 10.1 indicate which ones can.

Table 10.1. Special sector characteristics that can be transferred by appropriate changer actions.

Code	Characteristic
4	High damage and blink; only the damaging aspect of this characteristic transfers
5	Medium damage
7	Low damage
9	Award secret credit
11	High damage and end level
16	High damage

If the role model has other values from those shown in Table 10.1, the moving sector acquires a special characteristic of 0.

CHANGER EFFECTS

Table 10.2 gives details of the available changer actions. Note that the majority are of the simpler trigger-model variety and that not all of these actions will transfer a special characteristic from the role model, even if it is of the permitted variety.

Table 10.2. Available changer codes.

Floor movement	Role-model type	Special Transferred					
			Activation Category				
			W1	WR	S1	SR	G1
Up to next higher	Trigger	0	22	95	20	68	47
Up 24 units	Trigger	0	–	–	15	66	–
Up 24 units	Trigger	X	59	93	–	–	–
Up 32 units	Trigger	0	–	–	14	67	–
Down to lowest adjacent	1st Neighbor	X	37	84	–	–	–

Changers that do not transfer the special characteristic from the role-model sector do still change the special characteristic of their target sector. They set it to 0, nullifying any damaging characteristic the sector may have had.

Movements occur in an identical manner to the corresponding mover actions.

WAD SORTIE 22: USING CHANGERS

This Sortie builds on the WAD produced in the previous one. If you did not produce that WAD, you should use WAD21.WAD (DOOM) or D2WAD21.WAD (DOOM II) from the CD-ROM as your starting point here.

This WAD Sortie will show you how to use each of the two categories of sector changers. First of all, though, it will show you how you can utilize a changer as a straightforward mover, thereby expanding the range of available floor-moving actions at your disposal.

ALTERATIONS BEYOND THE LIFT

In my opinion, the sunken area of corridor in the green stone passageway is a little less than perfect in its operation. The small section of corridor immediately prior to the sunken section is fine while the sunken section is at its starting height, but it looks odd after the sunken section has been raised. It seems strange to have a lower section of corridor between the newly-raised sunken section and the corridor leading back to the lift.

The special line used to raise the sunken corridor currently invokes an action that raises the floor to the next higher adjacent floor—in this case, the floor of the alcove housing the switch. The immediate adjacent corridor section—the one that is upsetting me so—is currently used to isolate the sunken sector from the long corridor, which is only 16 units above the starting height of the sunken floor. If this were the sunken floor's next higher floor, it would not rise enough to enable the player to go on.

It would be nice to have the ability to raise the sunken floor by a fixed 24 units, rather than having to worry about arranging neighbors at suitable heights. However, the actions to do this are only available as walk-through triggers, and I'd like to keep this operation on a switch. Line-type 15 (S1 Change floor: trigger-model; up 24) will work, though; it provides a sector change in addition to the movement, but that will not matter here. Indeed, it won't even be noticed. This action uses the trigger-method to find the role model; because the sector that houses the trigger for the sunken sector currently has the same floor-texture setting, no visible change will ensue.

All that is needed here then is to change the special attribute of the appropriate trigger line (at the back of the small alcove off the sunken sector) to the value 15. After this modification, the offending short section of corridor can be raised 16 units to –320, so that its floor is no longer lower than the long corridor's. Put NUKE24 on the new texture surface that this exposes.

STARTING THE ARENA DEVELOPMENT

The remainder of this Sortie will concentrate on development of the open arena at the northern end of the WAD. Figure 10.6 shows how this area needs to be divided up. As you can see, there are a lot of additions here, even though this is but the first stage of the development of the arena. This Sortie concentrates mainly on the arena's western half. Each new area is detailed shortly.

Figure 10.6.

The first additions to the arena.

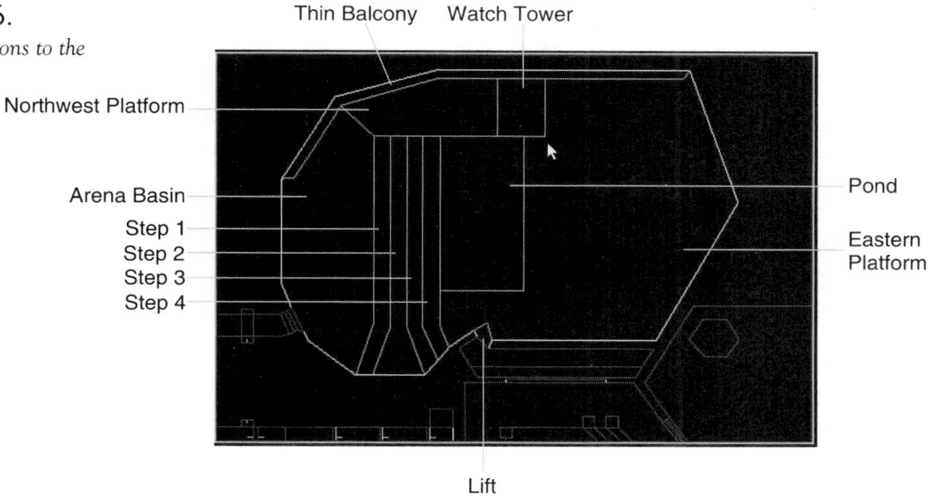

Thin Balcony   Watch Tower

Northwest Platform

Arena Basin

Step 1
Step 2
Step 3
Step 4

Pond

Eastern Platform

Lift

ADDING THE NEW AREAS

Start the modifications by using MULTI in LINES mode to change all of the major wall textures of this arena to WOOD5. Leave the faces of the lift in the southern wall as they are for now, though, so that it remains easy to find. Then enter Draw mode, select STARTAN1 as the default drawing texture, and add the lines for a thin balcony running along inside the northern rim of the arena.

Readers using DOOM II should substitute BRICK5 for STARTAN1 throughout this Sortie. (It's a much nicer texture anyway!)

Next, draw the square area that meets this northern balcony midway across the arena. (In Figure 10.6, the cursor is pointing to this area's southeastern corner.) This sector will eventually form a lookout tower. Follow these lines with those marking out the platform area to the west of the tower. Then mark off the area at the extreme west of the arena—this will form the low arena basin. East from this are four wide steps, formed from lines running between the northwestern platform and the southern wall of the arena; add these next. The steps will lead up from the arena basin, the top step adjoining the large eastern platform and a rectangular pond. The player's progress from the west will be halted here through the use of an excessive step height.

Make all of these sectors before going on. The settings are given in Table 10.3.

Table 10.3. Sector settings for the first additions to the arena.

Area	Lighting		Ceiling		Floor
Balcony	255	216	F_SKY1	152	FLAT1_2
Watch tower	255	216	F_SKY1	104	FLOOR4_8
Northwest platform	255	216	F_SKY1	–144	FLAT1_2
Southwestern door recess (from earlier Sortie)	255	–128	FLOOR4_8	–264	FLAT1_2
Arena basin	255	216	F_SKY1	–264	FLAT1_2
First step	255	216	F_SKY1	–240	FLAT1_2
Second step	255	216	F_SKY1	–216	FLAT1_2
Third step	255	216	F_SKY1	–192	FLAT1_2
Fourth step	255	216	F_SKY1	–168	FLAT1_2
Eastern platform	255	216	F_SKY1	–128	FLOOR0_1
Pond	255	216	F_SKY1	–200	NUKAGE1

The watchtower and northern balcony walls need WOOD5 on their essential textures to make them look like part of the main arena walls. Use BROWN144 on the risers of the steps and STARTAN1 on all remaining essential textures.

The southwest door's sectors should be changed a little from their earlier settings. Use GSTONE1 on the side walls of the door sector itself as well as the outer door recess. Apply a Y-offset of –16 to these wall sections. WOOD5 is required on the upper over the outer door recess, with its upper unpegged flag set. Put GSTONE1 on the lower essential below the outer face of the door.

DIVIDING UP THE POND

The nukage-slime pond in the middle of the arena is the area that will use the changers. The next step, then, is to add the additional sectors within the pond. Figure 10.7 shows the arena again, with the new areas required for the pond.

Start by adding the five shapes that are entirely contained within the pond. These are four square stepping-stones, 64 units or so in size, that lead out across the pond to a slightly larger rectangular island. The stepping-stones will appear to offer a way across the pond but will, in fact, sink below the surface when the player steps on them. (I'll explain just how this works in a moment.)

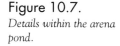

Figure 10.7.

Details within the arena pond.

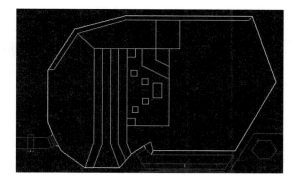

Make the sectors for these areas, using Make Sector on the pond sector itself again, afterwards. Then put line-type 37 on each line of each stepping-stone (but not the larger island—this will be somewhere for the player to stop and think). As you set its special attribute, tag each of these lines to its own stepping-stone sector—this way, the sector will sink regardless of which of its boundary lines the player crosses.

The floor settings for each island sector should be FLOOR0_1, at a level of –176. Set the brightness and ceiling values to match all of the other sectors in this area.

HOW THE STEPPING-STONES WORK

The stepping-stones will operate as follows. Special line-type 37 is a walk-through trigger, which invokes a first-neighbor model changer. This changer lowers a sector's floor to the height of the lowest adjacent floor, at the same time transferring a floor texture and special characteristic from an adjacent sector.

All of the stepping-stone sectors are completely surrounded by the main sector of the slime pond. No matter which of their lines was drawn first, therefore, their first-neighbor will be this pond sector. The main nukage-slime pond will thus act as the role-model sector, so that each stepping-stone will acquire the NUKAGE1 texture as well as the pond's damaging special characteristic as they move.

Of course, being the only adjacent sector means that the main pond will also provide the new floor setting for the tagged sector. The net effect, therefore, is that as a player steps onto one of the stepping-stones, it will sink to the level of the pond floor. This, combined with its texture change, will cause it to vanish into the slime.

LETTING THE PLAYER OUT

The main pond sector is currently 32 pixels below the arena's top step, its lowest adjacent sector. There is thus no escape from the pond. With such a clear invitation to enter it, players will find it annoying in the extreme if they are then caught there until they die. An escape route is needed here.

Escape shouldn't be made too easy, though, so make it possible only from the very corners. Add the two corner sectors, as in Figure 10.7, shown previously, using a floor height of –192 and a texture of FLOOR0_1. Once again, use STARTAN1 as the essential texture for all these new areas.

ADDING THE FINAL CHANGER

Finally, add another changer to provide an eventual means of progress across the pond to the eastern platform (and thence the lift). An angled causeway across the northeastern corner of the pond will provide this. It will lead from the northwestern platform (itself accessible from the top step), across the pond to the eastern part of the arena. Initially, though, it will appear to be part of the pond.

Draw the lines for this new sector and use Make Sector on it but do *not* use Make Sector to repair the pond sector. Notice how the addition of the new causeway sector has cut away a small corner of the original pond sector, isolating it from the main body of this sector. Ordinarily, this would be turned into a new sector, and given identical settings to the original. There is no need to do that though—DOOM does not insist that all parts of a sector be contiguous, merely closed.

There is nothing to prevent the small northeastern corner from belonging to the main pond sector. If you move the mouse cursor over the main pond sector with Make Sector active, you will see that the original lines of this corner piece do indeed light up at the same time.

Unfortunately, it is beyond the capabilities of Make Sector to find these isolated lines and gather them back into the fold, so you need to use Sec Define here instead. Before choosing Sec Define, though, you will need to enter LINES mode and make each of the new lines of the causeway sector two-sided by setting their two-sided flag. Then you can return to Draw mode, select Sec Define, right-click somewhere in the pond sector (even in the isolated northeastern corner), and then left-click each of the four new lines of the causeway sector in turn to add their left sides to the now disjunct pond sector.

Having done this, you should give the new causeway sector the same settings as the pond sector, making sure that both have a special characteristic of 7.

Finally, make the new angled piece into a suitable changer. Choose a convenient line to use as the trigger for this action—it doesn't matter which at the moment, because it is only a temporary arrangement to test the mechanism—and put a switch texture on it so that you will be able to find it easily when you play the WAD. Assign a special attribute of 20 to this line, tagging it to the causeway.

Special line-type 20 provides a switch-activated trigger-model changer that will raise the floor of the tagged sector to the next higher floor level. The floor texture of the sector on the right side of the trigger line is transferred to the sector that is moved. The special characteristic is not transferred but any existing special value is reset to 0.

The angled sector's next higher neighbor is the western platform sector. This sector therefore provides the new height for the moving sector's floor, just 16 units below the large eastern platform floor—sufficiently close to allow the player onto it.

The causeway's new floor texture will be whatever is on the right side of the switch-line that triggered the change. You can confirm this by putting a distinctive floor texture next to the switch and observing that the angled sector acquires it when it is activated. If you were to place the switch action on one of the pond's enclosing lines that has its right side facing into the pond, then the causeway's floor texture would not change as it rose. (I don't recommend that you do this—I'm merely pointing out possibilities!)

The harmful effect of the angled sector's special characteristic is nullified by the changer (whatever the role model is), making it safe for the player to walk across the new causeway.

The movement of the angled sector will generate some essential textures. Fix these by applying STARTAN1 to them.

TRYING OUT THE ADDITIONS

You are now ready to save the WAD (as WAD22.WAD) and try it out. Try running over the stepping-stones to the island and back. It's all fine as long as you keep moving, isn't it? Activate the causeway and confirm that it acquires the correct texture and becomes safe to walk over.

Did you manage to remember all of the essential textures? Figure 10.8 shows a view of the completed pond in my WAD22.WAD.

Figure 10.8.
Pond, causeway, and stepping-stones.

DRAGGING OTHERS ALONG

The final group of remote-controlled actions that produce moving sectors are the *entrainers*. These actions affect more than just their target sector.

DOOM'S DONUT

The first of the entrainers is, in effect, an extended changer. It works in a more complicated way than those described earlier, though. It is known as the *donut-eater* or *equalizer*. This action entrains an additional sector in its effect, as follows.

DOOM begins the action by inspecting all of the lines that make up the boundary of the tagged sector to find the linedef with the lowest number (the first-drawn line of this sector). If this line is single-sided, nothing further happens.

If the line is two-sided, however, DOOM inspects it to see which way it faces. If the right side faces *into* the tagged sector, then this sector's floor is moved to the level of the floor on the other side of the line. Motion downwards occurs at standard mover speed; movement upwards occurs instantaneously. Any special characteristic of the sector *adjacent* to the tagged sector is removed. The action is then at an end.

If, on the other hand, the first-drawn line's right side faces *away* from the tagged sector, then this neighboring sector is taken to be a "donut" sector. It is this sector that will be consumed (its settings, that is, not its extent; this will be explained shortly). Note that this sector doesn't actually

2
EPISODE

1
MISSION

10
ROOM

DOOM
PROGRAMMING
GURUS

need to be donut-shaped—it can be any shape at all—but it usually will be, with the tagged sector acting as the "hole" at the center. Figure 10.9 shows the usual arrangement: a central sector with a donut sector around it. The first-drawn line of the central sector is shown with its right-side tick.

Figure 10.9.
A DOOM donut.

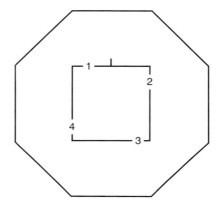

FINDING A ROLE MODEL

Having found a sector to be the donut, DOOM will proceed with the action by examining *this* sector to determine its lowest numbered linedef, *excluding* any that are shared with the original tagged sector. The sector on the other side of this further line (whichever way it faces) becomes a role model for the actions that follow.

USING THE ROLE MODEL

At this point, DOOM has all of the information it needs to consume its donut (you're relieved, I'll bet!). It does this by transferring the floor texture of the role model to the floor of the donut sector (*not* the original tagged sector, note), setting the donut's special characteristic to 0 at the same time.

Figure 10.10 illustrates this with a simple example: the central tagged sector acts as the hole to its surrounding sector's donut. This in turn supplies a role model through its lowest numbered linedef. The donut gains the role model's floor texture.

DOOM
PROGRAMMING
GURUS

10
ROOM

1
MISSION

2
EPISODE

Figure 10.10.
Consuming the donut.

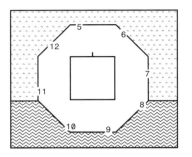
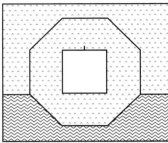

EQUALIZING THE FLOORS

At the same time as the floor texture and special characteristic are being changed, the game engine moves the donut sector's floor up to match the role model's. The original tagged sector's floor moves down to the same height. In common with all movers, any motion in the opposite direction to the one expected will occur instantaneously.

> If the engine does not find a role model for this action (because there is no sector on the other side of the donut's first-drawn line), all hell will break loose! Well, not quite, but random settings are taken for the role model—with suitably unpredictable consequences.

THE DONUT CONSUMED

The net result of this action is that both the tagged sector and its surrounding donut end up at the same floor height as the role-model sector—usually the sector that surrounds the donut itself. The donut's floor texture is changed and any harmful effect it had is nullified in the process. You have no doubt seen many instances of this effect in use. It is commonly employed to place goodies out of reach on a central platform, surrounded by a damaging sector, which is consumed when the appropriate switch is pressed.

Figures 10.11 and 10.12 show the result of a well-known donut-eater's action.

Figure 10.11.
Before....

Figure 10.12.
...and after.

IMPLEMENTING A DONUT-EATER

The easiest way to ensure that donut-eaters work correctly is to draw the whole structure at one time. The steps in the process are:

1. Start by drawing the complete inner donut-hole. The first line you draw must have its right side facing out from this sector, so draw this sector in a counter-clockwise manner.

2. Draw the outer donut sector next, starting with the line that will border the sector that is to act as role model.

3. Avoid splitting any of these lines in future edits. Most editors will assign new (later) line numbers to the new lines so created—this can mess up DOOM's identification of both the donut sector and its role model.

4. Locate a suitable switch line for the action: the donut-eater is only available as a single activation, space-bar-operated action. Tag this line to the inner donut-hole sector. Set the line's special attribute to the value 9.

FAULTY DONUTS

There are a number of problems that can occur to stop the donut from operating correctly. The causes of the commoner faults are listed in Table 10.4.

Table 10.4. Common donut faults and their causes.

Symptom	Cause
The switch refuses to operate.	The switch is not tagged to any sector; or the lowest-numbered line of the tagged sector is single-sided.
Only the tagged sector moves (although the donut sector loses its damaging effect).	The lowest-numbered line of the tagged sector has its right side facing in.
The donut operates but finishes at the wrong level and/or with the wrong floor texture.	The lowest-numbered line of the donut sector borders the wrong sector.

SELF-RAISING STAIRS

DOOM's other entraining action is the self-raising staircase. This action drags further sectors along with it, using an entraining method similar to the donut-eater's.

FINDING THE STEPS

The action starts, as always, with the tagged sector. This sector will become the first step of a new staircase. DOOM then looks for a two-sided line that has its right side facing into the tagged sector. If there are more than one of these, the one with lowest number is taken. The sector on the other side of this line becomes the second step of the staircase.

This process is repeated until one of the following conditions occurs:

- No two-sided line has a right side facing into the current sector.
- A sector is met with a different floor texture.
- A sector is encountered that is already part of this action.
- A sector is encountered that is currently locked out of floor height changes.

The sectors selected by this process all take part in the action that follows.

Figure 10.13 illustrates this entrainment process in operation. In each case, the sector marked with the solid circle is the initial tagged sector. The upper part of the figure shows a simple arrangement of sectors. The action's selection of sectors is brought to a halt by the lack of further inward-facing right sides after four sectors.

Figure 10.13.
The entraining of sectors in a rising staircase action.

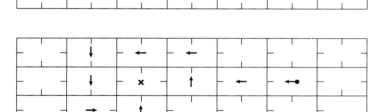

The lower portion of the figure shows a more complicated arrangement of sectors. The entrainment process has been made easier to follow here by careful manipulation of the way the lines face. Each participating sector has only one two-sided line with its right side facing into it—an arrangement that is recommended you adopt when building these structures yourself. Notice how the selection of sectors in the lower example is terminated when a sector that is already part of the action is revisited.

MOVING THE STEPS

The tagged sector's floor provides the reference height from which all of the other sectors' final floor heights are calculated. This first sector will be raised by a standard step-height—8 or 16 units, depending upon the type of staircase in use—from its starting position. Each sector in the sequence after this will finish one step-height above the previous.

Once the sectors for the entire staircase have been located, and their final floor heights are determined, DOOM starts the floors of all these sectors moving simultaneously, accompanied by appropriate sound effects. The result is a block of sectors moving together, with each successive sector stopping as its floor reaches its allotted height.

Any sectors of the staircase that start out above their finishing height are moved to their new height instantaneously.

Self-raising stairs will operate as crushing floors, doing harm to anything caught in the closing gap between their floor and ceiling. They are also capable of driving their floors up through their ceilings; it is probably not a good idea to let them.

BUILDING SELF-RAISING STAIRWAYS

From their description, self-raising stairs may sound complex to build. In reality, they are generally quite easy. The main steps (sorry!) involved are as follows:

1. Draw the sectors for the staircase, starting with the bottom step and working upwards.

2. Again starting from the bottom step, select each sector in turn, making sure that the line bordering the next step in the sequence has its right side facing into the selected sector. Make sure that all other two-sided lines have their right sides facing out from the sector. This saves you from having to worry about the numbering of lines, which is often beyond your control anyway. Leave single-sided lines with their right sides facing in, of course.

3. Make sure that all of the two-sided lines of the last sector in the sequence have their right sides facing into *other* sectors.

4. Make sure that all the sectors of the staircase have the same floor texture.

5. Decide on a suitable activation line for the staircase. You can use either a switch or a trigger. Set this line's special attribute to the appropriate value. (See Table 10.5.)

6. Tag the trigger line to the first sector to move: the bottom step of the staircase.

If you find that your staircase fails to operate correctly, check the direction of all of its lines—and watch out for those floor-texture changes!

SUMMARY OF LINE-TYPES FOR ENTRAINERS

Table 10.5 gives the codes for the donut-eater and self-raising stair actions.

Table 10.5. Entrainer codes.

Action	Activation Category			
	W1	WR	S1	SR
Donut-eater	–	–	9	–
8-unit, slow stairs	8	–	7	–
16-unit, turbo stairs	100*	–	127*	–

*Turbo stairs are only available in DOOM v1.666 and above.

WAD SORTIE 23: USING ENTRAINERS

This Sortie builds on the WAD produced in the previous one. If you did not produce that WAD, you should use WAD22.WAD (DOOM) or D2WAD22.WAD (DOOM II) from the CD-ROM as your starting point here.

This Sortie will develop the eastern end of the outdoor crescent-shaped area that lies beyond your blue-keyed door. It adds a new room with a donut-eater; a self-raising stairway will also provide another connection to the embryonic maze area.

ADDING THE DONUT-EATER

Figure 10.14 shows the general location of a new room, at the eastern edge of your WAD.

The new room will be entered through a short passageway, connected (via a new keyed door) to an alcove area towards the eastern end of the crescent. Figure 10.15 shows all the new lines needed for this area, with the cursor arrow pointing to the southeastern corner of the sector that will become the donut.

Figure 10.14.

The general location of the new room.

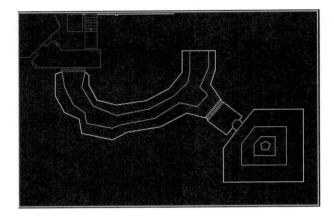

Figure 10.15.

Detailed lines for the environs of the donut-eater.

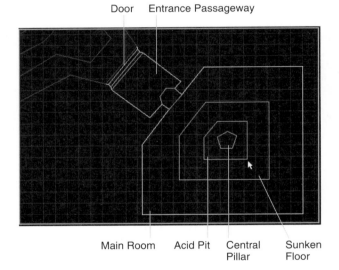

ADDING THE NEW DOOR AND ENTRANCE PASSAGE

Start this new development by building a red-keyed door off the crescent. It should have outer and inner recesses, as usual. Make the door as close to 256 units wide as you can for best alignment of the door texture. Don't forget to apply suitable textures to the side-walls of the recess to tell the player that the door needs a key. Use BIGDOOR2 on the door itself.

Next draw the two sectors of the entrance passageway. Use GRAYVINE on the walls of the larger of these, DOORBLU2 on the short walls of the small one beyond.

2 EPISODE   **1** MISSION   **10** ROOM   DOOM PROGRAMMING GURUS

THE DONUT ROOM

Next, draw all the new lines for the main room and donut. Use GRAY7 as the default line-drawing texture for the outer walls of the room. When you come to make sectors here, start with the central one and work outwards.

Table 10.6 gives the settings for all of the new sectors in this area. Note that some of the sectors use special characteristics—mostly of a damaging variety.

Table 10.6. Sector settings in the new area.

Area	Special	Lighting		Ceiling		Floor
Outer door recess	0	176	128	FLOOR7_1	0	FLAT1_2
Door	0	128	0	FLOOR7_1	0	FLOOR7_1
Inner door recess	13	224	128	FLOOR7_1	−8	FLOOR7_1
Outer passageway	0	128	120	FLAT22	−16	FLOOR7_1
Connecting sector	4	240	88	FWATER1	−40	FWATER2
Main area of room	0	176	168	FWATER3	−24	FLAT14
Sunken floor area	0	192	168	FWATER3	−48	FLAT14
Acid pit	16	192	168	FWATER3	−80	FWATER1
Central pillar	0	240	168	FWATER3	32	FLOOR1_1

Use GRAY1 on all essential textures, except for the lowers of the central pillar. Put GRAYDANG on a couple of these.

> DOOM II does not have GRAYDANG. Stay with GRAY1.

DOOM II NOTE

Finally, split one of the room's outer walls by adding another vertex 64 units from one of the corners, and put the SW1GRAY texture on the new short length of wall. (Don't worry about the alignment and vertical repetition of this texture—it is only a temporary arrangement.) Set the special attribute of this line to 9 (S1: Donut) and tag it to the central pillar sector. Make sure that all of the lines of the central pillar face out—this saves the worry about which is the lowest numbered—and that's the donut-eater made. Simple, in the end, wasn't it?

Before adding the stairs, you may want to save the WAD (as WAD23.WAD) and try out the donut-eater.

SELF-RAISING STAIRS

The area with a self-raising staircase will also be off the crescent-shaped courtyard. It will connect this courtyard to the embryonic maze area. Figure 10.16 shows what I am planning here.

Figure 10.16.
Connection from the crescent to the maze.

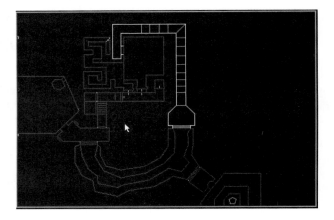

ADDING A NEW DOOR

Start by adding another red-keyed door off the currently closed northeastern end of the crescent, drawn to match the door's blue counterpart at the other end with BIGDOOR2 on the door face, and suitable recesses. You may need to rearrange the end of the crescent a little to get the door 256 units wide and to have it line up properly for a connection beyond it. Figure 10.17 shows a close-up view of the new door, with recesses outside, on the crescent side of the door, and inside next to a funnel-shaped entrance for a passageway.

Make the new door operate by using a special attribute of 28 (MR: Red Door: open and close) on the outer side, facing the crescent. The door should be one-way, however, so put no special attribute on its other, inner face. Use the DOORSTOP on the side walls of the inner recess as an indicator that the door doesn't open from this side. Then draw and make the sector beyond the inner recess using STONE2 as the default texture. Apply the settings in Table 10.7 to the sectors you have so far.

Figure 10.17.
Details for the new door.

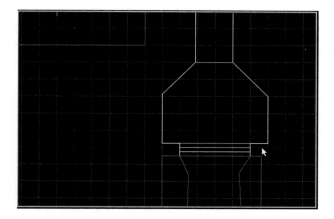

Table 10.7. Sector settings for the end of the crescent.

Area	Lighting		Ceiling		Floor
Outer door recess	144	144	CEIL3_5	0	FLAT1_2
Door	144	0	CEIL3_5	0	FLAT5_5
Inner door recess	128	112	FLAT10	0	FLAT5_5
Funnel-shaped sector	112	128	FLAT10	0	FLAT5_5

CONSTRUCTING THE CORRIDOR AND STAIRS

Figure 10.18 shows the number and arrangement of sectors beyond the funnel-shaped corridor section. They should all be drawn with the STONE2 wall texture.

Make the first of these sectors, setting its lighting level to 96. All of its other settings should be the same as the neighboring funnel-shaped sector. This is to be the first step of the self-raising stairway.

You can now start making the other steps. Note that the number of sectors used here is important, if the fully risen staircase is to end at the correct height. Another twelve sectors will be used, so that the final floor height of the top step will be 13×8 = 104 units above the current floor height.

Draw and make the next five sectors, taking the ceiling of the last of these up to 160 to increase the headroom available here. Then make the additional sectors up to the corner, where the ceiling needs to go up again, this time to 192. Make the last four staircase sectors, once again taking the ceiling up on the last of these, this time to 224. Notice how the ceilings here rise steadily to prevent the player from being crushed as the stairs rise. The increment used for the ceiling step is 32 units to ensure that the wall texture (which has a 32-pixel pattern repeat) stays aligned.

Figure 10.18.

Sectors for a corridor with self-raising stairs.

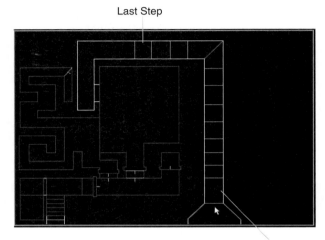

Last Step

First Step

Now draw and make the last of the corridor sectors, taking its ceiling up to 256. This sector will not be part of the rising staircase, so its floor needs to be at a suitable height. Set it to 112 to match the floor of the maze area close by. The top step will end its movement just 8 units below this, leaving a final step up to the end corridor section.

Now, to make the staircase work, go into LINES mode and select the line marking the entrance into the narrow area of the corridor. (The cursor arrow is pointing to this line in Figure 10.18.) Put a special attribute of 8 (W1 Stairs: 8-unit rising) on here, tagging the line to the first step sector to its north. Check that this line has its right side facing into the sector to its south, otherwise you will find the wrong sector becomes entrained into the raising staircase.

If you now examine all of the lines marking the risers for the remaining steps of the staircase, you should find that they already have their right sides facing into the step below them. This is what you want. Put STEP3 on the right lower texture slots of all of these risers—they are latent essentials, remember. The line connecting the last step with the end section of the corridor needs to be flipped so that its right side faces away from the last moving step. This will end the entrainment of sectors into the rising stair. Put STONE2 on the essentials of this line. Locate the lines where you changed the ceiling height, and put STONE2 on the upper essentials here, too.

2
EPISODE

1
MISSION

10
ROOM

DOOM
PROGRAMMING
GURUS

That completes the construction of the staircase, but you need to finish off the area before you can try it out.

COMPLETING THE CORRIDOR

Make a short sector to connect your new corridor to the right half of the maze area. You will find that as you do this, the new sector inherits a tag. Don't worry about this; this is what you want it to do. This sector's lighting level will now follow the right-half of the maze's. Set the new sector's ceiling to 112 (the same as its floor) and put a special attribute of 1 (MR Door: open and close) on the corridor face of this new door. Remember that this line-type does not need to be tagged to a sector, but it does need the line to face the correct way.

Put texture STONE3 on its upper texture facing the corridor (with a Y-offset of 16. You want a slight change of texture, not a lurch in the alignment.). Use a CRATE texture on the other side of the door, so that it is not noticeable from the maze. Do not provide any method of opening the door from this side, however, because I do not want the player to be able to leave the maze by this route. Complete the door by setting its side walls' lower unpegged flags, again using Y-offsets of 16.

MAKING AN EXIT FROM THE MAZE

This completes the additions to the map. Given the right keys, a player can now pass through the crescent section, up the new stairs, and into the maze—only to become trapped, of course, at the top of the marble stairs.

Let us arrange for players entering the maze by this route to trigger the removal of the impediment of the one-way stairs. You will recall that the trap on this staircase was created by placing two ceilings at special heights. We need, therefore, something to trigger the raising of these ceilings. Line-type 40 provides a walk-through action which raises a ceiling to the height of its highest adjacent ceiling. Position two of these triggers as you feel appropriate on suitable risers of the new back stairs into the maze.

Special line-type 40 is incorrectly categorized in WADED. It can be found in the FLOORS-3 list!

You will need to order these triggers correctly and space them out sufficiently to allow one ceiling to have moved fully before the other is triggered. And you will have to tag them to the correct marble staircase sectors, of course. Don't forget, too, that this will create a latent essential texture some-where on the marble stairs. Use MARBLE1 on this.

When you've done this, you can save the WAD (as WAD23A.WAD) and try it out.

SUGGESTED FURTHER MODIFICATIONS

There are a number of additional modifications that spring to mind for the areas you have just added.

MAKING THE STAIRS LESS OBVIOUS

You can make the presence of the corridor containing the rising stairs less obvious by raising the floor of the first step to 48. (You'll have an essential texture to deal with if you do this.) Use a special line-type of 23 (S1 Floor: lower to next adjacent) on one of the short walls adjacent to the door (the cursor arrow points to this in Figure 10.17, shown previously) with a suitable texture (SW1SATYR, perhaps?) and tagged to the newly-raised sector.

A LITTLE JOKE?

To balance up the areas around the door, you may wish to use the same (or another) switch texture on the other wall at the side of the door. There isn't much for this switch to do, but line-type 41 (S1 Ceiling: move to floor) tagged to the inner door-recess would convince the player that there really is no way out here. If you add this modification, change the upper texture over the recess to BROWN144 to match better with SW1SATYR, and set a couple of lower unpegged flags. In addi-tion, you will need to tag this sector to another trigger to raise it again, in case the player ever comes back through the door from the other side! You can do that by adding a trigger of type 40 (W1 Ceiling: raise to highest adjacent) to one of the stair risers.

TIDYING THE MARBLE STAIRS

Raising the ceilings to remove the one-way stair trap leaves the stairway's walls a little messy. You might want to try tidying them up. Anything you do will be a compromise, however—it's just about impossible to have this perfect for all contingencies here.

The example WAD23B.WAD (or D2WAD23B.WAD for DOOM II) on the accompanying CD-ROM has these modifications added.

EXIT: MOPPING UP AND MOVING ON

In this room, you learned about the most complex of DOOM's active sectors. You have learned how sectors behave when they are asked to move together; you have learned about role model emulation by sectors that move and change; and you have seen and used crusher chains, moving and changing platforms, donut-eaters, and self-raising stairs in your own WAD. In fact, you have now seen all of the active line-types that DOOM provides for sector movement and change.

The next room, "Let's Get the Hell Out of Here!", will present the few remaining special line-types—those that act on the player, rather than on elements of the map. Its WAD Sorties will have you adding some of the final components of the DOOM world to your almost completed WAD.

DOOM
PROGRAMMING
GURUS

10
ROOM

1
MISSION

2
EPISODE

ROOM 11

By Steve Benner

LET'S GET THE HELL OUT OF HERE!

The last few rooms have all concentrated on special line attributes that cause changes in targeted sectors. This room will look at the few remaining special types of lines and also revisit the sector's special characteristic. None of the actions examined in this room result in changes to sectors, however; they all act on players, monsters, or both.

The WAD that has been building in previous rooms will be developed further in this room in three more Sorties. The first of these will finally add an escape route to the embryonic maze area added several Sorties ago. The second of this room's Sorties will add an exit to the WAD as a whole, while the last will sort out the awarding of credits for the discovery of the WAD's secrets.

This room starts, though, with a trip through DOOM's teleport (also known as the "transporter").

TELEPORTS

You will already be familiar, no doubt, with the way a DOOM teleport operates: the player steps into it, vanishes, and rematerializes somewhere else. You have probably guessed by now that a teleport's action is provided by yet another special type of line. This is indeed the case. DOOM needs rather more than just the line, though, to implement a functioning teleport.

COMPONENTS OF A TELEPORT

To build a teleport, three things are required:

- **A teleport trigger line:** This is the line that the player steps over to "enter" the teleport and trigger the transportation action.
- **A destination sector:** This is where the player rematerializes.
- **A landing spot:** This marks the precise location within the destination sector where the rematerialization takes place.

Each of these three items must be in place and properly set up for a teleport to operate. Let us look at how each of these three items is provided.

TELEPORT TRIGGERS

Teleport triggers are provided through special line-types. (As the only really active component of a teleport, these lines are often just termed "teleporters.") Table 11.1 gives the codes for the various teleport triggers that are available.

Table 11.1. Codes for teleport triggers.

Action	Activation Category	
	W1	WR
Player/monster teleport	39	97
Monster only teleport	125*	126*
* Monster-only teleports are available only in DOOM v1.666 and above.		

These triggers act much like any other walk-through trigger line, with the action taking place as it is crossed. The familiar teleport "pads" are simply sectors with all of their passable boundaries set up as teleport triggers. When anything steps into the sector, it crosses an active line and is whisked away to the appropriate destination. This arrangement creates the illusion that the pad itself is active.

Unlike other walk-through actions, teleport lines can only be triggered from one side: their right. If you think about it, this makes a lot of sense. It allows a teleport pad to act as the destination from another teleport (a common arrangement) without having one of that pad's own teleport lines transport the player somewhere else as soon as they try to step from it.

To make a teleport pad active on entry and not on exit, all of its active lines should be arranged with their right sides facing out from the pad sector.

TELEPORT DESTINATION SECTOR

Like other special lines, each teleport trigger needs be tagged to a sector—in this case, to act as a destination. Each trigger should be tagged to only one sector; a player cannot be sent to multiple destinations simultaneously. If a trigger is tagged to more than one sector, DOOM will take the lowest-numbered one to be the destination.

It is possible, however, to have more than one teleport trigger tagged to the same sector. This allows all of a teleport pad's active lines (or, indeed, several different teleports) to deliver to the same location.

TELEPORT LANDINGS

DOOM needs to know more than just the sector in which rematerialization will occur, though—it needs the precise spot. This is marked by the placing of a special category of Thing within the destination sector: the teleport landing. Each teleport destination sector must have one of these, or the teleport will not operate.

Teleport landings use the same attributes and flags as all other categories of Thing. The facing-angle attribute is used to determine which way players and monsters will face as they materialize. The skill-level flags can be used to indicate whether individual teleport landings are present (or absent) at particular difficulty settings of the game. DOOM will only consider those present at the game's current skill setting when looking for a particular teleporter's destination. This can be used to vary the precise location (and/or facing) of a teleport landing with skill setting, although this variation can only take place within the one sector, of course.

If a destination sector contains more than one teleport landing, the one with the lowest number (usually the first placed) will be used. If no teleport landing can be located within the destination sector at the game's current skill setting, the teleport remains inactive.

BUILDING A TELEPORT

Here is a summary of the steps involved in implementing a fully operational teleport:

1. Choose a line or lines to act as the teleport trigger. If you are using a particular area as a teleport pad (and you don't have to, of course), then make sure that you use all of the passable lines surrounding the pad—unless you want players and/or monsters to be able to walk onto the pad from some directions without teleporting.

2. Flip all of the chosen trigger lines so that their right sides face the direction from which you want the line to be triggered. Typically, this will mean that all of the passable lines surrounding a teleport pad will have their right sides facing out.

3. Place a teleport landing where you want materialization to occur. Make sure there is sufficient head-room for players to arrive at this spot. Decide which way you want players and monsters to be facing when they arrive here and adjust the teleport landing's facing angle to suit.

4. Tag each of the teleporter lines to the sector containing the teleport landing.

These are the essential steps in producing a functioning teleport. You can, of course, arrange for more complex teleport pads that have their component triggers tagged to different sectors. Such teleports will then deliver to differing locations depending upon which line is crossed.

TELEPORT TRAPPINGS

Teleports may be as conspicuous or as invisible as you feel is appropriate in your WAD. It is often a good idea to mark teleport destination points with distinctive patterns, especially in WADs that are

designed for multi-player use. This provides players with at least some warning of potential tele-frag spots and discourages them from lingering there.

If you want your teleports to *look* like teleports, the GATE_ series of flats provides the classic set of ceiling and floor textures used in id Software's own levels. (See Figure 11.1.) There is no special trick to the use of these. Simply make your teleport pads a standard 64-units square, aligned precisely along grid lines.

Figure 11.1.
The GATE series of floor/ceiling textures.

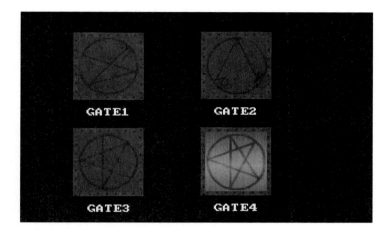

GATE4 tends to be used for teleporter landing pads that are not themselves active teleports; but there is, of course, no requirement that it be used in this way.

MONSTERS IN TELEPORTS

DOOM v1.666's monster-only teleporters are useful for enabling monsters to move around a WAD in a way that prevents players from following them. A discussion of the use of these, and other useful techniques for using teleports as monster-laden traps, appears in the next room, "Populating Your DOOM World."

The following WAD Sortie builds on the WAD produced in the last Sortie of the previous room. If you did not accompany me on that Sortie but would like to come along on this one, you should use WAD23B.WAD (DOOM) or D2WAD23B.WAD (DOOM II) from the CD-ROM as your starting point.

WAD SORTIE 24: USING TELEPORTS

Teleports are useful devices for getting players out of sticky situations without requiring a lot of additions to a WAD. To demonstrate this, this Sortie shows you how to add a simple way out of the maze. After that, I'll also show you how to use teleporter lines to make life a little trickier for the players.

A STRAIGHTFORWARD TELEPORT

Let us start by adding a teleport as an exit from the maze for players who have entered via the one-way marble staircase. Decide where you would like this to be. I've put mine at the end of one of the twisting areas in the left part of the maze, as shown in Figure 11.2, but it could be almost anywhere. All it needs is a single 64 x 64-unit grid square.

Figure 11.2.
Location for a teleporter in the maze.

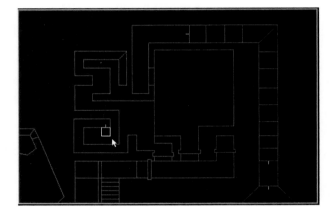

Be careful how you add to the maze, by the way. It is easy to wreck the special lighting operations here. If you add lines internally across an existing sector, you should incorporate the new lines into it using Sec Define, rather than with Make Sector. This will ensure that the sequence of sector numbers isn't changed. (Grouped-sector lighting effects are sensitive to this, remember.)

When you have your new teleport sector properly defined, apply appropriate settings to it—you will need to use a lighting value of 144 to keep the lighting tricks working, remember—with one of the GATE_ textures on the floor and the ceiling. Use whatever wall textures you fancy, wherever they are needed.

Next, make sure that all of the entrance lines to your new sector have their right sides facing out from it. Put line-type 97 (WR: Teleport) on them all, tagged to a suitable destination sector. This could be anywhere, but I feel it should be somewhere that the player has already visited, so that the teleport is viewed as a means of escape from the stair-trap, not as a way on to new locations. I recommend using the starting sector—the hexagonal room.

Finally, switch to THINGS mode, and select the Teleports category. Place a teleport landing somewhere in the destination sector. Save the WAD as WAD24.WAD, and then give it a whirl!

Teleport landings are termed *teleport destinations* in WADED.

SOME TELEPORT TRICKS

A more elaborate arrangement of teleports can be used to make whatever is located within the donut rather harder to obtain. Figure 11.3 shows five new areas around the sides of the donut room.

Figure 11.3.
New areas around the donut room.

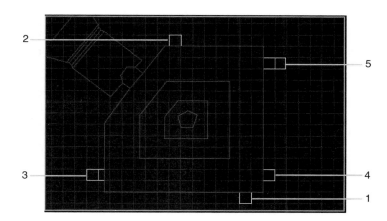

These new areas use an array of teleporters and switches to provide the player with a little puzzle. This operates as follows:

1. The switch to operate the donut-eater is in plain view on the rear wall of this alcove. This is also the only alcove that the player can enter from the floor of the room. All of the others are either raised too high or are hidden behind doors. The problem is that the entrance line to this alcove is a teleporter line. As players enter, they are immediately transported to Area 2, without any hope of reaching the switch.

2. This alcove has a switch on its rear wall to activate a small sector adjacent to Area 3 as a lift. The player will have to run across the room to catch this lift before it goes back up. The floor heights of areas 2 and 3 are such that the player cannot enter either of them from the main room's floor.

3. This area can only be entered using the lift activated from Area 2. The alcove contains no switch, but it does have a teleport trigger across its entrance from the lift, which transfers the player to Area 4.

4. This alcove houses another switch, this time to raise the door that has been hiding Area 5 (and which is not in view from here!). The player has five seconds to find it and get through it, before it closes.

5. Behind the secret door raised by the switch in Area 4, is another teleporter. This takes the player (finally!) back to Area 1 so that he may now press the switch to consume the donut—provided he can still remember what he was trying to achieve after all that.

Implementation of this puzzle is not complicated, merely a little tricky to keep track of. Start by drawing and making each of the new areas. Area 5's two floors should both be at the same height as the main room floor. Set the floor height for the first alcove 24 units higher; all of the others need to be even higher so that they cannot be entered directly. Choose the remaining sector settings for yourself. You may wish to consider how many of the teleports you want to have looking like teleports. Make sure you leave enough headroom for players not to become stuck when they materialize.

Use suitable members of the GRAY series of wall textures (with appropriate pegging) for all of the new walls. There are a couple of suitable switch textures to choose from. Don't forget that the door in front of Area 5 needs to be hidden. Careless texture alignment will give its location away.

Work round each of the switch and teleporter lines, placing appropriate special attributes and tags, making sure that each of the teleporter lines faces the correct way. Be sure to use repeatable actions for each of the switches that require the player to run to complete the next stage of the puzzle. Also, don't forget to disconnect (and hide) the temporary switch for the donut-eater before connecting in the real one.

Finally, place teleport landings in each of the destination sectors. Arrange these so that they face out from the alcoves, into the room. This means that the switches will always be behind the player as they materialize. Figure 11.4 shows the location of each of the teleport landings required. Note that the numbers in this figure show which of the areas in Figure 11.3 have trigger lines tagged to the indicated sector.

Figure 11.4.

Teleport destinations and other tagged sectors in the donut room.

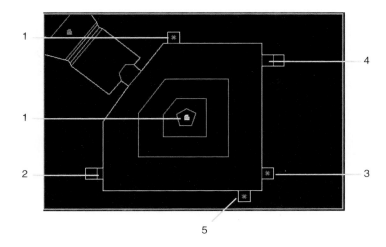

Notice that I've also added a key as the reward for solving the puzzle—a yellow one.

Save the WAD as WAD24A.WAD and see how well you did. Did you solve the puzzle of building it? How well does it play? Make whatever adjustments and changes you feel are necessary before going on. You might like, for instance, to reverse the way that the teleporter line of Area 3 faces. This will enable players to enter the sector without being teleported immediately. They will then probably hunt around in vain for some switch. Only when they give up and decide to leave will they be teleported on.

> Readers with DOOM v1.666 or later may like to make this room harder by using the turbo lift and door actions.

ENDING THE LEVEL

The final category of special line-types are the exits. These bring about the termination of the level in progress, displaying the appropriate intermission screen, with its tally of kills and so on. In addition to using special lines, DOOM also has another method of ending a level. Before looking at that, though, let us examine the way lines are used to signal the exit from a level.

EXIT SWITCHES AND TRIGGERS

DOOM provides two mechanisms for ending a level with lines: a walk-through exit, and a switch-activated exit. Naturally, these lines can only be activated once. Table 11.2 gives the codes that are available for producing exits.

Table 11.2. Exit codes.

Exit type	Activation Category	
	W1	S1
Standard exit	52	11
Secret exit	124*	51

* The walk-through secret exit is only available in DOOM v1.666 and later.

STANDARD EXITS

Standard exits take the player to the next higher level number (after the intermission screen) except for the last mission of the episode, of course, which ends the episode. Mission 8 is the last of each DOOM episode; Level 30 ends DOOM II. If an external patch WAD does not contain the subsequent map, DOOM will load the original from the IWAD file.

SECRET EXITS

Secret exits take the player on to the appropriate secret level (again, after the intermission screen). In DOOM, this is always Mission 9 of the current episode; in DOOM II it is either Level 31 or 32, depending upon which "half" of the game the current map is in.

All exits from the secret missions are hard-coded to return the player to the same subsequent map as in the original game.

FATAL EXITS

A final way of ending a level is provided through one of the special sector characteristics—11. This setting applies the high rate of damage to reduce the health of a player in the sector. When it falls below 11 percent, the level ends. Most WADs make it impossible to escape such a sector, to ensure that the mission does indeed end as a consequence of the player reaching this spot.

Although this action operates as a standard exit, taking the player on to the next mission, it makes more sense to use it as a device to end a complete episode—just as id Software does.

THE NEED FOR EXITS

It is desirable for all levels (especially those intended for single-player use) to have an exit; otherwise players will not know whether they have completed it or not. This may sound trivial, but remember that it is only through triggering an exit action that players are given their tally. Without this tally, they will not know whether all secret locations have been found, all monsters disposed of, or all goodies collected. Such things are less important in WADs designed primarily for Deathmatch play, but most players still like to see exits and use them to end the game.

Exits are also vital in multi-level WADs, of course, to enable the player to progress to the next mission. You can have as many exits in each map as you consider necessary.

MAKING EXITS OBVIOUS

In most players' view, it is also important that the role of a switch that ends a level should be obvious *before* it is pressed. There is nothing more frustrating than pressing a switch that you have fought hard to gain in the belief that it opens a door, only to discover that it ends the level instead! Few players will be impressed with exits such as this.

Once again, the designers at id Software have provided several textures for you to use to make your exits conspicuous. The most obvious is, of course, the large red exit sign. Less obvious, perhaps, but still recognizable to most DOOM players, is the distinctive techno-door texture that id Software's designers use on the doors to most of their exit anterooms. This is the EXITDOOR texture, shown in Figure 11.5.

Notice how this texture is a multi-function texture, by the way. The pattern for the face of the door only takes up one half of the pattern; the remainder includes three additional textures. These are intended for use on the reveals of the recesses to either side of the door. Figure 11.6 shows these in use. Note the symmetrical form of the patterns to the side of the door.

The pattern for the left reveal is obtained by using an X-offset of 64 pixels into the EXITDOOR texture; the pattern for the right reveal appears when an X-offset of 88 pixels is used. The lines for each reveal must be precisely 24 units long, of course, to take these patterns. If the lines are too long, the patterns will not repeat; there will merely be spill-over into the next part of the texture.

Figure 11.5.
The EXITDOOR wall texture.

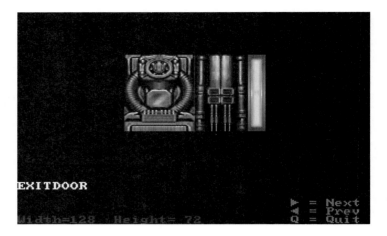

Figure 11.6.
EXITDOOR textures in use.

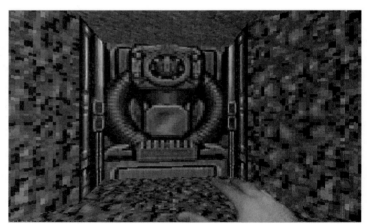

The last 16 pixels of the EXITDOOR texture provide an additional lighting-panel pattern. Use an X-offset of −16 to apply this to any suitably sized line. Incidentally, notice that the EXITDOOR texture is only 72 pixels high. It will therefore not tile correctly if applied to spaces that are too high for it.

WAD SORTIE 25: ADDING AN EXIT

> This Sortie builds on the WAD produced in the previous one. If you did not produce that
> WAD, you should use WAD24A.WAD (DOOM) or D2WAD24A.WAD (DOOM II)
> from the CD-ROM as your starting point here.

This WAD Sortie will add an exit to your WAD to enable a player to end the level and move on to
the next. This exit will be located in an area off the outdoor crescent, just to the west of the donut
room. It will be located beyond a new yellow-keyed door, requiring the player to successfully complete the donut-room's puzzle before being permitted to leave this level. Figure 11.7 shows the location and form of this new area.

Figure 11.7.
The exit from the level.

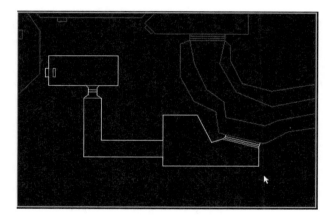

BUILDING THE WAY OUT

THE APPROACH

Start by building a yellow-keyed door off the southwest end of the outdoor crescent. Use suitable
recesses, a door width of 256 units and BIGDOOR2 on the door itself to match all of the other doors
off this area. Then use whatever wall textures and sector settings you feel are appropriate for the
areas beyond the door—an open chamber and a corridor leading on towards the exit room itself. My
WAD (WAD25.WAD or D2WAD25.WAD) used ASHWALL for the walls of the chamber and
STONE2 for the corridor. The corridor floor is 16 units below the chamber floor and has a much
lower ceiling. I've also set the lighting levels quite low.

DOOM
PROGRAMMING
GURUS

11
ROOM

1
MISSION

2
EPISODE

The corridor ends in a funnel-shaped sector (see Figure 11.8) that is designed to bring the corridor width down to 64 units and the height down to 72 to enable the EXITDOOR texture to be used on the door ahead. (The cursor arrow points to the face of this door in Figure 11.8.)

Figure 11.8.

Close-up of lines for the exit door and final room.

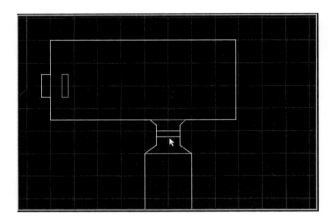

EXIT ANTEROOM, WITH CHARACTERISTIC DOOR

The two walls of the funnel-shaped recess sector use the EXITDOOR texture on them where they abut the door. The lines for these have been made 24 pixels long (they run north-south aligned to make this easier to arrange) and have the appropriate X-offsets to use the symmetrical door-reveal patterns of this texture, as previously discussed. The face of the door itself also carries the EXITDOOR texture on its upper texture slot. Figure 11.6, shown previously, is, in fact, a view of this door in my WAD25.WAD. Both sides of this door should be of special type 1 (MR Door: open and close).

Beyond the door (and an inner door-recess sector) is the main exit anteroom itself. The recess on this side of this door has short walls abutting the door sector. These are 16 units long and use the right-most portion of the EXITDOOR texture. The short lines that connect the inner recess to the main anteroom use the STONE2 texture, as do the rest of the walls beyond the door.

Ceiling and floor heights for the areas around the door to the anteroom are given in Table 11.3. You may need to adjust these (or those of the approach areas to the south) to provide a better tie-in with your corridor. The room heights should be maintained if you want the wall textures to align correctly.

Table 11.3. Ceiling and floor heights for main exit anteroom and door.

Area	Ceiling level	Floor level	Height
Recess south of exit door	48	–24	72
Exit door	–24	–24	0
Recess north of exit door	48	–24	72
Exit anteroom	72	–32	104

THE EXIT SWITCH

The switch that will trigger the end of the level is placed in an alcove in the western wall of the anteroom. This is a standard 64-unit wide switch alcove with the SW1STON1 texture on its back wall, with its lower unpegged flag set. The alcove should be 72 units high, with the same floor height as the rest of the room. Place a special attribute of 11 (S1: Exit) on this line. No tagging is necessary. This creates the exit switch.

AN EXIT SIGN

The fact that this is an exit switch needs to be signalled to the player. The EXITSTON texture could be used on the wall over the alcove—it provides the red EXIT lettering on the appropriate stone texture—but I prefer a sign suspended from the ceiling. To make this, another sector is needed, just east of the switch alcove. This sector should be 64 pixels wide by 16 pixels deep and located close to the western wall as seen in Figure 11.8, shown previously.

This sector has the same settings as the main room, except for the ceiling, which has been lowered 16 units to create a set of essential upper textures around it. The 16-pixel high EXITSIGN texture is used on all of these essentials, with X-offsets applied so that the appropriate parts of this multi-function texture appear correctly on each face (–16 on all faces).

FINISHING OFF

Finally, to save you from having to run around like crazy in the donut room to acquire the yellow keycard just to test this new area out, place another one in the crescent by the yellow-keyed door. Save the WAD as WAD25.WAD, and then go try it out. You should now be able to progress from your WAD to the standard second level of the game.

SECRET AREAS

Amongst the items reported on a level's final tally screen is the percentage of the secret areas of the map that the player successfully located. You may have noticed that no matter how many of your own "secret" areas you visit when you play your WAD, your secret tally is always 0 percent when you trip the exit switch. This is because DOOM does not yet know that your level has any secrets!

MAKING SECRET AREAS

You have seen the ways in which areas can be kept hidden from players. However, simply hiding doors and other entrance points to these areas does not make them "secret" as far as DOOM is concerned. An area's secret nature must be notified to the game engine if it is to be included in the reckoning of the final tally. This is done by setting a sector's special characteristic to the value 9. A player entering a sector with this special value will be credited with the discovery of a secret area.

Note that the use of their special characteristic in this way precludes such secret sectors from possessing other special characteristics, such as fluctuating light levels or damaging properties.

TALLYING SECRETS

The game engine calculates the final tally of secrets that have been located by counting up the total number of sectors with a special characteristic of 9 and determining what proportion of these have been entered by the player during the game.

To provide the player with a useful indication of what proportion of secret locations have been found, you should apply the secret credit characteristic carefully. Generally, you should only use one occurrence of the special value for each *area* that is hidden. Remember that players are generally unaware of the distribution of sectors—they see only rooms and such like. A room consisting of three sectors behind a hidden door should not grant more than one secret credit.

Furthermore, credits should be awarded sooner rather than later. The best location would be either the entrance sector itself, or the first sector beyond it. This way, the player is not forced to walk all around a secret area just to collect the credit for its discovery. Watch out too for secret areas that have more than one possible way in. Make sure that players will pass into the credit-awarding sector no matter what entrance to the area they use.

You should also ensure that players are given good reason to enter a secret area. If a player opens a secret door but does not enter because the small room beyond appears empty, DOOM will consider there to be an undiscovered secret area when the mission finishes. This will result in frustrated players wandering around trying to locate that last secret they have already found. The placement of a few bonuses in the room would have prevented this.

COMPULSORY SECRET DISCOVERIES

It is important for the correct feel of a game that players easily equate the secret credits they have been awarded with the locations they have found. You should not award secret credits for areas that players are forced into locating because of traps. Such areas are rarely seen as "secret" by players and you will therefore disturb their own mental count of how many secrets they have located by awarding credits unnecessarily. Finding a hidden exit from a room in which a player has been locked is usually its own reward!

Finally, even if your level doesn't use any secret locations, you should make sure that one sector does award a secret-discovery credit. Use either the start sector or the one with the exit switch—one that the player is guaranteed to pass through. This ensures that the tally screen reports 100 percent of secrets located, rather than 0 percent when the level ends. This simple addition to your WAD will save players much frustration from wandering around looking for secrets that are not there. (If only id's designers had taken this advice with DOOM II!)

WAD SORTIE 26: AWARDING SECRET CREDITS

This Sortie builds on the WAD produced in the previous one. If you did not produce that WAD, you should use WAD25.WAD (DOOM) or D2WAD25.WAD (DOOM II) from the CD-ROM as your starting point here. You should be aware that this Sortie assumes a fair degree of familiarity with the layout of this WAD. If you have not been following these Sorties in detail, you may wish to take a quick run through this WAD to familiarize yourself with its features and layout.

This final Sortie from the current room examines the WAD that you have built and makes recommendations about which of your current sectors should award secret credits.

SETTING THE SECRET AREAS

Some of the WAD's candidates for awarding secret-discovery credits are:

- The marble one-way stairs
- The hidden room at the top of these stairs
- The platform room
- The southern courtyard
- The hidden room in the southwest corner of the courtyard
- The crusher room
- The sniper's den
- The hidden room off the southwest staircase
- The string of rooms behind the shot-activated doors off the blood pool
- The room north of the blood pool
- The causeway across the pond
- The Imp ledge outside the northern window of the platform room

Let us consider the case for each of these areas in turn. To make a sector award a discovery credit, simply set its special characteristic to the value 9.

THE MARBLE ONE-WAY STAIRS

These stairs are currently located behind a secret door that is activated from a rather obvious switch. Currently, this area of the map is away from the main flow of the WAD. Decide for yourself whether it warrants inclusion as a secret area. If you decide in favor of it, I recommend using the entrance from the southwest passageway as the credit-awarding sector.

THE HIDDEN ROOM AT THE TOP OF THE MARBLE STAIRS

This room is only hidden in the sense that players may not notice it as they pass. Its opening is triggered from further along the corridor—at which point they will definitely discover its presence! They may not be able to fathom the way to get in there, though. On balance I would award a secret-discovery credit here.

THE PLATFORM ROOM

The entrance to the platform room is currently semi-hidden and its switch is not too obviously attached to it. It seems a little generous to award a discovery credit for this, though.

THE SOUTHERN COURTYARD

This area can only be gained once the player has located and tripped the switch in the hidden room. The area is hardly secret, however. How you view secret areas will determine whether you mark this as one or not. I probably wouldn't.

THE ROOM IN THE SOUTHWEST CORNER OF THE COURTYARD

This strikes me as a perfect candidate for a secret-discovery credit. By awarding a secret credit here, credit is effectively given also for finding the courtyard itself, because this credit cannot be collected until the way into the courtyard has been found.

THE CRUSHER ROOM

The string of crushers is located behind a door that is hidden and shot-activated. I would probably award a secret-discovery credit here. I would also let the entrance sector be the one that awards the credit. The discovery is awarded then, even if the player doesn't run the gauntlet of the crushers. (Just call me generous.)

THE SNIPER'S DEN

I would also award a credit here, too—that way the player earns extra credit for braving the crushers and noticing the door beyond. (Not that it's hidden, though. I said I was generous, didn't I?)

THE ROOM OFF THE SOUTHWEST STAIRCASE

The case for this room is similar to that for the room at the top of the marble stairs. It is easier to get into though—its door latches open—and there is the added complication that the special characteristic will already be in use if you left this area with flashing lights. As this particular room contains the switch that will permit access to other areas already marked as secret, there seems little point in awarding a separate credit here. I'd leave this area out of the secrets list.

THE CORRIDOR BEYOND THE BLOOD POOL

The discovery of these areas is a vital step in the completion of the arena section of the WAD. There is little point in awarding discovery credits here, in my opinion.

THE ROOM NORTH OF THE BLOOD POOL

The opening mechanism for this room is not obvious in its purpose and is sufficiently far from the room itself for careless players to miss it. It is not central to the overall scheme of the WAD—I suggest that this room should award a credit.

THE CAUSEWAY

There seems to be no point in awarding credit for finding the causeway across the pond: as things stand, this is the only escape from the lower area of the arena.

THE IMP LEDGE

It may not be immediately obvious why I have included this in the list of secret areas, as it may not seem particularly secret to you. Bear in mind, though, that this area does start out hidden from the platform room side. Also, if the lift up to it from the arena were to be made less conspicuous, players may not find this ledge. This, coupled with the fact that currently no secret credits are awarded at all for successfully attaining this area of the map—it involves the correct location of a number of switches, remember—means that I would probably award a secret-discovery credit to players who do manage it. (I may change my mind later, though!)

COLLECTING THE CREDITS

When you have decided which areas are to award credit for their discovery and have set all of the appropriate sectors' special characteristics, you should save your WAD as WAD26.WAD. Check that your Player 1 Start position is back in its normal location in the hexagonal room, and take a run through your empty WAD, to check that you can collect all of the secret credits. You may wish to revise your original opinions as to what should be secret after you've been to them all.

THE TIME SCORE

In testing out your latest WAD, you may have noticed that DOOM reports a ridiculously short Par time for the completion of this level. This is caused by the proximity of the exit switch to the level's starting position—if you check the map, you will see that they are, in fact, very close to each other in terms of map coordinates. If you want your levels to give more reasonable Par times, you should place their exit switches as far from the start position as you can. Most players, however, are used to DOOM's unreasonable expectations here and habitually ignore this element of the score.

EXIT: MOPPING UP AND MOVING ON

In this room, you learned about the last few types of active line and saw how to implement teleports and exits using them. You also learned how to make areas award secret-discovery credits.

By now, the geography of your WAD should be nearing completion. There are a few areas that need some final development but you should be able to complete these for yourself by drawing on the knowledge you have acquired so far.

Your WAD is still sparsely populated, however. It contains little to fight, nothing to fight with, and little to collect beyond some credits for locating the secret areas. The next room will put right these deficiencies: it will lead you through the process of placing the enemies that your players will have to fight on the way to your new exit. (See Figure 11.9.) And, of course, it will show you how to handle the provision of weapons, ammunition, and other goodies that they will need in order to survive the ordeal.

Figure 11.9.
All it needs now are some monsters!

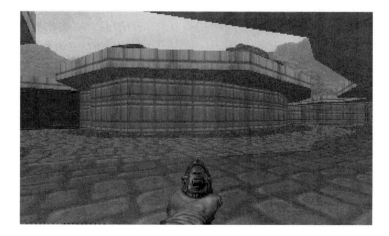

ROOM 12

POPULATING YOUR DOOM WORLD

By Steve Benner

By now, you should have a WAD in which the map is nearing completion. It will not yet have much of a population, however—a few monsters on the higher skill-levels to help you test out some areas, a suit of Security Armor, and a few keys is about all.

In this room, we will set about changing that. Here, you will be led through the steps involved in populating your WAD for real. First of all, you will be shown a strategy for deploying the enemy forces—and for laying out caches of arms and other supplies for dealing with them. Methods for implementing different difficulty levels will be discussed, and mention made of other uses for the game's difficulty settings. There are also examinations of the way in which DOOM's creatures behave and the way in which sound propagates through a WAD.

In addition, this room's final Sorties will provide you with practical experience in the initial stages of the process of populating your DOOM world.

This room considers the general principles which apply to the populating of DOOM WADs. WADs intended for multiplayer use—especially Deathmatch WADs—have additional considerations. These are covered in the next room, "The Finishing Touches."

PLANNING THE ASSAULT

Many designers spend long hours drawing up the geography of their playing arena, getting the layout and appearance just perfect, only to spoil everything with careless—one might even say thoughtless—selection and positioning of enemies and resources. The distribution of the creatures and artifacts that players will encounter is at least as important—many would say more so—as the layout of the geography itself.

As always, the key lies in the planning. You should aim to:

■ Plan carefully
■ Progress logically, and
■ Play-test thoroughly

Apply these guiding principles to the populating of your WAD as to every other aspect of WAD design.

PREPARING TO POPULATE THE WAD

By the time you start populating your WAD, you should have a clear picture in mind of the way you want the WAD to play. You should know what each of the areas in the map is like and what function each is to serve in the grand scheme of your level. You should have a fair idea of what is to happen in each area and in what order events should occur. If you don't know these things before you start laying out the denizens of your WAD, they are unlikely to contribute much to the way it plays.

So before you start placing any items, take a good look at the geography of your WAD, clearing up in your own mind how you want each area to contribute to the level as a whole. Sketch out the way that you feel play should progress. Then take a run through your empty WAD, trying to visualize the way it will all work. Only when you're confident that you know what you want should you set about trying to achieve it.

THE NATURAL ORDER OF THINGS

The secret to laying out a WAD successfully is largely one of sequence. One of the main difficulties in populating a WAD is achieving a balance between the forces that players will encounter and the means of disposing of them. You will find that it is much easier to achieve this balance if you do things in the right order. The sequence of placement that I recommend is:

- **Player starts and keys:** Begin by laying out player-start positions and keys. This determines the flow of the WAD from the outset.

- **Essential obstacles and artifacts:** Next, place those obstacles (and any artifacts) that are essential to the control of flow. These can be regarded as part of the geography. Leave out the decorations at this stage.

- **Enemies:** When the flow of the WAD has been established, place enemy forces in the principal combat areas. This enables you to see how the forces you envisaged behave in the space you have provided for them.

- **Weapons and ammunition:** Once you are happy that the monsters behave as you'd like, concentrate on providing the players with the weaponry needed to dispose of them.

- **Power-ups:** Having provided your players with creatures to fight, and the means of fighting them, you should now make sure that they can live long enough to do it.

- **Bonuses:** Most players see collecting the bonuses as secondary to slaying the monsters. Lay these out, therefore, after the main battle scenarios have been completed.

■ **Decorations:** Add any final atmospheric decorations that you feel enhance your WAD. Don't overdo it!

■ **Extras:** When you're happy with the main areas of your WAD, consider adding a few wandering extras to the enemy's principal forces, just to keep your players on their toes.

Each of these stages in the laying out of a WAD will be examined shortly. Between each stage, test thoroughly and don't be afraid to go back a stage or two if need be to change or refine things that you have doubts about.

EFFECTS OF OVERPOPULATION

Before you dash off to start filling your WAD with monsters, you should be aware of the consequences of overpopulating your DOOM world. Placing too many Things around your map can overload DOOM in two ways. The first is through *Sprite overload*. This occurs when there are too many Things in view at one time. The second problem you may encounter is *save buffer overflow*. This occurs when there are just too many changeable items in a WAD.

SPRITE OVERLOAD

Sprite overload is an unpleasant effect that can occur in areas that use a lot of Things—such as hordes of monsters all attacking simultaneously, or lots of decorations, or both. In laying out a WAD, you should always bear in mind that DOOM can only handle the display of 64 Sprites—enemies, decorations, ammunition (either on the ground or in flight!), bonuses and so on—simultaneously. If there are any more than this, you will find that they all wink in and out of existence during play. The more Sprites there are, the longer each spends invisible.

Avoid this effect by limiting the number of Things in view at any one time. Cut down on the number of monsters (you can make combat tougher by reducing armor, ammo, and health availability, or by increasing the toughness rather than the number of enemies) and resist dense pockets of unnecessary decorations.

A maximum of 64 Sprites in view may sound like a major restriction to the more bloodthirsty of you, but remember that, generally, the game engine will have slowed to a crawl, trying to keep track of all of these Sprites long before this limit is reached! However, if you really want these quantities of monsters, take steps to keep them spread out around the player so that they can never all be in view at the same time. The game will still slow down, but the WAD should not suffer from the disconcerting effect of winking Sprites!

SAVE BUFFER OVERFLOW

The buffer that DOOM uses when writing a saved game to disk is not very large. If your WAD provides the game engine with too many items that can change during the course of the game—basically any items that the player can acquire, kill, destroy, move or change in any way—you risk causing this buffer to overflow. The result is a game that cannot be saved—and some very frustrated players!

It is difficult to gauge how big a WAD can get before causing this condition, mostly because it is impossible to judge precisely just how much space DOOM will need. Developing your WAD by degrees, and regularly trying to save games while in play, will keep you assured that you are not over-stretching the engine's capabilities in this area.

USING THE DIFFICULTY SETTINGS

It is common for WADsters to feel that it is not necessary to create a design for each of DOOM's difficulty levels. They argue that most players will be using the "Ultra-Violence" mode anyway, so why bother? In my opinion, such a view is misguided.

Certainly there is little point in implementing an easy version of your WAD for first-time players. You can reasonably expect all of the users of your WAD to be seasoned DOOM players. (Why would they be playing an add-on WAD, otherwise?) Remember, though, that not all players have the same abilities or preferences. Your WADs will be better received if it is possible to vary the level of difficulty to suit a range of playing skills and styles.

Bear in mind, too, that you are not constrained to using DOOM's difficulty-level settings merely to vary the WAD's survivability. Used imaginatively, Things' skill-level flags can work constructively to prolong the useful life of your WAD, by providing players with scope for more varied play than graded WADs can provide.

GRADED PLAY

As already noted, the provision of graded play can make a WAD appeal to a wider audience. When working on such a WAD, it is often best to lay it out at skill-level 1 ("Hurt Me Plenty") and to play-test this first. Make this setting hard enough to push your own DOOM-playing capabilities—it should be a struggle to complete the level. Work out next what should appear at skill-level 0 ("I'm Too Young To Die" and "Hey, Not Too Rough") to produce something that is a comfortable play for you. Finally work on skill-level 3 ("Ultra-Violence" and "Nightmare"), making this very difficult for you to play.

DOOM
PROGRAMMING
GURUS

12
ROOM

1
MISSION

2
EPISODE

Laying a WAD out like this can be time-consuming and tedious. But you should find that the result is a WAD that will have at least one level to suit any player. Some tips on what you can do to give your players a harder time are given in later sections of this room.

There are only three difficulty-level settings for Things, remember.

VARIED PLAY

If you are more interested in producing a WAD which is uniformly tough to play at all difficulty settings, you can still use Things' skill-level flags to introduce other variations into your WAD. You can use the flags to control or vary the occurrence of most Things with skill level. Remember that this applies to obstacles, key-cards and teleport destinations, as well as the more obvious categories of monsters, weapons, and power-ups.

You can therefore use these settings to change the flow of a WAD completely from one difficulty setting to the next. You can use obstacles at some levels of difficulty to block corridors that are open at others; move the keys around and generally employ the skill-level flags as a cheap way of producing three different designs within the same basic map. This can greatly increase the lifetime of your WAD, providing its players with three WADs in one, with the need to find new ways of tackling each difficulty level.

You can also vary the game style, while at the same time keeping the play tough enough for even the most seasoned DOOMster. Use different mixes of monsters, weapons, and power-ups at each skill level to provide another element of variety for your WAD's players to select.

POSITIONING THE MISSION IN THE EPISODE

Another point you may need to consider when planning the population of your WAD is where it will be played within an episode. Most PWADs replace an episode's opening mission—few people will want to play all of the way through a familiar mission to begin a new one. You may, of course, be building a new multimission WAD either from scratch yourself or by contributing one mission to a collaborative project.

Planning for players arriving from earlier levels can be tricky. You do not know whether players will arrive barely alive and in need of some power-ups pretty quickly, or whether they will arrive fully armed and super-fit, having saved the previous level's Soul Sphere for last.

Usually, though, you will know what weapons were available to the player on the previous level. Generally speaking, you should assume that these have been obtained and can plan your own WAD around this assumption. If having those weapons then becomes vital to the completion of your own WAD—it doesn't have to, of course—you should make sure that your WAD will supply additional ones for players who missed them earlier.

The safest option is to make it immaterial how a player is equipped on arrival and to provide everything necessary to complete your own level.

A DEPLOYMENT STRATEGY

A suggested sequence for laying out the creatures and artifacts in a WAD was presented earlier. Each of the steps outlined then will now be examined in more detail, to enable you to see the overall strategy for the successful population of a WAD. Let's start by considering a map's flow of play.

CONTROLLING FLOW

Hopefully, your geography has been planned with consideration of its general flow in mind. Before you come to populate in earnest, though, it is worth taking a final run through it, looking at the way it all interconnects and imagining how the player might progress from one area to the next.

Consider what order players might choose to do things in. Can they try variations in the order in which areas are tackled? If they do, will this alter the way in which your planned encounters occur? It is easy to lose sight of the big picture when you are working on the geography of each room. Take the time, then, to try to imagine each area in use and how it fits in with what should happen in other areas; this will enable you to refine your thinking (and hence your design) of each area and maybe the WAD as a whole.

PLAYER START POSITIONS

When you are reasonably happy with the layout of the lines, decide where a player is to start—you should really have planned this from the outset, but you may want to revise your thinking after walking through the WAD a couple of times. Unfortunately, you *cannot* use the skill-level flags of Player 1 Starts to have the player begin the level in different places. If you attempt this, DOOM will use only the *last* of the Player 1 Starts that you placed, no matter what difficulty level is selected. Each of the other positions will be occupied by a static "projection" of the player. (See Figure 12.1.) These do not participate in the game—monsters appear not to be able to see them—but be warned that any harm they take will be passed on to the "real" player!

This restriction on the use of the skill-level flags applies to the other Cooperative-mode player starts, too. It does *not* apply to Deathmatch starts, however.

Figure 12.1.
Seeing double? I wouldn't pull the trigger if I were you!

KEY-CARDS

Use keyed doors to divide a WAD into self-contained areas, or to control the flow of play so that areas are tackled in an appropriate order—to ensure that the tougher monsters are not encountered until a player has had a chance to acquire some heavy weaponry, for instance, or to prevent a player from leaving until all of the WAD's puzzles have been solved.

Lay out the key-cards in the positions they need to occupy to facilitate the flow pattern you envisage. The locations of key-cards can be made to vary with skill level. Utilize this either to make the cards harder to obtain at higher skill levels, or to spring different traps as cards are acquired. If you wish, you can even alter the flow altogether by changing the order in which the cards can be obtained.

OTHER ESSENTIAL ARTIFACTS

At this stage you should also lay out any obstructions that are important to the flow of the game. You can use certain items of decoration—fire-sticks, columns, and so forth—as obstructions in gaps that you want to let players shoot but not pass through. Once again, you can control the use of these obstructions at the different skill-level settings, thus blocking off some corridors and opening up others to change the interconnections of your WAD.

Consider also whether any special power-ups might be needed for the successful playing of certain areas of your geography—Light Intensifying Visors for the dark areas, for instance, or Radiation Suits. Place these items at this stage to help your play-testing. Again, the skill-level flags can be used to control the available quantities as well as the locations of these items. You might want to reduce their availability (or remove them altogether) at the higher difficulty settings.

TESTING THE FLOW

Once you have laid out the various items that will control the flow of the game, try taking another run through it. Aim to make your way as quickly as possible from start point to exit, taking whatever route is required to collect all the keys and make it to the exit. Doing this at this stage may well identify areas that the player doesn't need to visit—and that therefore contribute little to the flow of the game. If you had intended those areas to figure more prominently in the game, you may need to redesign the flow. Try moving the keys around, or changing the way the doors are keyed, for instance. Or maybe you will just want to use those areas for the positioning of secrets. (Players shouldn't need to go everywhere in order to complete a mission, of course—only to complete it with a full score.)

After any redesign, run through your level again to check that everything flows as you had intended. Try to imagine the sequence of predicaments that players might find themselves in as they work through the WAD. By the time you have done this a few times, you should have a clear picture of the way your WAD is going to work and where most of the monsters should be.

DEPLOYING MONSTERS

The choice and deployment of the forces that your players will encounter require not only a full appreciation of each enemy's individual characteristics, but also an understanding of the basic behavioral patterns common to all monsters. Some of this knowledge you should already have gained from playing the game itself (as well as from elsewhere in this book). Some additional factors which influence the movements of monsters during play, and the options open to the designer for controlling them, will be covered in a later part of this room. For now, though, I shall just discuss in general terms tactics for the deployment of monsters in battle zones.

CHOOSING THE TYPES

The bulk of a WAD's monsters should be introduced in a structured way. Work around your WAD, implementing the main battle areas first. For each zone, determine the principal type of combat you wish to inflict upon your player. Decide the main mix of monsters and their quantities, taking into account their basic behavior and characteristics, the way they mix (or don't) with each other, and how much space they have around them in which to fight.

If the structure of your WAD forces areas to be tackled in a particular sequence, make sure that you keep this in mind as you place the monsters. Try to make each encounter harder than the previous one, and don't present players with the tougher monsters too early unless you also intend them to have acquired some heavy weaponry as well.

GRADED ENCOUNTERS

When using monsters to produce graded play, don't assume that just throwing more and tougher monsters into the fray will always make things harder for the player. It might, but more often than not, it won't. This tactic frequently produces an unstable mix of monsters who are happy to spend their time fighting each other rather than the player. Often a player will have little to do apart from keeping out of the way, and picking through the corpses afterwards!

There are better ways of making levels tougher than by loading them up with extra monsters, and you should resist the temptation to do this. In particular, don't use the skill-level settings simply to satisfy players who might want a bloodfest. Let them use "Nightmare" mode.

Remember, too, that giving some players certain types of monsters to fight will simply supply them with additional ammunition and weapons! Most players view Sergeants as just another supply of shotgun shells, for instance. On the other hand, Imps used in large quantities will give players a hard time. These are frequently employed because of their tolerance of their own kind's poor aim—and the fact that they provide the player with nothing afterwards.

As you populate each area, therefore, it is imperative that you try out the WAD to see how the mix of monsters you are using behaves.

TESTING THE MIX

Testing your mix of monsters should not consist of wading into battle with the full protection of degreelessness and lots of very happy ammo, just to see how easy it is to waste everything in sight. Rather, you should mostly be running amongst the baddies, shooting at them just enough to keep them interested in you, and observing how they behave together.

Use IDDQD to stay alive while you see whether any sort of status quo is maintained if you don't fight. Try to determine whether the monsters would quickly surround and overwhelm a player during proper play. Or will their buddies do all of the dirty work if a player can just keep moving? Check that you are giving the player the sort of hard time that you had planned.

ADDING VARIETY

When you think you have one area right, you can move on to populating the next. Aim for variety in encounters with monsters—not only in the types and quantities of enemies, but also in the character of the fight. Your geography should already have been designed to vary the sizes of combat arenas and to provide a mix of light levels. Make the most of these variations in your monster deployments. As well as rooms full of foes, arrange for some monsters to hunt for players while others lie in wait. (We'll look at some ways to arrange this shortly.)

Above all, don't make everything predictable—leaving a dark and twisting corridor altogether devoid of monsters can be a very effective way of raising a player's pulse rate. Aim to balance the suspense, the surprises, and the episodes of total carnage. Try to avoid the kind of shoot-'em-up WAD that bores players with its predictability long before they finish it.

WEAPONS AND AMMUNITION SUPPLIES

When you have most of the major battle zones populated with monsters, you can turn your attention to the weaponry that is required to deal with them.

GAUGING SUPPLY

One way to find out how much ammo you need to supply is to play each area in turn with the IDKFA code invoked (and IDDQD if necessary), taking note of your ammunition stocks before and after each main combat event. This gives you a chance to try the effects of fighting with different weapons, too. You may find that certain weapons make fighting easier, while others are a positive hindrance (such as the rocket launcher in confined spaces). Use this information to decide what weapons to make available at each difficulty level. Make levels harder by limiting the power or suitability of weapon supplies, as well as by reducing availability (and accessibility).

RELEASE RATE

Once again, consider the flow of your WAD in deploying weaponry—use the secret places for the real goodies, so that the more observant players benefit the most. Make sure, though, that players can obtain the weapons necessary for survival if they look and work hard enough for them.

In higher difficulty levels, you may want to leave it entirely to the monsters to supply ammunition and certain weapons such as the shotgun (and, in DOOM II, the chaingun). You can also make things tougher by limiting the amount of ammunition players can carry—do not provide Backpacks. This is a far more effective way of increasing the difficulty of a mission than increasing the monster-count—half a dozen Imps can be quite a challenge if a player is down to bare hands!

ADDITIONAL ITEMS IN THE ARSENAL

This stage of laying out the WAD is often an appropriate time to consider the placement of barrels. These are important elements of the players' (and the enemies') arsenal. Not only do they act as a powerful weapon, but barrels also represent extra hazards in confined spaces. They are useful for creating temporary obstructions that players can move (if they think to) and are a good way of preventing players from being able to creep about the WAD without waking any monsters who may be around.

Barrels are useful devices for creating variation across the skill settings. Place them close to monsters to favor the players—or next to likely hiding places to make players' lives more hazardous.

TEST IT ALL AGAIN

When you've completed the layout of your WAD's arsenal, try playing it again using only what you've laid out. Use the IDDQD code as necessary to stay alive, but don't award yourself any additional ammo at all. Refine your monster placings and oil-drum spacings, and adjust the weaponry available until the WAD is satisfying to play.

You can then start thinking about the power-ups.

POWER-UP ARTIFACTS

Power-up artifacts will be necessary for your players to survive the ordeals of your WAD. The correct deployment of these can often make or break a WAD.

GAUGING WHAT'S NEEDED

You can determine the amount of health that players are likely to expend in their battles by using the same technique you used to determine ammunition requirements—play the WAD without the IDDQD code and note how much health is consumed in each encounter. Lay a temporary stockpile of health power-ups—berserk packs are good here, because they give 100-percent health—somewhere central in your WAD so that you can grab a quick boost between each encounter. (Don't forget to remove these again when you've finished with them.)

Consider where you might place Stimpacks and Medikits to provide major replenishment of the player's health. Decide whether you want to provide the player with a health boost before a heavy encounter—this often acts as a warning of something bad ahead—or make them wait until (or if) they have survived the ordeal before offering the chance.

Generally, you should reserve the major bonus items, such as Soul Spheres and blue Combat Armor, as rewards at the end of large-scale combat, or tuck them away in secret locations.

Make levels harder by reducing available health. Provide a single large power-up quite early, say, and then only smaller boosts from then on. Players will then have to sustain little damage if they want to make it to the end of the mission.

SPECIAL POWER-UPS

Some of your planned encounters may require the more powerful artifacts, such as Blur or Invulnerability—make sure these are positioned appropriately (which is not to say easy-to-find or to easy-to-obtain, of course!). Do this at this stage, if you didn't do it earlier.

It is often a good idea not to place these too close to where the action that you think requires them will occur. Let them be squandered the first few times the WAD is played, by encouraging players to take and use them too soon. You can achieve this by positioning such artifacts in junctions, or close to secret connections to the appropriate battle area. This prevents players from associating the artifacts with the route to any particular area. Make it ambiguous how such artifacts might be needed. Give players the opportunity to try out their use in different ways. Don't forget to try all of these different ways out for yourself, too, of course!

BONUSES

Once the major items are in place, the Spiritual Armor and Health Potion bonuses can be sprinkled around as you feel necessary—usually either in secret locations, as an incentive to enter and collect the secret credit, or as a quick boost before the next major combat. Generally, you can set the same bonuses on all skill levels—they may be all that will keep the player alive in the upper settings! Indeed, you may already have placed most of these items when you laid out your medical supplies.

ADDITIONAL DECORATIONS

Finally, any additional decorations that you feel are necessary for atmosphere can be positioned around the WAD. You may add these purely for effect or to serve some other purpose—as warnings, for example. Pools of blood beneath crushers are common in many WADs, as are corpses outside particularly hazardous areas. (Or just scattered around to make players nervous!) Mostly, what you use will be a matter of personal taste. Use whatever you feel fits into the general design of your WAD but, as always, don't overdo it. Avoid too much decoration in areas with large numbers of monsters, or you will run the risk of Sprite overload, or of just slowing the WAD down to the point of unplayability.

At this stage of the design, try to avoid adding any items classed as Obstacles (see Appendix A, "Essential DOOM Thing Information," for a list of these), unless they are well away from the main action. Otherwise you risk upsetting the balance of play which you have worked so hard to produce. If you particularly want decorative elements to contribute to the hazards of a level, add them early, rather than late in the design, so that they are in place while you are testing the layout of their areas.

> Many items of gore are available in both obstructing and nonobstructing versions. Choose which you use carefully.

EXTRAS

At this stage, your WAD should be just about ready. Try playing it from beginning to end without any cheat codes at all. Ask yourself how it works as a whole. Is there enough variety? Are things distributed correctly? Are there any unnecessary holes in the action? Refine the way it plays by adjusting any of the elements already in place. You might also want to add a few new items to break up any unevenness in the way the WAD plays.

To add a little unpredictability to a WAD, you might consider introducing a few wandering monsters. Placed where they will be awakened early, either by seeing or hearing the player, but in an area where they will take a long time to appear, such monsters can be made to pop up unexpectedly in a slightly different place each time. (Ways of achieving this are discussed after the next WAD Sortie.)

FINAL REVIEW STAGE

When you are completely happy with the way your WAD is playing, pass it to someone else to play, and ask for their comments. If you can, watch the way they play it—you'll get a better feel for whether your traps and signals are working as you expected them to. If you can't be there to watch their game, ask them to record a demo of it. Watch this through a few times, making notes of what aspects of the WAD are working as you intended and which ones still need improvement.

Don't keep asking the same play-testers to look at your levels after each minor change, though—they'll most likely just get bored and not give it a full workout. Only pass it on again when you think you have made all the significant improvements you can think of and feel you have things as good as they can be.

The following WAD Sortie builds on the WAD produced in the last Sortie of the previous room. If you did not accompany me on that Sortie but would like to come along on this one, you should use WAD26.WAD (DOOM) or D2WAD26.WAD (DOOM II) from the CD-ROM as your starting point. If you have not been following the development of these sample WADs in detail, you may want to take a complete run through it to familiarize yourself with its layout before participating in the Sortie.

WAD SORTIE 27: CHECKING THE FLOW

By way of preparation to the real populating of the WAD, this Sortie will look at the steps involved in checking the flow of play through your WAD. It starts by considering the placing of the keys for those keyed doors.

THE INTENDED FLOW

It is time that I revealed to you my intended control of flow through the WAD you have been building. The keyed doors are already in place; I ought to tell you now where I planned to place the keys.

Currently, players can explore west from the starting room, by passing through the platform room, whence the whole of the western half of the map is accessible. Alternatively, a player may start by venturing east into the maze. The remaining areas of the map are locked away behind the blue-keyed door off the southeast passageway. One of the two accessible areas will need to hold a blue key-card, therefore.

In reality, two keys are needed before a player can progress much further. The blue key-card only grants access to the outdoor crescent area—all further doors are locked with red or yellow cards. I have used this arrangement to force players to tackle both the maze and the western area of the map before proceeding anywhere else.

The yellow key will need to be acquired before players can locate the exit from this level. The planned positioning of the keys is as follows.

- **Blue key:** Located just outside the north window of the platform room. This key will be accessible only after the player has successfully negotiated both the bottom corridor and the arena.
- **Red key:** Hidden in the maze. By locating the key to the "back entrance" of the maze in the maze itself, it becomes impossible for a player to use the back stairs until the maze has already been visited. Measures will be taken to ensure that the player does not leave the maze without having first located the red key—read on!

■ **Yellow key:** Located in the donut room, the yellow key requires that room's puzzles to be solved before it can be acquired. Before that, though, the two other keys will need to be obtained, to gain access to the donut room itself.

Once all three keys have been found, the player is free to leave the level.

It is worth considering the rationale behind the placing of these keys in a little more detail.

THE BLUE KEY

The blue key will be placed where a player will quickly see it—reaching it will prove to be the problem here. Offering an early sight of a key in this way provides players with an incentive to explore the area further. This key needs to be positioned where it will be visible from within the platform room—provided the northern window is open, that is! Call the locating of this key a reward, then, for approaching the upper level of the platform.

In my WAD (WAD27.WAD and D2WD27.WAD), the key has been placed on a pedestal so that it is conspicuous through the window of the platform room. It can be reached from the Imp ledge—if the player makes it that far, of course!

THE RED KEY

The red key is also to act as a lure—this time in the more usual way, to entice players over a trigger line. This trigger will not perform the expected trick of opening a monster-pen—it will, in fact, be used to open the teleport that acts as an exit from the maze. To achieve this, a slight modification to the current WAD is required. The teleport sector needs to have its ceiling lowered to its floor. This change ensures that the player cannot leave the maze without taking both the key *and* locating the teleport.

Maybe the trigger should open a monster-pen as well, to mask the sound of the teleport opening...

Once the teleport in the maze has been found, it provides the area with an easy exit, making the trips on the back stairs that open the one-way staircase redundant. They can be used, though, to add another little twist here. Consider what would happen if we were to add another trigger action to the self-raising stairs, this time to close the teleport sector again.

Remember that these stairs cannot be reached without the red key. Anyone entering the maze by this route will, therefore, already know about the teleport, and, in all likelihood, the trap of the one-way stairs. After arriving back in the maze by this route, a player will in all probability head straight for the teleport. Unfortunately, it won't be there any more!

A player's next logical move will be to head back to where the red key was located to try to reopen the teleport by retriggering the appropriate line. That approach needs to be foiled too. The line that opens the teleport sector as the red key-card is taken needs to be a once-only walk-through trigger. This will force the marble stairs to be used as the exit on this second visit to the maze—when the player eventually thinks of trying them!

THE YELLOW KEY

The yellow key is already in place as the prize for solving the puzzles in the donut room. No further consideration needs to be given to this item's contribution to the flow of the WAD.

TRYING OUT THE FLOW

You may like to place these various keys now, with suitable modifications to the appropriate areas of your own WAD.

When you've done this, see how it affects the flow of the WAD as a whole. Try running through from start to finish, visiting just those locations that are necessary to attain the exit.

Note that two areas do not need to be visited: the southern courtyard and the back stairs to the maze. The southern courtyard contains several secret areas. Their credits will remain uncollected until the player visits them. The player is not penalized at all for not using the back entrance to the maze, however. Figure 12.2 shows how this has been remedied by the addition of some further secret areas, with a cache of goodies off the corridor at the top of the self-raising stairs.

Figure 12.2.

Extra development to entice the player up the back stairs to the maze.

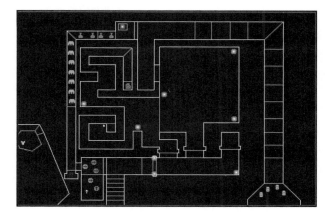

Also conspicuously undeveloped are the maze itself and the large open arena (which also still has temporary switching arrangements in place for the causeway across the pond).

ARENA DEVELOPMENT

Figure 12.3 shows how the arena might be developed further, as in my WAD27A.WAD (or D2WAD27A.WAD). The development here concentrates around the watchtower, north of the pond. A lift has been added to permit access to this watchtower, activated from a nearby switch. From the tower, an additional step provides access to the arena's northern balcony. The top of the watchtower has two switches. The more conspicuous of these will raise the ceiling trap in the green stone corridor, should that have been tripped. The second, hidden round the back of the first, will be the proper switch for raising the causeway from the pond—it will replace the temporary switch that was installed for testing purposes.

Figure 12.3.
Development of the watchtower in the arena.

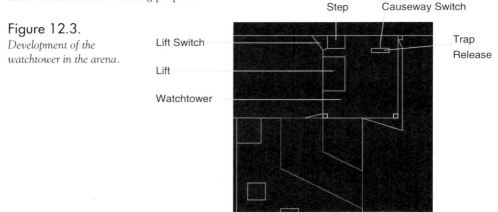

Allowing players onto the watchtower and the balcony compromises the impediment to progress caused by the pond—there is nothing to prevent players from simply leaping down from here. To rectify this, the southern and eastern edges of the watchtower and the south side of the balcony need to be set as impassable.

To explain the blockage, my WAD uses the MIDGRATE texture on both of the main textures of these lines. This creates railings to stop the player from jumping down to the eastern section of the arena. Additional sectors have also been placed around the watchtower to provide pillars to terminate these railings and to bring the ceiling down around them so that they look right from both sides. Figure 12.4 shows a view of the top of the new watchtower, looking east through the railings.

If you want to see this area in detail, you should examine WAD27A.WAD (D2WAD27A.WAD for DOOM II) from the CD-ROM. As well as trying it out to see how it plays, take a look at it in the editor to assure yourself that you understand how it operates.

Figure 12.4.
On top of the watchtower.

PUSHING THE LIMITS

Before going on to begin populating your WAD, add whatever further developments you want to the arena, as well as the maze. Note, though, that with the watchtower development just described, the arena is now about as complex as DOOM will permit. WAD27A.WAD will push v1.2 of DOOM over its maximum number of visible edges in this area—and some views within it will produce HOM, especially those that include all of the edges around the pond (with its stepping-stones). DOOM v1.4 and above should be okay for a little while longer.

Figure 12.5 shows how the eastern platform of the arena only needs a few tasteful decorations to complete it.

Figure 12.5.
*"Tasteful enhancements" to
the arena's eastern platform.*

UNDERSTANDING AND CONTROLLING THE ENEMY

The strategy for testing the deployment of monsters in the WAD was presented earlier. To be able to place the monsters properly in the first instance, though, it is necessary to understand something of the standard modes of behavior of DOOM's monsters and the ways in which these can be controlled through the layout of a WAD.

STANDARD MONSTER BEHAVIOR

As you will know from playing DOOM, the basic behavior of monsters is to stand at their posts asleep until something awakens them. Once awake, they will stand still no longer and will start to track the player. If a player is in sight, monsters who are capable of it will sooner or later start firing.

If within striking range, most monsters will bite players or rake them with their claws. Former Humans prefer to back off a bit, though, to carry on using their weapons.

There are three things that will awaken a "sleeping" monster:

- Catching sight of a player
- Hearing a noise made by a player
- Being hit by fire

Once awakened, monsters do not normally go back to sleep—although they will when a player resumes a saved game—a common form of cheating!

LINES OF SIGHT AND MONSTER FACING ANGLE

Very little in the world of DOOM works equally for players and monsters alike. You have been told earlier that monsters can see through all two-sided lines, regardless of texture. In fact, it goes further than that: monsters can see through all two-sided lines that have any air gap at all between their adjacent sectors, regardless of vertical displacement. This means that of the three configurations of adjacent sectors illustrated in Figure 12.6, only in the right-most case (*iii*) is the player (at upper right) out of sight of the monster (at lower left).

Players in cases *i* and *ii* of Figure 12.6 will awaken the monsters and will come under fire (although the fire will not reach the player in case *ii*). This trait will betray the presence of any monsters that you attempt to hide in trenches and such—bear it in mind when placing monsters.

2	1		12		DOOM PROGRAMMING GURUS
EPISODE	**MISSION**		**ROOM**		

Figure 12.6.

Unequal lines of sight.

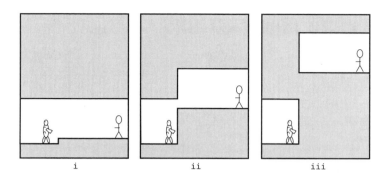

The Reject Map can be used to disable monsters' lines of sight between particular sectors, removing the inequalities of this aspect of DOOM. This is covered in a later episode of this book.

To a certain extent, you can use a monster's initial facing angle to compensate for this effect. Monsters look forward with a field of vision of about 30° to either side. Monsters do not stand perfectly still, though, even when asleep, and they will move a little from their starting angle as the game progresses.

USING DEAF MONSTERS

To prevent monsters from waking when they hear a sound, you can use the monster's deaf-guard option. Setting this flag will cause them to ignore all sounds, so that they only awaken when they catch sight of a player or are hit by fire—either from a player or from one of their fellows.

This option is also termed the ambush option, as it creates enemies that stay resolutely where they were placed (in hiding, usually), ignoring the sounds of combat around them, to surprise the player later. Most of the time, you will not want to set this option, for you will want to draw monsters from immediately adjacent areas, to make combat come to a player no matter how the level is tackled.

Usually, though, you will not want to draw monsters from too far away. It would be undesirable, to say the least, to have all of the enemies in a WAD zero-in on the player's first pistol shot! To learn how to control the way sounds draw monsters into the fray, you need to know something of DOOM's principles of sound propagation.

SOUND PROPAGATION

Once again, the way monsters hear noises differs from the way in which a player hears them. Monsters will only hear sounds made by a player's weapons discharging. (This includes the chainsaw and the fist!) Monsters will not hear players grunting as they walk into walls or jump off high platforms. They are also immune to the sounds of doors and lifts operating, as well as of their fellows firing or crying in pain.

Sounds from a player's weapons propagate through the DOOM world in a standard way. First, a sound will immediately fill the player's current sector, waking every nondeaf monster within it. It then travels across every line that has the two-sided flag set and where the arrangement of ceilings and floors leaves an air gap into an adjacent sector. Sound will not pass into sectors that are completely obstructed, such as a closed door or a sealed-off lift, for instance, or through any two-sided lines which have their two-sided flag clear.

You should be able to see that, left to its own devices, this propagation of sound could quickly have most of a WAD's monsters awake and on the trail of the player. Fortunately, DOOM provides a mechanism to prevent sound from propagating wildly throughout an entire WAD and waking your monsters prematurely: a line's Blocks Sound flag. Lines with this flag set impede the progress of sound from one sector to another.

This line does not operate in the same way as the Blocks Monsters or Impassable flag, however. It will not always prevent sound from crossing the line. First, it cannot stop sound spreading through an entire sector. Lines with the Blocks Sound flag set that are not between sectors will be entirely ineffectual. This flag is only examined by the engine when it determines whether or not sound can be propagated into an adjacent sector.

Further, sound is only stopped at the *second* Blocks Sound line it encounters. This means that sound will always pass into the sectors adjacent to the player's sector, provided there is a suitable air gap.

These lines are intended to allow sound to fade away through a level, rather than completely isolating sectors sonically from their neighbors. They also have no effect on the sound that the player hears while playing the game. That is handled completely differently.

TRACKING TALENTS

A further inequality between monsters and players is the monsters' ability always to sense the direction in which players lie. They use this sense to home in on players and to track them through the WAD. Fortunately (for the player), this ability is a straightforward homing talent—it often leads monsters into dead ends.

You may wish to impede monsters in their player-tracking and contain them in particular areas by setting the Blocks Monsters flags of some lines of your WAD. Remember, though, that such lines block the movement of all monsters, including the flying ones. If you only want to stop ground-based monsters from tracking through certain areas, consider using raised or sunken floors instead.

USING SOUND-PROPAGATION RULES AND THE TRACKING TALENT

The sound-propagation rules can also be used to awaken monsters that otherwise would never be awakened. This can be combined with monsters' player-tracking capabilities to create monster caches that deliver monsters into the game, either at irregular intervals to the keep the player on guard, or in a rush to overwhelm the player at inopportune moments.

This technique is used in many of id Software's own levels. Take a look at the extreme northwest corner of DOOM's E1M9 for an example of the latter type of cache. (See Figure 12.7.)

Figure 12.7.
The E1M9 monster cache.

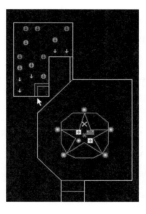

In this area, a thin open sector acts as a sound conduit into a room that is otherwise isolated from the rest of the WAD. The conduit carries the player's sounds into the isolated room, to awaken the horde of monsters waiting there. In the starting condition, the monsters are no threat to the player, because, apart from the thin conduit, the room is sealed.

A player who is lured into the room just to the south by the sight of the goodies there is in for a surprise, though. The edges of the star-shaped sector are tagged to open the thin sector in the corner of the monster-filled room (indicated by the cursor arrow in the diagram). This arrangement causes a teleport in the corner of the monsters' room to become accessible once a player has stepped into the star-shaped sector. Once this has occurred, their ability to track the player will draw the monsters one-by-one over the teleporter lines to materialize in the room with the player.

Sound conduits such as this are not always necessary to carry sound into a monster cache, though. The next WAD Sortie shows another way to achieve the same effect by utilizing the sound-propagation rules in a different way.

SUMMARY OF MONSTER-PLACEMENT CONSIDERATIONS

Here is a summary of the main points to remember when laying out monsters in a WAD.

- Use monsters' facing-angle option to watch (or not) the entrances to areas, so that the monsters are awakened as the player passes particular points in each area.
- Set a monster's deaf-guard option if you want a monster to wait until it sees a player before waking.
- Use a suitable array of lines with the Blocks Sound flag set to prevent all nondeaf monsters in your open combat areas from waking at the first sound the player makes.
- Use level changes or lines with the Blocks Monsters flag set to contain monsters within certain areas and prevent them from tracking the player in an undesirable way.
- Consider how the rules of sound propagation and monsters' player-tracking abilities can work to provide sudden monster releases or a steady stream of monsters into areas that players think have been cleared.

The next WAD Sortie gives some practical examples of these ideas in use.

WAD SORTIE 28: DEPLOYING THE ENEMY FORCES

This Sortie uses WADED to build on WAD27A.WAD (or D2WAD27A.WAD for DOOM II) developed during the previous Sortie. These WADs are available on the CD-ROM if you did not create your own version. You will need to be familiar with the operation of WADED to follow the first part of this Sortie.

This Sortie starts with a new development of the WAD: a monster cache. Figure 12.8 shows the form and location of this.

Figure 12.8.
The new monster cache.

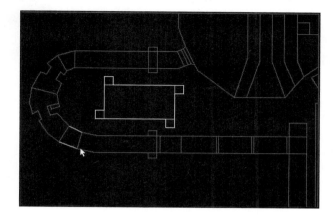

ADDING THE MONSTER CACHE

Notice where the new room is located, in the open space left by the curve of the western green stone corridor, beyond your first lift. To add this area, you should begin by drawing the main rectangle of the new room using GSTONE1 as the wall texture, but do not use Make Sector to turn it into a new sector. Instead you should add the new lines to an existing sector. I've used the short corner sector of the corridor, indicated by the mouse pointer in Figure 12.8.

To add the new lines to this sector, choose Sec Define, right click in the chosen corridor sector to highlight it, and then left click in turn on each of the new lines. You now have another disjunct sector, like the slime pond in the arena. There are, of course, no sector settings to change for the new area—it shares those of its disjunct part in the corridor. If you change one area's settings here, you will change the other's: this is all one sector, remember.

Because it is all one, any sound reaching the corridor section of this sector will immediately propagate through to its disjunct part. Sound from any shots the player fires in the green stone corridor—or indeed out in the arena beyond, if the door is open—will therefore penetrate through to the new area and will awaken any nondeaf monster that you choose to place there.

If you want sound to propagate through doors even when they are closed, add a recess on each side of the door as usual; then use the technique you have just seen here to make *both* of these recesses into *one* sector. Any sound reaching one side of the door will then be passed immediately to the other, without any need to pass through the intervening door sector.

Let us make use of our new monster cache by adding a route out of the new room for whatever has been awakened. Draw and make additional sectors off the four corners of the new room as shown previously in Figure 12.8. Make the lines across the entrances of these into teleporters, delivering monsters to various locations around the WAD. Make some of these deliver to points nearby, while others carry monsters further away. Use your knowledge of the way monsters in this room will follow the movements of the player to decide where each teleport will deliver.

As an additional twist, let us allow the player to vary the way in which this monster cache delivers its load. Start by making the heights of the ceilings of the two teleport sectors that deliver furthest from the corridor the same as their floors. Then tag each of these sectors to the switch line in the unused (southern) alcove located in the corridor near the bottom of the lift. Put the special attribute of 103 (S1 Door: open) on this switch. Now, until this switch is thrown, the new room will deliver monsters closer to, rather than farther from, the corridor. It may be quite a while before a player figures out what the switch achieves—and whether it is useful or not.

Finally, populate the new room with some monsters and place a few columns in the room to stop the monsters from moving too freely along the walls. This should slow down their arrival at the teleports. If you want to be able to get into the room and take a look at it, turn one of the lines of the corridor into an active teleport line that will take you there. Figure 12.9 shows the room with three Imps, four green columns, and a teleport destination in it to permit player access. Three of the room's own teleport delivery points can be seen in nearby corridor sections.

Notice, incidentally, how this addition has turned the corridor ceiling trap into something of a two-edged sword. Is it worth cutting off the line of retreat before entering the arena in order to prevent the propagation of sound to the new room? Probably. The last thing a player will need here is an additional attack from behind—as will occur if that ceiling is left up! This has provided players with an unexpected gain from an apparent trap. I wonder how many times they will need to play before they learn this though?

When you've saved the WAD (WAD28.WAD) and seen how it works—you should hear the monsters wake up when you fire a shot in the bottom corridor—reload it into the editor and remove the temporary teleport line from the bottom corridor. Leave the teleport landing in the new room, though—tagged instead to all of the lines surrounding the yellow key at the center of the donut.

This will cause any player who grabs the yellow key to be whisked away to the monster cache. (I just hope the monsters were enticed out earlier!) The yellow key should be close enough to the lines to enable the player to reach it just before a teleporter line does its stuff.

Figure 12.9.
Layout of things in the new monster cache.

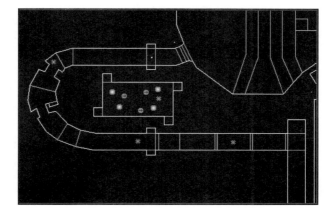

DEPLOYING THE REST

The final section of this Sortie considers an initial trial distribution of monsters throughout the WAD. It is meant to suggest the kind of monster layout that I had in mind when I designed the geography of the WAD. Add monsters at skill-level 1, as suggested forthwith, first. Resist temptations to vary the forces until you've tried it out like this.

HEXAGON ROOM

Leave the starting room as it is, with just a suit of armor on the platform. There will be plenty to fight later on.

SOUTHEAST PASSAGEWAY

Place a couple of Former Humans here. (The player still only has a pistol, remember.) Position one of them so that he will see the player heading for the suit of armor.

MARBLE STAIRS

Players heading up the marble stairs are going to need a better weapon to face what's up there. You'd better have a Former Human Sergeant guarding the bottom of the stairs to supply a shotgun!

SECRET ROOM AT TOP OF STAIRS

This room should have a good mix of nasty beasties in it: some Imps, a Demon or two, and some Spectres, perhaps. Place at least one Spectre, with its deaf-guard option set, hiding in the depths of the room. (We don't want the player to empty the room completely from the corridor, do we?) Put a chaingun in the depths of the room, too—the player will need it later.

MAZE

The maze isn't finished yet, so it is not a good place to populate right now. You may want to set some sound-blocking lines across the entrance to it, though, so that when the maze is used, it won't empty too quickly as a result of the fight that is likely to occur in the corridor outside.

Return now to the western part of the map.

PLATFORM ROOM

Remember that players can enter the platform room before venturing anywhere else, and may still be armed with only a pistol. Place some Former Humans around the floor level, along with a Sergeant or two, either on the platform or around the room. There should be some Former Humans on the platform, too, to encourage the player to go up there.

OUTSIDE THE PLATFORM ROOM'S NORTHERN WINDOW

There should already be some Imps waiting for the platform room's northern window to be opened. Set their Level 1 flags to bring them into the game.

SOUTHERN COURTYARD AREAS

The southern courtyard and its associated areas should still be populated from the test games. Change their skill-level flags to bring these Imps into the game, too, along with the sniper in his den. Put an Imp (or two) in the secret room off the southeast corner of the courtyard, with some barrels about the place. Leave the crushers as the only hazard in the southern corridor, at least for now.

Place another chaingun in the sniper's den, in case the player comes this way rather than going up the marble stairs. Put some barrels here, too.

If you're using DOOM II, try putting a Former Commando here as the sniper. That'll have your players dodging!

SOUTHWEST STAIRS

Try a couple of Lost Souls in the secret room off the southwest stairs, and maybe a Spectre or a Demon. Decide whether you want them to see the player as the door is tripped, or whether you'd rather have them wait until the player returns—or shoots to open the doors at the end of the corridor. Set one of them deaf anyway.

Leave the rest of the corridor empty.

STRING OF SHOT-ACTIVATED DOORS BEYOND THE BLOOD POOL

Place an Imp or two behind a couple of the doors beyond the blood pool. Don't let them get too close to the lift, though—you don't want to risk the monster cache being triggered too soon.

BOTTOM CORRIDOR

Leave the bottom corridor empty. Any shots fired here spring the monster cache, remember.

ARENA

The arena is planned as the main combat area. Start it out with a couple of Hell Knights: one on the northwestern platform, guarding the lift, and another on the eastern platform. Put some Imps and a Former Human or two in the basin and on the steps by the pond. You could put some Imps on the balcony and maybe on the watchtower, but you will need some monster-blocking lines to prevent them from coming down on the lift.

Finish this first attempt off with a deaf Cacodemon hiding behind the watchtower to catch players once they've found and crossed the platform.

Don't forget to set up a sound block between the arena and the platform room; otherwise you'll have these arena monsters awake long before the player makes it down there—which will spoil the layout. Don't forget that you will need two lines between the platform room and the arena in order to block the sound. You'll know whether you put them in the right place or not as soon as you open fire in the platform room.

GOING ON

When you've placed all of these, save the WAD (WAD28A.WAD) and see how the areas work. There are no extra ammunition or health stocks out yet, of course, so you'll need some cheat keys to make it to the end.

After you've looked at the way this WAD operates—pay particular attention to the way the arena plays and to the way the monster cache delivers up its occupants—I'll leave it to you to decide what more it needs and where. From now on, in fact, this WAD is entirely in your hands. Feel free to add whatever you think it lacks. Good luck—and have fun!

You'll find my final populated WAD (with one or two little additions!) on the CD-ROM as ARENA.WAD (or D2ARENA.WAD). Enjoy.

EXIT: MOPPING UP AND MOVING ON

In this room, you learned more about the behavior of DOOM's creatures, as well as the rules for sound propagation through a WAD. You were presented with a strategy for the population of your WADs. If you have been completing the Sorties, your own WAD should be nearly finished by now.

The next room considers some additional changes you might want to incorporate into your WAD for enhanced multiplayer use. It also looks at ways to improve its playing speed and shows you how you might produce WADs that contain more than one level.

ROOM 13

By Steve Benner

THE FINISHING
TOUCHES

Previous rooms have covered all the major aspects of the way the DOOM world operates and have shown you those elements that can be manipulated with a WAD editor.

This room presents the additional considerations that need to be given to the design of WADs intended for more than one player to experience simultaneously, either in Cooperative play mode or as a Deathmatch arena.

It also looks at what may lie beyond the realm of the pure map editor, as a precursor to the more advanced topics covered in the following episodes of the book.

MULTIPLAYER MODES

The WAD that has been developed during the course of this episode has grown very much as a single-player WAD—it was designed principally with single-player use in mind. Many players of DOOM prefer to play in groups, rather than alone, either in Cooperative play, where they gang up on the monsters and solve the WAD's puzzles together, or in Deathmatch, where the creatures and the puzzles can go hang. (Why frag a monster, when you can frag a friend?)

Each of these two types of multiplayer games have their own particular requirements and impose an extra layer of design criteria on the WADster.

COOPERATIVE PLAY

Many single-player WADs can be immediately suitable for Cooperative play. All you may need to do is check that all four Cooperative starts have been added to your WAD. Monster and power-up ratios can often be left as they are. Your single-player testing should have ensured that there is little spare health or ammunition lying around. In Cooperative play, these resources have to go further—balancing out the additional ease with which the monsters may be dispatched.

BATTLING COOPERATIVELY

Ironically, battles are often *not* easier for players in Cooperative mode—making sure their buddies don't get caught in friendly fire means they have to take a little more care where they spray their lead. The additional slight hesitations that result can make all the difference to the player's own survival.

TRICKS AND TRAPS

One aspect of a game that changes totally as soon as there is more than one player at large in a WAD is the possible flow through its areas. Many flow-control features—such as those in and around the maze in the sample WAD—rely on knowing where the player is at the point that a trap is triggered, as well as where they have been beforehand. In Cooperative play, the location of other players when one springs a trap cannot be known or unpredicted. Some traps can become disastrous in Cooperative mode—again, just consider the implications of allowing more than one player into the sample WAD's maze area, for example. The designer needs to give careful thought to the consequences for Cooperative play when adding traps and tricks to WADs.

TACKLING PUZZLES COOPERATIVELY

The preceding comments apply to puzzles, too, of course. Puzzles that are difficult in single-player mode can become trivial in Cooperative play. The donut room in the sample WAD is a good example here. With a little modification, this room could be made into a puzzle that *requires* Cooperative play to solve it; by making it impossible for a single player to run from one of the switches to the lift or the door, the WAD suddenly needs two players to solve it. There is another little multiplayer twist that could be added here, too: Arrange for each teleport line around the donut's center to deliver to *different* teleport destinations. Cooperative players may not always notice which side of this sector their buddies passed through in grabbing the key. When they try to follow, they could find themselves somewhere completely different! (This particular modification would also bring an interesting little twist to the single-player game, of course.)

Giving Cooperative players the need to work together as a team in this way can make play much more rewarding. It may also wreck the WAD as a single-player WAD, of course. You will need to decide which is more important to you.

DEATHMATCH

Many of the points just discussed in relation to Cooperative play apply equally well to Deathmatch mode. In Deathmatch, however, the situation is complicated by the very different nature of the play. DM players will be less interested in solving puzzles, and are likely to have little patience for traps and tricks. First and foremost, these players will want to find each and start trading lead.

Deathmatch DOOM is used to provide a virtual-reality environment where players set their own targets (usually their buddies!) and their own objectives. The designer's job here is to provide the environment but not the objectives. From this point of view, Deathmatch WADs can be easier to design and implement than single-player WADs. The designer does not need to consider flow or provide puzzles. Give the players a space to run around in, some weapons, and some ammo—and then leave them to it. If only it were that simple…

DEATHMATCH DESIGN CONSIDERATIONS

Single-player WADs rarely convert well to Deathmatch scenarios. It is usually better, if you want to design for Deathmatch games, to concentrate on that aspect of a WAD's design and develop a DM-only WAD. This prevents you from having to compromise both single- and multiplayer aspects, which is what usually happens with WADs intended to be used in either mode.

To put a good Deathmatch WAD together, you need to have an understanding of what makes a good Deathmatch arena. DM design can be every bit as challenging (and some would say much more rewarding) than producing a single-player WAD. Let us look at some of the more important points to consider if you wish to venture into this area of WAD design.

BALANCE

The overriding requirement in any Deathmatch WAD is to provide and maintain balance. Keep things equal for each player—which is not to say that you must keep things the *same* for each player. Strive to ensure that no player gains an unfair advantage over any other or is unfairly disadvantaged in any way. Sacrifice all other aspects of the design before compromising this principle. If you get this aspect of your design right, most players will forgive all of its other shortcomings. If you get it wrong, your WAD will probably be consigned to a black hole somewhere.

Keep this warning in the back of your mind as you consider the main design features of your WAD.

THE PLAYING SPACE

The playing space of a Deathmatch WAD needs to be given a lot of thought. As already stated, DM players like to get into action quickly. They also like to be able to ambush each other and to be capable of disappearing and reappearing suddenly in other places. This creates a number of design requirements and possibilities.

INTERCONNECTIONS

Deathmatch WADs must dispense with the largely linear design that can often benefit single-player WADs. You should provide geography that enables your players to move around in a large number of ways. Provide lots of interconnections between the areas of the WAD, but keep the interconnections short to enable players to travel through them quickly.

HEIGHT VARIATION

Try to keep your thinking away from the purely horizontal—use variations in height levels to produce areas which allow plentiful ambush spots and make players keep their eyes open. (Take a look at DOOM's E1M4 for a good example.) Again, use short interconnections between the various levels. Use steep stairs and lifts rather than gradual level changes down long corridors. Provide players with an interesting and varied hunting ground.

RANGE

In planning the extent of a Deathmatch WAD, keep the players' range in mind. DM players are unlikely to want to spend much time exploring the WAD itself. They will want to be able to appraise the immediate area quickly, grab some weapons, and then go in search of their opponents. Few players enjoy trudging for miles before they catch sight of anything.

Remember, though, that DOOM can support up to four players at once. Games with three or four players may need a bigger playing area than games with only two. And, of course, the more familiar players become with the geography, the smaller it will start to seem to them.

If it is a large WAD, you might want to place all of your DM starts fairly close together, so that everyone starts out in the same general area. You can then lay out some (similar strength) weapons in a way that draws the players together. Once they have located their opponents, players can decide for themselves whether they want to enter the fray right away or spend time hunting out some different weapons.

HIDING PLACES

The provision of hiding places is an important consideration in the design of Deathmatch WADs. Provide plenty of them (the interconnections of a DM level can be helpful here). Be careful, though. Secure hiding places overlooking exposed areas (particularly ones that players are forced to cross) encourage players to spend their time here in the hope of picking off their opponents in safety. Such features make for boring (or frustrating) play.

OPEN SPACES

Open spaces are useful for the exposure they can bring to players crossing them. Do not make them too large, though, or you make it impossible for the exposed player to work out where distant and better-hidden players are firing from.

DOOM
PROGRAMMING
GURUS

13
ROOM

1
MISSION

2
EPISODE

Make sure that open spaces do not work in favor of particular starting positions. It is often a good idea to aim for a fairly symmetrical map layout, with the open spaces in the center. DM regeneration locations can then be positioned in similar areas around the edges of the map, and all players will need to cross the central spaces to hunt the others. Be careful though that such areas do not prevent regenerated players from getting back into the game.

CHOICE OF TEXTURES

When choosing textures for walls in WADs intended for Deathmatch play, remember that each player is given a different colored suit: green, brown, indigo (black, actually), and red. Take care not to give any one player an unfair advantage by using textures against which they can hide—or placing them at a distinct disadvantage by having them conspicuous wherever they go.

The indigo player is virtually invisible against the ASHWALL texture, for example. The green player has a decided advantage against the marble wall textures—which the red player will hate.

Keep players' colors in mind as you design your WAD, and try to vary the surfaces so that you have no single overall color scheme. If you want areas that are predominantly one color, try to balance the WAD by providing areas that offer similar advantages to each of the other players.

OTHER MAP FEATURES

Elements of the map that a designer of single-player levels takes for granted can gain new significance in Deathmatch WADs. Many standard features need to be reappraised if they are to be used successfully.

DOORS

Many Deathmatch players dislike the presence of doors, because they slow progress from one area to another. They also signal a player's whereabouts through the sounds they make as they open and close. Certainly you should not include doors simply for the sake of the appearance of your WAD. They can be a useful feature, however, because of the risk that players can face from opening them.

You could provide a choice of tactic by connecting the same areas in different ways—a short interconnection using a door and a longer one without, say. Players can then either take the longer route quietly or risk signaling their presence to any opponents within earshot by taking the shorter one. Such arrangements also enable doors to be used as decoys and distractions; a player could open the door and then run around the long way in the hope of fragging from behind any opponents on the other side of the door.

KEYED DOORS

The presence of keyed doors is of complete irrelevance to DM players who always start out with all necessary key-cards in their possession. This feature can also be used to aid in the adaptation of a single-player WAD to Deathmatch use: If a WAD does not utilize one of the three colored keys in its single-player mode, then that color becomes available to supply an additional series of doors that only DM players can open. These extra doors can be used to bypass areas of the map that are un-suited to Deathmatch play or simply to provide extra connectivity, breaking up the enforced linear flow of the single-player game.

If you do use such a feature, you should *not* use the appropriate color coding by the side of the door to indicate that a key-card is required to open it. This would confuse single players who will think there is still a key somewhere for them to find. Instead, use the DOORSTOP texture to suggest to the single player that the door is merely decorative. (Although, of course, DOOM will tell them otherwise if they try the door—as most players will!)

An alternative way of preventing single players being confused by these doors is to provide them with the extra key once the WAD has been completed in the "prescribed" manner. The intercon-nections provided by the door might as well be used in the single-player game too, rather than leav-ing it as just so much wasted space.

TELEPORTS

Teleports are great devices for improving the interconnection of areas in Deathmatch WADs. Remember, though, that the sound and sparkle of a teleport in operation are conspicuous to other players. You may want to vary the exposure of teleport destinations with the skill level of the game by placing the lower skill-level teleport landings behind alcoves in the destination sector, for example.

DAMAGING SECTORS

Areas with harmful special characteristics or crushing ceilings tend to be unpopular with DM play-ers. Many feel that these features get in the way of Deathmatch play. Newer versions of the game have addressed the problem of suicides, but it is generally best to remove the temptation by keeping damaging areas in a Deathmatch WAD to a minimum.

DECORATIONS AND OBSTACLES

Decorations and obstacles can be used in Deathmatch WADs much the same way as in single-player games. Their use is governed by more or less the same rules. DM-only obstacles can be used to con-vert parts of a single-player WAD for DM play by blocking off areas that would not work well in multiplayer games. Make sure that areas that need to be blocked off have the obstacles properly placed and that players cannot work their way around their edges, or just bludgeon their way through.

Remember not to use barrels as such obstacles—they can be quickly disposed of! Also remember that barrels do not regenerate in `-altdeath` play. Generally, though, barrels can be employed much as they can in single-player games: to make areas more hazardous and to discourage players from hiding around particular corners.

SPECIAL FEATURES

As is the case with standard map elements, many of a WAD's special features need to be reappraised for Deathmatch use. DM WADs generally do not benefit from some of the features used to enliven single-player WADs but need their own particular kinds.

PUZZLES, PROBLEMS, AND TRAPS

As already noted, Deathmatch players rarely have the patience to solve puzzles and problems, whether to make progress through a room or to obtain the items they might be interested in (their weapons and ammunition). Traps that are intended to catch individual players can become a nuisance in Deathmatch WADs. Either keep such traps out altogether, or, again, if you're aiming for a multi-purpose WAD, make sure there are alternative ways around the traps for DM players.

Single-player WADs can also cause traps for DM players unintentionally. Doors that single players could only approach from one side may not have an opening mechanism from the other side. These doors will bar the exit of DM players who regenerate on the wrong side of them. If you lock your players in areas where there is nothing for them to do except wait until someone comes along and frags them, they are unlikely to be very impressed!

It is probably a good idea to make sure that every door can be operated from both sides (unless this defeats the design of the single-player game, of course—but then there should be another exit anyway), even though there may seem to be some redundancy in this from the single-player point of view.

SECRET AREAS

Whereas single-player games commonly have the majority of the goodies tucked away in secret locations, this is usually a bad idea in Deathmatch WADs. This can give any player who has a greater familiarity with the layout of the WAD a major advantage over the others. If you hide weapons, for example, the player who has played the WAD before will know where to dash to grab them all before the other players have even oriented themselves. Newcomers to the WAD will quickly become bored with it if they are fragged over and over again while they spend time hunting for a weapon so that they can join in against their more experienced colleagues.

While it can be argued that prior knowledge will always be to a player's advantage, this can be minimized by placing in plain view everything that is available. This doesn't mean that *obtaining* all items has to be easy—only the finding of them.

SIGNALS

Many DM players like features that signal the location of their opponents. This can be something as simple as the operation of doors and lifts giving audible signals, and the glitter and fizz of a teleport (or regeneration event). Or it can involve more complex arrangements, such as trips in one area triggering events in another—turning the lights on and off in one area to warn of a player in another, or the triggering of remote lifts, for example.

These features enable players to assess the whereabouts of their opponents and to plan interceptions, ambushes, or just a good old-fashioned chase to gain their frag. If you want to demonstrate your abilities as a DM WADster, dispense with single-player traps and tricks and aim for these sorts of features instead. Be aware, though, that they do tend to favor the more experienced players of your WAD. Once again, make them obvious, so that players with a knowledge of your WAD's features do not gain an unfair advantage over the newcomers.

OBJECT PLACEMENTS

The laying out of objects in a Deathmatch WAD is far more critical than it is in a single-player WAD. It is crucial that you keep an eye open for any imbalance you might be creating as you distribute items through the level. Don't have single, large caches of items such as weapons or health, as you might in a single-player WAD, or you could end up in a situation where one player will begin near a weapons cache, another gets the armor, while the third begins in the middle of nowhere with only a pistol and some useless Stimpacks.

Again, a symmetry of design can help here, enabling you to present each player with a similar array of objects wherever he or she starts.

STARTING POSITIONS

Deathmatch games can have up to 10 DM Start/Regeneration positions per difficulty level. Make sure that you have at least four, or DOOM will not be able to start a four-person session with your WAD. It is recommended that you use all 10 DM start positions so as to provide a greater variety of starting conditions for your players, and to make the restart process less predictable.

| DOOM PROGRAMMING GURUS | 13 ROOM | | 1 MISSION | 2 EPISODE |

As previously noted, the shimmer of a player's DM regeneration is conspicuous to the other players, and you may want to take this into account when you position the DM start positions. Unlike the single and Cooperative player starts, you can use the skill-level flags of DM rebirth positions to change their locations with the difficulty level of the game. Use this to shelter the regeneration of players using the lower skill settings, or to place them nearer to available weapons or armor.

In positioning regeneration spots, don't forget to allow your players to get back up to a reasonable strength quite quickly. If you don't do this, you will unfairly favor the players who make the early frags. Let regenerated players back into the game quickly, or you will find that they tend to leave for good!

WEAPONS AND AMMO

Acquiring weapons and ammunition will be the principal goal of most DM players—when not actually fragging the opposition, that is. Don't get carried away with the weapons that you make available to DM players, though. Most players will want something more powerful than the pistol fairly quickly, but you should limit the power of what you provide.

A popular tactic is to make a shotgun readily accessible from all DM start positions. There should be greater risk involved in reaching more serious weapons, such as the chaingun and rocket launcher. (Risk, in DM terms, usually means exposure, of course.) Weapons such as the chainsaw can be made available, too. The very powerful weapons such as the plasma guns—and the rocket launcher, some would argue—should only be available at the lower difficulty settings of the game, if at all (and preferably only then at considerable risk to the player). These weapons quickly destroy any balance the WAD had by making long-distance or indiscriminate kills too easy.

Similarly, ammunition needs to be distributed carefully in Deathmatch WADs. Keep players on the move to hunt for ammunition by spreading it around the WAD in small quantities. Additionally, limit the players' ability to stockpile ammunition by depriving them of Backpacks. This will prevent a player who has a plentiful supply of ammo from settling down in a good ambush spot and just picking off everyone who appears.

MONSTERS

Monsters serve a very different purpose in Deathmatch WADs from the roles they play in single- and Cooperative player games. Many players prefer to have no monsters in the way while they stalk their buddies; others like to have monsters around—as a supply of weapons and ammunition! The presence of monsters also provides additional signals for players. They can act either as lookouts for carefully positioned players, or, more usually, will provide clues to the whereabouts of other players through the noise and flashes of combat.

It is largely a matter of personal preference whether you use monsters or not. Use them in limited quantities, though, and confine yourself to the weaker types. The principal players should not find themselves upstaged by appearances of Cyberdemons and such. Use monsters only to make the main play a little trickier, or to provide a steady stream of ammunition.

As always, aim to keep things balanced, making sure that no particular start position will subject a player to more (or less) than his fair share of monster encounters. Players will not take kindly to finding their opponents have been waiting, weapons at the ready, while they fought their way past the hordes of Hell. Nor will the other players be happy to be robbed of their rightful frag if the hordes win!

BONUSES AND POWER-UPS

The distribution of power-ups is also more critical in DM WADs than in those intended for single-player use. Once again, an uneven distribution of these items will lead to an imbalance. Too much health or armor—or the correct quantity poorly distributed—can lead to unfair advantages (especially in `-altdeath` play), while too little of either can be disastrous for all players.

It is usually better to use more of the smaller power-ups than to provide large ones, although you may want to supply some Security Armor as standard close by each regeneration point, at least at the lower skill levels.

As with weapons, you may want to place a few of the more powerful artifacts in exposed positions—more as bait than as anything else, maybe. As always, aim for balance by providing an even distribution of them. In general, though, avoid the excessive power-ups such as Combat Armor, Blur and Invulnerability Artifacts.

It is always better to distribute a lot of the smaller power-ups, like the Stimpacks and bonus items, throughout much of your WAD, rather than use the bigger Medikits or Spheres. Unlike structured single-person WADs, remember you can't predict players' hunting patterns through your WAD; you can only guess at the likeliest encounter spots.

TESTING

The testing of DM WADs can be more involved than that of single-player WADs—largely because of the problems involved with hunting oneself! You can usually only inspect the technical aspects of the WAD with simple walk-throughs. To test how it works as a Deathmatch arena, you will need to make contact with other players and arrange some test sessions. If you're at all involved in DM play, though, this shouldn't be too difficult to arrange.

After that, play-testing and refinement is similar to the testing of single-person WADs—get it played and listen to the comments.

Don't be put off, though, if your play-testers initially complain that the level is too complex or too large. Wait until they've been trying it out for a while and have grown more accustomed to its playing space before you start to take that particular criticism seriously.

CONCLUDING DEATHMATCH COMMENTS

The production of Deathmatch WADs can be a major test of your abilities as a WADster. Provided you keep in mind the requirements of Deathmatch play, it need not be more difficult than the production of any WAD. As usual, plan your work, pay attention to the detail as you work, and try to arrange a test for playability at every stage. Aim to maintain balance throughout the WAD. The production of a good Deathmatch level can be one of the most rewarding of WAD-building experiences.

BEYOND THE MAP EDITOR

We are now just about at the limit of the range of things that can be achieved with a DOOM map editor. The next episode will concentrate on what more can be done to enhance your own levels and to change the way DOOM behaves. Before that, though, there are a couple of further topics that you may wish to know about and apply to the WAD you have built so far. They concern improving the speed of play and building multilevel WADs.

IMPROVING PLAYING SPEED

You may have found that your own WADs do not seem to play as smoothly as the original DOOM levels. Your major combat zones may play jerkily, and you may notice impaired play even when there are no monsters in the immediate environs.

This slowdown occurs because most map editors leave an important structure of the WAD—the Reject Map—in an empty state after editing the map. This particular WAD resource was mentioned briefly, way back in Episode 2, Mission 1, Room 2 "Reconnaissance Debriefing." Its purpose is to provide the game engine with some precalculated line-of-sight information between the various sectors of your WAD. It tells DOOM whether there exists a line of sight between one sector and another. Having this information at hand enables DOOM to know immediately if it is feasible for a monster to be able to see a player from where it stands.

Usually in a large WAD, the player will be out of sight from most of the WAD's monsters for most of the time. The Reject Map can quickly tell the game engine which monsters need to have their specific lines of sight checked to determine whether or not they can see the player. Knowing this saves the engine from carrying out a lot of unnecessary processing. Naturally, the game plays faster when it is spared these extraneous calculations.

Inter-sector line-of-sight inspections are not trivial to perform. As a consequence, most editors are not capable of providing a correctly completed Reject Map; they will, instead, produce one that is empty. Such a map in effect tells DOOM that all sectors can see all other sectors. The result is that the game must check *all* monsters' lines of sight for itself during play. WADs with many monsters will play slowly as a consequence.

Fortunately, utilities exist for you to generate a properly optimized Reject Map for your own WADs. The use of these utilities—Reject Map builders—is covered in a later episode of this book. If you find that your developing WAD is playing particularly slowly, you might like to investigate Reject Builders and see whether one can be used to speed up your WAD's play.

Some interesting special effects can also be produced via the Reject Map, but that is very much a topic for a later episode.

MULTILEVEL WADS

So far, this episode has concerned itself with the development of a single-level WAD to replace just one mission of the original game. If you try to cram too many ideas into one level, you will find yourself running out of resources of one type or another—either memory in the editor, or game resources during play. In such circumstances, you might consider splitting the WAD into smaller parts, making each part into its own level; or indeed, you may fancy emulating id Software by producing an entire episode of related missions.

Breaking WADs into smaller levels is a good idea for other reasons, too. It enables you to provide a greater concentration of items in each level, without pushing the engine so hard against its limits. It means that node trees compile faster—because each one is smaller. You may even find that your players appreciate being able to divide their play into smaller chunks, too.

The development of multilevel WADs requires no special consideration, beyond giving thought to how continuous you want the action to feel. The best way to develop a multilevel WAD remains to concentrate on one level at a time, working on each as if it were a stand-alone mission.

If you intend them to play as a continuous entity eventually—with the weapons a player acquires in one mission being necessary to the successful completion of the next—you will need to play-test each new mission with this in mind. One way is to put temporary caches of the appropriate weaponry near the start position during your final play-testing stages. Remove this cache when play-testing is complete.

Few editors will enable you to work on WADs with more than one map. Most strip single missions out of multilevel WADs for you to edit individually and then save these to new, single-level PWADs. If you want to create a multilevel WAD of your own, you will need to use a utility to fasten several single-level WADs together. Remember though that there is no need to connect WADs together into a single PWAD in order to play them in sequence. Multiple files can be supplied to DOOM through the `-file` command-line parameter; DOOM will load each WAD as the appropriate map as you progress through the game.

Usually you only need to join WADs together into one multilevel WAD for easier distribution to other players; or if you do not want to offer players the option of omitting particular levels from your WADs.

OTHER PWAD INFORMATION

In addition to the resources on which this episode has concentrated, there are other items of information which may be placed in a PWAD. These include:

- **Patches:** Graphical patches out of which new wall textures can be assembled.
- **Textures:** New ways to assemble either the id-supplied graphical patches or your own new ones (or a mix of both).
- **Graphics:** Various fixed graphical elements, like the player's face in the status bar, the skull menu-index, and all of the text characters used throughout DOOM, to name but a very few.
- **Music:** The musical soundtrack that plays while your players create mayhem and carnage.
- **Sounds:** Sound effects to replace those included in the main IWAD.

A shortcoming of DOOM is that floor and ceiling Flats, as well as Sprite graphics, cannot be successfully incorporated into PWAD files. To change these elements, it is necessary to alter the contents of the main IWAD file, making DOOM play differently until the original file is restored.

The manipulation of these aspects of a WAD is beyond the capabilities of a map editor and therefore outside the scope of this episode. You will learn more about these items in later episodes, however.

CHANGING DOOM

The final modifications you can make to the way your WAD plays involve the alteration of some tables of data tucked away at the end of DOOM's executable code. These tables provide the game engine with information on the way various aspects of the game operate. Coded here are the characteristics of all of DOOM's weapons, ammunition, and monsters, as well as various other bits and pieces, like lists of animated and switch textures and so on.

Note, incidentally, that the tables of information for all of DOOM II's extra Things (weapons and monsters) are contained within DOOM versions 1.666 and beyond. All that is required to make use of these items in your own WADs are some Sprite graphics so that they can be rendered on-screen. (If you add suitable Sprites, you must add your own graphics and not steal from the DOOM II IWAD— see the following cautionary note.)

Tinkering about in the DOOM executable is not a task for the faint-hearted—you risk damaging the game beyond repair and should be prepared to reinstall the game from scratch if things go wrong.

Hacking at id Software's executable code is an activity specifically prohibited by DOOM and DOOM II's license agreements. If you do change any of the data in the tables at the end of the DOOM.EXE file, you must *not* distribute the changed file. The same applies to changes to the IWAD file. Nor may you extract sections from these files to distribute with your own PWADs.

If you want to share PWADs with others, you must make sure that they contain no material which belongs to id Software. Stay within the confines of the techniques described in this episode if you want to be perfectly safe.

Again, this is a topic for later episodes.

EXIT: MOPPING UP AND MOVING ON

You have seen all of the basics of WAD construction using the elements supplied by the creators of the game, id Software. In this room, you learned about the additional considerations that need to be given to WADs designed for Deathmatch play. You were also given some tantalizing glimpses of what lies ahead in the Land of the Gods.

Before heading there, however, there is one more room to this episode. That room, "The Anomalies," is a Chamber of Horrors. It shows you what may go wrong with your WADs, tells you why, and gives some advice on preventing encounters with DOOM's anomalies.

ROOM 14

By Steve Benner

THE ANOMALIES

This room provides a short illustrated tour of the anomalies that can occur during your WAD editing. It looks at what can go wrong with your WADs and examines causes and cures. It starts with the most annoying anomaly of all: no map!

WHERE'S MY WAD?

Few things are more infuriating in the world of WAD editing than to spend hours perfecting a map, only to have DOOM start up with the familiar opening screen of E1M1 when you start a new game. Table 14.1 is a list of the common causes of this problem.

Table 14.1. Causes of DOOM not using your map.

The Cause	The Effect	The Cure
You forgot the `-file` parameter.	If you don't tell DOOM to use an external WAD, it won't bother. You will know when this is the cause, because DOOM won't pause to tell you that the game has been modified.	Always start DOOM with the `-file` parameter to use your own WADs. Use a batch file to start DOOM, with the `-file` command in it, so that you won't forget it.
You used an incorrect filename or path.	If DOOM can't find your WAD, it won't be able to load it; DOOM II will warn you if it is unable to load a WAD file; earlier versions of DOOM won't.	Check your typing carefully. Don't forget that if you're starting DOOM with a batch file, your default directory may not be what you think. DOOM insists that the full name of the WAD be given, including the .WAD extension. Again, use a batch file to manage these things for you.
You gave an invalid WAD name.	If DOOM doesn't recognize your file as a WAD, it won't use it.	WADs must have the .WAD file extension—always save WADs with one.

The Cause	The Effect	The Cure
You used a higher mission number in your WAD.	DOOM always starts a new game from the first game of the episode, unless you use the -warp or -wart command-line parameters. If you saved your map as a level with a higher number, DOOM will present you with the standard opening mission when you begin a new game.	Save the WAD with an opening mission number, or use appropriate command-line parameters (or IDCLEV) to reach it.

Another common complaint amongst those new to WAD editing is that their saved game won't restore after an edit. Remember that if a map has changed since the game was last saved, the new map will have a different collection of items. As a consquence, DOOM will be unable to reconcile the saved game file with the new map. Don't use save and load to try to advance quickly through a WAD that's under development. It won't work.

VISUAL ANOMALIES

Many of the visual anomalies that can occur in DOOM have been covered in earlier rooms. Some that haven't been discussed before are introduced here, and some old favorites are reviewed again.

PINK BUG AND TUTTI FRUTTI

If you have worked through the earlier rooms of this episode, you will be familiar with the causes of the two graphical anomalies known as Pink Bug and Tutti Frutti. (See figures 14.1 and 14.2.)

Pink Bug results from the use of short textures on spaces that are too large for them. In Figure 14.1, the 24-pixel texture STEPTOP has been used on a tall wall.

The Tutti Frutti effect results from the use of transparent textures as single-sided main textures. Note the streak of Tutti Frutti above the player's index finger in Figure 14.2. MIDGRATE should not be used on a one-sided line like this.

DOOM PROGRAMMING GURUS	14 ROOM		1 MISSION	2 EPISODE

Figure 14.1.
A wall with Pink Bug.

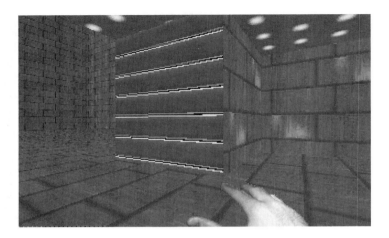

Figure 14.2.
Tutti Frutti.

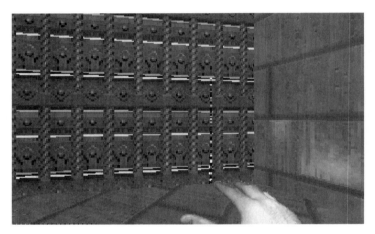

HALL OF MIRRORS

Perhaps the most infamous of all of DOOM's visual errors is the Hall of Mirrors (HOM) effect. It is unlikely that you will have completed this episode without encountering it somewhere in your WAD. Figure 14.3 is an example of how this effect appears.

The effect of HOM is much more spectacular than Figure 14.3 suggests. On a computer monitor, it flashes and flickers. This anomaly results from errors that leave DOOM with nothing to paint on part of the display. As a consequence, it leaves an area of the screen unrefreshed between updates of the view, and whatever was there before remains in the gap.

Figure 14.3.
A nasty attack of HOM.

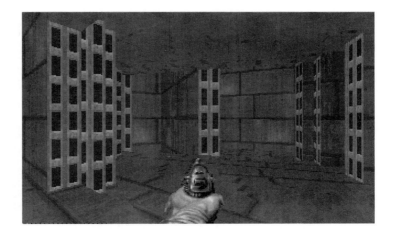

DOOM's video-buffering technique works by building a number of separate images in video pages out of sight of the player and cycling around these pages in turn to produce a smooth screen representation of the player's changing view. When an area of the display is not refreshed properly between these cycles (as occurs with any unpainted area), then earlier updates will not be overwritten, and the older images will flash before the player in turn, to cause the flickering effect associated with this anomaly.

There are a number of causes of the Hall of Mirrors effect, each producing a slightly different variation on the main theme!

HOM FROM MISSING TEXTURES

The most common cause of HOM, as you should know by now, is the omission of an essential texture, usually those of a line's main texture slot. The example shown in Figure 14.3 was caused by the omission of texture from the essential upper of a door face. While the door is closed—as in the figure—this texture slot will act in the same way as any of the adjacent main textures. When texture is omitted from this slot, the result is as you see here.

HOM FROM EDGE OVERLOAD

The problem known as *edge overload* was mentioned briefly while discussing stairs in Room 6, "Putting Sectors to Work," of this mission. The cause of this affliction is the graphics engine being given too many vertical surfaces to render in one update. The result is that it simply gives up after it has painted as many as it can, leaving the rest as they were. HOM will result in the unpainted areas of the screen.

Versions of DOOM earlier than 1.4 exhibit this problem sooner than do later versions. Figure 14.4 illustrates how this problem is beginning to affect the sample WAD when it is played with DOOM v1.2.

Figure 14.4.
Edge overload in a view of the arena.

The view shown here is from the extreme eastern edge of the arena balcony, looking back across the watchtower and the pond. If you consider the map, you will see that the view has been carved up into a lot of small sections by the many lines in this area. Look carefully at Figure 14.4 and you will see that the problem is at its worst in the areas over the pond—especially over the stepping-stones—and in the section over the switch that operates the lift (note the sky directly above the player's index finger in the figure).

HOM caused by edge overload can be distinguished from the more common effect of omitting texture by the inconsistency of the former's appearance. Edge overload will manifest itself in different places as the player moves (or merely looks) around an area of the WAD. HOM from missing textures appears only (and consistently) in the area of the screen that the missing texture should occupy.

In the example shown in Figure 14.4, when the player takes a single step forward from the point shown, the effect vanishes—presumably because the removal of the complex of lines making up the lift at the extreme left edge of the screen drops the number of edges in view back below the critical threshold value.

Edge overload can be difficult to avoid in large and complicated open areas like the arena, areas that have a vast number of lines in view. This problem is much reduced in later versions of the game, but the effect can still occur. When it does, the only solution is to cut down on those regions of a WAD that provide open vistas through the entire map or to make your maps less complex. Sorry, but that's the way it is.

> If your WAD ever requires DOOM to display more than 128 surfaces (collectively known as *visplanes*) simultaneously, a more serious error occurs: DOOM crashes back to DOS with an error message that reads "Too many visplanes!" This can also arise from wide open views across many sectors—another good reason to limit such views.

SLIME TRAILS

Another cause of HOM (one that is, thankfully, becoming rare) is a faulty nodes tree. Node generators are much better than they used to be, but node-tree faults can still arise from time to time. The nodes tree is essentially the structure from which all views are derived, so it is understandable that display anomalies result from faults in this structure.

HOM can result from nodes-tree faults that leave holes in the display information. The result is similar to that caused by missing textures. These anomalies always occupy the same place—and are always present—but they can be distinguished from a missing texture error by virtue of their almost invariably narrow form. They tend to appear as thin strips of some visual anomaly (usually HOM) on odd walls, usually in areas of complex shape.

In addition to causing HOM, a faulty nodes tree can give rise to spurious transparent areas on walls. Being thin, these effects usually show up as a silvery shimmer down a wall. This gives the effect its name—a *slime trail*. One such example is shown in Figure 14.5.

You should recognize this area—it is part of the sunken section of the western green-stone corridor in the sample WAD. Notice how the player is pointing to a transparent strip that runs up part of the right wall. The effect occupies only a small section of wall—much smaller than the smallest line used on the map hereabouts—so it cannot be an editing error.

It is, in fact, caused by a faulty build of the nodes in this area—in turn caused by the awkward angle at which the walls run here. The faulty build has led DOOM to believe that there is something to display beyond this section of line. Fortunately, DOOM found something there in this case: the corridor beyond. Had there been void beyond this wall, HOM would have been the result—just as if a texture was missing.

Figure 14.5.

A slime trail in the sunken sector.

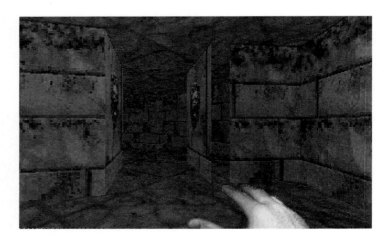

TRANSPARENT WALLS

Transparent walls are not a true anomaly in DOOM—they are a normal consequence of two-sided lines that have no texture on their main texture slot. Often, though, you can find that they crop up where you do not expect (or want) them. They can be caused by missing essential textures—if the void is thin enough, DOOM can sometimes display what is beyond—or by incorrectly set 2-sided flags.

More often though, transparent walls (or wrongly placed walls) are caused by DOOM getting confused about which way a line faces. Such confusion usually arises from faults in the nodes tree. The most common cause of these faults is forgetting to rebuild the nodes after a significant change to the map—such as a line being flipped around.

When this happens, the nodes tree may supply the graphical engine with incorrect information about which sidedef the player is viewing. The result, not surprisingly, is a view of the wrong side of the line. This particular anomaly can be exploited to produce some interesting special effects. Try using WADED's `Sec Define` facility to bind a sidedef to the sector on the "wrong" side of a line (or even both sidedefs to the same sector) if you want to experiment. This technique is fraught with pitfalls— but that's what you must expect if you start bending the engine's rules!

MEDUSA

An example of the dreaded Medusa effect is shown in Figure 14.6. As you will know if you have read Episode 2, Mission 1, Room 5, "The Low-Down on Textures," this is caused by using overlapping or vertically tiled textures on a two-sided line's main texture. The precise form of this effect differs depending on the texture in use; Figure 14.6 is what happens when BROVINE is used. The other consequence of this effect is that the game slows down to an absolute crawl. The problem becomes more acute as more of the screen is taken up by the faulty texture. The best way of escaping from Medusa when it occurs is to hit the Tab key to bring up the automap. The player can then be turned to face away from the offending wall, and proper control of the game will be restored.

Figure 14.6.
The Medusa effect.

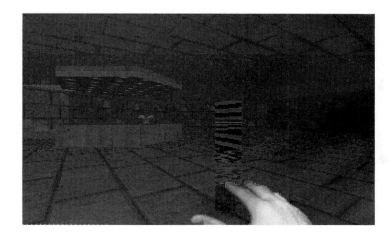

MOIRÉ, TALL ROOM ERROR, OR FLASH OF BLACK

Another effect that has not been discussed previously is a strange, annoying flash of black across the screen that can occur as the player moves into a new sector. This happens when moving between sectors with large differences of ceiling height (more than 559 units in DOOM v1.2, much higher in later versions). The taller a sector becomes, the worse the effect—hence one of its names: the Tall Room Error. Figure 14.7 shows what the effect looks like if the player passes through it slowly enough: a brown moiré pattern that sweeps across the player's view.

Make the transitions in your sector heights more gradual if you are plagued with this problem.

Figure 14.7.

A bad case of moiré.

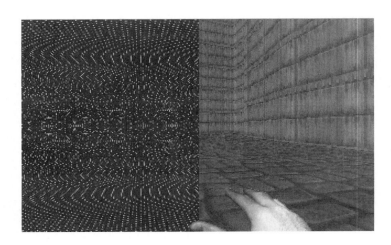

MORE ANOMALIES

The anomalies that can occur in DOOM are legion. Mostly, though, they occur irregularly, or as a result of breaches of the construction rules that have been explained throughout this episode. If you keep your edits small (and keep your wits about you), you should always be able to track the problems down to a fault in your map. If all else fails, restore to a previous version of the map and add the changes in smaller stages until you can identify the cause. Once you've done that, the solution will usually be apparent.

The further into DOOM editing you go, though, the more esoteric the errors and anomalies will become. Some you will be able to exploit and treat as deliberate features of your WAD. Mostly though, you'll be more interested in identifying and eliminating the causes.

EXIT: END OF EPISODE

This room brings the current episode of this book to a close. You have now seen all of the elements that are available for easy use in your own WADs and some of the consequences of getting things wrong. You have also been given a tantalizing glimpse of what else is possible, once you have mastered the art and become a true DOOM Deity.

Your training with me is over, but you still have a way to go yet, soldier! So, gird up your loins. Gather your wits about you and take a deep breath, as you move onwards, into Episode 3, "The Land of the Gods."

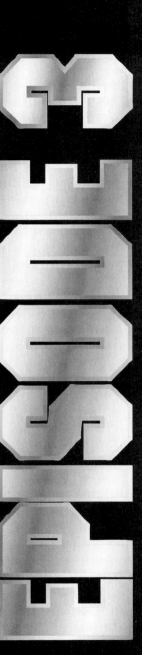

THE LAND OF THE GODS

MISSION 1:
FROM THE GURUS
OF GORE

ROOM 1

THE TOP FIVE WAD FILES

By Steve McCrea

This chapter will closely examine the five best homemade WAD files to learn how the designers achieved their goals. Having seen the effort that has gone into these WAD files, I hope that you will be inspired to continue your own designs and that you will pick up the gauntlet thrown at your feet, accepting the challenge to do better. Do not be disheartened—each of these WADs was created one linedef at a time by someone just like yourself (although possibly with more spare time). You can learn from their experience. Besides, level-editor technology continues to improve by leaps and bounds.

Unfortunately, I will also be spoiling any and all surprises that these levels would otherwise supply. So do yourself a favor and play them first.

ALIENS—TOTAL CONVERSION

Aliens—Total Conversion, or *Aliens*-TC, had a lot to live up to. The previous attempt (called *Alien DOOM*) at a DOOM episode based on the characters from the film *Aliens* was very impressive, with nine levels, a new weapon, a host of amusing sound effects taken from the film, and new bad guys rendered in 3D Studio. Even before *Aliens*-TC was released, the author was one of the most famous names in WAD design, thanks to a series of progress reports and screenshots on the Internet, each prominently displaying the line "by Justin Fisher."

So how does it live up to expectations? The level archive includes a patch for DOOM.EXE that must be applied with DeHackEd in order to modify the behavior of the bad guys and various objects. The WAD is again a full episode, this time closely following the plot of the film from the point where the Marines arrive at the base. And this is what sets it apart from every other DOOM level: The gameplay just feels *different*.

The scene is a landing pad outside a docking bay. The edges of the pad are rimmed with safety barriers that are painted with warning stripes. Lights course down short poles, and along chevrons on the ground, to guide ships in. Towards the horizon, large brown stones are scattered on the earth.

A door opens with a high-pitched metallic whine. A lift leads down into the bay, where barrels occupy the corners. Shooting a barrel results in a dribble of fluid running from a hole in the side. On a wall of the bay is the number 37, in bold print. The neon numbers flicker erratically.

The big stones blend perfectly with the mountainous backdrop to give a real sense of depth to the landscape. The flashing pole is set up as a three-frame animation in the object table using DeHackEd. The exploding barrel has been replaced with the more tame leaking barrel in the same way, to reduce the number of frames it occupies (DeHackEd cannot change the size of the table, and the extra frames are needed for another effect). The chevrons are new floor flats, replacing green slime.

The barriers are a transparent texture on an impassable, two-sided line. Although the ceiling is more than 128 units above the floor, the texture does not repeat, due to one of the inconsistencies of the DOOM engine. The floor level number on the wall is in a narrow recess textured in steel, which has the random flashing attribute covered by a transparent texture with cutouts for the digits.

The door-open sound is just one of 35 well-chosen sound effects from the film, ranging from the bleep of the motion detectors to the whine of the cargo loader, all of which enhance the feeling that this isn't DOOM anymore.

A passage is blocked with metal plates, ladders, and other scrap welded together. The automap indicates that the passage continues for some way beyond the hastily constructed barrier. Progressing down a darkened side passage, Apone barks: "Check those corners!" Entering a nearby room, the floor strewn with debris, someone comments: "Sir, this place is dead. Whatever happened here, I think we missed it."

Incredibly, the first level has no enemies. In a very brave move by the author, the player instead wanders around a deserted complex, discovering the changes made by the defending humans, and stumbling across evidence of alien activity. (He might also take the opportunity to stock up on ammunition and armor.) Lighting is expertly controlled, with an exceedingly good mix of dim and slightly flickering areas.

Occasional outbursts of dialogue are actually triggered at appropriate moments. For example, a "Check those corners" object is created by giving it the dialogue as a wake-up cry and then editing the frame table so that it is invisible and is removed from the game on waking up. So each time Sergeant Apone says "Check those corners," it is this type of object, placed nearby. A superb idea, and needless to say, the atmosphere it generates is tremendous. (This effect has since been "borrowed" for incidental sound effects in Heretic.)

The docking area is secure. The intermission screen indicates the next objective is to rescue the colonists from the atmospheric processor. A smart gun is available from the armory—this baby really rips out the rounds! As the lift descends into an area that shows all the signs of heavy infestation, Apone reminds you that there may be survivors out there. Fibrous green matter hangs off the walls, and here and there corpses are stored near open eggs.

The smart gun is a plasma-rifle replacement, where the plasma bolt has been replaced by a small bright dot of tracer fire. This actually makes the gun more pleasant to use, as the bolt no longer obscures what you are shooting at. Wisely, Justin Fisher left the shotgun unchanged, except for the pickup message: "For close encounters." The chaingun and rocket launcher have been cosmetically changed, and the chainsaw has actually become a cargo-bay loader, complete with Ripley's shout of "Come on!"(See Figure 1.1.)

DOOM PROGRAMMING GURUS   1 ROOM   1 MISSION   3 EPISODE

Figure 1.1.
Using the cargo loader in the Sulaco.

The alien-infested regions are very cleverly done. Justin extracted some of the skin and flesh textures from the Inferno episode and recolored them dark green. He then cut bits of corpses from various textures and pasted them in. Rib-like objects are arranged along the edges to roughen the passage. (See Figure 1.2.)

Finally, a dark shape rushes forward. The shotgun barks, and the alien explodes with a screech in a spray of deadly acid—the next one won't get so close. From the direction of a closed egg comes a gurgling sound, and suddenly a facehugger is scuttling rapidly into another shotgun shell. If only it wasn't so dark…

Alien behavior is well implemented though a DeHackEd patch. Some are basically Demons, with only a close attack, while others (with some artistic license) are Imps who spit acid at you. Facehuggers actually do hatch from alien eggs, and then behave like ground-based skulls.

After all the buildup, I found the aliens themselves a little disappointing. They behave well, they sound good, and they are better and more organic than the 3D Studio-rendered creatures in *Aliens* DOOM. However, the contrast in the graphics is too high, as they are basically black with a few highlights. Given the large number of dark grays and greens available in the DOOM palette, this is a great pity.

The first eight levels loosely follow the plot of the film *Aliens*, ending in a cargo loader showdown with the alien queen in the *Sulaco*. (There are also three bonus levels.) For example, on Level 3 there are more aliens than there is ammunition, so you must rush around closing security doors to prevent aliens getting in; on Level 6, Newt's watch is visible on the automap. All around, there are glowing blue maps on tables, facehuggers twitching in jars, and wires hanging from holes in the ceiling.

Figure 1.2.
Finding some of the colonists by an opened alien egg.

Aliens-TC is the most complete add-on to DOOM ever written, evoking those old feelings of fear and trepidation you experienced when you first played DOOM. Some people even put off playing DOOM II until they had finished *Aliens*-TC! It is, to my knowledge, the only WAD to provoke a public (if not official) response from id Software. In the words of John Romero, "*Aliens*-TC kicks ass!"

DOOMSDAY OF UAC

Doomsday of UAC, commonly known by its filename UAC_DEAD, is a massive single level, weighing in at nearly 400KB for the level data alone, with a starry sky patch completing the file. (In comparison, the largest—and my favorite—level in DOOM, The Spawning Vats, is a mere 184KB.) The setting is the headquarters of the UAC corporation in Jakarta, which has (surprise, surprise) been overrun by assorted Hellspawn.

You awaken inside a narrow aluminum container. The presence of three Medikits is somewhat disquieting, as is the total lack of visible features on the walls and floor. You throw open one of the walls to reveal a Demon and its Former Human Sergeant handlers in a narrow passage. Two or three Medikits later, you step out of the passage into a huge courtyard.

So far, nothing particularly inventive. It makes for a frantic start if the player is armed with only a pistol, as seen in a number of the original levels, such as The Spawning Vats. There are several more Spectres, Former Human Sergeants, and Imps around the end of the passage before the player has a chance to relax.

You glance back at the aluminum container. It is a truck trailer, turned on its side! The back door, emblazoned with the UAC logo, is hinged back, and the wheels are still spinning after the crash. Nearby are rows of similar trailers, in a more natural attitude.

Putting the trailer on its side was very clever, allowing the wheels and axle to be detailed immaculately with a single O-shaped sector. The tires are the DOORTRAK texture, given a scrolling effect to make them appear to spin. Rear lights on some of the other trailers are the thin, blue striplights in aluminum frames. However, this is just a warm-up for the spectacle to come.

Some distance ahead of the trailer you find the cab, also lying on its side with its wheels spinning. The engine cover has popped open to reveal a burning engine; but strangely, the headlights still cut a bright swathe through the gloom. From the bloodstains, you guess that the driver has been dragged away through the shattered windscreen. Angrily, you shoot the fuel tank.

It is hard to find fault in this piece of DOOM architecture, and very hard to believe that it is even possible, given the restrictions of the graphics engine. However, closer examination reveals that only one floor and one ceiling are visible in any one region of the truck. Excellent little touches such as the headlights and the barrel for a fuel tank complete the effect. Pools of blood are used throughout the level in a creative way.

You jog down a wide curving ramp to a circular courtyard, at its center is a fountain filled with blood. You make short work of the Imps hiding behind the stone sculpture of the letters UAC, then waste the Former Human Sergeants lurking in a dimly lit underground car park down another curving ramp. Fluorescent tubes flicker erratically on all sides of the regular lines of concrete supports. (See Figure 1.3.)

Similar floor and wall textures disguise the steps on the ramps, giving the immediate impression of a smooth slope. The center of the fountain includes a blood drooling gargoyle texture. The UAC lettering again makes the player wonder how it is done. In contrast to *Aliens*-TC, the flourescents are lit in the standard way, using a small flickering sector in front of the wall.

When you finally enter the headquarter buildings proper, a sudden urge overtakes you, probably because this place is making you nervous. You slip into a nearby room, and not wanting to squeeze between a line of soldiers, start looking under the doors for an empty cubicle. When you get in, though, you find that all it contains is a box of bullets, which you have to use on the soldiers.

The author, Leo Martin Lim, has used a not-so-well-known feature of doors: They can be initially partly open, just by setting the ceiling height appropriately. When the door closes again, though, it closes all the way to the floor. (In a subsequent level, called Cheese, the women's toilets contained not water but blood!)

Figure 1.3.

Picking off the hellspawn that are hiding behind the UAC statue.

You stagger, relieved, into a tall marble lobby. Large cylindrical columns hang from the ceiling, supporting spotlights. The guard Imp behind his security desk calls to his buddies on the level above, so you rush up to silence them. Taking a moving walkway, you enter a long room containing a low rectangular table. As you approach the table, shutters over the windows rise to reveal a heavily populated balcony.

There is a board meeting in progress in the next room, and the board members are concentrating heavily on their meeting briefs laid before them on the circular table. The walls are brightly illuminated, highlighting monitors and maps. The doors behind you remain hinged open, but instead you open the secret door behind the speaker's podium and venture into the hellish passage beyond.

The architecture in this level is highly effective, with the rooms and furniture slightly larger than life, which has the effect of intimidating the player. The huge columns supporting the spotlights look as though they came directly from the lobby of an expensive hotel. The walkway does not actually carry the player along, but otherwise it is realistic, and similarly the hinged doors are there even before the doors are opened; but the presence of a large collection of Cacodemons is a good distraction.

Narrowly avoiding falling into two deadly pits, you finally choose the correct path in the underground complex, and step out onto a ledge above a huge lake of lava. Ahead of you, you can see pairs of candles floating in the air, marking what appears to be a path across the chamber. "Hell with it," you think. "It worked for Indiana Jones in the Last Crusade." So you step off the ledge and onto…an invisible staircase! (See Figure 1.4.) Running across, you cannot help but notice the poor guy hanging in the rock formation to your right. He certainly has lost a lot of blood.

The invisible staircase is the trick in this level that made it so famous, and it is quite bizarre that it exists at all. I can only assume that Leo discovered it by accident, because John Carmack himself would have had a hard time predicting its existence. It works this way: Each step is the height and texture of the floor and contains a small inner sector with the required step height. The object-placement routines believe that your coordinates correspond to the small sector, whereas the drawing routines are blind to it. To set this up, just change the sector references of the lines making up the small sector so that both sides point to it.

Figure 1.4.
Facing the invisible staircase.

At the top of the staircase is a room, the door of which locks behind you. A Cyberdemon floats unmoving on the red key-card, surrounded by four skulls that hover above your dead buddies. Clearly some kind of Satanic ritual is under way. As you approach the Cyberdemon, Barons of Hell suddenly appear and attack you. In its death throes, one of the Barons completes the incantation, which awakens the summoned creatures. (See Figure 1.5.)

The monsters in the room are surrounded by invisible blocks, just like the staircase, which reach up to the ceiling. These are marked with the sector tag 666 so that they lower when the last Baron dies. (This level is E1M8.) The clever tricks around the Cyberdemon make up for its inclusion in such a small room, which I consider in most cases to be inexcusable.

Exhausted from the struggle, you finally find an escape shuttle powered up at the end of a runway, its engines roaring against a blast wall. Hopping in, you take off the brakes, allowing the ship to race towards the cliff edge.

COLOR GALLERY

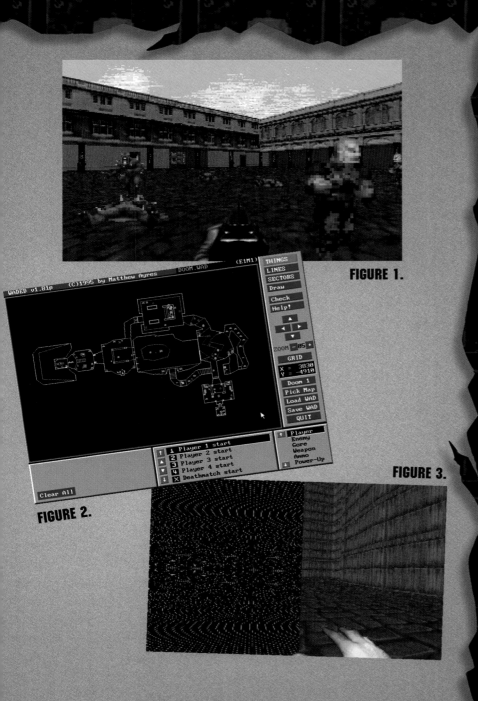

FIGURE 1.

FIGURE 2.

FIGURE 3.

FIGURE 1.
A SCUFFLE IN NEVILE'S COURT IN THE UNHOLY TRINITY

FIGURE 2.
WADED'S MAIN EDITING SCREEN, AS SEEN AT START-UP.

FIGURE 3.
A BAD CASE OF MOIRÉ—A FLASH OF BLACK—CAUSED WHEN THE HEIGHT OF ADJACENT CEILING SURFACES VARIES TOO MUCH (CAUSING A TALL ROOM ERROR).

FIGURE 4.
FINDING SOME OF THE COLONISTS, AND AN OPENED EGG, AS THE PLAYER MOVES THROUGH *ALIENS*-TC.

FIGURE 5.
CONNECTING A SELF-RAISING STAIRCASE FROM THE CRESCENT TO THE MAZE.

FIGURE 6.
THE SECTOR EDIT DIALOG BOX. ALL OF THE PROPERTIES FOR INDIVIDUAL SECTOR EDITING ARE DONE IN THIS DIALOG BOX.

FIGURE 4.

FIGURE 6.

FIGURE 5.

FIGURE 7.

FIGURE 7.
WALL TEXTURES THAT
TEMPT THE PLAYER IN
PRESSING THE SPACE
BAR.

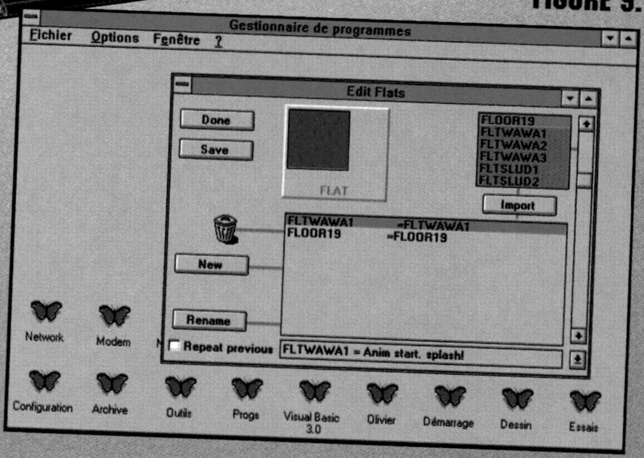

FIGURE 8.
EDMAP'S ABOUT BOX
SUPERIMPOSED OVER
A TOUGH LEVEL UNDE
DEVELOPMENT.

FIGURE 9.
THE FLOORS AND
CEILINGS EDITING
WINDOWS.

FIGURE 9.

FIGURE 8.

FIGURE 10.

FIGURE 12.

FIGURE 11.

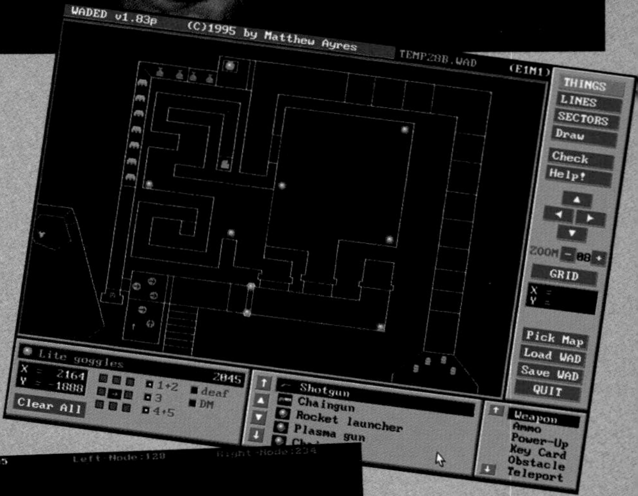

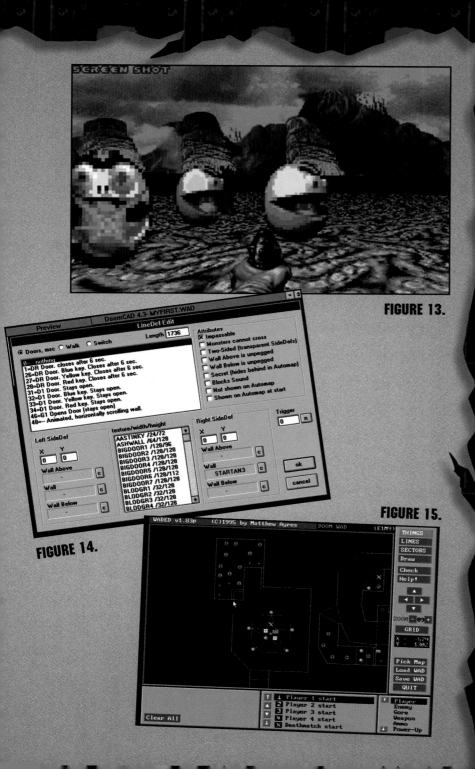

FIGURE 13.

FIGURE 13.
PACATTACK! THREE
PACS IN VARIOUS
STAGES OF ATTACK.

FIGURE 14.
THE LINEDEF EDIT DIA-
LOG BOX. ALL OF THE
LINEDEF PROPERTIES
ARE CHANGED ON THE
DIALOG BOX.

FIGURE 15.
A MONSTER CACHE IN
THE EXTREME NORTH-
WEST CORNER SHOWS
SOUND-PROPAGATION
RULES WHICH CAN BE
USED TO AWAKEN MON-
STERS—GREAT FOR
SURPRISING AND OVER-
WHELMING A VICTIM.

FIGURE 15.

FIGURE 14.

**FIGURE 16.
THE FRONT END TO THE
HONORIFIC TITLES HOME
PAGE.**

**FIGURE 17.
WADED'S DEMONSTRATION
OF MANIPULATING A SEC-
TOR'S SPECIFICATIONS.**

**FIGURE 18.
THE TEXTURE EDITING
WINDOW WHILE EDITING
A PART OF THE NEW
TRINITY FILM.**

Welcome to the DOOM Honorific Titles!

DOOM II, Level 07, Ultra–Violence, starting with a pistol, ending with 100% everything, 200% health and 200% armour.
This is the sort of thing that the DHT is about. If you play like this, the DHT is right for you!

1995 02 01: The new rules, DHT4, are out!
Tons of new titles, including ~~~~ II stuff.

FIGURE 16.

```
0  Normal.
1  Light level flickers, random period.
2  Light level strobes, fast.
3  Light level strobes, slow.
4  Light level strobes, -20% health loss, only -10% at skill 1.
5  Hell slime, -10% health loss, only -5% at skill 1.
6  Ceiling crush and raise
7  Nukage, -5% health loss, only -2% at skill 1.
8  Light level glowing.
9  Secret area discovery credit.
10 Door closes in 30 seconds.
11 End episode if player dies, -20% health, only -10% at skill 1.
12 Light level oscillates from normal and 0, slow.
13 Light level oscillates from normal and 0, fast.
14 Door raises in 5 minutes.
16 Super hell slime, -20% health, only -10% at skill 1.
17 Light fire flickering.
```

WADED v1.83p   (C)1995 by Matthew Ayres   PIGGY.WAD   (MAP01)

THINGS
LINES

CANCEL

SPECIAL   LIGHTING   CEILING
Make DOOR   LIST   APPLY   CEIL1 2
MULTI   FLOOR   CEIL3 1

FIGURE 18.

FIGURE 17.

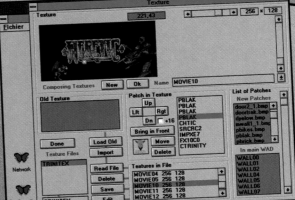

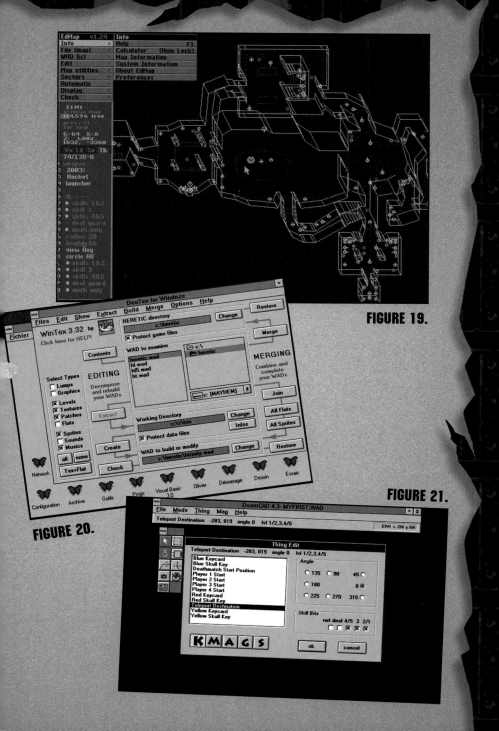

FIGURE 19.

FIGURE 20.

FIGURE 21.

FIGURE 19.
AN EDMAP DEMO
OF A NASTY LEVEL IN
PROGRESS.

FIGURE 20.
THE MAIN SCREEN
OF WINTEX.

FIGURE 21.
THE THING EDIT
DIALOG BOX.

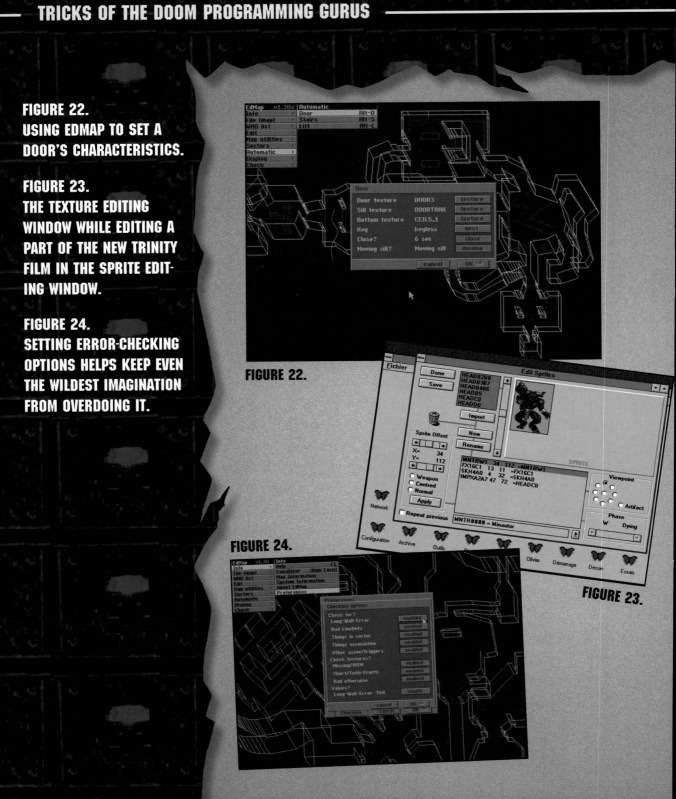

FIGURE 22.
USING EDMAP TO SET A DOOR'S CHARACTERISTICS.

FIGURE 23.
THE TEXTURE EDITING WINDOW WHILE EDITING A PART OF THE NEW TRINITY FILM IN THE SPRITE EDITING WINDOW.

FIGURE 24.
SETTING ERROR-CHECKING OPTIONS HELPS KEEP EVEN THE WILDEST IMAGINATION FROM OVERDOING IT.

FIGURE 22.

FIGURE 24.

FIGURE 23.

Figure 1.5.
The Barons do not appreciate you interrupting their Satanic ritual.

The level ends with another spectacular vehicle. At the other end of the runway there is a sector with ceiling texture F_SKY1 and a ceiling height equal to its floor height. The dividing line has no upper texture, and altogether this creates a cliff edge.

Doomsday of UAC features solid level design and interesting gameplay. What sets it apart is that every location is big, bold, and dramatic, and guaranteed to impress or baffle. As with many add-on levels, though, a fast machine is needed for the full experience.

ETERNITY

Eternity, or Serenity II, by Bjorn Hermans and Holger Nathrath, is a full episode that replaces the Shores of Hell. This, I think you will agree, is a huge undertaking when you consider that they have already released a highly acclaimed replacement episode for Inferno called Serenity. Having gotten some of the more bizarre ideas out of their systems in Serenity (for example, mazes with walk-through walls), the authors have settled down and designed a beautiful, traditional episode with an emphasis on playability.

You emerge from the end of the pipe into a bloody reservoir. At your feet lies a shotgun, which you snatch up gleefully before quickly wading forth. Some cannon fodder in a pipe a few steps to your right guards a radiation suit, and you rapidly clear the blockage in the pipe, off to the left, which leads to the main part of the complex.

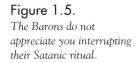

Here, the presence of the Radiation Suit fools the player into thinking that this bloody complex of passages is going to be huge and tortuous to navigate. The immense simplicity is then a great and unexpected relief (as well as an excellent design decision). Having gone to the trouble of selecting appropriate wall and floor textures, most designers would have made this section overly large, immediately frustrating the player.

On a more general note, acid floors in the episode are handled sensibly: They mostly are avoidable, a punishment for falling off a ledge, rather than being a necessity to run over. Where it is necessary, near the edges of the acid radiation suits can be found, often in hidden areas. There are perhaps too many acid floors for my taste, although they do add to the atmosphere and feel of the levels. The authors have ensured that is impossible to get trapped anywhere.

Down a pair of symmetrical stairways a passage stretches away, its lights flashing rhythmically. Between the stairways, an alcove sports a huge marble engraving of a Baron, illuminated by a pair of striplights. As you venture down the passage, a door suddenly opens just ahead of you and its occupants stream out and attack.

Many of the rooms in the episode display partial symmetry, broken only by the passages in and out, adding an element of realism to the architecture. The authors are not afraid to borrow an idea or two from the original id Software levels, such as the passage with its alternately dark and flashing light levels.

There are many recurring decorations, one of which is the Baron engraving. In contrast to the id Software levels—where the presence of this icon symbolized the imminent appearance of a Baron and hence served to set the player's nerves on edge—in this episode it usually is just decoration. Similarly the conventions of what are normally teleport pads have been upset, as quite often the pads are nothing more than placemats for keys. These and other details are at least consistent throughout and contribute to the unique feel of the levels.

In the majority of homemade WADs, when rooms full of bad guys open suddenly, those rooms are usually behind you, and Sergeants will make short work of your back. Not so here. This is typical of the fair play of the enemy. It is a rare moment in this game when you are not given the opportunity to shoot first.

Beyond the strobing passage is a marble-walled room, the marble broken vertically at regular intervals by rusting iron beams. In the center of the room, brightened by a large rectangular skylight, the yellow skull-key rests atop a platform. When you throw the switch facing the platform, however, parts of the balcony drop into the floor, revealing stairs down into the lower regions of the room.

The marble-and-iron motif crops up repeatedly in the levels, and it is one of the many original and imaginative combinations of textures that breathe new life into the old id Software graphics. Holes in the ceiling are made to accentuate the dramatic look of a room, contrasting sharply the edges of the room and its center.

3
EPISODE

1
MISSION

1
ROOM

DOOM PROGRAMMING GURUS

The playing sequence is not entirely predictable, but at the same time it is usually made obvious what to do next. It is clear that the levels are designed almost exclusively for single-player rather than Deathmatch mode. Travel from one point to another in a level is by a specific route. The effect of the switch, although unexpected, is both visible and audible from the switch location, and hence rewarding.

A line of archways splits the lower area in two, and at each end lies a door. Through the archways, strips on the columns of the arch cast overlapping cones of light onto suspicious-looking panels. (See Figure 1.6.) You nudge a panel open and find the blue skull-key. Meanwhile, one of the other panels has slid open, releasing more of the usual beasts to roam amongst the archways. You take the key with one hand while you pump the shotgun with the other.

Figure 1.6.
Lights affixed to beautifully constructed archways.

Wherever possible, the authors have added realistic lighting in the form of light coming in through windows and skylights, artificial light sources such as torches and wall strips, and the shadows cast by both. The effort they have expended was not wasted; indeed the lighting is one of the most eye-catching features of the episode. (See Figure 1.7.)

Just before the exit you come across a serifed capital R cut into the floor of a room and filled with glowing slime. The slime casts a faint reversed R on the ceiling. (See Figure 1.8.) Ignoring it totally, you sprint into the exit room, and having waited for the opposition to be crushed, you time your bid for the central column and freedom (at least until the next mission).

Each level has a letter prominently incorporated into one of the rooms in some way, so that over the eight levels the letters spell out *Serenity*. (The level just described was number three.) Fortunately, this did not influence the design of the levels as the rooms in question are just tacked onto the map. The final level recapitulates the letters and then adds the Y, which is also used to make the Cyberdemon easier to deal with by raising and lowering just enough to block his rockets when raised.

Figure 1.7.

The lighting was inspired by the starting room in id Software's Spawning Vats.

Figure 1.8.

The trademark of the episode, a letter which forms the centerpiece of a room on each level.

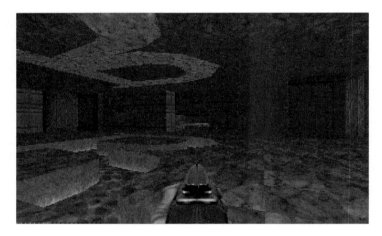

Also of note on the final level is a beautiful semi-transparent stained-glass texture that looks terrific with the hellish red sky visible through the gaps. Perhaps coincidentally, Heretic also features stained glass textures, although not transparent and not so realistic (the Eternity graphic appears to be a scanned photograph).

Eternity comprises eight varied yet consistent levels that have a unique and enjoyable feel, with the style of play allowing a mainly offensive approach. The difficulty levels are sensibly chosen, with "Hurt Me Plenty" about equivalent to "Ultra-Violence" in the original DOOM, and "Ultra-Violence" roughly the same as "Ultra-Violence" in DOOM II. A lot of care has been taken to make the levels look good and play better.

RETURN TO PHOBOS

When Michael Kelsey's Return to Phobos was released, it was one of the first full-episode replacements available, and it was eagerly received by the Internet community. There was much discussion about the excess of switches and puzzles (there are two new textures and both of them are switches), but there was no disputing that id Software itself would have been proud of this one. To this day no one has so successfully recaptured the spirit of Knee Deep in the Dead and placed it in a WAD.

You are outside a huge slab of a building. From the front, with its columns and overhangs, it is highly reminiscent of a museum. (See Figure 1.9.) The central entrance is a door formed from a thin metal panel stretched between a pair of thick beams. When you try to open the door beyond, it sticks. After a few attempts you open it enough for you to get under.

Figure 1.9.

The spectacular facade of the main building in Return to Phobos.

Doors in Return to Phobos are not always simply a rectangular sector with a picture of a door on it. Here we have a door with some meaningful shape followed by a one with an unpredictable character. The sticking door is a clever trick, relying on the standard door behavior of rising to just below the lowest neighboring ceiling. There is then a sector on the left of the door with a crushing ceiling. (The scraping sound is audible next to the door). The sector is hidden by a DOORTRAK texture on the two-sided line separating it from the door.

Although there are no examples on this level, lifts are also made more interesting, for example by having pillars with SUPPORT, DOORTRAK, or LITE textures cutting into the lift sector. Once you have seen one of these types of lift, standard DOOM lifts look plain and unrealistic.

DOOM PROGRAMMING GURUS   **1 ROOM**   **1 MISSION**   **3 EPISODE**

You make it out the back of the building, past the huge shallow pool set among tall columns. A set of stairs leads to the upper floors where from a window you can almost see over the perimeter wall. You take another flight of stairs even higher, and from here the view is spectacular. Beyond the wall irregularly patterned agricultural land stretches away to the base of the mountains. (See Figure 1.10.)

Figure 1.10.
Looking out of an upper window toward fields stretching away to the mountains.

The author has set aside almost one third of the area of the level for this one view out of a window. The fields are just any green flats; at long range, the details of the ground are lost. The edge of the map has been carefully positioned to avoid the sky texture wrapping around vertically.

Returning to the main building, you enter a cavernous area, the extents of which are hidden in darkness. Above the watery floor, small dimly lit rooms are cut into columns and steps lead variously up and down between them. As you move from column to column, you are knocked from a set of steps by an attacking skull. It is a short swim to the nearest teleport, which takes you back to one of the columns. (See Figure 1.11.)

This is the most impressive location I have ever seen in any DOOM level. The lighting is perfect; there is just enough to let you see the neighboring columns. The ground is far enough down that when there, none of the steps or little rooms can be seen. And it is great fun to rush up a set of stairs and blow an Imp out the far side of a column down into the water with the shotgun. To avoid the area slowing down excessively, it is irregularly shaped, with walls protruding from the edges and dividing the space into compartments.

You arrive on a wide balcony overlooking three sides of a large, chunky maze. From here you choose a route to the exit of the room and pick off its more obvious denizens before jumping in. Running swiftly to the end of the maze, you skip over some puddles of slime and throw a couple of switches, opening nearby doors. Only an Imp stands between you and the exit signs.

Figure 1.11.

Fighting on the steps between rooms cut into a series of columns high above some water.

I never liked mazes, even when I was playing Wolfenstein 3D. (I hated secrets, too, but the DOOM approach to secrets has tempered my opinion somewhat.) The overview of the maze is a novel approach though, and it works well. The acid puddles are just the right size so that you would be unlikely to be hurt when running over them, and even the switches are a lazy nod toward the designer's obsession with puzzles.

The first level is probably the worst offender in the puzzle department. To progress further than the fifth room requires the execution of a bizarre series of jumps and button presses, as follows.

You run down a slime trench, up some stairs, and across the top of two empty pillars, opening a secret door at the end of the run. In the secret room, you throw a switch that raises the pillars into recesses in the roof. Jumping back to the base of the pillars, you press a button that lowers them, and then you ride one of the pillars up into its recess. There are two buttons in the recess. You press the first one and hear a door open, finally. The other button lowers the pillar.

However, all the levels look excellent, thanks to good choice of textures and solid architecture. Everything feels right; columns are neither too fat nor too thin, passages are not overly cramped, doors are wide enough with tidy and functional-looking frames, stairs are never so steep as to make combat difficult, and transitions between textures on walls are always associated with an appropriate divider, such as one of the SUPPORT textures.

Once doors were doors, lifts were just plain old ordinary lifts, and WAD files were just single levels. When Return to Phobos was released, it greatly influenced all that. Now, doors are often all kinds of shapes, lifts run on tracks or up pillars, and level designers long for the free time to finish their episodes-in-progress. Others should follow Michael Kelsey's example and reexamine the features that made id Software's original levels so great.

THE UNHOLY TRINITY

The Unholy Trinity, by myself, Simon Wallm, and Elias Papavassilopoulos started life as a rather pedestrian map of Trinity College, Cambridge. Somewhere along the line, I decided that that would not be enough, and I took a camera over to college. When the level was completed, nearly all of its textures had been replaced by half a megabyte of scanned, retouched photographs and a couple of hand-drawn graphics. Add to this some entertaining tricks and challenging gameplay, and it could not fail.

You are looking out across a wide grassy courtyard criss-crossed by cobbled paths at a three floor ivy-covered building with a sloping tiled roof. Next to it is a tan-colored stone building with tall, ornate windows. The sky is almost clear blue, with only a few scattered wispy clouds breaking the monotony.

The walls across the court are 384 units high, and although DOOM textures normally repeat every 128 units, these walls appear to have a 384-unit-high texture. The truth of the matter is that there is a sector behind the wall, a floor height of 128 and a ceiling height of 256. The upper, middle, and lower textures are each a part of the tall texture. The line of the wall is marked impassable so that skulls and Cacodemons cannot accidentally wander into the hidden sector and disappear. The lines making up the sector are marked as hidden, and so they do not appear during the game in the automap.

SKY1 is redefined in the TEXTURE1 resource to consist of four patches, each 256 units wide. Therefore the sky texture is 1024 pixels wide and is unique through 360 degrees. Each patch is aligned with a main compass point; the patch at 0 is east, the patch at 256 is north, the patch at 512 is west, and the patch at 768 is south. Note that this means the sky is mirrored left to right.

To your right, a dark rounded doorway leads into the Porters' Lodge, according to the calligraphy above the door. You dash into the plaster-walled room, open the wood-paneled hatch in the counter, and steal the porters' supply of shotgun shells. They have no need of them anymore, as their corpses are sprawled at your feet.

Darkening the doorway sector disguises the inherent squareness of the structure so that the rounded graphic with its black base fits in. The plaster and wood paneling are the two hand-drawn textures. The hatch is simply a lift that is set one unit lower than the rest of the counter to make it visible to the observant player. Unlike doors, lifts return exactly to their initial height, and the position of the hatch is not lost.

Back out in the main courtyard, there are gatehouses set into three sides, their octagonal towers standing above the rest of the buildings. On one of the gatehouses you see a clock face partially obscuring arched windows. Below the windows, a sculpture of Edward III stands in a small alcove. (See Figure 1.12.)

The towers protrude from the wall to disguise the essentially two-dimensional nature of the structure. For an example, look at the wall at the start of Inferno, which appears to be a big sheet of cardboard, and compare it with the doorway in the courtyard of E1M1, which looks very solid indeed. The sector dividing off the taller part of the wall is thin, since you can see through the lower F_SKY1 ceiling to the wall behind.

Figure 1.12.
The Edward III gate in the Unholy Trinity, with the chapel on the right.

Details on each of the gatehouses are unique. Rather than having a full graphic for each of the walls, there are patches for windows, crests, statues, and the clock face, which are positioned over a plain stone background. Many of the textures in the level are handled this way, to save space in the WAD file. This level was the first to redefine TEXTURE1, and I had to write my own tools to do it. Now, though, you can just use DeuTex.

The chapel is packed with Imps arranging barrels under the supervision of a Former Human Sergeant. One or two shots takes care of them. On the altar lies one of your comrades. As you nudge the altar, the entire wall drops, revealing a hellish passage under the college. Down the passage is a chamber cut by a river of lava that runs between openings in the walls, and up to his waist in the lava stands a soldier.

There are several opportunities to kill monsters with barrels in the level, because I find it very satisfying when being attacked to single out and shoot the barrel in a horde of bad guys. Almost as much fun as the chainsaw.

The channel is basically one of those hideous glitches involving missing textures put to good use. A trench of the required depth is cut into the lava, and its sides are left untextured. The surface of the lava then extends over the region where the side wall should be, disguising the trench. The effect works quite well, except from certain angles where the bottom of the trench is visible. A much neater channel could probably be created by copying the technique of the invisible staircase from Doomsday of UAC, except with a step lower than the floor height.

When you attempt to go through a passage to the next court, the way is blocked by a door marked with the college coat-of-arms. Up some stairs, you find a Baron of Hell guarding a switch. The switch is slightly recessed into the plaster wall and flanked by copies of the same coat-of-arms. You throw the switch and return to the passage to find that the door has opened. (See Figure 1.13.)

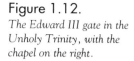

1
ROOM

MISSION

1

3
EPISODE

DOOM PROGRAMMING GURUS

Figure 1.13.
A scuffle breaks out in Nevile's court.

Identifying the switch with the coat-of-arms is a good way of associating it with the door. It is recessed into the wall to avoid having to redefine a switch texture to put a switch in a plaster-walled room. This is especially important if you want the level to be easy to include in a multi-author WAD file, for example a series of good Cooperative levels. The alternative is to widen a standard switch texture and add your patches on the right-hand side. For some reason, all the switches in Heretic are recessed into the wall.

You enter a small, darkened room packed with soldiers in neat rows. Through a window in one wall there is another player facing off against a Cyberdemon! During the scramble for the doorhandle, the words "CAMERA—PETER MORGAN" suddenly appear on the window, and the realization sinks in—it's only a movie. The player fires uselessly a few times before the Cyberdemon pulps him with a rocket. (See Figure 1.14.)

Figure 1.14.
The Unholy Trinity cinema.

One of the centerpieces of the level is this cinema screen showing the credits for the level in a 27-frame animation. Each frame is defined in sequence between SLADRIP1 and SLADRIP3. DOOM looks for these two textures and then animates whatever lies between them. The Cyberdemon, the player, and the rocket are simply the game sprites, since DOOM does not distinguish between sprites and patches in textures. Due to an inconsistency in the patch-caching routines in DOOM, the lettering had to be handled differently—each character was extracted and a new patch was made from it.

The Unholy Trinity was a ground-breaking level when it was first released because of the techniques it used, and thanks to the beauty of the buildings that it accurately portrays, it still looks good. As usual, however, complexity inevitably means it has a slow frame-rate in some areas. In "Ultra-Violence mode," it is challenging to complete quickly, and after some experience on the level, it still takes about 20 minutes to finish.

SUMMARY

In this chapter, I examined five WAD files, each with a unique style that makes it stand out from the many hundreds available. The levels all have well-tuned difficulty levels, in addition to Deathmatch and Cooperative starting points (even when they not specifically designed for Deathmatch or Co-op mode), in order to cater to the widest possible user base. I also explained the techniques and tricks that the designers used, so that you can implement them for yourself.

ROOM 2

By Justin Fisher

THE BEST SOUNDS

In DOOM and DOOM II, you have the ability to change the sounds, and there are a multitude of good WAD files available with new and creative sounds you can use. Following are two of the sound WAD files that stand out as being among the best. These are the (Monty) Python WAD and *The Evil Dead* WAD.

THE (MONTY) PYTHON.WAD

Obviously, with a sound WAD like this, whether you like it or not usually depends on how much you like the film/s, so this WAD won't appeal to everyone; but it is still well worth checking out. While many of the monsters (especially those that do not appear in the Episode 1 levels of DOOM) have not had their sounds replaced, pretty much all the environment sounds have been altered with fantastic sound effects, most made by the human voice box.

Of all the sounds, the most predictable was "Help help! I'm being repressed!" originally cried by a politically aware peasant as King Arthur tries to extract information from him. It is now cried by the Former Humans as you take them out. Other than that, this collection wasn't what I expected. Considering the Monty Python films and the number of good one-liners in them, I was pleasantly surprised to find that the creators of this WAD hadn't fallen into the trap of putting speech where it wasn't really suitable (such as when picking up items) and had used an array of (mostly vocal) sound effects where quotes would not be appropriate. The sounds of lifts and moving floor sections are great; it really does make DOOM seem like a Monty Python production. Doors, on the other hand, sound so clean, smooth, efficient, and new that they, too, are an amusing change.

Inevitably, a few new sounds require the player to have seen the films to understand them. Some examples are firing a pistol that goes "Neee!" or an exclamation of pain that says "'Tis but a scratch!" (The knight who originally uttered these words had just had his arm cut off.) Although these are movie-based sound patches, I think they would still be enjoyable to players who have not seen the films.

Other highlights include the player grunt after falling, the fireballs, the teleport, and the rocket launch sounds. The only one I didn't like was the burp at an Imp's death. It's a bit of a clichéd sound. The other death sound—"I've 'ad worse!"—is better.

Other than its subject matter, what makes this WAD stand out is how well the sounds go together, how they complement rather than compete with each other. There are not so many quotes as to be repetitive, and the sound effects have remained sound effects, providing genuine atmosphere rather than an opportunity to hear your favorite one-liners while playing DOOM. An example that worked well is the "Former Human nearby" sound: the troopers jeer "Chicken!" The effect is great as you wander deserted corridors in E1M2 and are taunted by unseen adversaries. An example that didn't work for me is the "Imp, spotting player" sound: "Honey, I'm home." Putting a speech quote on a monster's "spot player" sound is usually not a good idea, because when the player runs into a room full of identical monsters, you get a sort of Max Headroom/synthesized-voice effect, and if the quote is a long one, it will sound awful, especially if (unlike humans and Imps) there is only one "spot player" sound for that monster. (The obvious exception to this is when you are also building a level in the PWAD and thus are able to control how the creatures meet the player.)

The quality of the sampling is also good. I don't think there are any sounds which cut noticeably, and many sounds have so little background noise that they don't sound like they were sampled from a film. (There is an exception. "'Tis but a scratch!" doesn't sound well sampled, due to background noise. It's probably the worst, quality wise, but is nothing to complain about.)

Overall, this is a great sound patch, mainly because of how well it adds the Monty Python flavor to DOOM, especially the sound effects (such as environment sounds that are not quotes), which change the atmosphere as well as the action.

THE EVIL DEAD WAD (EVILSND.WAD)

This is a patch of new sounds digitized from *The Evil Dead*—one of the movies that inspired DOOM in the first place. My initial impression as I selected the appropriate options in the menu was that I had the wrong WAD, that this was the *Terminator 2* WAD. The pistol's sound has been replaced with what seems to be the pistol sound from the *Terminator 2* WAD. (This is a fantastic sound. It includes not just the pistol firing, but the bullet hitting something soft. Using this sound, the chaingun sounds incredible.) After playing a while, it would also seem that the door open and close sounds are sampled from *Aliens*. These sounds would have been good, except that the door-open sound cuts out halfway through opening, and the door-close sound doesn't seem to be quite the right length when closing. There may be other sounds that have been sampled from different movies, but those were the only ones I picked up.

As with many movie-based sound patches, most of the sounds this PWAD adds are memorable quotes or suitable snips of dialogue. There are a few cases of overuse of speech, but not many. There are very few quotes used for "monster spotting player" sounds, because there are so many perfectly suited demonic roars and screeches from *The Evil Dead* to use instead. The Demon's "spot player" sound is an exception to this. ("There's something out there," sounds good when you meet a lone demon, but too often they hunt in packs, thus producing a repetitive babble.) My favorite is the Cacodemon's demonic scream "I'll swallow your soul!" which sounds great, especially since Cacodemon's rarely appear in packs.

Most of the player sounds have not been changed. The shotgun sounds good, with a bit more kick to it (read: bass), and the plasma also sounds good. Item-pickup has been changed to "Let's go," which doesn't work very well in levels with a normal amount of items to be picked up, especially if there are a lot in a single room. I didn't like the new player-death sound either. It is a dialogue quote with a lot of background noise, and the player-oof (when you fall and hit the ground) is nothing I can decipher. It sounds like someone has dropped a duffel bag on a microphone, but it sounds quite good as a "you need a key to open this door" sound. (The other occurance when this sound is played.)

Monster death sounds mostly are replaced with quotes, supposedly said by the player. This can get repetitive after you've killed your 14th Imp. But combined with item-pickup and weapon-pickup ("Groovy"), an atmosphere of invulnerability starts to build, as each line is delivered with that same detached tone, as if the idea of these creatures posing a threat to you was inconceivable. (This combines well with the new monster sounds of EVILSND.WAD, which induce fear more readily than many of the original sounds.)

Unfortunately, some of the dialog lines came out sounding fairly tacky. For example, a Trooper's death sound is accompanied by the player sneering, "Swallow this." When this sound is played, the tense is wrong (the Trooper has already "swallowed" it), and thus the line just sounds dumb. Other death-sounds—"Come get some" and "You want a little?"—have the same flaw. These sounds only really work when you are in a room full of bad guys and in the middle of battle, where you can assume these wisecracks are directed at someone or something else. The more generic, "Hail to the King, baby," (as you nail an Imp) works in all situations.

The audio quality of many of these sounds could be better. Many also have a lot of background noise. (There isn't much that can be done about that except to drop the sound altogether, which isn't a very useful solution; however, you do need to draw the line somewhere.) The biggest problem throughout the PWAD is the number of sounds that cut in, or cut out, or have a spike at the end. These problems are very easily fixed in very little time—sometimes with your sound card's software.

If you ever intend to integrate sampled sounds or dialog into a WAD of your own, it is vital that background sound flows as smoothly as possible. In many respects, the ear distinguishes continuity better than the eye. If the level of background noise suddenly changes and the player becomes aware that he just heard a sound clip, the illusion of the game is destroyed. If a sound clip has background noise, it must be faded in and out to minimize the discontinuity. In practice, all sounds should be faded if possible.

The EVILSND.WAD patch works nicely, but there are quite a few things that could have worked better, and the actual number of sounds replaced is smaller than in many other sound patches. The source media used—*The Evil Dead*—has its own appeal, which adds greatly to the patch's effectiveness. Overall, it is great fun.

DOOM
PROGRAMMING
GURUS

2
ROOM

1
MISSION

3
EPISODE

ROOM 3

By Justin Fisher

THE BEST GRAPHICS

In DOOM and DOOM II, you have the ability to change the graphics. There are a multitude of good WAD files available with new and creative graphics you can apply. Many of the best WADs were seen in Episode 3, Mission 1, Room 1, "The Top Five WAD Files." Following are two more graphics WAD files that stand among the best. These are the Simpsons-2 graphics patch and PacDoom, an Imp Sprite replacement.

SIMPSONS-2 GRAPHICS PATCH (STEVE BLAUWAMP AND CHUCK FUOCO)

Simpsons-2 is a graphics (and sound) patch for both DOOM and DOOM II. It replaces most of the Sprites and sounds, as well as a few extra graphics such as the start screen and your face on the status bar. It changes the monsters into characters from *The Simpsons* and the player himself into Homer.

Each monster is transformed into a character it is suited to (or perhaps more accurately, the character it is least unsuited to), which is very impressive considering the 60-odd Sprites per monster and that all the monsters of both DOOM and DOOM II are changed. (Obviously, there are many more Simpsons characters when you use this patch in DOOM II, as there are seven additional monsters, all of which have been changed.) Virtually all the characters and personalities from *The Simpsons* are there, from Grandpa Simpson to Mayor Quimby. The only exceptions I can think of are Maggie and Lisa—I assume because they just don't fit the role of psychopathic cannon fodder. (I think the creators were right in not using these two.) Most characters have their own special means of attack, and this is one of the best parts of this patch. Patty and Selma blow thick clouds of choking cigarette smoke at you. Mr. Burns throws lumps of nukage at you from a waste container, and (my favorite) Willie, the Scottish caretaker from Springfield Elementary rips open his shirt and bares his chest, whereas Grandpa Simpson just lets rip with a chaingun and seems to be enjoying himself.

The Sprite graphics were hand-drawn (on paper), because rendered models would look nothing like the cartoon and drawing them on computer would take longer (assuming the artist was even able to sketch so well when using a computer interface). Sketching 60 frames on paper, with each frame coming out the same size, and the animation frames being similar enough to work, would obviously take a huge dedicated effort, let alone doing this for several monsters, so several shortcuts have been taken in Simpsons-2. The most noticeable is that rather than having each frame of the animation be a new drawing, usually only one frame (and its rotations) are drawn; each subsequent frame uses the original as a base, with some areas changed—especially legs and feet—so that in DOOM you will see its legs moving as it walks, but most of its body will not change. In many cases, this does not look good. When you start the game (DOOM II) and you are looking at Moe with his back turned, the only movement at all is a small move of his ankle—just enough to let you know there *should* be movement, but there isn't.

Another shortcut takes this same idea one step further. The best example of this is the Lost Souls featuring Krusty the Klown. The Pain Elementals are televisions, out of which blares Krusty. The same image is used, and not changed at all, for all the frames (except the pain frame) and for several rotations of each frame. The Lost Souls probably have the least Sprites of any monster (a little more than 30), and for the Simpsons-2 patch each Sprite was replaced with one of only five images of Krusty. This does not look good; even scenery items have better animation. Doing this (effectively cutting a monster from 30 down to five Sprites) enables you to change a monster's graphics quickly and easily. The result is not pretty, but if it is part of a larger conversion like Simpsons-2, it's usually better to do it this way than to not do it at all.

Overall, the big problem with the images in the Simpsons-2 patch is a lack of anti-aliasing, and I think this is due mostly to the method in which the images were made. According to the SIMPSONS.TXT file, the images were first drawn, then scanned, then colored in a painting program before being imported to DOOM. The stumbling block is most likely in the coloring—assuming the images are colored after scanning, then you will probably be scanning a monochrome pencil or pen sketch. A scanner naturally adds anti-aliasing as it works, but if you are scanning a mono image, anti-aliasing is going to prevent you from being able to color it properly later, so you need to stop the scanner's anti-aliasing (cut it down to 1bit—black and white), and thus all anti-aliasing is gone. The resulting image will look extremely blocky in DOOM. If you had a color scanner and were able to color the sketches before scanning, the problem would be solved—but how do you get consistent color across so many sketches? As you can see, no way is perfect, but anti-aliasing is so vital to DOOM graphics (due to their low resolution) that it is worth a lot of extra hassle to check out all the options available to you, and to seriously consider those that offer anti-aliasing, even if they are more difficult or time consuming. The Sprites in Simpsons-2 not only have no anti-aliasing, but the lines are drawn in black, with areas filled in with color. (Curved black lines on flat, light tones is where anti-aliasing is needed most.) Consequently, the Sprites look about as blocky as they could, and this is the weakest point of the graphics. The actual drawing, however, is great—all the characters look just like the ones on television, and are instantly recognizable.

> The issue here is anti-aliasing. Anti-aliasing is possibly the single most important factor in determining how good a graphic will appear once it has been imported into DOOM. Since Sprites can be greatly enlarged when you get close to them, if they lack anti-aliasing they will look extremely blocky and ruin what might otherwise be a great image. The easiest ways to get anti-aliasing is by using a color scanner on art, a 3-D modeling and rendering program, or a video-capture system. All of these systems anti-alias automatically. If you are using a different method, or have had to remove existing anti-aliasing, a simple blur filter is quick and will help a lot; but, like everything else, it has drawbacks.

In this sense, the graphics are fantastic—every last character is drawn true to the original. The sounds are good too. Almost all are dialogue quotes, and these do get repetitive, but they fit the characters and usually work well.

There are many other graphics too. All the graphics of the weapons you are using have been changed so that it is Homer who is holding them. (While the weapons themselves are not changed, the effect is nice, especially the clean yellow fists with the grimy metal knuckle-dusters.) Health and armor have been replaced with donuts and beer (alcohol depresses the nervous system), but in most cases, the Sprites were made too large. In the room with the end-level switch in M1 of DOOM II, there are three Medikits and an Imp (three boxes of donuts and Ned Flanders). If you have 100-percent health and thus can't pick up the Medikits, you are rendered practically blind, as you can see nothing but donut boxes while somewhere Ned Flanders lurks, hurling Bibles at you. (Many of the monsters also have Sprites larger than the original. This can be annoying when shooting down from a ledge at a monster you can clearly detect but nonetheless keep missing because, while the graphics are in view, the monster isn't. There is a DeHackEd patch that comes with the Simpsons-2 patch, which may fix the problem; I didn't check.)

Other things of note: the death scenes for the characters are in typical DOOM fashion, with lots of blood and even the odd eyeball or two. (That's something you won't see in *The Simpsons*.) (See Figure 3.1.) The artist has also demonstrated that his ability is not limited to the Simpsons characters alone, as there are a few surprises in the secret levels.

Figure 3.1.

You won't see anything like this in The Simpsons.

Overall, the sheer magnitude of this patch has to impress you, along with the great artwork in drawing the Simpsons characters. Added to the graphics are sound and .EXE patches, but the graphics patch—even on its own—is worth getting. The graphics do look blocky, but considering the time it must have taken to change so many Sprites, I doubt it would be possible to do much better.

PACDOOM IMP-SPRITE REPLACEMENT (BILL NEISIUS)

PacDoom is an Imp-Sprite patch that turns the Imp into a huge PacMan. It is one of the older graphics patches for DOOM, but it is done well and it still looks good.

The version I got to review was a .ZIP file containing about 60 PPM image files (PPM is the format used in the DOOM WADs) and a copy of DMGraph, along with a batch file to extract and backup the original Imp Sprites and then import the PacMan Sprites. I was expecting a PWAD, as these are easier and much safer, but there are advantages to this format (namely not needing a 2.5MB Sprite WAD), and many Sprite patches seem to use it.

In terms of Sprite quality, PacDoom does well; the PacMan is a fairly simple monster and looks like it was rendered with a 3-D modeling program, giving it plenty of good shading and anti-aliasing, despite there being few rich yellows in the DOOM palette.

The animation is good during the walking sequence (TROO rotation Sprites A through D) with the mouth opening and closing smoothly. There are slight lighting variations in each frame to prevent the areas that don't move from looking static. (This is a good idea if you are rendering from a 3-D program or using some means of video and a physical model. It must be subtle, but Sprites do look a lot worse if only a part of them changes, especially if there are areas that go unchanged during the entire four-frame loop.) The only thing I don't like about the moving sequence is that the PacMan's lower lip is the only part that opens and shuts. Its upper lip stays where it is. Perhaps the eyes are so close as to restrict movement. This results in a munching movement that looks a bit like a goldfish's. (This is one of those things that is hard to predict before seeing it finished or previewed.)

If you don't have some sort of animation software, you can end up having to finish the entire sequence and installing it into DOOM before you can get any idea how good it will look, or whether you have made mistakes. Finding some means of preview, especially if you are doing a lot of monsters and other animations, is usually worth it in the time saved, and well worth it if you are trying to achieve something particularly tricky or precise.

The attack sequence is not so good, as there is effectively *no* sequence. All the Sprites in all four frames are the same as in the first frame of the moving sequence. The exception is that in the front view of the middle two frames, a fireball (like a Pac pill) is forming. (It looks good, too.) Then the Imp's fireball is launched. What that means is that if an Imp (PacMan) attacks another creature, it will simply stop, completely unchanging, with its mouth wide open. No pills are fired, but Imp fireballs appear in front of it. The last frame, when viewed from the front, is the "in pain" Sprite. Usually, however, the PacMan is attacking you, and you only see it from the front, which looks good, especially since the PacMan floats at exactly the right height so that the pill/fireball forms in his throat and comes out in exactly the right position for the Imp's fireball to take over. (See Figure 3.2.)

Figure 3.2.

PacAttack! Three Pacs in various stages of attack.

Obviously, making 60 or so Sprites is a lot of work, and by reusing Sprites you can often use the time saved to make the overall product better, despite the repeating frames. In this case, however, using a rendered model would not take much extra time per frame (unless you significantly touch up each frame by hand afterwards), and having all the frames in the attack and pain sequences identical can look pretty awful if you ever see it from the side.

That said, PacDoom is still one of the best-looking monster-Sprite replacements out there. Its sheer simplicity of form is a great asset. There are many similar patches for DOOM; Bunny3D, for example, is a Sprite replacement for Former Human Sergeants, turning them into the Energizer battery Bunny. (Bunny3D was rendered in 3D Studio by David Lobser in a similar way to PacDoom.) The Sprites in Bunny3D are more detailed, and no Sprite is used twice—a good example of how today's patches are getting even better as DOOM programmers gain experience. (See Figure 3.3.)

Figure 3.3.

Welcome to Bunny3D.

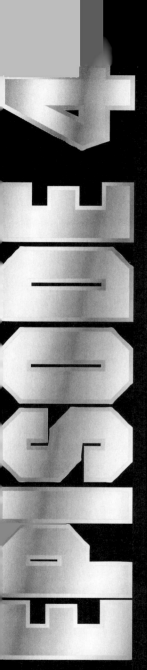

THE TOOLS OF THE GODS

MISSION 1: UNLEASHING YOUR DEMONS

ROOM 1

By Raphaël
Quinet

DEU

INTRODUCTION

The DOOM Edit Utility (DEU) project started soon after the release of DOOM 1.0. The first version of DEU was released in January 1994 by Brendon Wyber. At the time, it was only a Things editor: You could change the enemies, weapons and decorations but not the shape of the rooms. Two months later, Raphaël Quinet released DEU 5.0, which was the first DOOM editor that was able to create new levels. Since then, lots of people have contributed to this project, and DEU has evolved from an experimental hacker's tool to a real editor. At the time of this writing, DEU is available for various systems:

- **DOS:** The 16-bit version (compiled with BC) can run on any PC, even the 286s, but can only use the usual 640KB of standard DOS memory. The 32-bit version (compiled with GCC) can access the extended memory and run in protected mode, thanks to the GO32 DOS extender. It is faster and able to edit huge maps.

- **Windows:** Renaud Paquay created WinDEU, which is also available in 16-bit and 32-bit versions. It offers the same features as the DOS version in a windowing environment. You may find it easier to use as it comes with a very useful on-line help.

- **UNIX and X Window:** With DEU-X, you can use the full power of your workstation to create your maps faster and without any memory problems. It has been tested on SunOS, AIX, Linux, and several other UNIX systems.

- **Linux and SVGAlib:** If X Window is too heavy for your Linux box, you can use the SVGAlib version of DEU.

- **OS/2:** A port to OS/2 is under way and should be available soon.

There are two ways to use DEU. Like the hundreds of people who have already released their own levels, you can use it to create new WAD files. But since the source code is available, you can also modify it and add new features to the editor. This is another way to use DEU. If you send your code to the original authors, it could be included in the next release of the program, and everybody will benefit from it. This room will only deal with the "normal" use of DEU: the creation of WAD files. If you want to edit the code and contribute to the project, read the files contained in the distribution of DEU for more information.

If you are using DEU for the first time, read the next section of this room. It is a tutorial and guided tour to some of the features of the map editor. If you have already tried DEU before, you can skip this section and go directly to the next one which explains how to create a new map from scratch.

The following sections contain the list of commands available from the main menu, a description of the map-editor menus in each editing mode and the list of options for the command line or configuration file. This is where you should look if you are unsure about what some command or option does and how to use it.

The last part of this room will give you some hints and tips for building better maps easily. It also describes some common problems and how to solve them.

BECOMING FAMILIAR WITH DEU

STARTING THE PROGRAM

Before creating large and complex maps, let's begin with something simple: viewing and editing an existing map. First, you have to start DEU. If you have installed DEU in the same directory as DOOM, you just have to type DEU to start the program. If your main WAD file (DOOM.WAD or DOOM2.WAD) is not in the current directory, you can use the command-line option -main to give the path where this file can be found. For example:

```
deu -main C:\GAMES\DOOM\DOOM.WAD
```

Alternatively, you can edit the configuration file DEU.INI and add a line like this one:

```
Main = C:\GAMES\DOOM\DOOM.WAD
```

When DEU starts, your screen should look like in Figure 1.1. The last line shows the DEU prompt; the program is awaiting your command. If you want to see what commands are available, type a question mark followed by Enter. This text-based interface is not very pretty, but you will spend most of your time in the map editor which is more user-friendly, so don't worry about it.

The first command that we will use is Edit, to view and edit an existing map. Just press **E**, followed by Enter. DEU switches to graphics mode and displays a list of existing maps (if DEU reports an error when switching to graphics mode, refer to the last section of this room for troubleshooting tips). If you are using DOOM, your screen should look like Figure 1.2. If you are using DOOM II, you will see MAP01, MAP02, etc., instead of E1M1, E1M2, and so forth. Let's begin with the first map. Press Enter to select it.

Figure 1.1.
The opening screen of DEU.

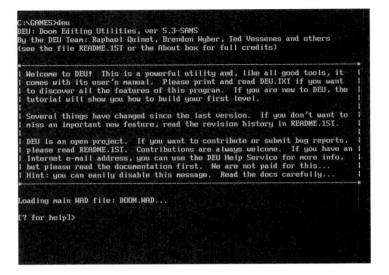

```
C:\GAMES>deu
DEU: Doom Editing Utilities, ver 5.3-SAMS
By the DEU Team: Raphael Quinet, Brendon Wyber, Ted Vessenes and others
(see the file README.1ST or the About box for full credits)

*--------------------------------------------------------------------------*
| Welcome to DEU!  This is a powerful utility and, like all good tools, it  |
| comes with its user's manual.  Please print and read DEU.TXT if you want  |
| to discover all the features of this program.  If you are new to DEU, the |
| tutorial will show you how to build your first level.                     |
|                                                                           |
| Several things have changed since the last version.  If you don't want to |
| miss an important new feature, read the revision history in README.1ST.   |
|                                                                           |
| DEU is an open project.  If you want to contribute or submit bug reports, |
| please read README.1ST.  Contributions are always welcome.  If you have an|
| Internet e-mail address, you can use the DEU Help Service for more info,   |
| but please read the documentation first.  We are not paid for this...     |
| Hint: you can easily disable this message.  Read the docs carefully...    |
*--------------------------------------------------------------------------*

Loading main WAD file: DOOM.WAD...

[? for help]>
```

Figure 1.2.
*Choose a map number
for editing.*

Depending on the version of DOOM that you are using, your screen should be similar to Figure 1.3 or Figure 1.4. Most of the screen is filled by the map. It shows all the walls (like in the automap) and all the objects in the level.

The objects (or Things, as they are called in DOOM) are displayed in different colors, depending on their type: Monsters are in bright red, weapons in brown, bonuses in bright green, Player Start positions in dark green, decorations in white. In the bottom-left corner of the screen, you see the information box that contains the description of the currently selected Thing. If you move the pointer over an object, the information box will automatically be updated and you will get the description of this Thing.

Figure 1.3.
The first map of DOOM (E1M1).

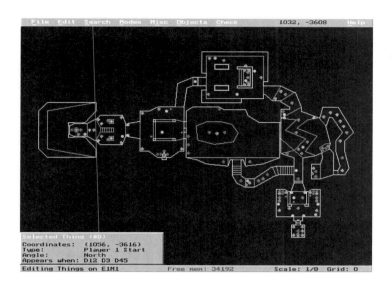

Figure 1.4.
The first map of DOOM II (MAP01).

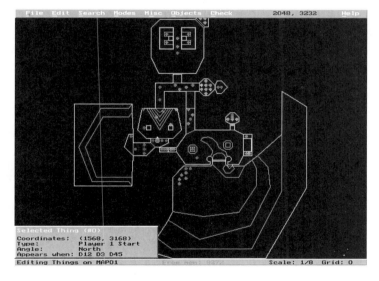

There are four different editing modes. You can press Tab or Shift+Tab to cycle through them. Notice how the information box changes to display the properties of the different types of objects. The four editing modes are as follows:

- **Things mode:** Changes the position and type of enemies, weapons, bonuses, decorations and player starting points.
- **Vertices mode:** Defines the endpoints of the walls.
- **Linedefs & Sidedefs mode:** Modifies the lines where walls and triggers are; changes the texture of the walls.
- **Sectors mode:** Defines the rooms or areas by modifying the texture, height or brightness of the floors and ceilings.

EDITING THE OBJECTS

As a first example of how to use DEU, we will replace some enemies by other objects and change some wall textures.

Go into Things editing mode (press **T** for a shortcut) and move the cursor over one enemy (displayed in bright red). You can see the type of the selected enemy in the information box. In both versions of DOOM, the first map contains mostly Imps and Troopers. If you press Enter, this will open the Thing editing dialog box, as shown in Figure 1.5, which enables you to change the properties of any object. In the center, you see the image of the thing as it appears when you play the game. On top of it, you have several lists of Things: enemies, weapons, and so on. On the left of the image, you see a kind of compass, which shows the initial orientation of the Thing. On the other side, several checkboxes control the difficulty setting(s) on which the Thing will appear.

If you have a SVGA card and are using a video driver that supports 256 colors, you will see the objects as they appear in the game. If you are using the standard VGA mode or a driver that only supports 16 colors, the images will be displayed with the best approximations among the 16 colors available.

The configuration of the video driver and the problems that may arise are discussed in the last two sections of this room.

Figure 1.5.
The Edit Thing dialog box.

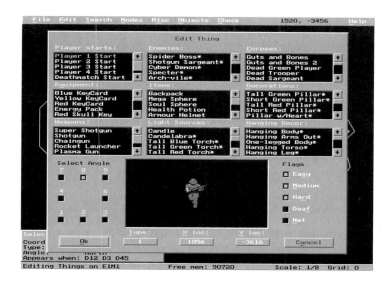

You can use the Tab key or the mouse to move from one field to another in the dialog box. The current field is always highlighted by a yellow frame. You can, for example, change the enemy into a rocket launcher or a blue key. You can also replace it by another monster, although it would not be wise to put a Baron of Hell in the first level of the game. When you are satisfied with the new settings, press Enter or click the OK button to accept your changes.

You can easily change the position of the objects: If you select a Thing and press **D** or the right mouse button, you will activate the drag mode. If you move the pointer, the object will also move. Press **D** again or release the right mouse button to drop it. An interesting thing to try for your first map is to move the starting position of the first player into another room. You will immediately notice the difference when you play.

Now, let's modify the walls. Switch to the Linedefs & Sidedefs editing mode by pressing Tab twice (or **L** for a shortcut). The information box at the bottom of the screen is much larger and shows the properties of the walls. Select one of the lines on the map, for example one of the walls in the starting room and look at the information displayed. The first box describes the line itself (or, more exactly, the vertical plane based on this line). The two other boxes describe what is displayed on the face(s) of the wall.

If you press Enter to edit this line, a dialog box will appear. (See Figure 1.6.) Choose "Edit First Sidedef" to edit the face of the wall and you will get another dialog box which shows the texture of the wall, as in Figure 1.7. You can scroll the list and you will see the different textures available. Choose something very different from the original walls so that it will be easy for you to see what has changed. When you are done, press Enter or click OK to close the dialog box. Close the first dialog box too. Now, if you look at the information box at the bottom of the screen, you will see that the name of the "normal" texture has been updated.

Figure 1.6.

*The Edit Linedef &
Sidedefs dialog box.*

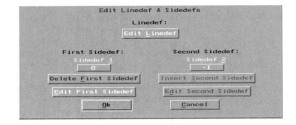

Figure 1.7.

*The Edit First Sidedef
dialog box.*

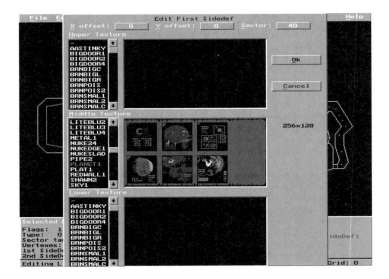

You can change the texture of several walls at the same time, by selecting a group of walls and applying the same changes to all of them. To mark a wall, you have to move the cursor over it and press **M** or click the left mouse button. The line will then be highlighted in green. If you press M or the left mouse button a second time, the line will be un-marked. Select for example four or five walls in the starting room and change their "normal" texture. All of them will be modified. This feature exists in all editing modes. You can always select multiple objects and apply the same changes to all of them in one operation.

TESTING YOUR NEW LEVEL

You probably want to test your first level now. First, you have to save it: You can either press Alt+**F** to open the File menu, and then select Save, or just press F2 for a shortcut. DEU will prompt you for the name of the file in which you want to save your level. Accept the default or type any name of your choice.

In order to play with your new level, you have to exit DEU and run DOOM (future versions of DEU may have an option to do that directly from within the map editor). Exit the map editor by pressing **Q** or Escape, then quit the main menu by typing **Q** followed by Enter. DOOM uses the parameter `-file` to load your level. For example, if you saved your map in a file called E1M1.WAD, you should start DOOM with the following command:

```
doom -file E1M1.WAD
```

In the game, go in the rooms in which you have modified the wall textures or the placement of monsters and check the differences with the original levels. If you replaced one of the enemies by a very powerful monster, you will probably be in trouble.

ADDING NEW ROOMS

When you want to edit your level again, you will have to reload the file in DEU. One way to do it is to start DEU with the same command-line parameter as DOOM. For example:

```
deu -file E1M1.WAD
```

Another way to load your level in DEU is to start the program in the usual way, then use the **R**ead command for the main menu as in this example:

```
[Type ? for help]> R E1M1.WAD
```

Type **E** followed by Enter to go in the map editor and continue your work. Now we will try something more interesting: adding a new room to the map. The easiest way to build a new room is to use the Objects menu. Move the cursor a bit below the starting room (this is where you will create the new one) and press Alt+**O** to bring the Objects menu. In this menu, select the polygon. A dialog box will appear, asking for the dimensions of the polygon. You can accept the default values or change them. When you press Enter to confirm, the new room appears on the map.

DOOM PROGRAMMING GURUS

1 ROOM

1 MISSION

4 EPISODE

You can easily change the shape of this room: Go into Vertices editing mode (press Tab or **V**) and drag the vertices (press **D** or the right mouse button and move). You can give any shape to your room, as long as the lines do not intersect. While you are at it, you can also modify the shape of other areas in the map.

Now you have to connect your room to the rest of the map if you want to be able to enter it. If you want to connect your room directly to another one, without door or corridor, then proceed as follows: Select one vertex from your new room and move it on top of one of the walls from the nearest room. DEU will ask you if you want to split the line that defines the wall (if the dialog box does not pop up, then you are not exactly on the line; zoom in using the + key and try again). Press Enter or click the OK button to accept. Do the same for the next vertex in your room: Move it on top of the same line, not too far away from the first vertex. In addition to the first dialog box, DEU will also tell you that two lines are superimposed and should be merged. Accept the proposed action.

Switch to Linedefs editing mode (Press Tab or **L**) and look at the map. It should be similar to Figure 1.8 if you are using DOOM II. (DOOM has a different map, but the principle is the same.) You will notice that all walls in your new room are displayed in white, which means that you cannot cross them. But the line between your room and the other one is displayed in gray. This line is not a wall, but only a separation between two sectors.

Figure 1.8.

Your new room may look like this.

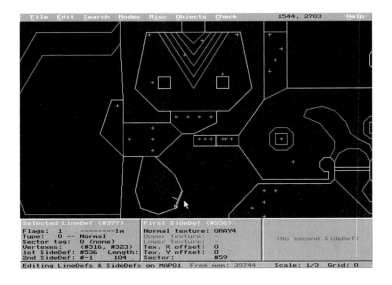

Select this gray line and look at its properties. DEU has automatically set the textures on both sides to -, which means transparent. Thus you will not see a "false wall" between the two rooms. If you see the name of the upper or lower texture displayed in red, this is because DEU has detected a missing texture. When two adjacent rooms do not have the same floor height or ceiling height, the "lower" or "upper" part of the linedef becomes visible (the lower part is like the side of a step, the upper part is the equivalent for the ceiling). If these parts are visible, they must have a texture; DEU warns you about this by displaying the texture name in red. In order to fix this, press Enter to bring the Linedefs & Sidedefs editing dialog box and edit the corresponding sidedef. We will see later that DEU has some powerful consistency checkers and can detect and fix these errors automatically.

Now, let's say that you want to create an acid pool in the middle of your new room. Here is how to do it: First, move the pointer inside your room, then use the Objects menu to insert a small rectangle. DEU will automatically detect that you are inserting an object inside a sector (the menu is different), and it will create a hole (void space) surrounded by walls instead of creating a new sector. In DOOM, this rectangle would look like a big pillar in the middle of your room.

In order to transform this pillar into an acid pool, you only have to press Ins while the linedefs are still selected. A new sector is created, replacing the hole. DEU also sets the textures of the walls to "transparent" and copies the properties of the outer sector to the new one.

HOW TO DESIGN A NEW LEVEL

In this section, we will see how you can create rooms, doors, stairs, and other objects. DEU offers several ways to do it, from the most automated ones to the most basic ones which give you more control over the structure of the WAD file. You will probably find that the automatic methods are easier to use for the initial layout of the rooms, while the "manual" ones are better for fine details and special effects.

ROOMS

When you start with an empty map (using the Create command from the main menu), the first thing you will have to do is to create some rooms. The easiest way to build them is by using the Objects menu: Position the pointer where you want to insert the new object, then press Alt+O or F9. Choose the type of object and enter its dimensions; DEU will then create the vertices, linedefs and sector that define your new room. The default values will be used for the wall textures, floor and ceiling height, light level, and so on.

You can easily change the shape of a room or split it in several parts. In Vertices editing mode, you can drag any vertex to a new position. If you add a new vertex on top of an existing line, DEU will ask you if you want to split the linedef in two. Confirm this and then move the new vertex to change the shape of the walls. Another way to do this is to select the line (in Linedef editing mode) and split it using the Split Linedef option from the menu of miscellaneous operations. For example, if you want to create a star-shaped sector (five points), you begin with a 10-sided polygon and you move every second vertex towards the center. You could also begin with a five-sided polygon, switch to Linedef editing mode while keeping all sides selected and split all lines using the appropriate option in the Misc menu. This menu contains several other options that could be useful to you.

Another way to create new rooms is to use the freehand drawing mode introduced in DEU 5.3: press Ins while in Linedef editing mode (with no objects selected) and then click the left mouse button or press Enter or Ins to insert a new vertex. DEU will add lines between the vertices and create a new sector as soon as you click one existing vertex (thus closing the polygon).

You can also create new rooms by duplicating existing ones or copying them from other WAD files. In order to duplicate parts of your map, you have to switch to Sector editing mode, select the room(s) that you want to copy, then press Ctrl+**D**. If you want to copy the rooms from another WAD file (which could be a library of common shapes), you have to use the Merge option in the File menu.

Last, but not least, is the "manual" way of creating the rooms. Although this was the only method available in the first versions of DEU, it is not recommended for beginners. First, you create several vertices, then you select them and press Ins. (When you press Ins and several vertices are selected, DEU adds linedefs between them.) Keep the lines selected and press Ins one more time to create the sidedefs and sector that define the room. This is a bit tedious, but if you are and experienced user and you know what you are doing, you can use this method to create some special effects by introducing errors (incorrect references) on purpose.

CORRIDORS AND PASSAGEWAYS

You may now wish to connect these rooms in order to be able to move from one to another when you play. Again, there are several ways to do this. The easiest way is to create a new rectangular room between two existing ones (use the Objects menu for this). Switch to Vertices editing mode and drag two vertices from one end of the rectangle on top of the wall in which you want to open the passage. (See figures 1.9 and 1.10.) DEU will ask you if you want to split the linedef and merge the middle part of the wall with the edge of the rectangle; confirm all these operations. DEU will change the attributes of the middle part of the wall so that it is transparent and passable. You now have your corridor connected at one end, as shown in Figure 1.10. Repeat this operation for the other end and the player will be able to move from one room to another (provided that the two rooms have the same height; if not, you will have to transform this corridor to a staircase).

Figure 1.9.

Create a corridor by inserting a rectangle…

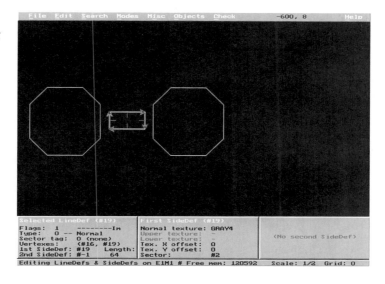

Figure 1.10.

…and join one edge of this rectangle with the wall of one room.

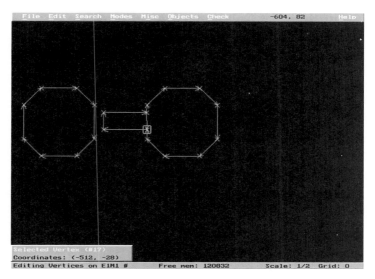

You can of course use the same procedure to connect two rooms together without a corridor be-tween them.

THE MAIN MENU

?

Help. This command displays a list of commands with their valid command syntax.

B *<OutIWadFileName>*

Build new IWAD file (all 10+ MB of it) with the given file name.

> Do not name your file DOOM.WAD, or you will overwrite the existing DOOM.WAD file
> and you will have to re-install DOOM to get back your original file.

C *[episode] [mission]*

Create and edit a new (empty) level.

D *object_name*

Dump gives an hex/ASCII dump of any object in the main directory (WAD file).

E *[episode] [mission]*

Edit a level.

G *OutPWad_FileName*

Group all opened PWAD files in a compound PWAD with the given file name. Using this option, you may put several levels, graphics, sounds, demos, and so forth in a single file.

I *datafile wad_filename_for_object*

Include a raw binary file in a PWAD. You can use this to replace certain DOOM objects. You should read DMSPEC13 (DOOM Specs 1.3) or higher to know what to call the objects. But beware—replacing DOOM objects is *not* for novices!

L *OpenedWad_FileName OutputFile*

List the structure of the directory of a opened file. If an output file is given it will write the list to that file.

M *[OutputFile]*

List the **M**aster directory of the IWAD and any PWAD files, all mixed together. If an output file is given it will write the list to that file.

`Q`

Quit to DOS.

`R [file]`

Read a previously saved patch WAD file. NOTICE: If you load a PWAD with multiple levels (or sounds, demos, graphics, and so on) and edit a level, THE SAVE COMMAND WILL ONLY SAVE THAT MAP, not any other levels, graphics, and so forth. *Do not* name it the same as the multilevel PWAD.

`S DirEntry WadFile`

Save one object to a separate file.

`V [Spritename]`

View Sprites. Spritename is optional. Use arrow keys to scroll through Sprite list. Scroll through the bosses fast and see them dance for you!!!

`WADS`

List all the opened WAD files.

`X object_name datafile_name`

Extract a DOOM object into a raw binary file.

COMMANDS OPTIONS OF THE LEVEL EDITOR

KEYBOARD COMMANDS

Table 1.1 is a quick reference to the keyboard commands available with DEU. Table 1.2 is a more extensive explanation of the DEU keyboard commands.

DOOM
PROGRAMMING
GURUS

1
ROOM

1
MISSION

4
EPISODE

Table 1.1. Keyboard quick reference.

Key	Description
Q	Quit
Escape	Exit (no save)
Arrows	Move pointer
Scroll Lock	Autoscroll on/off
Space	Scroll slow/fast
+, −	Zoom in or out.
Tab	Next mode
Shift Tab	Previous mode
N	Next object
P	Previous object
J	Jump to object #
M	Mark/Unmark object
C	Clear all marks
O	Copy Object(s)
D	Drag mode toggle
G	Set grid scale
H	Hide/Show grid
Enter	Edit object(s)
Ins	Insert object(s)
Delete	Delete object(s)
F1	Help
F2	Save
F3	Save As
F4	Search
F5	Preferences
F8	Miscellaneous operations
F9	Insert predefined objects
F10	Check consistency

Key	Description
1,2,...,9,0	Direct Zoom setting
T	Things mode
V	Vertices mode
L	Linedef/Sidedef mode
S	Sector mode
>	Next object
<	Previous object
#	Jump to object #
Shift+H	Grid Scale = 0
I	Info Bar on/off
R	Ruler/Normal cursor
Shift+Ins	Insert lines and close sector
Shift	Move pointer without selecting new object
Shift+[Mark]	Box object selection

Pull-Down Menu Keys	Meaning
Alt+F	File menu
Alt+E	Edit menu
Alt+S	Search menu
Alt+M	Mode menu
Alt+I	Misc menu
Alt+O	Objects menu
Alt+C	Check menu
Alt+H	Help menu

Table 1.2. Keyboard commands full description.

Key	Description
Q	Quit saving changes. You will be asked for the name of the PWAD file. Note: If you load a PWAD with multiple levels (or sounds, demos, graphics, and so on) and edit a level, the Save command will only save that map, not any other levels, or graphics. *Do not* name it the same as the multilevel PWAD.
Escape	Exit without saving. If you have unsaved changes, a warning message will be displayed. May also be used to CANCEL accidentally selected functions.
Arrows	Move the pointer.
Scroll Lock	Turn on/off the autoscroll feature.
Space	Toggle slow/fast movement speed and the scrolling speed.
+, −	Zoom in or out. (Change the map scale.) ZOOM levels range from 1/20 scale (smallest) to 4/1 scale (major magnification).
1,2,…,9,0	Set Zoom level from 1 to 10 directly. (1/1 – 1/10)
Tab	Switch to the next editing mode.
Shift+Tab	Switch to the previous editing mode. If objects are marked, the objects they are built from remain marked.
T	Switch to the Things editor.
V	Switch to the Vertexes (Vertices) editor.
L	Switch to the Linedefs/Sidedefs editor.
S	Switch to the Sectors editor.
N, >	Select the next object. This will only work if the pointer is not on an object.
P, <	Select the previous object. This will only work if the pointer is not on an object.
J, #	Jump to a specified object (enter number).
M	Mark/Unmark current object. (See also the Shift key listed forthwith.) * Objects stay marked until you un-mark them. *
C	Clear all marks.
O	Copy objects. After pressing O move the copy to where you want it and press Escape to drop it there.
D	Toggle Drag mode.

Key	Description
G	Show the grid and change its scale. Press it again to increase the number of grid lines thus decreasing the scale. Use Shift+G to increase the scale.
H	Hide/Show Grid. This only controls whether or not grid lines are displayed.
Shift+H	Set grid scale to 0.
I	Show or hide the info bar at the bottom of the screen.
R	Toggle between Normal Cursor and Ruler Cursor.
Enter	Edit current object or group of selected objects. A menu will pop up and you will be allowed to change attributes in the object(s).
Ins	Insert a new object at the current cursor position. This will copy the last selected object or insert a default object. There are two special cases: When a group of vertices are selected and you press "Ins": the editor will add new linedefs between the vertices and will put you in the Linedefs editor. The editor will create linedefs for all but the last line. (Use Shift+Ins if you want to close the polygon). When a group of linedefs are selected and you press "Ins" a new sector will be created and one sidedef in each linedef will be bound to this Sector and the edit mode will switch to the Sector editor.
Shift+Ins	Use this when selecting groups of vertices and want the editor to close the polygon.
Delete	Delete the current object or group of objects. All objects bound to the current object will also be deleted. (in other words, if you delete one Vertex, this will also delete the linedefs that used this Vertex). Except for Things, you will be asked for confirmation before the object is deleted.
Shift	Hold the Shift key while moving the cursor to prevent the pointer from selecting a different object.
Shift & Mark	Hold the Shift key while pressing M (or the left mouse button) to drag a selection box around several objects and select them all at once. This is *great* for mass selection of any objects.
F1	Help screen.
F2	Save level in a PWAD file.
F3	Save As... (Change Episode and Level Number.) This will enable you to reassign the episode and level number of a map. Enter a filename, then select the episode/level number.
F4	Search for object (Not yet implemented).

continues

Table 1.2. continued

Key	Description
F5	Preferences. Use this to change the default values for wall, floor, and ceiling textures, and floor and ceiling heights. These defaults are for your current DEU session only. You may change the defaults for all DEU sessions by editing DEU.INI.
F8	Miscellaneous operations. The options that appear on this key vary depending upon which editing mode you are in (as listed forthwith.) However, the first option is constant, no matter which editing mode you are in.

F8 Options for All Modes:

1. Find First Free Tag	This will locate the first tag number that has not yet been used in this map. The number it returns will be the lowest available tag number.

The rest of the miscellaneous options that are available vary by mode and are as follows:

F8 Options for Things Mode:

2. Rotate and Scale Thing(s)	Move marked Things by the degree of rotation and a percentage scale. This will enable you to rearrange Things by spinning them around (change rotation angle) or moving them closer to each other (scale < 100 percent) or further apart (scale > 100 percent).

F8 Options for Vertices Mode:

2. Rotate and Scale Vertices	Move marked vertices by the degree of rotation and a percentage scale. This will enable you to rearrange vertices by spinning them around (change rotation angle) or moving them closer to each other (scale < 100 percent) or further apart (scale > 100 percent).
3. Delete Vertex and Join Linedef(s)	Delete the marked vertex and joins linedef(s) that were previously connected to it.
4. Merge Several Vertices into One	Same as #3, but with multiple vertices.
5. Add Linedef and Split Sector	You must mark exactly two vertices from the same sector before calling this command. This will add a linedef and a new sector.

F8 Options for Linedefs & Sidedefs Mode:

2. Rotate and Scale Linedefs   Move marked linedefs by the degree of rotation and a percentage scale. This will enable you to rearrange linedefs by spinning them around (change rotation angle) or moving them closer to each other (scale < 100 percent) or further apart (scale > 100 percent).

3. Split Linedef (Add New Vertex)   Splits the selected linedef(s).

4. Split Linedefs and Sector   Splits the selected linedefs by adding a vertex at the midpoint, connecting the new vertices with a linedef which divides the original sector.

5. Delete Linedefs and Join Sectors   Remove the selected two-sided linedef(s) that divide sectors and make them into a single sector.

6. Flip Linedef   Flip the linedef(s) start and endpoints, thus reversing the side the first and second sidedefs are on.

7. Swap Sidedef   Swap the sectors that sidedef(s) 1 and 2 are tied to.

8. Align Textures (Y Offset)   Align the textures on the Y offset. The first linedef selected is used as the reference point. This is for Up/Down alignment.

9. Align Textures (X Offset)   This may be used on a group of linedefs that follow each other. The first linedef selected is used as the reference. This is for left/right alignment.

F8 Options for Sector Mode

2. Rotate and Scale Sectors   Move marked sectors by the degree of rotation and a percentage scale. This will enable you to rearrange sectors by spinning them around (change rotation angle) or moving them closer to each other (scale < 100 percent) or further apart (scale > 100 percent). This will *not* move the "Things" in the sector. After rearranging the sector, you may have to go into Things mode and select them and do the same rotation/adjustment on them.

3. Make Door from Sector   To use this, select a sector that is between two other sectors and then activate this function. The linedefs, ceiling height, textures, and so on, will be modified accordingly.

continues

F8 Options for Sector Mode

4. Make Lift from Sector	To use this, select the sector that is to become the lift and then activate this function. The linedefs, textures, and so forth will be modified accordingly.
5. Distribute Floor Heights	This function will take the difference in floor heights between the first and last sector selected, divide it by the number of sectors in between and then distribute the result across the floor heights of the in-between sectors. This is very useful for setting floor heights on stairways.
6. Distribute Ceiling Heights	This function will take the difference in ceiling heights between the first and last sector selected, divide it by the number of sectors in between and then distribute the result across the ceiling heights of the in-between sectors. This is very useful for setting ceiling heights on stairways.
F9	Insert a predefined object. This function has two different modes depending upon where the pointer is located. The two conditions are 1. Inside of a sector and 2. Outside of sectors (not inside any sector).

F9 Options for Outside of Sectors:

1. Insert a Rectangle	Enter the width and height (length) of the rectangle and DEU will automatically insert the vertices, lindefs+sidedefs, and sector at the current pointer location. Think of this as adding a rectangular room.
2. Insert a Polygon (*N*-sided)	Enter the number of sides and a radius and DEU will automatically insert the vertices, linedefs+sidedefs, and sector at the current pointer location. You can do anything from a triangle to a 32-sided polygon. Think of this as adding a *N*-sided room.

F9 Options for Inside a Sector:

1. Insert a Rectangle	Same as outside a sector, but first sidedefs will be set to the sector they are contained in. Think of this as inserting a rectangular pillar. Note that pressing Ins after inserting the rectangle will create a new sector

4
EPISODE

1
MISSION

1
ROOM

DOOM
PROGRAMMING
GURUS

	inside the rectangle and cause the walls to be changed to transparent. Use this to define a new area inside a sector.
2. Insert a Polygon (N-Sided)	Also the same as outside a sector, but the first sidedefs will be set to the sector they are contained in. Think of this as inserting an N-sided pillar. Note that pressing Ins after inserting the polygon will create a new sector inside the polygon and cause the walls to be changed to transparent. Use this to define a new area inside a sector.
3. Stairs	Insert a stairway. (Not yet implemented.)
4. Hidden Stairs	Insert a hidden stairway. (Not yet implemented.)
F10	Check level consistency (diagnostics). When using the following diagnostics if an error is reported, you can press return to continue checking or press Escape to select the problem object.
1. Number of Objects	This option gives a count of the number of Things, vertices, linedefs, sidedefs, and sectors. It also displays the amount of bytes needed to store this information in a PWAD file (rounded to the nearest kilobyte).
2. Check if All Sectors are Closed	This will test all sectors and make sure they are closed. If they are not closed it reports the number of the unclosed sector.
3. Check Cross References	Verify the integrity of the level and help locate possible problem areas. This will help to locate orphaned sidedefs, etc. This will also remove extraneous linedefs if there are two linedefs between the same vertices.
4. Check for Missing Textures	Report any sidedefs that may need to have a Normal/Upper/or Lower texture defined.
5. Check Texture Names	Some other editors will let you enter texture names which are not correct. This function will help fix their mistakes.

MOUSE COMMANDS

If you have a mouse, the following actions are available:

Left button	Mark/Unmark object (same as M)
Middle button	Edit object (same as Enter)
Right button	Drag object (like D when you press or release the button)
Move mouse	Move the pointer

You can change the buttons using the -sb (swapbuttons) switch when starting DEU or in the DEU.INI file. Swaps the left and middle buttons

THE MENU BAR

Along the top edge of the Level editing screen there is a pull-down menu bar with a number of options, including File, Edit, Search, Modes, Objects, Misc, and Help. These menu options can be pulled down by either pointing and clicking on them or by holding down the Alt key and pressing the underlined letter from the menu bar. Once the menu is pulled down, press the highlighted letter of the command in order to use it.

The functions on the pull-down menus are as follows:

FILE (ALT+F)

Save	Save the level as a WAD file.
Save As	This will enable you to reassign the episode and level number of a map. Enter a filename, then select the episode/level number.
Print (Not yet implemented)	Print a picture/description of the map.
Quit	Exit the level editor. Save file if changes have been made.

EDIT (ALT+E)

Copy Object	Used to copy (groups of) Things, vertices, linedefs and sidedefs, or sectors.
Add Object	Same as Ins key from keyboard.
Delete Object	Same as Del key from keyboard.

Preferences
Use this to change the default values for wall, floor, and ceiling textures, and floor and ceiling heights. These defaults are for your current DEU session only.

SEARCH (ALT+S)

Find/Change (not yet implemented)	Search for a specific object type.
Repeat Last Find (not yet implemented)	Perform the search again to find the next match.
Next Object	Go to next object.
Prev Object	Go to previous object.
Jump to Object #	Go to a specific object number.

MODES (ALT+M)

(Changes current editing mode.)

Things Mode	T
Linedefs & Sidedefs	L
Vertices	V
Sectors	S
Next Mode	Tab
Last Mode	Shift+Tab

MISC (ALT+I)

(Same as F8 keyboard command. See description of F8 key.)

OBJECTS (ALT+O)

(Same as F9 key in Keyboard commands. See description of F9 key.)

CHECK (ALT+C)

(Same as F10 key in Keyboard commands. See description of F10 key.)

HELP (ALT+H)

Keyboard & Mouse	Same as F1 key.
Info Bar	Turn on/off Info Bar at bottom of screen. This bar displays editing modes, grid size, and Zoom levels.
About DEU… (not yet implemented)	Brief information about the DEU programmers and the contributed work from the Net.

LINEDEFS ATTRIBUTES

Some abbreviations have been used for the linedef attributes:

Im (bit0)	Impassable by players and monsters.
Mo (bit1)	Monsters cannot cross this line.
2S (bit2)	Two-sided wall/may shoot through.
Up (bit3)	Upper texture is "unpegged." Try it with moving ceilings or doors.
Lo (bit4)	Lower texture is "unpegged." Try it with moving floors or lifts.
Se (bit5)	Secret. This line appears as normal on the map.
So (bit6)	Blocks sound. The sounds won't travel past this line.
In (bit7)	Invisible on the map. Even with the "computer map" power-up.
Ma (bit8)	Already on the map at startup.

LINEDEF TYPES

The first two letters in each linedef type give its features.

The first letter can be one of the following:

D	Door	Press the spacebar to open it.
S	Switch	Press the spacebar to activate this linedef.
W	Walk	Walk across this linedef to activate it.
G	Gun	You need to shoot that linedef to activate it.

Except for doors (**D**) and the "end level" linedefs, all linedefs that activate a sector need a "sector tag" number and at least one sector with the same tag number to operate.

The second letter can be one of the following:

R   Repeatable.

1   Works only once.

Abbreviations are also used in the type name. They refer to what happens to the Sector when triggered by this linedef, as follows:

O   Stays Open. Used only for doors.

N   Neighbor. Usually this means that the floor rises or lowers until it reaches the floor height of an adjacent sector on its way. In the menus, I have used **Ne** instead.

T   Texture and Type change. Same as above, but the texture and type of the sector are also changed. The new sector floor texture and type are copied from the Sector where the switch or walk-though linedef is, not from the adjacent sector(s).

C   Ceiling. This means that the floor rises until it reaches the ceiling height of one adjacent sector.

<,>   Used as modifiers for the above letters. **<N** means that the floor will stop just below a neighboring floor.

COMMAND-LINE PARAMETERS

This section describes the options that you can set from the command line or in the configuration file (DEU.INI). Some of them have a shorter equivalent that can be used on the command line (but not in the configuration file).

When you use these options on the command line, they have to begin with a hyphen (-). The effect of the Boolean options (-i, -s0 and others) may be reversed by using a + instead of a -. For example, +i means "no info bar." In DEU.INI, these have to be followed by an equal sign and their value. For Boolean options, the possible values are true/false or on/off.

DEU.INI can be modified with any text editor. The default configuration file that is distributed with DEU has all its options commented out. So in most cases you will only have to remove the comment sign (#) to activate the option that you want. Some of these options can also be changed and saved from within DEU. For example, the preferences for the textures or BSP builder can be saved directly to DEU.INI without leaving the program. If you are working with several versions of DOOM (or Heretic), you can have one configuration file in each directory.

Table 1.3 contains the list of options that can be used as command-line parameters or in the configuration file. If you are a programmer, you can also have a look at the files `d_config.h` and `d_config.c` in the source code.

Table 1.3. Command-line parameters for DEU.

Option name (and abbreviation)	Description
`-help`	View command-line options without entering DEU.
`-addselbox` (`-a`)	Additive selection box. Objects will be added to the current selection (when you use the selection box) instead of replacing the current selection by what is in the box.
`-debug` (`-d`)	Debug mode. Will produce a log file of warning messages to help track down linedefs that have problems. The number of the bad linedef will be listed. This file will be called DEU.LOG. The log file will also have timestamps.
`-expert` (`-e`)	Expert mode. Doesn't ask for confirmation of some operations (such as deleting an object or rebuilding the nodes).
`-infobar` (`-i`)	Infobar. Displays the info bar.
`-swapbuttons` (`-sb`)	Swaps the left and middle mouse buttons.
`-quiet` (`-q`)	QUIET! suppresses the sound made when you select or mark an object. Use it if you are in a library.
`-quieter` (`-qq`)	QUIET^2! Complete silence. DEU will not make any sound, not even for warnings. Enjoy the silence…
`-zoom` *zoom* (`-z`)	Zoom. Specify initial Zoom setting.
`-color2` (`-c`)	Use the alternate color set for displaying the Things.
`-main` *main_wad_file* (`-w`)	Specify name of main WAD file (such as DOOM.WAD).
`-file` *pwad, pwad, ...>*	Load patch WAD file(s), just like with DOOM. Note that patch WAD files may also be loaded from the main menu.

Option name (and abbreviation)	Description
-pwad *pwad* (-pw)	Add ONE patch file to be loaded.
-bgi *video_driver_name*	Use another BGI video driver for hi-res modes. (Default = VESA.)
-video *video_mode_number* (-v)	Set the default video mode for the extended video driver. (Default = 2; this is 640 x 480 x 256 colors for the VESA driver).
-fakecursor (-fc)	Use a "fake" mouse cursor. This option is useful if your mouse driver is not compatible with SuperVGA resolutions.
-splitfactor (-sf)	Adjust scale on the nodes builder. This parameter is for those techie types that like to fiddle with Things. There is no need for the average user to worry about this parameter. (The default value of 8 is the same value that id software uses. A number less than 8 means "more balanced" and a number higher than 8 means "least splits." Use this parameter at your own risk. We recommend the default value of 8.) -select0 (-s0) Select object 0 when switching modes.
-config *ini_file*	Specify an alternate DEU configuration file other than DEU.INI

PREFERENCES

```
-walltexture texture
-lowertexture texture
-uppertexture texture
-floortexture texture
-ceiltexture texture
-floorheight units
-ceilheight units
```

HINTS, TIPS, AND TROUBLESHOOTING

GENERIC EDITING TIPS

Save your work often: (with different file names) and test it every so often to make sure it's looking like you want it to. DEU makes a .BAK file but if things get really messed and you saved twice with the same file name you may lose your work.

Inserting linedefs: When marking vertices to add linedefs, do so in *clockwise* order. This will make sure that the normal (or first) side of the line is on the inside of your sector. DEU likes this better, and so will you!

Use clockwise order if you want to add a new sector outside (not inside any sector). This is the case most of the time.

Use anti-clockwise order if you want to add an obstacle inside an existing sector. (In other words, all first sidedefs will be on the outside of the area you just defined.)

Texture alignment: All the texture sizes (ceilings, floors, and walls) are based on multiples of 8 pixels. You can use the grid feature to help align the length of linedefs. You might even try mathematics (I know, it's scarier than DOOM...) See the TUTOR.DOC file for an example of using the texture alignment fields.

Tag numbers: Sectors may have a tag number associated with them. A linedef that has the same tag number can be used to activate the sector by walking across it or pressing it like a switch.

The tag numbers are an independent table that is used to link the actions of linedefs and sectors together. The fact that the tag numbers are independent means that a single tag number can multiple lindefs to a sector.

Add Things in order: Add a Player 1 Start as soon as you've built your first sector. Wait until your done building all the sectors before you add enemies and weapons. This way you won't have to waste time killing them every time you go to test out your creation. Decorations should also come before the enemies. (This will save you time, but, if you feel the need to kill something every time you test your level, go ahead and satisfy your desire for carnage.)

Suggested order for vertices, linedefs, and sectors: First add all major rooms using the F9 options. Then use F9 to insert obstacles or different areas inside these rooms. Connect the rooms by selecting two vertices from each (in clockwise order) and press Ins twice. Now go ahead and add more walls or sectors using the vertices method. Drag some walls on top of some others if you want to join two rooms. Then set the textures of walls and ceilings and height of sectors. Add a player 1 start thing and compile it and take a walk through it. Then go back and fix things and add decorations. Add enemies last so you don't have to deal with them every time. Remember to add enemies based upon difficulty level.

Stairs: The maximum difference between floor heights for stairs is somewhere close to 24. Typical values for the height differ by 16 units. (Most of id Software's stairs use 16, although some of id's stairs go by 8.)

GENERAL TIPS

Good things come to those who *work*!

It takes *time* to build a good WAD file. The first really cool WADs we've seen produced with DEU took in excess of 15 hours. Granted, that included time to learn the latest release of DEU, but we expect that it will take somewhere between six and 20 hours to churn out a really good level. Don't be discouraged. You can start out with a simple level and expand on it as time permits.

An important consideration is the *theme* of your WAD And a little continuity wouldn't hurt either. We've made a couple WADs without any continuity or theme and found that they looked, well, amateurish. The sample levels in the tutorial have little continuity and are in no way meant to demonstrate what a good level looks like; rather, these were built to show how things work.

Including your own demo in a PWAD:

```
> doom -devparm -record E1M1 -file E1M1.WAD > deu
> R E1M1.WAD
> I E1M1.LMP DEMO1
> R DEMO1.WAD
> G MYLEVEL.WAD
> doom -file MYLEVEL.WAD
```

Special tag numbers: The only special tag number we know of is tag number 666. It is used to lower a sector after all the Barons of Hell have been eliminated on E1M8. We haven't tested to see if that works on any other ExMx levels. Let us know!

Death of bosses ends level: This is only true at the End Levels (ExM8). When all of the bosses that are tougher than a Baron of Hell die, the level ends.

Exits for single, Cooperative, and multiplayer modes: It *is* possible to create a level suitable for single-player games *and* protect the exit in Deathmatch games so that players must cooperate in order to exit. There are many ways to do this, and most of them are based upon when Things are available. (See the "When Appears" option in Things mode.)

One simple way is to have two doors that lead to the exit.

In multiplayer mode: Door "A" could be blocked by having a lamp in front of it. Door "B" would require a distant switch to be pulled so that the player pulling the switch couldn't reach it by themselves.

In single player (and Cooperative) mode Door "A" would not be blocked by any object nor require any switch to be pulled. This is just one of many possible ways to make a WAD playable by a single player but require cooperation to exit in Deathmatch mode.

DEU/DOOM LIMITS

Maximum size of a WAD file created with DEU 5.2: This depends on how much base memory you can free up. The more free RAM, the bigger the WAD can be. If you are using the GCC version of DEU, you will be able to create a WAD as big as your total memory (standard + extended): you can create a huge WAD file with this…

X,Y locations of vertices: Somewhere in excess of –10,000 to +10,000. It could be –32768 to + 32767. Note however that DEU might get a little weird if your vertices are too far apart.

Maximum number of sector tags: 255

Maximum number of enemies/Things that can be displayed at a time: Somewhere near 64. We've seen that when there are too many some of them will disappear and reappear. This looks really bad.

The DOOM engine (v1.2) can handle floors and ceilings from –32768 to +32768 as long as the difference in a sector is not more than 1000. DEU imposes a limit of 16384 as a safety feature and will check for the ceiling/floor difference when you run the 'check textures' test.

The Maximum 2S linedefs that you can see from any point before DOOM engine limit causes Hall of Mirrors (HOM) effect: Somewhere near 16.

Maximum stairs you can climb: 24 units.

Minimum floor-to-ceiling distance that you can walk through: Near 60 units.

Minimum wall distance you can squeeze through: 34 units.

TROUBLESHOOTING SITUATIONS

CANNOT SWITCH TO GRAPHICS MODE

If the program crashes with the following error: `Mode not supported on this card`, or simply hangs after having displayed the message `Switching to graphics mode`, then you have a problem with your video driver.

If your card's BIOS is not VESA-compatible, then you will need the UNIVESA driver, available on many FTP sites. This TSR provides a good VESA emulation for the most common VGA and SuperVGA cards.

If that still doesn't work, try using a different BGI driver or video mode (the command-line parameter `-v 0` forces DEU to use the standard VGA modes only).

POINTER IS NOT DISPLAYED

Your mouse driver is not compatible with SuperVGA resolutions.

Try the following, in this order:

- Upgrade your mouse driver, if possible.
- Add `fakecursor = true` to the DEU.INI file (or whatever config file you use).
- Add `video = 0` to the DEU.INI file.

HALL OF MIRRORS (HOM) EFFECT

The Hall of Mirrors effect is an indication that something is wrong with your map.

Two common causes of this problem are as follows:

- You forgot to give a texture to one part of a wall.
- You have a transparent line which is shared by two sectors, but you forgot to set the two-sided (2S) flag for the linedef.

You should run all tests from the F10 menu to check for these errors.

If everything appears to be correct (no warnings during the checks), then maybe you have too many two-sided linedefs in the same room. There is a limit in DOOM's graphic engine on the number of two-sided linedefs that can be displayed at the same time. Solution: Delete some of them. (Sigh.)

But it may also be a problem with DEU's nodes builder. You may try to use different values for the "splitfactor" command-line parameter, and see if that solves the problem (use positive values; 8 is the default; 16 or more may solve some problems). If that still doesn't work, you will have to wait for the next release of DEU or use the excellent BSP program, available on most DOOM-related FTP sites (look for BSP11X.ZIP).

THE RULER CURSOR LEAVES GARBAGE ON THE SCREEN

This is a bug in the EGAVGA.BGI driver. It does not support XOR mode for circles. Solutions: use another driver (VESA, for instance) or recompile DEU with the symbol NO_CIRCLES defined. This will draw squares instead of circles.

ROOM 2

By Jeff
Rabenhorst

EDMAP

EdMap is a DOS-based map editor that can create and play map files (PWADs) that can be used in the original DOOM, DOOM II, and Heretic. Total Conversions (TCs) are also supported (such as *Alien*-TC, by Justin Fisher). This text will explain how to use many of the tools and features EdMap has to offer, and along the way examples will be provided. The outcome of the sum of examples will be a fully functional DOOM map. Before you learn how to use EdMap, however, it must first be installed.

OVERVIEW

REQUIREMENTS

EdMap requires little more than the game itself to run. A mouse is required and the line `FILES=40` (or more) must be in your CONFIG.SYS file.

FILES

The EdMap package (as of version 1.40, EDMAP140.ZIP) includes 31 data, text, and program files, all of which can be handled automatically; the only file that ever needs to be run is EDMAP.EXE. Usually, for information on any *.EXE file, running the file with /? as the only parameter will display a description of what the program does and how to use it.

PROGRAM

EDMAP.EXE and EDMAPSYS.EXE make up the main editor program. EDMAP.EXE automatically handles EDMAPSYS.EXE; EDMAPSYS.EXE is not to be run independently. Running `EDMAP /?` will list the command-line parameters. (See Table 2.1.)

Table 2.1. EDMAP.EXE parameters.

Parameter	Description
pwad file …	Specifies what map files, if any, to load; more than one may be included. If none are listed, then either the last WAD file saved will be loaded (if auto-loading is on), or the first map in the main IWAD will be loaded.
/M:*mapnumber*	Determines which map is loaded. Two formats are acceptable: ExMy (DOOM and Heretic), where *mapnumber* is from E1M1 to E3M9; and MAPxx (*DOOM II*) where *mapnumber* must be from 1 to 32.

Parameter	Description
/C:*config_file*	Uses *config_file* instead of EDMAP.CFG. Different game configurations are allowed: EDMAP /C:DOOM and EDMAP /C:DOOM2 may both work.
	Use EDMAPCFG.EXE to create configuration files (EDMAPCFG DOOM2, for example).
/D...	Lists the directory and resource information about the specified PWAD file. (EDMAP /DIR > PWAD-DIR.TXT will redirect the listing to the file PWAD-DIR.TXT.) /D? for more information.
/Q	Quiet mode; same as the No text on startup option in EDMAPCFG; suspends the status text when EdMap is loading.
/L	Disables auto-loading the latest PWAD. If auto-loading is not enabled, this option has no effect.
/X	Disables XMS, extended memory use. If the XMS is to be reserved or causes problems, this will prevent EdMap from accessing it. (All XMS is already unloaded during play-map and building.)
/S	Disables memory to XMS/disk swapping. Swapping is used to free memory for use by EdMap, but it requires more XMS and/or disk I/O.
/?	Displays help text (describing parameters, and so forth).

EDMAPCFG.EXE, creates a configuration file (*.CFG) that specifies where to look for certain files and saves the user's settings. (See Figure 2.1.) This utility also compiles data files when necessary. If there is no configuration file when EdMap is run (as the first time, out of the package), EdMap will ask whether it should load EDMAPCFG to create a configuration file and any necessary data files required, then EdMap will try again to start up. Running EDMAPCFG without parameters will use the default configuration file, EDMAP.CFG. To use a different file, specify the filename. EDMAPCFG MYWAY will create MYWAY.CFG. EDMAP /C:MYWAY will run EdMap according to the MYWAY.CFG configuration. To build the data files used by EdMap, run EDMAPCFG REBUILD. To rebuild the data files for MYWAY.CFG, run EDMAPCFG REBUILD MYWAY. While in EDMAPCFG, the line at the bottom of the screen describes how to edit the current field. A description of each field is given in Table 2.2.

The first three entries are directories; the game, data, and PWAD directories. The game directory can be filled automatically by searching the disk drive for DOOM, DOOM II, or Heretic. Press Page+Up/Down to select what game to search for and press Control+Enter to scan. The number just to the left of the entry specifies what occurrence was found on the disk (pressing Control+Enter three times will use the third occurrence of that game on the hard drive, if there happens to be three copies installed). Game parameters specify any additional parameters to pass when using the play-map feature. Grid and snap sizes determine the size of the dot grid and the snap grid (when dragging objects). Press + and − to edit these fields. There are 12 options that may be toggled on and off by pressing Enter. Directory tree and Information provide additional information.

Figure 2.1.
EDMAPCFG.EXE.

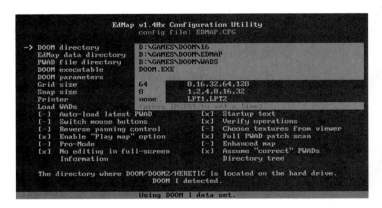

Table 2.2. EDMAPCFG field descriptions.

Field Name	Description
Game directory	EdMap must know the directory where DOOM, DOOM II, or Heretic is located. After changing this entry, EDMAPCFG will create the necessary data files if they do not already exist. Press Control+Enter to search the entire disk.
EdMap data directory	Location of the supplementary data files. If specified, files in this directory will be used instead of the default data files in the program directory. Pressing Insert will create a subdirectory in the EdMap program directory. This feature is useful for TCs (Total Conversions).
PWAD file directory	Directory to load and save PWAD map files.
Game executable	Defaults to the normal game program (DOOM.EXE). Specify an alternate program to run here. (ALIEN\ALIENTC.EXE for example, will run ALIENTC.EXE in the ALIEN subdirectory of the game directory). Only *.EXE and *.BAT files are acceptable. Running batch files

Field Name	Description
	(*.BAT) requires slightly more memory to run. (See Figure 2.2.)
Game parameters	Additional parameters passed to DOOM when run from EdMap (during a play-map).
Grid size	Size of the tiny blue dot grid when in EdMap. The grid may be adjusted or turned off from within EdMap.
	(**D**isplay, **S**nap/grid to change the sizes; **D**isplay, **G**rid-on/off to toggle the grid.)
Snap size	When dragging objects, the snap grid determines how accurately to follow the mouse. Low values mean more precise maps, but high values tend to be easier to work with as merging objects becomes easier. This may also be changed from within the editor.
	(**D**isplay, **S**nap/grid to change the sizes.)
Printer	This is not implemented yet, but will specify the location of the printer (LPT1, for example).
Load PWADs	If an ADD text file exists (EDMAP.ADD is the default), the PWADs specified on each line of this file are loaded when EdMap starts up and during play-map. This field can be used to create/edit the ADD file. Pressing insert appends a PWAD to the list, page up and page down scroll through the lines. "Adding" PWADs is a feature primarily used for editing TCs. See Listing 2.1. for a sample.
Auto-load latest PWAD	This option will cause EdMap to load the last *.WAD file to be edited when EdMap starts up. This greatly simplifies editing one map.
	(/L parameter disables auto-loading.)
Switch mouse buttons	Swaps left and right mouse buttons. If it exists, the center button (simulates pressing Enter) is not affected.
	References in this text to left and right clicking assume the default unswitched buttons.

continues

Table 2.2. continued

Field Name	Description
Reverse panning control	Holding the second mouse button and moving the mouse pans across the map. The normal panning direction is the same as the mouse; if the mouse slides right, the map will pan to the right, exposing the left. This will reverse that.
Enable Play-Map option	If this is off, the play-map feature will be disabled. Use this if for some reason the game does not run properly from EdMap. (INFO.BAT was included to solve such a problem; press Info, System, Info.bat.)
Pro-Mode	Pro-Mode allows more direct control/editing over objects and, most notably, enables object editing via the Pro-Mode object panels. This strays from the automation provided by EdMap; the user becomes more responsible for maintaining the map structure.
	(This option is only recommended for those who are knowledgeable of DOOM mechanics.)
No editing in full-screen	Many keys are reserved for editing by the object info bar; pressing 1 in Thing mode, for example, selects a Thing type. In full-screen mode, the entire display is reserved for the map by removing the menu, info box, and the object info bar. If this toggle is on, pressing 1 in full-screen mode will do nothing to prevent accidental changes.
	Pressing Display, Full-screen (or Ctrl+S) toggles between full and normal screen sizes.
Information	This line is not an actual field; pressing Enter here provides information about the the system and configuration.
Startup text	When the editor is loading, it displays status messages. Toggling this will disable this text. The text usually disappears quickly, since the screen goes to graphics mode immediately after loading the PWAD.
	(/Q parameter disables text on startup.)
Verify operations	This option controls whether some operations (mostly inserts and deletes) are verified. This can also be toggled from the Preferences Panel.

Field Name	Description
Choose textures from viewer	Usually wall, floor, and ceiling textures are chosen from appropriate panels, but textures may alternately be selected directly from the viewer by enabling this option. This may also be toggled from the Preferences Panel.
Full PWAD patch scan	Whenever a PWAD file is loaded, it is tested for external graphics resources. If Full patch scan (which may be slow) is off, only the alternate detection test is used. The alternate test uses string #162 of TEXTLIST.TXT as a reference. If any entry is found in the PWAD that matches one of those specified in string #162, the PWAD is noted as containing external graphics.
	If PWADs are not expected to contain graphics, or those that do have known header-entries (such as PP_START), then this option may be turned off.
Enhanced map	When enabled, the enhanced-map option adjusts the map view according to altitudes, in order to give a 3-D feel to the map. The additional lines also provide more information than the normal view. Enhanced map is slower, however; try panning across enhanced and normal views.
	(Display, Enhanced-map and Ctrl+E toggle enhanced mode.)
Assume "correct" PWADs	PWADs are examined when loaded to test for maps, graphics, sounds, and so on. This is usually instantaneous, but it may take a moment to examine a large PWAD. Allowing these tests to assume the WAD is properly structured can speed up these tests. (A proper WAD has, for example, the same number of x_END entries as x_START entries.)
Directory tree	Like Information, this entry displays information instead of inputting it. Directory tree provides a reference for the structure of the current drive, to aid in filling the three directory entries.

Figure 2.2.
EDMAPCFG.EXE with ALIENTC.CFG loaded.

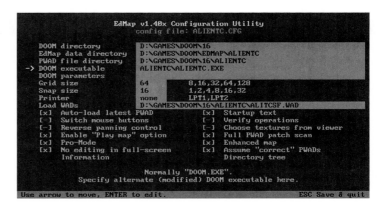

Listing 2.1. A sample ADD file: `ALIENTC.ADD`.

```
D:\GAMES\DOOM\16\ALIENTC\ALITCSF.WAD
D:\GAMES\DOOM\16\ALIENTC\ALITCWAD.WAD
D:\GAMES\DOOM\16\ALIENTC\ALITCSND.WAD
```

BATCH FILES

BUILD.BAT will "build" the BSP data for the specified PWAD. To build a PWAD called OUTPOST.WAD, type BUILD OUTPOST at the DOS prompt. EdMap automatically runs BUILD.BAT to build the BSP data.

INFO.BAT displays information about the system. This batch file is run from the Systems Resources panel in EdMap to examine the shell EdMap provides for child processes (such as running DOOM and BUILD.BAT).

UTILITIES

DOOM2WAD.EXE converts PWADs between the DOOM/Heretic and DOOM II formats. This is not a full converter; it only changes the map-entry format, and it does not change the textures in any way. This utility is used for building maps on a builder that does not recognize the DOOM II entry format. Since the included builder, WARM11, supports DOOM II PWADs, this utility is not used. If a new builder is installed, however, which only reads DOOM maps, DOOM2WAD.EXE would be necessary. To make a DOOM II map THISMAP.WAD readable by a utility lacking DOOM II support, run DOOM2WAD THISMAP 0. To again make the map playable under DOOM II, run DOOM2WAD THISMAP. A map number may be specified (DOOM2WAD THISMAP 32), or it will be calculated. DOOM2WAD run without parameters will provide instructions.

EPISODE 4 | MISSION 1 | ROOM 2 | DOOM PROGRAMMING GURUS

STUFFBUF.EXE inserts keystrokes into the keyboard buffer as if the keys were actually pressed. Typing STUFFBUF DIR! at the DOS prompt, for example, will type the letters DIR and press Enter. (The ! instruction will activate Enter.) This utility is used by BUILD.BAT to avoid requiring input from the user.

VGA50.EXE increases the number of rows (to 50) to fit twice as much text on the screen. This is run from INFO.BAT to display more information.

BUILDER

WARMDOS.EXE; WAD Auxiliary Resource Manipulator (WARM) Version 1.1 of January 1995 by Robert Fenske, Jr. (rfenske@swri.edu) is the node-builder used to "build" the BSP (Binary Space Partition) data for each map. The complete package is available as WARM11.ZIP.

WARM11.TXT is the documentation included in the WARM package.

EMU387 is the floating point emulation library required by WARM if a math-coprocessor is not installed.

INSTALLATION

Installing EdMap is almost completely automated. If the package is still "zipped," put EDMAP140.ZIP (or EDMAP???.ZIP, where ???=version) in the directory where EdMap is to be run, and unzip all the files. Run EDMAPCFG.EXE (running EDMAP.EXE will prompt whether to run EDMAPCFG), and supply the necessary information. (See the previous section for a detailed description of EDMAPCFG.) Press ESC to save EDMAP.CFG and create the necessary data files from the given DOOM IWAD. Once back at the DOS prompt, run EDMAP.EXE to make sure the installation is complete.

USING EDMAP

EdMap was designed to be easy enough for the user to immediately create playable PWADs without any prior knowledge of DOOM mechanics, but more importantly, it was written to provide an environment efficient enough to create complex maps in only a few minutes. The editing environment mimics MS-Windows or a NeXTstation in its use of graphic panels, buttons, and the menu system. Several differences are the product of the "simplicity = efficiency" design philosophy. There are no scroll bars on any panels; all options are always listed to be selected immediately using the mouse. Editing a field or selecting a menu requires only one touch of one key—for example, to select the File menu, press **F**; to change a Thing, press **1**. The basics of DOOM mechanics are handled automatically; the tedious chore of placing vertices, attaching linedefs, then assigning a sector has been simplified to merely placing complete sectors that may be easily managed into any shape. Probably the most effective aspect is the concentration of control on the mouse. Mode control, inserting, moving and editing objects, panning, zooming, and other controls are based on the mouse. After typing EDMAP at the DOS prompt, all editing functions (even loading the game) may be done by using the mouse, or occasionally pressing Enter or holding the Ctrl key.

DISPLAY ARRANGEMENT

It is important to first become familiar with the display. Most of the screen is allocated for the map display. White lines are walls (one-sided linedefs) and dark lines are two-sided linedefs that separate two sectors and usually enable things to pass (or at least shoot) through. Green linedefs trigger an action. Unless in Things mode, tiny x's mark where all the Thing objects are placed. The menu, mode, and other information is on the left of the screen. First is the main menu. Next is the information bar.

Above the gray mode selector is a status box, below it is data specific to the current object and mode. The status box has three lines at the top, three at the bottom, and a message area in between. The firsts list information about the editor, map identification, PWAD name, and free memory. Map identification means which map (E1M1, for example), and it adds an asterisk ('*') if the map has been changed since the last save. PWAD name is the filename where the map is saved to. "Original map" means the current map was loaded directly from the main IWAD; EdMap will not save to the IWAD, so if an original map is edited, it would have to be saved as an external PWAD file (**W**ad list, **S**ave as PWAD). The third line in the status box displays the amount of free memory under 640KB. Figure 2.3 shows 79.66KB available with E1M1 loaded. The green portion of the line shows how much of 640KB is still available (so it would never be near all green). If memory is low, EdMap will begin to sacrifice fast routines for memory-saving alternatives (like memory to disk-swapping and direct screen graphics).

The center space in the status box usually says Press F1 for help, but it is reserved for messages (which appear as bright white text over red). The last three lines provide information about the display. G and S on the first line indicate the grid and snap sizes, and Z is the zoom factor. The last line shows the immediate (snapped) coordinates of the mouse with respect to the map. If the provided map view is (somehow) not large enough, it may be expanded to fit the entire screen. Press **D**isplay, **F**ull-screen or press Ctrl+S to switch between normal view and full screen. In full screen, of course, the menu, status box, and information bar are removed. The menu still operates normally when using the keyboard (there is nothing for the mouse to click on), and editing the object information bar may be toggled in EDMAPCFG. Messages that would have appeared in the status box will appear at the top of the screen in full-screen mode.

Figure 2.3.

EdMap. First run out of the package.

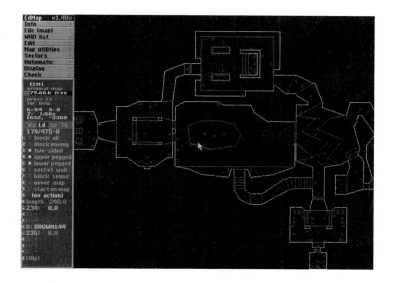

Using the menus has been simplified so that the most complicated function requires only two keys. To select from any menu (even in full screen), press the first letter of the desired selection. From the main menu, pressing **I** will expand the Info menu. Pressing **H** from the Info menu will select Help, and the Help panel will appear in the middle of the screen displaying the text for the keyword HELP. (Feel free to look around in the on-line Help system. Pressing F1 at any time will open the Help panel for the current topic.) If an entry from the main menu is accidentally selected, hitting the backspace key will revert to the main menu. The mouse may also be used to select from the menus. Click the bar of any menu entry to select it. Left clicking will activate that selection; right clicking will display a Help panel for that entry. To begin our PWAD, we will need a new map. Press **F** to open the **F**ile (map) menu. Note the hotkeys listed on the menu bars (a general key description is given in Table 2.3). Press **N** to select New map.

Table 2.3. General key functions.

Key	Function
Num Lock	Popup Calculator
F1	Popup Help
F2	Save
F3	Load

continues

DOOM PROGRAMMING GURUS

2 ROOM

1 MISSION

4 EPISODE

Table 2.3. continued

Key	Function
F4	WAD list
F5	Checking
F7	Tag linedef to sector
F8	Align/texture
F9	Build/Play
F10	Viewer
Enter	Accept
Escape	Abort

USING THE PANELS

List selection, text reading, and most editing is done from panels (windows). The top gray border of any panel is reserved for the title, the center blue space is for text, and the bottom border often has control buttons for the mouse. OK and Cancel buttons are usually provided, to accept or abort editing done on the panel. These buttons, as with most buttons, mimic a keyboard response; OK is equivalent to pressing Enter, and Cancel is Escape. Buttons are sometimes in the blue space, mixed with the text. These buttons always say what they refer to, and they are usually associated with the line they are on. If the panel consists of a list of selections, click the entry to select it. Two common list panels are the texture-selection panels, Choose a Wall Texture, and Choose a Floor/Ceiling Texture. (See Figure 2.4.)

Text descriptions are given (which may be edited) for floor and ceiling textures, because it would be difficult to remember what every texture looked like. Still, there is no replacement for actually seeing the images, so a viewer is provided to browse through all wall and ceiling/floor textures as well as sprites and patches. (See Figure 2.5.)

The viewer may be activated by pressing F10 either in normal editing mode or from either texture panel. The texture panels may even be replaced by the viewer via the Preferences panel. (This is described in detail later.)

Figure 2.4.

Choose a Floor/Ceiling Texture. This is one of the two texture panels.

Figure 2.5.

Selecting a new floor texture. The original was FLOOR4_5; shown is FLOOR5_1.

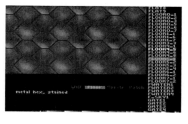

POPUP HELP AND CALCULATOR

Two popup panels are available. Pressing F1 will open the Help panel, with help on the current topic. As shown in Figure 2.6, the Help panel lists the active topic at the top; in this case, it is EdMap Basics.

Beneath the title is the text concerning that keyword. On the panel bar, four buttons are available: Basics, Previous, Search, and OK. Basics will return to the Help page displayed in Figure 2.6. Previous returns to the last topic shown, if one exists. Search opens a search panel to look for a specific keyword. If letters are typed at this panel, all keywords starting with those letters are listed and may

DOOM PROGRAMMING GURUS

2 ROOM

1 MISSION

4 EPISODE

be selected using the mouse. Pressing **C**, for example, will list 10 (only the first 10 are shown) keywords that begin with the letter C. If CHECK is typed, only keywords starting with the word "check" are listed. Press Enter or select with the mouse to search the Help file for the given keyword.

Figure 2.6.

Help: EdMap Basics. The on-line Help is activated by pressing F1.

The second popup utility is the calculator. (See Figure 2.7.) This is a simple four-operation (+, -, *, /) tool designed for convenience when no handheld calculator, adding machine, or 80 x 86-based operating system is readily available. Since Num Lock toggles the calculator, the numeric keypad may be used for input. The 17 keys on the keypad are the only keys used, in fact, by the calculator. Both the calculator and the Help panel are almost always available.

Figure 2.7.

The popup calculator.

MOUSE CONTROL

Although the keyboard offers control for almost everything, using the mouse control is usually faster, especially once the controls are memorized.

The second mouse button controls the map display. Holding the second button and moving the mouse will pan across the map. Normally, holding the second button and moving the mouse to the right will pan the map to the right, exposing the left. (This direction may be reversed from EDMAPCFG.) While holding the second button, pressing and holding the first button enables zoom control; pushing forward zooms in, pulling back will zoom out.

The first mouse button handles objects and mode control. Tapping the first button will "pick up" the closest (highlighted) object for dragging. Click again to drop the object (or press ESC to abort the drag, returning the object to its original position). Holding the first button and tapping the second (add/split) inserts an object, as if Insert were pressed. Be sure to hold the first button when the second is tapped, since holding the second and then hitting the first initiates zooming control. Holding the first button and moving the mouse will bring up the mouse pad, where releasing the button will select one of the options. (See Figure 2.8.)

Figure 2.8.

The mouse pad. In the background is everything provided with a new map: one sector and one Thing-object.

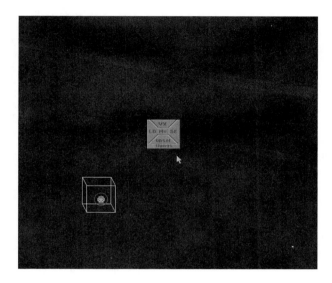

The four directions represent the four modes; for example, holding the first button, sliding the mouse to the right, and releasing will switch to Sector mode. The Unsel option unselects all multiple-selected objects.

HANDLING OBJECTS

The nearest applicable object is normally highlighted. This is the current object. The current object may be edited from the object-info bar. Ctrl+Enter selects the current object. The object-info bar will always refer to the selected object, if there is one. Pressing Ctrl+Enter again unselects the selected object, and the object-info bar again follows the current (closest) object. If Enter is hit alone, or the first mouse button is tapped while the Ctrl key is held, the current object is multiple-selected. When a multiple-selection list exists, the object-info bar still refers to the current object. Editing

DOOM
PROGRAMMING
GURUS

2
ROOM

1
MISSION

4
EPISODE

via the object-info bar always alters that object, unless that (current) object is multiple-selected; then all the multiple-selected objects reflect the change to the current object.

MODES

Editing is done in four modes: vertex (VX) and linedef (LD), sector (SE), and Thing (TH) modes. Vertices and linedefs may be edited simultaneously since EdMap will automatically switch between vertex and linedef modes. Objects may be inserted and deleted, edited or moved.

INSERTING, DELETING, AND DRAGGING

Selected/current (single) object inserting and deleting.

Mode	Insert (Add/Split)	Delete
Vertex	Vertex-break	Deletes lone vertices
Linedef	Splits the linedef into two halves, and adds a vertex in between	Deletes linedefs whose sides both face the same sector
Sector	Adds a sector	Deletes the sector
Thing	Adds a Thing	Deletes the Thing

Multiple-selected inserting and deleting.

Mode	Insert (Select Supporting)	Delete (Merge)
Vertex	Multiple vertex-break	Future?: Vertex-merge
Linedef	Selects all supporting vertices	Creates a new sector using the selected linedefs (sector split)
Sector	Selects all supporting linedefs	Merge or delete sectors
Thing	Adds a Thing	Deletes selected Things

Inserting and deleting Thing objects is the simplest. Pressing Insert in Thing mode creates a copy of the current thing. Delete will delete any current/selected Things.

Try it. Press Tab until it is in Thing mode (or press Page Down), move the mouse to any place on the map, then hold the first and tap the second mouse button (and release both buttons). A new Start 1 object will be created under the mouse pointer. Now delete it; highlight the new Start 1 and press Delete.

Moving (dragging) any object is a simple task; just click the object to pick it up, drag it to the new location, and click again to place the object. Two rules apply (which are not checked automatically for the sake of speed): First, no linedefs may ever cross, and second, sectors may not be dragged from their native surroundings. The first rule seems intuitive; if Sectors A and B exist independently, it makes no sense to place a vertex supporting Sector A inside Sector B, thus crossing two linedefs. The second rule means that if Sector A exists outside Sector B, you cannot drag A into B; all sectors must stay in the area where they were created. A sector created in the void may be dragged anywhere as long as it remains in the void, and a sector created within another sector must remain somewhere in the surrounding sector. There are ways around this: since any vertex may be vertex-broken, adjacent sectors may be broken apart to border the common void. Let's say that Sector A exists inside Sector B, for example. Sector A may be multiple-selected and inserted three times (twice to multiple-select all supporting vertices, a third to break all supporting vertices). Sector A now exists in the void that exists in B, but the void is common, so A may be dragged to the void surrounding B. Future versions should include checking or support for either or both of these cases. (Probably checking for the first, support for the second.)

SECTOR MODE

In Sector mode, Insert creates a sector using the current sector style. (Styles are explained later.) New sectors are created either in the void or in another sector. Delete removes that sector, leaving a void in its place. Even if the sector was created in another sector, deleting the inner sector leaves a void—empty space inside the remaining sector. If sectors are multiple-selected, deleting may also be used to merge the sectors with the current sector. If sectors are merged, they will be represented by the same sector-data structure; it becomes one non-contiguous sector. Merging sectors is not recommended (only 26 bytes are saved in the final PWAD file by merging a sector). A merged sector can be unmerged by using the sector-splitting utility.

Now we'll add a new sector and attach it to the first. Go to Sector mode by either pressing Shift+Tab or by hitting the End key. Besides simplifying the map display with depth, enhanced-map mode also makes attaching sectors easier by clarifying sector boundaries. Press Ctrl+**E** to toggle enhanced map drawing. The single sector should now appear, more appropriately, as a box rather than a square. Now (back to adding a sector), move the mouse so that the pointer is on the map, but not in the original sector (the sector-info bar should say "empty space." Insert a sector by hitting Insert. A new sector will appear and become the current object. The two sectors should have the exact same dimensions. Tap the first mouse button to pick up the new sector. Drag it so the bottom two vertices of that sector are on the two top vertices of the original sector. (The vertices will be marked when the mouse moves after picking up an object, in order to make merging vertices easier.) Click again to place the sector. Now do it again so there is a column of three equal sectors. The final product should look like Figure 2.9.

Figure 2.9.

*Three attached sectors.
Enhanced mode clarifies
which linedefs are walls and
which are open.*

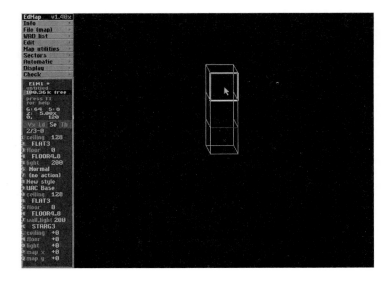

LINEDEF MODE

Linedefs, supported by vertices and supporting sectors, function with respect to these related structures. Pressing Insert on a single linedef, for example, splits the linedef, adding a vertex between the
two halves. Pressing Delete will remove a linedef, if both sides of that linedef face the same sector
and the linedef is not needed for something else (such as blocking sound or triggering an action).
Pressing Insert while linedefs are multiple-selected will select all the supporting vertices of those
linedefs. Pressing Delete with multiple linedefs selected will create a new sector supported by those
linedefs (sector-split). A continuous line of linedefs must be selected in order to form a new sector
this way. This is used to split sectors.

Now let's move and split some linedefs. Go to Linedef (Vertex) mode, and highlight the two-sided
linedef bordering the top and center sectors. (This should be Linedef 6 of 10, according to the first
line of the linedef-info bar.) Click to pick up, then drag it down below the center of the three sectors (albeit still above the lower linedef), then drop the linedef. (See Figure 2.10.) Now split (highlight and press Insert) the two longest linedefs (first split 7, then 8). Then drag the top halves (9 and
11) down and out, as shown in Figure 2.11.

Figure 2.10.

Dragging a linedef. Note the boxes around the vertices.

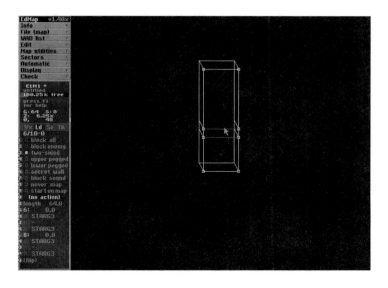

Figure 2.11.

Dragging another linedef. This linedef (11) will come down just as the left side did (9), so the map is symmetrical.

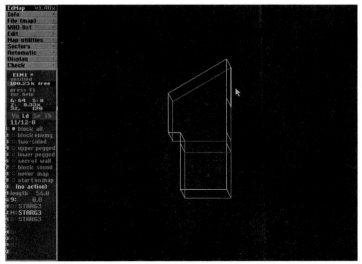

VERTEX MODE

Vertices, the simplest structure in the DOOM environment, offer a complicated set of tools for inserting and deleting. On a single vertex, Insert will perform a vertex break. This splits and recedes each adjacent sector from the original point. This is useful for making corrections; after fixing or removing the problematic sector, the vertices can be reconnected. Delete will remove vertices if the current vertex does not support any linedefs. Since it is impossible for EdMap to create a "lone vertex," this feature does not get much use, but if one existed, this would certainly be the way to remove it. To delete a supporting vertex, either use the info bar to set an adjacent linedef length to 0, or drag the vertex onto another vertex; either way, the two will merge into one vertex, and the linedef between the two would be deleted. If vertices are multiple-selected, Insert will break each of the selected vertices. Vertex-merging is the counterpart of vertex-break. A vertex that has been broken may be reassembled by multiple-selecting all the receded vertices and then deleting.

EDITING WITH THE OBJECT INFO BAR

The blue bottom half of the left bar is the object-information bar. Current object, mode, and other related data are displayed here. The top line is always reserved for the object number. The next few lines describe the current object, and the last are specific to that mode. Most of this data can be edited. Each line (after the first) of the info bar is associated with a key on the keyboard, from 1 to Q. To edit a field, press the respective key or left click that line with the mouse. To get help on any particular field, right click that line.

Editing a line may either switch a toggled option, open a panel of possible options, or bring up a control panel. Toggled fields are denoted by a white circle. If the circle is filled, the option is on; empty is off. If the circle is replaced by a dash, the toggle is no longer applicable. If editing the field opens a window of options, use the mouse to highlight the desired item and click it, or press ESC to abort the panel. Editing may also open a control panel for information or user input.

EDITING VERTICES

The vertex-object information bar (see Figure 2.12) displays only two lines specific to the current object; X and Y coordinates, neither of which is editable via the vertex-info bar.

The remainder of the info bar describes these supported linedefs. From line G, these linedefs and their lengths are listed. Above this list is a diagram of the current vertex and the direction of these linedefs. The length of each linedef may be entered by editing that line (pressing **G** for example, will edit the length of G, the first linedef). Pressing ESC will abort changing any values. After the new length is entered, the current vertex will shift accordingly. Since vertices are based on integer positions, the final length of the linedef will rarely be exactly what was entered, but it should be within half a unit. Entering a length of 0 will merge the current vertex with the vertex at the other end of the linedef whose length would be 0 (this linedef, of course, will be deleted). When dragging a vertex, this panel remains active for updated info on linedef lengths.

Figure 2.12.
Vertex mode.

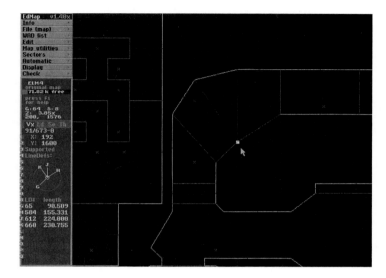

Let's move some vertices. Select Vertex 8 by marking any vertex and pressing Ctrl+**G** (or **E**dit, **G**o to object) and enter **8**. Press **H** to enter a new length; enter **300**. Select the next vertex by pressing **>** (Shift+period). Type **H300** and press Enter. (See Figure 2.13.) Press Enter again to unselect vertex 9.

EDITING LINEDEFS

While the vertex-info bar offered two lines of object data, the entire linedef information bar is dedicated to the current object (sort of). (See Figure 2.14.)

Lines 1 to 9 toggle the attributes of the linedef. Bit #3, two-sided, and (if the linedef is one-sided) Bit #1, block all, are handled automatically by EdMap and cannot be edited except in Pro-Mode. Field 0 specifies the linedef type or action. Press **0** to select a new action or no action. Press F7 to tag that linedef to a sector. Line B displays the length of that linedef. This line is not editable; to specify the length, highlight one of the two supporting vertices, and use the vertex-info bar. Lines G through P refer to the associated sidedefs; G through K are the first sidedef and, if it exists, L through P are for the second sidedef.

Figure 2.13.
Editing linedef lengths from the vertex-information bar.

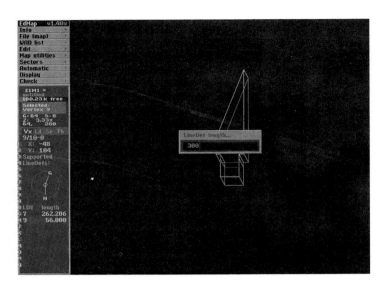

Lines G and L show the sidedef number and X and Y texture offsets. Pressing either of these will activate the sidedef panel for that sidedef, where object associations and texture sizes and offsets are listed. Both X and Y texture offsets may be specified here (although using the viewer is much easier). The sidedef panel provides even more information about related objects. Figure 2.13 shows the sidedef panel. Notice the action (Line 0) in the object-info bar; 14:8, St:rise 8 means trigger 14, type 8: Stairs rise 8 units each step. Also note that two textures are given, even though only one texture is required; the "above" texture on the first sidedef (line H).

The six texture entries (lines H, J, K, N, O, and P) refer to the six (or three, if the linedef is one-sided) possible locations for bitmapped textures along that linedef. The A: texture slot refers to the texture on the wall above the lower ceiling of the sector on the opposite side. B: defines the lower texture, between the floor of the facing sector and the higher floor of the opposite sector. M: is the main texture; this texture specifies what texture is used between the floor and the ceiling. The required texture slots are lit up in the info bar, while unnecessary entries are gray. The built-in checker will verify that appropriate textures are used. Two-sided linedefs may be flipped (swapping vertex references) by pressing Q.

EDITING SECTORS

Current sector, styles, and progression data are available on the sector-information bar.

Lines 1 through 7 refer to the current sector. 1 and 3 specify the height of the ceiling and floor levels, respectively. 2 and 4 determine what textures are used on the ceiling and floor. Entry 5 is the light level within that sector, ranging from 0 (total darkness) to 255 (maximum brightness). 6 refers to the sector type; to make the current sector blink randomly, press **6**, and select Light blinks randomly. Line 7 displays the tag number of that sector and what action a linedef will trigger, if any. Mult. actions indicates that more than one linedef acts on that sector. Press **7** to change the tag number associating the sector. Lines 8 through K refer to the current sector style. New sectors are created according to the sector style (styles are discussed later). Pressing **8** will select another style record from the style file. 0 through J mimic entries 1 through 5 but alter the style instead of the current sector. K specifies the wall texture used by the sector style to create new sectors.

Figure 2.14.
Linedef mode, sidedef panel.

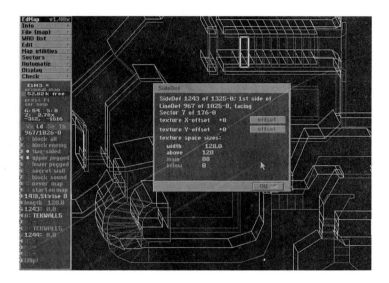

The fields L through Q are progression variables. Each time a new sector is created, the current style and map are incremented by these values. For example, if O (light) is set to –10 and three sectors are created, the second will be 10 darker than the first, while the third sector will be 20 darker. Pressing P, then, and entering 80 will shift the map to the left after a sector is inserted. Hitting Insert five times will place five sectors in a row, each 10 darker than its left neighbor.

For our map, we'll change the ceiling height of sector 0 and select a new texture for the sector style. Mark sector 0, and enter 172 (1 to edit the ceiling, 72 to specify how high). Press **B** to choose a new ceiling texture for the new sector style. Instead of using the mouse to pick a texture name, press F10 to look through the viewer. The Up and Down arrow keys scroll through the list of texture names, and Page Up and Page Down jump half a screen. The letter keys on the keyboard will also jump to the next texture starting with that letter. Press ESC to abort or Enter to select. Go to TLITE6_1 (try just pressing **T**), and press Enter to select it. Press the space bar. The panel that appears is a

Pro-Mode object panel. (See Figure 2.15.) If Pro-Mode (from EDMAPCFG) is disabled, this panel is just for looking, but if enabled, any object may be edited by clicking the byte column or by toggling any bit in the object.

Figure 2.15.
The Pro-Mode panel,
showing a sidedef.

EDITING THINGS

Lastly, lines 1 through H in the Thing object bar refer to the current thing, while J through Q determine how Things are displayed on the map. (See Figure 2.16.)

Any entry from 1 to 5 selects the type of Thing currently selected. Entry 6 determines which of the eight directions the object faces, if applicable (some things, such as barrels, are omnidirectional). 7 through B toggle the attribute bits of the Thing. 0, if the Thing is a monster, marks it a deaf guard; otherwise this entry is disabled. The other bits determine when the Thing is present in a game (difficulty and Deathmatch). G and H show the radius and height of that particular Thing. These two entries are not editable. J switches between View Any and View Equal. Use this with the toggles L through Q to discriminate what things are displayed on the map according to the attribute bits. Entry K switches between Circle All and Circle Foes.

Let's add a Thing or two to our map. Move the pointer to coordinates 0,72 (just north of the start position) by moving the mouse and watching the last line of the status box. While in Things mode, press Insert to add a Thing-object, then press **1** and select Foe:Imp. Then move to 0,200 and add a Former Human Sergeant. While the Sergeant is highlighted, tap **6** and make him face south. Now when he sees you, he'll fire and hit the Imp. The map should look like Figure 2.17.

Figure 2.16.
*Things mode. Everyone
should recognize this room.*

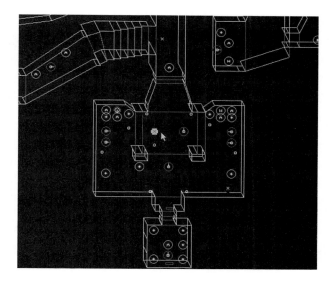

Figure 2.17.
The map so far.

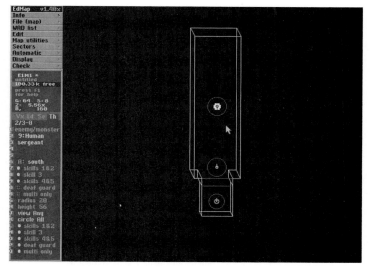

TAGGING SECTORS

Linedefs trigger tagged sectors to perform actions. To tag the current linedef to a sector, press F7. If the linedef does not already specify an action, a panel will appear listing the available linedef types. The map will then highlight sectors, as if in Sector mode. Mark the desired sector, and click it. The

DOOM
PROGRAMMING
GURUS

2
ROOM

1
MISSION

4
EPISODE

linedef is now tagged to that sector. The first number in the object info bar on the line describing the action (line 0 in Linedef mode, 7 in Sector mode) is the trigger number associating the linedef to the sector. To associate another sector to act on the same trigger, remember this trigger number, press **7** when the second sector is highlighted, and enter the trigger number.

Before adding actions, let's add another sector or two. For now, we'll work with enhanced map off; press Ctrl+**E** to toggle. First we'll add a sector inside Sector 2 near the top, but not touching anything. 0,280 is a good spot; go to 0,280 first, then press Insert to create a sector within Sector 2. Highlight the lower linedef of this new sector, and press F7. Select #77, CrshC: fast hurt, then tag the sector just created (number 3). This will make the ceiling above crush anything under it when that linedef is crossed. Return to Sector mode, press **0**, and enter **192** as a new ceiling height. Enter **G64** to make new sectors with a floor at 64. In the void, create another 64x64 sector and place it under the lowest sector so that the top two vertices merge with the bottom two of the original sector. While highlighting this new sector, enter **3128** to set that floor to 128. Create two more sectors in the void. Move the first just above the top of the current map and place the second above that one so the vertices merge. Go to linedef 7 and break it twice. Move both new vertices up so that they merge with the two bottommost vertices of the sectors created a moment ago. The map should now look like Figure 2.18. Move the pointer to 0,–64 and create a Former Human Sergeant. He is now on the raised floor behind the start position, which will lower when triggered.

Figure 2.18.
After adding a bunch of sectors.

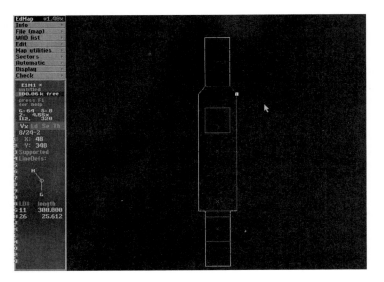

AUTOMATICS

To aid in map creation, four automatic construction routines are included for building commonly used devices. Lifts, doors, stairs, and teleporters may be created using respective panels, available from the **A**utomatic menu or by pressing Alt+**L**, Alt+**D**, Alt+**S**, or Alt+**T**. Changes to any of these panels are saved to the active configuration file to be available the next time that panel is used.

AUTO-LIFT

The automatic lift-construction panel is the simplest to create, using only four fields. (See Figure 2.19.)

Figure 2.19.
The Lift panel.

First highlight the sector to be the lift. The floor of this sector should be set at the lift's highest raised position. Press **A**utomatic, **L**ift or Alt+**L** to open the Lift panel. If the Repeatable button is pressed, the lift may be used more than once; click this button to toggle between this and only one use. Side Texture indicates the texture on the wall behind the lift that is seen when it lowers to the current floor. If the Use Floor? button is pressed, the floor texture of the lift will be replaced with the given floor texture; otherwise the floor texture in this panel is unused. Floor Texture, if used, determines what texture the floor of the lift uses. Activate lifts in the game by pressing the Use key while touching the wall of the lift.

Highlight the second-highest sector and press Alt+**L**. There's nothing to change, so just press Enter to accept the panel and create the lift.

AUTO-DOOR

The automatic door panel has six fields (or seven for DOOM II), but still remains simple. (See Figure 2.20.)

Figure 2.20.
The Door panel.

Like the lift, the sector to become a door must first be highlighted, then the door panel may be opened (**A**utomatic, **D**oor or Alt+**D**). The first three entries determine the texture used by the new door. Door Texture is the wall texture that specifies what the door itself will look like. The Sill Texture is used where the door meets the wall to form the frame, only to be seen when open, below the raised door. The texture used on the bottom of the door (the ceiling of the door sector) is specified by the Bottom Texture. The Key entry may be set to keyless, blue, yellow, or red (green in Heretic). The Close option toggles whether the door closes again in six seconds. Moving Sill may add an effect to the door by scrolling the sill textures up and down with the door itself.

Highlight Sector 1 and press Alt+**D**. Release the Close button so the door will stay open. Change the door texture to `DOOR1`; it fits in the 64-unit wide space. When everything looks good, press Enter. Now highlight Sector 1. Line 7 should read, `1:mult. actions`. The 1 is the trigger number that raises the door. `mult. actions` means that more than one linedef can activate that sector (via the trigger number). In this case, both sides of the door may open it. For our map, let's change that other side of the door to trigger lowering the floor behind the start position. Mark that linedef (number 6), and press **O**. `31, MDoor: open` should be lit, indicating the original value. Select `#38: Flr: down to min adj`. Highlight the linedef again and press F7 to re-tag this linedef to Sector 4 (the bottommost sector). (See Figure 2.21.)

AUTO-STAIRS

Unlike the lift and door functions, which alter existing sectors, the automatic-stairs feature creates an entire staircase. Figure 2.22 shows the auto-stairs panel.

From Sector mode, press Alt+**S** or press **A**uto, **S**tairs. Ten entries configure how the staircase will look and operate. Some of the values are related; after changing the number of steps, for example, the staircase length will be recalculated. Some arrangements are also impossible (such as a rising staircase that creates steps 4 units high) so fields may be limited to specific values. The first two buttons select what texture is used on the top and side of each step. Settings for Step Rise, Depth, and Width specify the dimensions of each individual step. Step Rise is the final height of each step relative to its predecessor. This number cannot be more than 24 (in order for the player to step over it), and even though the player may fall any amount, the minimum Step Height value is –32. If the staircase is designed to rise when triggered, the Step Rise value is limited to 8 units in DOOM, 16 units in DOOM II (if it is a fast-rising staircase), or either 8 or 16 in Heretic.

Figure 2.21.
Still a very simple map, but now it does stuff.

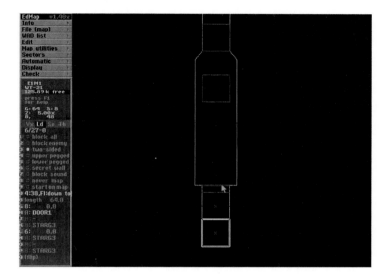

Figure 2.22.
The Stairs panel.

Ceiling Height is the constant height of the ceiling above the entire staircase, measured from the highest step. The number of steps must be from 1 to 128. The direction of the staircase may be either north, east, south, or west. To direct the staircase in any direction, multiple-select the steps (at least every other step, and both ends) and sector-rotate the entire structure. The last entry determines whether the staircase is a fixed structure or if the steps are triggered to rise out of the floor sequentially to 8 or 16 units above the preceding step. In DOOM II, the last entry may also specify fast-moving steps.

After accepting the values by pressing Enter, you must place the staircase itself. As with dragging, an outline of the staircase will follow the mouse until it is placed or ESC is pressed. The staircase may be either created within another sector or in the void. If created within a preexisting sector, only the steps will be added, using the textures specified in the Construction panel. If the staircase is placed outside, the steps will follow the textures outlined in the Stairs panel, and additional textures (such as the walls and ceiling) will be taken from the current sector style.

A rising staircase would fit nicely in our map. Press Alt+**S**, and change Step Width to 64 and Step Depth to 16. (See Figure 2.21, shown previously.) After pressing OK, place the staircase so that the bottom of the staircase is just above the top of the existing map. Then move the uppermost linedef (but just below the staircase) up so that the two vertices supporting it merge with the two bottom vertices of the staircase.

AUTO-TELEPORTER

Teleporters may be constructed in either linedef or sector mode. If Alt+**T** (or **A**utomatic, **T**eleporter) is pressed while in linedef mode, the current linedef will teleport to the point specified. Just mark the linedef to teleport, press Alt+**T**, then place and select the direction of the destination (if a destination does not already exist in that sector). In sectors, mode teleporters are constructed using the Teleporter panel. While simple linedef teleporters merely transport players to new locations, the Teleporter panel creates two new teleporter pads, which may perform specific functions. (See Figure 2.23.)

Figure 2.23.

The Auto-Teleporter panel.

The first field, Two Way, toggles whether to place two teleporters or just one. If enabled, the receiving direction must be specified in the second field. The third field indicates the destination direction if entered through this site. The texture used will be the pattern on the teleporter floor and possibly the ceiling. Texture Ceiling toggles whether the ceiling should be retextured like the floor. Sector Type allows for additional effects, such as pulsating light. Press OK to close the panel and place the two teleporter pads. The pads will automatically snap to the 64-unit grid so the pad textures are aligned properly. We'll add teleporters later; for now let's take a break from map construction.

4 EPISODE   **1** MISSION   **2** ROOM   **DOOM PROGRAMMING GURUS**

FILE HANDLING

F2 will save the file. If the PWAD already has a name, pressing F2 will quickly save the file with no panels to verify. A filename must be entered if the PWAD is untitled, and it must be verified if a file already exists by that name. Pressing Ctrl+F2 (Save as PWAD) will save the PWAD under a different name. (This has nothing to do with Rename map.) There is also a timed save option, controlled from the Preferences panel, which is discussed later. Press F2 to save this file. To keep things consistent, let's call it WALKTHRU.

Loading a map may be done in different ways. Pressing F3 alone will open a panel listing all the WAD files in the PWAD directory. If a file is chosen, it will be added to the WAD list (F4) and loaded as the current map. (The first map will be loaded). A map may also be loaded by its map designation by using the WAD list. Shift+F3 will open a panel displaying all the available maps in a game (27 for DOOM and Heretic, 32 for DOOM II). Press F3. (No, we're not going to reload the map; we're just looking.) The Load PWAD panel will list all the WAD files in the PWAD directory (as specified in EDMAPCFG). Two mouse buttons are available: Time and Name select how the files are sorted. If only one file is listed (WALKTHRU), these two controls should not do too much. To the right of each file is the date when the file was last saved. If a file is highlighted, the size of the file is listed at the bottom of the panel. Press ESC to close the panel.

The map may also be built. Pressing F9 will run the builder (via BUILD.BAT) with the current PWAD file. Press F9 now. If everything worked, the map is ready to run. Press Info, Map-Information. Among the data provided, the last line should say, This map is ready to run. If the build failed, a message would have noted so upon returning to EdMap. If the map is ready to run, try playing it (Ctrl+F9). The Play-map panel offers different ways to play DOOM (or DOOM II or Heretic). (See Figure 2.24.)

Figure 2.24.
The Play-map panel.

Buttons labeled No Monsters, Sound, Music, and Sound Effects are self-explanatory; if you want them removed from the game (for this session), disable the appropriate buttons. Respawning monsters revives dead monsters randomly after their death. Fast Monsters speeds up game play. Turbo scale specifies an increase (or decrease) in player movement (Figure 2.24 shows a 50 percent increase). Deathmatch and Alt-/Deathmatch 2.0 simulate a Deathmatch game. Altdeath respawns items. Try playing with the settings in Figure 2.25 for a fast-paced game. (These options are described in more detail in the README.TXT file included with the game.) Additional parameters may be added using EDMAPCFG. Each time the Play-Map panel is used, the settings are stored in the configuration file. Press a number from 1 to 5 to specify the level of difficulty and load DOOM. Don't forget to quit to return to EdMap.

PREFERENCES

By now, you probably have a feel for things. Let's take a look at how to adjust various options for personal flavor. The Preferences panel extends the configuration options beyond functionality to alter normal operation of EdMap to individual taste. Press Info, Preferences to open the panel, as shown in Figure 2.25.

Figure 2.25.
The Preferences panel.

From this panel, mouse control, verifications, timed saving, and other options may be controlled. Additional options panels are also accessible from the Preferences panel. The Checking Options panel offers control over the integrated checking utility. (See Figure 2.26.) Snap Options and the color palette panels are also available.

First on the Preferences panel is the Use Panel? Skill? (Play-Map) option. If this button is enabled, the Play-Map panel will open before loading the game. Disabling this switch will skip the Play-Map panel and run the game at the skill level specified. The last used settings from the Play-Map panel will be used, but pressing Ctrl+F9 will immediately run the game (the builder first, if necessary).

Figure 2.26.

The Checking Options panel.

Three mouse fields are available to adjust the mouse control. To change X or Y sensitivity, click the button and enter what percent sensitivity the mouse should have. After entering a number, the value entered may be adjusted to the nearest usable setting. The double-speed threshold for the mouse may also be adjusted, if the mouse driver supports this function.

The editor options alter the normal operation of the program. The error list toggles between Full and Fast checking. This option should be set to Full unless error checking takes too long, as on a slow machine. The checking routines test for genuine errors as well as generally accepted problems even though they do not necessarily influence game play. Listing warnings will test for these problems. Although picking textures from the available panels is faster, often there is no alternative for seeing the actual texture. The Viewer button skips the texture panels completely, switching to the viewer whenever a texture must be chosen. For convenience, a simple popup calculator is available. Usually pressing Num Lock activates this calculator, which remains active as long as Num Lock is on. If using Num Lock to toggle the calculator is a problem, disable the Num Lock button on the Preferences panel.

If the Always Save? option is enabled, the function that asks `This map has been modified, do you want to save?` will always assume the map should be saved. A timed saving feature is also available. Click this button to specify the interval between saves. If `0` is entered, this feature will be disabled. Otherwise, between two and 59 minutes may elapse between saves.

The Additional buttons open panels, which can be used to specify checking and snapping options, as well as adjust the color palette of the screen. All changes to these panels, as with the other preferences, are saved for the current configuration. Editing the color palette is done by adjusting the red, green, and blue components of each color. The palette is saved to a *.PAL file with the same name as the loaded configuration (*.CFG) file. Snap options determine which operations (in inserting, constructing, and dragging) use the snap grid.

Clicking the Checking button will open the Checking Options panel. Each of these toggles determines which errors are reported. Each controls several tests, not necessarily restricted to a specific check (from the Check sub-menu). The last field specifies a value. If Long-Wall-Error (the first toggle) checking is enabled, all non-orthogonal linedefs longer than this value will prompt a warning. Click OK to integrate these changes into the checking routines. These options are saved, of course, to the active configuration file.

CHECKING

To ensure maps are created free of errors, EdMap offers integrated checking routines. Pressing **C** will expand the Check menu. Check All searches the entire map for any errors (determined by which tests are enabled in the Checking Options panel in Preferences). If an error is found, the map will pan to the problematic object, select it, and report the error in a panel at the bottom of the screen. From this panel, the Next button will resume searching for another error, and OK will stop checking, leaving the object selected. Quick Check is similar to Check All, but more time-consuming tests are skipped. Error List compiles a list of all errors detected on the map. This list performs the same checks as Check All (or Quick Check, depending on the Error List: Full/Fast entry in the Preferences panel). The only difference is that instead of stopping at every problem, Error List adds occurrences to a list, and when the check is done, the list is presented in an Error List panel. The other menu entries under Check test for a specific kind of problem.

Still have WALKTHRU loaded? Press Ctrl+**L** to see the list of errors. (See Figure 2.27.)

Figure 2.27.

Error list. There seems to be a bad upper texture here.

Let's examine these errors. `Missing start-x things`, just means this map could not be played in multiplayer-Cooperative mode. `Missing Deathmatch starts` cannot be played in Deathmatch mode. `No exit` means we never added an exit to the next level. Oh, what's this? Linedef 6: `Bad upper texture size: 'tutti-fruitti.'`

Check All provides a clearer description of such errors; press Ctrl+F5, then press **N** three times to skip the first three errors. You will then get the following error explanation. `'Tutti-fruitti' effect: this upper texture had a height that does not divide evenly when tiling a wall taller than it`. A check of the linedef-info bar tells us that the only required texture is the upper texture on the first sidedef (DOOR1), line H. Press Enter, let's change that texture to match the walls; press

H, and select STARG3. Press **C**heck, **E**rror List to see if this fixed the problem. We'll add an exit later; for now, let's add more rooms to this map.

SECTOR UTILITIES

POLYGON CREATION

A sector may be shaped into any form by splitting linedefs and dragging vertices; but constructing a large polygon sector using only the vertex coordinates would require a steady hand, patience, and lots of math. A polygon-sector creation tool is available to simplify such a task. Select **S**ectors, **P**oly-gon (Ctrl+**P**) to create an *N*-sided polygon. The Polygon panel asks for the number of sides (from three to 64) and the measure of the radius (from the center to each vertex along the edge). The polygon can then be placed, just like auto-stairs.

For our map, we'll add a huge round room to the right of our current map. First zoom out (to about 1.5x), as the new room will be about 2,000 units across. (See Figure 2.28.) Open the Polygon panel, enter `1000` for the radius and `40` for the number of vertices. Place the center of the room around 1200,0. Next we'll add an acid pool to fill most of this new room and a circle platform in the middle of the acid. Again, we'll use the polygon utility, this time making a circle of 20 points that is 800 units in radius at 1200,0. To make this sector an acid pool, lower the sector (`3-16`, Enter), change the floor texture (press 4) to `NUKAGE1`, and set the sector type (press 6) to –5% Health. The island/platform will consist of 15 vertices, with a radius of 300 units at 1200,0. Let's raise that island to 16 units high (`316`, Enter).

SECTOR RESIZING AND ROTATING

Sectors, along with basic dragging, may also be resized or rotated. Both resizing and rotating are forms of dragging, so the target sector must still be clicked first to pick-up and again to place. Pressing **Z** toggles resize-dragging (so pressing **Z** twice enables resize dragging then reverts to normal dragging). When resizing is enabled, clicking the sector will pick it up, and place the mouse at the lower right corner of the sector. Moving the mouse now changes the dimension of the sector because the lower-right corner of the sector will follow the mouse. Right clicking on the mouse will move the mouse back to return the sector to its original shape, and hitting ESC will abort the operation. Information is given (in the status box under the menu) that shows the percentage change in both axes. Click again to place ("drop") the sector. **R** toggles rotating. Like resizing, rotating attaches the lower right corner of the sector to the mouse. The information provided while rotating is the angle-change in degrees. (Rotating should apply to any object; it follows that appropriate Thing objects may also be rotated. Pressing **R** in Thing mode is equivalent to pressing 6 to select the angle.) After any kind of drag, the normal move-drag is restored. Neither resizing nor rotating uses the snap grid; to snap the sector, click once to pick it up, then again to drop it in the same place, snapped to the grid.

Figure 2.28.

The map so far.

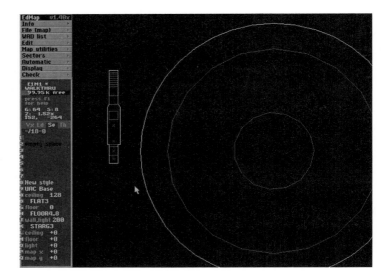

Let's see what we can do with our map. Sector 2, the main hallway with the Imp and the Sergeant. Press Enter to multiple-select it, and multiple-select all the sectors below it (sectors 2, 1, 0 and 4 should all be selected). Press **Z** and click one of those sectors to resize them all. Enlarge the X axis to about 350 percent, but keep the Y axis at 100 (careful, it cannot intersect the round room to the right). Click again to drop. (Wasn't that fun?) It should look like Figure 2.29. Press Control+Enter to unselect the four sectors.

SECTOR STYLES

The textures and attributes defined in the sector style are used in creating new sectors. This simplifies making maps by keeping commonly used style records, which may be edited and saved (as SESTYLE?.DAT in the data directory). The current style is edited just as the current sector is; by pressing the appropriate key for the field to edit in the information bar (this was discussed previously, in the "Editing Sectors" section).

Figure 2.29.

Moving right along.

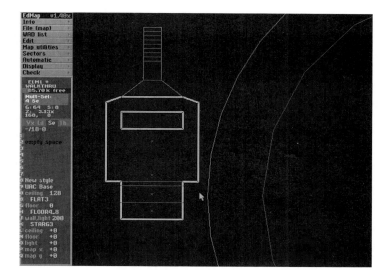

TEXTURE STYLE

Sector, **T**exture Style will replace the textures of the current sector with those of the sector style. The floor, ceiling, and walls are all retextured (even unnecessary sidedef textures).

GRAB STYLE

The opposite of Texture Style, Grab Style takes the textures of current sector and copies them into the current style. The sector attributes, ceiling and floor textures, are defined by the sector itself and stored in the style record. The wall texture used is the "best guess" since a sector is bordered by many walls (usually the most common main texture is used).

EDIT STYLES

All editing of the style records file is done using the Edit Styles option (Ctrl+F8 or **S**ectors, **E**dit styles). To add or delete records, select a linedef (even if no style is to be added) and press Ctrl+F8. A temporary style is created using that linedef. A panel will open describing the new style. (See Figure 2.30.) From this panel, the temporary style can be saved or a specified record may be deleted. To reorder the records in the file, press Ctrl+F8 while in sectors mode. The two selected style records will be swapped with each other in the file. The first record in the file is loaded at startup as the default style.

Figure 2.30.

Saving a sector style.

BACK TO WALKTHRU

Let's return to WALKTHRU; we'll insert a sector, then add a few teleporters. First add another 64 x 64 sector, and attach it to the end of the staircase. Adjust the ceiling and floor heights (1192, Enter, 3128, Enter). Now highlight the linedef bordering that new sector and the staircase; we'll make this teleporter manually. Press F7 (tag), select 39, Telpt: teleport once. and tag the nukeage ring in the circle room. Now add a Thing-object in that sector around 1200,–400. Press 1 and select t.dest: teleporter destination. (It should already be facing north.) That's it—a one-shot, one-way teleporter. Now for the teleporter back. While in sector mode press Alt+**T** and release the two-way button (to make it one-way), then press Enter. Place the first pad in the center of the round room, and put the destination somewhere in Sector 2, the enlarged square room. It should look similar to Figure 2.31.

Figure 2.31.

Almost done; WALKTHRU in things mode.

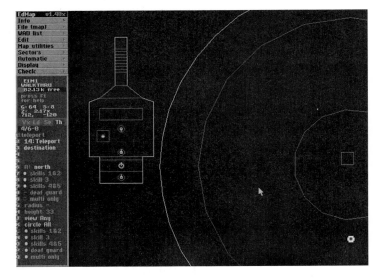

WALKTHRU still needs a way out of the big oval room. Pick a vertex near the top of the oval, and press G128 to move the vertex to make the linedef on the right (close to) 128 units wide. Mark the linedef whose length is now about 128 and press F7 to give it a function. Select 62, Lift: lower for 4sec, then tag the center island (sector 17, not the teleporter pad). Now we need to change the texture of the trigger linedef to look like a switch. Highlight that linedef and press **J** to select SW1STARG. Now there's a way out, but we still need an exit to the next level. Select (Ctrl+Enter) the top horizontal linedef above the stairs. Press **J** and select SW1STARG again. Press **0** and choose 11, `Exit: next level`. Now the level is exitable. Ctrl+**L** tell us the following: `Missing start-x things` and `Missing Deathmatch starts`. Looks like we're adding a few things. Add four or more Deathmatch starts and a Start-2, Start-3, and Start-4 Thing in the round room. While we're at it, add a whole mob of monsters and an arsenal of Things in the oval room. Ctrl+**L**: `No errors detected`. (See Figure 2.32.) WALKTHRU is now a fully functional map, but there's still one more thing to do.

Figure 2.32.
The completed map (shown in full-screen).

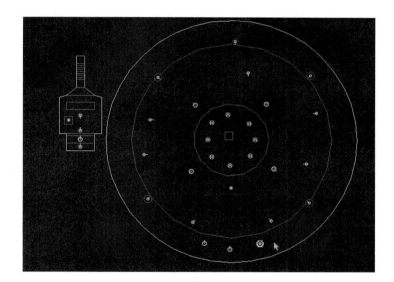

TEXTURE ALIGNING

For maps to look convincing, the wall textures must be aligned so that similar adjacent textures flow evenly into each other instead of meeting at an ugly seam. There are two automatic-aligning features, and using the viewer, individual textures can be aligned. Pressing F8 in Sector mode will adjust the offsets of each texture in that sector. This works best if the walls surrounding that sector are mostly one-sided. Otherwise, there will be a seam on the one-sided wall where the sector being aligned follows a two-sided linedef. Aligning along the one-sided wall is usually more useful. Do this by marking a one-sided linedef and pressing F8. Starting with the that linedef, textures will be aligned to the right (if you face the wall) until one of two cases occurs. First, it will stop if a wall is reached where none of the textures of the next wall match any of the textures of the previous wall (to the left). The second case stops aligning along the one-sided linedefs when the first linedef is reached (which it will, if the first case is never met). Aligning can adjust the X, Y, or both offsets. Specify what to change by using the Configure Texture Align panel, which is accessed by pressing **S**ectors, **C**onfigure Align. The Sectors submenu specifies what axes are adjusted for aligning on the Align Textures bar; Align Textures (X,Y) means both X and Y offsets will be shifted according to adjacent textures.

Now we'll align the textures in WALKTHRU. First press **S**ectors, **C**onfigure Align. Ensure that both X and Y offsets are enabled. Each of the sectors in the big round room may be aligned from Sector mode, but this should be unnecessary because polygons are made with prealigned textures. Now highlight the linedef to the right of (and below) the linedef that exits the level (this should be linedef 127). Press F8. The textures in that entire room are aligned, except for the switch texture. Highlight the exiting linedef and press **J** to open the texture panel. Press F10 to go to the viewer. The switch texture should be shown, and a box should enclose part of the texture. The numbers on the keypad shift the box on both axes. (Press Num Lock, or hold Shift; otherwise you'll scroll through the textures.) Move the box to surround the switch itself. Press Enter to accept this change. Repeat this for the switch in the oval room. Save the file and enjoy—the map is done!

ADVANCED TOPICS

CUSTOMIZING

EdMap has been designed to be very user-customizable. Most of the data files may be edited to personal preference; if the text is not descriptive enough, there is no reason it cannot be changed.

As part of the startup procedure, data (*.DAT) files are checked against their text sources (*.TXT); if a source file is found to have been edited, the data file is then recompiled. This system also allows for easy updates; just replace the outdated file. Data files may also be created manually by running EDMAPCFG.REBUILD. If an alternate data directory is specified (in EDMAPCFG), files found in that directory will be used instead of the normal files found in the current (EdMap) directory.

The beginning of each text file provides a brief description of the required format for that text, but a more verbose explanation is given here. All text files allow remarks; if the line begins with a semicolon (;), that line will not be read as data (this is how the file description is inserted). Some files use a [2] or a [H] to indicate a line specific to DOOM II or Heretic. Because EdMap uses proportional text there is no set length for text descriptions, so text strings should not be too long. (A long string is not dangerous, it may just look bad if it runs off some border.)

FLORLIST.TXT

The descriptions of floor and ceiling textures (in the Choose a Floor/Ceiling Texture panel and the viewer) are taken from FLORLIST.TXT. Lines have the texture name and the texture description. If the texture is specific to DOOM II or Heretic, a [2] or [H] must be added before the description (this file also determines which textures are available to choose from). Unmarked lines are used for DOOM and DOOM II; Listing 2.2, for example, shows one DOOM texture, two DOOM II textures and one Heretic texture. From FLORLIST.TXT, FLORLST?.DAT is compiled. FLORLST1.DAT is used for DOOM, FLORLST2 is for DOOM II and FLORLSTH for Heretic.

Listing 2.2. Lines from FLORLIST.TXT.

```
;FLORLIST.TXT
…
FLOOR0_1        tan patchwork
SLIME01   [2]   brown sludge
FLAT504   [H]   weathered grey tile
…
```

SETYPES.TXT

Like FLORLIST, SETYPES.TXT contains descriptions. This file defines what sector styles are available. If a line does not begin with a semicolon, first comes the sector type number, followed by a colon, then two descriptions separated by a comma. Sector type descriptions must be enclosed in double-quotes. The first text string is the long description listed in the Choose a Sector Type panel and the second is the brief description shown in the sector information bar on line 6. A [2] or [H] may follow the line. Unlike most other TXT files, this file is not used to create a data file; instead, SETYPES.TXT is read at startup. Listing 2.3. shows a few lines from SETYPES.

Listing 2.3. Lines from SETYPES.TXT.

```
;SETYPES.TXT
…
16:"-20% health","-20% hlth"
17:"Light blinks (fire)","fire flckr" [2]
42:"Wind, East (Strong)","HardWi:E" [H]
…
```

THINGS.TXT

THINGS.TXT and SETYPES.TXT are the only two text files read at startup without a data file. All Thing-object data is read from THINGS.TXT. First is the Thing number, then the radius and height, followed by the name of the Thing-object, and lastly, the optional [2] or [H]. All data is separated by commas, and the name is enclosed in double-quotes. The first letter in the name is used to define what kind of Thing it is. (See Table 2.4.) If this letter is uppercase, the Thing is animated. The list should be read in order of the Thing number, it will be sorted by kind and name when the file is read at startup. Heretic things do not need to be sorted with DOOM things, since only one set is read for any configuration, other lines are ignored. While editing Heretic maps, for example, only lines with [H] are read. (See Listing 2.4.)

Table 2.4. Kinds of Thing-objects.

Kind type	Description
X	(nothing)
S	Start position
K	Key
W	Weapon
A	Ammunition/Backpack
B	Bonus (health, Radiation Suit, and so on)
E	Enemy/monster/foe
T	Teleporter object
O	Obstacle
D	Picture/decor
N	Sound (Heretic), N=hacked DOOM II sound

Listing 2.4. Lines from THINGS.TXT.

```
;THINGS.TXT
;<number>,<radius>,<height>,"<kind><name>" [?]
1,16,32,"sstart 1"
5,16,33,"Kblue keycard"
43,16,33,"ogray tree"
65,20,56,"Ehuman chaingunner" [2]
82,20,16,"wsuper shotgun" [2]
```

```
0052,0,33,"Tglitter (exit/blue)" [H]
1204,1,0,"nheartbeat" [H]
...
```

ACTIONS.TXT

Linedef types (actions) are taken from ACTIONS.TXT. The line format in this file is slightly more strict: if a letter is missing the line may be unreadable. Fortunately, any errors found are clearly defined with the line number. The linedef type number leads the string, followed by two or more spaces. Next follow three letters: first is the game used (H for Heretic, 2 for DOOM II, and . (a period) for original DOOM and DOOM II). The second character is S if the action is a switch-action (requiring the Use key to be hit in the game), otherwise . usually indicates a line activated by walking over it. The third character determines whether the action is repeatable; R means the linedef may be retriggered, . indicates a linedef type which may only be used once. A space follows, then a brief description, a semicolon, and lastly a verbose description. Usually the brief string consists of the kind of action and the action itself. (See Table 2.5.) This string is shown on line 0 of the linedef information bar and in the Choose an Action panel. The long description is used at the bottom of that panel to provide a full explanation of what each action does. (See Listing 2.5.) ACTIONS.TXT is used to make ACTSLIST.DAT.

Table 2.5. Kinds of linedef actions.

String	Kind of Action
M'Door	Manual Door: player must "use" the door to open.
R'Door	Remote Door: the door may be opened from a remote linedef.
Telpt	Teleporter: teleports a player or monster to another location.
Flr	Moving floor: floor raises or lowers.
Ceil	Moving ceiling: ceiling raises or lowers.
CrshC	Crushing ceiling: starts/stops crushing ceilings.
CrshF	Crushing floor: starts/stops crushing floors.
Stair	Triggers successive sectors to rise into a staircase.
Light	Alters the light value in a given sector.
Exit	Ends the level, begins next or secret level.
Scroll	Scrolls the wall texture.

Listing 2.5. Lines from ACTIONS.TXT.

```
;ACTIONS.TXT
000   ... (none); no action
001   .SR M'Door: 6sec;ceiling behind rises, then returns to floor after 6 sec.
107   2.R R'Door: fast close;Turbo close Remote-Door
048   H.. Scroll: left;Wall texture scrolls left
011   HS. Exit: next level;Exit switch to next level
...
```

TXTRCONV.TXT

Texture Replace (**M**ap Utilities, **T**exture Replace) replaces all occurrences of a given texture with another. TXTRCONV.TXT may be used alternatively to replace a list of textures. The included TXTRCONV can be used to replace all the original-DOOM-only textures with textures available in DOOM II, so DOOM PWADs may be run in DOOM II. This file may be edited to convert DOOM textures to Heretic equivalents, for example. The basic format for each line in this text file is the searched-for texture name followed by a greater-than sign (>) and the replacement texture name. (See Listing 2.6.) This is not a genuine data file as it is not even required to run, so there is no related *.DAT file.

Listing 2.6. Lines from TXTRCONV.TXT.

```
;TXTRCONV.TXT
AASTINKY >REDWALL
ASHWALL  >ASHWALL2
BLODGR1  >BLODRIP1
BLODGR2  >BLODRIP1
...
```

TEXTLIST.TXT

In order to save memory, many text strings were moved out of the program code and stored in this external text file. Almost 200 strings are references in this file; map names, error messages, warnings, general information, and various data are kept here. Some strings are meant to be user editable; string #162 defines patch header names. Why edit any of the system strings? If `There is no *?* key to open this door` is not descriptive enough, it easily can be changed to `You forgot the damn *?* key, idiot!` Editing TEXTLIST is simple; only the text within double quotes is recorded, so remarks need not be prefixed with a semicolon. The only rule is that strings may only take one line.

Although this file is read directly, TEXTINDX.DAT is compiled to quickly reference locations in the text. See Listing 2.7 for an example.

Listing 2.7. Lines from TXTRCONV.TXT.

```
TEXTLIST.TXT for EdMap v1.40
1=E1M1: "Hanger"
2 "Nuclear Plant"
3 "Toxin Refinery"
...
116: "Floor height\Not all ceilings above new floor level."
117: "Light value\Out of bounds; should be between 0 (total dark) and 255 (brightest)."
118: "One of the selected sectors already has a trigger.  Retrigger it?"
...
146: "This LineDef has a transparent *?* texture."
147: "Only one teleporter destination may occupy a sector."
148: "There cannot be more than *?* scrolling walls in a map."
...
162:EXTERNAL PATCH HEADER NAMES: "[P_START ][PP_START]"
163: "Patch check\Not enough memory to perform a full external patch scan."
...
```

HELP.TXT

Even the help file can be edited. HELP.TXT is the most structured of all the text files because it contains all the help data; keyword, text, and related topics. The general format is: a divider-line, the topic/keyword, another divider-line, the actual text, and an optional related topics list. The divider-line is simply a line consisting of equal-signs (====).

The keyword name must be exactly as it appears in references; Level begin & end is not the same as Level begin and end. This line is not case-sensitive; it will be made uppercase to simplify searching.

The topic text cannot have any returns except to end paragraphs; entire paragraphs must be written on one line. This is because with proportional text, new lines are not determined by the number of columns. (A line of 10 i's is shorter than a line of five W's.)

Most help screens have a group of related-topic buttons in the blue below the text. In HELP.TXT this is done by adding a see_also line and listing the related topics on a separate line. Each line will become a mouse button to lookup that keyword.

The text and keyword buttons must all fit in the same panel. If the text is too long, page the topic; TEXTURES and TEXTURES, PAGE 2. Like HELP.TXT (like TEXTLIST.TXT) is read directly with the aid of a data file, HELPINDX.DAT.

DOOM PROGRAMMING GURUS

2 ROOM

MISSION 1

4 EPISODE

"TOTAL CONVERSION" SUPPORT

In addition to supporting DOOM, DOOM II, and Heretic, EdMap can be used to create "TC"-based PWADs. Total Conversions involve taking the normal game engine and changing the maps, graphics, sounds, and the game program itself. The result can pit you deep in an alien hive wielding your trusty pulse rifle as eggs around you hatch Facehuggers. Normally, a simple upgrade file will automatically install a TC configuration; just put the *.INS file in the EdMap directory, and run EDMAP /C:<TC-name>. If such a thing is unavailable, however, manually installing is not hard.

We'll install an *Alien*-TC configuration. (Is it obvious I like *Alien*-TC? Who wouldn't love those sneaky little guys?) First, we'll need a new config file (let's call it ALIENTC.CFG); this is done by running EDMAPCFG ALIENTC. Enter the DOOM directory and the PWAD directory. For the DOOM executable, the hacked file must be specified. Enter @ALIENTC, this will search the disk for a file called ALIENTC.EXE, and use its full path.

Similarly we'll need to search for files to make the ADD file. The ADD file contains PWADs loaded at startup and to play the map. In this case, these are files containing the replacement maps and graphics (and optionally sounds, music or anything else) required to run the TC. Go to the Load WADs line and press Insert. Enter @ALITCWAD; this will create an ADD file to load ALITCWAD.WAD at startup and when playing the map. Press Insert again and Enter @ALITCSF and @ALITCSND. Go to the EdMap data directory, press Insert, and enter ALIENTC to create a new data directory. After the new configuration file is saved, three files will be made in the data directory: WALLLST1.DAT, PATCIDX1.DAT, and FLORLST1.DAT.

We'd need new text-based data files, too; copy FLORLIST.TXT and THINGS.TXT into the new directory. These files will have to be edited. Cacodemons no longer exist; they're eggs in *Alien*-TC. Unless you have a list of Thing-objects changed for any given TC, this step will require experimentation. FLORLIST.TXT should also be edited, since some of the floor textures have changed. Use any text editor to modify these files. (Editing the data files was explained in the previous section, "Customizing.")

That's it; to edit *Alien*-TC WADs, run EDMAP /C:ALIENTC.

UPGRADING DOOM (OR DOOM II OR HERETIC)

If the game is updated to a newer version, some of the data files become outdated. These files will be detected as outdated at startup and recompiled. This is different from normal auto-updating because IWAD-referenced data files cannot depend on the timestamp of the source file (the IWAD, in this case). Some data files that reference PWADs are also updated this way.

If configured to use two versions of the same game, one version configuration must use a separate data directory, so version-dependent files are not recreated each time a different version is used. If both DOOM version 1.2 and 1.9 are used, for example, the data files for the earlier version could go in a v12 subdirectory.

INSTALLING A DIFFERENT BUILDER

EdMap loads COMMAND.COM (as specified by COMSPEC) and runs BUILD.BAT to build the BSP data using an external builder. (See Listing 2.8.) As of v1.40, EdMap uses WARM11 by Robert Fenske, Jr. (rfenske@swri.edu) as the BSP node-builder. Installing a different builder requires changing the BUILD.BAT file. A list of parameters passed to BUILD.BAT is given in Table 2.6.

EDMAPCOM.EXE is used to change the variables governing process-control. In Listing 2.8, for example, under the BUILDFAILED label, EDMAPCOM is used to abort a play-map and report that the build was unsuccessful. Three variables are available, shown in Table 2.7. EDMAPCOM must be called with %4 and %5 as the first two parameters and, all in uppercase, one of these variables followed by =TRUE or =FALSE. See Listing 2.8 for examples.

Listing 2.8. A simplified BUILD.BAT.

```
@echo off
set GO32=emu EMU387
copy %1.wad backup.wad > nul
echo Building BSP data...
:BUILDNOW
if "%2"=="ALTBUILD" goto ALTBUILD
WARMDOS -z -n -b %1.WAD
goto DONEBUILD
:ALTBUILD
WARMDOS -n -b -r %1.WAD
:DONEBUILD
if errorlevel 1 goto BUILDFAILED
echo Finished building PWAD; %1.WAD is now playable.
if "%5"=="" goto END
EDMAPCOM %4 %5 BUILT OK
goto END
:BUILDFAILED
copy backup.wad %1.wad > nul
if "%5"=="" goto FAILTEXT
EDMAPCOM %4 %5 PLAYMAP=FALSE
EDMAPCOM %4 %5 ERROR BuildFailed
:FAILTEXT
echo BUILD FAILED!
echo PWAD RESTORED
:END
```

Table 2.6. Parameters passed to BUILD.BAT.

Parameter	Action
%1	PWAD full path and filename: `C:\GAMES\DOOM\WADS\HANGER18` (no .WAD extension).
%2	ALTBUILD; `%2"=="ALTBUILD` is true if the alternate build (ALT+F9) is to be used.
%3	Used by DOOM2WAD for DOOM II <–> DOOM/Heretic conversion.
%4,%5	Used by EDMAPCOM to communicate back to EdMap.

Table 2.7. EDMAPCOM switches.

Switch	Response
BUILD	Was the build successful?
PLAYMAP	Load the game?
RETURN	Return to EdMap?

To install IDBSP version 1.0 of Ron Rossbach's (`ej070@cleveland.freenet.edu`) port to DOS of id Software's BSP builder, only minor changes to BUILD.BAT are required. (Version 1.0 is outdated; the latest version requires even fewer changes, but for this example we'll use a builder that does not recognize the DOOM II map entries.) First, the builder program (IDBSP.EXE) is required in the EdMap directory. This earlier version of IDBSP cannot take WAD files as input so WAD_DWD.EXE, included with the IDBSP, is required to convert the PWADs to DWD format, which IDBSP understands. Since IDBSP was released before DOOM II it does not recognize DOOM II map entries, so DOOM2WAD.EXE will have to be used (described earlier). Using these new files, BUILD.BAT should look like Listing 2.9.

Listing 2.9. BUILD.BAT modified for IDBSP.

```
...
:BUILDNOW
DOOM2WAD %1.wad 0
WAD_DWD %1.wad tmp.dwd
 if errorlevel 1 goto BUILDFAILED
erase %1.wad > nul
IDBSP tmp.dwd %1.wad
 if errorlevel 1 goto BUILDFAILED
DOOM2WAD %1.wad %2
```

```
goto DONEBUILD
 if errorlevel 1 goto BUILDFAILED
echo Finished building PWAD; %1.WAD is now playable.
if "%5"=="" goto END
EDMAPCOM %4 %5 BUILT OK
goto END
:BUILDFAILED
...
```

SUMMARY

This text covers many of the features EdMap has to offer, but accounts for only those tools necessary to create a simple map. There are many other features not described, (the Find panel, the Map Utilities menu, WAD list management, the directory function, and so on). Additionally, with new improved versions being released so often, the copy included on this CD-ROM is sure to be outdated by the time this book hits bookstores. Who knows what the next version will do? EdMap combines flexibility with simplicity in an effort to produce the most useful map-editing environment possible. Driven by user appreciation and guided by suggestions it has grown into what is presented here. (And more.)

ROOM 3

By Geoff Allan

WHAT DOOMED DOES

DoomEd is a comprehensive editor for Doom and will soon be available for Heretic as well. Using DoomEd, you can create your own maps, place your own textures on the walls, ceiling, and floors, and completely define the locations of all the items. Your maps can range from the simplest two-room configurations to very complex mazes—even more complex than the original DOOM levels.

DoomEd is a Windows program, and it requires Windows 3.1 or greater. If your video card allows it, you should be running 256 colors, at 800 x 600 resolution. DoomEd works with all versions of DOOM, but you are only allowed to modify the registered versions.

HOW DOOMED CAME ABOUT

My first experience with game editors came with id Software's Wolfenstein 3D. After spending several frustrating hours with a shareware editor, I decided to write my own. Painful months of struggling resulted in a rather dismal editor that was never released.

In the spring of 1993, rumors of DOOM began circulating all around the BBSs. This new game would have several features that seemed rather ambitious. For instance, your bullets would leave marks in the walls, and you would be able to walk up to a computer terminal and interact with it. Preview pictures showed the player apparently riding around in a little tank, or maybe wearing a computerized helmet. Finally, in summer of 1993, I was able to play with an "alpha" version of DOOM.

This alpha version was widely circulated to magazines for review, and several of the gaming magazines fueled the fire. The monsters were unable to move, and there was no sound, but the potential for the game was instantly obvious—DOOM was going to be FUN!

When DOOM was finally released on December 10, 1993, I was one of those people who jammed the Internet in an attempt to get a copy. It took me about three days to complete all of the shareware levels, and then I wanted more. More challenges, more levels, more bad guys, more weapons. My registered version was obtained shortly after.

It didn't take too many more days before I was ripping apart the structure of the WAD file. I was using Microsoft's Professional BASIC, but it soon became obvious that even one part of one map was bigger than BASIC enables you to load into memory. So I switched to C. Yes, I learned how to program in C and Windows by writing DoomEd.

Throughout the months from January to April 1994, I was decoding the WAD file format to the best of my abilities. I had an editor that enabled the user to move things around and even change wall textures, but any changes to the map resulted in garbage—the dreaded "Hall of Mirrors" effect. I still needed to figure out what those "nodes" were for.

In April, I discovered a program called the DOOM Edit Utility, by Raphaël Quinet and Brendon Wyber. Magically (it seemed to me), they had written a "node builder." I checked the source code and found that they were allowing anybody to use this code, so I integrated it into my almost complete editor.

Finally I had a tool that enabled you to build your own maps. I soon released my program as shareware.

Over the next few months, I completely rewrote the program, including writing my own node builder. The version of DoomEd that is included with this book is the result of about a year of full-time work. As I have learned more about C programming and Windows programming, DoomEd has improved to the point you see it now. A new version, Version 5, should be available by the time you read this. It will be a total rewrite, using a new tool for Windows programming that I wrote specially for DoomEd. Full details of the improvements are listed at the end of this room.

USING DOOMED

DoomEd was designed to be as simple to use as possible. Feel free to experiment. As long as you save often, you won't damage your computer or DOOM files.

INSTALLATION

To install DoomEd, run the file called Setup. From the Windows Program Manager, select File, then Run. Click the Browse button, and search through the CD until you find the DoomEd directory. Click the SETUP.EXE file, then OK. Click OK again, and Setup will begin.

Setup will attempt to determine where you are installing from, where you are installing to, and where your Windows directory is. If you wish to install to a different directory, click the Change button and enter a different directory name in the proper place.

When you click the "All Right, Install It!" button, DoomEd will be installed to your hard drive. Also, a file called CTL3DV2.DLL will be placed in your Windows system directory. It is extremely important that this file *not* be placed in your DoomEd directory. If it is, DoomEd will not run (but it will give detailed instructions on how to fix the problem).

If, for any reason, you are unable to use the Setup program, copy all of the files into their own directory, except CTL3DV2.DLL. Place this file in \Windows\System if it does not already exist there. Then, add DoomEd to your Program Manager. (See your Windows documentation for this step.)

You should now be able to run DoomEd by double clicking its icon in Program Manager.

DEALING WITH WAD FILES

When you first run DoomEd, you will be asked for the location of the main DOOM.WAD file. This is critical. If you do not get this correct, you will have to manually edit the DOOMED40.INI file (which is in your Windows directory). If you have DOOM, this file will be called DOOM.WAD, while DOOM II uses DOOM2.WAD. The DOOM.WAD file contains all of the required resources for DoomEd, such as the colors, images of things, and the picture in the About box.

As is explained elsewhere in this book, WAD files contain all of the maps, images, sounds, and music for DOOM. By creating your own WAD file containing only a map, you can "fool" DOOM into thinking that your map is one of its own. You can do the same with sounds and music; however, this version of DoomEd does not enable you to work with graphics.

Select the File menu and Open. You will be opening a WAD file. If you have never used a DOOM editor before, try opening the DOOM.WAD file (as described previously). This file contains all of the regular maps, so you can edit something that you know. (You *do* know all of the DOOM maps, don't you?)

To edit any map, simply double-click its name in this WAD file directory. To get the directory to show again later, select the File menu, then Contents. Alternately, you can click the left-most icon on the toolbar. This icon represents looking at the things inside of a file.

EDITING MAPS

DoomEd's map editor is *sector-oriented*. This means that the basic unit of manipulation is a sector. Every door, room, each step on a staircase, and every window is a sector. A sector has lines surrounding it, and each line can be a part of either one or two sectors.

SECTORS

A sector is where you define the floor and ceiling textures, the light level (brightness), and the floor and ceiling altitudes. The simplest possible map contains two sectors, making one single room. This is the map that you start with when you click the Add Map button in the directory listing.

To create a new sector, hold the right mouse button while drawing a box *outside of any other sector*. (You can move it inside another sector later.) You can also hold the Shift key to make this box perfectly square, or the Ctrl key to make the start point the center of the box, or both. The status bar displays the width and height of the box as you draw it. When you release the button, a menu will appear, giving you several options for your new sector.

The simplest option is Rectangle. This makes your newly drawn rectangle into a four-walled room.

4	1		3		DOOM
EPISODE	MISSION		ROOM		PROGRAMMING GURUS

The next option is Elliptical. This makes your new sector into a circle if it is square, or an ellipse if it is a rectangle. You will also be asked how many segments constitute this ellipse. But beware: because of some limitations of DOOM, you should keep this number as small as possible. If you have too many circles with too many segments, DOOM may be unable to properly run the map. Also, try to keep this an even number, and, even better, a multiple of four. This way, you can more easily attach entrances and exits from this sector at north, south, east, and west points.

The third option is Star, which creates a properly proportioned five-pointed star. Since the theme of DOOM is somewhat demonic, it made sense to include this as a basic shape.

Fourth, you may elect to create Steps. Read the Steps dialog box carefully when you first start using this tool—it requires the Lowest height, the Highest height, Rise per Step, and Number of Steps. The Rise and Number are adjusted as you change them. (Try it, it's easy.) The Runner Texture is the texture that will be placed on the front of each step, so try using the textures that start with "STEP." Finally, the Rise Direction should be fairly obvious. If you want to create an angled staircase, create the steps first, then use the Rotate tool. Using the Steps tool will create more than one sector.

Finally, you can select Cancel, which cancels the creation of any sector.

Your new sector (or sectors, when creating steps) is now created. You will see that it is a different color than any others, since it is now the "currently selected" sector. If you need to move it, simply hold the left mouse button down (inside the new sector) and drag it into a new position.

Double-click the sector to pop up an attributes window for this sector. This is called a "modeless" dialog box, and it can remain displayed while you do other things. If you change any of the items in the dialog box, they are instantly changed in the sector (or sectors) that are currently selected. Expanding the dialog box using the ">>" button will enable you to see the floor and ceiling textures that are assigned to the sector. Selecting new textures will cause the display to instantly reflect the change.

Deleting sectors is easy. Just select them and then press the Delete button on your keyboard. To select more than one of anything, hold down the Shift key while selecting sectors. Or, using the left mouse button, draw a box around the group of sectors you wish to select. You can combine both of these shortcuts.

You can also use the Shift key or "box" selection technique to select multiple sectors, and then move them around together.

Sectors can be placed into other sectors. In fact, you will find this to be an essential part of map building; therefore, good technique is required.

When you place the new sector (or sectors) inside another sector, no edges can "stick out" over the edges. If you place a sector inside another sector and then remove it, lines will remain where the sector was just moved from. These lines are the "border" lines and can be easily removed using the Lines tool.

You can also place a sector within a sector within a sector. DoomEd is doing several things at this point: adjusting the wall textures so they line up, for example, and adding "border" lines (something which is required and automatic, and which you don't need to worry about). The best way to learn these techniques is through experimentation.

If you click a sector with the right mouse button, a different menu appears. This menu allows further customization of the sector (or group of sectors). When you have sandwiched a sector between two others, you can select Make Sector a Door to handle all of the gritty details. You may wish to adjust the texture, since it is always just a basic door texture.

The Rotate and Scale options enable you to do just that. Rotating always centers around the logical center point of all selected sectors. Scaling expands or shrinks from the center point also.

You can even Duplicate a sector or group of sectors, and the new ones will be placed off to the side.

Again, the best way to become skillful at these techniques is to experiment. Try to do something, and if it isn't exactly what you intended, try to figure out why, so your next attempt will be more successful.

LINES

Lines, or *linedefs* (short for line definitions), are where wall textures are stored. Each line has a front and back. The front is indicated by the direction of small "pointer lines." Exterior walls, for example, have all of these pointer lines pointing "in." If there is no sector on the other side of a line, then it has no back (and thus no second texture).

Although you can drag lines into new locations, it is not recommended that you do so. If you move a line that forms part of a sector and you don't close the sector, then your node build will fail (meaning you can't run the map). You may, however, delete a line by pressing the Delete key while a line is selected. After doing so, you must manually reconnect the affected sectors (see the section on Vertices) to close the sector. This feature was primarily included as an aid in fixing "broken" maps.

When you double-click a line, a modeless dialog box appears, showing details of this particular line. Here you will find such specifications for the line as whether monsters or players can cross, whether the line blocks sounds, and more. If you expand the dialog box using the ">>" button, you will see the wall's textures. Clicking the texture-selection combo boxes will bring up yet another dialog box, which shows the currently selected texture.

4
EPISODE

1
MISSION

3
ROOM

**DOOM
PROGRAMMING
GURUS**

Wall textures are broken down into three sections: *main*, *above a lower ceiling*, and *below a higher floor*. DOOM can place textures along a line that joins two different sectors, even if those sectors are at different altitudes. Just remember to watch the front and back, and think as though you were in the game and looking at the line. Are you seeing the front? If so, is the next sector's ceiling lower? If so, then you must place a texture in the *Above A Lower Ceiling* box. A dash (—) indicates no texture will be shown.

One of the most common mistakes when building DOOM maps is forgetting to place textures where sectors join. DoomEd automatically places these textures, although they may not always be the ones that you want. Even if you change the height of a sector's floor or ceiling, DoomEd is intelligent enough to add or remove these textures as required. The only time you may need to change this is when you are manually adding an elevator or some other special feature of DOOM. Some other actions can also cause texture "failure," which appears to the player as a bleeding-through of other textures (such as the ceiling). If this happens, simply ensure that a texture exists on the offending wall.

Lines can also *control* sectors. This is the key to the dynamic nature of the DOOM environment. By crossing, activating, or shooting a line (or wall, remember), you can cause some action to occur to a sector. DoomEd enables you to define "tags" to any line, and any sector. One line can trigger multiple sectors, and one sector can be affected by multiple lines. The only exception to this is doors, which have a line action but no sector connected.

DoomEd offers a rather large list of special-action possibilities (141 for DOOM II). These include "Blazing" (fast) doors, doors that require keys, a ceiling that lowers to the floor (effectively sealing off a room), and teleportation. Scroll through this list to see just how flexible DOOM is. The list is sorted alphabetically and grouped in logical sections.

VERTICES

Lines are connected to vertices. A vertex is simply a point with an X, Y coordinate. DoomEd handles all creation and deletion of vertices automatically; however, you can use this tool to *move* the vertices. Simply drag the corner of some sector and you will see how easy it is.

While editing vertices, you may find it useful to break a line in two, essentially adding a new vertex in the line. To do this, hold the right mouse button while the pointer is over a line. The line will be broken, and you can move the new vertex at will (by continuing to hold the right mouse button). Use this for fine-tuning the positions of sectors and lines.

You will also use this tool when connecting two sectors. If one is larger than the other, then you must break the lines where they join. Any two vertices that are moved into the same position will become one, and all of the lines that connect to either vertex will be attached. If this causes two or more lines to be joined, DoomEd will automatically adjust the line textures and make one single line.

You can select multiple vertices the same way as sectors and lines, and you can move them as a group if desired.

THINGS

Every thing is a Thing. The player-start positions, blue bottles, a shotgun, and an Imp are all examples of Things. You may double-click any Thing to bring up a dialog box showing what the Thing is and even showing a picture of it. (Click the Expand button, ">>".)

To create a new Thing, click the right mouse button. The new Thing will be exactly the same as whatever the last Thing was that you clicked, so it is easy to create many copies of the same type of Thing. Things can also be grouped, dragged, and deleted the same way as sectors, lines, and vertices.

MAP-BUILDING TUTORIAL

Although DoomEd is easy to use, it will certainly help to walk through this little tutorial in order to get a "kick start." Once you have actually followed along on your computer, these basic techniques will soon become second nature. You may find, however, that the process becomes addictive and that spending 100 hours building maps for your own episode is not unthinkable.

BUILDING A MAP

If you have ever used one of those "other" DOOM editors, you will be pleasantly surprised at how much of the mundane drudgery of map building is done for you by DoomEd.

First, start DoomEd. Click the File menu to pull down a list of choices. Select New to create a new WAD file. You will be asked for a directory location and filename for your WAD file, so for now just call it Test. A directory listing will appear, which will be empty.

Click the Add button to add a new map. You will be prompted for the name of the map. If you are running DOOM II, type in

```
MAP01
```

For the original DOOM, type

```
E1M1
```

Whatever name you entered will appear in the directory listing. Double-click the name in order to bring up the map editor.

You should now see a screen that appears something like Figure 3.1.

Figure 3.1.

The DoomEd window.

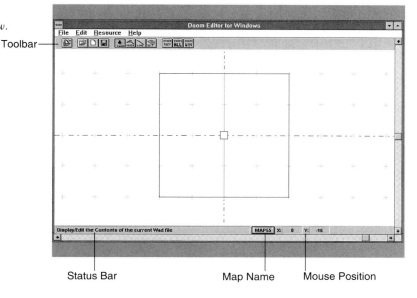

Toolbar

Status Bar   Map Name   Mouse Position

This is the common editing screen, and all of the most important aspects of DoomEd appear here. First, let's take a look at the toolbar buttons.

Referring to Figure 3.1, the first button is the Show Directory button. The icon represents looking at the contents of a file, and that is exactly what this button lets you do. Click this button to select another map or other object to work with.

The second is the Open File button. Use this button to open a different WAD file to work with.

The third button is a clean sheet of paper and is the shortcut for creating a new, empty WAD file. (You could have clicked on this button to create your new WAD file instead of selecting **F**ile, **N**ew.)

Fourth, a picture of a diskette represents the Save function. You can't select it right now, because you can only save if you have made changes. The "unavailable" status is indicated by the way it is grayed out. Clicking this button saves your work, so after you have something to save, get in the habit of clicking it every few minutes.

The next group of four buttons selects which aspect of the DOOM map you are currently editing: Things, Vertices, Lines, or Sectors. Each button, when pressed, has a different color. After using these for a while, you will be able to tell just by the color what tool is currently selected. In this case, the Thing tool is currently selected.

Still referring to Figure 3.1, the rightmost three buttons enable you to zoom into a specific section of your map. By clicking Zoom All, the map will be shrunk so that all of it is visible in the window. Zoom Win(dow) enables you to draw a box around a section of your map. The screen will be resized to fit that section into the display. Zoom Prev reverts the view to whatever it was before you used one of the other Zoom buttons.

You can also zoom into and out of your map by pressing Alt+**Z** to zoom in, and Alt+**X** to zoom out. These keys were chosen to be easy to hit with your left hand, assuming that your mouse is in your right hand.

The bottom of the window is called the status bar. This portion contains mostly informational data. At all times, the mouse location is indicated with the X: and Y: indicators.

Finally, the Map Name is also a button. If you click this button, you can change the name of the current map.

Now that you know where everything is, let's start looking at the actual map. The small "plus" signs that are scattered about are the Floor/Ceiling grid indicators. Since each floor and ceiling tile is exactly 64 x 64 pixels, that is the size of this grid. If you want a teleporter to be exactly right, you should line it up on one grid square. These marks also help you to determine quickly how large a particular area of your map is. Again, once you get into editing your own maps, you will find this to be a valuable tool for quicker, easier building.

Oh, yes, the blue dashed lines are simply the origins for the X and Y axes. If you move the mouse around, you will see that the X and Y location is exactly zero on these lines.

Notice that the large square, which is a room, is divided into two rectangles, left and right. That is because DOOM cannot run a map which has only one sector, so we divided this starting sector into two. Each side is actually a sector on its own. To prove this, pull down the Resources menu and select Statistics. You will see two sectors.

First, let's add a third sector. Click the Sector button, then use the right mouse button to draw the outline for your new sector. See Figure 3.2 to see that the newly dragged-out sector is highlighted.

After you release the right mouse button, a menu will pop up with some choices. For now, simply select Rectangle. The new sector is created. Now, move the mouse cursor inside of the new sector and hold down the left mouse button. You will be able to drag the sector about. Place it approximately where it is in Figure 3.3.

4
EPISODE

1
MISSION

3
ROOM

**DOOM
PROGRAMMING
GURUS**

Figure 3.2.

Adding a new sector.

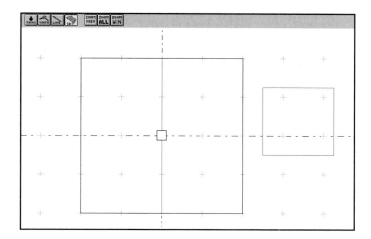

Figure 3.3.

Placing a new sector.

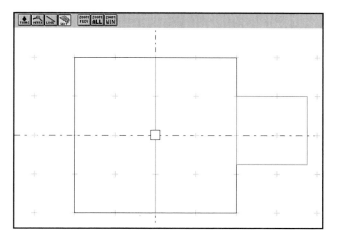

Now, although you have moved the sector, it has still not been attached to the original sector. To do that, you must do some vertex connecting. Click the Vertex button, and use the right mouse button to break the original sector line. (See Figure 3.4.)

Then, using the left mouse button, drag the new vertex until it is exactly where the first connecting point is. You can tell when it is exact, because the vertex changes color. (Try it, you'll see.) You could also combine these two steps. Use the right mouse button to break the line above the new sector, and while holding the right mouse button, move the new vertex into place on the second connecting point.

Figure 3.4.

Connecting vertices.

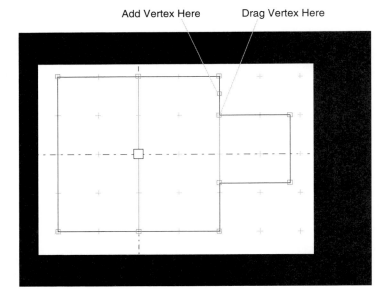

Congratulations—you have just connected a new sector to a previous sector. Save this map by clicking the Save button, then run DOOM to see this map in action.

To start DOOM while loading a WAD file, type:

```
doom -file test.wad
```

The `-file` keyword tells DOOM that it should add any maps, sounds, music, or graphics that are in the named WAD file in place of whatever DOOM has in its own WAD file. Of course, the file "TEST.WAD" must be in the same directory that you start DOOM from. If not, just add the full pathname like this:

```
doom -file c:\DoomEd\WadFiles\test.wad
```

ADDING A TELEPORTER

Our next goal will be to put a teleporter into this newly added sector. For this, you will need to create another new sector. This one should be exactly 64 x 64, since it will be our teleporter. Create this new sector outside of any other, then drag it into place as shown in figures 3.5 and 3.6.

Figure 3.5.
Creating the teleport sector.

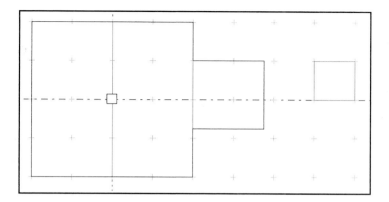

Figure 3.6.
Placing the teleport sector.

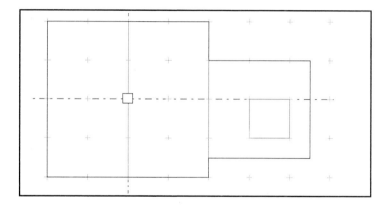

Now, while still in Sector mode, double-click the sector that will receive you when you teleport through. This will bring up the sector-editing dialog box. On the bottom, you will see a section called Tag. Click the Add button here.

Now you will see a new dialog box. This one is for entering tag information. For this purpose, simply note which tag number is here, and click the OK button.

Select the Lines tool, and double-click the line that will trigger your teleport. This is the highlighted line in Figure 3.7.

Since you double-clicked this line, you will see the line-editing dialog box. Adjust the bottom two entries so they look like Figure 3.8.

Figure 3.7.

Selecting a line.

Selected

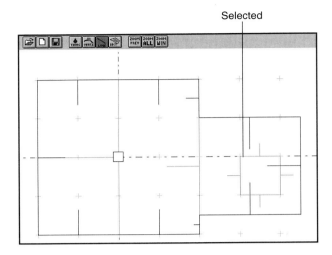

Figure 3.8.

Selecting the teleport action.

Use whatever the Tag number was for the destination sector. You may want to duplicate this for whatever other lines could possibly be crossed to teleport you, such as the top line of the teleporter pad.

Finally, simply defining the sector is not enough to teleport you there. You must select the Things tool, and place a new Thing somewhere within the destination sector. (Right click to add.) Make this new thing a "TeleportMan." The TeleportMan object is where you will actually be sent. DOOM only looks for this Thing inside of the destination sector.

It is possible to make a teleporter pad the destination of another teleporter pad. Lines that teleport only do so if you cross them from front to back so that you can exit a teleporter without being banished to some other teleporter.

CREATING DOORS AND WINDOWS

Doors and windows are actually just sectors, sandwiched between two other sectors (remember to connect the vertices!), and they must be attached in a special way. A little bit of logic should help here.

For doors, ensure that the sectors on both sides of the door have the same floor height. This is important. A door will not be created if you don't do this. If you examine the DOOM maps, you will see that wherever a very tall sector has a doorway, there is also an extra sector between them. This is called a buffer sector, and is to prevent the entire wall from moving upwards as a door.

After creating the sector that will become a door and attaching its vertices correctly, right-click the sector. A menu will pop up from which you can select Make Sector a Door. This will automatically adjust everything required, including the door texture, side texture, and actuation.

Windows are similar, except you don't need a buffer sector. Simply sandwich a thin sector between two other sectors. Make sure that the window sector has a floor and ceiling altitude which will make it a window, not just an opening. (See Figure 3.9.)

Figure 3.9.

Example of a window from DOOM II's Map03.

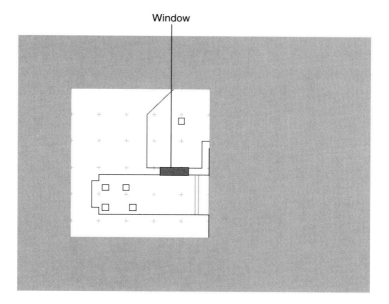

Window

ELEVATORS (LIFTS)

The first thing you need to remember about elevators is that they are simply another sector. The only difference is that crossing or activating something makes them lower to match their nearest neighbor for about five seconds and then return to their original height.

Examine the elevators that appear in the DOOM maps to see how easy they are to design. Other than tagging the sector and defining a line to activate it (Platform Down, Wait, Up, Stay), there is nothing special required. (See Figure 3.10.)

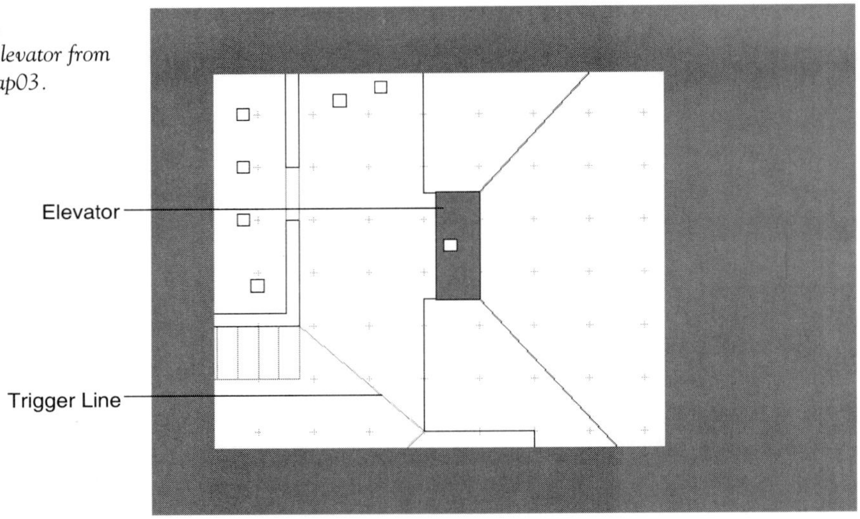

Figure 3.10.

Example of an elevator from DOOM II's Map03.

Elevator

Trigger Line

TUTORIAL SUMMARY

The most important part of building DOOM maps is to **experiment**. Creating a new map to test a new theory requires very little disk space. If you see something in a WAD file that is not discussed here, load that map up and see how it works. Any WAD file that DOOM can read can be viewed and edited by DoomEd.

Since people have been creating their own DOOM maps, several new tricks and techniques have been developed. Maybe even id Software doesn't know how to do one of the things that you will learn or invent!

Always remember: DOOM is a *game*. As such, it should be relaxing, entertaining, and fun. The goal of DoomEd is to enhance that fun, by enabling you to create anything you want with the ultimate of ease. Be creative, and try to avoid placing huge pockets of monsters where they will be impossible to defeat. Try to give your players plenty of ammo and health. Experiment with concept levels, where the goal is not just to finish but to see how fast you can finish, or to see what percentage of kills or secrets can be attained.

MISCELLANEOUS FEATURES

BITMAP VIEWER

The Bitmap Viewer enables you to view the items in the DOOM.WAD file. These include the "sprites," pictures that are designed to move around (such as monsters, players, fireballs, and so forth), panels (also called patches, which are sections of wall textures), textures (the actual graphics that go on the walls), and tiles (floor and ceiling textures). You can view any graphics in the WAD file, either at normal or double size. In addition, sprites contain a "lock point," which is the location of the floor. By selecting the Locked option, you can see how high the sprites are above the floor (represented as a dashed line).

To export graphics from DOOM for other uses, use the WAD file viewer. Click a graphic, then click the Export button. A standard Windows BMP file will be written, which you can use for anything you wish. Try making creative Windows Wallpaper so your co-workers know what your favorite pastime is!

3-D VIEWER

The 3-D viewer provides a simple perspective view of your map. You can use this powerful little viewer to help visualize your map as you develop it. While displaying a 3-D view, you can use the mouse to change the current view, as follows:

Both mouse buttons:	Move left to **back away**, move right to **move in**.
Left mouse button:	Move up, down, left, or right to change the location of the **viewer**.
Right mouse button:	Move up, down, left, or right to change **where the viewer is looking towards**.

Press the **H** key to remove hidden lines. If you have the hidden-line removal mode on and then use the mouse to alter your position, the map will return to "wireframe" mode until you release the mouse button(s).

This hidden-line removal feature works by sorting all of the panels needed to draw your map and by drawing them from farthest to nearest. Thus, the nearest walls will block the farthest. Because the rectangles are sorted from their center points, sometimes a far wall will cover a near one. This is a minor problem that will not affect your map in any way.

WHAT'S NEXT

DoomEd Version 5 will have even more great features. Users who buy retail version 4.0 or 4.2 or register their shareware versions will receive this upgrade when it is ready (expected date: mid-1995).

In addition to the map editor, DoomEd 5 will have a full graphics editor built-in. This editor will enable you to modify existing graphics or to create your own. You can even use a scanner to convert artwork to the DOOM graphics format.

You will be able to load several maps at once and copy sections from one to another. This means that you also could have several maps showing for quick comparison.

Full support for the new game Heretic will be built-in, and you will be able to copy DOOM maps into Heretic. If (or when) id Software releases other games based on this engine, DoomEd 5 will have a mechanism to enable upgrading the editor to the new game. Mostly, this affects the descriptions of tag actions and Things (including their pictures), since the actual game engine is identical.

And since DOOM is now a worldwide sensation, international-language versions are being prepared. Look for French, German, Dutch, and Spanish editions of DoomEd in the future.

ROOM 4

By Matthew Ayres

WADED

WADED is an intuitive, easy-to-use map editor for DOOM, DOOM II, and Heretic. WADED enables you to manipulate already-made levels and to create your own. As one of the easiest editors to use, it includes many features that make level-editing and level-building a snap.

OVERVIEW

Back in 1994, after the registered version of DOOM was released by id Software, there was a definite need for a map editor. Matthew Ayres started on a project that is still in progress today: making an easy-to-use and easy-to-understand editor to build levels from scratch. With the release of WADED 1.83b, easy level-editing and level-building have been achieved.

WADED is programmed in QuickBASIC v4.5 using a few routines written in Assembler. A typical screen from WADED is shown in Figure 4.1.

Figure 4.1.

A typical WADED screen.

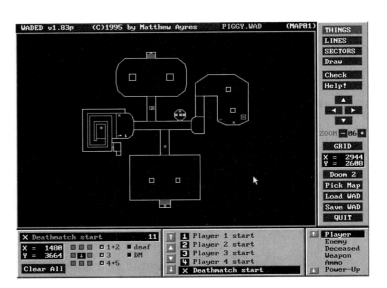

INSTALLING WADED

Installing WADED is a snap. You can place WADED anywhere on your hard drive, whether it be in the DOOM directory or a directory specifically for WADED.

Unzip the WADED.ZIP file into the target directory. To set up WADED for your system, simply run the WADED setup program from the command line. WADED will bring up a setup screen where you are asked for the locations of your DOOM, DOOM II, and Heretic games. To work, WADED only needs to know where one of them is, but you must have a registered copy of each game you plan to edit. (See Figure 4.2.)

Figure 4.2.

The WADED setup screen.

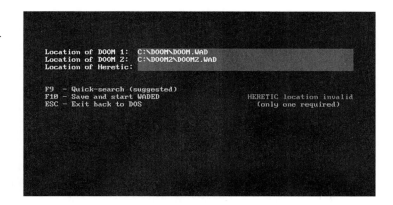

Once in the setup screen, you can have WADED search your hard drive for DOOM, DOOM II, and Heretic by hitting F9, the quick-search key. If WADED is unable to find a registered copy of DOOM, DOOM II, or Heretic, it will leave all three fields blank. From here you will have to manually type in the paths. Once you are done telling WADED the location of your games, hit the F10 key to start up WADED. WADED will not let you proceed unless you have at least one of the games specified. Notice that you only need to give WADED the location of *one* of your games.

If at any later time you need to tell WADED a different location of your game, you can load the setup program from the command line by typing waded -c. The locations of all your games are stored in the WADED.CFG file.

After you've finished with the configuration screen, you will be greeted with an introductory screen informing you how to register WADED and telling you little about the program. After the timed delay, WADED will bring you to the first map of either the DOOM.WAD, DOOM2.WAD, or HERETIC.WAD files, depending on which games you own.

If you have more than one game on your hard drive that WADED supports, you can start WADED up directly from the command line to that particular game.

waded *mywad.wad*	DOOM
waded -2 *mywad2.wad*	DOOM II
waded -3 *mywadh.wad*	Heretic
waded -h *mywadh.wad*	Heretic

FILE OPERATIONS

WADED supports DOOM, DOOM II, and Heretic map editing. You can either bring up the desired game from the command line (as described previously) or you can switch to another game after WADED has been loaded into memory. Switch to other games by clicking the left mouse button on the button directly below the arrow buttons. (See Figure 4.3.) The name on this button is the current game you are working with. When you click the button, WADED will bring up a list of games that you have set up for use with WADED. Switching games will erase all that is currently on the screen. WADED will ask you if you are sure, just in case you do not want to switch games.

Figure 4.3.
Switching to other games.

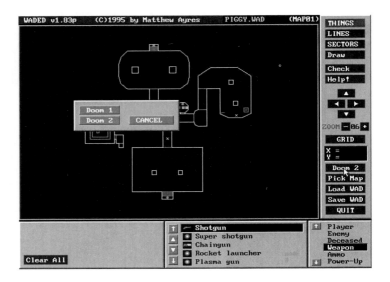

Because WADED is loading up a large file with multiple levels in it, after you switch games, WADED will prompt you for which map or level you wish to view or edit. Click the level that you would like on the screen. If you are working on an external WAD file from a different game platform, you must first switch WADED to that game before loading the file. For example, if you are editing the first level of DOOM and want to edit a new DOOM II level, you must first switch to DOOM II and then load the external level.

If you have a WAD file that has multiple levels in one WAD file, WADED can pick out a map from the main WAD. After you have loaded the WAD file with more than one map in it, WADED will bring up a menu of all the available maps contained in that WAD. Select one of the levels by clicking the left mouse button on the button with the level you want.

To load external WAD files, click the left mouse button on the Load button, or press the **L** key on the keyboard. WADED will bring up a list of all the files in the current directory with the extension of .WAD. Simply click the actual WAD name, or press the **L** key again to type in the complete path and name of the WAD file. If you load up a WAD that has multiple entries, WADED will ask you which level you want to view first. You can switch later with the Pick Map button.

To save a map that you have been working on, click the left mouse button on the Save button or press the **S** key. WADED will bring up the save window. (See Figure 4.4.) This is where you tell WADED what you want to call your map file and what level to save it as; for example, E1M1 (Episode 1, Mission 1). When saving a WAD, you can have WADED build the nodes before saving or you can choose not to. The current directory is where the file will be saved unless you change the path field. You can change the path by clicking in the path field, or by pressing the **P** key. If you are saving over an existing file, WADED will prompt you if you would like to proceed. If you do save over an existing WAD file, WADED will make a BAK file out of the old file.

Figure 4.4.
The Save PWAD window.

To exit out of WADED, click the left mouse button on the Quit button. You can also exit with the **Q** and Escape keys. Before exiting, WADED will ask you if you are sure you want to exit. Click Yes to exit or Cancel to return to WADED.

MAP MOVEMENT

When you are editing a level in WADED, it is helpful to be able to move around on the map that you are working on. You can move in the four basic directions: up, down, left, and right.

If you prefer using the keyboard to the mouse, you will probably want to use the arrow keys on your keyboard. Tap any of the keys to scroll the map in that direction just a little bit. Hold down a direction key to scroll around quickly.

If you like to stick with just mouse movements, you can use the movement buttons located on the right side bar. (See Figure 4.5.) Simply click the proper direction-arrow button. Click and hold to move around quickly.

If you want to get in closer to your map for more precision editing, it's easy. Use the plus key (+) to zoom into the map, or use the minus key (−) to zoom back out. Your other option is to use the Zoom buttons located on the right side bar, located under the movement buttons. (See Figure 4.5.) You can just click the mouse on the + or − buttons on the main screen. In-between the Zoom buttons, you'll find the current Zoom factor. WADED enables 15 different Zoom levels.

Figure 4.5.
The WADED feature keys.

Movement Buttons ─
Zoom Buttons ─

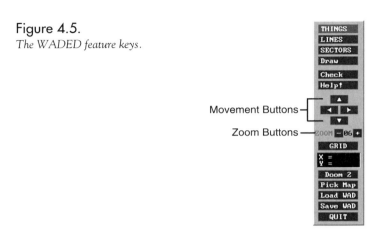

To make WADED center your map on the screen, just press the Home key on your keyboard and WADED will center the map at any Zoom level.

THINGS MODE

WADED's Things mode enables you to add, move, remove, and position Things. The name "Things" actually came from what DOOM calls them; however, they actually consist of all enemies, player-start positions, obstacles (that are not walls), and items. They will still be collectively referred to as "Things."

Most Things in WADED have a small depiction of the real Thing within the game. Some do not, and these are shown simply as shaded blue circles. Weapons and ammunition are shown as shaded red circles if they don't have a depiction. Each different type of enemy has a different color in WADED. Some have a white box around them, due to the fact that there are more types of enemies than colors to choose from. At higher Zoom levels, all enemies will have an arrow in them that points in the direction in which they start.

MOVING THINGS

To move a Thing, click and hold the left mouse button down while the cursor is over the Thing. As long as you continue to hold down the left mouse button, moving the mouse around will drag the Thing around the map. Release the mouse button to drop the Thing at its new location.

REMOVING A THING

Deleting Things is simple. You can delete Things by either clicking the right mouse button on a Thing or by selecting a Thing with the left mouse button and pressing the delete key. You can remove all the Things on the map at once with the Clear All button in the Things bar. (More information on clearing multiple items at one time follows.)

INSERTING A THING

Before you insert a Thing, you need to select which Thing you would like to insert. Do this by selecting the category of the Thing first. The category selection window is located at the bottom right of the screen. (See Figure 4.1, shown previously.)

There are many categories to pick from. DOOM, DOOM II, and Heretic each have different sets of categories. All of this can be customized by editing the WADED.T configuration file.

Once you've selected the category of your choice, look at the window to the left of the category-selection window. This selection window enables you to pick the actual Thing you'll be inserting. (See Figure 4.6.)

Figure 4.6.

WADED's Things selection window.

Move the cursor onto the map area and click the right mouse button everywhere you'd like to place the Thing you selected. Be sure not to click an already existing item since that will delete the Thing already there.

SELECTING A THING

Position the mouse over an existing Thing on your map. Click the left mouse button to select that Thing. A green highlight box will appear around the Thing. Once a Thing is selected, you will see its name and attributes in the bottom right information window.

CHANGING A THING'S ATTRIBUTES

Things have many attributes that affect when, where, and how they appear in the game. Focus your attention on the bottom-left corner of the screen. There you'll find the Things information and attributes window.

At the top left of the Things selection window you'll find a picture of the currently highlighted Thing. (See Figure 4.6, shown previously.) Just to the right of it, you'll find its name. And farther right you'll find the number for that Thing. (This is the actual number that DOOM uses to keep track of Things; you need not worry too much about it.) Below all of this, you can find the X and Y coordinates of the Thing on the map. You can only change a Thing's X and Y coordinates by moving it around on the map.

In the middle of the Things information window you'll find eight small buttons. These are only important for enemies and certain items. In the middle of the eight buttons, there is an arrow that shows the current orientation of the Thing you have highlighted. Click any of the eight direction buttons to change the direction that the arrow will face. The direction you select here will tell the game which way to face the item in actual game play.

Toward the right side of the Things information window you'll find five more small buttons. These are all toggles that can either be turned on or off. Buttons that are toggled on are marked with a small white box within the small button. The first three toggles are marked "1+2," "3," and "4+5." Toggling the "1+2" button will determine if the Thing will appear in difficulty levels 1 and 2 while playing the map. Similarly button "3" is to set difficulty 3, and "4+5" is to set difficulty 4 and 5. These difficulty settings apply directly to the five choices of difficulty you have when you first start DOOM, DOOM II, or Heretic.

The last two buttons in the Things information window are marked "DM" and "Deaf." Toggle "DM" on if you want a Thing only to appear during Deathmatch play. Toggle the Deaf button if you want a Thing to be deaf. (The Deaf toggle, of course, only logically works with enemies.)

CLEARING THINGS

Within the Things information window, you'll find a button marked Clear All. Click this and it will do exactly what it says! It will clear all Things from your map. A confirmation window will pop up first, just in case you accidentally hit this button and didn't mean to. (See Figure 4.7.)

Figure 4.7.
The Clear ALL Things confirmation window.

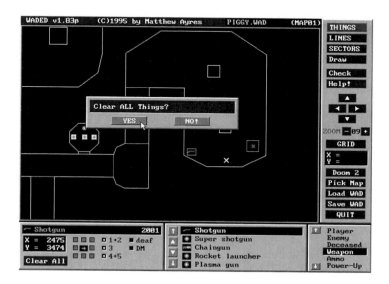

Also within the Things information window is a button marked Clear Sec. Click here if you're interested in clearing all Things from a particular sector. WADED will then wait for you to select the sector you'd like cleared. There is no confirmation on this, so be careful that you select the proper sector.

LINES MODE

WADED's Line mode enables you to select lines and modify all of their attributes. In Line mode, you can assign textures to walls and add special tags. You can also assign sectors to lines with specials.

LINE COLOR CODES

Lines in WADED are colored different depending a some important factors. Single-sided Lines are bright white. Double-sided lines appear gray. Doors are bright cyan. The currently selected line will be red, and any of its tagged sectors will be green.

SELECTING A LINE

To select a line, move your mouse cursor over any line on the map. Click the left mouse button to select that line. The selected line will be highlighted red. Only one line can be selected at a time unless you are using multi mode, which is explained later.

INFORMATION WINDOW

Located in the lower information bar is the Line information window. (See Figure 4.8.) When you select a line in your map, WADED will display information on that line in this window. The length, angle, and number of the line are displayed in the window. (See Figure 4.9.)

Figure 4.8.
The Line information window.

Figure 4.9.
Selecting a line.

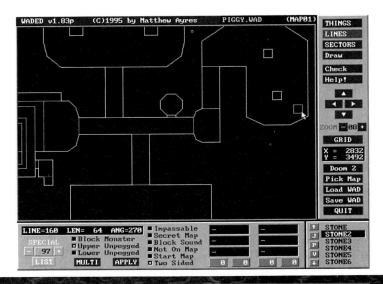

4 EPISODE   **1 MISSION**   **4 ROOM**   **DOOM PROGRAMMING GURUS**

CHANGING A LINE'S ATTRIBUTES

Once you have selected a line on your map, you can change the attributes of that line. You can change or add line specials to lines, or change the selected line's attributes.

A line can be either one- or two-sided, depending on whether you can walk over it in the game. You can only walk on a line if there is a sector on either side of it. You can make a line two-sided or one sided with the Impassable and Two-Sided buttons. If you want to flip a line's direction, select a line from the map and hit the **F** key. You can also assign toggles to a line that can block the sound from entering a room, or which can block an enemy. Other toggles include whether a line appears on the overhead map when you first start the level, and whether passing over the line will give the player secret credit.

To add line specials, doors, lifts, and so on, first you must select a line on the map. Next select a special that you would like to use for that line. You can do this by using the + and – buttons next to the Special area. A line with no special assigned has special number 0. You can either adjust the special value with the + and – buttons or by bringing up the list and selecting it from there. Click the left mouse button on the List button and WADED will bring up a list of all the specials available to you. The specials are divided up into categories by what they do—Doors, Floors, Lifts, and Misc. You will see that in front of every special on the list is a set of numbers and letters. These letters stand for how the line is activated and whether or not it can be activated more than once. If the code includes a W, the player must walk over the line to activate the special. If the code includes an S, the line is activated by the player hitting spacebar near the line. If the code includes a G, the player must shoot the line to activate the special. The character following this part of the code will either be a 1 or an M. If the character is a 1, the line can only be activated once, and if it is an M, the line can be activated multiple times.

SELECTING A TRIGGER SECTOR

If you want a line to have an effect on a sector—for instance, a door or an elevator—you must tag a sector or sectors to the line. Once you have a line selected, use the right mouse button to select a trigger sector for the currently highlighted Line. Click the right mouse button in any sectors you want to tag to the line. You may tag as many trigger sectors as you'd like. Tagged Sectors will be green on the map. Click the right mouse button on a green sector and WADED will deselect the sector.

LINE TEXTURES

On the bottom Lines bar are six boxes. (See Figure 4.8, shown previously.) These boxes are split up into two groups: the left and the right. When you select a line on the map, the line will have a small stick on one side of the map. The side with the stick is the right side, and the side without the stick is the left side. The left three texture boxes stand for the "left" side of the line. The three texture boxes on the right are the boxes for the "right" side of the line. The top two boxes are for an upper texture, the middle boxes are for a main texture, and the lower boxes are for lower textures. If any of the six boxes are highlighted red, this means that they need to be defined or else you will get an error in your level. Double-sided lines should never have a main texture defined, except in rare cases where you want a wall that you can walk through. Single-sided lines should always have a main texture defined, no matter what.

There are two toggles that you can select for a line that will affect how a texture will appear in the game. These are Lower Unpegged and Upper Unpegged. Each texture in the game has a definite bottom and a definite top. If you select the Lower Unpegged toggle for a line, the game will automatically line up the bottom of the texture with the floor of that room. If you select Upper Unpegged, the game will align the top of the texture with the ceiling.

SELECTING TEXTURES

To assign textures to a line, you have to first select a texture from the lower-right list. (See Figure 4.8, shown previously.) Once you have the texture selected, you can click the left mouse button in any of the six texture boxes. Clicking the right mouse button in any of the six texture boxes will make that texture clear; in other words, it will delete the texture. If you want to view a texture, you can click the right mouse button on the texture name or select the texture with the left mouse button, and click the **V** button. By clicking the **P** button, WADED will bring up a large texture list, where you can pick the texture you want to use. You can also view textures from this main list. (See Figure 4.10.) The last function in the lower-right texture bar is the **J** button. (See Figure 4.11.) This button will let you jump to a certain part of the list. WADED will prompt you for the first letter of the texture you want to jump to. For instance, if you type in c, WADED will jump to the first texture that starts with the letter C.

Figure 4.10.
The main textures list.

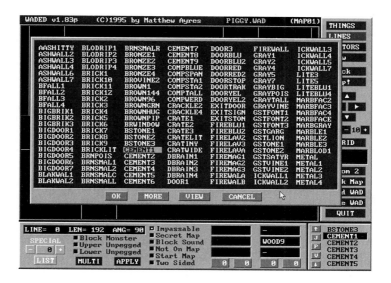

Figure 4.11.
Using the J button.

CHANGING MULTIPLE LINES

WADED features a simple way to manipulate attributes of multiple lines. To start, click the MULTI button. All attributes in the Line information window will be reset. The attribute toggles will contain small green marks, and the texture boxes will contain "XX."

Now use the left mouse button to select all the lines you'd like to change. Each line you select will be highlighted red. Click the line again to deselect it.

Now you can tell WADED which changes you want to make on all the selected lines. Change the attributes in the Line information bar. Only change the attributes you want changed on *all* the selected lines. Any attribute you leave unchanged (green mark for attribute toggles and "XX" in texture boxes) will leave the line how it was.

Once you're satisfied with your selections, click the APPLY button to make the changes take effect. (See Figure 4.12.) If you don't want to make the changes, click the MULTI button to cancel the operation.

Figure 4.12.
Applying textures.

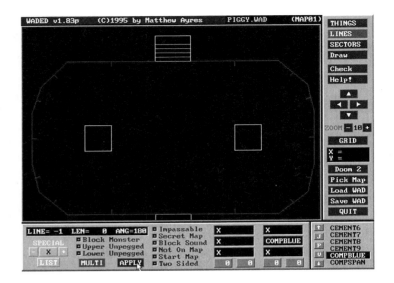

SECTORS

WADED's sector mode is used to assign or change attributes to sectors in your map. When you are in sector mode, you can change ceiling and floor heights, assign specials, and change the textures of the ceilings and floors.

SELECTING A SECTOR

In order to edit a sector's attributes, you must first select it. Click the left mouse button within any sector in the map to select it. (See Figure 4.13.) The sector that is selected will be outlined with flashing red lines. Now you can change anything related to that sector. If the sector you have selected has a special line attached to it, the line will appear green on the map.

Figure 4.13.
Selecting a sector.

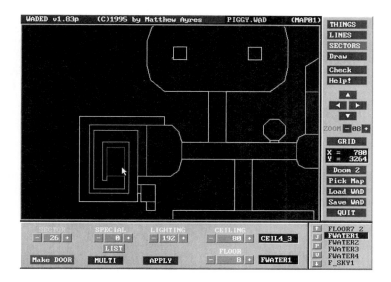

EDITING SECTOR ATTRIBUTES

Changing floor and ceiling heights is easily done. First select a sector to change. Now change the number values for the heights. There are two ways to change the height of floors and ceilings. One is to use the + and – buttons next to the ceiling or floor height box. If you want to change the height to a specific number you can click the number itself, and type in a new value. Changing sector light levels is edited exactly the same way as ceiling and floor heights.

Changing or adding sector specials is done in the same way as changing floor and ceiling heights. You can change the value with the + and – buttons, or type in your own value. To get a quick list of all the sector specials, click the left mouse button on the LIST button under the special number.

To change or add textures for the ceilings and floors, first select the texture you want to use from the lower-right list. You can now click the left mouse button in the ceiling texture box or the floor texture box. If you want to use a clear texture, simply click the right mouse button in the floor or ceiling texture box. This will insert the sky texture used by DOOM. WADED can view textures from the main WAD files. View textures by clicking the right mouse button on a texture name, or by selecting the texture in the lower-right box and clicking the left mouse button on the **V** button. The **J** button will prompt you for the first letter of a texture. The **J** key is used to quickly jump around on the texture list by letter. The **P** button will bring up a complete listing of all the textures where you can either choose, or view each texture. Click the left mouse button on the APPLY button and the changes will be implemented. (See Figure 4.14.)

Figure 4.14.

Applying textures to ceilings and floors.

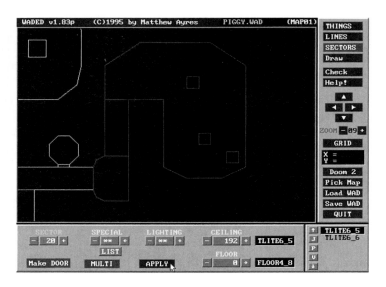

CHANGING MULTIPLE SECTORS

Editing multiple sectors is similar to editing multiple lines. Simply click the left mouse button on the MULTI button to put yourself in multi mode. All attributes will be X'ed out. Now select all the sectors that you want to be affected. Selected sectors will be highlighted in flashing red. After the sectors are selected, you can now edit the attributes that you want to change. You can change the ceiling and floor heights and textures, the lighting in a sector, and sector specials. After all the changes have been made, click the left mouse button on the APPLY button, and the changes will be implemented. To cancel changes before they are applied, click the MULTI button again.

MAKE DOOR

To make a door out of any four-sided sector, select the Make Door button from the sectors section. (See Figure 4.15.) Click the left mouse button anywhere in the sector that you want to make the door out of. WADED will define the two longer sides of the sector as special 1 (door) and default the textures of the doors, to BIGDOOR1. WADED will also make the inside tracks of the door have the texture called DOORTRAK.

Figure 4.15.
Making a door out of a four-sided sector.

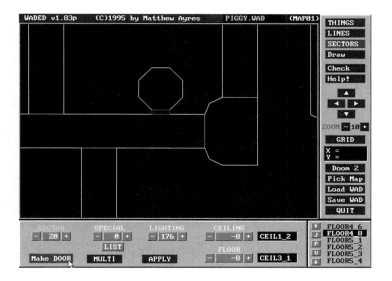

DRAW MAP

WADED's Draw mode is used for editing existing maps by changing vertices, lines, and sectors. Draw mode is also used for creating levels from scratch. While in Draw mode, you can add, move, and delete vertices, lines and sectors. The Draw mode also contains the utilities to define sectors in your map out of existing lines and vertices. You can also do precise editing of the placement of walls in your level.

There are three main ways to draw new parts to your map. These are the Line, Lines, and Room modes. In any one of these modes, it is helpful to use the GRID feature of WADED. The grid is always 64 x 64 pixels at any zoom level. If you line up your lines on top of the grid, most textures in the game will match up exactly with the surrounding textures. Most Floor and Ceiling textures will also be aligned. Since most of the wall textures—and all of the ceiling and floor textures—are 64 x 64 pixels, using the GRID feature will perfectly align your walls and floors.

WADED's Draw: Line feature is used to draw a single line from one point to another point on the map. This feature is mainly used to add to an existing level. Line is used to connect two existing vertices or to make an entirely new line. To use Line, simply click the left mouse button on a point where you would like the line to begin. Drag the mouse pointer to the desired ending point of the line. Click the left mouse button again. WADED will put down a line on the map from the first point to the second point. (See Figure 4.16.) You can use the Line feature to draw a room by adding each side of the room individually. To do this start the next line with the trailing vertex. However, if you want to make room-drawing easier, using the Lines feature (described forthwith) will save you a lot of time.

Figure 4.16.
Drawing a line.

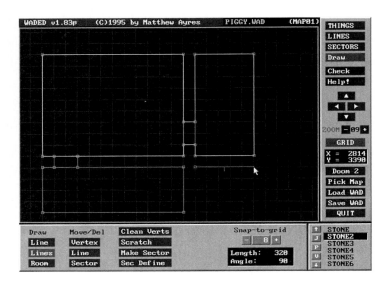

WADED's Draw: Lines feature is similar to the Line feature, but it adds a few helpful features. When you are in Lines mode, click the left mouse button at the point where you want to start a line or in the corner of a room. Drag the mouse pointer to a new location and click the left mouse button where you want to end the line. You will notice that now, when you move the mouse again, WADED will automatically start drawing a new line. Drag the mouse to a new destination and click the left mouse button. Repeat this process until you are happy with the number of walls for your room. You will notice that we now have the beginnings of a room. To complete any room, drag the mouse to another existing vertex or to the original vertex, and WADED will stop the drawing process.

DRAW: MOVE/DELETE

WADED's Draw mode also enables you to move and delete existing vertexes, lines, and sectors. When you are in Draw mode, click the type of thing you would like to move or delete by clicking one of the three middle buttons in the lower Draw bar. WADED will let you move and delete the three items from this menu: Vertices, Lines, and Sectors. The commands for moving and deleting Vertices, Lines, and Sectors are basically the same.

4 EPISODE   1 MISSION   4 ROOM   DOOM PROGRAMMING GURUS

To move or delete a vertex, first select the vertex button by clicking the left mouse button on the vertex button under the Move/Del title. You are now in vertex-editing mode. Moving vertices to a new location is easy. Click and hold the left mouse button on any vertex and drag it to its new location. Let go of the mouse button and the vertex will be placed down on the map. Notice that in Figure 4.17, the top-right vertex of a room is being moved out to the right. If you move a line straight out in any basic direction—up, down, left, or right—WADED will tell you if the line is lined up with the GRID by highlighting the line yellow. If you move a vertex over another existing vertex, WADED will ask you if you want to merge these two vertices. Merging vertices will simply combine the vertices into one. To delete a vertex, move the mouse cursor over an existing vertex until WADED highlights it. Next click the right mouse button on the vertex. The vertex is deleted. Take note that deleting a vertex that has more than one line attached to it will effectively delete those two lines. A line needs two points to exist. While in vertex mode, you can also add vertices on the map. You can add vertices as reference points for later drawing, or you can split an existing line. You can place vertices down on the map by positioning the cursor and clicking the right mouse button. To add a vertex to an existing line, move the mouse cursor over a line on the map. The line will flash red. Clicking the right mouse button will add a vertex to the selected line. You can now move this new vertex to make two walls from the original one.

In Figure 4.18, a line is selected. WADED highlights the line red. The right mouse button is clicked where the new vertex is to be added. (See Figure 4.19.) WADED adds the vertex at the point of the mouse. Now the user can move the vertex to a new position. (See Figure 4.20.)

Figure 4.17.

Moving a vertex.

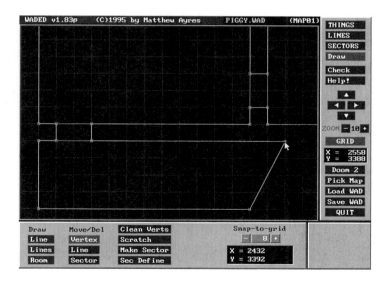

Figure 4.18.

Selecting a line.

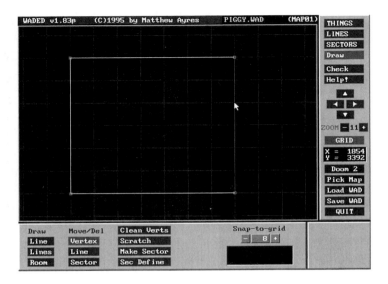

Figure 4.19.

Adding a vertex with a mouse click.

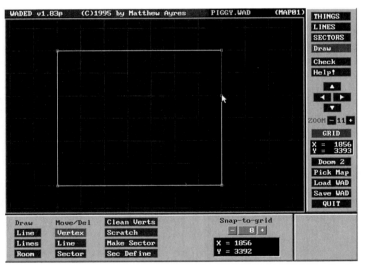

Figure 4.20.
Moving the vertex.

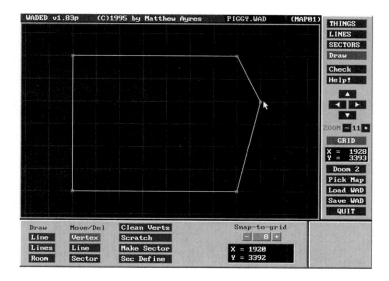

To move or delete lines, select the Line button under the Move/Del title. You can now move and delete existing lines on the map. To move a line, click and hold the mouse button on an existing line and drag the line to a new position. Letting go of the mouse button will drop the line on the map. Figure 4.21 shows a line being moved from right to left on the map. When moving lines, be sure not to overlap any lines, since this will cause problems with making sectors and building nodes later. To delete lines on the map, click the right mouse button on an existing line. Make sure if you delete a side of a room, to somehow make the sector closed. An open sector cannot be made into a sector.

Moving sectors is done in the same way as moving lines. Select the Sectors button under the Move/Del title. You now can move and delete sectors on the current map. The left mouse button will move any existing sector, and the right mouse button will delete that sector. Again, make sure not to have overlapping lines on your map, or WADED won't be able to complete the map.

Figure 4.21.

Moving a line on the map.

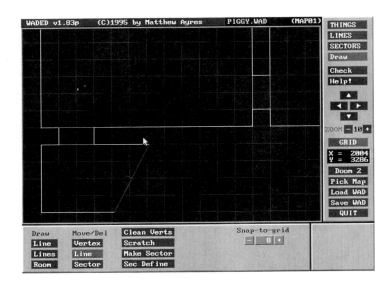

CLEAN BUTTON

If you want to get rid of all those excess vertices, the ones not attached to any lines, click the Clean Verts button and WADED will remove them all. Be sure to rebuild the nodes if you do this, however. The final WAD file has extra vertices that the game uses to decide what to view. If you clean them and save the level without regenerating them, your level won't work! To build these extra vertices that DOOM requires, use the node builder; either hit B or select "Yes" for node build when saving your WAD.

SCRATCH BUTTON

The Scratch button does exactly what you would expect it to. Click the left mouse button on the Scratch button and WADED will clear the entire map. (See Figure 4.22.) The Scratch button clears all Things, lines, sectors, and vertices off the map. With a clean slate, you can work on your own WAD made from scratch.

Figure 4.22.
Starting from scratch.

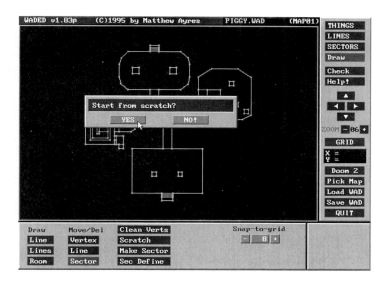

MAKE SECTOR BUTTON

After you have drawn out all your lines, you'll want to use WADED's Make Sector feature to define the sectors on your map. (See Figure 4.23.) Lines not currently assigned to a sector will appear purple in color. In Figure 4.23, the mouse is over an undefined sector. All the lines of this sector appear purple in color. When the left mouse button is clicked from this position, the sector will be defined. If you move the mouse around the map, WADED will highlight the sector the mouse is over. If your mouse is over a sector, and it's not highlighted red, or only certain walls of the sector are highlighted, you need to use Make Sector to "fix" the sector. To do this click the left mouse button in a sector. Your newly-defined sector will highlight red. You should continue Making Sectors until all unde-fined purple lines are gone off your map, and all sectors are completely enclosed areas.

Do not try to use Make Sector on a sector that is an open ended figure or that has overlap-ping lines. All sectors must be closed polygons.

Make Sector can sometimes take a little while on complex or large sectors, so be a little patient. Clicking in the area outside the existing map will do nothing.

DOOM
PROGRAMMING
GURUS

4
ROOM

1
MISSION

4
EPISODE

Figure 4.23.

WADED's Make Sector feature.

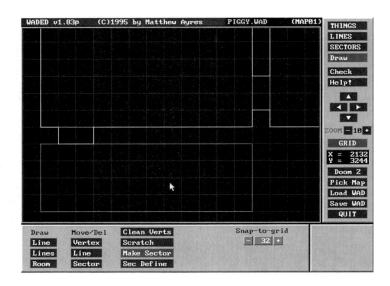

SECTOR DEFINE

WADED's Sector Define feature is used to manually define sectors instead of using the Make Sector button. (This function was used before the advent of Make Sector.) Sec Define is mainly used to fix up your map if Make Sector has not built the room correctly. You must first select the offending sector in sector mode, and then go back to Draw mode. Next select Sec Define from the lower Draw bar.

Click any line in the selected sector to redefine it. WADED will prompt you for which side you would like the line to be added to. This feature is not complete, as Make Sector will practically do sector defining for you flawlessly.

SNAP-TO-GRID

WADED's Snap-to-Grid feature is used to control how close together you can draw or move lines and vertices. For instance, if the snap-to-grid setting is set on 64, you can only place vertices and lines 64 pixels or larger apart (64, 128, 192…). If Snap-to-Grid is set at 4, you can place vertices and lines 4 pixels or larger apart (4, 8, 12…). Figures 4.24 and 4.25 show how to use Snap-to-Grid. In Figure 4.24, the Snap-to-Grid is set on 64. The vertex will not stray from the grid line intersections. In Figure 4.25, the Snap-to-Grid is set to 32. The vertex can now be moved in between the two GRID intersections. You can adjust the sensitivity of the mouse down to 1 pixel.

Figure 4.24.
Snap-to-Grid at 64.

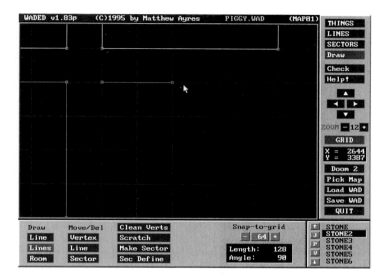

The Snap-to-Grid number is not the amount of pixels on the screen; rather, it is the number of pixels that will appear in the game.

Figure 4.25.
Snap-to-Grid at 32.

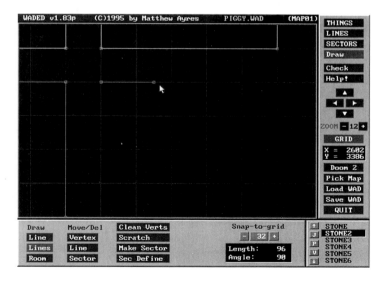

KEYBOARD EQUIVALENTS IN WADED

The following tables list the keyboard equivalents in WADED. Table 4.1 lists the global keyboard equivalents. Table 4.2 includes the keyboard commands available for editing lines. Table 4.3 contains the keyboard commands for editing sectors.

Table 4.1. Global WADED commands.

F1	Things
F2	Lines
F3	Sectors
F4	Draw
F5	Draw: Line
F6	Draw: Lines
F7	Draw: Room
F9	Move/Del: Vertex
F10	Move/Del: Lines
F11	Move/Del: Sectors
Home	Center map
C	Consistency checker
H	Help!
B	Build nodes
I	Information on level
R	Redraw/reset mouse
G	Grid on/off
M	Map pick
L	Load
S	Save
+	Zoom in
–	Zoom out
Q	Quit
Esc	Quit

Table 4.2. Line keyboard commands.

P	Pick texture from list
V	View textures
F	Flip
T	Two-sided
Del	Delete

Table 4.3. Sector keyboard commands.

P	Pick floor/ceiling tiles
V	View floor/ceiling tiles
Del	Delete

USING WADCAT

Included with the release of WADED version 1.83 is WADCAT 0.7. With this program you can easily put multiple levels into one main WAD file. This is extremely useful if you are making a set of levels that you want to follow each other, as in an episode. To use WADCAT, load up the program from the command line by typing wadcat.

First, type in the name of the main WAD that is going to include the sub WADs. From here, you must tell WADCAT which WADs to use. WADCAT will prompt you for each level that you want to include. Type in the names of the WAD files for each level until you have added all the WADs you want to include. Now press Enter on an empty line. WADCAT will now ask you which map you would like to save the level as. You can save each level as any map. This way you can spread out your levels over the existing ones, or if you typed the WAD names out of order, you can place them in a new order here. After you tell WADCAT where to put all the WAD files, WADCAT will write to the main output WAD file and exit.

FILE LIST AND DESCRIPTIONS

Table 4.4 lists the file names and descriptions for WADED.

Table 4.4. WADED file names.

WADED.EXE	Main WADED executable file
WADED.T	WADED Things file—contains information on items
WADED.DOC	Documentation on WADED
WADED01.FAQ	WADED Frequently Asked Questions v0.1
WADCAT.EXE	WADCAT v0.7—WAD concatenater
WADCAT.DOC	Documentation on WADCAT 0.7
WHATSNEW.183	WADED revision history up to 1.83
FILE_ID.DIZ	Description file of WADED for BBSs

REGISTRATION

If you decide you like WADED and you plan to continue using it, you should register it with the author, Matthew Ayres. You are required to register WADED if you continue to use it for more than two weeks. Registration cost is $20 US. Cash and checks only, please.

Registration will eliminate the beginning delay. It also compensates for the author's time and hard work. If you register WADED, you will receive a personalized program called WADEDREG. Your personalized WADEDREG will work on any version of WADED, and it will place your name in the opening and ending screens.

Mail registrations to:

Matthew Ayres
977 E. Stanley Blvd., Unit 349
Livermore, CA 94550

ROOMS

By Matt Tagliaferri

USING DOOMCAD

My goal as the author of DoomCAD was to create a system that enabled its users to create levels for DOOM as easily as possible. After studying the DOOM level specifications, I realized what a challenge this was going to be. DOOM levels consist of a set of extremely complicated data structures. A level consists of many individual, interrelated elements, and each must relate to the other elements in a precise way or DOOM will not be able to display the level properly.

The goal of this room is to explain these elements, their relationship, and how to use the program DoomCAD to create usable DOOM levels. We will do this by creating a small level together, step by step. Between each step, I will try to explain what we just did in terms of the DOOM definitions you will need to know. (I chose to intersperse the definitions within the actual tutorial to assure myself that you wouldn't skip the dry glossary stuff and get right to the meat of this room!) It is very important to read the explanatory text between each step so you have a good understanding of what you just created. Once you have this understanding, you will be able to create levels that are much more complicated and imaginative than the one we'll create here. With that in mind, let's get right to work and make our first DOOM level.

YOUR FIRST LEVEL

When you first start DoomCAD, it will ask you for the location of the DOOM.WAD file that came with DOOM. This large 10MB file contains all the maps, graphics, and sounds that the game uses. DoomCAD needs this file to load wall and floor texture names, and some other information. DoomCAD will ask you for the location of this file only once, unless you delete DOOM and reinstall it in another directory on your hard drive.

Some users experience a "Subscript out of Range" error during the initial load period after specifying the location of the DOOM.WAD. If this happens, try reinstalling DOOM to get an unaltered DOOM.WAD file. Many DOOM utilities actually alter the contents of the DOOM.WAD file, and DoomCAD has trouble reading some of these altered WAD files.

After specifying the filename, you will see a map of the first level in DOOM.WAD. Our object, however, is to create a brand new level. Start this process by selecting New from the File menu.

When you start a new level, you will see a large square that takes up the entire map display area, as shown in Figure 5.1. This square encloses an area of space that a DOOM player or monster can walk on. An enclosed area of space is called a *sector*. Sectors are the most important concept to understand when creating DOOM levels. A sector has the following properties:

- Ceiling altitude
- Floor altitude
- Floor texture
- Ceiling texture
- Brightness
- "Special" flag

Figure 5.1.

Starting a new level.

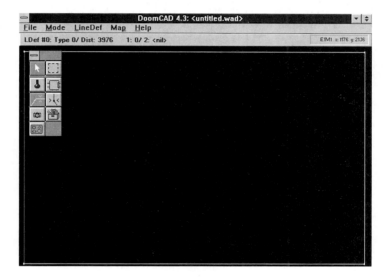

We will cover these properties one by one as we go through the tutorial. The default sector given when you start a new level has a floor altitude of 0, a ceiling altitude of 104. It is given some default textures, a brightness of 128 (values can be from 0-255), and no special attributes.

DoomCAD cannot properly build a level that consists of only one sector, so our first task is to create a second sector, attached to this first one, so we can try the level out in DOOM. To create the second sector, follow these steps:

1. Go into Vertex mode. A *vertex* is a point in space on the map defining an X,Y coordinate. Vertices (or, as id Software calls them, vertexes) serve as the connecting points for the walls that make up sectors. The Vertex mode button is on the toolbar. It is the third button down, second button across.

2. Make the default sector smaller. To do this, drag each vertex inward more toward the center of the map. As you drag each vertex, you will change the shape of the sector. Make the sector smaller, and leave some room to the right of it so we can add the next sector. Don't worry about making the sector perfectly square; it's easy to align vertices to each other later.

3. Add two vertices. To do this, go into the Vertex menu and select Add vertex. This begins Vertex Add mode. While in this mode, clicking anywhere on the map will add one vertex to the spot you click. You can add as many vertices as you wish. When you have added all the vertices you need, right-click the mouse anywhere on the map. This terminates Vertex Add mode. Add the two vertices to the right of default sector, as shown in Figure 5.2. Don't worry about the exact orientation of vertices; we will make all the lines straight in a later section. The first step is to "rough out" the level as shown.

Figure 5.2.

Your level after resizing the default sector and adding two new vertices.

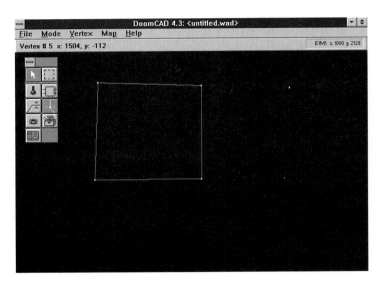

4. Go into Sector mode. The Sector mode button is right above the Vertex Mode button. It is an icon that looks like a little room with hallways coming out of it.

5. Add the new sector. To do this, select Add Sector from the Sector menu. Then, click the uppermost new vertex. After you click this vertex, move the mouse around a bit. You'll notice a red line tracing from the vertex you just clicked on to your mouse pointer. Now, move the mouse down to the other new vertex and click that. You'll have just created a line between the two new vertices. Continue clicking vertices, now going leftward to the southeastern most vertex of the original default sector. Next, click the northeastern most

vertex of the original default sector. (Ignore the fact that there's already a line drawn between these two vertices: draw over it, anyway.) Finally, click back on the vertex you started with, the uppermost new vertex. You will have traced a complete square. To end the Add Sector process, right click the mouse.

There are two extremely important things to remember when adding sectors. Over half of the technical support e-mail I receive is due to the failure to remember one of the two items. The two key things to remember are to

- Always create sectors clockwise. The reason for this will become apparent when discussing linedefs below.

- Always travel in a complete closed path when creating sectors. Note that in our little two sector level above, when we drew the third line, there was already a line drawn between two of the vertices (the easternmost wall of the original default sector). We drew over that line a second time, pretending it wasn't there, in order to make a complete closed path and end up on the vertex we started from.

The last step is to make sure that there's a place for Player 1 to begin. We do this by setting up a Player 1 Start *Thing* somewhere on the level. A Thing is defined as any object that the player can come in contact with. Things include monsters, weapons, other players, and keys, as well as scenery objects such as torches, barrels, and candles.

The default level already has a Player 1 Start Thing on it—we just need to make sure that the Thing is still somewhere within the two sectors we just defined. To do this, complete the following steps:

1. Go into Thing mode. The Thing mode button is the first button in the second row. It looks like a blue potion bottle.

2. The Player 1 Start Thing will appear as a gray dot on the screen. If it is not somewhere in one of the two rooms you defined, simply drag it to be in one of the rooms.

SAVING YOUR LEVEL

Finally we can test our mini level in DOOM. To save your level, select Save As from the menu. You will be prompted for a filename. Choose the name MYFIRST.WAD, and make sure to save it in the same directory that DOOM is in. You will be prompted for a game and level to save your level as. Choose Game 2, Level 1. You should get a message that states, `Highlighted Linedefs are marked as Impassable but have no textures (warning only)`. Ignore this warning message for now. If you built the rest of the level correctly, you should see DoomCAD build the level by displaying a series of cyan, white, and red boxes. If you get another type of error message, you must have made a mistake in the preceding steps. Go back and try building the level again.

Once DoomCAD succesfully builds the level, you can go into DOOM and try it out. From the DOS prompt, start DOOM by typing the following command line:

```
DOOM -DEVPARM -FILE MYFIRST.WAD -WART 2 1
```

This command line tells DOOM to read the file you just made (MYFIRST.WAD) and replace DOOM's regular map data with the data found in this file. The -WART 2 1 tells DOOM to skip over the opening credits and warp directly to Game 2, Level 1 (which is what you saved your new level as).

If you've done all this correctly, you should be standing inside your first DoomCAD-created DOOM level. Feel free to wander around and check everything out. When you're done, it's time to start the next phase.

> In addition to saving your level and trying it out periodically, it's also a good idea to copy your level to a backup name in case of disaster. (DoomCAD also copies your current level to the name OLD.WAD right before it saves, providing an additional level of backup.) Level-building is a complicated process, and it's pretty easy to make mistakes along the way. Having one or two of the previous versions of the level is important in this case. (I have even known DoomCAD users who save *every* version of their level.)

SECTOR AND LINEDEF EDITING

It might have been hard to notice, but when you were walking around your first level, you couldn't tell when you moved from one sector to the other. The reason for this is that the two sectors we defined are exactly alike. That is, all the sector properties are the same. When adjoining sectors have every property the same, there is no way to tell when the player steps from one sector to another. Let's change the properties of one of the sectors so we can tell them apart.

Start DoomCAD up again. You'll notice that MYFIRST.WAD comes up right away, so you won't have to load it. First, go into Sector mode. You can select a sector by clicking one of its walls. (If you click the center line that connects the two sectors, it will highlight the *first* sector that that line defined. Clicking that line a second time will designate the second sector as the current one.) The selected sector appears red on the screen. Experiment with this for a while until you're used to highlighting sectors. After you're comfortable with this, select the rightmost sector and then right click. You should see the Sector Edit dialog box pictured in Figure 5.3. All of the properties for individual sector editing is done in this dialog box. Textures are changed by dragging them off of the scrolling listbox and dropping them in the Ceiling or Floor Texture box. All of the other properties are selected (as radio buttons) or typed in manually.

Figure 5.3.

The Sector Edit dialog box.

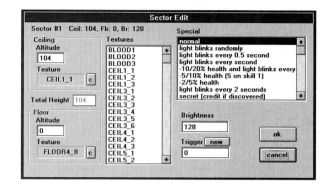

There are locations for editing all of the sector properties described above. Make the following changes to this sector:

- Ceiling Texture: FLAT1 (Change textures by dragging a name from the list box marked Textures and dropping it on the appropriate box.)
- Floor Texture: BLOOD1
- Ceiling Altitude: 96
- Floor Altitude: 16
- Brightness: 255 (255 is the fully bright; 0 is fully dark)
- Special: Light blinks every second

When you have made these changes, click the OK button. You won't see anything different on the map, but the changes you have associated with this sector have been made. (The status bar under the menu gives a brief description of the sector; you can see some of the changes you made there.)

Now we need to redefine the adjoining line between the two sectors so that the player can walk through it. All of the lines displayed on the map are called *linedefs* (short for "line definitions"). A linedef can be defined as a connection between two vertices. Linedefs have the following (major) properties:

- They have length.
- They have a "right" side.
- They sometimes have a "left" side.

DOOM PROGRAMMING GURUS

5 ROOM

1 MISSION

4 EPISODE

- They can define up to six textures along their surface.
- They may trigger some action by either pressing against them (like a door or switch), or by walking over them.

Our default level up to this point is made up of seven linedefs: three solid ones for each of the sectors and one that adjoins the two. This adjoining linedef is called a *two-sided linedef* because there's a sector on both sides of it. Notice that the other six linedefs help to define a sector on one of their sides, but essentially have "nothing" on their other side. These are *one-sided linedefs*.

In addition to a linedef having either one or two sides, we also define those sides as being the "right" and "left" sides. How can we tell which side is which? Imagine, for a moment, when you traced out the lines to define the second sector of our level. For each of the lines, you started on a vertex (call this the "from" vertex) and drew a line to the second vertex (call this the "to" vertex). If you can imagine a player standing directly on the "from" vertex, looking along the linedef in the direction of the "to" vertex, the right side of the linedef would be at the player's right hand.

The concept of the right and left side of linedefs is a difficult but essential concept to understand. Our next step will be to assign textures to our linedefs, and we will have to be able to tell the right from the left sides to properly place the textures. Imagine standing on the "from" vertex, looking toward the "to" vertex, along the linedef. The right side would be at your right hand. Three linedefs are pictured in Figure 5.4. The arrow indicates the direction the linedef was drawn, and the right and left sides are shown.

Figure 5.4.
Determining the right side of linedefs.

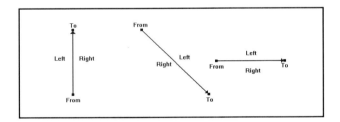

There is a feature in DoomCAD that displays the right side of linedefs. Select Direction Marks from the Grid menu, and a small line will point in the direction of the right side of each linedef.

To edit individual linedefs, go into Linedef mode. The Linedef mode button on the toolbar is the leftmost button in the third row. Once in Linedef mode, select linedefs by clicking near their center (the center is where the direction mark connects to the Linedef). Once you have selected the center linedef, right click the mouse button. The Linedef Edit screen will be displayed. (See Figure 5.5.) All of the linedef properties are changed in this dialog box. Textures are assigned by dragging them from the textures listbox and dropping them on the desired texture edit boxes. Textures are cleared by hitting the small "c" button near the texture edit box.

Figure 5.5.
The Linedef Edit dialog box.

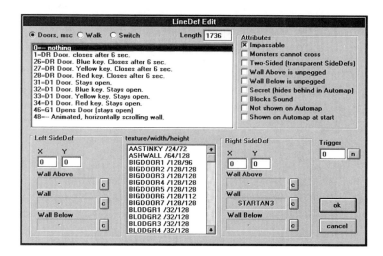

All we want to do now is deselect the check box marked "Impassable" and check the box marked "Two-Sided, Transparent." Do this now, then click the OK button.

If you highlight some other linedef, deselecting the center one, you will notice that the color of the center | linedef is now yellow. This is the visual cue that the linedef is marked as transparent.

Before we can save our level and look at it, there's one more thing we need to do. Remember that our two default sectors have different ceiling and floor heights. This means that when the player travels from the left sector onto the right sector, he will be stepping up. We need to define a texture that the player will see on the front of the step as he crosses between the sectors. In addition, we made the ceiling of the right sector lower than the ceiling of the left sector. Therefore, we need to define the texture that the player will see on the drop-down portion of the ceiling as he crosses into the right sector. These two textures are called the WallBelow and WallAbove textures. A WallBelow texture is needed on any two-sided linedef whose two sectors have different floor heights. Likewise, A WallAbove texture is needed on any two-sided linedef whose two sectors have different ceiling heights.

Remember, a two-sided linedef by definition is one that has a sector on each side of it. These are the two sectors used to compare floor or ceiling heights for WallAbove/WallBelow textures.

Since our level so far has two adjoining sectors, and these sectors have both different floor *and* ceiling heights, a WallAbove *and* WallBelow texture are both needed on the linedef that connects them. We now need to determine which side of the linedef these textures need to be on (the right or left side). To determine on which side a WallBelow texture is needed, determine which side of the linedef points to the sector with the *lower* floor. This is the side that needs the WallBelow texture. To determine on which side a WallAbove texture is needed, determine which side of the linedef points to the sector with the *higher* ceiling. This is the side that needs the WallBelow texture.

There is a feature in DoomCAD to help find missing WallAbove or WallBelow textures. This feature is called the Integrity Check. The Integrity Check tries to find problems with your level. One of the things it looks for is missing WallAbove or WallBelow textures. To run the Integrity Check at any time, press the F12 key. When you do so, a gray listbox will be made visible in the upper left corner of the map window. Errors will be displayed in this listbox. As you click each error, DoomCAD will show you the location of each error. To close the Integrity Check window, press the small c button next to the gray listbox.

If you hit F12 now, the Integrity Check will tell you that a texture is needed for the right side WallBelow on the center linedef. This matches our WallBelow definition: Since the center linedef is two-sided, a WallBelow texture is needed on the side that faces the sector with the lower floor.

This is a good time to revisit the definition of the right vs. the left sides of a linedef. In our example level, the *right* side of the center linedef actually faces the *leftmost* sector, and the *left* side of the linedef faces the *rightmost* sector. This seems counterintuitive, but if you have the Direction Marks feature turned on, you can verify that this is so. The right side of a linedef has nothing to do with its orientation on the map; it has more to do with the direction you drew the linedef when you defined the sector.

To fix the center linedef's missing textures, go into Linedef mode, highlight the center linedef, and right click. At the bottom of the linedef edit dialog box, you will see areas for textures for the right and left *sidedefs*. (A sidedef is the official name of the side of a Linedef.) We need to add a texture to the right side WallBelow. Find the texture STEP4 in the texture listbox, click it, drag it to the right side WallBelow box, and drop it. (I chose STEP4 because it is 16 units tall, and the floor-height difference between our two sector is also 16.) In addition, the right-side Wall Texture (between the

WallAbove and WallBelow texture boxes) may have a texture in it. Since this linedef is transparent, we don't want a texture on it. To clear this texture, click the button marked "c" at the right of the Wall Texture box. The texture should be replaced with a hyphen, indicating there is no texture there. When you have done this, click the OK button.

To see if the level looks alright now, perform the Integrity Check again (F12). It should tell you that a texture is needed for the right side WallAbove on the center linedef. Again, this follows our definition: Any two-sided linedef needs a WallAbove texture on the side facing the sector with the higher ceiling.

To add the WallAbove texture, right click to bring up the Linedef Edit dialog once again. Drag texture STEP4 from the texture box to the right sidedef WallAbove Texture box. Click OK to end the operation.

Finally, our level should be ready to play! Perform the integrity check one more time to make sure. If it returns with the message "Level looks OK!", you're ready to save it. Follow the save and test procedures given earlier in the room. Your level should look much different in DOOM now. You should be able to easily discern the differences between the two sectors you created. Note the WallAbove and WallBelow textures as you pass from the leftmost to the rightmost sector.

INTO THE PIT

The next type of sector that we want to make is a pit of the green "nukeage" that damages the player when he's standing in it. This sector will be different than the other two in that it will lie wholly inside another sector. We'll choose the westernmost room of our two-room level to put the pit in. For reference purposes, we'll start referring to this westernmost sector as *the PitRoom*.

To begin making the pit, go into Vertex mode. Place four vertices in a rough square inside the westernmost sector.

Then, go into Sector mode. Select Add Sector from the menu. Trace clockwise around the four vertices, making a complete closed path. Right click when this is done. You just made four (one-sided) linedefs that define this new sector.

The next step is to make these four linedefs two-sided. They need to be two-sided because they will help to define both the new sector (the pit), *and* the sector in which the pit is contained (the PitRoom). Another way to think of this is that these linedefs will have to be transparent (so the player can walk into the pit). *All* transparent linedefs must be two-sided, by definition. (Put yet another way, if a linedef is transparent and the player is standing in a sector looking through the linedef, then there must be something on the other side to be looking at. This "something" must be another sector.)

DOOM PROGRAMMING GURUS

5 ROOM

1 MISSION

4 EPISODE

Since the four new linedefs already help to define the pit, we need to make them define the "parent" sector (the sector that makes up the PitRoom). To do this, select that sector by clicking one of its linedefs (you should still be in Sector mode). Once that sector is highlighted, select Edit Current sector's linedefs from the menu. This function works exactly like Add Sector, except that it creates linedefs for an existing sector instead of creating a new sector.

Trace over the four new linedefs a second time. Make sure to make a complete closed path. When you are done, right click.

To see that these four new linedefs are now two-sided, click one of them (while still in Sector mode). The sector making the pit should highlight. After a short pause, click in the same spot again. The "parent" sector (the PitRoom) should now highlight.

To make this new sector a nukeage pit, highlight it in Sector mode, and then right click. Choose a floor altitude of –16, make the floor texture NUKAGE1. Under the Attributes box, select one of the "Health Minus x/y %" attributes. (The x refers to the health lost on difficulty 1, the y refers to health lost on other difficulty levels.)

Finally, go into Linedef mode. We need to mark these four linedefs as two-sided, transparent, and define a WallBelow texture for the step up seen as the player walks out of the pit. There is a way to change all four linedefs as once. While holding down the Shift key, click each of the four linedefs. Each one should highlight itself in red. Once all four are highlighted, right click. Change the following attributes:

- Clear the right-side wall texture if it's not a hyphen.
- Add the texture NUKDGE1 to the right-side WallBelow. (Why the right side? Review the preceding section if you need a reminder.)
- Remove the Impassable bit.
- Select the Two-Sided (transparent) bit.

Figure 5.6 shows how the level should look so far. If it does, run an Integrity Check, save the level, and go try it out in DOOM. If you get any error messages, you'll need to fix them before you can play the level.

If you ever receive the error message `Partition Node not found, Nodes will be inaccurate` during the level save process, this is an indication that your sector/linedef relationships are not correct. Most of the time, this error is pointing out that you have a linedef that needs to be defined as two-sided but isn't. DoomCAD doesn't tell you exactly where the problem is, but the cyan, red, and white lines that form boxes during the level-save process will sometimes give you an indication of where the problem might be. These boxes are created from larger sizes down to smaller sizes, traveling from one specific area of the level to another. If you can see where the boxes were being drawn before the error occurred, this should be near the problem spot on the level. Until you fix this error, DOOM will *not* be able to display your level. Look for sectors within sectors (such as the pit mentioned previously) where you forgot to go back and make the new linedefs point to the "parent" sector, or sectors where you forgot to trace over adjoining linedefs a second time to make them two-sided.

Figure 5.6.
Our three-sector level so far.

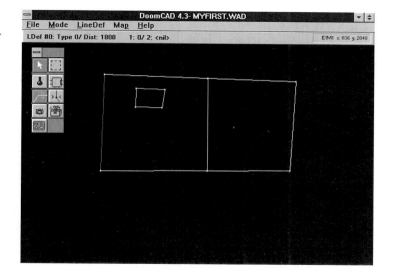

UP ON THE ALTAR

In the other (easternmost) room on the level, we're going to make an altar. This altar will be a sector inside the east room, with a raised floor. The interesting thing is that you will make the altar in almost the same way that you made the pit in the previous section. Follow the next steps carefully to make the altar.

1. Go into Vertex mode. Add four vertices in a rough square inside the easternmost room.

2. Go into Sector mode. Select Add Sector. Trace clockwise around the four new vertices. Right click when you have made a complete, closed path.

3. Select the "parent" sector. (The original easternmost sector.) Choose Edit Current Sector's Linedefs from the menu. Trace around the four new vertices a second time. Right click when done.

4. Select the new sector. Right click to bring up the Sector Edit dialog. Make the ceiling height 96, the floor height 32, and choose a new texture for the floor. Click OK when done. (Note: The maximum floor difference that the player can step over is 24 units. A difference of 32 units is too high to negotiate.)

5. Go into Linedef mode. Select the four new linedefs by Shift-clicking them. Right click to bring up the Linedef Edit dialog. Clear the Impassable bit, set the Transparent bit, clear any wall textures, and choose a texture for the *left* side WallBelow (Why the left side? Use the direction marks to figure this out). Also, in the large listbox in the upper left of the screen, find Attribute 48 (Animated, Horizontally Scrolling Wall).

Run an Integrity Check, save the level, and try it out in DOOM once again. Your level should now look like the level in Figure 5.7.

Figure 5.7
Our level after adding the altar.

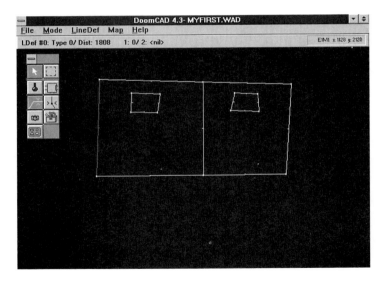

QUICK HALLWAYS

Our next step is to make a hallway exiting the PitRoom on the south wall, similar to Figure 5.8. This is easily accomplished by splitting the south linedef twice, adding two new vertices, and tracing a new sector around the four newly created vertices. Complete the following steps to accomplish this.

Figure 5.8.

Adding a hallway to the south of the PitRoom.

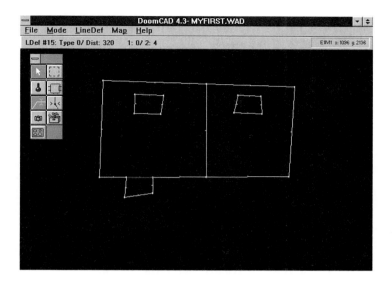

1. Go into Linedef mode. Choose the southernmost linedef of the PitRoom. Select Split Linedef from the menu. This function divides the current linedef into two identical linedefs, placing a new vertex directly between the two vertices that made up the original Linedef. The two new linedefs will have the exact same properties as the original linedef. After splitting the linedef once, select Split Linedef a second time. What you should have now are three linedefs making up the south wall of the PitRoom. There should be two new vertices created by the two linedef splits.

2. Go into Vertex mode. Add two vertices directly below the two new ones that were created by the two split actions in the last step. These four new vertices should form a rough square.

3. Go into Sector mode. Select Add Sector. Travel in a clockwise direction between the two vertices you just made and the two created by the split operations. Notice you trace over one of the south linedefs that makes up the PitRoom while creating this sector: this existing linedef will be two-sided after this sector is made.

4. After creating this sector, right click to bring up the Sector Edit dialog. Choose ceiling and floor heights of 128 and 0, textures, a brightness, and any special attributes that you want for the hallway. Click OK when done.

5. Go into Linedef mode. Select the linedef that the player would walk over when going from the PitRoom to the hallway. Make this linedef transparent, remove the Impassable bit, clear the Wall textures, and add any WallAbove or WallBelow textures you might need.

(The textures you will need, and what sidedef they will be on, depend on the ceiling and floor altitudes you choose for adjoining sectors. Review the sections above if this is still confusing to you. Don't forget you can use the Integrity check to help you determine what textures you will need.)

When you're done with this sector, make sure it looks similar to the level pictured in Figure 5.8, shown previously. If you want, save your level and check it out in DOOM.

PREFAB MODE

DoomCAD has a method of automatically creating many of the common structures you find yourself creating over and over, eliminating much of the repetitive work involved in creating DOOM levels. This feature is called Prefab mode (as in Prefabricated structures). The Prefab mode tool icon is in the fourth row on the right side, and appears like a small toolbox. Go into Prefab mode now.

In Prefab mode, you can click and highlight sectors just as you can in Sector mode. For many of the Prefab options, you will need to define a "parent" sector to enclose the item you're creating. To do this, you will highlight the existing sector before selecting the Prefab menu option, and this will become the "parent" sector.

For now, we are going to use the simplest of the Prefab options: the PreFab Room With Hallways. This option creates a rectangular room with up to four hallways coming off of its walls. Prefab mode automatically creates the two-sided linedefs between the room and the hallways, and properly places WallAbove and WallBelow textures based on the ceiling and floor altitudes you provide.

Choose the menu option Prefab Room With Hallways now. You will see the dialog box, shown in Figure 5.9. Use the following values to build your room:

- Turn on a North and East hallway.
- Room Ceiling = 255
- Room Floor = 0
- Hallways' Ceiling = 128
- Hallways' Floor = 0

After you click the OK button, you will be dragging a rectangular box around the map. Place the box due south of the hallway created in the last section, and click the left mouse button. DoomCAD will automatically create the structure you just described! Once you've created these new sectors, you can go back and edit them just like any other sector. Feel free to change textures on the walls or floors/ceilings, brightness levels, or sector attributes.

Figure 5.9.

The Prefab Room with Hallways dialog box.

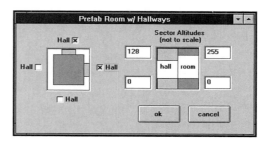

Before you save and try out this new structure, you will need a way to get into it, since there are no entrances into it. It's time to make one of the most complicated structures in DOOM: a door!

THE DREADED DOOR

Before we start the Door, make sure your level looks similar to Figure 5.10. Our goal will be to make the door between the south hallway coming off the PitRoom and the north hallway leading from the Prefab room made in the last step.

Figure 5.10.

Our level after adding the Prefab Room with hallways.

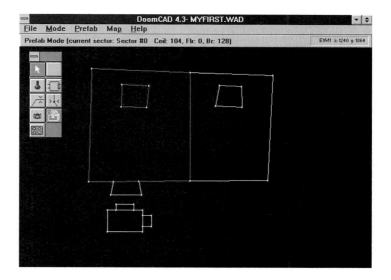

The first thing to learn about doors is that *a DOOM door is an entire sector, not just a linedef.* The common DOOM door is a rectangular sector made up of four vertices. The two long linedefs that make up this sector are the linedefs that contain the door graphic. The two short linedefs make up the door "track," or the sides of the door.

DOOM
PROGRAMMING
GURUS

5
ROOM

1
MISSION

4
EPISODE

The first step, then, to making the door, is to make a rectangular sector. We do this the way we made all the other sectors above, except that we don't need to make any new vertices; the four vertices we want to use are already in place. So then, to start the door, go into Sector mode, select Add Sector, and trace a clockwise complete path around the four vertices and right click. If you're doing this right, you should be tracing over two existing linedefs, (the Door part of the sector), and you should be making two new linedefs (the door tracks).

Staying in Sector mode, highlight the new door sector and right click to bring up the Sector Edit dialog. Make the following changes:

- Floor Altitude = 0
- Ceiling Altitude = 0

Why make the floor and ceiling heights the same? This brings us to the second part of our definition of a door: A door is a sector whose ceiling height is equal to the floor height. The act of opening a door is actually the act of raising the ceiling of this sector up so that the player can walk under the raised ceiling.

To complete the door, go into Linedef mode. Select the two long linedefs of the door by Shift+clicking them. Then right click. In the linedef edit dialog, set the following attributes:

- Set the linedef attribute (the big listbox in the top left of the Linedef Edit dialog) to "1=Door. Closes in 6 sec."
- Clear the Impassable bit.
- Set the Transparent (two-sided) bit.
- Clear the Wall texture.
- Add the texture BIGDOOR2 to the right sidedef WallAbove. (Why Wall*Above*? Remember that the ceiling of this sector is resting down on the floor. The door graphic is going *above* the ceiling level.)

Click OK, Shift+click to select the two door track linedefs (the short ones), and right click. Set the following attributes:

- Wall Texture: DOORTRAK.
- Set the "Wall Below is Unpegged" bit. This bit stops the door-track graphic from moving with the sector. The best way to describe this is to simply see it. The next two times you're ready to save and play your level, leave this bit for these two linedefs at different settings, and watch the sides of the door as the door opens and closes. With the unpegged bit off, the door track will move. With the bit on, the door track will stay stationary. Your choice

for this bit is purely preference. It applies only to sectors that move up and down (doors, lifts, and so forth).

The last part of the definition of the door is that the *right* sidedefs of the long linedefs of the door sector must point *out* of the door. The door we just made already complies to this rule, because our long linedefs had already been created by the time we made the door sector. If you make a door sector first and attach hallways to it later, however, the linedefs will point *into* the door sector, and the DOOM player won't be able to open the door. To fix door linedefs that are facing inward, go into Linedef mode, select the linedef, and choose Flip Linedef from the menu. This will swap the left and right sides of the linedef. You can only flip two-sided linedefs; one-sided linedefs can't be flipped.

In review, to make a door:

1. Create a sector with two long and two short linedefs.
2. Make the sector's ceiling and floor height the same.
3. Make sure the long linedefs' right side faces *out* of the sector (Put another way, the long linedefs' left sidedef should face the door sector).
4. Make the long linedefs transparent. Put a DOOR texture (BIGDOORx) on the right side WallAbove. Clear any Wall textures.
5. Add a door-track texture (DOORTRAK, DOORBLUE, DOORBLU2, and so forth) to the short linedefs Wall texture. Optionally, mark these linedefs as "WallBelow is Unpegged".

The next time you save your level and try out the door, you may notice that the door texture repeats itself across the linedef. This will be true if your door is longer than the width you chose for the door texture (usually 128 units). Most doors are an exact width to prevent this effect. To make a linedef an exact width, select it in Linedef mode and right click. Near the lower left of the Linedef Edit dialog is an edit control where you can specify an exact length. DoomCAD adjusts the linedef by moving the "to" vertex of the linedef, so keep in mind that if this vertex is also being used for other linedefs, those linedefs' lengths will change as well.

Door textures will also repeat upward if the door is facing a sector higher than the texture chosen for the door. For this reason, most doors are not placed in rooms with high ceilings. Instead, a hallway is made to lead out of the room, and the door is placed in this hallway.

VERTEX ALIGNMENT

This would be a good time to "pretty up" the level we have so far. I usually rough out between a half dozen and a dozen sectors at a time, save the level and try it out in DOOM, and then go back and make those sectors perfect by choosing the textures I want for the walls, floors, and ceilings and aligning the vertices.

Since you already know how to change textures, we won't do that here. We will cover vertex alignment, however. To align vertices, perform the following steps:

1. Go into Vertex mode.

2. Choose the Multi-Select tool. This is the second tool button in the righthand column of the toolbar. It looks like a rectangle made of dashed lines.

3. Click and drag a rectangle to enclose the vertices you want to align. Make sure not to catch any stray vertices. (Zooming in the map may help here. To zoom in, press the + key.) After you create the rectangle, the selected vertices will highlight in red.

4. Right click the mouse. The Vertex Align dialog box will appear. In it will be the average X and Y values for the selected vertices. You may change these numbers if you wish.

5. Then, select either "Align X" or "Align Y" and click the OK button. The selected vertices will align to the value specified.

Don't align a group of vertices to *both* X and Y, or all the vertices will occupy the same point in space. Because the present version of DoomCAD doesn't have an Undo feature, this mistake is really a mess to fix. You'll have to drag all the grouped vertices one by one back to their intended spots to fix this condition.

With a group of vertices selected in this manner, you can also "nudge" them eight units in any direction by pressing the arrow keys. This is good for minor alignment. Or, for major vertex movement, you can click inside the box you created and drag it to a new spot on the map. The selected vertices will move to that spot.

After aligning vertices, your level should look like Figure 5.11.

LIFT ME UP

The next step in our tutorial will be to turn the short east hallway in the Prefab room into a lift. First, lets make a sector at the end of the east hallway for the lift to lead to. In order to do this, follow these steps:

1. Go into Vertex mode. Add to vertices east of the east hallway of the Prefab Room, so that these new vertices and the two easternmost vertices of this hallway form a rough square.

2. Go into Sector mode. Select Add Sector. Trace a clockwise closed path around these four vertices. Right click when done.

Figure 5.11.

Our level after cleaning it up a bit.

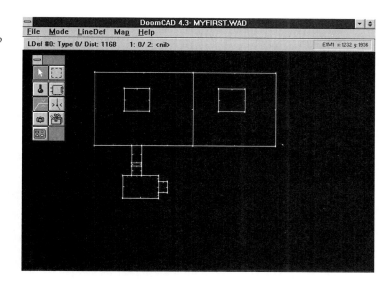

3. Highlight the new sector. Right Click. Set the following properties:

    ■ Floor Altitude = 152

    ■ Ceiling Altitude = 408 (Note that this sector is high above the other sectors.)

4. Go into Linedef mode. Make the westernmost linedef of the new sector Transparent. First, flip the linedef (the right sidedef needs to point out of the lift, as in doors). Now, bring up the Linedef Edit dialog. Click off the Impassable bit. Change the attribute to "088=WR Floor lowers quickly for 3 sec, then rises." You may need to click the radio button marked "Walk" to find this attribute. Then, go to the edit box marked "Trigger" and click the little button marked "n". This means to create a new trigger number in the box. (The number should be 1, since there are no triggers on your level yet. The next time we need a trigger, the number will be 2.) Whatever the number is, remember it for the next step. Click the OK button.

5. Now highlight the westernmost linedef of the lift sector (it used to be the east hallway of the Prefab room). Right click. Give this linedef the attribute "62=SR Floor lowers for 3 sec, then rises". (You will have to click the radio button marked "Switch" to find this attribute). Also, set the following attributes for this linedef:

    ■ Trigger Number = (1) (or whatever number you assigned to the preceding linedef)

    ■ Right Side WallBelow Texture = PLAT1

6. Go back to Sector mode. Highlight the lift sector. Make the following changes:

- Floor Altitude = 152
- Ceiling Altitude = 408
- Trigger = 1 (Or whatever number you assigned to the above two linedefs).

This would be a good time to save and try out the lift in DOOM. It should look similar to Figure 5.12.

Figure 5.12.

After adding the lift.

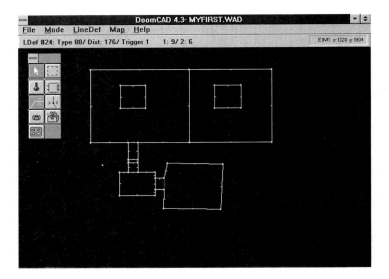

You may notice that after you lower the lift in DOOM, the walls behind it may demonstrate a "Hall of Mirrors" effect. This effect is exhibited when a wall needs a wall texture but has none assigned. The reason DoomCAD didn't discover these missing textures through its Integrity Check is because the lift sector is in the "Up" position at the start of the level. DoomCAD uses its Integrity Check only on the starting positions of sectors, not any movement that might occur during game play. It is left as an exercise for you to determine which walls need textures and to place them there.

TRIGGERS/ATTRIBUTES

We need to go back and explain exactly what we just did to make the lift in the last section. All of the sector movement functions, as well as some other functions (like teleportation and end of level switches), are handled through the use of linedef *triggers*. These triggers are in the large listbox at the upper left of the Linedef Edit dialog box. The triggers are separated into three major classes, handled by the "Door, misc.," "Walk," and "Switch" radio buttons above the listbox. These classes are described as follows:

- Walk: Sector(s) with a trigger number matching the trigger number on this linedef will be activated when the player walks over this linedef. The player must walk from the right side of the linedef to the left side. All linedefs containing a Walk-activated trigger should be transparent, so that player can, in fact, walk across it to trigger the action.

- Switch: Sector(s) with a trigger number matching the trigger number on this linedef will be activated when the player walks up to the right side of this linedef and presses the activate button. Many of the linedefs having this graphic should have a texture with a Switch graphic on it. These graphics have names that begin with SW in the texture box. This graphic can also be on the WallBelow or WallAbove texture, in the case of an overhang or altar whose WallBelow or WallAbove area is at the player's level to activate the switch.

- Door: Sector on the left side of current linedef raises up ceiling to match neighbor ceiling. A key may be needed. (Doors were covered in a previous section.)

There are also a few triggers activated by shooting the current linedef with a weapon, and one linedef that makes the wall texture scroll horizontally. These linedefs are listed in the "Door, misc." category.

The first two letters given for each linedef trigger describe that trigger. The "D", "W", "S", "G", refer to a Door, Walk, Switch, or Gun (shoot)-based trigger, as described previously. A "1" as the second character means that the action will happen only once, while an "R" means the action will happen repeatedly.

To review our earlier lift, we used a trigger called "62=SR Floor lowers for 3 sec, then rises" on the west side of the lift. This enables a player to push against the wall of the lift to lower it to his level. On the east side, we used a trigger called "088=WR Floor lowers quickly for 3 sec, then rises". That way, when the player walks over this linedef (onto the lift), it lowers down.

Note that our first two triggered linedefs happen to be attached to the sector that the linedefs help to make up, but this need not always be the case. You can have a switch somewhere in a level that opens up doors, lowers lifts, or raises bridges on the complete other side of the level. The trigger number is what ties a triggered linedef with the sector that the linedef activates. (The exception to this rule is doors, where the door sector is by definition the sector on the left side of the current linedef.)

In addition, one linedef trigger can affect many sectors at once. If a linedef is given trigger-number n, any and all sectors with trigger number n will be affected by the action described by the linedef Attribute. You can therefore make the player walk into a room and have five secret doors open up all around the room, having monsters attack from all directions!

When you highlight a linedef that has a trigger number (in Linedef mode), DoomCAD will show you the sectors with that same trigger number by drawing them in cyan. Likewise, while in Sector mode, when you highlight a sector having a trigger number, the linedef with the same trigger number will highlight in cyan. Again, doors are handled slightly differently since they don't use trigger numbers. If a linedef has a door trigger, the sector pointed to by the left side of that linedef is shown in cyan.

I'm not going to cover each of the individual linedef triggers here. The best way to learn about them is to experiment with them. Most of them have to do with either sector ceilings or floors lowering or raising. This allows for lifts, bridges, crushing ceilings, trap doors, and other related goodies. Some of the other triggers, such as "011=S1 End level. Go to next level," are self-explanatory. We will cover the teleport triggers in the next section.

TELEPORTERS

The red evil-glyph teleporters in DOOM are actually a fairly complex connection of linedef triggers working together. We will make a teleporter now.

The first thing to understand is that the act of teleporting has nothing to do with red square sectors, it really has to do with a simple teleport linedef trigger (triggers 39 and 97). Both of these are Walk-based triggers, so walking over a linedef causes the teleport. To make one of the red evil-glyph teleporters, then, we simply need to make a square sector made up of four linedefs that all have one of the two above triggers.

There is a Prefab option in DoomCAD for making square teleporters. Let's put a teleporter in our newest room (the room east of the lift). Follow the steps below to make a Prefab teleporter.

Go into Prefab mode. Highlight the sector east of the lift. Then, select Add Prefab Teleporter from the menu. You will see a small box following your mouse cursor around. Place the cursor somewhere completely inside the highlighted sector, and click. DoomCAD will build the teleporter at the spot you specified (using linedef trigger 97, the repeating teleport trigger). In addition, it will give you the following message:

```
To complete the teleporter, you must now:
"1. Select a destination sector and give it trigger number 2"
2. Place a 'Teleport Destination' thing (#14) in that sector.
```

What this is telling you is that DoomCAD just built the actual red teleport sector. You now need to set up the place where the teleporter is going to send the player. Let's choose the PitRoom as the destination sector. Go into Sector mode, highlight the PitRoom, and right click. Fill the Trigger Number edit box with the number 2 (or whatever number the preceding message gives you).

Lastly, go into Thing mode. Select Add Thing from the menu. Place the cursor somewhere inside the PitRoom and click. Then, right click. (You could add many Things at this point, but we only want to add one for now.) Select the newly placed Thing by clicking it. Then, right click to bring up the Thing Edit dialog. (See Figure 5.13.)

Figure 5.13.
The Thing Edit dialog box.

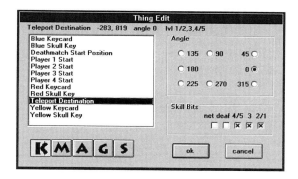

You can change the type of this Thing by using a combination of the listbox and the buttons under it that spell the word "KMAGS". These letters stand for Keys (and Misc.), Monsters, Ammo/weapons, Goodies, and Scenery. We want to turn this new Thing into a teleport destination Thing, which is in the Misc. List (button "K"). Hit button "K", then select the teleport destination Thing. You can also change the way the object is facing, which will affect the direction the player faces when he or she teleports to this spot.

Try out the teleporter in DOOM now. You may notice that the ceiling and floor texture for the teleporter is mapped funny. The reason for this is that picture ceiling and floor tiles must be on 64 unit boundaries for their texture to map properly. To easily accomplish this, go into the Grid menu and select Set Grid Snap. Choose a value of 64 for both x and y. Then, select Snap to Grid from the same menu. Now, go into Vertex mode and move the four teleporter vertices around slightly, and you see them snap to 64 unit values. This will properly align the texture. You'll need to perform this process on any floor or ceiling texture that has a picture on it.

Making two teleporters that teleport to each other is a similar process. You will need to place teleport destination Things inside each of the teleporter sectors. Teleporter A's linedefs and Teleporter B's sector will have trigger number *x*, while Teleporter B's linedefs and Teleporter A's sector will have trigger number *y*. See Figure 5.14 for making teleporter pairs.

Figure 5.14
Making transporter pair A and B.

THING EDITING

We covered the concept of Things in earlier sections, so most of this section will be a review. There are a few concepts that didn't come up in the previous sections, however, so I wanted to give Thing editing a revisit.

A *Thing* is defined as any object that the player may come in contact with during the game. Things can be monsters like Imps or Former Humans, power-up objects such as radiation suits or computer maps, scenery objects such as torches or pillars, keys, and various other special objects.

The complete property list of a Thing is:

- The Type of Thing (key, computer map, and so on)
- Location. Given in X,Y map coordinates.
- Direction Facing. Applicable only to monsters, players, and a few special Things. Other objects face every direction at once (they look the same from every angle).
- Skill Bits: These include the game difficulty levels the Thing appears on, as well as a "deaf" bit for monsters.

To add a new Thing, follow these steps:

1. Go into Thing mode. The Thing toolbar button looks like a blue potion bottle. If you know what type of Thing you want to add, and a Thing of that type already exists somewhere on your map, select it by clicking it. The reason for doing so is that when you select Add Thing in the next step, the Thing that you add is a copy of whatever the currently select Thing is. This makes it easy to copy Things. If you are adding a Thing that is *not* on your map yet, you can skip this step.

2. Select Add Thing from the menu. Place the cursor to the spot on the map you wish to add the Thing and left click. A Thing of the type selected previously will be added (or a dummy type if no Thing was selected). You can add as many Things of this type that you want by clicking the map in multiple places. When you are done adding Things of this type, right click to end Add Thing mode.

3. Select the Thing (or one of the many Things) you just added by clicking it. Now right click. The Thing Edit dialog will appear. (See Figure 5.13, shown previously.) You can change the Thing type using the list box at left. As stated above, the KMAGS buttons divide the Things into (K)eys (and Misc), (M)onsters, (A)mmo/Weapons, (G)oodies, and (S)cenery. Change the facing orientation by clicking one of the direction radio buttons at the right of the dialog. The "Skill Bits" check boxes are used as follows:

- 1/2: Thing will appear on Skill Levels 1 and 2.
- 3: Thing will appear on Skill Level 3.
- 4/5: Thing will appear on Skill Levels 4 and 5.
- Deaf: Monster will not react to nearby sounds (gunfire, and so forth), and must see the player to attack. Good for ambush spots.
- Net: Thing appears on multiplayer game only.

You can finish the tutorial level by populating it with as many Things as you wish.

THREE-DIMENSIONAL PREVIEW

As you create your level, you can get a rough idea of how it will look in DOOM by using the 3D Preview Tool. 3D Preview gives you a wireframe black-and-white perspective drawing of your level, from any camera angle. It is particularly useful for looking at relationships between the heights of nearby sectors.

To use the 3D Preview tool, click the 3D Preview tool in the toolbar. (The tool button looks like a camera.) A blue line will appear on the map. This line represents a camera line of sight, with one side representing where the viewer is standing, and one side being the spot the viewer is looking at. To move this line, grab either side and drag it to the desired location. The status bar will tell you which side you're moving. When the camera is at the desired location, right click. The 3D Preview window will appear, and the level will be displayed from the spot you specified. The initial altitude of the camera is above the level. To lower the height of the camera location, move the slider marked "Loc" down. The second slider controls the height of the camera viewpoint. When you are done using the 3D Preview tool, hit the Exit button.

SUMMARY

We have covered the basic steps of DOOM-level creation using DoomCAD. You should now have the basic tools for complete levels of any complexity. If any new questions come up, remember that one of the best sources of ideas and information are the 27 original levels that come with DOOM. You can load any of these levels in DoomCAD and study how it works. Not only this, but there are literally *hundreds* of homemade levels available online. All of these are great sources for ideas and assistance.

Finally, if you have any DoomCAD related questions, feel free to e-mail me at `matt.tagliaferri@pcohio.com`.

4
EPISODE

1
MISSION

5
ROOM

DOOM
PROGRAMMING
GURUS

ROOM 6

By Ben Morris

DCK

Welcome to the DOOM Construction Kit (DCK)—one of the easiest and most powerful map editors for DOOM, DOOM II, and Heretic.

While it can't do everything for you, DCK can automate the simple and oft-repeated tasks involved in creating a DOOM level. DCK affords you complete control over the design of your maps while it retains a level of usability that makes it very quick and intuitive to use.

Getting started with DCK is simple: if your copy came on a disk or a CD-ROM, run the install program in the DCK directory and follow the instructions. After doing so, run the batch file DCK.BAT and select the video driver for your system.

The first time you run DCK, it will search your system for any of the three games that it recognizes by default. If it can't find any of them (for shame!), you won't be able to run DCK—it requires data from at least one of the games.

INTERFACE

DCK's interface is similar to that of many modern GUIs (Graphical User Interfaces), such as Windows. The layout of DCK's screen remains largely the same, no matter what you're doing at the time. The screen is separated into three distinct parts, presented here in top-down order:

> **The Menu Bar:** This bar, at the top of the screen, contains the titles of several submenus. Submenus are organized by the subjects of the features they activate, so, for example, the File menu facilitates loading and saving files.

> **The Map Display:** Between the menu bar and the status bar, the map display takes up most of the screen. As the name implies, it's where the map you're working on is displayed.

> **The Status Bar:** At the bottom of the screen, the status bar displays information about DCK's status, such as which features are turned on, information about the map you're editing, and details about the area of the map the mouse cursor is in.

DCK's interface is centered around the mouse. Most of DCK's features can be activated by a click or two and moving the mouse around.

DCK'S MENU SYSTEM

The menu system can be used either with the mouse or the keyboard. Move the mouse to the menu you want to activate, and hold down the left mouse button. Move around the mouse to access each different menu, and release the button to activate the highlighted feature.

Press ESC (Escape) to activate the menu from the map editor and ESC again to deactivate it. Use the cursor keys to navigate the menu, and Enter to choose the highlighted selection. Any other keys will activate the item with the same hotkey, which is displayed in red.

THE MAP DISPLAY

The map display is where most of the work in DCK is done. DCK always displays the lines in the map, but it makes bright only the parts of the map that can be edited with the current tool. The tools are as follows:

- With the Line tool, you can edit each line and change its textures and attributes, such as settings for "Blocks Sound" and "Impassable." Press **L** or choose Line mode from the Edit menu to change to this tool.

- The Vertex tool enables you to add and delete vertices, and to drag existing vertices to new locations. Press **V** or choose Vertex mode from the Edit menu to select this tool.

- With the Sector editor, you can change the sectors' floor and ceiling textures, and set their floor and ceiling heights. Press **S** or choose Sector mode from the Edit menu to change to this tool.

- The Thing tool enables you to place new Things and move existing ones around. You can also edit Things' settings, such as the settings for which skill levels the Thing appears on, and settings for making monster Things deaf. Press **T** or choose Thing mode from the Edit menu to select the tool.

Except the for the Vertex editor, each tool enables you to edit the settings of more than one object at a time using "marked" objects. This is explained in detail in the section titled "Marking and Editing Objects."

In addition to the four main tools, there are two other tools—the Rectangle and Polygon creators—that you can use to add to the map quickly. These tools are discussed in the sections titled "Rectangle Tool" and "Polygon Tool."

The mouse plays an important role in each mode: each mouse action's results vary, depending on which tool you're using at the time. For example, double-clicking in Vertex mode adds a vertex to the closest line, and double-clicking with the Thing tool adds a Thing at the current mouse position.

Moving the mouse around in any of the modes, DCK will highlight the object that is closest to the cursor and display information about it on the bottom status bar. You can edit this information by clicking and releasing the right mouse button.

DIALOG BOXES

Throughout DCK, dialog boxes are displayed into which you must enter information in order to proceed. You can navigate them with the keys as outlined in Table 6.1.

Table 6.1. Navigating dialog boxes.

To do this...	...press this key
Move to the next field	Tab
Move to the previous field	Shift+Tab
Toggle a checkbox or radio field	Spacebar
Text: Move around	Left and Right arrow
Text: Previous and next word	Ctrl+Left and Ctrl+Right
Text: Start and end of text	Home and End
Text: Delete cursor letter	Del (Delete)
Text: Delete previous letter	Backspace
Save the dialog box and proceed	F10 or OK
Cancel the dialog box	ESC or Cancel

Some of the fields in a dialog box may be blank. This usually happens when you're editing multiple objects and they don't share the same data for a particular field. For example, if you were editing several Thing objects, each of different types, the Thing Edit dialog box would display a blank Thing Type field. If you set any field to be blank, DCK will ignore the field and not make any changes to the data represented therein.

CREATING MAPS WITH DCK

Creating maps is quick and easy using DCK's powerful drawing tools. With the tools, creating new areas on your map is as easy as a few mouse clicks and moves. You can easily do the following:

- Make a pit of monsters that rises when the player walks over a line
- Create a hidden staircase that rises with the flick of a switch
- Make a walkway in a pit of lava that starts to sink as soon as the player steps onto it

Areas that you create with the tools look the same as the areas around them—so it's easy to make additions to the map without having to make sure the appearance is consistent. And once you get into seriously detailing your map, DCK's editing tools make the job quick and easy. It's a simple feat to do any of the following:

- Change the texture on a set of walls with a few keystrokes
- Add dimension to your map with architecturally detailed areas
- Make nasty monster arrangements that are sure to surprise the player

WORKING WITH FILES

When you load an existing map or create a new one, you must choose the game that the map is to be used with. When you load a map, DCK examines the map's tag and searches its list of games for a matching tag. If it finds that the tag is valid in more than one game, it displays a menu of the possible choices for you to select from. If the map tag is unique to one game, DCK loads the map without any prompting.

Creating a new map requires that you choose a game before beginning to edit the map.

DRAWING TOOLS

DCK features three drawing tools, each suited for a certain job: the Region tool, the Rectangle tool, and the Polygon tool.

THE REGION TOOL

The Region tool is accessed by pressing **L** and doubles as the Line Edit mode.

Using the tool, you draw a series of lines. The entire series is called a *region*. The region can be of any shape and size—for example a square, a diamond, or the outline of the Taj Mahal. When you're done drawing, DCK analyzes what you've drawn and turns the region into *play space*, by creating the game objects (such as vertices, linedefs, and sidedefs) that are needed by DOOM in order for the map to run properly.

Since DCK is not an artificial-intelligence program (yet!), there are some limitations to the Region tool. In fact, there are defined sets of "rules" that you should follow in order to get the results you want. These rules are explained in detail later.

The Region tool looks to the mouse for instructions:

1. Double-click the left mouse button to start a new region.
2. Click the left mouse button once to finish the line you're drawing and start a new one.

3. Click the right mouse button once to complete the region.

The start- and end-points of the region (that is, where you start and finish drawing) are very important when DCK is deciding what to do with the new area. For example, if you start and finish on an existing line, DCK assumes you want to create a new area connected to the line, and it makes sure that the line can be passed through by the player.

> You can't start and end the region in different ways; that is, if you start on a line, you must finish on the same line, and if you start by not touching any lines, you must finish on the first point of the region.
>
> The only points of the region that can touch existing lines are the start- and end-points. *Note: All points drawn between the start- and end-points must not touch anything!*

REGIONS THAT DON'T TOUCH EXISTING LINES

When you create a region that doesn't touch any existing lines, the following results:

- If the new region is outside of any existing sectors, the area lines will be one-sided; the player cannot pass from the new area into "blank space."
- If the new region is inside an existing sector, the area lines will be two-sided; the player can move into the new area from the surrounding sector.

REGIONS THAT TOUCH EXISTING LINES

When you create a region that touches an existing line, DCK splits the line (the *contact line*) at the start- and end-points of the region.

If the new region is outside of any existing sectors, the area lines will be one-sided; the player cannot pass from the new area into "blank space." The contact line will be made passable, so the player can move into the new area from the contact line's sector.

If the new region is inside an existing sector, the area lines will be two-sided; the player can move into the new area from the surrounding sector. The contact line will remain "as-is." For instance, if it was originally impassable, it will stay impassable.

> All regions created inside an existing sector take on the appearance and floor and ceiling heights of that sector. Likewise, regions that touch existing sectors (but are essentially "outside" of any sector) will take on that sector's attributes.

THE RECTANGLE TOOL

Press **R** to access the Rectangle tool, or select the rectangle icon from the mouse toolbox.

The advantages of the Rectangle tool are many: it can overlap as many lines from as many sectors as you wish, and it will always produce a valid new area. For example, you can use it to create a window between two sectors simply by drawing a box between the two that touches their lines—an operation that would require many more clicks and movements with the Region tool.

The disadvantage is that the Rectangle tool can only draw four-sided boxes. Although the tool is very useful in this respect—when you *need* a rectangle—maps drawn entirely in 90° angles tend to be a little boring. The other two tools—Region and Polygon—are much better suited to starting abstract areas.

Using the Rectangle tool is simple: hold down the left mouse button, drag out the rectangle that you want, and release the button. If the rectangle overlaps any existing lines, DCK will make them passable so that the player may move into the new area. Make sure none of the rectangle lines cross any existing lines.

In addition, you can hold down the right mouse button to move the origin of the rectangle while you're drawing the rectangle.

THE POLYGON TOOL

Press **N** to access the Polygon tool, or select the polygon icon from the mouse toolbox.

The Polygon tool is used in the same way as the Rectangle tool, but it can create a shape with from three to 64 sides. The tool also splits and combines any lines it overlaps.

The following actions can be taken while you're drawing a polygon:

- Hold down the right mouse button to move the origin of the polygon.
- Hold down the Ctrl key to constrain the polygon to a circle instead of an oval.
- Press **Q** to decrease the number of sides in the polygon.
- Press **W** to increase the number of sides in the polygon.

MARKING AND EDITING OBJECTS

Except for vertices, each type of object has a series of attributes that you can modify to give the object a different appearance and function.

A line that borders two sectors, for example, can be set to be impassable so that the player cannot move across it. This is useful for those lines where you've set up a middle "bar" texture, which can normally be walked straight through.

In addition to editing a single object, DCK enables you to change an entire set of objects by first marking the objects you want to change and then editing them all together.

Marking objects is simple: move the mouse cursor over the object you want to mark and click the left mouse button once. Marked objects are outlined in Red.

You can unmark all the objects by pressing **C**, for "Clear Marks."

DCK includes a Box Mark and Unmark mode, where all the objects in an enclosing box are affected. To mark all the objects in a box, hold down the left mouse button and drag out the box. To unmark, hold down the right mouse button until the toolbox disappears and drag out the box.

To edit the marked objects, press Enter or click and release the right mouse button. A different edit screen will appear depending on the type of object you've selected.

USING THE TEXTURE BROWSER

DCK includes a browser that displays multiple textures, including floor and ceiling textures, for you to choose from. The browser also enables you to search the list of textures.

You can access it directly by selecting the Textures menu item and pressing the Browser button. Or, you can press F2 in one of the dialog box fields that gives you access to the browser—such as the sidedef textures in the Line Edit box, or the floor and ceiling textures in the Sector Edit box.

To search for a texture using part of its name, press Alt+**F** and enter the string to search for. Press **/** to search forward again, or **** to search backwards.

If you pressed F2 to access the browser, press Enter to choose the highlighted texture, or press Escape to cancel the selection and keep the original texture. Alternately, double-click the mouse on the texture you want to use, or click the right mouse button to keep the original.

EDITING LINES

The main parts to the Line Edit dialog box are, from the top-down: the line's type, its attributes (flags), and its sidedef(s).

The line type consists of three fields: a text field where you can type in a partial line type or the type's number (if you've memorized it); a list of line-type categories, split into sections such as "door open," "door close," "teleporters," and so on; and the line types contained in the highlighted category.

The line's attributes are a series of checkboxes reflecting the flags that DOOM interprets for each line. You can set and unset these attributes freely: the Two-Sided and Impassable settings must be heeded according to the rules of the DOOM engine, which are discussed earlier in this book.

The line's two sides are the most complicated part of the dialog box. Only one is displayed at a time, to make room for the textures on each side. The three texture fields can be used to type in a texture's name directly, or you can press F2 to access the texture browser and pick one from there. The other three fields are: the X and Y offsets of the texture, and the side's sector reference.

If the line has no second side, DCK will give you the option of adding a second side by pressing a button. Conversely, you can delete the line's second side by pressing the Delete button after selecting side two. In either case, DCK will set or unset the Impassable and Two-Sided attributes to reflect the change.

EDITING SECTORS

Each sector has settings for its type, its floor and ceiling textures and heights, and its light level and sector tag.

The line type is fairly simple: choose the type you want from the list, or select the Normal type if you want a plain sector.

Scroll through the floor and ceiling texture lists to select a texture, or use Alt+**F** and the search keys (/ and \) to find a texture using a partial name. Or, you can use the texture browser by pressing F2.

The light value can be from 0 to 255.

The sector tag associates the sector with all the lines having the same tag. When one of those lines is activated, its type is "applied" to the sector and the sector is modified according to the type. This relationship is discussed in detail earlier in the book.

EDITING THINGS

There are three parts to the Edit Thing dialog box: the Thing type, the angle it faces, and its attributes.

The Thing type consists of three fields: the type string, where you can type in a partial name, such as "Player 1"; the Thing type category list, which breaks the lower Thing-type list into distinct sections; and the type list itself, which contains all the Thing types in the highlighted category.

The Thing's angle is a set of radio buttons; that is, only one can be selected (of course.) For monsters, this angle is only relevant until the monster is activated, at which time it starts moving around and its direction becomes unpredictable. If none of the buttons is set, it means that the multiple objects you're editing do not all face in the same direction.

The Thing's attributes consist of settings for when the object appears (that is, for which skill level it appears), settings for whether the object only appears in netgames, and, for monsters, the "Deaf" setting, which means the monster will not respond to sound.

DRAG-AND-DROP

One of DCK's most useful features is its drag-and-drop function. You can use it to move any number of objects to a new location quickly—no muss, no fuss, and a money-back guarantee.

Start dragging by highlighting an object and holding down the left mouse button. While holding down the button, move the mouse until the objects are in the desired position; then release the button to drop them.

If any objects are marked, they will also be moved.

If you're using Snap to Grid, the highlighted object is the only object that is snapped. The rest of the objects remain at their original distances from the highlighted object.

Other things to know about:

- You can press Escape at any time to abort the drag operation.
- All of DCK's basic features can still be used during dragging: for example, zooming in and out, moving the map around, changing the grid size and snap-to-grid, and so on.
- The coordinates at the top-right of the screen are displayed in red when the objects are dragged back to their original positions.
- When you're dragging Things, press Home or End to toggle between copying the Things and moving them.

- When you're dragging other kinds of objects, DCK displays the lengths of the lines that are stretched by the operation with color-coded boxes and numbers on the status bar.

- If you decide you liked where the objects were before you dragged them, press Alt+Backspace to reverse the operation.

DELETING OBJECTS

Although deleting objects is a fairly straightforward procedure, there are a few things you should know about how DCK handles it.

Deleting vertices automatically joins the lines they separate. This can be a little surprising when you delete a series of vertices, expecting the lines that they connect to be deleted also—the result is not usually the desired one. If you want to delete lines, the best way is to do it from Line mode, where DCK does not attempt to join anything.

Deleting lines is the best way to remove entire chunks of your map. From Line Edit mode, simply mark all the lines that you want to remove and press Del. If there are any leftover vertices (such as vertices that are no longer connected to any lines), they will also be removed.

Deleting sectors: DCK examines each line that references the sector, and makes a decision based on what kind of line each is, as follows:

- If the line is a one-sided line, DCK deletes it.

- If the line has two sides, DCK removes the side that references the deleted sector and reverses the direction of the line if necessary.

Again, the best way to delete entire parts of your map is by deleting all the lines in the area you want to remove. Deleting vertices and sectors are specialized functions and should be used for specific cases.

OTHER TOOLS

DCK features many automated tools designed to make short work of many of the details in designing maps. These tools include the following:

- The Format Painter, which copies an object's attributes to all the marked objects.

- The Automated Tag feature, which associates the marked lines or sectors with an opposite object, for use with moving floors and ceilings and the like.

- The Vertex Editor, with which you can add vertices and split lines, delete vertices and join lines, and so on.

■ The Automatic Door, Lift, and Stair creators.

These features and others are discussed in the following sections.

AUTOMATED TAG FEATURES

This tool enables you to visually set a "tag" relationship between a set of sectors or lines and an opposite object. Using the tool is straightforward: mark the objects you want to tag, activate the auto-tag feature and select the opposite object.

If the opposite object already has a tag, DCK will give you a menu choice: you can use the existing tag, or DCK can set a new one.

Activating the auto-tag can be done in several ways:

1. Choose it from the Object menu
2. Activate it from the keyboard with Ctrl+**T**
3. Select it from the mouse toolbox—it's the tags icon

THE VERTEX TOOL

With the vertex tool, you can split existing lines by adding vertices to them at any point, you can join two lines separated by a vertex, and you can drag around existing vertices to make small changes to the structure of your map.

To select the vertex tool, press **V**, or choose Vertex Mode from the Edit menu. Alternately, select the vertex icon from the mouse toolbox.

Using the tool to add a vertex is simple: double-click the left mouse button to add a vertex to the closest line at the cursor position. DCK will split the line by creating a new one that begins at the new vertex and ends at the original line's endpoint.

Press the Del (Delete) key to delete the vertex under the cursor and join the two lines it separates. If the vertex is connected to more than two lines, the results may be unpredictable; DCK searches for the first two lines that the vertex separates and merges them into one line.

AUTOMATIC DOOR, LIFT, AND STAIR TOOLS

These tools automate creating some simple map structures. They don't create new areas; they work by changing existing areas into the type of object you select (a door, a lift, or a staircase).

THE DOOR TOOL

The Door tool turns an existing sector into a door by setting its floor and ceiling heights to the floor height of the neighboring sector with the lowest floor.

Activate it by marking all the sectors you want to turn into doors (first switching to Sector mode) and pressing Ctrl+**D** or by choosing Create Door from the Object menu. DCK will display a menu of available door types for you to choose from.

One-sided lines in the door sector take on the "Door Trak" motif texture. Two-sided lines take on one of the door textures. Lines shorter than 65 take the Small door texture, and lines longer than 64 take the Large door texture. The exception is the Secret door type, whose sides take on one of the surrounding textures.

Finally, the two-sided lines are made to face out of the door sector, and their line types are set to the type you choose from the menu. In addition, the Secret door type sets the Secret flag on all two-sided lines.

THE LIFT TOOL

The Lift Tool turns an existing sector into a lift by setting its floor and ceiling heights to that of the highest neighboring sector's.

Activate the tool by marking all the sectors you want to turn into lifts (first switching to Sector mode), and pressing Ctrl+**L** or choosing Create Lift from the Object menu.

Two-sided lines that border the sector are set to have a platform line-type based on how the player can use the line: if the player can walk over the line *into* the lift sector, the line type is set to Walk-Repeatable Platform. if the player cannot walk over the line (because, for example, the lift sector's floor is higher than the neighboring sector's floor), the line receives the Use-Repeatable Platform type—meaning the player has to press the Use button to activate the line.

THE STAIR TOOL

The Stair tool is the most complicated of the three, but its flexibility makes it very useful. To create stairs, you must select two lines, which will become the sides of the stairs. That is, the stairs run between the lines and along their length.

After selecting two lines (from Line mode), press Ctrl+**Z** or choose Create Stairs from the Object menu. DCK will display a dialog box in which to enter information about the stairs. This dialog box contains a simple preview of the direction of the steps; the green circle indicates the first step, and the red circle indicates the last. The fields in the dialog box are as follows:

1. **Number of Stairs:** Enter the number of stairs you want to create.

2. **Step Height:** Enter the height of each step. If you want to create a descending staircase, enter a negative value (such as –8).

   - **First Stair Floor:** Enter the height of the first step. DCK automatically sets this when you press Ctrl+**Z**, and you can change it to another value if you wish. If you change the Last Stair Floor field, this field is automatically updated based on the number of steps and the step height.

   - **First Stair Ceiling:** Enter the height of the first step's ceiling.

   - **Last Stair Floor:** Enter the height of the last step's floor. DCK automatically calculates this when you press Ctrl+**Z**, or when you change the First Stair Floor, Number of Stairs, or Step Height fields.

   - **Last Stair Ceiling:** Enter the height of the last step's ceiling. If the "Stair Ceiling" checkbox is not set, this field is ignored and all stairs have the height of the first stair's ceiling.

Options for the Stair tool are in checkboxes, as follows:

1. **Reverse Direction:** Check this box to flip the direction of the steps.

2. **Stair Ceiling:** Check this to stair the ceiling as well as the floor. If unchecked, the stairs will all have the same ceiling height as the first stair.

3. **Hidden:** Check this box to make the staircase "hidden," so that it can be made to rise from the floor. In this case, DCK sets all the stair-floor heights to the same as the first step's floor.

After you've entered all the options, press F10 or click OK to create the stairs. DCK will split each of the lines you've chosen with as many steps as you've specified and create the step sectors with incremental floor and (optional) ceiling heights.

Make sure that the lines you've selected form part of a whole sector. DCK creates the step sectors in between and along the lengths of the lines, which become the sides of the staircase.

The lines should have nothing in between them when you start the stairs. This does not include Things, but other objects such as protruding lines will make the staircase wonky.

If the staircase isn't exactly what you wanted, press Alt+Backspace to delete what you've done and try again.

TEXTURE ALIGNMENT

Proper texture alignment is a tricky issue, and DCK's automated feature will not handle every situation. However, for common scenarios, it does the job quickly and easily. Activating it can be done one of two ways:

- Select Align Textures from the Object menu
- Press Ctrl+**W**

For example, suppose you had a circular room painted with a texture (from DOOM) such as SKINSYMB, which does not repeat very well. Where each line ends and a new line begins, there will likely be a visible seam where the first line's texture ends and the second line's texture starts. This effect can be nullified by setting the lines' sides' Texture X offset, so that the room's walls form a seamless pattern of textures.

In simple cases such as this, the Sector Alignment tool will probably do the job. Simply switch to Sector mode, move into the sector you want to align, and activate the aligner; DCK does the rest.

In those cases where the lines you want to align do not reside in a single sector—the sides of a staircase are a good example, because each step is an individual sector—alignment from Line mode is the only way to go. Switch to Line mode, and mark the series of lines that you want to align. Then activate the aligner.

In either case, DCK will prompt you as to which type of alignment you'd like to perform: Horizontal, Vertical, or Both.

THE FORMAT PAINTER

Most often used with sectors, the Format Painter is useful for ensuring consistency in appearance where it's needed. It works like this: mark the objects you want to change, activate the Format Painter, and select the object you want to copy *from*. Activating the Format Painter can be done one of several ways:

- Choose it from the Miscellaneous menu
- Activate it from the keyboard with Ctrl+**P**
- Select it from the mouse toolbox—it's the paint-can icon

After selecting the object to copy from, DCK will give you a menu of combinations to copy, based on common situations. At this time, you can select one of the combinations or press ESC to abort the Format Painter operation.

OTHER FEATURES

DCK also includes other useful features, such as the ability to run DOOM from within itself, and the ability to combine single levels and virtually any data from your disk into a single WADfile. It also includes one of the most powerful and comprehensive map checkers available at the time of this writing.

THE MAP CHECKER AND DEBUGGER

Over time, little errors may creep into your map. Most of them won't cause any big problems, but it's always nice to know that they're easily found and fixed. With DCK's error checker, most are.

After it is activated, the checker runs through every object in the map and checks it against a series of rules that have been set up to detect flaws in the map's structure: deviations from the rules set down by the DOOM engine's limitations, situations that may have undesired effects, and so on. (A list of all the errors the map checker catches can be found at the end of this section.)

Those objects that DCK finds as problematic are added to a list of errors, which is displayed when all the checks are complete. From this list, most of the errors can be zoomed in on and fixed with a couple keystrokes. However, some errors (such as the "Sector is not closed" error) cannot be fixed automatically because of their complex nature.

To activate the checker, choose it from the Miscellaneous menu or press Alt+**C**. The dialog box that is subsequently displayed is a list of options for the checker. It will only perform the kinds of checks that are selected here.

The checker displays the list of errors, from which you can do the following:

- Get help on the current error by pressing F1. This option displays a detailed description of the error, explaining how it is fixed or how to fix it manually.

- Jump to the object that is in error by pressing **G**. DCK will switch to the appropriate edit tool and zoom in and center on the object. This option is not always available; for example, the error `Too few player starts` is a general error and cannot be zoomed in on.

- Fix the error by pressing **F**. If the error is a simple one, such as a line missing a texture, DCK will fix it and change the error list to reflect the fixed object. If you want to get information on what automatically fixing a particular error does, press F1. Some errors can't be fixed because of their complex nature, such as `Sector is not closed` and `Too few DEATHMATCH starts`.

Table 6.2 includes a complete list of the errors that DCK's map checker can pinpoint.

Table 6.2. List of performed error checks.

Performed Error Checks

Line Checks

Linedef is two-sided but has no second sidedef.

Linedef is *not* two-sided but has a second sidedef.

Linedef's vertex references are the same.

Linedef has no first sidedef.

Linedef has a line type but no sector tag.

Linedef has a sector tag but no line type.

Linedef's tag is not shared by a sector.

Side Checks

Sidedef *n* is missing upper/lower textures.

Sidedef *n* is missing a full texture.

Sidedef *n*'s full tex not "transparentable."

Sidedef *n* has a bad texture.

Sidedef *n*'s transparent full texture is too high.

Sector Checks

Sector is not closed (ends at vertex *n*).

Sector's tag is not shared by a linedef.

Sector's floor texture is invalid.

Sector's ceiling texture is invalid.

Thing Checks

Thing is not in a sector.

Thing is too high for its sector.

Thing collides with other Things.

Thing collides with a line.

Unknown Thing.

continues

Table 6.2. continued

Performed Error Checks
Miscellaneous Checks

No Player 1 Start.

Too few player starts.

Too few Deathmatch starts.

Missing an exit line.

Tele-line's tagged sector has no Tele-exit.

Vertex n is at the same point as vertex n.

THE WAD MANAGER

Accessible from the File menu or by pressing Alt+**W**, DCK's WAD manager enables you to edit and view WAD files much like you'd do with a DOS directory navigator. With it, you can do the following:

- Add entries to a WAD file from data in other WAD files or from raw files anywhere on your system
- Rename existing entries in WAD files
- Delete existing entries from WAD files

The WAD manager works with a Source list and a Destination list. The Source list is the list of files in the current directory, or the list of entries in a WAD file. The Destination list is the directory of the final WAD file, which is what is manipulated and saved at the end of the session.

Navigate the Source list with the arrow keys, and change to a new source location with Enter. If you press Enter while the Source list is highlighting a WAD file, the contents of the file will be displayed for you to browse and add to the destination, if you wish.

Build up the Destination list by copying data items (files or WAD entries) from the Source list into the destination. You can load an existing WAD into the Destination list by pressing Alt+**L**, and save the Destination list to a WAD file with Alt+**S**.

To view an entry in either of the lists, press Enter. If the entry is a map, it will be displayed. Otherwise, DCK will give you the choice of displaying the entry as a "binary dump" or as a game picture.

To add the highlighted Source entry into the Destination list, press **P** or click the Put button. DCK will, by default, save the data under its original name. If it's a file, it will use the filename without the extension; if it's a WAD entry, it will use the name from the .WAD.

If the entry you're placing in the Destination list already exists, and the "Replace Entries" checkbox is not set, DCK will ask you if you'd like to overwrite the existing entry, rename the new one, or not save it at all.

To save an entry from either the Destination list or the Source list to a raw file, press **X**.

REFERENCE: EDITING COMMANDS

The list of commands in Table 6.3 are for your reference. Please note the conventions used in the table:

- Ctrl+Key means hold down the Ctrl (Control) key and press the specified key; for example, Ctrl+N means hold down the Ctrl key and press N at the same time. The same applies for Alt+Key.

Table 6.3. Editing commands reference.

Feature (what to do)	Command (how to do it)
System Commands (File and Menu)	
Save the current map	Alt+**S**
Edit a different map	Alt+**E**
Configure DCK	Alt+**N**
File Manager	Alt+**W**
Exit DCK	Alt+**X**
Playtest the current map	F9
Menu system	Escape
Changing the size and position of the map display	
Move the map around	Arrow keys
Center the map	Ctrl+**G**
Zoom in or out on the cursor	+ (in), – (out)
Zoom presets	1 through 9
Fast zoom	**Z**

continues

Table 6.3. continued

Feature (what to do)	Command (how to do it)
Toggles, Grid and Marking Commands	
Fine mode toggle	' (beside the '1' key)
Auto-join mode toggle	J
Crosshair cursor toggle	*
Grid display toggle	G
Change the grid size	[and]
Snap to grid	P
Mark the object under the cursor	Left Mouse Click
Clear all marks	C
Clipboard and Delete Commands	
Copy marked objects to the Clipboard	Ctrl+Insert
Cut to the Clipboard	Ctrl+Delete
Paste from the Clipboard	Insert
Delete marked objects	Delete
Editing Commands: All Edit Modes	
Scale (resize) marked objects	Ctrl+A
Rotate marked objects	Ctrl+O
Align objects horizontally	Ctrl+X
Align objects vertically	Ctrl+Y
Snap objects to the grid	Ctrl+V
Format Painter	Ctrl+P
Editing Commands: Thing Edit Mode	
Create a new Thing	Double Left-Click
Copy marked Things	Double Left-Click+Drag
Toggle Thing Origin	O
Toggle Thing Graphics	T
Adjust Thing display	D

Feature (what to do)	Command (how to do it)
Editing Commands: Vertex Edit Mode	
Split a Line with a new vertex	Double Left-Click
Join lines separated by a vertex	Del
Editing Commands: Line Edit Mode	
Split lines	Ctrl+C
Apply the current motif to lines	Ctrl+E
Flip lines	Ctrl+F
Flip side references	Ctrl+R
Add required textures	Ctrl+I
Remove unrequired textures	Ctrl+U
Normalize lines (remove tags/types)	Ctrl+N
Automatic tag-set	Ctrl+T
Align textures	Ctrl+W
Create stairs from two lines	Ctrl+Z
Edit first side	Alt+1
Edit second side	Alt+2
Search and replace textures	Alt+R
Editing Commands: Sector Edit Mode	
Create door	Ctrl+D
Create lift	Ctrl+L
Apply current motif to sectors	Ctrl+E
Raise/lower sectors	Ctrl+H
Normalize sectors (remove tags)	Ctrl+N
Automatic tag-set	Ctrl+T
Align textures	Ctrl+W

ROOM 7

By Jack
Vermeulen

DEEP / HEEP

DeeP is a precision DOOM and DOOM II editor running under DOS or in a DOS box in Windows. The Heretic version of DeeP is called HeeP.

SYSTEM REQUIREMENTS FOR DEEP AND HEEP

DeeP requires a 386 processor or higher and 540KB of base RAM. A math co-processor and 615KB of base RAM are highly recommended. With a math co-processor installed, the node builder, DeePBSP, will build nodes about four times faster than without. DeeP uses conventional memory and DeePBSP uses extended memory.

DeeP requires a video card that supports VESA with a minimum of 512KB of video memory. If DeeP will not display anything, refer to the section entitled "Troubleshooting" later in this room. A program called UNIVBE has been included and may solve video problems.

DeeP requires very little hard-drive space, only about 1.4MB. However, additional levels made using DeeP will require much more disk space, usually about 3MB.

A mouse is very strongly recommended to run DeeP. Although DeeP will function without a mouse, levels are much harder to construct without one. DOS 6.2 is also recommended, although not required. If your system has more than 4MB of RAM, SmartDrive should also be running. Many of the tasks DeeP performs run much faster with disk-caching software.

When running SmartDrive, keep in mind that any memory that it uses takes away from the extended memory DeePBSP could use. If DeePBSP runs out of extended RAM while building a level, simply reduce the size of the cache.

INSTALLING DEEP/HEEP

From the DOS command line (`C:>`), follow these steps to install DeeP and HeeP. (Sample commands for each step have been enclosed in parentheses.):

1. Change to the DOOM or DOOM II directory. (`CD \DOOM` (or `CD \DOOM2`))
2. Make a directory to hold the DeeP files. (`MKDIR DEEP`)
3. Go to the location where DEEP.ZIP is located. (`CD \DEEPDIST`)
4. Use PKUNZIP to install DeeP in the directory created in Step 2. (`PKUNZIP DEEP.ZIP C:\DOOM\DEEP`)
5. Change to the directory where DeeP was just installed to run DeeP. (`CD\DOOM\DEEP`)

To install HeeP, follow these instructions:

1. Change to the directory where the Heretic software is located. (`CD \HERETIC`)
2. Make a directory for installing HeeP. (`MKDIR HEEP`)
3. Change to the directory where DEEP.ZIP is located. (`CD \DEEPDIST`)
4. Use PKUNZIP to install DeeP to the directory created in step 2. (`PKUNZIP HEEP.ZIP C:\HERETIC\HEEP`)
5. Change to the directory where HeeP was just installed. (`CD \HERETIC\HEEP`)

THE .INI FILES

Before running DeeP or HeeP, edit the DEEP.INI or HEEP.INI file to match the current locations of DOOM or Heretic. The default is set for `C:\DOOM2` (DeeP) or `C:\HERETIC` (HeeP).

From the `C:>` prompt in the directory where DeeP and HeeP are installed, type the following command:

`EDIT DEEP.INI`	Type this if DeeP is to be installed
`EDIT HEEP.INI`	Type this if HeeP is to be installed

This brings up the DOS Edit program, a text editor suitable for editing small files. The contents of the .INI files are explained in the .INI files. Normally all you are concerned with at this moment is the location of your DOOM/DOOM II or HERETIC file. You may wish to change the default path where you are going to read and save levels. Set this in the .INI files also.

STARTING DEEP

To start DeeP, change to the directory where DeeP is installed and type `DEEP command_line_parameters`

The command-line parameters are explained forthwith. (These are not normally needed for your first session.)

STARTING HEEP

To start HeeP, change to the directory where HeeP is installed and type `HEEP command_line_parameters`. The command-line parameters for running HeeP are explained later. As with DeeP, these are not normally needed for your first session.

COMMAND LINE OPTIONS

Command-line parameters for DeeP can be defined by entering H and then pressing Enter while at the character mode DeeP prompt `Deep [?=Help]>`.

If you are running from a CD-ROM, the `-config` option must be entered as a parameter so DeeP will know where to find the DEEP.INI file. Copy the DEEP.INI file to a convenient location (perhaps in a DEEP directory as described previously). Edit the DEEP.INI file as discussed before and enter the following command line: `>D:\CDROMdir\DEEP -config c:\mydir\DEEP.INI`

This instructs DeeP to look for the file DEEP.INI in the directory *mydir*. We suggest you make a small batch file containing the preceding line (adjusted for your actual directory names, of course). If you do run from the CD-ROM, please add the appropriate directory information to the instructions that follow.

The `-v` and `-n` options are also useful to know.

The `-v` option temporarily overrides the video-resolution setting in the file DEEP.INI. Experiment with this to find the setting appropriate for you. The default is `-v 2` (640 x 480, 256 colors).

For example, entering `> C:\DEEP\DEEP -v 3` will test your video for 800 x 600 resolution and `> c:\DEEP\DEEP -v 4` will test your video for 1024 x 768 resolution.

The `-n` option erases all memory of any files you have loaded. Since the shareware LITE version has a limit of six files at once, load DeeP with this option to start over. You can also reset all the levels in edit mode by selecting Alt+**F** (the File menu) and then selecting Reset Level.

TROUBLESHOOTING

If either HeeP or DeeP fail to run, refer to the following solutions and to the latest DEEPFAQ.DOC file.

Problem: When editing a level, DeeP does not display the map or locks the system.

Solution: This is most likely caused by a video BIOS that is not VESA compatible. Try running the included UNIVBE driver and then running DeeP again.

Problem: DeeP does not display 256 colors or the colors look funny.

Solution 1: The .INI file has an incorrect statement. Change the line that states VIDEO=0 to VIDEO=2 (the default and see if the problem persists. If it does, the next solution may work.

Solution 2: This problem occurs when the video BIOS is not VESA compatible. Try running the UNIVBE driver and run DeeP again.

Problem: The maps and graphics refresh very slowly.

Solution: There are three common causes:

- If video shadowing has been disabled to run DOOM, the performance of DeeP may suffer. Re-enable video shadowing and check to see if the video speed improves.

- You accidentally slowed down the video. Try pressing the [key while in the map editor to change the speed of the video. The bottom status bar has a number that will change each time the button is pressed. The lower the number, the faster DeeP displays the map. Change this number to 0 and the video speed should increase if it was not 0 before.

- You are not running SmartDrive. Disable the display of pictures, press **I**.

Problem: When I move the mouse around the screen, the map moves too fast.

Solution: On Pentium machines or when making a new level, the video frequently displays too fast. Use the [and] keys while running the map editor to adjust the speed of the video. The bottom status bar displays a number which will change when the button is pressed. The higher the number, the slower the map will display each time it is drawn.

Solutions to other problems are offered in later sections of this episode.

THE DEEP MAIN MENU

DeeP contains online documentation that will help you start it. From the main menu, type **?** and press Enter. This will bring up the help screen that explains what all of the options do. The help can be printed to a printer by pressing the Print button. To scroll down one page, press Continue. To end viewing help at any time, press Escape.

This is a help file, not a manual. It has compressed information, suitable for reference. Although we recommend browsing the help file, each section is dedicated to explaining the functionality of a submenu and may appear disjointed when "read" from end-to-end.

THE DEEP MAP EDITOR (WHERE THE FUN BEGINS)

To run DeeP's map editing utility, type **E** at the DeeP character command prompt (DEEP [?=Help] >) and press Enter. If you are running the shareware version, the introduction screen appears. Press Enter.

The next selection enables you to choose the level to edit. In DOOM and Heretic these are organized into episodes and mission (for example, E1M1) while in DOOM II they are organized into maps (for example, MAP01).

Once you select a level, DeeP displays what the map looks like from an overhead view. The first order of business should be to customize DeeP to suit your needs. Hold down the Alt key and press F5. This brings up a list of options you can customized. All are explained in the online help, which can be accessed by holding down the Alt key and pressing **E**.

In the Edit menu accessed above, refer to the other options for setting the mouse movement speed, click speed, colors and more. Browse through these now, so you get a feel of the possible things you may wish to change. That's the beauty of DeeP, you can personalize it!

Once you have customized DeeP to suit your tastes, you will be ready to edit the level.

COMMANDS IN THE DEEP MAP EDITOR

DeeP's online help is context-sensitive. To view help on a particular subject, use the built-in F1 command. For example, to view the help for the File menu, hold down Alt and press F. Then press F1 and online Help will appear about the File menu.

DEEPBSP

DeePBSP is DeeP's nodebuilder. DeePBSP was derived from Colin Reed's BSP 1.2 and made much faster. It is about four times faster than BSP and builds levels without error.

DeePBSP requires that HIMEM.SYS has been loaded from CONFIG.SYS and is running. If HIMEM.SYS hasn't been loaded, then DeePBSP will not work. Also, make sure that the line `FILES=xx` in CONFIG.SYS has the xx at 20 or higher. DeePBSP may not function if `FILES=` is less than 20.

If you have QEMM, please remove QDPMI.SYS from your CONFIG.SYS. It's usually not required and QEMM installs this if you did a default install. DeePBSP will NOT work if this is present.

DeePBSP operates independently from DeeP. When you save a level, DeeP automatically sends the correct command-line parameter to DeePBSP instructing it to build the level. Note that DeePBSP can be run from DOS by typing `DEEPBSP Input_file Output_file`

The preceding is used normally to test the functioning of DeePBSP on your system.

Please enter the command DEEPBSP by itself to make sure that it works. If you do this from within DeeP, it is difficult to see any error messages, because they go by so fast! The message, filenam.wad not found from DeeP indicates that DeePBSP failed. Other file error messages may occur.

> Do *not* make the input and output files the same. (DeePBSP will not allow this.) Do not name the input or output file-HEEP.WAD or ~DEEP.WAD. Doing so will result in the destruction of your level. Whenever possible, run DeePBSP from within DeeP to avoid any problems.

Do not substitute another node-builder in place of DeePBSP. When building the nodes on a grouped PWAD file or a PWAD with added textures, most other node-builders will destroy the WAD file. In addition, although it is not important now, DeePBSP leaves the REJECT resource alone!

When DeeP prompts you whether or not you wish to clear the REJECT, select Yes.

If you want to have fun, customize how the monsters interact with players. Go into the File menu and select Build Nodes. This will bring up more options when building the Reject. To view the help on this, press F1 while in the File menu.

If DeePBSP fails to run, go to the section entitled "DeePBSP Troubleshooting," later in this room.

DEEPBSP AND WINDOWS

If you plan to run DeePBSP under Windows, please read this section.

DeePBSP requires the files 32RTM.EXE and DPMIVM.OVL to be in the directory where DeePBSP was installed. If these files are in the correct location, then the next step is to edit your SYSTEM.INI file, located in the C:\WINDOWS directory (the directory where Windows is stored).

The following steps detail how to run DeePBSP in Windows.

1. CD\WINDOWS (Change to the WINDOWS directory.)
2. EDIT SYSTEM.INI (Use the DOS Edit program SYSTEM.INI.)
3. Search for the phrase [386Enh] and enter the following lines directly below it:

    ```
    ;Device required to run DeePBSP (Borland DPMI program)
    DEVICE=C:\DOOM2\DEEP\WINDPMI.386
    ```

Change this line to reflect where DeeP is stored. Once this line has been added, DeePBSP can be run under Windows.

DEEPBSP AND QEMM

If you are using QEMM, the driver QDPMI.SYS will cause DeePBSP to crash and give error messages. If you are must use QDPMI.SYS, create a multi-config option (preferred) or a boot disk that has all the settings *except* the line that reads:

```
DEVICE=QDPMI.SYS
```

This line must be deleted or DeePBSP will not run. It is even possible that all of your applications will function without this driver, although I am still not certain of this. The file QHINTS.DOC, included with QEMM, can help you decide if you need this driver loaded. Additional information is currently being sought into this matter and will be posted in a future version of DeeP.

DEEPBSP TROUBLESHOOTING

If DeePBSP builds nodes for a level the first time it is run and then gives an error message, please review the preceding notes, read README.DOC and see more suggestions that follow.

UNIVBE DRIVER

Although DeeP requires that a video board have a VESA BIOS, the included UNIVBE driver can provide VESA support for many boards and enable you to run DeeP.

The UNIVBE driver comes in a .ZIP format. To unzip this file, go to the directory where DeeP is stored and type `PKUNZIP UVBE50BD.ZIP` This unzips the driver into your DeeP directory.

To look at UNIVBE's help file, type `NIVBE /?`. This brings up a list of options that are available to run UNIVBE. Once this driver is loaded, try running DeeP again.

UNIVBE is *not* made by Sensor Based Systems, Inc. It is a product of SciTech Software. If you experience problems with this driver, consult SciTech Software.

OTHER EXECUTION PROBLEMS

If DeeP locks up or quits to DOS for no apparent reason, this section offers some solutions.

Problem: DeeP appears to lock up randomly. The mouse does not work and Ctrl+Alt+Delete will not reboot the machine.

Solution: This problem normally stems from having the DRAM wait state in the BIOS set to a value that is too low. Other common symptoms of this problem include Windows generating "General Protection Faults" and DOOM crashing. Try increasing the wait state of the DRAM by one. If this does not solve the problem then restore the wait state to its original value.

Some systems that have been "tweaked" (the clock speed was increased from the factory default) will be incompatible with DOOM and DeeP. If the system clock speed has been increased, lower it to the original value and run DeeP again. If the problem persists, then restore the original clock speed.

You may also have memory-resident programs that are misbehaving. Use the DOS command MEM /c/p to view what is loaded.

Problem: I have an ATI video card and DeeP locks up my system.

Solution: The ATI board does not appear to be 100 percent VESA compatible. Load the UNIVBE driver to solve this problem.

THE DEEP FAQ

DeeP includes a FAQ (Frequently Asked Questions) list that serves as a quick reference card for users who don't want to spend time sorting through Help. The most commonly asked questions about the mouse and customizing DeeP are answered in this text. The file is called DEEPFAQ.DOC and is located in the DeeP directory. To print this file type DEEPFAQ.DOC > PRN from the DOS prompt. This file should answer most of the basic questions concerning DeeP.

FUTURE RELEASES

DeeP is an expanding product. Every day changes are constantly made to make the interface more user friendly and the Help easier to access. There have been frequent requests for many options, and the following is a list of features that will be seen in the not-so-distant future:

- A clipboard, so items from one WAD can be placed in another.
- More complete DIR viewing box in the editor.
- Addition of more pre-built items, such as rotating stairs and rising stairs.
- DPMI support. This is one of the top priorities, and DPMI support will be available in DeeP 6.3.
- Replaceable graphics.

All of these features will be available in DeeP 6.3, which is planned for Spring 1995.

HOW TO CONTACT ME

If your questions were not answered in the DeeP help files or you have suggestions that would help to improve DeeP, we would like to hear from you.

CompuServe members can send e-mail to Jack Vermeulen, at 75454,773. America Online members can send e-mail to JACKV56036. If you subscribe to Internet services and would like to send us e-mail, use either of the following two addresses:

```
75454.773@compuserve.com
JACKV56036@aol.com
```

THE DEEP TUTORIAL

This tutorial is suitable for beginners who would like to construct their first level. DEU tutorial v1.5 PWADs were used as reference for this tutorial. The file TUTOR.DOC has step-by-step information for those who like the nuts and bolts.

We assume that you have a copy of TUTOR.WAD in your DeeP directory and that DeeP has already been successfully installed.

MAKING YOUR FIRST ORIGINAL LEVEL

This document and the accompanying TUTOR.WAD file should help you to see what you need to do to build a level. This is a hands-on explanation and trying out the different commands is encouraged.

There are two ways to read the file TUTOR.WAD:

- At the character command prompt, type R C:\yourdir\TUTOR.WAD.
- In the graphical Edit mode, select the File menu with the mouse (or Alt+F) and select Read PWAD.

Enter the same name in the box provided.

We recommend setting the Patch directory to yourdir then the path is not required (the .WAD is always optional).

The sample levels just loaded were made for DOOM. It is also compatible with DOOM II with the following changes.

The texture COMPUTE1 does not exist in DOOM II. For MAPs 5 through 12 (inclusive), use the F10 option c to change the texture automatically to DOOM II. (Save any changes F10 makes so you don't have to do it again, see shareware note below).

Everywhere you see episode/mission (EeMm) DOOM references, substitute mission (MAPxx) numbers for DOOM II.

Items appearing in braces {} indicate that there is a sample level available you can edit to follow along and see how to do things. Edit the example level by selecting File from the top menu bar and Edit Level.

Select the editing mode(s) indicated and move the pointer around to touch things and look at how they are structured.

Some adjustments you may wish to make now:

- Screen redraw speed ([and])
- Mouse speed (how fast it moves across the screen)
- Mouse click speed,(determines response times)
- Grid lines/size
- How quickly DeeP will select an object

These and many others are all user definable. You may also wish to turn on auto-start now. Select Alt+**E** and then "Load Options". This option starts DeeP in Edit mode right away. You do not have to enter **E** at the character prompt.

Additional options are available. Please set these to your comfort level. As you get more experience, you may wish to change them again.

You will probably be zooming a lot, so set the Zoom range for **Z** also. You can also use the +/- buttons on the top menu bar to control zooming.

Set the Zoom (scale) size to at least 1000 using the + and – keys. The grid looks bad at less than this (switch to solid lines) and it's hard to make things out.

Be sure to use the [and] keys to slow down your display speed for these tiny levels (the delay is displayed on the bottom bar), otherwise you'll fly all over the place!

DeeP defaults to Snap-to-Grid 8. If you want to see the grid, press **H** or click the top button h. In Edit Options, change the grid to a solid line (default is dashed) depending on your Zoom level and monitor.

The lines you draw are forced to the intersecting lines on the grid when snap-to-grid is active. This is recommended for clean drawing and a better match with the textures.

After you play around, press Escape (or Alt+F4) to quit and say you want really want to quit even though you didn't save it.

Use the **J** command and then enter the number described in the box that pops up. The object centered on the screen is the object selected. Refer to the bottom screen information boxes to see the description, and so on.

Shareware Note

The shareware LITE version has a limit of six external PWAD files you can edit.

Five files if you save, because the save temporarily becomes a sixth file as a backup (if you save twice).

In addition, the shareware will not save a grouped PWAD (that's what TUTOR.WAD is, a collection or "group" of levels), but it will save one level at a time.

Use the -n load option to reset all the files: > DeeP -n or use the reset level menu option under File. If you forget, you will get the message "Limit of 6 files exceeded."

CREATING A NEW LEVEL

To create a new map level, follow these steps:

1. First, start by selecting File (Alt+**F** or use the mouse and left click).

2. Select New Level (you can also press Shift+F3 and do it all).

3. Select level E1M1 (or MAP01).

You are now creating a new map and the screen is blank!

Select Vertex edit mode (press **V**). Now press Ins. (You can also quickly double-left mouse click instead of pressing Ins.) The top of the screen displays a help line. This help line means you are in create mode. Position the cursor where you want to start drawing a line. Next, press the left mouse button.

A blue square is placed where you have started creating a vertex. (You can change the color in Edit/ Options)

Move to the right some distance and press the left mouse again. You have just created a linedef!

You will need a minimum of three lines (linedefs) to create an enclosed area (called a polygon).

Move the mouse some more and press the left mouse button again. Form a square or any type of room you want, just keep clicking.

The last linedef connecting (or closing) the polygon is made by pressing the right mouse button.

HOW TO CONNECT AREAS

Move vertices on top of existing vertexes to connect areas. Experiment with the different ways you can connect lines. We will describe one method here.

You are still in Insert Mode, aren't you? Look at the top menu line to be sure. Keep clicking the left mouse button and repeatedly make more nice areas, as many sides as you want for now. We are not trying to make anything special here, just get the hang of how clicking and creating works.

To restart at any time, repeat the instructions we started with the preceding step 1.

CONNECT TWO AREAS

Start with a rectangle that you created previously. Move the cursor on top of one of the existing vertices and left click. Move away from it and then loop back in a clockwise direction to make a second area. This connects automatically to the first area.

Each time you finish an area, a sector is also created (the default one). The left square is Sector 0 (numbers start at 0) and the second one is Sector 1.

You can go back later in Sector mode (press **S**) and edit the height and textures of the floor and ceiling. Similarly, for the lines we drew (linedefs), enter Linedef mode (press **L**) and edit the wall textures.

We will do this soon.

We call a *room* an area that has only one side and you never see the other side. An *object* is something you draw that is placed inside a *room*. It may be viewed from one or two sides.

For rooms, move in a clockwise direction, for objects in rooms normally move counter-clockwise.

To quit creating, press the right mouse button again (just after you made your last area) and now you are back in basic Edit command mode.

SOME CLEANUP STUFF

If you don't like the size, shape or location of what you drew, use the Drag feature to fix it!

To move anything in DeeP, select the object to move and press the right mouse button. When you move the cursor, the object follows the cursor like a well-trained puppy.

To move only one object at a time, move the cursor on top of the object (it lights up), press the right mouse button and move. The object will move with you.

To move many objects at the same time, move the cursor on top of each object to move and left click. The color changes. Now click the right mouse button and they *all* move.

To clear the selections, press **C**.

Each editing mode moves a different set of objects. In vertex mode (where we drew the lines just now), you can move a point at a time or many at once.

Experiment with each mode to see which one is appropriate for what you had in mind.

If you don't like something, press the Delete key. Be careful if you are deleting vertices, lines or sectors. It is best not to do deletions yet. When you delete, you usually create "holes" in a structure (unless you go rid of it all). This has to be "fixed" to follow the rules. When starting out, it is not obvious how to make it all work, so for now is discouraged.

Always run the check (F10, option B) to make sure that you have made no mistakes.

4 EPISODE   **1** MISSION   **7** ROOM   **DOOM PROGRAMMING GURUS**

MORE "MOVING STUFF AROUND"

You can "soft" select by clicking the right button when the object to move lights up or you can select a whole bunch of them by left clicking each object and then doing a mass move.

Be sure to keep the cursor on one of the "active" objects, otherwise it will switch to your new one and discard (clear) all your selections.

The latter is a handy feature, but it can be puzzling in the beginning.

If you press the left button down for over 0.25 of a second (or whatever you set the mouse speed to), a select box is created with the origin at the cursor location. Move the box to enclose all objects you want to select. All editing can do done to all the objects selected (they will all light up).

TEXTURE AND LINEDEF CHANGES

If you have any lines that are shared by two sectors (that's the two areas we drew above) and they are at a place where you cross from room to room set the flags to Two-Sided and turn off the Impassable flag.

Press **L** to enter linedef edit mode and then press Enter or right click to edit the line. The line created previously when we joined automatically was made this way. Check it out!

If you joined them while making it all, it should be OK, but just in case you want to know how to fix it afterwards, this is how.

You will probably want to get rid of any of the Normal/Upper/Lower Textures that are on lines that you walk across. This is done by entering a texture of -, which means nothing. If want to create the illusion of walking through a wall, leave a texture in place! Remember, the linedef attribute of Impassable controls whether you can "walk through" a wall, not the texture.

EXAMINING SOME OF THE LEVELS IN TUTOR.WAD

Check out linedef #1 in E2M2 (MAP03). (Press **L** to enter linedef editing mode.) To change the way the walls look, select a line or a group of lines and change the normal texture on some of the sidedefs.

Take a look at linedefs #0,2, and 3 in E2M3 (MAP05). To change just the texture and nothing else, select the linedef to change by moving the cursor to the line. When it lights up, press the shift key (to keep the linedef "locked") and click the left mouse button over the linedef texture displayed on the bottom that you want to change. The shift key temporarily keeps DeeP from following the cursor movement and selecting a different linedef. You can make it always not follow by pressing the **A** key and turning auto-select on/off. Look at the bottom of the screen when you do this and view the box with Delay.

You can also press the right mouse button on top of the active linedef and go into complete linedef edit mode or press Enter. Now you can change all the options listed.

Press the right mouse button to exit any of the menus. You can also press Escape or move the left/ right arrow keys. The latter doesn't work when data has to be entered by you.

CHANGE THE FLOOR AND CEILING TEXTURES IN A SECTOR

To go to Sector editing mode, press **S**.

Look at Sector #1 in E2M4 (MAP06) and compare it to the default in Sector 0. The same editing options explained for linedefs apply for Sectors. You can change the Floor or Ceiling look by clicking the bottom picture.

ADD A PLAYER1 START THING

Press **T** to go to Thing editing mode.

Press Ins and a Thing object is added at the current cursor spot. Each time Ins is pressed, another Thing is created. You can also double-click the left mouse button.

If you press **T** again when in Thing mode, a picture of the Thing is displayed. Pressing **T** again reverts back to the circle with the direction arrow. You can change the background color (from dark gray) in the Edit submenu selection for colors.

For cooperative play you need to add Player2, Player3 and Player4 start Things. If you want to play in Deathmatch mode you must have a MINIMUM of four Deathmatch start Things.

Examine E2M5 (MAP07). That's where you start and the direction you're facing. The same editing options explained for linedefs apply for Things. You can directly change the direction of things, by selecting a Thing and pressing the < or > keys.

CHANGE THE LINEDEF TYPE OF ONE OF THE LINES

You need an exit to leave the level. There are other choices, but "Special—Ends level goes to next level." is the easiest for now. Look at E2M6 (MAP08) and examine Line 5. The texture was changed to one of the SW1*xxxx* textures so it looks like a switch, too. If you wanted a "secret" switch you would use a plain texture, so choose anything special here. Edit the linedef (as explained earlier) and change the normal texture to see what the texture looks like.

Press F2 to save your changes. Answer **Y** to the question about building the nodes, and so on. (Be sure you read README.DOC about testing your system for compatibility with DeePBSP.) If you have the shareware version, press Alt+F4 to quit DeeP. Otherwise, under File, select the test level option and off you go (next step is automatic). Fire up DOOM and try it out!

Type in c:\DOOM>DOOM -FILE *yourfile*.WAD -warp e m

If you have already started doom and forgot the add the -warp on the command line and you are working on a level higher than E1M1 you can go straight there by typing IDCLEV*em* (after you start the level) where *e* is the episode and *m* is the mission number.

MORE ADVENTURES

Now that we have a level, we can fill it with details to make it appear more interesting and real. We will show one possible way to construct some special Sectors, such as doors, stairs, and lifts.

Please note that there are other ways to do them because there are many different types of doors and lifts, and so on. Also, you're a little more experienced at making vertices, lines and Sectors already so we are not going to have as many WAD files to demonstrate the structures, just one or two to show each structure.

In the following examples, the changes made are discussed as a, b, and so on, describing the objects that were added and changed.

Use the **J** command to jump to the object number described. Press J and then enter the number in the box that pops up. Toggle the information boxes displayed on the bottom by pressing the **I** key. This will speed up the display as required for some systems, since it takes a bit to show each linedef texture.

ADDING A DOOR PRECISELY

This is a very easy way to make doors (see TUTOR.DOC for a more detailed method).

You may want to add some more vertices and lines to build a sector on the other side of the door so you've got somewhere to go once the door is open. View E2M7 (MAP09). There's no door here yet, practice making one using the following guide:

We're going to assume you have a hallway already and want to put a door in it.

Snap-to-Grid normally helps place the vertex on top of a linedef. However, if the linedef runs at a slant, it may be easier to turn snap-to-grid off (/) so you can place it wherever you want.

Enter Vertex mode (press **V**), press Ins, and then do as follows:

1. Place your first vertex right on top of L1 where you want the door by pressing the left mouse button. Move over to the right (width of door) and left click again to place the second vertex. Press the Ins key to finish. This prevents a 2-sided linedef from being created and must be done.

2. Place your third vertex right on top of L2 where you want the door by pressing the left mouse button. Move over to the right (width of door) and left-click again to place the fourth Vertex. Press the Ins key to finish.

3. Place your cursor right on top of the vertex 3 and press the left mouse button.

   a. Move on top of vertex 2, left click.

   b. Move on top of vertex 1, left click.

   c. Move on top of vertex 4, left click.

   d. Move on top of vertex 3, left click.

   Press the Ins key to finish. Do *not* right click!

4. Press the right mouse button (or Ins) again to exit Vertex Create mode.

5. Go into Linedef mode and select the four linedefs a, b, c, and d (left mouse click them one at a time).

6. Select Misc, Create Door from four linedefs and press Enter for the selection.

ADDING A DOOR PREDEFINED OBJECT

This is easier than the method described previously, because you do not have to understand as much. It could be more work in the end, since you have to move it around more.

1. Press Alt+O or F9 and select Door.

2. Enter the width and height (length) of the Door and DeeP automatically inserts the vertices, linedefs and sidedefs, and the sector at the current pointer location. Everything is made for a door.

3. Drag the door over where you want it. Rotate it as required (using the < or > keys) or drag the vertices. The easiest way to connect it to a hallway is to select the door ends and drag them on top of the hallway linedef one at a time.

4. If everything is aligned on the grid then Snap-to-Grid helps you. If not, turn snap off.

5. Fix any missing textures as appropriate. This displays on the bottom panels as "missing".

Look at E2M8 (MAP10). Does you door looks like this? Don't worry about the different textures, etc. That's all up to you.

THE STAIRWAY TO THE SKY OR DUNGEON

You can build automatic stairs, in two easy ways. Refer to the TUTOR.DOC for a step-by-step sequence.

24 DOOM units is the maximum for a stair you can climb. You can make it as small as 1.

Increment for stairs going up, decrement for stairs going down.

1. Make stair from two selected linedefs.

2. Select two linedefs that will be come the stair sides. Then press Alt+I or F8 and select Make Stairs from two linedefs.

3. Supply the step height and number of steps.

The linedefs, ceiling height, textures, and so on will be modified accordingly.

The word *bottom* indicates the bottom of the stair by default. Reply **Y** to the next prompt to make the bottom the *top*.

Enter a negative value to make the stairs go down. This is similar to reversing the stair direction, but the steps are created for going down instead of up.

You are need to check that the stair did not overlay some existing area. Sometimes you may need to fix the final sector, if the steps end up overlaying an existing linedef.

The *top* of the stair changes the floor height of the old sector. So anything that that connects to the old sector should be raised to match the new floor. Make the stairs first to avoid extra work.

MAKE STAIRS IN THE MIDDLE OF A ROOM

Press Alt+O or F9 and select Stairs. This makes a stand-alone stair that you can place in the middle of a room or extend out from a room.

Both types of stairs are initially created inside a sector. The bottom step connects to this sector for reference. You need to complete the top step by connecting it the sector desired as follows:

1. Switch to Vertex mode and place the last two vertexes on the target linedef and reply Yes to the split linedef message. You can also do this by dragging the stair on top of the linedef you want it to connect to.

2. Finish by changing the linedef just created by the split-linedef to point to the sector of the last stair step (sector reference).

Be sure to move a room stair out of the sector.

NEED A LIFT?

A lift gives the appearance of an elevator. Go into Sector edit mode (press B) and select a sector to make into a lift. Now press Alt+I or F8 and select Make a Lift. Done! Look at the lifts in E3M1 (MAP12).

TELEPORT PAD

(For the next few examples you will want to also try out the WADs to see how they look in DOOM)

Press Alt+O or F9 and select make a Rectangle object. Place the cursor where you want to create the teleport. Make the object a pedestal type that is 64 x 64. To make a teleport pad, follow these steps:

1. Open E3M2 (MAP13).

2. Edit the line type and change it to 97: WR (Transport to other Sector) by going to line type, then special; or change it to 39: W1 if you want it to work only once.

3. Set the sector tag number of the lines to an unused number.

4. Next, you'll need to decide where you want to transport. Select a sector and set the linedef tag to the same as above.

5. Lastly, add a transporter exit Thing somewhere in the destination sector. Go to edit Thing mode (press **T**) press Enter (or click Change Type), select Player Start/Teleport and then Teleport Landing.

This is where you will appear when teleporting from the linedef to the sector.

MORE FINISHING TOUCHES

Examine E3M3 (MAP14). It should appear similar to the previous section but with textures aligned. Now you know the reason for that weird texture.

WHAT IS TEXTURE ALIGNMENT?

Textures have patterns. The patterns start and stop for each linedef. On some patterns, you can see a visible mismatch where two walls meet.

The alignment feature of DeeP does X and Y alignment automatically. However, DeeP does not "see" the texture and you may have to compensate for the visual effect desired.

Stairs and windows are common areas where your talents come into play. The following levels have some simple samples.

Read TUTOR.DOC for a detailed explanation of "what and why" you do either. Most of the time you do not need to do this, but it depends on how fussy you are.

SUMMARY

You'll find DeeP and HeeP to be a powerful DOOM, DOOM II, and Heretic editor family. In addition to the steps you've worked through to create your special levels, you'll find experience to be the most important learning tool. Also, you should check out the following test areas which demonstrate important points:

E1M1 (MAP01)	A test WAD that needs a LOT of alignment work!
E1M2 (MAP02)	An aligned version of E1M1 (MAP01)
E3M4 (MAP15)	A different version of E1M1 (MAP01) but using a different alignment method with "unpegged" settings.

EPISODE 4

THE TOOLS OF THE GODS

MISSION 2: HACKING THE DOOM CODE

ROOM 1

By Gregory A.
Lewis

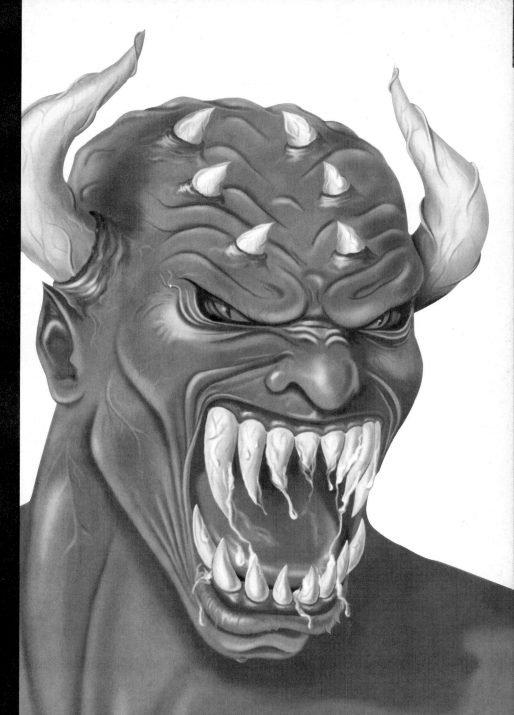

DEHACKED

DeHackEd (pronounced dee'-hak-ed), the DOOM.EXE Hack Editor, is a utility written to edit the Doom.executable file to produce results that cannot be obtained any other way. It enables you to change such things as enemy hit points, the monsters' speed, and graphics by changing a few specific values in the EXE file. It also enables you to alter your weapons and ammo to do extreme amounts of damage in mere seconds. You can change any text in DOOM to personalize it to your liking, or modify a monster's behavior in strange ways with the Frame editor. Although some improvements remain on the "wish list" of things that could be done, many new creations are now possible that could never be accomplished by editing the WAD files alone.

BACKGROUND

The first spark of an idea for DeHackEd came soon after the "DOOM.EXE Hack Specs," written by Matt Fell, were released to the Internet. The "DOOM.EXE Hack Specs" (which are now merged with the "Unofficial DOOM Specs") revealed and explained some parts of the data section of the DOOM.EXE file. (The file is available on the `ftp.cdrom.com`, in `/pub/idgames/docs/editing`, with a filename of DMSPEC16.ZIP.) Using information gained from that document, the first version of DeHackEd was born, which was the first easy way to edit some of the newly found information. Subsequent versions added new editing capabilities and other major improvements, such as the creation of a file format to store the edited information in. Lengthy modifications before the release of DOOM 1.666 changed DeHackEd's cryptic, unfriendly interface into the more useable interface found in DeHackEd v2.0. Two minor revisions later, DeHackEd now includes full editing for seven major portions of the EXE data, works with all versions of DOOM from 1.2 through 1.7a, and includes mouse support.

To best use DeHackEd, it's important to learn a little about how it works its magic. DOS executable files such as DOOM.EXE consist of several different parts that all work together to create the program that you see when you run them. Without getting too technical, the DOOM.EXE file consists of three main sections: the DOS extender, the code section, and the data section. The DOS extender is a program added to the beginning of the DOOM.EXE file that makes use of more advanced 32-bit instructions in order to manage memory quickly for DOOM. The code section is the heart and brains behind DOOM and controls everything that is displayed onscreen. The data section is the section that DeHackEd modifies to create all the cool effects. This section contains many pieces of data, in no particular order, which the code section uses when it needs information. The parts that have the most impact on the actual playing of the game are the Thing table, the Frame table, and the Text section. (These sections and others are covered in more detail later in this room.) DeHackEd edits a total of seven parts of the data section, although the DOOM.EXE file contains much more information than that. Data on miscellaneous DOOM details, such as the placement of menus, the cheat codes, and some precalculated math tables, can also be found in the EXE, although DeHackEd does not modify that data.

PATCH FILES

Modification of the DOOM.EXE would not be as much fun if the changes could not be saved and used again at a later date. DeHackEd can save the changes that are made to the DOOM.EXE file to *patch* files, which contain the information from the DOOM.EXE that DeHackEd edits. Patch files, which normally have the extension .DEH on them, are entirely different from WAD files. WAD files (especially the DOOM.WAD file) contain the sounds, graphics, and level information that you see when you play DOOM and are used easily with the `-file` parameter. Modifications to the EXE are not nearly as easy to carry out. DeHackEd is, as of this writing, the only program that can load a patch file into the DOOM.EXE file.

Patch files contain all the information that is in the sections of the EXE file that DeHackEd edits. Older types of patches, which are still fairly prevalent, contain information on only three of the seven parts. DeHackEd converts those older patches on the fly when they are loaded. Conversions normally should not present a problem; however, if the patch does some unusual modifications, there may be difficulties. The new format of patch files is compatible between all versions from DOOM v1.666 through DOOM II v1.7a, except for DOOM II v1.666. Because the DOOM II v1.666 EXE is different in the Text section, that section cannot be transferred to other versions. The most important sections—Things, Frames, and Weapons— transfer fine between all the versions.

GETTING STARTED

DeHackEd does not require much computer hardware to run. If your computer can handle DOOM, it can run DeHackEd. DeHackEd must locate the main WAD file for either DOOM II or registered DOOM to run; it will not work with the shareware version of DOOM. A mouse is optional, since all commands can be entered as easily with the keyboard. A Sound Blaster-compatible sound card is also optional for those who wish to hear the various sounds in DOOM.

THE DEHACKED.INI FILE

DeHackEd comes with an INI file that enables you to customize your copy of DeHackEd for your personal use. It is recommended to create a separate directory for DeHackEd and place all of the necessary files in that directory, in order to keep your main DOOM directory less cluttered. As long as the DEHACKED.INI file is in the same directory as your main DEHACKED.EXE file, it will read the defaults from that file. You can then place the files wherever you'd like.

The INI file consists of a series of variables that can be set to different values. Any lines that begin with the pound sign (#) are comment lines that are ignored when the file is processed. Be sure to keep a space on both sides of the equal signs for the values, or DeHackEd will not read the values correctly.

The doomexe and doomwad parameters tell DeHackEd where it should look for the main DOOM files on your computer. You may want to make a copy of your DOOM.EXE file (calling it something like DOOMOLD.EXE) and then refer to that file in the DEHACKED.INI file. That way, there will always be a clean copy of the DOOM.EXE file to use under its normal name, and yet you can still edit a copy to your heart's desire. The DOOM.WAD file reference must also be correct or DeHackEd will not run. The WAD file is used for two reasons: to make sure that you are using a registered or commercial version of DOOM, and to play or show the Sounds and Frames when required.

Two additional parameters, doompath and doomargs, determine how DOOM is run from within DeHackEd. The doompath determines which directory DeHackEd runs DOOM from when DeHackEd is not in your main DOOM directory. The doomargs line controls which parameters are passed to DOOM when it's run from within DeHackEd. If, for example, you are working on creating a custom WAD file and a patch to go along with it, you can specify

```
doomargs = -file newlevel.wad
```

and DOOM will automatically load the new level when you run it inside DeHackEd.

The patchdir variable lets you specify where you want your patch files to be kept. This directory is used every time you load or save a patch file in DeHackEd. If this is not present, the current directory is used.

Three options enable you to specify the configuration of your Sound Blaster sound card. sbaddr is the address for the sound card, sbirq is the IRQ that the sound card uses, and sbdma is the DMA channel for the card. Specify a value of -1 for the sbdma to have DeHackEd attempt to auto-detect your DMA channel. These options default to an address of 220, an IRQ of 7, and auto-detection of DMA.

The remainder of the options in the DEHACKED.INI file are entirely optional and will need to be modified only in unusual circumstances. You *must* set the doomver variable if you specify any of the following optional arguments. Valid values for doomver are 0 for DOOM 1.2, 2 for DOOM II v1.666, and 1 for every other version (DOOM v1.666, DOOM II v1.7, and DOOM II v1.7a). The doomsize is just what it appears to be, the size (in bytes) of the DOOM.EXE file you're editing. It can be changed to prevent any error messages that occur if you have a DOOM.EXE file with a strange size. And finally, the thingoff, soundoff, frameoff, spriteoff, ammooff, weaponoff, and textoff are offsets in the DOOM.EXE file where the information can be found. Values are given in decimals from the beginning of the file. *Play with these at your own risk.* (If they are changed incorrectly, DeHackEd will almost certainly crash. Incorrect changes also could corrupt the EXE file.)

MAKING A BACKUP PATCH FILE

The first thing you should do before using DeHackEd is save a backup patch file containing the information in your clean, unmodified EXE file. This will be a file that you can turn to at a later time when you want a clean copy of your DOOM.EXE. DeHackEd will also need to access this file whenever you merge patch files together. (Merging is explained later in the section called "More About Patch Files.") After making sure the DEHACKED.INI file is configured the way you want, you can save a backup patch file with the following command:

```
dehacked -save filename
```

where `filename` is a name from the following list:

```
NORMAL12.DEH For Doom 1 v1.2
NORMAL16.DEH For Doom 1 v1.666
NORMAL20.DEH For Doom 2 v1.666
NORMAL17.DEH For Doom 2 v1.7
NORML17A.DEH For Doom 2 v1.7a
```

You can save the backup files under whatever name you wish, but when DeHackEd attempts to merge a patch file, it will look for a file with a name from the preceding list for a given version of DOOM. It is also a very wise idea to save one backup for each version of DOOM if you have more than one that you plan to edit.

Even making a backup patch file is not a 100-percent guarantee that you can return your DOOM.EXE file to its original state. The updates that id Software releases to upgrade DOOM from one version to another also check the date/time of the DOOM.EXE, which will not be correct even if you load the backup patch. Always make sure to keep a copy of your DOOM.EXE file zipped up safely, so that it can be unzipped whenever you need an original copy of the EXE file.

USING DEHACKED

By now, you should have DeHackEd set up to your liking, so that it can find all the components that it needs in order to work correctly. It's time to start the program now and dive into the editing part

DOOM PROGRAMMING GURUS

1
ROOM

2
MISSION

4
EPISODE

of the program. Change to the directory that you have DeHackEd stored in (if you haven't already), and start the program by typing

`dehacked`

by itself at the prompt. A few lines will appear briefly as DeHackEd locates the files it needs. If the files cannot be found, a message will appear showing you what the problem is. If the DOOM.EXE or DOOM.WAD files can't be found, check your DEHACKED.INI file and change the settings for your `doomexe` and `doomwad` variables.

After finding the proper files, DeHackEd will switch to a 50-line VGA screen and bring up the main Thing editing screen. An introductory status box will show up first, displaying the credits for DeHackEd in the top box and a small status summary in the bottom box. If you are ever uncertain about where the patch files are being saved or which DOOM version you are editing (if you have more than one), you can easily return to the About window by pressing the **A** key or clicking the program's name on the bottom line of the screen.

BASIC NAVIGATION

Pressing a key or clicking the mouse button removes the About box, leaving you at the editing screen to begin work. Every editing screen has at least one editing window (the Thing screen has five different windows itself) and a line at the top and bottom of the screen to aid in mouse navigation. Almost every part of the screen is clickable, meaning you can do everything with the mouse that you can do with the keyboard, and usually it's quicker. The best way to learn what each part does is by simply clicking to find out.

A navigation bar at the top of the screen provides an easy way to move from one editing screen to another. The function keys F2 through F8 are the keyboard shortcuts to switch screens. Alternately, you can click the word or function key and move to the screen instantly.

The bar at the bottom of the screen serves a similar purpose. It is a reminder of the keys for keyboard users and a shortcut bar for mouse users. Clicking F1 Help will bring up the Help page to explain what the various keys will do. Clicking Esc Exit or pressing the Escape key will exit the program (and ask if you want to quit if you have unsaved changes).

A FEW TERMS

A brief explanation of a few terms is in order to make it easier to explain the workings of DeHackEd. When referring to these terms, I will continue to capitalize the first letter when I'm referring to the object in the specific context of DeHackEd to differentiate any general sound from a specific Sound entry in DeHackEd. A *Thing* in DOOM is any object that's in the game, such as the monsters, the player, the health items or weapons, and decorations such as bodies and lamps. A *Frame* is one specific picture in DOOM and a few pieces of information associated with it. For example, the picture of a Baron of Hell with his arm back, ready to throw a fireball, is one Frame. A *Sprite* is a group of Frames that belong to one Thing and is usually referred to by a four-letter name in capital letters. For example, all of the pictures dealing with the Baron are, collectively, the BOSS Sprite. A *Weapon* is a particular weapon of the Marine, along with information on the ammunition that weapon uses. And finally, a *Sound* is one sound that a Thing makes, such as a Baron's roar when it's killed.

DEHACKED COMMANDS

Actual editing with DeHackEd isn't all that difficult; it's only a matter of selecting the correct fields and typing in the new values that you want. To make the best use of the program, though, it's best to know some shortcuts that make editing a lot faster and easier. If you ever forget what key performs some action while editing, press the F1 key for a key summary. The key actions are also summarized in Table 1.1.

Table 1.1. A summary of available keys.

Key	Action
Escape	Exits to DOS, and leaves input boxes and Help screens.
Enter	Edits the current field.
Space	Views or play the current field (when applicable).
C	Copies data from one object to another.
D	Changes to the Decimal number system.
G	Goes to a specific Thing through an alphabetical list of Thing names.
H	Changes to the Hexadecimal number system.
J	Jumps to the information in the current field, in its respective editor.
L	Loads a patch file and replaces all information with the data from the file.
M	Merges a new patch file with the information already in DOOM.
R	Runs DOOM from within DeHackEd.
S	Saves a patch file to a specified filename.

continues

Table 1.1. continued

Key	Action
U	Undoes all changes and return to the most recent Writes to the DOOM.EXE file
W	Writes all changes to the DOOM.EXE file.
F2	Switches to the Thing editor.
F3	Changes to the Frame editor.
F4	Brings up the Ammo/Weapon editor.
F5	Goes to the Sound editor.
F6	Changes to the Sprite editor.
F7	Switches to the Text editor.
F8	Brings up the Thing List (a quick-reference list for the Things).

HOW TO GET AROUND

The standard arrow keys on the keyboard navigate around the editing screens. When editing one of the lists of information, the right and left arrow keys move between columns, and the up, down, page-up, page-down, home, and end keys move between the various objects. On the Thing and Weapon editing screens, the up and down keys move between the various fields, so the page-up, page-down, home, and end keys are used to change the Weapon or Thing that you are editing.

A quick way to move to a different Thing is via the Go-To window. Pressing the **G** key brings up a list of all the Thing names in alphabetical order. Select the name that you want to see (using the arrow keys), press enter, and that Thing becomes the active Thing. Mouse users can also bring up the Go-To window by clicking "Thing Name" or the name itself in the upper left window on the Thing editing screen.

Another method of navigation that becomes useful when you start understanding the relationship between all the various data that DeHackEd edits is by using the **J** key to jump from one piece of information to another. If the field that is currently highlighted refers to a different table, pressing the **J** key will change to the referenced editing screen and highlight whichever piece of information was shown. For example, if the "Far Attack Frame" of a Thing is 285 and you press the **J** key, DeHackEd will switch to the Frame editor with Frame number 285 highlighted. It saves time because you don't need to go searching for that specific Frame to edit it.

Once you have the correct field highlighted, editing it isn't difficult. Press Enter to bring up a small box in which you type the new value. If it turns out you didn't want to select that field after all, Escape exits the input box without making changes. Left-clicking a field with the mouse will bring up the same input box, and a right-button click will leave the box if you change your mind about editing it.

Pressing the Escape key or clicking the right mouse button always leaves input boxes, Help screens, or even the frame viewer. They are identical, except that a right click will not exit DeHackEd, whereas hitting the Escape key will. Mouse users need to click the "Esc Exit" text on the right side of the bottom line of the screen to exit (to prevent errant right mouse clicks from exiting accidently).

OTHER BASIC COMMANDS

Some people may prefer to work in a hexadecimal numbering system rather than the standard decimal system. DeHackEd can display all of the data in hex format if you wish with a press of the **H** key. Switch back to decimal notation by pressing the **D** key. Mouse users can toggle back and forth by clicking the "Base" line in the box in the upper left corner of the screen.

A copy command is available to help with major editing jobs. Press the **C** key and two input boxes will pop up, asking which object (Thing, Frame, and so on) you wish to copy from and which you wish to copy to. A clipboard is available as Thing #138 (or Thing #104 if you are editing the DOOM 1.2 EXE) for use when copying Things. The clipboard isn't stored in the EXE and is just available for temporary storage when copying Things from one to another (if you want to use it). When copying the information from one Thing to another, the Thing name and number will *not* change. Those pieces of information are present to make it easier to edit the data and aren't really stored in the EXE. Text strings cannot be copied due to the stringent length restrictions on the strings. (See the section on the Text editor for more information on Text strings.)

After editing whatever material you are interested in changing, there is one last step before you can take DOOM for a test run. You will need to update the changes in the DOOM.EXE file with the changes stored in DeHackEd. This is done by hitting the **W** key to write the changes. If you attempt to exit without writing the changes, a box will appear to confirm whether you really want to quit without saving the changes.

Sometimes when editing, you will want to discard the changes that you've made and return to the data that's stored in the EXE file. Use the **U** key to undo the editing that has been done so far in an editing session, back to the most recent **W**rite of the DOOM.EXE file.

It's always fun to quickly give DOOM a test run as you are editing to see how the changes you've made will affect DOOM. Although you can certainly leave DeHackEd and run DOOM from DOS, it's easier to use the run function that's built into DeHackEd. Simply press the **R** key to run DOOM.

DeHackEd will switch to the DOOM directory, as specified in the DEHACKED.INI file, and run DOOM with any parameters that you provided in the INI file. (For more information on the INI file, see the previous section entitled, "Getting Started.") Remember to **W**rite the changes to the EXE before you try running it, or the results might not show up correctly. Note: Running DOOM inside DeHackEd might be a bit "iffy" if you are low on conventional memory.

SEEING WHAT YOU'VE GOT

When working with the pictures and sounds, it is a good idea to be able to see and hear the data rather than just go by the cryptic names that are found in the EXE. After all, who would know off-hand exactly which sound "dbopn" is? (It's the sound used for the reloading of the combat shotgun.) DeHackEd provides easy playing and viewing capabilities at the press of the spacebar (or a left click of the mouse on the name you wish to see or hear, such as dbopn). If you highlight any Sound or Frame in the Thing or Weapon editors and press the spacebar, you will see or hear the selected object. In the Frame and Sound editors, the current Frame or Sound will be played when the spacebar is hit. Note: If the Next Frame is highlighted in the Frame editor, the *next* frame will be played—not the current one. The spacebar also displays the full text of strings in the Text editor. Some strings are longer than one line in the list of text and can only be seen entirely by pressing the spacebar.

Some frames are only one of a series of frames that DOOM displays, such as the soul sphere. When frames such as these are displayed, pressing the spacebar (or left-clicking) will cycle through the frames in the order they are processed. Pressing Escape exits the Frame viewer. The Frame viewer closes automatically if the last Frame in a series (such as a Trooper's death sequence) is played.

As of this writing, the sound-playing capabilities are not functioning 100-percent correctly in DeHackEd. The first sound will play normally, but any sounds after the first one are stored in a buffer and played in a continuous stream after a certain point. This may be corrected in a future version of DeHackEd.

MORE ABOUT PATCH FILES

And last, but not least, DeHackEd can take the information in your EXE file and save it to a patch file for easy distribution. Press the **S** key to bring up a box that asks for the filename for the patch file. Files are stored in the patch directory that you specified in the INI file. Entering a specific path along with the filename will override the patch directory and store it in the one you type. If another file of the same name already exists, you will be given the option of overwriting it or aborting the save. Using the **S**ave option from within DeHackEd is equivalent to using the line

```
dehacked -save patchname
```

from the command line. (See "Command Line Parameters" for more information.) Also, when editing the 1.2 version of the DOOM.EXE, the saved patch file will be an older format to make it backward-compatible with older versions of DeHackEd (previous to 2.0).

Loading a patch file is very similar to saving one. The **L** key will load a patch file into DeHackEd. Type in the name of the patch that you want to load, and DeHackEd will check your patch directory to see if it can find the file. Type in the full path and filename if the patch file is located somewhere other than the patch directory. Keep in mind when loading files that you will still need to **W**rite the changes before exiting in order to make them permanent. The **L**oad command by itself merely brings the information into DeHackEd's memory. Older patch files (from DeHackEd v1.3 and older) will be converted into the newer formats on the fly. Using the **L**oad command inside DeHackEd is equivalent to entering

```
dehacked -load patchname
```

on the command line (see "Command Line Parameters" for more information), with the exception that the **W**rite command must be used afterward in DeHackEd.

Sometimes loading a patch won't always be the best way to add the patch's information into DOOM. For instance, if you already have a patch installed that changes the Troopers into missile-shooting maniacs, and you want to load the super-weapons patch too, loading the patch won't work correctly. It would give you the super-weapons, but in the process it would overwrite the new Trooper information. The way to overcome this problem is by using the **M**erge operation in DeHackEd. Pressing **M** brings up an input box similar to that used for loading a file. Type in a filename and DeHackEd will attempt to merge the old file with the information already in DOOM. To aid in the merging, DeHackEd looks for the backup patch file (see "Making a Backup Patch File," earlier in this room, for more information), and the merge will abort if the correct backup patch isn't found. After finding the backup patch, the information that's being loaded is compared with the backup patch to decide what information has been changed and what information is the same. The changed data is loaded into DeHackEd, while data that's the same remains unchanged. This way, in our previous example, the Trooper information would not be overwritten when the super-weapons patch is merged over it since the super-weapons patch does nothing to the Trooper information.

COMMAND LINE PARAMETERS

DeHackEd was designed to make it simple to use in batch files. The full command line syntax is the following:

```
dehacked [doompath] [-load patch1 patch2 . . .] [-save patch]
```

DOOM PROGRAMMING GURUS 1 ROOM 2 MISSION 4 EPISODE

The [*doompath*] is optional. If you run DeHackEd in a different directory from the one DOOM is in, you can give the path to your DOOM directory here. This value will override any path and name specified in your DEHACKED.INI file.

The `-load` *patch1* *patch2* . . . option will update the DOOM.EXE file with the patches called *patch1*, *patch2*, and so forth and return to the DOS prompt. The first patch is loaded normally (equivalent to typing a **L**oad command in DeHackEd), and all other patches listed after it (if there are any) are merged with the first one. The patch directory given in the INI is the directory where DeHackEd checks for the files unless you specify an explicit path along with the filenames.

Conversely, the `-save` *patch* option will save the current DOOM.EXE status to a patch file named *patch* and return to the DOS prompt. This is identical to typing **S**ave in DeHackEd and entering the filename.

An example command line:

```
dehacked c:\games\doom -load suprwep6.deh army1.deh
```

This will start DeHackEd, using the DOOM.EXE (or DOOM2.EXE) file found in C:\GAMES\DOOM, and load in the information from the SUPRWEP6.DEH patch file. Then it will merge in the patch file ARMY1.DEH and return to the DOS prompt.

THE THING EDITOR

The first screen you see when you start DeHackEd is the Thing editing screen, shown in Figure 1.1. It is a main area of the program, used to create many of the special DeHackEd effects. On this editing screen, general Thing characteristics such as hit points, height, and width are displayed, along with special toggles for such Things as invisibility or the ability to walk through walls.

Note that DOOM uses the Player entry a little differently than the other Thing entries. Fields such as Speed and Hit Points are NOT changeable through DeHackEd; they are controlled elsewhere in the EXE and aren't easily accessible. Most of the rest of the Player entries can be changed like any other Thing.

Table 1.2 contains information on all the fields that can be edited on the Thing screen. Things have, by far, the most information concerning them, with a total of 23 different pieces of information (detailed in the next section). One of those 23 fields, the Bits field, has information for another 30 or so attributes (as described in the section "The Lowdown on Bits"). Many interesting effects are possible by editing all this information.

Figure 1.1.
The main Thing editing screen.

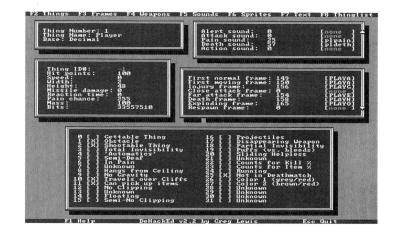

Table 1.2. Fields on the Thing editing screen.

Field Name	Description
Thing Number	The (somewhat arbitrary) number of the Thing.
Thing Name	A short descriptive name for the Thing.
Thing ID#	This is the Thing's identification number used in level development (WAD files).
Hit Points	How much damage this Thing can sustain before dying.
Speed	How fast the Thing goes.
Width	The radius of the Thing.
Height	How tall a Thing is.
Missile Damage	How much damage a projectile does when hitting a target. Note that Lost Souls have this set to 3. (They become projectiles when attacking.)
Reaction Time	Reaction time for monsters. Lower makes the Thing quicker to attack, higher makes it slower to attack.
Pain Chance	The chance out of 256 that a monster's attack will be interrupted if it is injured.
Mass	The Thing's mass. Set a Trooper's mass to 1 and watch him fly! The Cyberdemon has a high mass, and rockets don't budge him much.

continues

Table 1.2. continued

Field Name	Description
Bits	This is the numeric equivalent of all of the bits displayed in the bottom window on the Thing screen. Change this one number if you want to set all of the bits at once.
Alert Sound	The Sound made when a monster first spots the player or when a projectile is launched.
Attack Sound	The Sound made during an attack by a monster, such as the demon "chew" sound.
Pain Sound	The Sound played when a monster is injured.
Death Sound	The Sound of the Thing dying (or exploding, if it's a projectile).
Action Sound	A Sound played randomly when the monster is wandering around.
First Normal Frame	The Frame displayed for inactive Things, or monsters that are not yet active. All frame numbers refer to the Frame table.
First Moving Frame	The first Frame played when a monster becomes active. Usually this is the first in a sequence (several Frames alternate for the "walking" effect).
Injury Frame	The Frame played when a monster is shot and injured.
Close Attack Frame	The beginning Frame depicting the up-close attack of a monster, such as an Imp clawing at the player.
Far Attack Frame	The first Frame showing the far-away attack of a monster, such as an Imp winding up to throw a fireball.
Death Frame	The starting Frame of the sequence shown for a Thing's death.
Exploding Frame	The first Frame of the series for an exploding death. This is only available for Imps, the player, and the human undead characters, because only those creatures can have an exploding death.
Respawn Frame	The Frame shown when a Thing is resurrected by the Arch-Vile. This field does not exist in DOOM 1.2 and won't be shown when editing that DOOM version.

A DESCRIPTION OF THING FIELDS

The first two fields listed (Thing Number and Thing Name) are not editable and are displayed to give more information about the current Thing. The Thing Numbers are ordered according to how DOOM stores the Things in the EXE. They are different between DOOM 1.2 and any of the newer DOOM versions. The Thing Name is also not stored in the DOOM.EXE file. It will always remain the same. Thing #23 (the Pain Elemental) will always be described as a "Pain Elemental," even if you modify that Thing to look or act like something entirely different.

The Speed field begins to give unpredictable results if you set too high a speed. Monsters begin to move so fast that they blink in and out of sight and become impossible to hit. Projectiles start to drift distinctly off target at high speeds (a Speed of 50 is about the upper limit for a useable weapon). This is due to a loss of precision in the DOOM calculations and is unavoidable.

The Width of a Thing is half of its actual width, in pixels. To fit a Thing through a narrow passage-way, you need to have a passage slightly wider than twice its width. Thus, a passage must be 33 pixels wide to allow the player through, though the player's actual width is 16. Narrow Things are also harder to hit.

The Height setting of a Thing is how tall that Thing is, in pixels. The Height is used to calculate how tall sectors must be for the Thing to enter them. No matter what the height of a Thing, one Thing can *never* walk over another. The Height also does not influence the location of the player's "eyes." No matter what height the player is, the view onscreen will always be the same distance above the floor.

A Thing's Pain Chance dictates how often an attacking monster will stop its attack when injured. Each time a monster gets injured, DOOM picks a number between 1 and 256. If the number it picks is lower than the Pain Chance for that Thing, the monster stops its attack; otherwise, it continues what it was doing without interruption. The Lost Souls will always stop flying at the player when shot (Pain Chance of 256), whereas the Spider Mastermind does not stop his attack very often when shot (Pain Chance of 40).

THE LOWDOWN ON BITS

The Bits field listed at the bottom of the middle window on the left side of the Thing editing screen is interpreted differently from any of the other fields. Each bit in that field contains information about an option that is either on or off for a particular Thing. The purpose of some bits is still not known (if they do indeed have a purpose). The bits that aren't known are numbers 7, 13, and 21. Bits 28 through 31 are probably unused. Each bit field and meaning are listed in Table 1.3.

Table 1.3. Explanation of the bit fields.

Bit Field Name	Description
0. Gettable Thing	A Thing that can be picked up by the player, such as an ammo clip.
1. Obstacle	A Thing that cannot be walked through.
2. Shootable Thing	The Thing will take damage if this is set. Barrels also have this bit set because they are shootable.
3. Total Invisibility	The Thing cannot be seen in any way. It won't even show up on the auto-map with the cheat codes.
4. "Automatics"	Necessary for certain automatic elements in DOOM (still not fully understood).
5. Semi-Deaf	Monsters activate if they hear a sound and are in a direct line-of-sight to the player.
6. In Pain	Used internally by DOOM if a Thing is in pain from being shot.
7. Unknown	???
8. Hangs From Ceiling	Used for those gory legs and mangled bodies. This determines where the picture is drawn and if Things can walk under it.
9. No Gravity	This Thing will not fall if it's in mid-air. For example, the Cacodemons have this set.
10. Travels Over Cliffs	A Thing that can go from a higher sector to a lower one, no matter what the drop-off is. Most monsters cannot jump off a cliff higher than about 16.
11. Can Pick up Items	This Thing (such as the player) can pick up Gettable Things.
12. No Clipping	The same as the cheat codes IDSPISPOPD and IDCLIP, but also effective for monsters.
13. Unknown	???
14. Floating	For floating monsters, such as the Lost Soul or Cacodemon.
15. Semi-No Clipping	Similar to Travels Over Cliffs, except that with this bit set the Thing can walk up any size cliff (normally the player cannot walk over steps higher than 24). Also, walk-over linedefs are not triggered.

Bit Field Name	Description
16. Projectiles	Set for Things that are projectiles. Without this bit, projectiles such as rockets explode as soon as they are fired.
17. Disappearing Weapon	Used for weapons such as the shotguns that sergeants drop when they die, which disappear when picked up. Normally used only internally by DOOM.
18. Partial Invisibility	The same effect as a Spectre, only permanent.
19. Puffs (versus bleeds)	When this bit is on, the Thing has a puff mark when shot. When off, the Thing shows a blood spot when shot. The barrel is normally the only Thing with this set.
20. Sliding Helpless	???
21. Unknown	???
22. Counts for Kill%	This Thing counts as part of the Kill% displayed at the end of a level.
23. Counts for Item%	This Thing counts as part of the Item% displayed at the end of a level.
24. Running	???
25. Not in Deathmatch	A Thing that is not present in Deathmatch mode, such as keys and normal player starting spots. (Deathmatch spots are used instead.)
26. Color 1	Changes green colors in the Thing to a different color.
27. Color 2	Changes green colors in the Thing to a different color.
28-31. Unknown	These are likely unused bits.

A few of the more complex or confusing bits need a little further explanation. One such bit is the Semi-Deaf bit (Bit 5). This is a separate type of deaf from the type that can be set in the WAD files. When this is set, the monster acts deaf (it won't activate) if the player is around a corner and makes a sound. The monster *will* activate when there is a direct line of sight between the player and monster, and the player makes a sound.

Bits 26 and 27 control a limited form of color changing. There is actually only one Sprite of the player (wearing a green outfit) in the DOOM.WAD file. In multiplayer games, DOOM manipulates these bits to create players of red, brown, or gray clothing. The same method can be applied to any creature with green in its picture. If both bits are off, any greens in the Thing remain green. If

Bit 26 is set, the greens turn to indigos. If Bit 27 is set, the greens change to browns. And if both bits are set, the greens change to dark red.

THE FRAME EDITOR

The Frame editor displays all of the editable Frame information. It's arranged in a list format with the data for one Frame on one row of the table. The Frame editor is probably the most powerful of the sections that are editable. Every good patch that has been released has involved tweaking of the Frame table. If you're serious about doing an awe-inspiring patch, be sure to learn the Frame information well. Table 1.4 briefly explains each column in the Frame editor.

Table 1.4. Description of the Frame columns.

Column Heading	Description
Frame Number	The number of the current Frame. The Frame fields in the Thing editor refer to this column.
Name	The name that DOOM looks for in the DOOM.WAD file when it needs to display this Frame (not editable).
Sprite Number	The Frame is a member of this Sprite (found in the Sprite table).
Sprite Sub-Number	This tells which individual picture of the Sprite to use for this Frame.
Bright Sprite	A Frame that is always displayed at its full brightness, even in dark rooms. Examples include Lost Souls and plasma bullets.
Next Frame Number	Which Frame to play after this one is finished.
Duration	How long this Frame is shown before moving on to the next one.
Code Pointer	An offset in the DOOM.EXE file that shows what code should be executed for the Frame. After more digging, it appears this value is not used by DOOM and that changing it is pointless.

The Sprite Number and Sprite Sub-Number fields both narrow down exactly which Frame the current Frame is. For example, let's say the current Frame has a Sprite Number of 42 and a Sprite Sub-Number of 7. A quick check of the 42nd element of the Sprite table reveals this to be the BOSS Sprite (the Baron of Hell). Each Sprite Sub-Number is matched to a letter of the alphabet, starting at 0 being A. Sprite Sub-Number 7 gives the letter H, which is appended to the Sprite name, giving the name BOSSH. That is the Sprite that DOOM looks for in the DOOM.WAD file to show the

4	2		1		DOOM PROGRAMMING GURUS
EPISODE	**MISSION**		**ROOM**		

Baron of Hell in pain. (It's a little more complex than that because a suffix is attached to the name BOSSH to tell whether to show the front, back, or side of the baron.)

The Next Frame field is one of the most useful fields. DOOM accomplishes more than one action in a row by stringing them together with the Next Frame field. Consider the injury sequence for an Imp. When an Imp is injured, DOOM looks at the Thing entry for an Imp and finds the Injury Frame (455 in DOOM 1.7a). That Frame (showing an Imp in pain) is played for a certain time (specified by the Duration of Frame 455), and then DOOM moves to the next frame. For Frame 455, the Next Frame is 456, so DOOM moves on to that Frame and plays it. The Next Frame of 456 is 444, which is the Frame of an Imp walking. DOOM then keeps showing the Frames of an Imp walking (in a cycle) until another event occurs, such as the Imp attacking or getting shot again. It's easy to make DOOM change its course of action. You could, for example, change the Next Frame of Frame 456 (when the Imp is injured) to 452, the first Frame in the Imp's attack sequence. Then whenever an Imp is injured, it will immediately attack its opponent.

THE WEAPON EDITOR

The Weapon editor provides information and enables changes to the weaponry in DOOM, including what the weapons look like and the ammunition they use. The information on weapons damage is *not* stored in the same location, and thus there is no way to change how much damage a given weapon will do per shot. (It *is* possible to edit the projectile weapons in the Thing editor.) Table 1.5 gives a short explanation for the fields in the Weapon editor.

Table 1.5. Explanation of Weapon screen fields.

Field Name	Description
Weapon Name	The name of the Weapon being modified (not editable).
Ammo Type	The name for the type of ammunition this Weapon uses. To change this, change the Ammo Number of the Weapon.
Ammo Number	The ammo type for this Weapon.
Max Ammo Cap.	The starting maximum capacity for the type of ammo this Weapon uses.
Ammo Per Item	Amount of ammo gained when a power-up of the current ammo type is picked up.
Deselect Frame	The Frame shown when another Weapon is selected and the current Weapon drops off the screen.

continues

DOOM PROGRAMMING GURUS

1 ROOM

2 MISSION

4 EPISODE

Table 1.5. continued

Field Name	Description
Select Frame	The Frame shown when the player switches to the current Weapon and it rises onscreen.
Bobbing Frame	The Frame of the current Weapon bobbing back and forth.
Shooting Frame	The Frame played when the Weapon is shooting.
Firing Frame	A Frame that shows the actual "flames" coming from the Weapon. It accompanies the Shooting Frame.

The Ammo Number is an arbitrary number that DOOM uses for each type of ammunition. The numbers 0 through 3 stand for bullets, shells, cells, and rockets, respectively. Both the fist and chainsaw (which do not need ammunition) use Ammo Type 5. Ammo Type 4 is unused, although at one time there may have been plans for a different type of weapon.

The Max Ammo Capacity is the maximum amount of a certain type of ammo that the player can carry. (For instance, for bullets the maximum is initially 200.) Picking up a backpack will automatically double this limit. Ammo Per Item shows how much ammunition the player gains when ammo of that type is picked up in the game. For bullets, whenever the player picks up a clip, he gains 10 bullets (20 if playing on the "Nightmare" or "Don't Hurt Me" skill levels). The large ammo power-ups (such as boxes of bullets, boxes of rockets, and so forth) automatically give five times as much ammunition. Both of these fields display "N/A" when the Ammo Type is a value other than 0 through 3.

THE SOUND EDITOR

The Sound editing screen enables you to edit the Sound information in the DOOM.EXE. The Sound information is still unexplored ground; not much is known about the Sound fields. The Sound Number is the number used in the Thing fields to indicate a certain Sound. The Text Offset is the location in the Text section where the Sound Name is found. DeHackEd looks at that location and displays the Sound Name from the information that is found there. The other two columns, labeled 0/1 and Value, contain the rest of the information in the EXE. It is not known what changing those values will do, but they're editable in case someone figures it out. Overall, this screen does not contain much fun information to play with.

THE SPRITE EDITOR

The Sprite information in the DOOM.EXE is nothing more than an arrangement of offsets that point to the Text section. Each Frame refers to one of these Sprites, which in turn points to a four-letter name in the Text area. The Sprite Numbers, Text Offsets, and Sprite Names are listed for each Sprite, should you wish to edit the offsets yourself. Playing with this information will not accomplish too much.

THE TEXT EDITOR

The Text section is another fun collection of information to play with. The Text editing screen contains all of the text found in the DOOM.EXE, along with the offset that the information is found at. Any of the text can be edited to personalize your copy of DOOM or to poke fun at the unfortunate player who plays it. (Be sure not to change any of the copyright or piracy notices!)

Most of the text strings are quite short, but some are longer than the 60 characters that fit on the screen. Those that are too long have an ellipsis displayed at the end of the line to show that they continue. A tilde symbol (~) is shown for non-printing characters such as tabs or new lines.

If you wish to view the entire text for one of the lines that runs longer than 60 characters, simply hit the spacebar. A window will pop up containing all of the text, formatted much as it would appear onscreen in DOOM. A new line is shown by a \n in black, and tabs are shown by \t in black.

To edit the text, hit Enter; the view window along with an editing window will appear. (See Figure 1.2.) Enter the new text in the edit window. When you are done entering the text, hit Escape. A window will appear asking if you wish to save the changes to the text. If you want to save the text changes, answer yes and the old text will be replaced with the new.

Due to the method DOOM uses to store the text in the EXE file, there are stringent limits on how long the replacement text can be. The maximum and minimum lengths for the replacement string are shown at the top of the edit window, along with the current length of the text you are typing. Strings cannot be saved unless they are between the listed lengths. If the new text you wish to add is shorter than the text which you are replacing, it's usually easy to add spaces to the end of the text to reach the minimum length. There is no way around the maximum limit though, so you must choose the replacement text carefully. The text editor is not a full-fledged word processor, so the only movement key you have is the backspace. There are no arrow keys, macros, or spell checkers included.

Figure 1.2.

A Text string being edited in the Text editor.

```
This is the current text string:
You've done it! The hideous cyber-\n
demon lord that ruled the lost Deimos\n
moon base has been slain and you\n
are triumphant! But . where are\n
you? You clamber to the edge of the\n
moon and look down to see the awful\n
truth.\n
\n
Deimos floats above Hell itself!\n
You've never heard of anyone escaping\n
from Hell, but you'll make the bastards\n
sorry they ever heard of you! Quickly,\n
you rappel down to the surface of\n
Hell.\n
\n
Now, it's on to the final chapter of\n
DOOM! -- Inferno.

         6032   MT_LAB_4
         6040   ZOMBIEMAN

Enter new text. ESC quits, 464 chars min, 467 chars max. Current len:      64
You've done it! The hideous chicken-\n
lord has been de-feathered!

F1 Help               DeHackEd v2.2 by Greg Lewis              Esc Quit
```

THE THING LIST EDITOR

The Thing List editing screen is a rehash of the familiar information of the main Thing editing screen. Because the main Thing screen has so much information available within it, it's sometimes hard to get a look at the important data, such as hit points or speed. This screen concisely lists each Thing along with that Thing's Name, ID Number, Hit Points, Speed, and Missile Damage. These are the same fields that appear on the main Thing editing screen (see "The Thing Editor" section, earlier in this room, for more information on those fields); there is no new information presented on this screen.

A WALK-THROUGH OF THE SUPER-WEAPONS PATCH

Included with every version of DeHackEd is a copy of the newest super-weapons patch available. The inspiration for this patch originally came from a small program written by a fellow named Chris Gillespie. It was released a few days before DeHackEd was created and accomplished the same thing as this patch. The patch has proven to be a favorite of DOOM users because of the incredible fire-power it gives the player. Every weapon has been overhauled to give an amazing increase in firing speed and ammo capacity, making the pistol or even the fist a daunting weapon. A look at its design may give insights and ideas that you can use in patches of your own. This example will use DOOM version 1.666, although it should also apply to any of the DOOM II versions.

| 4 | 2 | | 1 | | DOOM |
| EPISODE | MISSION | | ROOM | | PROGRAMMING GURUS |

The best place to start is by checking out the Weapon editing screen to see what information we can learn about the weapons. We can start by optimizing the regular shotgun and then applying whatever we learn in that process to the rest of the weapons. Press page-down or click the down scroll arrow to move to Weapon 3, the shotgun. The Select, Deselect, and Bobbing Frames are listed as Frames 18 through 20. The Shooting and Firing Frames start at 21 and 30, respectively. Now that we know where to look for the information, highlight one of the Frames and press **J** to jump to the Frame editor.

The quickest and easiest way to speed up the shotgun is by changing the Duration column of each Frame. For each Frame from 18 through 31 (all of the shotgun Frames), edit the Duration and change it to 1 (unless it already has a value of **0**). If you wish, you can **W**rite the changes and try running DOOM to see the improvement. You'll find that instead of pausing briefly at each picture of the shotgun, DOOM cycles through the pictures very quickly and the firing rate speeds up proportionally. You'll also find that the normal ammunition that comes with the shotgun gets used up very quickly. The next thing we can do is fix the ammo capacity for the shotgun.

Leave DOOM (if you ran it) and return to the Weapon editor in DeHackEd. Highlight the Initial Max Ammo field and change it to some large number such as 100,000. You could complete DOOM several times over with that much ammo. You'll also want to change the Ammo Per Item field; otherwise, the player will have a maximum ammunition limit of 100,000 shells but still only pick up four at a time. It's a good idea to change it to 100,000 also, so that every shell you pick up takes your ammunition to the max.

There is still one more important tweak that can be done to speed up the shotgun markedly. Another look at the firing sequence for the shotgun (Frames 21 through 29) shows that those Frames are all strung together using the Next Frame column. Each Frame points to the next one, and the last has a Next Frame pointing back to the normal bobbing Frame. A glance at the Code Pointers for those same Frames also shows that many of them do not do anything (they have a Code Pointer of 0) and are only included for a smooth-flowing cocking of the shotgun. Instead of letting it show all of those pictures, we can change the Code Pointer of Frame 22 to go back to Frame 18 and skip most of the animation. Note that Frame 29 does have a Code Pointer, but we're skipping it anyway. This can be done, but sometimes skipping the wrong Frame will cause DOOM to lock up. Here it does not seem that skipping Frame 29 causes any problems, so we can try it. If you wish, you can try running DOOM again to see the improvement. The speed increase should be noticeable. The improvements made to the shotgun can be used on all the other weapons to give the same sort of speed improvement.

There is one other thing included in the super-weapons patch that is tricky. Notice when using the patch that the BFG 9000 is an automatic weapon, like the plasma gun. I'm still unsure why the following trick works, but since it does, I'm not going to complain. Skip the last Frame in the plasma gun Frame sequence by changing the Next Frame of Frame 77 to 74. Then change the Next Frame of the last Frame of the BFG sequence (Frame 87) to point to Frame 78, the one we just skipped. Change the Next Frame of Frame 78 (the Frame we are inserting into the BFG sequence) to 81 to complete the sequence. Finally, change the Sprite Number of Frame 78 from 12 to 14, so that the Frame looks like a BFG. After making the rest of the speed-up changes to the BFG, you'll find that it is a continuous fire weapon. Great for those tough situations!

One last thing that can be changed to improve the super-weapons is to alter the Duration of all the BLUD and PUFF Frames. If these are left the way they normally are, DOOM will slow down on *any* computer when using the super shotgun on a close wall or a nearby monster because of the huge number of bullet puffs or blood splats that need to be drawn. The BLUD and PUFF Frames are Frames 90 through 96.

SUMMARY

By now you should have a good sense of how to use DeHackEd and the power and capabilities that it gives you over a unique aspect of DOOM editing. The key to finding cool tricks for editing the EXE is experimentation. The DOOM engine has all sorts of quirks that no one to this day knows about, and they are just waiting for you to discover them. Some people have turned monsters into players, turned players into monsters, and done even wilder things. Try your hand at it, and see what interesting effects you can create!

EPISODE 4

THE TOOLS OF THE GODS

MISSION 3:
NOXIOUS NODES

ROOOM 1

By Jens
Hykkelbjerg

RMB

RMB is short for *Reject Map Builder*. The reject map can be very important for your WAD if you want it to play fast (with a high frame rate). You need to have a good reject map if your WAD has grown big and has many monsters in it. Apart from being a good reject-map builder, RMB can also make all kinds of special effects with the reject map. In short, RMB gives you perfect control of what your monsters can and can't see.

The RMB package also contains two small utilities, Inspect and Effect. Inspect is used to check the efficiency of the reject map in any WAD, and Effect is a small and fast program to make simple special effects with the reject map. In the following these three programs will be described, and examples of their use will be given.

THE REJECT MAP

The reject map is a sector by sector table of bits (with values of either 0 or 1). If there is a 1 at position (X,Y) in the table and the player is in Sector Y, the DOOM engine will never make any Line-Of-Sight (LOS) calculations for monsters in Sector X. The DOOM engine will simply assume that it's impossible for any monsters in Sector X to see anything inside Sector Y. On the other hand, if there is a 0 at position (X,Y), the DOOM engine will not know if it's possible for the monsters in Sector X to see into Sector Y. In this case additional difficult calculations have to be carried out for each monster in the sector. Thus a reject map that consists entirely of zeroes can always be used. In large WADs, a reject map with zeroes at all positions will force the DOOM engine to perform a lot of calculations for each monster in the entire WAD. These calculations are needed to check if the monster should wake up or try to shoot at you.

A reject-map builder is a program that analyzes your WAD to find pairs of sectors wherein it is impossible to see from one sector to the other. In Figure 1.1 it is clear that it is impossible to see from sector one to three. This means that it's safe to add the pairs (1,3) and (3,1) to the reject map. The more such pairs a reject-map builder can find, the more efficient it is. It should be clear that the more 1s there are in the generated reject map, the better the DOOM engine performs. This leads to the definition of reject-map efficiency: The efficiency of a reject map is the percentage of 1s in the table.

4
EPISODE

3
MISSION

1
ROOM

DOOM
PROGRAMMING
GURUS

Figure 1.1.
A simple WAD.

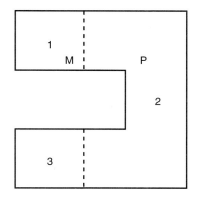

Applied to the WAD in Figure 1.1, RMB will generate the reject map shown in Table 1.1.

Table 1.1. An example reject map table.

X/Y	1	2	3
1	0	0	1
2	0	0	0
3	1	0	0

RMB is a very efficient reject-map builder, but as already mentioned, this is not all that RMB can do. RMB can also introduce special effects through the reject map. It is a special effect if a sector pair is marked with 1 in the reject map when there actually is a line-of-sight between those two sectors. Look at Figure 1.1 again. If the reject map marked it as impossible to see from Sector 1 to Sector 2, and there was a monster at the M, that monster would be unable to see the player if he was at position P, or anywhere inside Sector 2. Of course the monster will see the player and wake up if he enters Sector 1, and if the monster pursues the player into Sector 2, it can suddenly see the player, and will shoot him. Notice that *all* RMB special effects apply to specific sectors, not directly to the monsters. In this case all monsters currently positioned in Sector 1 will be unable to see anything in Sector 2, whether they started out in Sector 1 or just wandered there by chance. Maybe you don't think that this special effect sounds very useful or is very desirable, but later you will see more useful examples. But let's take a look at the utilities in the RMB package first.

THE INSPECT UTILITY

The Inspect utility has two main uses. It can be used to count the number of bits set in the reject map and at the same time calculate the efficiency of the reject map by dividing with the total number of positions in the reject map. To do this to your WAD, write:

```
C:> INSPECT path\filename.wad
```

Inspect can also be used to test for special effects present in the reject map. If the reject map has no special effects, all monsters will behave just as they do in the original levels from id Software. If the WAD has some reject-map special effects, some monsters might behave as if they were blind or nearsighted, or they might just stand and wait until the player enters a specific sector. To test for special effects such as this, type

```
c:> INSPECT path\filename.wad test
```

As a result, Inspect will report whether it detects any special effects. This is useful if you want to apply RMB to other people's WADs. If Inspect reports that there are special effects in the WAD, you should not use RMB on it, as that would destroy all the special effects. If Inspect doesn't find any special effects it's usually safe to use RMB with the WAD.

THE EFFECT UTILITY

The EFFECT command enables simple special effects to be applied to WAD files through the reject map. The syntax of the EFFECT command is

```
EFFECT WADfile [level_id] {SAFE, BLIND} {0,1} {sector_number, ALL}
```

Don't forget the .WAD file extension to the WADfile parameter. The optional level_id is either a DOOM episode and mission number such as E2M3, or a DOOM II map number such as MAP03. EFFECT will process the specified map or, if none is specified, the first level in the WAD.

The Safe option makes sectors safe for the player to be in. As long as a player is in a safe sector, he can't be seen; monsters thus won't wake up or attack. The other available effect is Blind. This blinds a sector so that monsters in it will be prevented from seeing the player, wherever he might be.

The parameter immediately following the Safe or Blind keyword specifies the degree of safety or blindness that the EFFECT command will produce. Currently only 0 or 1 are supported here. Their meanings are:

SAFE:

> 0   Sector is completely safe. Players in a completely safe sector cannot be seen by *any* monsters.
>
> 1   Sector is safe only from other sectors. Monsters within it can still see the player.

BLIND:

> 0   Sector is completely blind. Monsters in it can't see the player, no matter where he is.
>
> 1   Sector is blind only to other sectors. Monsters within will attack the player only if he enters the blinded sector.

In each of these four cases, you can use ALL instead of the sector number for the last parameter. With a degree setting of 0, this will make all sectors totally safe (or blind; there is no distinction between the two, the table being filled with 1's either way): All monsters will be total pacifists. A degree setting of 1 creates a level full of near-sighted monsters who will only notice players in the same sector as themselves.

Making all monsters blind will make for a very dull game, but it may be useful for play-testing a WAD to check, for instance, that all monsters are placed correctly (but do remember that noises will wake them up and cause them to move around) or to see what the absolute maximum reject speed-up of the WAD would be like.

Although this command is quite powerful, it is really only intended as a quick way of applying the occasional special effect. For a more comprehensive application of special effects, as well as special processing (speed optimization), it is recommended that the RMB command be used, in conjunction with an options file; see the next section.

Be aware that if you use the RMB command on a WAD after it has been processed with EFFECT, you will remove all of the added effects. (Most editors and node-builders will happily do this for you, too.)

HOW DO I USE RMB?

If all you want to do is optimize the reject structure in your WAD, just type the following:

```
c:> RMB input.WAD output.WAD
```

For multi-level WADs, you need to give the level identification of the level you want to process. In DOOM and Heretic, this level identification is, for instance, E2M3; for DOOM II, an example would be MAP03. To process "Episode 2, Mission 1" of a WAD, write

```
C:> RMB input.WAD output.WAD E2M1
```

If you don't give the level parameter to RMB, the first level in the WAD will be processed.

During the processing of a WAD, a map of the level being processed is shown on the screen, with the number of the sector currently being processed given in the top left corner of the screen, together with the total number of sectors to process in the level. The map may look a little different from the view of the WAD that you are used to seeing; all two-sided linedefs appear initially in blue with a selection of one-sided linedefs in white. As the program looks at each sector in turn and works round all the sector's two-sided linedefs, lines on the map will turn red (to show that they're being processed) and then cyan (when finished). From the current (red) linedef, it will be possible to see other two-sided linedefs. The first of these out from the sector being processed will show yellow on the display for a while, finally turning magenta as processing on it completes. As the program progresses, there should always be a red and a yellow line, showing where the program is currently processing LOS calculations. The sector count will rise steadily; processing finishes when all sectors have been examined.

When processing is complete, the program will create the specified WAD file, writing the new reject map to it, along with the rest of the WADs resources. The final efficiency of the reject map will be reported, and RMB will beep to let you know that it has finished.

WHY USE SPECIAL EFFECTS?

By using RMB or the Effect utility, you can make all kinds of special effects. In the section about the Effect utility earlier, it has already been explained how to make a few simple special effects. Using RMB, you will have perfect control over which sectors the monsters should be able to see. However, it is not obvious why it's a good idea that the monsters can't see everything around them. The last thing you want is your monsters making a sit-down strike. To avoid this, you have to think twice before applying too many special effects.

To realize why it's a good thing to have some reject-map special effects in your WAD, consider why there are deaf monsters in DOOM. The answer is that a small amount of deaf monsters surprises the player. It doesn't sound too wise to have deaf monsters in a game, but the result is that the deaf monsters don't wake until they see the player. By placing deaf monsters in places where it's difficult for the player to spot them, the monsters gain an advantage over the player, and the player gets surprised when he is suddenly attacked.

4	3		1		DOOM PROGRAMMING GURUS
EPISODE	MISSION		ROOM		

With RMB it is now possible to have the monster wait until the player enters a specific sector. To do this you normally need to hide the monsters a little better than simply around the nearest corner.

HIDING MONSTERS

Generally, to hide a monster one of the following places or strategies can be used:

- In the dark
- Around corners or in alcoves
- Behind two-sided walls with texture on at least one side
- High up where the player can't see

It is, of course, possible to use a combination of these good hiding spots if necessary. Normally a hidden monster will wake up the instant it sees the player, but with RMB it's possible to construct much more fiendish ambushes. RMB is able to make the monsters hold their fire until the player is in a really difficult position—for instance, halfway across a narrow bridge. Some of these setups can be constructed without RMB, only with much more difficulty and with a lesser degree of precision. The point is that RMB makes it easier to control your monsters and it allows for effects impossible to achieve in any other way. Technically it is possible to make the monsters ambush the player when he enters the sector of your choice.

This type of special effect makes life harder for the player. But it's also possible to make other kinds of special effects to make life a little easier.

REALISTIC SPECIAL EFFECTS

When I started playing DOOM, I thought that the monsters sometimes were a bit unfair. It seemed that the monsters had perfect vision, no matter how dark it got. When I stumbled around a dark sector and found it difficult to see the end of my own shotgun, the monsters were still able to shoot at me with remarkable precision. With RMB, it's now possible to impair the vision of the monsters in dark areas. A list of such realistic special effects follows:

- Safety (or partial safety) in the dark
- Safety in trenches
- Safety behind two-sided walls with texture

This list of possible special effects is by no means complete. In the following sections the options used to implement special effects are described, and examples of their use are given later.

APPLYING SPECIAL EFFECTS

To apply special effects to your WAD you need to make a specific option file for the WAD. The option file should be placed in the same directory as the WAD and should have the same name as the WAD, only with an .REJ extension instead of .WAD. RMB will detect the presence of the option file when you run it, and the options in the file will be processed.

RMB option files do not need to have a particular structure beyond being straightforward ASCII text files, with a single RMB option statement on each line. (Empty lines are permitted.) Options can be entered in upper- or lowercase. Options can appear in the file in any order; the only exception is that options intended for particular levels in multi-level WADs must be grouped together under a heading for that level. The first part of the file before the first level identifier contains the default options, which RMB will always use.

AN EXAMPLE OPTION FILE

A sample REJ option file should make this clearer. (Full details of the RMB options used in this example are given shortly.)

MYWAD.REJ:

```
# This is an example of a multilevel option file, for use with MYWAD.WAD.

# The first lines are the defaults.
# These options will always be used.

Perfect

# Now comes the options used to process E1M1:

E1M1
# ^ This marks the end of the defaults, and the beginning
#   of the options that apply to e1m1.
#   Use MAPxx for options to levels in DOOM2 WADs

Left 311
Right 217

E1M2
# ^ Here end the options for episode 1 mission 1:
#   options for episode 1 mission 2 begin.

Blind 3 (5 6)

E1M1
# ^ Here the options for E1M1 take over again.
```

```
INCLUDE (4) (6)
EXCLUDE (2) (3)

# If RMB is called with a mission that is not in the options
# file (e.g. "e1m3" here), only the default options at the beginning of
# the file are used.

# ==END OF OPTIONS==
```

To summarize: If you want to apply different options to different levels in a multi-level WAD, you must divide your WAD_*FILENAME*.REJ option file into sections started by a line containing nothing but the level ID. For WADs containing only one level, you can just use the default options without worry.

A LIST OF RMB OPTIONS

A full list of the available options, with a short explanation of the function of each, is given here. Detailed descriptions of the operation of the most important options will follow in the next sections.

#	Marks a comment line in the option file.
BAND	Makes "bands" of blindness/safety; see the manual for further details.
BLIND	Makes sector(s) blind (or partially so).
BLOCK	Stops monsters from seeing through a pair of specified lines.
DISTANCE	Specifies how far that monsters can see generally (horizontal distance).
DOOR	Specifies the maximum number of doors that monsters can see through generally.
EnMy	Marks start of options for a particular DOOM or Heretic level.
EXCLUDE	Forces exclusion of view from one sector to another.
GROUP	Merges sectors into one. (Sectors get the same reject maps.)
INCLUDE	Forces inclusion of view from one sector to another.
INV BLIND	Makes sector(s) long-sighted.
INV SAFE	Makes sector(s) invisible to monsters nearby (but not distant ones).
LEFT	Makes a two-sided line into one-way see-through (from left to right).
LENGTH	Specifies how far (by sector) monsters can see generally.
LINE	Makes a two-sided line impossible to look through for monsters.
MAPxx	Marks start of options for a particular DOOM II map.

NODOOR	Marks sector(s) as not being counted as a door. (Used only with DOOR option.)
NOMAP	Removes the graphical display; reports progress as dots instead.
NOPROCESS	Only applies special effects; no processing done. Very fast.
ONE	Same as BLOCK, but only operates in one direction.
PERFECT	Generates a perfect reject map. (Forces processing of all sectors.)
PREPROCESS	Groups sectors to gain processing speed. (The efficiency drops.)
PROCESS	Forces processing of specified sector(s).
REPORT	Reports long lines of sight to file.
RIGHT	Makes a two-sided line one-way see-through (from right to left).
SAFE	Makes sector(s) invisible to distant monsters.
TRACE	For debugging only; use is not recommended.

INV is short for INVERT. Any option can be abbreviated to its shortest unique form. If you wish, Safe can be abbreviated S, as no other options begin with an S. Preprocess can be abbreviated PRE, but not PR, because Process also begins with PR.

In the following sections, the most important options will be described. If you want to know about the options not described here, you can read the manual supplied with the RMB package. The options described here should be enough for most of the special effects you will ever think of.

BLIND

The syntax of Blind is

```
BLIND distance sector_list
```

This is a similar option to the Blind parameter in the EFFECT utility, but with more flexible usage. It turns all of the sectors in the *sector_list* blind for the specified *distance* (by sector). A value of 0 for *distance* will produce a sector in which monsters can see nothing at all. A *distance* of 1 prevents monsters from seeing out of the sector. With *distance* 2, monsters can see their own sector and all immediately neighboring sectors, and so on. The option

```
BLIND 3 (5 7)
```

will enable monsters in Sectors 5 and 7 to see up to 3 Sectors in every direction (counting their own sector).

This option is useful if you want to restrict monsters' viewing range in certain areas, to allow for low light intensities, perhaps; or just to prevent them from waking too soon.

SAFE

The syntax of the `Safe` option is:

```
SAFE distance sector_list
```

This option operates much like the `Safe` parameter in the `EFFECT` command, but with more flexible usage. The `distance` parameter enables you to specify how close (in sectors, of course) monsters must be in order to see into the specified sector(s). Distance is reckoned exactly the same way as for the `Blind` option: `Safe` 0 indicates that a sector is completely safe; `Safe` 1 sets a sector that can be seen only by monsters actually in the sector; `Safe` 2 indicates that a sector can be seen by monsters in it, and in its immediate neighboring sectors, but not from further away. In general, `Safe` makes a sector safe from sectors located further away than `distance`.

EXCLUDE

The syntax of `Exclude` is:

```
EXCLUDE sector_list1 sector_list2
```

This option enables you to specifically exclude particular inter-sector lines of sight. Its action is to make it impossible for monsters in any of the sectors in `sector_list1` to see any of the sectors in `sector_list2`. Note that `Exclude` operates only in one direction (affecting just a single bit in the reject map for each sector pair), and that it overrides *all* other option settings for the specified sector pairs.

`Exclude` can be used to make small adjustments after the wider application of other options, or to make minor modifications to a reject table. It is particularly useful for setting small "safe" areas within larger rooms. The option

```
EXCLUDE (1 2) (4 5)
```

will exclude all the LOS pairs: (1,4) (1,5) (2,4) and (2,5). In this example the monsters currently in Sectors 1 and 2 will be unable to see the player if he is in one of the Sectors 4 or 5.

INCLUDE

The syntax of the Include option is:

INCLUDE *sector_list1 sector_list2*

This option enables you to force particular sight-lines to be examined at game-time. It marks it as feasible for monsters in *sector_list1* to see a player in any of the sectors in *sector_list2*, no matter what all the other options say. Include overrides all other options except Exclude. The option

INCLUDE (1 2) (5 6)

will include the following LOS in the reject map: (1,2) (1,5) (2,5) and (2,6). In this example, it is marked as possible for the monsters currently in Sectors 1 and 2 to see the player if he is in one of the Sectors 5 or 6.

Include can be used to make special effects like this: Blind a sector completely with Blind 0. Put a lot of monsters in it, then make a platform in sight of the blinded sector. Use the Include option to make the monsters able to see the platform and nothing else. If it is difficult for the player to see from the platform to the blinded sector, the player will be surprised when he is suddenly attacked.

LEFT

The syntax for Left is

LEFT *line_number*

This option makes a two-sided linedef, specified through its *line_number*, into a line through which monsters can only see from its left side. This option is useful if you have a wall (or curtain) that has a solid texture on one side, but not on the other, and you want monsters to respond logically to it. (Normally, monsters can see through all two-sided linedefs, regardless of their textures.)

Note that for this option to be applied successfully, the specified line must be on an inter-sector boundary. Internal lines cannot be specified; if you need to apply this type of block to a particular line within a sector, you will need to divide the sector into additional sectors along this line using your WAD editor, before applying RMB.

RIGHT

This option works exactly the same as Left, except that it enables monsters to see through the line from its right side only.

PERFECT

Ordinarily, RMB will treat all sectors that are totally enclosed within another sector as part of the enclosing sector (provided they have no one-sided linedef). In most WADs, this greatly cuts down the number of sectors that RMB needs to consider, but it also leads to a less-than-perfect reject map. Use the Perfect option to prevent RMB from taking this processing shortcut and make it consider all sector-to-sector sightlines. Be prepared for long processing times, however, if you have a large WAD.

Note that all sectors referenced in a Safe, Blind, Block, One, Left, Right, or Process option will be processed, regardless of whether Perfect has been specified. However, sectors that are internal to the sectors referenced in the Safe or Blind options will not be treated separately from their enclosing sector, unless Perfect has been specified or Process has been used for these specific sectors. (See the section on Process below). If you don't use Perfect or Process, any sector specified as Safe, say, will have all its internal sectors marked safe as well. Don't be tempted to use Perfect just to prevent the Safe and Blind options from working in this way over a small area, especially if you are processing a larger WAD. You will add a large processing overhead to prevent only a small number of unwanted effects; it is better to identify the areas that will be treated incorrectly (to your way of thinking) and force their inclusion in RMB's processing with a Process option. Using Perfect on large WADs can add considerably to RMB's processing time for very little gain in reject efficiency.

You may find it beneficial to think in terms of rooms rather than sectors when planning and applying your special effects. In the default mode of operation (without Perfect), if you apply the Safe option to a sector that encloses other sectors (a room), you will make all the "decorational" sectors in that room safe too; this is usually what is desired. By and large, you will usually find that the default operation of RMB (such as without Perfect) will give more desirable handling of the Safe and Blind special effects.

PROCESS

The syntax of this option is

PROCESS *sector_list*

This option forces RMB to process fully the sectors specified in the *sector_list*, regardless of whether they happen to be contained wholly within another sector. The option is designed to force processing in areas where you are applying special effects, where you wish to prevent the grouping of enclosed sectors with their surrounding sector, or where you need rigorous optimization of the reject map. Naturally, its use is entirely superfluous if you also use the Perfect option.

EXAMPLES OF SPECIAL EFFECTS

In the following sections, it will be explained how to implement some of the special effects that RMB can make. Not everything is covered here, but go ahead and make experiments yourself.

SAFETY BEHIND TWO-SIDED WALL

In a Deathmatch WAD, two-sided walls with textures on only one of the sides can be used for great ambush spots. Achieving the effect that the player can hide from the monsters behind a wall such as this can only be done by altering the reject map. The monsters can normally look through any two-sided wall. The only way to make sure that the monsters don't shoot through the wall will be to use the Left or Right option for that linedef. That way the monsters will only be able to see one way through the wall.

SAFETY IN TRENCHES

A trench is easy to make. Just make a hole in the floor and you have a trench. It's much harder to convince the monsters that they shouldn't shoot you from far away when you are in the trench. To achieve this, you might have to make a sector around the trench, where the monsters should be able to see into the trench. Now you have a choice. You can make the trench sector Safe 2, which would make monsters farther away than the neighboring sectors blind to the player in the trench. You can also make the trench Safe 1, and then Include the sectors outside the trench that should still be able to see into the trench. An example of a room with a trench is shown in Figure 1.2. Here Sector 4 should be a little higher than the normal floor height, and Sector 3 should be a little lower. Sector 3 should be the trench. Sectors 5 and 6 is used to make the steps in a stair leading from the trench to normal floor height. Place some nasty monsters in Sector 4. For the player to be safe from the attack of the monsters in Sector 4, he has to jump into the trench. There he can sit in relative safety, while he shoots the other monsters in the room, until finally he makes a run for the door in the other side of the room (Sector 8).

To make the trench safe against the monsters in Sector 4, the following option is applied:

```
SAFE 2 (3)
```

This means that only the immediate neighboring sectors can see into Sector 3. Supplied with the RMB package you will find a small example WAD that demonstrates this special effect precisely. The name of the example WAD is RMB1.WAD.

Notice that RMB1.WAD is a DOOM WAD. If you have DOOM II, you should look for WADs with the suffix D2.WAD instead; in this case, the filename is RMB1D2.WAD. All example WADs replace the DOOM level E2M1 and the DOOM II map MAP01. All WADs are supplied with an option file. In this case the option file is RMB1.REJ for DOOM and RMB1D2.REJ for the DOOM II WAD.

Figure 1.2.
A room with a trench (RMB1.WAD).

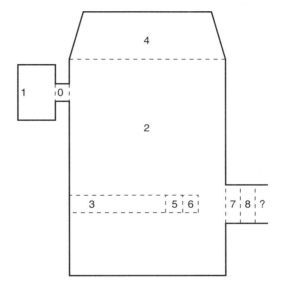

SAFETY IN THE DARK

In dark areas you may want your monsters to have limited visibility. Remember that the player won't be surprised if *all* your dark sectors have limited visibility. It is however your decision if you want to surprise the player or not. It's quite easy to achieve the limited vision: just use the `Safe` *x* option, where *x* is the number of sectors that you want your monsters to be able to see. Note that monsters in light areas will also find themselves unable to see into the dark area if they are more than *x* sectors away. An example of this is supplied with RMB on the CD-ROM. Take a look at the WAD called DARK.WAD. Here a big dark room has been divided into many small sectors, and `Safe` 3 has been applied to every sector in the dark room. The result is that the monsters will stand and wait until you get close enough for them to wake up. Just remember that a special effect like this is a little tedious to make, as you have to divide the big room into many smaller sectors.

TRICKS AND TRAPS

I said previously that RMB could be used to make traps for the player. Let's look at a simple trap. In Figure 1.3 you will see a drawing of a map. You should easily be able to make a map like this in any editor. The player should start in Sector 0. Sector 7 and 15 are doors, and Sectors 4, 5, 9, 10, 11, and 12 should have a very high floor height. The switch in Sector 6 should open the door made by Sector 15. Now put some monsters in Sector 1. We want the player to be attacked from behind when he goes through the door (Sector 7). To do that we need to hide the monsters in Sector 1, but that's easy. We just apply a texture on the side facing Sector 0. Now the player won't expect to be attacked by the monsters when they are hit. The problem is, of course, that normally the monsters will charge as soon as they see you. To make them wait until the player enters Sector 3, you need to use RMB. All you have to insert into the option file is the following:

```
BLIND 1 (1)
INCLUDE (1) (3)
```

Now you will surprise the player when he is suddenly attacked from behind as he is entering the new room. Inside Sector 3, you can also place one or two monsters. This way the player is attacked from two sides at the same time.

Figure 1.3.
A simple trap
(RMB2DL.WAD).

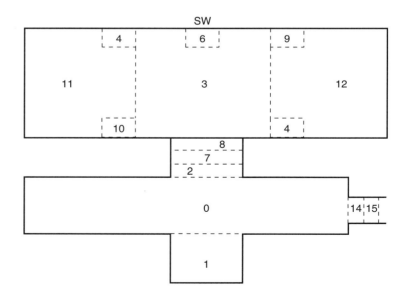

When the player has entered the room and fought off the monsters, it's time to find some more things for him to do. Make sure that the high sectors to the left and right of Sector 3 are so high that the player thinks they are walls. Now place some monsters in Sectors 4, 5, 9, and 10. You want these monsters to start attacking when the player presses the switch. It's impossible to make them wake up at that very moment, but we can make them wake when the player enters Sector 6. To do that, all you need to add in the REJ file is the following:

```
BLIND 1 (4 5 9 10)
INCLUDE (4 5 9 10) (6)
```

Now all you need is to put some bonuses in for the player to pick up and decide what should happen behind Sector 15 (the exit door), and suddenly your WAD is taking shape. This small example WAD is included in the RMB package under the name RMB2D1.WAD.

WHAT TO DO NEXT

Now you have seen how to use RMB to optimize your WAD for speed. You have also seen examples of different kinds of special effects, and you have learned how to write option files for your WADs to create these special effects. Now it's time for you to make your own experiments with reject-map special effects. Just take the time to consider what you want the monsters to see, and you should be able to implement it using a combination of the options mentioned here. You should find that RMB helps you control the monsters' behavior in your WAD, and if your WAD is large, RMB will even speed it up, too.

ROOM 2

By Frank Palazzolo

NODENAV

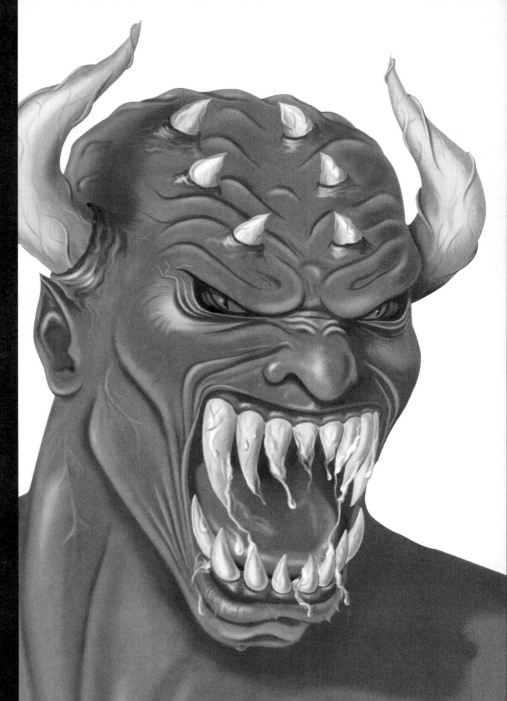

NodeNav is a program that can be used to graphically display level information from a DOOM, DOOM II, or Heretic WAD file. Although it was originally designed to explore the Nodes resource, it can be easily modified to read and display any coordinate-based data from the file.

BACKGROUND

When DOOM was first released, almost everyone was impressed by its graphics capabilities. Even if DOOM was a boring game (and this is certainly not the case), the speed and flexibility of the design would still be impressive. NodeNav was developed in an effort to understand how the designers of DOOM had managed to accomplish this.

Immediately following DOOM's release, people began dissecting its WAD file. This file contains almost all of the graphics and sound resources used in the game. These dedicated people reverse-engineered nearly the entire file format, which is documented in Matthew Fell's "Unofficial DOOM Specs." This provided a common source of information for anyone interested in creating his or her own levels, or just understanding how DOOM works internally.

While many of the WAD file resources are straightforward, some of the information seems mysterious. The linedef and vertex resources provide sufficient information to draw a 2-D diagram of a level. These are simply the points and lines visible on the map. The sidedefs enable the walls in DOOM to be "two-sided," which is important because some walls look different from each side. However, the segs, ssectors, and nodes resources are more difficult to understand. Segs are smaller portions of the linedefs. Ssectors indicate groups of segs that form polygons. Finally, the nodes resource (along with the ssectors and segs resources) form a special kind of binary tree structure called a Binary Space Partitioning (BSP) Tree.

If you simply want to play a modified DOOM level or generate one of your own, it's not really necessary to understand the details of nodes, segs, and ssectors. This is because there are plenty of level editors and automated tools for generating them from the linedefs, sidedefs, and vertexes. However, examining these resources in a graphical way offers some insights into the structure and function of the graphics engine.

When rendering a 3-D view, a program spends a lot of time deciding which walls are visible and which are not. In DOOM, the use of a BSP Tree significantly speeds up this process (known as Hidden Surface Removal). Creating the BSP Tree is a relatively time-consuming process. However, once the BSP Tree is created, it's much easier to determine which walls to draw (from any viewpoint). In other words, using a BSP Tree trades a time-consuming preprocessing step for a much faster rendering time. Since the BSP Tree is created by the level maker, it doesn't matter if it takes a while. It is stored in the nodes, ssectors, and segs resources of the WAD file. Then, when the game is running and the screen is being drawn, the decisions about what to draw happen very quickly.

USAGE

NodeNav is a DOS program that requires two command-line arguments. The first is the name of a particular level resource in a WAD file. For DOOM or Heretic, this is of the format EXMY, where X is the single-digit episode number, and Y is the single-digit mission number. For DOOM II, the first argument is MAPXX where XX is the two-digit level number. The second argument is always the filename (and optional path) of the WAD file, such as C:\DOOM\DOOM.WAD.

When you run NodeNav, it will display the top view of the level in the middle of the screen, along with some additional text information along the top and bottom lines. (See Figure 2.1.) In the map area, there is the light-gray map, a red rectangle, a blue rectangle, and a green line segment.

Figure 2.1.
NodeNav 1.0. A view of DOOM level E1M1.

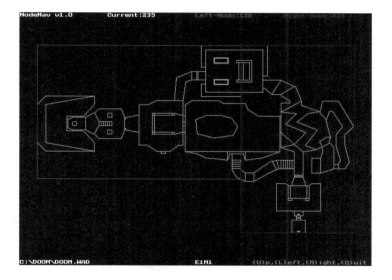

Along the top row, there are three pieces of data, labeled Current, Left- (in red), and Right- (in blue).

The program begins at the top of the BSP Tree, with the current node being initialized to the root node. Each node is associated with three graphical entities: 1. A green line segment, which represents a bisecting line on the map; 2. A red rectangle, which encloses the left subtree; and 3. A blue rectangle that encloses the right subtree. This is how it works: first, imagine the green line segment extended across the entire map. Now, everything on one side of the line and inside the red rectangle forms the left-child part of the tree. Likewise, everything on the other side of the green line and inside the blue rectangle makes up the right-child part of the tree.

You may now switch nodes by descending into the left- or right-child region. To do this, type L or R. The map then changes as the child node becomes the new node, complete with a new green bisector, and new left- and right-child regions. Note that the view automatically zooms to show you the maximum portion of the area of the map affected by the current node.

When you reach the bottom of the tree, the "leaves" are the SSECTORS. The left- or right-child description on the top line will change from "Node:" to "SSeg:" to indicate this. To move back up to the previous parent node, use the U command. When finished, you may exit via the Quit command.

PROGRAM DETAILS

As stated previously, NodeNav is a DOS program. Version 1.0 is a 16-bit program, but the data structures are defined so that it can be compiled as a 32-bit program with minimal changes. This is not surprising, because NodeNav v0.8 was a 32-bit program. It was changed in order to make it easier for a wider audience to compile it, because it no longer requires a DOS extending compiler. As a 16-bit program, two changes were required. In order to handle arrays of resources bigger than 64KB, NodeNav uses huge pointers to point to them, and dynamically allocates them using the `farmalloc()` call.

NodeNav v1.0 is also dependent on the Borland Graphics Interface routines for drawing, but it should be easy to make it work with any compiler. It is written mostly in C, but it does need to be compiled under C++, as I am using some C++ conventions.

The file NODENAV.H contains declarations of all of the data structures of interest from the WAD file. These include the file header WadHeader, a directory entry DirEntry, a linedef, a sidedef, a vertex, a segment, an ssector, and a node. These data structures came directly from the "Unofficial DOOM Specs," and are declared so that they will compile to the same sizes in both 16- and 32-bit environments. The file NODENAV.CPP contains the main routine, which is essentially a file reader, and a rendering section.

THE READER

The file reader uses the command-line arguments to open the file and look for the given mission resources. First, I will describe the two utility routines, `seek_entry` and `read_resource`, which make this a little easier. Here are their prototypes:

```
DirEntry *seek_entry(FILE *fp, DirEntry *entry, char *name);
int read_resource(FILE *fp, void *array, int size, DirEntry *entry);
```

4
EPISODE

3
MISSION

2
ROOM

DOOM
PROGRAMMING
GURUS

Seek_entry() starts from the current directory entry, and looks for the entry whose name matches the name argument. If successful, it returns the new directory entry information. If not, it returns null. Read_resource() requires a pointer to enough free space to hold an array of resources. (It is the calling program's responsibility to manage this memory.) It also requires the size of an element of the array, and the directory entry of the resource. It returns the number of resources successfully read.

First, the program calls seek_entry() to find the directory entry for the resource whose name is the mission (EXMY or MAPXX). Then it calls seek_entry() again for each graphics resource of interest. These calls must occur in the same order as the resources appear in the file, because each seek starts where the last one ended.

When NodeNav finds a directory entry for a matching resource, two things happen. First, it dynamically allocates enough memory to hold an array of these objects, based on the resource size in the directory entry. Then, it calls read_resource() in order to fill up the array with the actual resource data from the WAD file. This process continues until the program has read in all of the resources of interest.

THE RENDERING SECTION

This section of the program draws the level map on the screen, along with additional data on the first and last lines of the display. The first thing NodeNav does is create and initialize one more array called up_node[]. For each node, this array returns the index of its parent node. This is a convenient way to hold onto the parent node information at all times, which makes it easier to travel "up" the tree.

Secondly, NodeNav calculates the X and Y extents of the two bounding child regions. It uses the maximum, minimum, and midpoint calculations along with the Zoom factor to determine the proper offset and scaling for this part of the level. It draws the whole level by indexing through all the linedefs. Then it adds the bisector line segment in green and the two rectangles in red and blue. Finally, the program updates the text information to indicate the new node and/or ssegment numbers.

ENHANCEMENTS

One of the best features of NodeNav is that it's very easy to modify and enhance. For example, suppose you want to change NodeNav to find the exit location on a certain level. First, the reader must be modified to load in the Things resource. All that is required is an additional structure declaration and definition, an additional memory allocation, and a call to read_resource(). As long as the program calls for each resource in the order that it appears in the file, this works just fine. Once the

DOOM
PROGRAMMING
GURUS

2
ROOM

3
MISSION

4
EPISODE

Things resource is added to the reader section, it is very easy to display any item you wish. The renderer must be changed so that it searches for the exit and draws it as a yellow square on the screen. This is an easy exercise for users who want to customize NodeNav for themselves. Of course, you could always use a full-fledged level-editor to get this information, but it's still kind of fun to do it yourself.

If you would like to try exploring on your own, there are several other things to try. Here are a few ideas: you could extend the green bisector to the edges of the red and blue rectangles. You could add direct panning and zooming via the arrow and + and – keys. If you have a good algorithm for tree-drawing, you could even add a full tree display on another page.

FOR THE REALLY AMBITIOUS...

When DOOM is running, the BSP Tree is used during every frame to determine which walls are visible and which are obscured by other walls. It is possible to modify NodeNav to get an idea of how this might work. Let's assume that we are at some arbitrary point on the level called our "viewpoint." Here is the beauty of the BSP Tree: by walking through the tree in a particular order, based on our viewpoint, we can draw all the segs on the level in front-to-back or back-to-front order. From our top-down viewpoint in NodeNav, it will appear as though the level is being drawn from our viewpoint "outward" or from the edges "inward" toward the viewpoint.

How would these modifications be made? First of all, we must pick a viewpoint. One way to do this would be to use the entry or exit point from the Things resource. Then, we would need to do what is called a "modified in-order walk" of the tree. A normal in-order tree-walking algorithm looks something like this:

```
ProcessNode(&top_node);

void ProcessNode(NODE *X)
{
    Delay();    // to see the individual ssectors get drawn
    IF X is a SSECTOR
    {
        Draw all SEGS in the SSECTOR;
        RETURN;
    }
    IF I is a NODE
    {
        Process_Node(X->Left_child_node);
        Process_Node(X->Right_child_node);
        RETURN;
    }
}
```

This would draw all of the segs in some arbitrary order, as `Process_Node` is recursively called once for every node. (Recursive programming is a little hard to get used to, but it is a powerful technique for doing things such as this.) Notice that if we changed this code slightly to process the right subtree before the left one, this would draw the segs in exactly the opposite order. (Try it, you'll see.)

We have one more piece of information to factor in: whether or not the viewpoint is on the left or right side of each node's bisector. We can change the order so that we switch subtree order (left or right first), based on this additional factor. From the viewpoint, this becomes a front-to-back or back-to-front drawing algorithm.

```
Viewpoint V;
ProcessNode(&top_node);

void ProcessNode(NODE *X) {
    Delay();    // to see the individual ssectors get drawn
    IF X is a SSECTOR
    {
        Draw all SEGS in the SSECTOR;
        RETURN;
    }
    IF I is a NODE
    {
        IF (V is on the left(or right) of X->bisector) THEN
            Process_Node(X->Left_child_node);
            Process_Node(X->Right_child_node);
        ELSE
            Process_Node(X->Right_child_node);
            Process_Node(X->Left_child_node);
        RETURN;
    }
}
```

Of course, we are still drawing all of the walls when we know that this is unnecessary in the real game. There are additional optimizations in DOOM that correct this as well. Specifically, the DOOM engine renders the screen in front-to-back order, making sure not to overwrite sections that are already rendered. Also, it does all of this while checking each node to see if its bounding region is visible. This is easy to do, because we already know the direction we are facing, the angle that is visible, and the X and Y extents of the node bounding region. If this bounding region (a rectangle) does not fall within the current view region (a triangle), then the subtree under this node may be skipped entirely. As you can imagine, this speeds up the rendering process significantly.

FINAL THOUGHTS

NodeNav may not be as big and powerful as other sophisticated level-editors available today. But, as a flexible, extensible framework for gaining insight into the WAD file resources, I think it does just fine. And with a little effort, it can do whatever you want it to do.

DOOM
PROGRAMMING
GURUS

2
ROOM

3
MISSION
4
EPISODE

THE TOOLS OF THE GODS

MISSION 4: MUTATIONS IN DOOMSPACE

ROOM 1

By Michael
LaFavers

DMGRAPH

DMGraph (version 1.1) enables you to change the look of DOOM. It won't let you change the layout of the game or where items or monsters are located. You can, however, replace graphics with your own files.

The graphic images in DOOM are numerous. Depending on what you want to change, it can be rather easy or downright tedious to customize your environment. Walls are easy to change because changing only one graphic may be adequate. To change one of the monsters, however, you need to create a different graphic for each of the new creature's movements and each of those from eight different angles.

SYNTAX AND OPTIONS

The syntax for using DMGraph is as follows:

```
DMGRAPH graphic_name [-s input_file] [-e output_file] [-i x,y] [-v] [-d] [-b] [-t type]
                     [-f pwad_file] [-r] [-c]
```

The following options may be invoked. (A more detailed description of the options will follow.)

Option	Description
graphic_name	Name of the desired graphic.
-s input_file	Stores a graphic (input_file) in a WAD file.
-e output_file	Extracts a graphic (output_file) from a WAD file.
-i x, y	Insertion point X,Y.
-v	Verbose list of image information: size, insertion point and allocation.
-d	Displays graphics on the screen.
-b	Uses black for background color.
-t type	Graphics format (GIF or PPM).
-f pwad_file	Name of PWAD file.
-r	Removes graphic from an alternate WAD file.
-c	Lists the contents of the WAD file, including nongraphic elements.

GRAPHIC___NAME

This is the name of the graphic you wish to act upon. There are many different graphic images in the WAD file. Unfortunately, there is no easy way to find out what the different graphics are. DMGraph doesn't have a list option, such as -l in DMAUD and DMMUSIC. The only source for graphic names is the -c option, which lists all elements in the WAD file, not just graphic names. The only way to determine that a name refers to a graphic is to try to extract it.

-S INPUT__FILE

This option stores a graphic into the WAD file from the specified `input_file`. DMGraph supports two image formats: GIF and PPM. The format used is determined by the file's extension or the -t option.

-E OUTPUT__FILE

This option extracts a graphic from the WAD file into the specified `output_file`. If the file already exists, it will not be overwritten. You must specify a new file. The file will be extracted in either the GIF or PPM format, depending on the output file's extension or the -t option.

-I X,Y

This option sets the insertion point in the graphic. The insertion point determines the position of the image when it is drawn in the game. This can be adjusted to manipulate the placement of the image relative to its placement on the screen.

Some images require precise placement on the screen. The graphics on the panel don't move around on the screen. These static images have negative numbers for their insertion point, which represents an absolute position from the upper-left corner of the screen.

If this option is not specified, the insertion point is assumed to be the middle of the bottom line *x/2,y*.

-V

The -v option displays information for the specified graphic. It lists the type, size, insertion point, and allocation.

The type is one of four numbers:

Type 0 = miscellaneous (letters, numbers, panel graphics, menu items, static images)

Type 1 = sprites (monsters, missiles, most other images)

Type 2 = wall texture

Type 3 = floor texture

The size is listed in width-by-height format. The insertion point is listed as *X*, *Y*.

The allocation value lists how much space in the file is allocated to the graphic.

-D

This displays the graphic on the screen. To see the title screen, type

```
DMGRAPH TITLEPIC -d
```

-B

When you extract a graphic, the background color of the image is cyan. To change the image to use black as the background, use the -b option. (See figures 1.1 and 1.2.)

-T TYPE

Graphic images may be stored or extracted in either GIF or PPM format. If the file you wish to extract to or store from has no extension or uses a different one, use this option to tell DMGraph what format the graphic is in. Set *type* to either GIF or PPM.

-F PWAD___FILE

This specifies the name of a PWAD file to use instead of the WAD file. This enables you to make the changes in the PWAD file and leave your original WAD file intact. If the PWAD file doesn't exist, it will be created. The file must have .WAD as the extension.

To play DOOM with a PWAD file, start DOOM by using the -file option:

```
DOOM -file pwad_file
```

Some graphics cannot be stored into a PWAD file. Sprites (type 1) and floor textures (type 3) don't work properly when placed in a PWAD file. If they're present, DOOM will either ignore them or abort. They can, however, be placed in the WAD file with no problem.

Figure 1.1.

It may be easier to see the image with the cyan background.

Figure 1.2.

A black background makes it hard to see the edges of the figure.

-R

This option must be specified if you are extracting a graphic from a PWAD file. It is not required to store a graphic.

-C

The -c option lists all the separate elements in the WAD file.

THINGS TO KNOW ABOUT ADDING GRAPHIC IMAGES TO DOOM

In order to make the background of a graphic invisible, set the background color to cyan. To do this, set the red value to zero, and maximize the green and blue values to 255.

Graphics must be no larger than 320 x 200.

Some graphics may cause an error if the size or placement is changed. For example, TITLEPIC (the title screen) must have 0,0 for the insertion point, and STFGOD0 (the player image on the panel in degreeless mode) must not be larger than 31 x 31.

To completely change one of the monsters in the game, you must change all of the images associated with it. The Imp creature, for example, requires 52 images. These images show each of the creature's movements from eight different angles: front, back, left, right, and four diagonal views. There are also three sets of death images. These are shown from only one angle. The first has the creature reeling from a gun shot. The next shows the creature dying from the gun shots and ends with it lying bloody on the ground. The last shows the creature blown to smithereens by some massively destructive weapon.

Many of the graphics are numbers and letters that DOOM uses to specify various statistics of the game, such as how many bullets you have or how healthy you are. If you change these to different numbers or make them unrecognizable, it may be difficult to understand what's going on in the game.

A LIST OF GRAPHIC ELEMENTS

Because DMGraph doesn't provide a list of all the graphics in a WAD file, you may want to make a list yourself. Keep in mind, this is a *very* laborious process. What you must do is make a DOS batch file to create the listing. You'll need a text editor that can read and write ASCII text files and has macro capabilities or can store keystrokes and play them back using a hot key. Make sure you don't have files called LISTGRPH.BAT or GRAPH.LST in the directory you'll be using.

STEP 1: LIST ALL THE ELEMENTS OF THE WAD FILE

The `-c` option lists all the different elements of the WAD file. Some of them are graphics, some are not. You can't tell which. Start by listing all the elements to a file. Type the following:

```
DMGRAPH -c >listgrph.bat
```

The `>listgrph.bat` part tells the program to write the list to the file LISTGRPH.BAT.

STEP 2: MAKE THE BATCH FILE FROM THE LIST OF ELEMENTS

This is one of the tedious parts. Edit LISTGRPH.BAT in your text editor. Notice that on each line is the name of a different WAD element. Make a macro to do the following for each line:

> Copy the element name to the clipboard.
>
> Add `echo` before the name and `>>graph.lst` after it, leaving a space before and after the element.
>
> Go to the end of the line and press the Enter key to create a new line.
>
> Type `DMGRAPH`, leaving a space after, and paste the element name from the clipboard here.
>
> After the element, type `-v >>graph.lst`.
>
> Move to the next line.

This takes a line such as

```
AGB128_1
```

and creates two lines such as

```
echo AGB128_1 >>graph.lst
DMGRAPH AGB128_1 -v >>graph.lst
```

The first line prints the element name and appends it to the file named GRAPH.LST. The next line runs DMGraph using the `-v` option to list the characteristics of the graphic and again appends it to GRAPH.LST.

Try the macro out on a few of the lines. You may find that it doesn't work the first time. You may have to tweak it a little to get it right. Once the macro works properly, repeat it for each line in the file and save the file.

STEP 3: RUN THE MACRO

At the DOS prompt, type:

```
listgrph.bat
```

This will create a file called GRAPH.LST.

STEP 4: MODIFY THE LIST

Load GRAPH.LST in your text editor. Some entries will just have the element name and some will have a description. Part of the file looks like this:

```
END1
END2
END3
END4
END5
END6
TITLEPIC
type: 0; size: 320 x 200; insert point: 0,0; allocation: 68168
CREDIT
type: 0; size: 320 x 200; insert point: 0,0; allocation: 68168
BOSSBACK
AMMNUM0
type: 0; size: 3 x 5; insert point: -1,0; allocation: 48
AMMNUM1
type: 0; size: 2 x 5; insert point: -1,0; allocation: 32
```

END1 through END6 and BOSSBACK are not graphics. The rest are graphics. What you must do now is delete the elements that are not graphics. This is another very slow process. There are thousands of elements.

To avoid manually modifying the graphic listing, instead of listing the attributes you could change the batch file to extract the graphic. Change the macro to create the following line:

```
DMGRAPH graph_name -e graph_name.gif
```

EXAMPLE

Before trying this example, make a backup copy of your original WAD file.

There are many barrels on each level. Change the barrels to paper sacks. A paper sack is pretty easy to draw and there aren't very many images that need changing. If you don't want to change them yourself, check the disc that came with this book for the necessary GIF files.

STEP 1

Find the images you need to change.

4	4		1	DOOM PROGRAMMING
EPISODE	**MISSION**		**ROOM**	**GURUS**

This usually means searching through all the images with the -d option until you find the ones you need. To save time, I'll just tell you what they are.

There are seven images that need to be changed. There are two images for the stationary barrel: BAR1A0 and BAR1B0. (See figures 1.3 and 1.4.) DOOM cycles between them to simulate a barrel containing a sloshing toxic fluid.

Figure 1.3.
This is BAR1A0.

Figure 1.4.
This is BAR1B0.

The exploding barrels are represented by the five remaining images. (See figures 1.5 through 1.9.) The first image resembles the stationary ones. The next seems similar, but you can't see the fluid. The last three show the barrel exploding.

Figure 1.5.
This is BEXPA0.

Figure 1.6.
This is BEXPB0.

Figure 1.7.
This is BEXPC0.

Figure 1.8.
This is BEXPD0.

Figure 1.9.
This is BEXPE0.

STEP 2

Use the -v option to find out the information for each image. Type

```
DMGRAPH BAR1A0 -v
DMGRAPH BAR1B0 -v
...
DMGRAPH BEXPE0 -v
```

You'll find the information for these images is as follows:

Graphic	Size	Insertion Point	Allocation
BAR1A0 Type 1	23x32	(10,28)	944
BAR1A0 Type 1	23x32	(10,28)	944

BEXPA0 Type 1	23x32	(10,28)	944
BEXPA0 Type 1	23x31	(10,27)	924
BEXPA0 Type 1	40x36	(19,32)	1584
BEXPA0 Type 1	56x50	(27,46)	2696
BEXPA0 Type 1	60x53	(29,49)	3420

STEP 3

Extract the existing images using the -e option. Type

```
DMGRAPH BAR1A0 -e bar1a0.gif
DMGRAPH BAR1B0 -e bar1b0.gif
...
DMGRAPH BEXPE0 -e bexpe0.gif
```

STEP 4

Change the images to look like a paper sack. Start by drawing a brown rectangle and adding two parallelograms, one for the side and one for the open top. Touch it up a little and add the green toxic waste. For the exploding images, you really only need to make the parts of the barrel a flat brown color. Remember to use cyan for the background color. (See figures 1.10 through 1.16.)

Figure 1.10.
This is BAR1A0.

Figure 1.11.
This is BAR1B0.

Figure 1.12.
This is BEXPA0.

Figure 1.13.
This is BEXPB0.

Figure 1.14.
This is BEXPC0.

Figure 1.15.
This is BEXPD0.

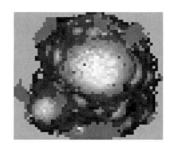

Figure 1.16.
This is BEXPE0.

STEP 5

Store the images back into the WAD file. (Since these images are Sprites (type 1), they cannot be put into a PWAD file.)

If you modified the old images files, the insertion point should still be in the image and you won't need to specify it. If you created new images from scratch, you'll need to use the -i option, as follows:

```
DMGRAPH BAR1A0 -s bar1a0.gif -i 10,28
DMGRAPH BAR1B0 -s bar1b0.gif -i 10,28
...
DMGRAPH BEXPE0 -s bexpe0.gif -i 29,49
```

STEP 6

Run DOOM. Once in the game, find a barrel. It should look like a paper sack filled with toxic waste. Now, stand back and shoot it. It explodes like the old barrels did.

OTHER THINGS TO TRY

1. Change the gender of the face in the panel to female.
2. Change the radiation suit on the fourth level (Command Control) to a clown suit.
3. Make a birthday version of DOOM: put party hats on all the monsters. Put streamers on the walls. Change the tall candle holders and other objects into cakes and presents.

ROOM 2

By Olivier
Montanuy

DEUTEX AND WINTEX

Do any of the following statements describe your ambitions as a DOOM designer?

- You've been thinking of a new level, but the textures in DOOM or Heretic just don't fit the mood.
- You'd like to leave your name in your WAD.
- You're a wanna-be artist, and you want to tag a wall that will be seen worldwide—in a cool WAD.
- You dream of slicing monsters with an elegant light sword rather than a disgusting chainsaw.
- You're wondering what Justin Fisher used for his *Aliens*-TC graphics.
- You want to reuse those cool textures that make Trinity so attractive.
- You don't want to be limited to editing maps, something any newbie with a good editor can do.

AN INTRODUCTION TO DEUTEX AND WINTEX

If you intend to create a WAD with custom graphics, Sprites, sounds, music, floors, and especially with custom wall textures, you should take a look at DeuTex. It can help.

DeuTex will decompose an existing WAD into a set of entries that can be edited with common graphics- and sound-editing tools. DeuTex will compose a WAD according to your written desires and the various entries you give to it, such as pictures, sounds, music, texts, and lumps (LMP files), and then DeuTex will check your creation. (See Figure 2.1.)

Figure 2.1.
The DeuTex logo.

WinTex will do all this, but more easily, using a special interface, under MS-Windows. (Unless otherwise indicated, all references to DeuTex in this discussion apply equally to WinTex.)

This set of tools is my original contribution to the DOOM fanship. Why did I write them? Because they had no equivalent at the time, and even now some of their features have no equivalent. I never had in mind to design a quick and dirty hack, but I also never imagined it would take so long. The project that these tools were built for is still on my disk, unfinished forever. But who cares? DeuTex/DeuSF will provide you more fun than just another WAD would have. But I mainly hope that they'll help you build the best DOOM/ Heretic patch ever.

WHAT USE ARE DEUTEX AND WINTEX?

DeuTex or WinTex will never let you create a new level map. There are tools for this—the level editors—and they do the job very well.

DeuTex was written to do a job that no single tool could do correctly at the time: easily decomposing and recomposing WAD files. WAD files have a special format, and the data inside has an even more special format, so there is no chance that the common sound and graphic editors might be able to read those tricky formats. Therefore you need a converter between the available tools and the WAD internal. If you need to treat a lot of data, then DeuTex is your best ally, although maybe not the easiest one to handle.

DeuTex will enable you to build (and install) patches to WADs that modify:

- The wall, floors, ceilings, and sky textures
- The Sprites (appearance of monsters, weapons, and objects)
- The graphics (menu texts, title screens, and status bars)
- The sound effects (monsters screams and weapons noise)
- The music

It will also let you combine separate levels, or any other entry, in any way you want, and of course it will give you easy access to the inside of the WADs that you like most, so that you can modify them to suit your desires.

There are a few tricks in WAD composition that DeuTex was designed to handle, and generally it will do all that can be done automatically. Alas, lots of things still require that you make the right decisions.

Even now that New Wad Tool (NWT) is out and working fine, I'm still tempted to say that only DeuTex does the WAD-composition job correctly, because with DeuTex you never handle the WAD internals yourself. Hopefully, with WinTex you'll be able to summon all the power of DeuTex without having to fight with a command-line interface.

Wad Tools, Wad Master, and above all New Wad Tool are very powerful tools in the hands of an expert; but for a wanna-be guru, their apparent simplicity is deceiving. You'll be tempted to do things that may end up crashing your WAD, and you'll never know why. With DeuTex, you're never supposed to put your hands inside the WAD structure itself.

WHAT IS THE DIFFERENCE BETWEEN DEUTEX AND WINTEX?

DeuTex is quite powerful and has been ported to many operating systems, such as DOS, OS/2, Linux, and UNIX; but to make it portable, I had to make it a command-line program. To use it, you need to be computer literate (at least literate enough to know how to use a command line).

I knew that the stipulation of computer literacy would leave most people out, and I could imagine that the best artists were not necessarily good with computers (although Fisher, with his *Aliens*-TC, is a notable exception).

So I wrote WinTex. It's no less powerful than DeuTex, because it is DeuTex presented in another way. Indeed, it's even more powerful than DeuTex, because it can compose textures and play or retrieve single entries in the main WAD.

Despite the very different presentation of the two, WinTex and DeuTex are the same tool, they work the same way, and you will use them in exactly the same way. The only difficulty is to understand the way you're supposed to use those tools, and that's what this part of the book is for. It will explain the operation of DeuTex and WinTex at the same time.

Most of the technical details of DeuTex and WinTex vary with the different versions, so if you got a version of these tools that doesn't behave exactly as described here, don't be disappointed. I'm writing with version 3.4 in mind.

WinTex 3.4 is the second public release of this tool, it has improved quite a bit since the first release, and two persons even wrote a tutorial for it that I included in the help file. I really did my best to make this tool usable for you, despite some tricky limitations of Visual Basic. Still it can improve, of course. Especially if you propose improvements!

USING DEUTEX AND WINTEX

This is the real important part. All the rest is technical information that you'll find in the on-context help of WinTex or the manuals of DeuTex. You need not bother with boring technical information until you really need it. Read this room, make some personal experiments, and then come back for the additional information.

HOW A WAD FILE IS TRANSLATED INTO MANY SMALL FILES

On your disk, a WAD file looks like a single big file. But it's a trick—it's one big file because DOS would be unable to handle so many separate data files. In fact, internally, a WAD file is made of a lot of smaller entries.

Before you can modify any of these entries, they must be extracted from the WAD and put into a plain file. These are the lumps, or LMP files, a representation of a single DOOM internal entry as a DOS file.

There are many entries in a main WAD—more than 4,000 of them. It is, of course, out of question to put all those entries in a single directory—you would not be able to browse that directory efficiently.

The choice made in DeuTex is to put all the entries in separate directories, according to their type, or, in other words, their role in DOOM.

There are nine major entry types:

- **Levels**   Everything that defines a level map, including the special NODE and REJECT structures
- **Sounds**   The sound effects, as sampled in a format such as WAV or VOC
- **Music**   The music, in a special MUS format
- **Textures**   The description of the wall textures, made out of many patches
- **Patches**   The pictures that are used as components of the wall textures
- **Flats**   The floors and ceilings
- **Sprites**   The monsters, players, weapons, and objects
- **Graphics**   The menus, title screens, and the like
- **Lump data**   All the rest

THE SUBDIRECTORY STRUCTURE

The principle of DeuTex and WinTex is that for each entry type, a special subdirectory will be used to contain all the entries of a given type. To make things simpler, the subdirectory will bear the name of the entry type, as defined previously.

All the operations concerning a given type of entry will happen in the relevant subdirectory.

When DeuTex or WinTex will need to store WAD data of a given type, it will put it into the corresponding subdirectory.

When DeuTex will need data of a given type, it will look in the corresponding subdirectory.

When WinTex will try to edit data of a certain type, it will use the same assumptions as DeuTex. So that when editing Flats, for examples, you'll be in fact modifying the Flats subdirectory.

I thought it was an easier to organize that way, and experience shows that people get used to this real fast—once it's explained plainly. I considered it logical that things of different type should go into different subdirectories. After all, you use a special subdirectory for DOS stuff, for DOOM stuff, for Heretic stuff, so it's nothing new to you. The advantage of using subdirectories is that you will know where to look if you try to modify your entries with other tools, like raytracers or graphic editors.

THE WAD DESCRIPTION FILE

There is another little trick: the WAD description file.

It would be just nice if DeuTex could store WAD data only as files, but it just isn't so, because there is a little more information in a WAD file than there is in a bunch of files.

What is missing?

- The entry names, which can be different from the filename. Think about what happens when you're redefining an Imp to become Homer Simpson. You want your files named HOMER-something, for clarity, but DOOM will require that the entry be named TROO-something, because it's hard-coded in the program.

- The graphic offsets for some pictures. These are tricky numbers that are used by DOOM to position your Sprites on the screen.

- You might no wish to use all the entries available in your directories. You will want to declare only those you want to use.

- You might be tempted, if you have a series of similar entries, to use the compression tricks that consist of giving a template entry and then saying some of the following entries are the same as the template entry. (That's the kind of trick that I used to reduce SIMPSON2 from 4.5MB to just 1.8MB).

- To redefine the animations for floors and ceilings, you need to declare the entries in a special order, since all the animated frames must be contained within the beginning and ending of the animation.

So you can see there is quite a lot additional information to store, which somewhat describes the internal organization of the WAD.

The choice in DeuTex and WinTex is to store all those information in a special file called, by default, the WADINFO file. Under DeuTex, you'll have to edit that file, but WinTex handles all this editing for you. Sometime, however, you will want to have direct access to this file, because WinTex is not always fast enough. You can modify it with text editors, but don't touch it before you know you have understood its structure.

THE ORGANIZATION OF THE WADINFO FILE

The organization is very simple: For each entry type there is a special section, whose name is the same as the name of the entry type and thus the same as the subdirectory that will contain the entries.

Each entry starts with a header that indicates which section we are in, and thus which entry type is concerned. This header is a name with brackets ([]) around it. For instance, the [SPRITES] header introduces the Sprites section (this is the same convention as in INI files). After this header comes a certain number of lines, each line giving information on one entry.

The format of the entry's information is always the same:

- First, a name, which will be the name of the entry.
- Then, an X and a Y offset. Of course, this is relevant only for graphics and patches. They are optional and are ignored if not needed.
- Then, an equal sign (=), followed by a filename (just the root name, without extension) of eight letters maximum. This name is optional.
- Then an asterisk (*), which is just here to indicate that no file defines that entry and it's just the same as the previous entry. Of course, if you use that sign, it's useless to specify an X or Y offset, or a filename, as they will be ignored.

Examples of valid LEVEL sections:

```
[LEVELS]                        ; level headers
E1M1                = TRINITY   ; level for Episode1 Mission1
E3M4                = MAYAN     ; level for Episode3 Mission4
```

Explanation: the level section defined here contains the definition of two levels, E1M1 and E3M4. The E1M1 is build from the file TRINITY.WAD in the LEVELS subdirectory (and MAYAN.WAD for E3M4). Note that the first level found in those WADs will be used, so it's no use to put many levels inside the WADs.

Examples of valid SPRITE sections:

```
[SPRITES]                       ; sprites header
TROOA1 123    45      = HOMER_1  ; file HOMER1, with offsets X = 123 and offset Y = 45
TROOB1 *                        ; TROOB1 is the same as TROOA1
```

Explanation: the Sprite TROOA1 (TROO is an Imp, and A1 means that it's walking, and seen from front) is defined by the file HOMER_1.BMP (or .GIF) in the SPRITES subdirectory. The aserisk (*) after the Sprite TROOB1 is to declare that TROOB1 is the same as the preceding Sprite, TROOA1. Use this trick when you don't want to draw all the phases or views of a Sprite, and want to save on the WAD file size.

SOME SPECIAL TRICKS OF THE WAD INFORMATION FILE

The definitions of wall textures are not contained in the WAD Information file. They are contained in text files, whose names are referenced in this file. The Textures information are not in that file because it would become too big for easy editing.

There is no TEXTURES entry, but rather a TEXTURE1 and possibly a TEXTURE2 entry (DOOM and Heretic only, not DOOM II). The texture entries don't directly define the textures. They refer to files that only contain textures. Of course, I should have put the textures directly in the WAD information file, but then it would have become too big and difficult to handle. I assumed that people will tend to keep their texture definitions in separate files, because a texture definition can be real big, and it need not change very often.

Also, the texture files only define your new textures. All the textures in the main WAD files are automatically imported from the main WAD, and they will be used unless you redefine them in your files. This is to sidestep a bug in DOOM and Heretic that concerns the usage of new textures. With earlier versions of DeuTex, no such strategy was employed, and some people encountered the bug. So I decided to take some preventive action.

There is no definition of wall patches (the components of wall textures) in the WAD Information file. This is because the DeuTex handles the patches automatically. Any patch that is defined in a texture and referenced in the PATCHES subdirectory will be loaded. What DeuTex has to do is obvious, in terms of the composition of texture, so why ask you to write it? Like the composition of the PNAMES list, all the obvious operations are automated. (This is not the case in other tools.)

Concerning the levels, you cannot use the asterisk (*) to indicate that a level is similar to the preceding one. Repeating a level would not be really wise. However, I hope in future versions to implement another trick that will allow you to create a WAD working with DOOM and DOOMII, by duplicating only the entries defining the object, sectors, and lines sides.

You will also sometime notice that a given section header, such as [SPRITES], happens many times in the WAD. DeuTex and WinTex treat this as a unique section, even if it looks like different sections. Why this tricky thing? Because it makes my life easier when programming the entry extraction routine. I don't have to reorganize the file each time I add a new entry.

THE DEUTEX DIRECTORIES AND FILES

To work correctly, DeuTex will need to know the following:

- The directory where you have put your main WAD file
- The working directory, where all the subdirectories containing the entries will be created
- The name of the WADINFO file

Default values:

- The main WAD directory is the current directory, unless you have set the DOOMWADDIR variable. (This is a facility meant for Linux and UNIX, but it can also work under DOS.)
- The Working Directory defaults the current directory.
- The WADINFO file defaults to WADINFO.TXT in the working directory.

Changing the default value:

This is easy under WinTex, since the main WAD and the working directory are indicated on the screen, and you just need to press the Change button to select another one. The name of the WAD information file can be directly modified on the screen, but you will seldom need to modify it.

Under DeuTex, use these options on the command line:

```
-doom directory    To specify a new main WAD directory
-dir directory     To specify a new working directory
```

The WAD information filename need only be specified when you use commands like Extract and Make. It is just another parameter of those commands.

THE FORMAT OF THE DATA FILES IN THE SUBDIRECTORIES

The LUMP subdirectory: The LUMP subdirectory contains files with no special format—or rather, with formats that DeuTex can't handle, because I didn't bother to write the code for this, since they are so seldom modified.

One exception is the end text of DOOM and Heretic, as well as the start-up text of Heretic. Those Lumps have a special format that an editor called TED can modify. TED is included in the WinTex package, but you can use another one. It's always nice to put your name and a few friendly messages there, and maybe a nice ASCII picture if you can.

Another exception is the Start screen of Heretic. The gods of Heretic have decided that it would not be coded like the other graphics, but would be under a special picture format.

The LEVELS subdirectory: The LEVELS subdirectory contains actual WAD files, which should contain the data for one single-level map.

Why WAD files? Because that way your level editors can directly handle those files. Most level editors, if not all, take WAD files as input, since levels are made of eleven parts, and the best way to store those parts is a WAD.

Why single level? So that you can reorder them and rename them easily. Oh, you say you have a WAD with many levels and can't use it here? Well, just extract all entries in that WAD, and you will get the single-level WADs you need.

Note that with DeuTex and WinTex, the single level WAD files are meant to contain only level data. If you are using custom textures or custom flats, they are not supposed to be in those level WAD files. If they are, they will be ignored.

It seems that now most programmers of level editors agree that the texture and flats WAD files should be distinct from the level WAD file, at least during the WAD conception phase. This is because no level editor is yet able to create texture and flat files, but of course I'm doing my best to have those WinTex features included in better-known level editors.

The SOUNDS subdirectory: This subdirectory shall contains sound files. They are used to modify the sound effects, such as the monsters' screams.

Those sounds effects can be recorded and stored as mono (not stereo) sounds, using 8 bits per sample, and no compression. All the good sound utilities can provide that kind of sound, but it may necessitate a conversion if you are using a 16-bit sound card.

I'm sorry for those requirements, but they are due to the format of sounds in DOOM and Heretic, and you certainly know that you had better not expect miracles from the sound code in those games.

You may store your sounds under three file formats: the default Windows format, WAV, which is the only one WinTex can handle; the VOC format of Creative Labs, because it is widely used; and the AU format of SUN Microsystems, because there is a version of DeuTex that runs on SUN. Note that only the most basic versions of those formats are supported. You can't expect a freeware tool to support every variant of the formats.

If you can, use an 11,025 sample-per-second mode, because DeuTex will convert to that rate—via a not very clever method. Expect background noise if you don't use 11,025 samples per second. I'm not a sound expert, and DeuTex is not supposed to be the ultimate sound editor.

If you have trouble with the sound capapbilities of DeuTex, it might be for one of several reasons: because your sounds are too big, because you used stereo sound, or because you use VOC format and your sound editor defines tricky stuff such as comments or skipped silences. DeuTex won't eat that—because DOOM or Heretic won't eat that either, and DeuTex doesn't know how to convert them, since I didn't bother to write the code.

The MUSICS subdirectory: The MUS files are in fact LUMP files, under the MUS format. That format is not read by DeuTex because Joachim Erdfelt, who wrote MUS2MIDI, didn't write the code clearly enough so that it can be reused in another tool. Hopefully, MUS2MIDI works fairly well, so it's not a real concern.

The TEXTURES subdirectory: The textures files come as TEXT files. You might be surprised by this, but texture files only describe the way the wall patches are to be placed in order to compose a wall texture. This is so because if there was a picture for every texture, that would make too many pictures. Think, for instance, of the switches, which need to be set against different backgrounds. Thus the patches are graphic elements, and texture files only define how to assemble those elements. The format of the texture files is trivial. It is the same as the one used by New Wad Tool, and almost the same as the one used in DoomTex.

Each texture starts with a line that defines its name, width, and height. Then come one or more lines, which begin with an asterisk (to distinguish them from a texture name) and which define a patch name, followed by a patch offset. Example: BIGDOOR7, a 128 x 128 texture made of two patches.

```
BIGDOOR7          128    128        ; width=128  height=128
*      W105_1      -4     -4         ; patch W105_1 at offset (-4,-4)
*      W105_2     124     -4         ; patch W105_2 at offset (124,-4)
```

When this texture is used, the game engine knows that the BIGDOOR7 texture, is a 128x128 texture, and thus has to be repeated horizontally every 128 pixel, if the wall is bigger than 128.

Vertically, all textures are repeated every 128 pixels, whatever their size, so sizes above 128 are useless, and sizes below 128 are dangerous, if used on high walls.

The game engine also knows, from the above definition, that there are two patches to place in this 128 x 128 space: one that is called W105_1 (what a name!) that is to be placed in the upper left corner at position (–4,–4), and the other one W105_2 that needs to be placed at position (124,–4). That only means that W105_1 will define the left side, and W105_2 will define the right side of the Door. But you certainly wonder what happens to the top left corner of W105_1, which is at (–4,–4), so obviously outside of the texture space? Well, it is ignored. As if it didn't exist. Only the parts of the patches that fall within the texture space can be displayed.

All the above certainly appears quite confusing. That's why WinTex has a great Texture Editing window, where you will never bother about those tricky numbers, but rather place your patches as you feel they should be placed, and contemplate the result. But of course, the principles remain the same.

The SPRITES, GRAPHICS, PATCHES, and FLATS subdirectory: All you need to know is that those sudirectories contain the picture files that define Sprites (the objects and monsters), Patches (the components of wall textures), Flats (the floors and ceilings) and Graphics (the menu entries, the fonts, the title screens, and all general-purpose pictures).

Only three graphic formats are supported by DeuTex. These are the default Windows format, BMP, which is the only one that WinTex can display; the GIF format of Compuserve, that is a very widely used format; and the PPM raw format. The PCX format is not supported because I don't use PCX, and I'm too lazy to code something that I won't use.

THE RIGHT USE OF DEUTEX, WINTEX, AND NWT

I'm tempted to say that the right way to use these tools is the way that I use them. This is the way they were written to be used. But is it really the best way? I can't tell. Most of you will do more WAD editing in your lifetime than I ever have. So these are only suggestions, which you will read, assimilate, and forget about after that.

You may be wondering when to use WinTex and DeuTex in relation to other tools. If you like, you can think of DeuTex as the WAD equivalent of a compiler and New Wad Tool as the WAD equivalent of an interpreter.

If you intend to make only small modifications to your WAD, then use NWT—it does this better.

If you intend to build a WAD with many entries, and if you know that some entries (such as Sprites generated by a raytracing software) will need to be re-created quite a few time before you get the animation right, then think of DeuTex.

As you probably know, compilers do a better job than interpreters—but the compilation pass is slower.

You may sometime have to make frequent modifications to some parts of your WAD file. This is common practice, especially when you are building a WAD containing Sprites, and you have to adjust each frame in relations to the others.

Then it may be real unconvenient to rebuild your entire WAD file every time, because it's a lengthy process. My suggestion is to make two temporary WADs: one that contains the entries you have to modify, and one that contains the entries you want to see but don't have to modify.

Adjusting Sprite frames requires yet another trick. Due to a bug in DOOM and Heretic, all the Sprites must absolutely be contained in the same WAD file. So the fastest method to edit Sprites is to create your WAD file, merge it into the main WAD with WinTex or DeuTex, see if the Sprites are correct, and if they are not, restore the main WAD, modify the Sprites, rebuild the Sprite WAD, and repeat the process. That will mean modifying your main WAD, but in a reversible way. This is much safer that the traditional method of using the old DMGRAPH tool to patch the main WAD, because DMGRAPH is not reversible.

However, the WinTex 3.4 Sprite Editing window now has some special tricks that make it especially suitable to guess how your Sprites will animate, without having to run the game. By playing with the phase and viewpoint indications, you can make your Sprite rotate or animate. However this is rudimentary, since WinTex cannot guess how the Sprites need to be animated. Use the great DeHackEd tool to view that kind of animation.

Note that DeuTex is especially meant for large projects, such as DOOM total conversions. It is good practice to provide the sound, level, music, and Sprite WADs separately. If you intend to do so, I recommend that you make one special working directory and one WAD information file per component of your project. When building your WAD, this is easier than playing with the entry-type selectors.

If you only want to modify levels, get a level editor; DeuTex won't help you a lot. It can only check some textures in your levels and tell you which textures are really used in your level (something that most level editors won't tell). Keep in mind that many level editors are not able to run a DeuTex-generated WAD, because DeuTex can do things that the programmer of the editors never imagined. But even in those worst cases, if you merge your WADs into the main WAD, the level editor will recognize it. This is DeuTex's special way to trick the level editors, because those limitations of the level editors were easy to forecast. Even DEU was limited in that respect, but it was a bug of DEU 5.21, certainly not a lack of imagination on the part of the DEU team.

Oh, and if you really want to make some very limited modifications, use New Wad Tools. DeuTex works fine, but it really works better in combination with a tool such as NWT. And I dare say that the reverse is true, since it's out of the question to extract more than a few dozen entries with NWT— you have to do all the operations by hand.

THE TRICKS OF TEXTURE COMPOSITION
TEXTURE SIZES

WinTex simply assumes by default that your textures have a width (in pixels) that's a power of 2, such as 8, 16, 32, 64, 128, 256, 512, and that the height of your texture is 128 pixels maximum. DeuTex will complain if it isn't so.

If your texture is less than 128 in height, you won't be able to tile your texture vertically, so avoid it.

Use 128 x 128 and you'll always be safe. But you can use as much as 4096 x 128 in DeuTex, and 2048 x 128 in WinTex.

Note that when making a texture, you should be aware that since the texture will be repeated on big walls, the left and right border should be very similar. Otherwise, players will notice that the textures repeat every 128 pixels (for instance) and it makes the texture a real pain for the eye. Even a WAD as beautiful as TRINITY has this small defect. I hope you will notice the difference in my conversion of TRINITY to Heretic.

SKY TEXTURES

Yes, the sky is indeed a kind of wall texture. Under DOOM, it was a plain 256 x 128 texture, which could easily be extended to 1024 x 128 to create a non-repeating sky pattern, as demonstrated in TRINITY. (See the clouds.)

Use a serial of four consecutive 256 x 128 patches to make the sky. Under Heretic, use four consecutive 256 x 245 patches. This is because a height of 128 wasn't enough in DOOM, but nobody noticed—until Heretic let you use the Wing of Wrath to fly all around. The 256 x 245 trick was found by Dan Teeter while testing early versions of WinTex.

TOO MANY PATCHES IN TEXTURE

The early textures built by id Software contained many patches. The later textures don't contain as many. Under Heretic, they really don't contain a lot. It's the evolution of the DOOM engine that makes it unable to handle a lot of patches in textures. For instance, if you want to put a nice text on your texture, don't do like in Trinity—don't use letters separately. Group all your words into a single patch. It's especially true for the sky textures.

ANIMATED TEXTURES

Under DOOM or Heretic, you can't create new wall animations; you can only redefine existing ones. This is because the animation names are hard-coded in the game program. What is coded are the two extremities of the animation sequence. Under WinTex, they are indicated as the Start of Animation and End of Animation.

So, you assign a Start of Animation, you add a few textures, then you add an End of Animation, and there it is—you have defined a new animation cycle. An animated cycle made of 24 frames is very close to the limit of DOOM and beyond the limits of Heretic. You have a lot of chances to crash the game during the startup sequence. Sorry, but the actual limit somewhat depends on the version of the game; you will have to experiment by yourself.

Of course, to compose your animations, you might wish to use WinTex. It used to be slow, but now that the patch cacheing is implemented, it is only slow when displaying a texture the first time. For an example of animation using WinTex, see the movie screen, beyond the yellow door, in my conversion of Trinity to Heretic.

PARTLY TRANSPARENT TEXTURES

For a texture to be partly transparent, or to be used on a false wall (a pass-through wall), it must contain just one patch. Put two patches on a transparent wall, and either the game will slow down painfully, or it will display random garbage.

TEXTURES WITH TRANSPARENT COLUMNS

Textures with a column not covered by any patch are not allowed by DOOM or Heretic. The sanction is a game crash. If, when checking your texture WAD, DeuTex tells you that you have a void column, which means you are in trouble, and the solution is to put a patch in that column. If you really want a transparent column, then it's the patch itself that must be transparent at this very place. For an example, look how the grids are done in Heretic.

THE TRICKS OF GRAPHIC COMPOSITION

The following remarks are valid for the flats, textures, patches, and Sprites that you will build with DeuTex and WinTex.

COLOR PALETTES

This is a general trick for graphics. DeuTex has some built-in palette matching, but due to speed considerations, the color matching is not always the best. It is designed to be real fast if your picture respects the DOOM or Heretic palette perfectly. If you have problems with colors, a programs such as Paint Shop Pro enable you adapt your picture's color to the DOOM or Heretic palette (which you can extract from any representative game picture). If you use a sophisticated picture-drawing tool, it is quite certain that your tool can find the best colors to represent your picture in DOOM or Heretic.

Generally, rely on DeuTex. If a picture doesn't go right, then use a specialized tool to adapt the colors.

Note that most picture editors use the RGB format (millions of colors), whereas WinTex can only read 256 color pictures, because palette patching would be much too slow. So if you find that WinTex reads your bitmap as transparent when it isn't transparent at all, then you know that you have made the mistake of using an RGB picture instead of a 256-color one.

SMOOTHING AND BLURRING YOUR PICTURES

You should smooth your pictures so that they appear as slightly blurred when you seen them normally. That way, they will keep looking fine even at a distance. A light blur will enable it to display fine at a small distance, but if it needs to be used in wide open areas, you had better smooth it a lot. Otherwise, it will display fine when you don't move but will seem to be flashy whenever you start moving.

AVOID REPEATING PATTERNS IN PICTURES

Repeating patterns can be a real texture killer. Never make a repeating pattern, especially not on flats and textures that will be seen at a distance. The worst examples are in *Aliens*-TC (which is also one of the best WADs, but for other reasons). The kind of stuff you must absolutely avoid include stripes, grids, and meshes. And the thinner they are, the greater the contrast between the stripes, and the worse the effect is. The kind of stuff you should prefer includes random or semi-random patterns. If you need stripes, don't make them straight.

REMARKS ABOUT ALIASING

The picture reduction done by DOOM and Heretic is simplified, as in Windows. It kills some lines and columns. That's why you need to smooth your pictures and avoid repeating patterns in patches.

Don't worry if you have some trouble understanding the logic of the previous statement. Despite the fact that we use digital sound in our phones and CD players, the aliasing effect is not really intuitive to us. But you have probably heard of anti-aliasing devices, and the preceding suggestions about blurring and about avoid repeated patterns are very crude anti-aliasing techniques, albeit for pictures rather than sounds. (It's only bytes in both cases. Just ask your PC.)

THE TRICKS OF SPRITE COMPOSITION
MAKING SMOOTH AND NATURAL ANIMATIONS

You must be careful that there is generally no more than four frames per animation cycle. That means that to look smooth, the movements of your Sprites will need to be minimal. Avoid long arms and legs rushing back and forth.

Another important consideration when drawing or designing Sprites is that when people move, they don't only move their legs. If you create something that only moves its legs back and forth without its body moving up and down, you'll have a mechanical rabbit—ugly to the eyes and an insult to your talent.

AVOIDING PLAIN FRONT VIEW

In real life, you almost never see a person directly from the front in symmetry. Likewise, your Sprite will look flat if shown this way. Do like id Software: always display the Sprites as seen slightly from the side.

ADDING MULTIPLE VIEWPOINTS

With DeuTex, you can declare eight viewpoints for a Sprite that normally only has one (or the reverse, if you want to save on the frame table, for future hacks).

The eight-viewpoints stuff works, but it's not real great for fixed objects, because the object will switch from one viewpoint to another very brutally. See my PCBAR demonstration patch for an example of a barrel transformed into an eight viewpoint PC. (Normally, a barrel is only one viewpoint.). The landing ship in *Aliens* DOOM II also has this behavior (although the WAD builders didn't use DeuTex, so they had to sacrifice eight frames instead of one). It really looks strange.

DOOM
PROGRAMMING
GURUS

2
ROOM

4
MISSION

4
EPISODE

USING EXTERNAL SPRITE AND FLATS WADS

You can't directly feed a file to DOOM that contains some Sprites or flats. But there are a couple alternate methods.

First Method: The WAD must be completed, so as to contain all the Sprites and flats of DOOM. DeuTex provides a command that will work with every version of DOOM and DOOM II, even with Heretic. The problem with Heretic is that the game will crash anyway, because there is a bug in the game.

Of course you don't distribute your completed WAD. You only distribute the base WAD—along with DeuSF, a little utility of 30KB compressed that does the job. (See Episode 4, Mission 7, Room 1, "DeuSF: A WAD Installation and Combination Tool," for more information.)

Second Method: Instead of completing your WAD, which can take up to 4MB of disk space, you may prefer to merge your WAD into the main WAD. In fact, with Heretic, this is the only solution. But of course, there is a command to restore your main WAD to its original state, including even the time stamp. This is one of the best tricks I have designed for DOOM, and you better believe that I'm quite proud of it, because it works great!

MORE TECHNICAL INFORMATION ABOUT WAD EDITING

This book will not try to give you the latest editing tricks. It will only enable you to become a DOOM and Heretic guru like the rest of us. We hope and expect you'll soon be better than us—because then we will be happy to use those great tools you will make and to play those marvelous levels you'll have built! For a DOOM guru, nothing is closer to Nirvana.

So if you want to know the latest tricks of DeuTex, WinTex, and DeuSF, you won't find them here. You will find them in the DeuTex manual, which was written by Kevin McGrail, the author of the amazing VOIDSHIP, a WAD that put a real strain on DeuTex (for the textures), RMB (for the reject map), and of course the node builders—not to mention the level builder. Kevin had RMB specially debugged so that it would accept his VOIDSHIP, and he learned so much about DeuTex that he could write a manual better than me. (I can't imagine what may have happened to the poor guys who wrote the node builder and the level editor.)

WinTex comes with its very own Help file (which in version 3.3 was written by me, because no one else had ever used the tool before) and Help system, so that clicking anywhere and pressing F1 when you're in trouble should get you more help than you actually need.

WINTEX, AN INTEGRATION TOOL FOR WINDOWS
WHAT MOTIVATED THE CREATION OF WINTEX?

WinTex only exists because I needed to learn Visual Basic, because I felt like training myself in the use of the graphic user interface, and because—well, because of the great tool NWT. I wanted to prove (essentially to myself) that I could do at least as good as Denis Moller.

Of course, I had to do something real new, under Windows (for graphics and sounds that were independent of hardware); but at the same time, I couldn't let down DeuTex, alhough it was obvious that the lame Windows programming environment would not permit DeuTex to remain a reliable tool.

So the answer is WinTex—a shell for DeuTex and an integration tool.

It's a shell because Visual Basic is too slow for anything else, despite the libraries written in C, and because it's the more reliable DeuTex DOS version that runs in the background, doing the serious business.

It's an integration tool because I knew there were many tools around, programmed by many people from different cultures using different approaches and languages, and the perfect integration tool was only a dream. I can only hope that someday such a tool will exist. It will be called DEU 6.0—or perhaps DoomEd.

Anyway, a shell such as WinTex can call DeuTex, but it can also call other tools, provided they are able to run under Windows and can be called from a command line or something similar.

WinTex 3.4 can directly call your default windows tools that edit the bitmap, wave and MIDI files. However, there is no default Windows tool for WAD files, so you will need to indicate to WinTex what tool you want to use, when you need one. Under WinTex 3.4, this is quite easy as when it runs a tool for the first time, WinTex asks you the file name that corresponds to the executable.

The hard part is that most tools need special command lines or adaptations before they can run correctly. Some level editors require so many indications that support for those editors has been hard-coded in WinTex. Some tools like RMB, REJECT, or BSP require a special command line, but WinTex can recognize them and provide the correct command line.

However, if you want to use a tool that I never heard about, it is possible, but you will have to edit the command line provided to this tool. This command line is written in the WINTEX.INI file. You will find it just behind the name of your tool. Composing a correct command line is tricky but explained in the Help file.

WinTex works with external reject builders, node builders, end-text editors, text editors, graphics editors, sound editors, MIDI file editors, MUS-to-MIDI, and reverse converters—it's real easy!

Of course, it could be easier, but keep in mind that the authors of most of these tools never imagined that another program would be designed to use them automatically.

A QUICK OVERVIEW OF WINTEX

Figure 2.2 was taken while I was rebuilding Trinity for Heretic. The display is that of WinTex version 3.3, which may change in future versions, if it is found to be inconvenient.

Figure 2.2.

The main screen of WinTex.

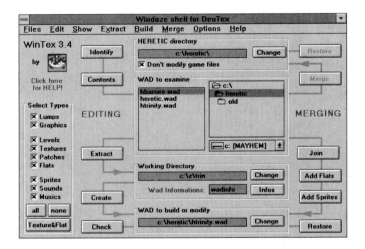

WinTex has one main screen with lots of button and menus. From top to bottom, this is where you will indicate the following:

- Where to find the DOOM or Heretic files. (Here it's written in the Heretic directory.)
- The WAD you want to examine. (Here it's HERETIC.WAD itself.)
- The working directory. (Here it's C:\Z\TRIN, my Trinity directory.)
- The WAD to be built. (Here I'm about to build HTRINITY.WAD.)

Notice that you can specify (on the left part of the screen) that only levels, textures, patches, Sprites, and music will be put in the HTRINITY.WAD. Then all I have to do is press BUILD and press CHECK to see that there are no errors.

The right part of the screen deals with WAD merging. (See Episode 4, Mission 7, Room 1 for more information.)

Pressing the BUILD, CHECK, EXTRACT, and MERGE buttons will in fact call DeuTex, with all the right parameters on the command line. (No need to plunge deeply into the manual of DeuTex here.)

On the menu bar, you will see the Edit menu. This menu enables you to invoke the various editing forms. There is basically one form per entry type, just as in DeuTex there is one directory per entry type. When you are under the Edit menu, DeuTex doesn't work, but other tools will be invoked when needed.

Figure 2.3 shows the texture editing window while I was editing MOVIE11, a texture part of the new Trinity film.

The upper part of the screen displays the texture, defining its name, MOVIE11, and size, 256 x 128. The frame in the center of the screen deals with the patches that compose that texture. You can notice the list of patches composing the texture, with their cryptic names like PBLACK or IMPXF7.

On the lower right part of the screen, you can see two lists. One list contains BMP files, (the list of the custom patches). The other list (on a gray brackground) is the list of graphic entries contained in the main WAD that can be reused as patches. To add a new patch, you just need to pick one from one of the lists and drop it on the texture.

Figure 2.3.
The texture editing screen.

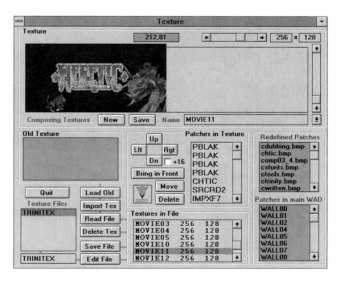

Figure 2.4 shows the WAD browser of WinTex, which lets you view (or listen to) the entries in a given WAD. Here I am viewing the Minotaur in HERETIC.WAD. The use of this windows is pretty obvious, and it is quite convenient.

Figure 2.4.
The WAD browser.

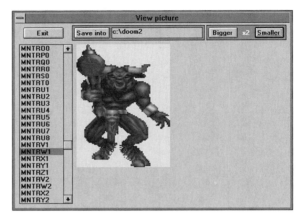

Note that I can save the picture, as a bitmap, into the DOOM II directory, as indicated previously.

Figure 2.5 shows the Sprite editing window. In the center, you can see the Sprite that is being edited, which is referenced in the Sprite list below as SRCRB2. Below the Sprite list is a drop box that tells which monster or object the Sprite is actually used for, since it is not always obvious from the name. Here, SRCR means that it's D'sparil riding his pet.

Figure 2.5.
The Sprite Editing window.

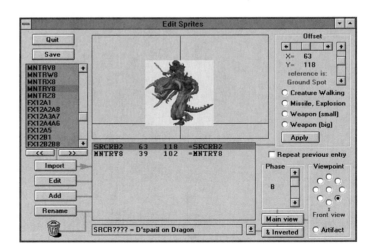

On the right of the Sprite, you can see a windows dedicated to setting the Sprite position on the screen, a position that directly represents the way it will be displayed by the game. Here, it is X=63, Y=116. That means the Sprite is positioned relative to the point where it stands on the ground, and that point is represented in WinTex as the intersection of the two black lines you can see behind the Sprite. Notice that the feet of the Sprite are in fact below the ground, but that's normal.

On the right of the Sprite list, there are two panels that show the Phase and Viewpoints. These are directly related to the Sprite name, and they indicate when the game is supposed to use that picture to represent the Sprite. Here Phase is B, and Viewpoint is 2, which means the Sprite is seen from the left front.

The left part of the screen is only the list of Sprites present in the main WAD file. This is very useful when you redefine Sprites and want to check that you replacement will actually make sense to the game. Remember that in DOOM or Heretic, only the Sprite name is important, not the picture displayed. So if you draw a picture of a guy walking, you had better give it a name that corresponds to the picture of a walking monster.

Double-click your Sprite name, and your favorite graphic editor is invoked with the Sprite file as argument.

Figure 2.6 represents the window used to edit floors and ceilings, usualy referenced as the flats. This window is a simplified version of the one used to edit Sprites.

Figure 2.6.
The Floors and Ceilings editing windows.

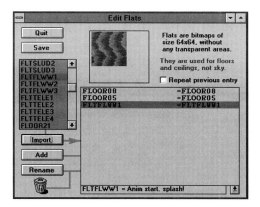

Note that the name of the select flat has been identified by WinTex as an animation start. (Here it's the start of the water animation.) "Splash" indicates that the monsters will splash water if they fall on such a floor.

I hope by now that you're convinced this tool is worth the try. Although it's a bit strange at first sight, it is in fact really easy to use.

Keep in mind that WinTex is a test bench. Despite all my efforts, it's still a Windows utility, and unless you add a second 100Mhz processor with 4MB of cache, it will remain desperately slow. Of course, I know how to make it run slightly faster—but the point was rather to test some new configuration while waiting for Denis Moller or another DOS coder to write the ultimate integration tool that won't need Windows (because DOOM doesn't run well under Windows).

Anyway, the use of the texture, Sprite, and flat windows is detailed in the WinTex tutorial, available in the help file. It may not be complete, but you will certainly want to thank Avery Andrew and Drake O'Brien who managed to write those tutorials before the last version of the program was actually finished.

SUMMARY

I know from the e-mail that I have received that I didn't do a bad job on DeuTex and WinTex. But of course, it will mean nothing at all if it's not used by people like you. The only satisfaction the author of a freeware tool can expect is to see that tool used and recommended. Of course, someone could write an even better program. The more features you add to a program, the more people will request it, and the continual upgrading and superceding of old products is perfectly normal. I can only hope the existing features of DeuTex and WinTex will give you some satisfaction. I did my best, and I do have a day job to worry about. (Some of you won't believe it, considering the time I spent on these programs. Well, let's make it clear: I said I had a job, but I don't pretend I have time for a life!)

As mentioned in WinTex 3.4, I wish I could get a simple postcard from all the people who will use my program and who think I deserve a friendly note for the work I did. It's an additional motivation for future work. If you don't have a few cents to waste on a postcard, then I'm sorry I'll never hear from you. But I'm even more sorry when thinking of the kind of outdated 386 that you probably play DOOM with!

4
EPISODE

4
MISSION

2
ROOM

DOOM
PROGRAMMING
GURUS

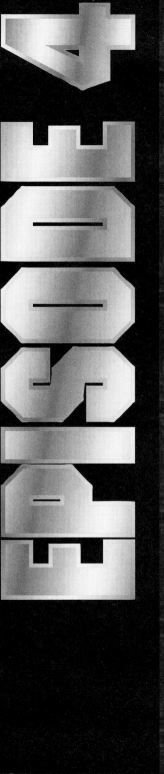

THE TOOLS OF THE GODS

MISSION 5: VOICES OF THE DAMNED

ROOM 1

By Michael LaFavers

DMAUD

DMAud (version 1.1) enables you to modify the sounds in DOOM. With this utility you can make your favorite monster sound like Curly from the Three Stooges or customize the player character with your own voice.

DMAUD SYNTAX AND OPTIONS

The syntax for using DMAud is as follows:

DMAUD *sound_number* [-s *input_file*] [-e *output_file*] [-l] [-q] [-x] [-f *pwad_file*] [-r] [-c]

The following options may be invoked. (A more detailed description of the options will follow.)

Option	Description
sound_number	Number of the desired sound sample.
-s *input_file*	Stores a sound sample (*input_file*) in a WAD file.
-e *output_file*	Extracts a sound sample (*output_file*) from a WAD file.
-l	Lists the samples in the WAD file.
-q	Don't play the sound.
-x	Enables you to add a sound sample larger than the current size.
-f *pwad_file*	Name of PWAD file.
-r	Removes the sound from an alternate WAD file.
-c	Lists the contents of the WAD file, including non-sound elements.

SOUND__NUMBER

This is a number between 1 and 61 that tells the program which sound file to refer to. DMAud always plays the sound when you run the program. To simply hear what a sound sounds like, type DMAUD with the *sound_number* as the only parameter. For example, to hear the sound of the pistol firing, type

DMAUD 1

A description of the sound is also displayed.

To extract or store a sound file without hearing it, use the -q option.

Numbers 50 through 61 are only available when you use a WAD file from the commercial version of DOOM.

-S INPUT FILE

Use this option to specify the name of the sound file you are storing in the WAD file. DMAud supports many sound formats, including AU, VOC, WAV and SND. Regardless of the sound's sampling rate, DMAud will automatically convert it to a rate of 11,025 samples/second.

-E OUTPUT___FILE

This option extracts a sound from the WAD file into *output_file*. DMAud always extracts sounds in the WAV format. If the file already exists, it will not be overwritten. You must specify a new file.

-L

This lists a description of all the sound samples in the WAD file. Sounds listed with an asterisk (*) before the description are not available in the public domain version of DOOM.

It's a good idea to use this option first and send the output to a file or the printer for future reference.

-Q

If you don't want to hear the sound you're referencing when you run DMAud, use this option. It also suppresses the sound description that is printed.

-X

If your sound sample is larger than the sample in the WAD file, it will be truncated to the same size as the sample in the WAD. To allow for a larger sample, use the -x option. This will allocate more space for the sound.

Using the -x option may increase the size of your WAD file when it makes room for the larger sound. Once the size is increased, however, using -x with a smaller sample will not decrease the size.

-F PWAD___FILE

This specifies the name of a PWAD file to use instead of the WAD file. This enables you to make the changes in the PWAD file and leave your original WAD file intact. If the PWAD file doesn't exist, it will be created. The file must have .WAD as the extension.

DOOM PROGRAMMING GURUS

1 ROOM

5 MISSION

4 EPISODE

To play DOOM with a PWAD file, start DOOM using the `-file` option, as follows:

```
DOOM -file pwad_file
```

-R

This option must be specified if you are extracting a sound sample from a PWAD file. It is not required to store a sample.

-C

The `-c` option lists all the separate elements in the WAD file.

EXAMPLES

Before trying these examples, make a backup copy of your original WAD file.

EXAMPLE 1

To change the sound of the pistol to the Windows DING.WAV sound, follow these steps:

1. Copy the DING.WAV file from your Windows directory to your DOOM directory. (If you don't have DING.WAV, find a short sound effect in any sound format. Use that file wherever this example refers to DING.WAV.)

2. Go to your DOOM directory and type

   ```
   DMAUD 1 -s ding.wav
   ```

   1 is the number for the pistol firing. The `-s` option stores the sound in the WAD file.

3. Run DOOM. Once in the program, fire the pistol. It should make a ding sound.

EXAMPLE 2

To change the sound the player makes when he tries unsuccessfully to open a door, follow these steps:

1. If you have a sound capture board, capture your voice saying "Open Sesame!" Save the sound as OPEN.WAV and copy it to your DOOM directory. If you don't have a sound capture board, look on the compact disc supplied with this book for a file named OPEN.WAV.

2. Go to your DOOM directory and type the following:

```
DMAUD 47 -s open.wav -x
```

47 is the number for the sound of the player pushing on a wall. Since the new sound is much longer than the original grunt, the -x option has to be used.

3. Run DOOM. Once in the program, go to the nearest wall and try to open it. You should hear your own voice saying "Open Sesame!"

OTHER THINGS TO TRY

- Replace all weapon sounds with cartoon sound effects.
- Give all the dying monsters some famous last words from historical figures or TV or movie characters.

ROOM 2

By Michael
LaFavers

DMMUSIC

DMMusic (version 1.0) enables you to extract music from (and insert music into) a WAD file or PWAD file. With this program, you can kill monsters to your favorite rock or classical music. DMMusic only accepts music in the MUS format. There are conversion programs available to convert other formats, such as MIDI to MUS.

DMMUSIC SYNTAX AND OPTIONS

The syntax for using the DMMusic utility is as follows:

```
DMMUSIC music_name [-s input_file] [-e output_file] [-l] [-f pwad_file] [-r] [-c]
```

Table 2.1 includes the options that may be invoked. (A more detailed description of the options will follow.)

Table 2.1. DMMusic Options.

Option	Description
music_name	Number for the desired music entry.
-s input_file	Stores a music entry (input_file) in a WAD file.
-e output_file	Extracts a music entry (output_file) from a WAD file.
-l	Lists the music entries in the WAD file.
-f pwad_file	Name of PWAD file.
-r	Removes the music from an alternate WAD file.
-c	Lists the contents of the WAD file, including non-music elements.

MUSIC__NAME

This is the name of the music entry to act upon. There are 27 music entries whose names have the following format: D_EXMY, here X is a number between 1 and 3 and Y is a number between 1 and 9. D_E1M1 is the music for level 1, D_E1M2 is for level 2, and so on.

There are four other music entries: D_INTER, D_INTRO, D_VICTOR and D_INTROA. These represent music not associated with any particular level. For example, D_INTRO is the music for the title screen.

4
EPISODE

5
MISSION

2
ROOM

DOOM
PROGRAMMING
GURUS

-S INPUT FILE

Use this option to specify the name of the music file you are storing in the WAD file. DMMusic supports only the MUS format. To store any other format, such as MID, the file must first be converted to MUS.

-E OUTPUT FILE

This option extracts a music entry from the WAD file into the specified *output_file*. DMMusic always extracts music in the MUS format. If the file already exists, it will not be overwritten. You must specify a new file.

-L

This lists a description of all the music in the WAD file.

It's a good idea to use this option first and send the output to a file or the printer for future reference.

-F PWAD FILE

This specifies the name of a PWAD file to use instead of the WAD file. This enables you to make the changes in the PWAD file and leave your original WAD file intact. If the PWAD file doesn't exist, it will be created. The file must have .wad as the extension.

To play DOOM with a PWAD file, start DOOM using the -file option, as follows:

```
DOOM -file pwad_file
```

-R

This option must be specified if you are extracting music from a PWAD file. It is not required to store music.

-C

The -c option lists all the separate elements in the WAD file.

EXAMPLE

Before trying this example, make a backup copy of your original WAD file.

Change the music from Level 1 to your favorite MUS file. Let's call it SONG.MUS for the purpose of this example. To change the music, follow these steps:

1. Copy SONG.WAV to your DOOM directory.
2. Go to your DOOM directory and type

   ```
   DMAUD D_E1M1 -s song.mus
   ```

   D_E1M1 is the name of the music for the first level. The -s option stores the sound in the WAD file.
3. Run DOOM. Notice that the music has changed to the music in SONG.MUS.

OTHER THINGS TO TRY

1. Change all the music to easy listening to have a nice, relaxing massacre.
2. Replace the music with songs from the 1970s and pretend you're killing the inhabitants of a disco.

EPISODE 4

THE TOOLS OF THE GODS

MISSION 6:
ENTERING THE ABYSS

ROOM 1

By Grant
Willison

DOOMMENU 12

The DoomMenu program is a front-end shell for DOOM that will run your favorite WADs without the hassle of DOS. DoomMenu organizes your WADs and performs all the cryptic commands to play your favorite game without you having to worry about anything. If you're like me, you have about 20 MB of WADs sitting around, and the only way to play them is via command-line options. If the author of the WAD didn't include a note telling you what level to play at, you have had to go hunting. DoomMenu is a quick way to bypass the hassle; choose your WAD with the mouse, and it automatically selects the correct level.

INSTALLATION

From the DOS prompt, change into your DOOM directory.

```
c:\> cd\doom
```

On the distribution CD-ROM that comes with this book, there exists a file called DMU02.ZIP. Type in the following command: (it is assumed your CD-ROM drive is d:. If it is not, replace the d: with your CD-ROM drive letter)

```
c:\doom> d:pkunzip d:dmu02.zip
```

This will extract two files into your DOOM directory: DOOMMENU.EXE and GODOOM.BAT.

THE SIMPLE WAY

To run it, install the program to your DOOM directory as described above, and type **GoDoom** (it is not case-sensitive) in the DOOM directory. This will call DoomMenu and pull up the WAD listing in your DOOM directory. If you get the message "there are no .wad files in .\!", you are going to have to type **GoDoom -d d:**, where the d: is your CD-ROM drive. You should now be on a screen which has a list of all your WADs you can play with. The first item in the list of wads will be highlighted. By pressing the four arrow keys, you will be able to highlight a different .wad file. Search around and pick a WAD by pressing the Enter key.

If there is more than one level available by the WAD, the program will ask for which level you want to play. Generally, you can simply press enter at any question at this point on and be just fine. If you want to play a particular level though, this screen gives you that option. Using the arrow keys, highlight your desired level, then press Enter. Finally, a pick list comes up asking for what difficulty level you want to play. After you choose, DOOM will run with your choices.

4
EPISODE

6
MISSION

1
ROOM

DOOM
PROGRAMMING
GURUS

USING THE OPTIONS

If you want to actually use subdirectories and other organized ideas, DoomMenu will handle that, too. Typing in `GoDoom /?` will give you an idea what type of options you have. Basically all the options you could type into DOOM you can forward through DoomMenu. The options are as follows:

-d *dir*	Specify WAD directory. An example could be `-d .\wad` or `-d c:\incoming\doomstuf`.
-s *level_#*	Specify skill level. Since I always play at (Nightmare - 1), my batch file has: `-s 4`.
-r …	This is how to pass on other options to the game. After -r is read, the rest of the command line is sent as is to DOOM.
-BATCH	Environment switch. Mainly for internal use and is explained later in this section.

UNDERSTANDING DOOMMENU

You may be wondering by now why you are running GoDoom instead of DoomMenu. DOOM (as you may well know) takes up a lot of memory. So it is necessary to exit DoomMenu, because a shell would not leave enough memory free. GoDoom then runs another little batch file called WORKING.BAT. The WORKING.BAT file, created by DoomMenu, runs DOOM with all the command-line specifications that were specified from the DoomMenu program. The setup enables you to edit GoDoom at will, so you can set option preferences to be permanent. The best way, of course, is to just enter your settings into your boot menu that runs GoDoom, so you can play with it there.

You can run DoomMenu directly, and it will notice that you are not calling via the batch file. It will then push the text string `working` to the DOS prompt. When the program ends, WORKING.BAT will run just as if you typed it yourself. If you are calling DoomMenu in your own batch file (without the -BATCH option), the text will not be processed until the end of your batch file. The -BATCH option prevents the program from pushing `working` to the DOS prompt. Finally, I require the file MINUS.WAD with my DOOM sessions (I've changed DOOM around so often I've long lost track of what I've done to mess it up to require this file). MINUS.WAD does not do any damage if it's not needed, so if the file exists, the program automatically includes it. The file must be in the DOOM directory. If you do not know what MINUS.WAD is, it's just a little patch id Software produced to make some versions compatible.

HOW DOOMMENU WORKS

DoomMenu was written in Turbo Pascal v6.0, with Turbo Professional v5.5 (which is why I can't compress the stack enough to run DOOM inside of the menu—the extended DOS unit won't compile in v6). If you are interested in the source code to DoomMenu, just e-mail me at grantgw@unixg.ubc.ca and ask.

I first wrote the code without any idea of how to determine at what level the designer of the WAD placed his/her game, and I used WADNAME.EXE (copyright 1994 by ASRE). I just linked it to my program, and it would choose for me. It was fine for me, but when I thought of releasing the software, I thought there might be some copyright violations somewhere in doing that. So I e-mailed the writer of WadName, and he sent me the C code. I thought, "Hey, no problem—I know both languages, so conversion should be easy." I was wrong. Pascal has limited power when dealing with binary files. C, on the other hand, allows almost anything.

Before the first pickwindow, the program pulls all the WAD files out of the specified directory. I used code directly out of the Turbo Pascal examples file. (See trick #1.) Then, using code from an old program (see trick #2), I put it into a pickwindow, which comes from Turbo Professional. When choosing a WAD, DoomMenu validates it and finds out what levels it supports. I translated ASRE's code into Pascal for that task. (See trick #1). I thought of letting people add both game WADs and sound WADs, but in my experience, I've never found just one WAD that had all the sounds I wanted. So I've taken all the good sounds out of add-in sound WADs and included them directly into DOOM.WAD.

If the program finds that the number of supported levels in the game WAD is greater than one, it displays another pick list so you can choose what level you want to start at. Then if you didn't specify via command-line options, you must choose your skill level. Finally, the program writes the file WORKING.BAT. This is what actually runs DOOM. If you want to know exactly what is being sent to DOOM, you can type out this file and look at it.

TRICKS AND TRAPS

I like the idea of doing a small amount of work for a large result. As in other fields of endeavor, DOOM programming has tricks and traps that can make your life easier or harder.

4 EPISODE

6 MISSION

1 ROOM

DOOM PROGRAMMING GURUS

TRICKS

1. Always use someone else's code if possible.

2. Employ modular code. If you do it right, you can use the code again without having to re-understand it.

3. Don't use C if you can help it.

4. Read the newsgroups.

TRAPS

1. Believing you will be satisfied with just "a little program."

2. Thinking you will remember, in your head, all the code you have written.

The preceding list gives some basic point form suggestions that I always try to follow when programming. I'll go through that list again, but this time I'll explain myself:

1. Remember: Someone else's code is already debugged, and it takes considerably less time to import code than to design it yourself. As long as you can't be sued for it, use it! It's the same principle as why you would copy a school import code than design it yourself. As long as you can't be sued for it, use it! It's the same principle as why you would copy a school assignment off a friend. If no one knows how you accomplished the assignment, your grade can be as good as your source's, but with considerably less work involved. The number-one help in programming for me has been the extended units in Turbo Pascal. For designing a DOOM add-on, I knew there were hundreds of megabytes of programs out there relating to it. The most challenging part of the program was deciphering all the WAD files—finding the levels, verifying the file, and so forth. Someone else already did it, so why should I have to? When I mentioned the problem to my friends, they told me about the WADNAME.EXE program supplied by ASRE. It took just one e-mail message to receive the C code. It can't get much nicer than that.

2. This sort of follows trick 1. I wanted to reuse the directory window from DoomMenu for a point-of-sale program I'm working on. When I copied it over, I realized that I had to change it to accept more than just WAD files, and I (gasp!) used global variables, which (because I was lazy) included the new program. If you ever clone any part of your code,

you'll feel very happy about not having to retype another hundred lines of code. I have this terrible tendency to hack code together, yet understanding my own hacked code is impossible. A guy wanted an interface changed in a program; I actually spent three hours on about 300 lines, and then I just gave up and re-wrote the entire piece (modularity!).

3. Yes, I know about C's power and the computability across platforms, but any language that allows

```
for (p=++s--;--(*p)++ = (*p =="\n") ? "\0" : " ";p++);
```

just cannot be trusted. Because of Pascal's structure, you take a few more lines of code, but you will never be confronted with the words *segmentation fault*. Pascal also has the nicest range of extended libraries. There's Turbo Professional, Object Professional, Turbo Wheels, and so on.

4. If you want to create a program, you need to do two things. One is to make it useful, and the other is to do it before someone else does. Since the DOOM newsgroup gets about 3,000 messages a day, occasionally there will be someone griping about a shortcoming in a DOOM-related program or even in DOOM itself. For instance, the command-line options can be somewhat cryptic for users. The DOOM FAQ sheet required several pages to cover them all. Like most front-end programs, mine bypasses the necessity for the user to know these options. The newsgroup enables you to know the market you are working towards. In comparison, the cheapest market survey you can get for commercial purposes costs about $900.

5. When I started this program, all it was going to do was give me a pick list and push that through into DOOM for me. Then, after that worked, my brother asked for an option for different difficulties. (Not only is he in God mode half the time, but he plays at easier levels, too.) Then I got some WADs that contained nine levels, and I found ASRE's WadName program did not have enough error handling for me to use unless I included it directly. Also, nine levels take a while to play; I needed an option to start halfway through an add-on WAD. Then my D: drive ran out of space, and I put all the game WADs onto C:. Therefore I added the different-directory option. My friend got a new DX/2, so we had to play against each other with his new machine. I wasn't going to add any more code at this point, so I added the -r option. Around this time, I thought that it would be cool to place the program on the Internet. Well, to do that, I had to put in more error checking and handling, as well as a Help screen, which any good program should have. The point of all this? *Know where you plan to end the program!*

6. Having programmed many assignments throughout the years, I have found an amazing assortment of routines hiding on my hard drive—most of them are programs I don't recognize anymore. After five years, I might remember most of what a program did, but I don't have a clue of what the code actually is. If you want to follow tricks 1 and 2, you need to make a list. Make a file within your IDE (integrated development editor), and cut and paste the first line of all your procedures and functions into the file. After each one, write *one* line describing the procedure. If you need more, you probably didn't write modularly enough. A real description would go with the function itself. The description here is just to get you interested enough to look it up.

ROOM 2

By Christopher
M. Badger

DOOM-IT V5.4 SETUP UTILITY

If you're tired of playing DOOM and DOOM II by the same old rules and want something to spice it up a little, you're in luck. With a program called DOOM-IT you can access features of DOOM and DOOM II not available through the normal setup program. With the use of these features you can change nearly every aspect of the game to your preference. DOOM-IT also simplifies some of the basic setup procedures by allowing you to save your modem, serial, and network game settings. All this, and an easy-to-use interface, makes DOOM-IT a must for any DOOM or DOOM II player.

DESCRIPTION

DOOM-IT is an alternate setup program for DOOM and DOOM II. When using DOOM-IT to start single or multiplayer games, one can take full advantage of command-line parameters. These parameters enable you to load multiple WAD files, record a game, start from any level, turn on development mode, and much more. The 5.4 version of DOOM-IT provides complete support up to DOOM v1.666 and DOOM II v1.7a.

INSTALLATION AND REQUIREMENTS

Installation of DOOM-IT from the CD-ROM is simple and painless. Simply UnZip all files within DOOMIT.ZIP into any directory on your hard disk. DOOM-IT requires about 175KB of disk space and 200KB of conventional memory. The memory requirement increases for each WAD file DOOM-IT reads (about 18 bytes each). All of this memory will be freed once the program exits to run DOOM.

To start the program, type DOOMIT at the DOS prompt and press Enter. You must use the DOOMIT batch file for DOOM-IT to work correctly. You cannot run DMLOAD.EXE.

CONFIGURATION

When you run DOOM-IT for the first time you need to configure the program to work with your hardware. Before you run a Network, Serial, or Modem game, you need to specify the PORT and COM settings. To access the hardware configuration menu, press the Alt key from the main menu. This will bring up a menu bar located near the top of the screen. Use the arrow keys to highlight the word CONFIG, then select one of the three connection types. (More information on each of these is given later on.)

The next step in configuring DOOM-IT is to make sure the path statements correctly point to the appropriate directories on your hard disk. They tell DOOM-IT where to find the DOOM, WAD, and DeHackEd files. (DeHackEd is a helpful utility that will be discussed forthwith.) To modify these settings, choose PATH from the menu bar then select one of the three file locations to modify.

You must select DOOM 1 or DOOM 2 from the initial menu before accessing the menu bar. This is done so DOOM and DOOM II will have separate settings.

NETWORK SETUP

When you are playing a network game, you and all the other players must have an identical port number chosen. To configure DOOM-IT with a port number, choose the network category under CONFIG on the menu bar. By selecting different port numbers, more than one multiplayer game can be played over the same network. The default port number is set to 0, which should work in most cases.

SERIAL SETUP

Before you start a serial game, you must specify which COM port the serial cable is plugged into. To change this setting, choose the serial category under CONFIG on the menu bar. Most computers only have an external COM 1 or COM 2 port for serial connections.

On the same serial-configuration menu, you are given the option to choose a baud rate. If you use this feature, it will override the setting in your MODEM.CFG file that DOOM normally reads from. If you don't want to override the baud rate setting, choose Default.

The final option on the serial-configuration menu determines whether or not to set the UART to 8250. If you have a faster I/O card and it's not working properly at the higher speed, you might try using this option to use the slower setting.

MODEM SETUP

Before starting a modem game, you must specify which COM port your modem is connected to. To do this, choose the modem category under CONFIG on the menu bar. Most external modems can only use COM1 or COM2. Most internal modems can be setup to use COM ports 1 through 4.

As with the serial setup described previously, you can specify a baud rate for the modem which overrides the settings in your MODEM.CFG file. You can also set the UART to 8250 if you are having problems at the higher speed.

Once you have your modem configured correctly you can provide the phone number to dial in one of two ways. You may use the built in phone book (which is discussed later on) or you may type in the phone number manually each time. If you choose to be the dialer when starting a modem game, then you will be given the option.

USING WADS

WAD files are an easy way to add your own levels, graphics, or sounds to DOOM and DOOM II. When loaded, they temporarily replace some of the information usually found in the main WAD file (DOOM.WAD or DOOM2.WAD).

If you tell DOOM-IT that you want to load WAD files, then you will be presented with a list of all files with a .WAD extension in the WAD directory you configured DOOM-IT for. You can select up to nine different files to load at one time. To select more than one WAD, highlight each file and press the space bar to mark it. You will then see an asterisk character next to the file. Once you have your WADs marked, you can press the Enter key to continue.

If you chose to load a WAD containing a new level, the program will ask if you want to warp directly to that level. Doing this will skip the process of choosing an episode or level number and instead use the WAD's level. If you have marked more than one WAD level to load, the program will warp you to the one that occurs earliest in the game.

There are a couple of other features you can use from the WAD-selection menu. If you wish to change the episode or level number of a WAD level, then highlight the file and press F1. You will then be prompted to enter in the new information.

It is also possible to scan through a large list of WAD files by pressing a key from **A** through **Z** to jump to the first WAD in the list beginning with that letter. This is very helpful if you have a hundred or more WADs to look through.

USING DEHACKED PATCHES

There is a great utility for DOOM called DeHackEd that was created by a fellow named Greg Lewis. This excellent program enables a person to modify the DOOM or DOOM II executable file. By doing this, you can alter every last detail about DOOM, such as the speed of weapons, the behavior of monsters, and the amount of health or armor the player starts with. Episode 4, Mission 2, Room 1, "DeHackEd v2.2," discusses the DeHackEd utility in detail.

To load a patch file created with the DeHackEd utility, press **P** from the final setup menu. This will bring up a list of all files with a .DEH extension in the directory specified in your DEHACKED.INI file. Make sure the DeHackEd directory path for which you configure DOOM-IT contains both the DEHACKED.EXE and DEHACKED.INI files. DOOM-IT reads the DEHACKED.INI file to determine where your patch files are located.

Because DeHackEd patch files permanently change the information in the DOOM or DOOM II executable file, I recommend making a backup of these settings. This way you can restore the original settings within DOOM-IT by simply loading a default patch file. To make a patch file called DEFAULT.DEH, type the following at the DOS prompt:

```
DEHACKED -SAVE DEFAULT.DEH
```

This should be done before making any alterations to your original executable files.

DEFINING DEFAULTS

If you find yourself choosing the same settings over and over for a single or multiplayer game, you can automate the process by defining a set of custom defaults. This way you can load the settings you want with the press of a button rather than going through every menu each time you play.

DOOM-IT enables you to customize five sets of defaults. To edit these settings, select the Defaults category under MISC on the menu bar. Choose one of the five available slots and press Enter. You now have the option to give your settings a menu title. Once you have chosen a title, press Enter again. You are now presented with a screen showing nearly all of the game options. Customize the settings to your liking and press Enter a final time. The settings will be saved permanently for future use.

To load these defaults, press **D** from the game-selection menu. When the list appears, highlight the desired settings and press Enter. The only thing left to do to is select a game type and decide whether or not to use WADs.

PHONE BOOK

The built-in phone book enables you to store the name and phone number of up to 10 different people. To add a name to the phone book, choose the Edit category under PBook on the menu bar. After you have done this, you are able to pick one of 10 slots to modify. Highlight a slot and press Enter. Type the person's name and press Enter again. Now type his or her phone number and press Enter a final time to go back to the original menu.

RECORDING DEMOS

To keep those great frag feasts for posterity, DOOM-IT enables you to record and play back your single or multiplayer games.

If you choose to record your game, you will be prompted to enter in a filename to save the demo into. When typing in the filename, use no more than eight characters and leave off the file extension. DOOM will use .LMP as the file extension automatically. For example, if you provide DOOM-IT, the name DEMO1 for recording, DOOM will save it as DEMO1.LMP.

If you are using DOOM v1.666 or DOOM II, you can record multiplayer games. You can also specify the maximum size you want DOOM to reserve for the recording. This is done by using the -MAXDEMO parameter followed by the number of kilobytes to reserve. Since DOOM-IT v5.4 doesn't directly address the MAXDEMO feature, you must add it manually to the ADD PARAM list under MISC on the menu bar. If you enter -MAXDEMO 1024, for example, DOOM will reserve 1MB for the recording.

When recording multiplayer games, make sure all players choose the Record option and specify the same MAXDEMO size. The recording of your game begins right when you start DOOM. To end the recording, press Q or exit the game.

Once you have recorded your demo, you can play it back within DOOM-IT by selecting the PLAY DEMO category under MISC on the menu bar. If you recorded the demo from a WAD level, you must load that same WAD again for the demo to play back correctly. After doing this, you will be prompted to enter in the demo filename. Type it in the same way as before, leaving off the file extension.

MOUSE INTERFACE

DOOM-IT provide an interface for using a mouse in addition to the keyboard. You can use the right and left buttons of any Microsoft-compatible mouse to perform the same functions as the keyboard. In general the left mouse button is used to make menu selections and the right mouse button is used to back up a menu (the same as pressing the ESC key).

On a single-list menu, use the left mouse button to make your selection. After doing this, the program will take you to the next menu. On a multi-list menu (such as the modem config menu), use the left mouse button to change the settings in each box. Then click the left mouse button on the parenthesis box in the upper-left corner of the menu.

On the WAD selection menu, use the left mouse button to mark or unmark each file you want to load. You can also use the left mouse button to click the up and down arrows to scroll through the WAD file list.

On menus that require a yes or no answer, click the left mouse button on the word YES or NO to specify your answer.

ID SETUP

If needed, you can run the SETUP.EXE program that comes with DOOM or DOOM II within DOOM-IT. To do this, choose the ID SETUP category under MISC on the menu bar. This option is given just in case you need to change your hardware settings at the last minute. Make sure you exit the setup program and return to DOOM-IT before starting DOOM.

RESPONSE FILES

Since DOOM-IT uses command-line parameters to pass the settings you choose to DOOM, the size of the parameter list must not exceed the DOS limit of 128 characters. One way around this limit is to use a response file. A response file is a feature available in DOOM v1.666 and DOOM II that enables the command-line parameters to be written to a text file, which is then passed to DOOM.

CUSTOM PARAMETERS

DOOM-IT enables you to define your own parameters if needed. This might be necessary if you have an alternate SERSETUP or IPXSETUP file that can accept non-standard parameters, or if you want to use parameters not addressed by DOOM-IT. To define them, you need to select the ADD PARAM category under MISC on the menu bar. You can type up to about 50 characters of your own parameter text. These parameters will always be added to the settings you choose when starting a game.

OTHER PARAMETERS

There are other parameters DOOM accepts that are not necessary to directly address in DOOM-IT. Many of these are listed in the following table. If you wish to use any of these, you may add them to the custom parameter list.

Version	Parameter	Description
1.2	-config <filename>	Specifies an alternate config file.
1.2	-devparm	Is needed to allow certain parameters. With -devparm enabled, you can press F1 during the game to save the screen as a PCX file.
1.2	-recordfrom <#> <name>	This is only available in DOOM v1.2. It enables you to record a game from a saved game (Example: -recordfrom 1 demo).
1.666	-irq <number>	Sets the IRQ for a COM port.
1.666	-port <number>	Sets the COM I/O port that SERSETUP uses for your modem (Example: -port 0x3f8).

A more complete description of many of these parameters can be found in the README file that comes with DOOM or DOOM II.

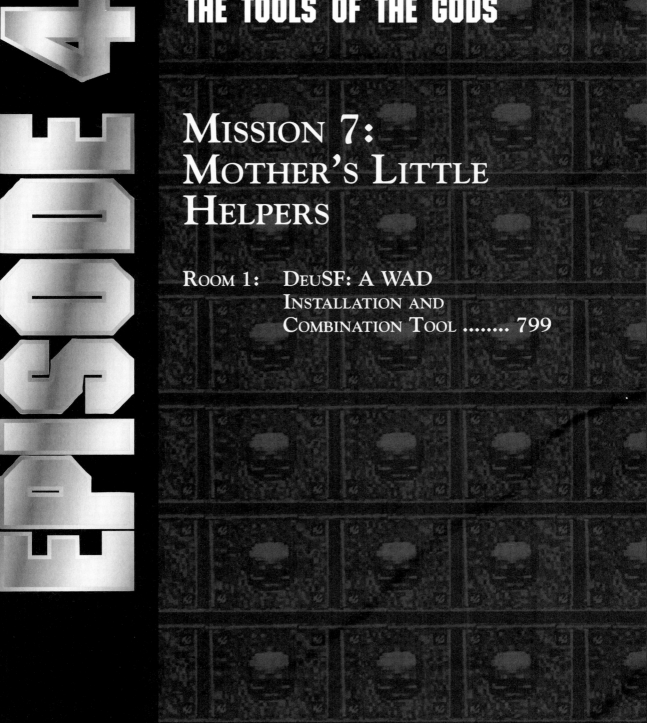

EPISODE 4

MISSION 7:
MOTHER'S LITTLE
HELPERS

ROOM 1

DEUSF 3.4: A WAD INSTALLATION AND COMBINATION TOOL

By Olivier Montanuy

DeuSF is a simplified version of my more general tool DeuTex and is meant to be used by people wanting to have fun with DOOM, DOOM II, and Heretic. With DeuSF, you can easily combine WADs that have been built by other programmers.

Don't be afraid to use this tool. It's not more complex to use than DOOM or Heretic themselves. If you have already played a custom WAD with DOOM or Heretic, then you know enough DOS to be able to use DeuSF.

This tool is made for ordinary players, not for gurus or even apprentice gurus; so don't expect boring technical discussions here.

Note that you need version 3.4, which is on the CD-ROM included with this book. Earlier versions of the program didn't work so well.

WHERE DEUSF CAN BE USEFUL

Check whether you have already encountered any of the following scenarios. If yes, DeuSF can help. Just apply the command line listed therein.

(Remember: These are only example of command lines. The name of the specific WADs will need to be adapted to your situation.)

- *Aliens* Sprites are great! I don't wanna ever see another Demon!

  Want to modify DOOM/Heretic definitively? DeuSF can merge any WAD into your main file. Merge your favorite *Aliens* patch and you'll never see normal monsters again.

  ```
  > deusf -merge ALIENGFX.WAD
  ```

  DeuSF was the first ever tool to implement this. At first, Elias Papavassilopoulos, one of the greatest DOOM gurus, told me the idea was ridiculous. Four months later, Denis Moller found it so cool he added it to New WAD Tool! New WAD Tool (NWT) is a DOS-based tool. NWT version 1.03 is on the `ftp.cdrom.com pub/doom/newstuff`.

- My little brother doesn't like *Aliens*. I'll have to re-install DOOM.

  Changed your mind? Then discover one of the craziest features of DeuSF: Whatever job it did, it can undo. It will restore your DOOM/Heretic file to it's original state, with file size and time stamp preserved, so that you can even apply id Software's patches after that. An example of the undo command is as follows:

  ```
  > deusf -restore DOOM.WAD
  ```

  The file you merged into the main DOOM/Heretic file is even regenerated.

  DeuSF was the first tool to implement this reversible modification of the main files. No other tool will spit back the files you've fed into your main DOOM/Heretic files. (And yet, months after the first DeuSF release, people still keep patching their files with DMGRAPH—a nice tool, but not reversible at all.)

■ When I install *Aliens* DOOM, a huge file is generated.

This is because when you want special custom Sprites but don't want to modify your main DOOM files, you need to generate a file with all the Sprites. In fact DeuSF can do that, but it can even do better: Instead of generating a new file, it just appends to your existing Sprite file only those Sprites that are necessary to play DOOM. Hence, the file size increase is minimal. (It can't be less.)

```
> deusf -sprite -app ALIENGFX.WAD
```

```
> doom -file ALIENGFX.WAD
```

DeuSF was the first tool to implement this file-completion feature. (It was also the first feature Denis Moller copied from DeuSF into his NWT tool.)

■ I hate Barney! I hate Homer! I want to blast them both at the same time!

You say you've got that cool Barney patch and that other cool Simpsons patch, and you can't play them at the same time? Hey, guy, that was before DeuSF 3.1! DeuSF now has a command to join two separate PWADs together, as follows:

```
> deusf -app HOMERDOOM.WAD
```

```
> deusf -join HOMERDOOM.WAD BARNEY2.WAD
```

```
> doom -file HOMERDOOM.WAD
```

This is another unique feature of DeuSF, once again copied into the lastest version of NWT. Some other tools let you merge files, but none is yet as powerful as DeuSF. None can detect Sprite viewpoints that are not in the main files.

■ On second thought, Barney should suffice after all.

As usual, what you can do with DeuSF you can undo. The restoration command not only works on the main DOOM/Heretic files, it also works on any files you modified with DeuSF.

(Oh, by the way—with DeuSF 3.4, even if you modify your file with another tool, DeuSF should be able to restore the file. Of course, if your tool made a real mess, restoration won't be perfect.)

■ I'd like to make a compilation of DOOM files, but Trinity and Mayan666 can't work together, Trinity and Mayan both redefine textures of DOOM. Only one of them can be put in a compilation file, because one needs to supercede the texture of the other one to set up it's own textures.

That was before DeuSF 3.4. For the heck of it, I coded a texture merger into the join command. Now, provided your files don't redefine the exact same textures, they can coexist. Still, since most WAD creators are still afraid to use new names for their textures, it could be that two textures are conflicting, and one will have to be sacrificed.

```
> deusf -join TRINITY.WAD MAYAN.WAD
```

- Hey, I have DOOM 1.9—this won't work!

Yes it will. DeuSF is independent of the version of DOOM or Heretic. But of course, if your favorite patch replaces the Arch-Vile, trying it under DOOM might not be a wise idea.

- Simpsons DOOM is cool, but the file is too big to upload.

From time to time, some newbie discovers he can make a working patch out of the complete list of DOOM Sprites. Great—3MB or 4MB dumped onto the net so that people can contemplate the big red nose he put on those soldiers.

DeuSF can't help you reduce the size of such a file by magic, but you can tell the author about DeuSF and he might at least realize that there is a much better way to distribute Sprites on the net.

- I'm playing under OS/2 (or Linux or Unix!). I can't install any graphic patch.

Didn't you realize DeuSF was there, waiting for an occasion to help you? DMGRAPH or NWT were never ported to anything but DOS, but that's not the case with DeuSF. The command lines listed in this room can be used with all versions of DeuSF, whatever the operating system they were built for. DeuSF runs under DOS, DOS extended, OS/2, Windows, Linux, and any Unix brand, from SUN O/S to the Silicon Graphics and even the Unix for DEC Alpha processors. This was not done for fun. Porting the program to so many operating systems was one of the best ways to detect possible bugs in the programming. DeuSF was programmed for maximum security, because it is supposed to modify WADs that may be painful to rebuild or reinstall.

CREDITS AND ADDITIONAL INFORMATION

DeuSF is a tool I derived from DeuTex's merge command, following a request by Dewi Morgan of the DEU Team when DOOM 1.666 came out. It was originally an enhanced version of DMADDS, the great tool by Bernd Kreismeyer that permitted AliensDOOM 1.0. The idea of Sprite and flat completion is not mine, but I took great care to implement it in the most reliable and convenient way. DMADDS required a tricky directory structure and generated another file. This meant 2MB to 3MB of wasted disk space, and it was impossibile to port to other versions of DOOM or to Heretic. Still, credit goes to Bernd.

Oh, I forgot—additional credit for DMADDS, DeuSF, and the like should go to id Software. It was a bug in the handling of Sprites and flats by DOOM that compelled us all to create these tools in the first place. You should have been able to add Sprites as you added levels with the `-file` command. The folks at id Software tried to correct the bug—and failed. So Bernd had to design a trick to correct the problem; I only refined this trick later.

With Heretic, the situation was even worse than in DOOM. No external Sprite WADs are allowed with Heretic 1.0, and I'd bet it's yet another bug of the program, because it's certainly not id Software's intent to limit the capabilities of this great game. But because you can use the `-merge` command of DeuSF, it's not such a problem after all.

That's the basics of what you need to know about DeuSF. I hope it will be useful to you.

EPISODE 5

THE DAY AFTER THE APOCALYPSE

MISSION 1:
SHARING THE PAIN

ROOM 1

DISTRIBUTING YOUR DOOM

By Piotr Kapiszewski

Undoubtedly part of the great success of DOOM can be attributed not only to an interesting engine design, which allows almost an infinite number of scenarios, but to the distribution channels that are used.

DOOM has been on the Internet since its beginnings. The shareware version was released there first, and thus the craze began. The ease with which the information can be exchanged over the Net has allowed a wealth of information sources to spring up. As you will see in Episode 5, Mission 1, Room 2, "Places to Go and People to See," there are many interesting places to visit and people to talk to who are involved in design, distribution, coordination, and help services. The best part of the whole thing is the fact that all of this lies at your fingertips—and most importantly, it is free.

"Why would you want to distribute your work?" you might ask. There could be many reasons. However, instead of trying to spell them out, let me give you some interesting numbers.

Site: `ftp.cdrom.com:/pub/idgames/levels/doom`

Archive Directory	Number of Files
1-9	42
a-c	262
combos	14
d-f	236
Deathmatch	389
g-i	133
j-l	93
m-o	153
p-r	129
reviews	4
s-u	298
v-z	82

The left column represents an archive section from DOOM's primary FTP site (section number), and the numbers on the right show the number of files in each of the directories. As you can clearly see, there is plenty to choose from.

The number of homemade add-on levels is constantly growing. Sharing your level with others will no doubt enrich the number of scenarios that are available and perhaps even make you famous.

As a first step, let me give you some ideas on what can be distributed.

WHAT CAN BE DISTRIBUTED

The idea of "distribution" sounds very formal. Do not worry about it. It's just a term used on the Internet to talk about copying files over the network. It refers to complete documents, references, or archives that are placed by their authors on machines connected to the Net for others to enjoy. In our case, distribution will refer to any DOOM-related items you choose to package.

Let me give you some ideas of what is currently available.

- **Game elements:** Including various patches to sound, music, graphics, characters, and scenarios.
- **Documentation:** In the form of Frequently Asked Question (FAQ) documents, cheats, technical specs, and so on.
- **Reviews:** Descriptions and evaluation of various add-on levels that are available.
- **DHT exams:** DOOM Honorific Titles and demos of famous tourneys or Deathmatches.

Whether it is a new level, a help file, or a review, each time you contribute something many people benefit. Your name becomes known thoughout the world, and ultimately if you continue to provide the support or expertise, people turn to you for help or suggestions. And believe me, there is no greater feeling than when someone either thanks you for something you have done or asks you a good question relying on your knowledge and expertise.

In the following sections, you will find a more detailed look at some of the items you might choose to work with.

DEHACKED PATCHES

Greg Lewis (gregory.lewis@umich.edu) created a utility that is known as DeHackEd. It enables you to create patches against the DOOM.EXE file that can enhance the weapons, change the appearance of various elements and much more.

For more information see

- ftp.cdrom.com:/pub/idgames/utils/exe_edit/dhe22.txt
- (Section 13-2, 14-6)
- See the section entitled "FTP Sites" in Episode 5, Mission 1, Room 2, "Places to Go and People to See," for a description of the FTP tree.

DEMOS (LMPS)

One of the great features of DOOM is its ability to record everything that takes place during the game. This feature enables you to save to a file all events that take place during a given episode. Once it is saved, it is possible to play the file back later so you can analyze your own and your opponents' moves (or simply enjoy the action of past escapades and impress your friends).

For more information see

■ `ftp.cdrom.com:/pub/idgames/docs/misc/doomhelp.zip` (demomake.hlp by Ian Mapleson (`mapleson@cee.hw.ac.uk`))

■ `ftp.cdrom.com:/pub/idgames/docs/faqs/dmfaq66.zip` (Section 14-5)

■ See the section entitled "FTP Sites" in Episode 5, Mission 1, Room 2 for a description of the FTP tree.

DOOM HONORIFIC TITLES

The rating system created by Frank Stajano (`fstajano@cam-orl.co.uk`) enables DOOM players to earn titles based on their performance and through LMP recorded files.

The following files from `/pub/idgames/lmps/dht-exams/` should give you a good basic understanding about submission of your recordings and the rules that apply.

For more information see

■ `ftp.cdrom.com:/pub/idgames/lmps/dht-exams/`

DHT4-TXT.TXT	This file
DHT4.TXT	The complete DHT4 rules, PGP-signed, in ASCII format
REQUEST.TXT	Form to request a challenge
DESCR.TXT	Form to describe your completed exam
COMPLET.TXT	Form to announce that your exam is available for download

■ `http://www.cam-orl.co.uk/~fms/dht.html`

PWADS

Perhaps the most noteworthy things that can be distributed are new levels. By now you should have a good idea of what that is like and perhaps you already have a level to distribute. PWAD files can contain whole scenarios, new graphic elements, sounds, and textures. You can distribute not only complete levels but also smaller items such as sound replacements or graphics patches. A wealth of information is available on this topic, and you should probably obtain a copy of at least some of the documents mentioned in the following list. They will answer some of the questions you might have and should give you some ideas as to where to look for more information.

For more information:

- `ftp.cdrom.com:/pub/idgames/levels/{doom, doom2, heretic}` (see the following section on FTP stuff)
- `ftp.cdrom.com:` `/pub/idgames/docs/faqs/dmfaq66.zip`
- `ftp.cdrom.com:/pub/idgames/docs/editing/design12.faq`
- `ftp.cdrom.com:/pub/idgames/docs/misc/doomhelp.zip` (PWADMAKE.HLP by Tom Neff (`tneff@panix.com`))
- See the section entitled "FTP Sites" in Episode 5, Mission 1, Room 2 for a description of the FTP tree.

SOUNDS

There are lots of different sound-effect patches available. To get an idea of what they are and how they change the game, take a look at the sites listed here.

For more information:

- `ftp.cdrom.com:/idgames/sounds/`
- See the section entitled "FTP Sites" in Episode 5, Mission 1, Room 2 for a description of the FTP tree.

MUSIC

Not only can you change the sound effects but also the music tracks that play in the background and add to the overall atmosphere. To see some of them in action, take a look at the existing collection at the sites listed here.

For more information:

- `ftp.cdrom.com:/idgames/music/`
- `ftp.cdrom.com:` `/pub/idgames/docs/faqs/dmfaq66.zip` (14-4)
- See the section entitled "FTP Sites" in Episode 5, Mission 1, Room 2 for a description of the FTP tree.

GRAPHICS

Changing textures and characters enables you to completely change the appearance of the game. Graphics, apart from sounds, are the key elements of what makes the game so much more fun for the player.

For more information:

- ■ `ftp.cdrom.com:/idgames/graphics/`
- ■ See the section entitled "FTP Sites" in Episode 5, Mission 1, Room 2 for a description of the FTP tree.

LEVELS

Complete levels usually contain not only new floor layouts but also graphical elements, sound effects, new music, monsters, and many other things. The best way to get an idea of what's good in a new level and what's not is to listen to the users and to see some of the existing ones.

For more information:

- ■ `ftp.cdrom.com:/pub/idgames/levels/{doom, doom2, heretic}`
- ■ See the section entitled "FTP Sites" in Episode 5, Mission 1, Room 2 for a description of the FTP tree.

REVIEWS

With so many add-on levels out there it is becoming more and more difficult to choose which ones to get. Since reviews offer some aspect of what the level is like, they are always a great addition.

For more information:

- ■ `ftp.cdrom.com:/pub/idgames/docs/misc/reviewer.app`
- ■ `ftp.cdrom.com:/pub/idgames/levels/{doom, doom2, heretic}/reviews/`
- ■ `http://doomgate.cs.buffalo.edu/~williams/`
- ■ See the section entitled "FTP Sites" in Episode 5, Mission 1, Room 2 for a description of the FTP tree.

TEXT

Miscellaneous documentation is available online, ranging from "HOW TOs" to technical specs to answers for common questions. There is wealth of it already available, but if you see that there is something that needs to be written or updated, then either write it yourself or contact the author about updates.

For more information:

- `ftp.cdrom.com:/pub/idgames/docs/`
- See the section entitled "FTP Sites" in Episode 5, Mission 1, Room 2 for a description of the FTP tree.

HOW TO DISTRIBUTE

FTP

So, your level is complete and you can finally share it with others. In order to share the ideas that you have come up with, you are going to have to upload your files to some public, well-known Internet site. From there, other people will be able to FTP (transfer) it to their computers.

As you know, there are many hosts on the Internet that distribute DOOM-related work. Which one should you choose to upload your level to? The answer is quite simple. Always choose what is commonly called a "primary" FTP site. The primary FTP site, is at the moment, `ftp.cdrom.com`. By common agreement, this site accepts uploads and then other sites mirror it. Mirroring enables other machines on the Internet to have identical files distributed thoughout the world. The mirror sites make copies—mirror images—of the primary site, thus keeping everything up to date. It is therefore important to always upload new items to the primary site; this will ensure that all your work will propagate thoughout the world and will not be erased by the next mirror.

Because of space constraints and changing fads, the primary site changes from time to time. The DOOM primary FTP site has changed three times over the course of the last year. In case of a change, information will always be posted to all relevant newsgroups and mailing lists, so if you even sporadically read some of the forums, you will surely find out what the current site is at the moment.

Now, without further ado, let's go through the steps you will need in order to upload your new level.

1. Fill out the WAD Authoring Template. (See the following section.) It is crucial to have some standardized way of recording various aspects of your level. This template is used by all authors, and it covers all aspects of your level in a consistent fashion.

2. Save your filled-out template to a file with the same prefix as the name of your WAD file. For example:

```
mylevel.txt
```

3. Compress your WAD file with PKZIP to make it smaller and easier for transport

```
pkzip mylevel.zip mylevel.wad
```

Now you should have two files ready for distribution:

```
mylevel.txt
mylevel.zip
```

4. Establish an FTP connection to the primary FTP site. Since there are so many different ways in which you can be connected to the Internet, I am going to assume you know what steps are involved in doing so. If you experience problems, don't be afraid to ask about it. Just always make sure you have read all the avaiable documents that can potentially explain the process. If you are still not sure how to proceed, then post your questions to a wider audience. This will very likely save you from being flamed by others. Establish the connection as follows:

```
ftp ftp.cdrom.com
```

5. Log in to `ftp.cdrom.com`. For example:

```
Name (ftp.cdrom.com:kapis-p): anonymous
331 Guest login ok, send your complete e-mail address as password.
Password: YOURNAME@YOURHOST
230-Welcome to wcarchive - home ftp site for Walnut Creek CDROM.
230-You are user 371 out of 400 possible.
[parts deleted]
```

6. Change the directory to the one you will be uploading your file to. It is typically called "incoming." For example:

```
ftp> cd pub/idgames/incoming
250-*** please do not upload 1.9 patches. they are in ***
250-*** /pub/idgames/idstuff                          ***
250-
250-uploads to the doom/doom2/heretic sections of this ftp site
250-will remain here until they have been cleared and moved to
250-/pub/idgames/newstuff.
250-
250-for the convenience of people downloading files to floppy
250-later on, please try and keep the maximum filesize under 1.44 megs.
250-
250-please send a .txt file along with what you are uploading, failure
250-to do so can cause rejection of your files here.
250-
```

5
EPISODE

1
MISSION

1
ROOM

DOOM
PROGRAMMING
GURUS

```
250-if problems arise, send e mail to both pitts@ssax.com _and_
250-jschuur@ftp.cdrom.com. thank you.
250-
250 CWD command successful.
```

7. Now you are ready to send your file. Make sure you change the mode to BINARY before
   starting in order to ensure that your binary ZIP file uploads without errors. For example:

```
ftp> binary
200 Type set to I.
ftp> put mylevel.txt
200 PORT command successful.
150 Opening BINARY mode data connection for test.
226 Transfer complete.
local: mylevel.txt remote: mylevel.txt
1 bytes sent in 0.0012 seconds (0.79 Kbytes/s)
ftp> put mylevel.zip
200 PORT command successful.
150 Opening BINARY mode data connection for test.
226 Transfer complete.
local: mylevel.zip remote: mylevel.zip
1 bytes sent in 0.0012 seconds (0.79 Kbytes/s)
```

As each file is uploaded and transfer completes, you should receive a confirmation saying that the
transfer completed successfully. It is important to check this, so as not to upset others when they try
to download your level only to find out that it doesn't work.

Now your files are on the primary distribution FTP site. Within a few days they will be moved into
the right place in the directory tree, and others will be able to use it.

Since there are so many levels out there, it is important—if you want yours to be noticed—to inform the DOOM community on the Internet about your upload. The best way to do this is to post
the MYLEVEL.TXT file (or whatever) to the rec.games.computer.doom.announce newsgroup. You
can also mail it to the wads@doomgate.cs.buffalo.edu mailing list. From there you will have to wait
and see what the users think about it. Be patient—it sometimes takes a while before anyone decides
to mail you or comment on your level on a public forum.

In case you don't have FTP access to the Net but still would like to distribute your contributions,
there are many people out there who can help. The best way is to ask for help on one of the newsgroups
and see what possible ways are available. The IRC (see the following section) is another great way
to get someone to walk you through the process.

DOOM
PROGRAMMING
GURUS

1
ROOM

1
MISSION

5
EPISODE

WAD AUTHORING TEMPLATE

```
WAD Authoring Template V1.4   (Clip this line)
================================================================
Title               :
Filename            : xxxx.WAD
Author              : Your name here
Email Address       :
Misc. Author Info   :

Description         : Set the mood here.

Additional Credits to   :
================================================================

* Play Information *

Episode and Level #   : ExMx (,ExMx,...)
Single Player         : Yes/No
Cooperative 2-4 Player: Yes/No
Deathmatch 2-4 Player : Yes/No
Difficulty Settings   : Yes/Not implemented
New Sounds            : Yes/No
New Graphics          : Yes/No
New Music             : Yes/No
Demos Replaced        : None/1/2/3/All

* Construction *

Base              : New level from scratch/Modified ExMx/xxx.WAD
Editor(s) used    :
Known Bugs        :


* Copyright / Permissions *

Authors (MAY/may NOT) use this level as a base to build additional
levels.

(One of the following)

You MAY distribute this WAD, provided you include this file, with
no modifications.  You may distribute this file in any electronic
format (BBS, Diskette, CD, etc) as long as you include this file
intact.

You MAY not distribute this WAD file in any format.

You may do whatever you want with this file.
```

```
* Where to get this WAD *

FTP sites:

BBS numbers:

Other:
```

SUMMARY

In this section, you have learned about the various types of items you can distribute and share with other DOOM players around the world. You have also seen what steps are necessary to FTP your file into a public place. You now know what is involved in distribution of your work. Let's now go meet some of the people who are contributing to the DOOM phenomenon.

ROOM 2

PLACES TO GO AND PEOPLE TO SEE

By Piotr
Kapiszewski

FORUMS

Finding out answers to questions on the Internet sometimes takes a lot of patience and can even get you in trouble if you ask the questions on the wrong forums. It is thus imperative that you get some idea of what forums are available and what topics they pertain to. Finding out what is available also is interesting, since in the long run it will limit the amount of time you have to spend looking up answers to those crucial questions. When you know who to ask for help, you are one step closer to getting the right answer the first time you ask.

To start you off, I would greatly recommend the "DOOM FAQ" by Frank Leukart. It is probably the most detailed document about the game. As you become familiar with it and find answers to your basic questions, keep on reading to see what else is available.

WORLD WIDE WEB (WWW)

DOOMWEB

Some time back in the beginning of 1994, a group of people got together and decided to consolidate forces on development of a project they called DoomWeb. DoomWeb is a collection of hypertext documents that can be accessed via World Wide Web (WWW) browsers such as Mosaic or Netscape.

In order to provide a common reference point to the whole project, the group now has a dedicated host on the net (`doomgate.cs.buffalo.edu`), thanks to the help of Steve Young (`syoung@doomgate.cs.buffalo.edu`), Ken Smith (`kensmith@cs.buffalo.edu`), and Davin Milun (`milun@cs.buffalo.edu`). DoomWeb provides information about all aspects of the game, along with information about Heretic and the upcoming game Quake. In the following section, you will find a list of nodes that participate actively in the developments of the DoomWeb, as well as a list of all known DOOM-related nodes around the world.

DOOMWEB CREATORS

Piotr Kapiszewski	`kapis-p@cs.buffalo.edu`
	`http://doomgate.cs.`
	`buffalo.edu/`	

T.J Kelly	`TJ@hmc.edu`	`http://www.cs.hmc.edu`
		`/people/tkelly/`
		`http://venom.st.hmc.edu`
		`/~tkelly/doomfaq/`

Tim McCune	`trm@ksu.ksu.edu`	

Sven Neuhaus	sven@ping.de http://www.ping.de/ ~sven/doom/	
Martin Price	vhold@netcom.com	ftp://ftp.netcom.com /pub/vh/vhold/doom/doom.html
Joost Schuur	joost.schuur@ student.uni- tuebingen.de	
John M. Troyer	troyer@cgl.ucsf.edu	http://www.cmpharm.ucsf.edu /~troyer/sgidoomfaq.html
Paul Falstad	pjf@cts.com	http://www.cts.com/~pjf/

DOOMWEB CURRENT MEMBERS

Ronald Kinion	rkinion@eecs.wsu.edu http://www.eecs.wsu.edu /~rkinion/	
Joerg Findeisen	h8700707@obelix.wu- wien.ac.at	
Jonathan Matthies	matthies@ cs.colostate.edu	http://www.colostate.edu /~matthies/
Brad Robbins	brad@ onyx.pvcc.cc.va.us	http://onyx.pvcc.cc.va.us /~brad/doom/.html
Myles Williams	williams@ http://funnelweb.utcc. utk.edu martha.utcc.utk.edu	/~williams/bestwads.html
John Evans	lgas@cs.umd.edu	http://www.cs.umd.edu /~lgas/computers/doom.html
Randal Wilson	deftly@catt.ncsu.edu	http://www.catt.ncsu.edu /users/deftly/www/doom.html
Kerry Leanne Smith	klsmith2@eos.ncsu.edu /eos/users/k/klsmith2/ mosaic/	http://www2.ncsu.edu
Tony Lezard	tony@mantis.co.uk http://www.mantis.co.uk/ doom/	
Ian C.R. Mapleson	mapleson@cee.hw.ac.uk	http://www.cee.hw.ac.uk /~mapleson/doom/doom.html

Kent Ng	kentng@ee.UManitoba.ca	
Marco M.A. Rotelli	mmar1@york.ac.uk	http://www.york.ac.uk /~mmar1/doom /doom_level_design.html
Raphaël Quinet	eedraq@ http://www.montefiore. ulg.ac.be chapelle.eed.ericsson.se/~quinet/games/doom-en.html	
Frank Stajano	fstajano@cam-orl.co.uk	http://www.cam-orl.co.uk /~fms/dht.html
Steve Benner	S.Benner@ lancaster.ac.uk	http://cres1.lancs.ac.uk /~esasb1/doom/
Steve VanDevender	stevev@efn.org http://www.crayola. cse.psu.edu	http://jcomm.uoregon.edu /~stevev/Linux-DOOM-FAQ.html /~bielby/

Perhaps the most useful aspect of WWW is its ability to integrate not only textual information but also graphics and sound via hypertext. Documents can be linked together across the world, creating a single resource, even though the actual data resides on many different computers. They can be maintained by different individuals who are sometimes thousands of miles apart geographically.

This certainly is the case with DoomWeb. All the people who participate in the project are literally on opposite sides of the planet. Only a few of us have ever met face to face, and the only way of communication is e-mail and IRC. As the results show, it is possible to create and maintain large-scale projects in such environments and to carry the ideas through without regard for distance or language barriers.

Because of the graphic nature of the game, it is important not only to provide information but also images of what it is all about. WWW is the ideal environment. Using WWW browsers, you can not only read the textual information but also see the images of characters, screen shots, maps, and various other types of interesting bits. You can also download files of interest directly from within the documents and leave comments.

Large documents such as Frank Leukart's (ap641@cleveland.freenet.edu) DOOM FAQs are well-suited for this type of medium, where, from the table of contents, you can immediately jump to the right section by simply clicking on the appropriate line of text. There are other documents and resources that are available from DoomWeb. You have to check them out for yourself to truly appreciate the work that is being put into their creation.

When looking at the list of all known WWW sites that carry relevant information, you should keep in mind that the list is constantly growing. By the time this book sees the light of day, there are surely going to be a few more sites that are worth visiting. To obtain the latest list of sites, check out the `rec.games.computer.doom.announce` newsgroup for information, or point your viewer at DoomGate (`http://doomgate.cs.buffalo.edu/`). Both sources should always have updated information.

ORGANIZATION OF DOOMWEB NODES

It is difficult to describe in detail the layout of each of the nodes since they are constantly changing. New updates to various documents or changes based on user feedback force each node to frequently update its pages. All of it is done with users in mind. For example, many of us have relatively slow access to the Internet via modems. This causes major delays when large image files need to be downloaded and displayed on our monitors. Because of that, many nodes are now providing only small amounts of graphical information, and in cases when there is no other way, links are clearly marked to tell users that lots of images are going to be displayed. Images are a great addition and make the pages unique, so definitely check them out when you get a chance.

Now let's get back to the organization of the nodes. The easiest way to access the DoomWeb is through its front door (or portal, if you will) called DoomGate. DoomGate can be reached at `http://doomgate.cs.buffalo.edu/` and is divided into the following sections:

DOOM

(`http://doomgate.cs.buffalo.edu/doom/`)

Forums

(`http://doomgate.cs.buffalo.edu/doom/forums/`)

This URL includes FAQs, supported platforms, newsgroups, IRC, mailing lists, BBS DOOM servers, screen shots, spoilers, themes, and WADs.

Editing

(`http://doomgate.cs.buffalo.edu/doom/editing/`)

This URL includes information about writing your own levels, node and reject builders, sound and music, graphics, front ends, and miscellaneous items.

DOOM II

(`http://doomgate.cs.buffalo.edu/doom2/`)

Forums

(http://doomgate.cs.buffalo.edu/doom2/forums/)

Editing

(http://doomgate.cs.buffalo.edu/doom2/editing/)

HERETIC

(http://doomgate.cs.buffalo.edu/heretic/)

Forums

(http://doomgate.cs.buffalo.edu/heretic/forums/)

Editing

(http://doomgate.cs.buffalo.edu/heretic/forums/)

QUAKE

(http://doomgate.cs.buffalo.edu/quake/)

Information or speculation on the upcoming game Quake.

FTP

(http://doomgate.cs.buffalo.edu/ftptree/)

Access to a mirror of ftp.cdrom.com at DoomGate.

NEWS

(http://doomgate.cs.buffalo.edu/news/)

UNDER CONSTRUCTION: A project is in the works to provide access to DOOM-related newsgroups to those who do not have USENET news.

USAGE

(http://doomgate.cs.buffalo.edu/wusage/)

Usage statistics of the DoomGate WWW server.

NEWSGROUPS

USENET carries several newsgroups of interest to all you DOOM players out there. Below you will find a list of the ones that are available at most sites and which carry lots of useful information.

`rec.games.computer.doom.announce` (moderated)

Subject: assorted announcements

Moderator: Tony Lezard (`doom-request@mantis.co.uk`, `doom@mantis.co.uk`)

Information, Frequently Asked Questions (FAQs) documents, and reviews about DOOM. A must read for both new and adept players and developers. It carries all the latest updates to all important documentation that is available. It covers games from id Software as well as games (such as Heretic or Quake) based on the same technology and/or licensed from id by other companies.

`rec.games.computer.doom.help`

Subject: DOOM Help Service (new players welcome)

Volunteer coordinator: Ian Mapleson (`mapleson@cee.hw.ac.uk`)

This newsgroup is where new players should go for flame-free help and info. Example topics include:

- How to solve a particular level, find a key, get 100-percent of the secrets, and so forth.
- How to patch DOOM (II) to v1.9 (or whatever the current version is).
- DOOM setup questions. ("I get such-and-such an error when I start DOOM.")
- Problems/suggestions re: DOOM setup programs (ser6, d!, and so forth).
- Non-DOS version (Linux, SGI, and so on) setup questions.
- Finding FTP sites, WWW sites, multiplayer BBSs, and so on.

`rec.games.computer.doom.misc`

Subject: Talking about DOOM and id Software

Volunteer coordinator: Richard Ward (`rrward@netcom.com`)

This newsgroup is where miscellaneous topics are appropriate, including:

- Status of WinDoom, Jaguar, and other "ports" of DOOM.
- Quake, other id Software-related "in-development" topics.
- Previous id games (Wolfenstein 3D, and so on) and DOOM-engine games (Heretic and so on).
- "DOOM, the Movie", Ferrari Testarossas, other stuff about id.

DOOM PROGRAMMING GURUS

2 ROOM

1 MISSION

5 EPISODE

- Comments about magazine/newspaper/TV stories about DOOM or id.
- GT Interactive, general DOOM sales/distribution topics.
- Piracy, viruses, and illegal copies of DOOM.
- Commercial (pay-for-the-product) DOOM-related advertisements.
- Mouse versus keyboard debates, SB versus GUS debates, and so forth.
- "What's the best ethernet/video/mouse/computer for DOOM?"
- Benchmarks and timedemo.
- Favorite music, monsters, weapons.
- Other topics not dealing with actual game playing or editing.

`rec.games.computer.doom.editing`

Subject: Editing and hacking DOOM-related files

Volunteer coordinator: Raphael Quinet (`eedraq@chapelle.eed.ericsson.se`)

This newsgroup is where technically-oriented discussions on editing DOOM and DOOM-related files take place. Topics include:

- Hacking the DOOM EXE file, editing saved games and LMPs.
- PWAD design techniques (how to do this, how was that done, and so forth).
- Design problems or limitations (HOM, Medusa, and so forth).
- Questions about the popular editors (where to get, bug reports, and so on).

Comments or questions about playing user-written PWADs (opinions, keys, secrets, and so forth) should not be posted here—post in `rec.games.computer.doom.playing` instead.

`rec.games.computer.doom.playing`

Subject: Playing DOOM and user-created levels

Volunteer coordinator: Mike Newton (`mik@netcom.com`)

This newsgroup is where all aspects related to playing DOOM are discussed, including topics such as:

- Anything about playing DOOM and DOOM II levels and user-written PWADS (secrets, strategies, bugs, where to get specific PWADs, and so forth).
- PWAD upload announcements, reviews of PWADS, PWAD lists, and so forth.
- Unusual experiences, Deathmatch strategies, boasts, LMPs, and so forth.
- Keyboard/mouse movement techniques.

5
EPISODE

1
MISSION

2
ROOM

DOOM PROGRAMMING GURUS

- Side-effects of playing DOOM.
- "Looking for another DOOM player in area code XXX."
- Lists of people wanting to play multi-player modem/net DOOM.
- Tournament discussions and multi-player topics.

Non-play-related topics go in the .misc group. (This includes Quake.)

The following is a partial list of the people who have organized and made help available on the newsgroups:

John Van Essen (`vanes002@maroon.tc.umn.edu`)

Tony Lezard (`tony@mantis.co.uk`)

Ian Mapleson (`mapleson@cee.hw.ac.uk`)

Richard Ward (`rrward@netcom.com`)

Raphaël Quinet (`eedraq@chapelle.eed.ericsson.se`)

Mike Newton (`mik@netcom.com`)

Frans P. de Vries (`fpv@xymph.iaf.nl`)

Doug Barton (`bartdoug@pwa.acusd.edu`)

David Damerell (`djsd100@hermes.cam.ac.uk`)

The archives of the newsgroups, along with all current versions of assorted FAQs that are regularly posted, are available from `ftp://ftp.mantis.co.uk/pub/doom`, a site maintained by Tony Lezard (`tony@mantis.co.uk`).

MAILING LISTS

There are quite a few mailing lists related to various aspects of DOOM. Some of them generate quite a bit of traffic, so don't be surprised when your mailbox suddenly becomes full after you subscribe to them. To subscribe to any of the following lists, you will have to send mail to an automated service that will do the actual subscription.

Here is what you have to do. Send mail to `majordomo@HOST`—where *HOST* is mentioned in parentheses next to each list—with no subject, and in the body of the message say `subscribe LIST`, where *LIST* is the name of the list you are trying to subscribe to.

Example:

```
mail majordomo@doomgate.cs.buffalo.edu
```

Subject:

```
subscribe dooml
```

DOOML

```
(doomgate.cs.buffalo.edu)
```

Maintained by: Steven Lorch (`lorchs@wasc.egginc.com`).

The original general-purpose DOOM, DOOM II, and Heretic discussion list.

DOOML-DIGEST

```
(doomgate.cs.buffalo.edu)
```

Maintained by: Steven Lorch (`lorchs@wasc.egginc.com`).

A digest version of the DOOM list, which is mailed out once a week for those who do not like to receive daily traffic.

DOOMGATE-ANNOUNCE

```
(doomgate.cs.buffalo.edu)
```

Maintained by: Piotr Kapiszewski (`kapis-p@cs.buffalo.edu`).

Announcement-only list dealing with various new things that take place on DoomGate. New additions to the Web or FTP archives, and general changes and improvements that the DoomWeb group is bringing out.

DOOM EDITING

```
(nvg.unit.no)
```

Maintained by: Steve Benner (`S.Benner@lancaster.ac.uk`).

Advanced DOOM editing list. Topics of discussion focus mainly on design issues. Heavy traffic.

QUAKE

```
(doomgate.cs.buffalo.edu)
```

Maintained by: Joost Schuur (`jschuur@doomgate.cs.buffalo.edu`).

QuakeTalk newsletter mailing list.

UTIL ANNOUNCE

(`doomgate.cs.buffalo.edu`)

Maintained by: Piotr Kapiszewski (`kapis-p@cs.buffalo.edu`).

Announcement-only list dealing with new utilities and add-on tools to help you stay informed.

WADS

(`doomgate.cs.buffalo.edu`)

Maintained by: Piotr Kapiszewski (`kapis-p@cs.buffalo.edu`).

General descusion forum for issues related to new level development. Critique, comments, and reviews regarding existing and newly released levels.

IRC-DOOML

(`doomgate.cs.buffalo.edu`)

Maintained by: Joost Schuur (`jschuur@doomgate.cs.buffalo.edu`).

Discussion of various issues that take place on `#doom` on IRC.

IRC

The Internet Relay Chat is a replacement for (and also an improvement to) Talk. A traditional UNIX tool, Talk enabled two people to conduct a conversation in real time. IRC expands on the concept to enable literally thousands of people to talk to one another through various channels.

For DOOM-related topics, several active channels exist. They are `#doom`, `#doom2`, `#heretic`, and `#doomgate`. As the names imply, they deal with various aspects of each game. However, you will most likely find the most traffic on `#doom`. Here you will be able to meet people who not only play the game but also those who actively participate in DOOM development (including, on occasion, people from id Software).

FTP SITES

FTP sites are probably the single most important resource of the Internet. They enable you to access files on remote computers for both download and upload. This means that you can obtain files and deposit files at public places.

In the case of uploads, you can put a file on an FTP site and others will be able to download it. If you take your new WAD file and upload it to say `ftp.cdrom.com` (as discussed previously), other people around the world will be able to download it from there and play it on their own computers.

Currently the primary site for all DOOM related materials is `ftp.cdrom.com`. It is managed by Joost Shuur (`jschuur@doomgate.cs.buffalo.edu`) and Jim Pitts (`pitts@ssax.com`). From there, all the other sites mirror or copy the new files and enable the users to access them. In order to distribute the load equally among sites, always use the site that is nearest to you geographically.

The organization of any FTP site in terms of its directory structure is important because it enables you to quickly get to the files you need and to download them to your computer. Recently, Joost Schuur has taken various steps to ensure that the directory structure pertaining to the DOOM hierarchy is cleaned up and made more accessible for users. Changes such as this do not happen often, since they involve a lot of time and work for the administrators. (See Figure 2.1.)

Figure 2.1.
*The `ftp.cdrom.com`
directory hierarchy.*

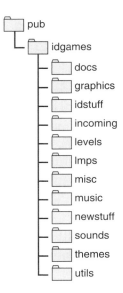

All the games made by id Software, such as DOOM, DOOM II, and Heretic, are included in this tree. The shareware versions of the games can be found in the .idstuff directory. Other directories pertain to graphics patches, various levels, demos, music and sound patches, themes, and many utilities.

Some of the directories are explained in the following sections. Figures 2.2, 2.3, 2.4, 2.5, and 2.6 show the subsequent directory levels at the `ftp.cdrom.com` site.

Figure 2.2.

The docs hierarchy.

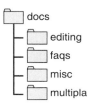

Figure 2.3.

The levels hierarchy.

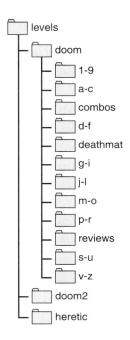

Figure 2.4.
The Imps hierarchy.

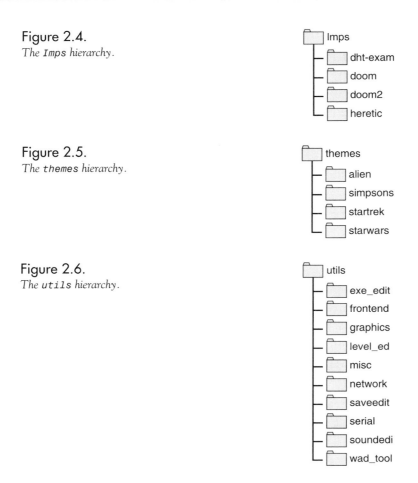

Figure 2.5.
The themes hierarchy.

Figure 2.6.
The utils hierarchy.

The following is a partial listing of sites that carry DOOM-related information. For more complete and up-to-date information, you should look at an FTP/WWW FAQ document by Mike Newton (mik@netcom.com). It is posted regularly to rec.games.computer.doom.announce.

List of Sites

California	`ftp.cdrom.com`	`/pub/idgames`
California	`ftp.pht.com`	`/pub/games/doom`
Austria	`flinux.tu-graz.ac.at`	`/pub/doom`
England	`ftp.dungeon.com`	`/pub/msdos/games/doom`
Oregon	`ftp.orst.edu`	`/pub/doom`
Montana	`ftp.coe.montana.edu`	`/pub/mirrors/doom`
Taiwan	`nctuccca.edu.tw`	`/pub/PC/games/doom`
South Africa	`ftp.sun.ac.za`	`/msdos/doom`
Germany	`ftp.uni-erlangen.de`	`/pub/pc/msdos/doom`
Netherlands	`ftp.sls.wau.nl`	`/pub/msdos/doom`
Sweden	`ftp.luth.se`	`/pub/doom`
Kentucky	`ftp.thepoint.com`	`/pub/msdos/games/infant2.doom`
Kentucky	`ftp.iglou.com`	`/doom`
Wisconsin	`ftp.uwp.edu`	`/pub/games/id/home-brew/doom`
Australia	`ftp.next.com.au`	`/pub/mirror/`
Pennsylvania	`smb130.rh.psu.edu`	`/pub/doom`
Missouri	`ftp.wustl.edu`	`/pub/MSDOS_UPLOADS`
New York	`doomgate.cs.buffalo.edu`	`/pub/idgames`
id Software	`ftp.idsoftware.com`	`/pub`

FTP BY E-MAIL

For those of you who do not have direct Internet access, there is a service that enables you to receive various DOOM-related files and documents by e-mail. A detailed document on how this service works is available in the form of a FAQ. It is maintained by John Van Essen (`vanes002@maroon.tc.umn.edu`) and is posted on a regular basis to `rec.games.computer.doom.announce`.

DOOM
PROGRAMMING
GURUS

2
ROOM

1
MISSION

5
EPISODE

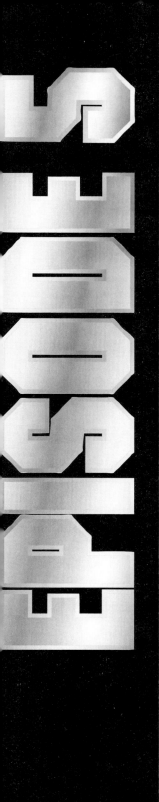

THE DAY AFTER THE APOCALYPSE

MISSION 2: ONLY FOR THE DOOMED CD

ROOM 1

THE DOOMED CD

HOW THE CD IS ORGANIZED

Level editors and general utilities which are discussed in this book can be found in the directories /EDITORS and /UTILS. All other editors, tools, and utilities are located in /BONUS. Example levels created by various designers are located in the /WADS directory. They are separated into three main categories—DOOM levels are in /DOOM1, DOOM II levels are in /DOOM2, and Heretic levels are in /HERETIC. WADs designed for more than one game version will be included in all appropriate directories. For instance, levels that work for DOOM and DOOMII appear in both directories. Type DOOMCD at your CD-ROM drive prompt to examine the contents of the CD.

USING THE CD

Most of the editors and utilities and some of the level files included on this disc must be copied to your hard drive to function properly. Refer to the respective rooms in this book and the documentation files accompanying the files on the CD for detailed instructions. To make playing the WADs from the CD easier, the WAD files for each game appear in /WADS/DOOM1/PLAY, /WADS/DOOM2/PLAY, and /WADS/HERETIC/PLAY. Use these CD directories as the locations of WAD files in front-end DOOM loading tools like DOOM-IT. The /PLAY directories include only those WADs that can be played from the CD without configuration. To install DOOM-IT to your hard drive, type DOOMCD from your CD-ROM drive prompt and follow the directions provided. Also, if a converted WAD does not exist for your game version, try the conversion programs located in /BONUS/UTILS to convert them yourself.

INSTALLING WINDOWS APPLICATIONS FROM THE CD

To install the Windows applications from the CD-ROM, do the following:

1. Start Windows.
2. Select File from the Program Manager menu.
3. Select Run from the File menu.
4. Type N:\SETUP, where N is the letter of your CD-ROM drive.
5. Follow the instructions provided by the setup program.

The program will create a Program Manager group named "Doom Utilities," which contains icons for installing the windows programs included on the disc.

THE DAY AFTER THE APOCALYPSE

APPENDIXES

APPENDIX A

By Steve Benner

ESSENTIAL DOOM
THING INFORMATION

the important characteristics of each of the Things which are contained in DOOM and DOOM II's main IWAD files. Table A.1 lists all of the available Thing types, ordered by category. The table gives each Thing's code number, its four-letter sprite prefix, together with the order in which the Sprite-frames cycle, and a summary of the Thing's basic characteristics.

NOTES ON THE TABLE ENTRIES

Some Things do not display using Sprites—these have a blank Sprite entry in the table. Other Things have a complex Sprite display cycle—these are denoted with a * after the Sprite prefix in the Sprite Sequence column.

Things which count as bonuses are marked —any of these which remain uncollected at the end of a level will be deducted from the Bonuses score. Things marked with can also be picked up by players, but will not contribute to the final tally. Things marked can be killed—these contribute toward final Kills tally.

Some Things act as obstructions, blocking the progress of playeers or monsters: these are marked . Unless marked otherwise, (with), Things will stand on the floor of the sector in which they are located.

Finally, some Things are only available in DOOM II: these are marked .

Table A.1. Table of DOOM Thing codes, Sprites, and characteristics.

Things	Code	Sprite sequence		Characteristics
		Player start positions		
Player 1 start position	1	PLAY	*	
Player 2 start position	2	PLAY	*	
Player 3 start position	3	PLAY	*	
Player 4 start position	4	PLAY	*	
Deathmatch start position	11			
		Enemy start positions		
Former Human	3004	POSS	*	
Wolfenstein 3D SS Officer	84	SSWV	*	
Former Human Sergeant	9	SPOS	*	

Things	Code	Sprite sequence		Characteristics
Former Human Commando	65	CPOS	*	
Imp	3001	TROO	*	
Demon	3002	SARG	*	
Spectre	58	SARG	*	
Lost Soul	3006	SKUL	*	
Cacodemon	3005	HEAD	*	
Hell Knight	69	BOS2	*	
Baron Of Hell	3003	BOSS	*	
Arachnotron	68	BSPI	*	
Pain Elemental	71	PAIN	*	
Revenant	66	SKEL	*	
Mancubus	67	FATT	*	
Arch-Vile	64	VILE	*	
Spider Mastermind	7	SPID	*	
Cyberdemon	16	CYBR	*	
Boss Brain	88	BBRN	*	

Miscellaneous

Teleport landing	14			
Boss Shooter	89			
Spawn Spot	87			

Weapons

Chainsaw	2005	CSAW	A	
Shotgun	2001	SHOT	A	

continues

Table A.1. continued

Things	Code	Sprite sequence		Characteristics
Weapons				
Combat shotgun	82	SGN2	A	
Chaingun	2002	MGUN	A	
Rocket launcher	2003	LAUN	A	
Plasma gun	2004	PLAS	A	
BFG 9000	2006	BFUG	A	
Ammunition				
Ammo clip	2007	CLIP	A	
4 Shotgun shells	2008	SHEL	A	
Rocket	2010	ROCK	A	
Cell charge	2047	CELL	A	
Box of Ammo	2048	AMMO	A	
Box of Shells	2049	SBOX	A	
Box of Rockets	2046	BROK	A	
Cell charge pack	17	CELP	A	
Backpack	8	BPAK	A	
Power ups				
Stimpack	2011	STIM	A	
Medikit	2012	MEDI	A	
Health Potion	2014	BON1	ABCDCB	
Spiritual Armor	2015	BON2	ABCDCB	
Security Armor	2018	ARM1	AB	
Combat Armor	2019	ARM2	AB	

Things	Code	Sprite sequence		Characteristics
Mega Sphere	83	MEGA	ABCD	
Soul Sphere	2013	SOUL	ABCDCB	
Invulnerability Artifact	2022	PINV	ABCD	
Berserk Pack	2023	PSTR	A	
Blur Artifact	2024	PINS	ABCD	
Radiation Suit	2025	SUIT	A	(up to v1.2)
Computer Map	2026	PMAP	ABCDCB	
Light Amplification Visor	2045	PVIS	AB	

Keycards

Blue key-card	5	BKEY	AB	
Red key-card	13	RKEY	AB	
Yellow key-card	6	YKEY	AB	
Blue skull key	40	BSKU	AB	
Red skull key	38	RSKU	AB	
Yellow skull key	39	YSKU	AB	

Obstructions

Barrel	2035	BAR1	AB	
Burning barrel	70	FCAN	ABC	
Tall green Pillar	30	COL1	A	
Short green pillar	31	COL2	A	
Tall red pillar	32	COL3	A	
Short red pillar	33	COL4	A	

continues

Table A.1. continued

Things	Code	Sprite sequence		Characteristics
Obstructions				
Candle	34	CAND	A	
Candelabra	35	CBRA	A	
Short green pillar with heart	36	COL5	AB	
Short red pillar with skull	37	COL6	A	
Evil Eye symbol	41	CEYE	ABCD	
Floating Skull	42	FSKU	ABC	
Burnt, gray tree	43	TRE1	A	
Stalagmite	47	SMIT	A	
Tall Technocolumn	48	ELEC	A	
Large brown tree	54	TRE2	A	
Tall blue firestick	44	TBLU	ABCD	
Tall green firestick	45	TGRE	ABCD	
Tall red firestick	46	TRED	ABCD	
Short blue firestick	55	SMBT	ABCD	
Short green firestick	56	SMGT	ABCD	
Short red firestick	57	SMRT	ABCD	
Tall technolamp	85	TLMP	ABCD	
Short technolamp	86	TLP2	ABCD	
Floor lamp	2028	COLU	A	
Impaled human	25	POL1	A	
Twitching, impaled human	26	POL6	AB	
Skull on a pole	27	POL4	A	
5-skull shish kebab	28	POL2	A	

Things	Code	Sprite sequence		Characteristics
Pile of skulls and candles	29	POL3	AB	
Hanged victim, twitching	49	GOR1	ABCD	
Suspended victim	50	GOR2	A	
Suspended victim, 1-legged	51	GOR3	A	
Hanging pair of legs	52	GOR4	A	
Hanging single leg	53	GOR5	A	
Hanging victim, no guts	73	HDB1	A	
Hanging victim, no guts/brain	74	HDB2	A	
Hanging torso, looking down	75	HDB3	A	
Hanging torso, open skull	76	HDB4	A	
Hanging torso, looking up	77	HDB5	A	
Hanging torso, no brain	78	HDB6	A	
Hanging Billy	72	KEEN	*	

Non-blocking Gore

Things	Code	Sprite sequence		Characteristics
Exploded player	10	PLAY	W	
Exploded player (as above)	12	PLAY	W	
Dead player	15	PLAY	N	
Dead Former Human	18	POSS	L	
Dead Former Human Sergeant	19	SPOS	L	
Dead Imp	20	TROO	M	
Dead Demon	21	SARG	N	
Dead Cacodemon	22	HEAD	L	
Dead Lost Soul (invisible)	23	SKUL	K	
Pool of blood and guts	24	POL5	A	

continues

Table A.1. continued

Things	Code	Sprite sequence		Characteristics
		Non-blocking Gore		
Suspended victim, arms akimbo	59	GOR2	A	
Hanging pair of legs	60	GOR4	A	
Suspended victim, 1-legged	61	GOR3	A	
Hanging single leg	62	GOR5	A	
Hanged victim, twitching	63	GOR1	ABCD	
Pool of guts	79	POB1	A	
Pool of blood	80	POB2	A	
Pool of brains	81	BRS1	A	

Many of the hanging items of gore are provided in two varieties: blocking and non-blocking. Use the non-blocking type wherever there will be room for a player to pass beneath the object, otherwise your players will encounter an invisible barrier as they try to move under it. On the other hand, if you hang these items in low-ceilinged areas, you should use the blocking variety for added realism.

Many editors have some of these items incorrectly described. If the particular items of gore that you want in your WAD are important to you, you should check the code numbers that your editor uses.

Table A.2 gives the sizes of the above Things—remember that although these are quoted as a radius (or as a diameter—both figures are given here for convenience). Things are really square in their extent.

Table A.2. Table of DOOM Thing sizes.

Things	Radius	Diameter	Height	Initial Health
Player	16	32	56	100
Former Human	20	40	56	20
Wolfenstein 3D SS	20	40	56	50
Former Human Sergeant	20	40	56	30
Former Commando	20	40	56	70
Imp	20	40	56	60
Demon	30	60	56	150
Spectre	30	60	56	150
Lost Soul	16	32	56	100
Cacodemon	31	62	56	400
Hell Knight	24	48	64	500
Baron of Hell	24	48	64	1000
Arachnotron	64	128	64	500
Pain Elemental	31	62	56	400
Revenant	20	40	56	300
Mancubus	48	96	64	600
Arch-Vile	20	40	56	700
Spider Mastermind	128	256	100	3000
Cyberdemon	40	80	110	4000
Boss Brain	16	32	16	250
Billy	16	32	72	100
Gettable items	20	40	16	–
Barrel	10	20	42	20
Large brown tree	32	64	*	–
Other obstacles	16	32	*	–

*For collision detection purposes, all Things classified as obstacles are deemed infinitely tall.

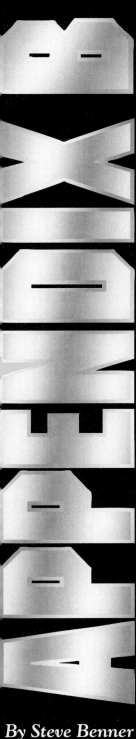

APPENDIX B

By Steve Benner

SPECIAL LINE-TYPES

This appendix provides a complete list of all of DOOM and DOOM II's special line-types. Table B.1 provides the codes of special line attributes, arranged by function; Table B.2 provides a complete ordered list of codes. The operation of each of these is covered in detail in various rooms in Episode 2 of this book.

In these tables, the following codes are used:

*	Indicates that the action is only provided in versions of DOOM beyond 1.4. It is safest to assume that v1.666 is needed in these cases.
Italics	Codes in italics does not use the sector tagging mechanism
S	Space bar operated action
M	Manual operated action (space bar, without sector tagging)
W	Walk-through activated trigger
G	Impact activated trigger
1	Single-use trigger
R	Repeatable action trigger
†	Trigger can be activated by monsters

Table B.1. Special attributes arranged by action.

Doors

	Activation Category						
Action	M1	MR	W1	WR	S1	SR	GR
Door: open, pause, close	–	*1*†	4†	90	29	63	–
Door: open and stay	*31*	–	2	86	103	61	46
Door: close	–	–	3	75	50	42	–
Door: close for 30s, open	–	–	16	76	–	–	–
Turbo Door: open, pause, close	–	*117*	108	105	111	114	–
Turbo Door: open & stay	*118*	–	109	106	112	115	–
Turbo Door: close	–	–	110	107	113	116	–
Door: open, close (blue)	–	26	–	–	–	–	–
Door: open, close (red)	–	28	–	–	–	–	–
Door: open, close (yellow)	–	27	–	–	–	–	–
Turbo door: open (blue)	32	–	–	–	133	99	–
Turbo door: open (red)	33	–	–	–	135	134	–
Turbo door: open (yellow)	34	–	–	–	137	136	–

Lights

Action	Activation Category		
	W1	WR	SR
Switch lights off (brightness level 0)	35	79	139*
Switch lights on full (brightness level 255)	13	81	138*
Switch light level to match dimmest adjacent	104	78	–
Switch light level to match brightest adjacent	12	80	–
Make light blink on every 1.0 seconds	17	–	–

Lifts (Elevators)

Action	Activation Category			
	W1	WR	S1	SR
Standard lift	10	88	21	62
Turbo lift	121*	120*	122*	123*
Perpetual lift start/resume	53	87	–	–
Perpetual lift pause	54	89	–	–

Moving floors

Action	Activation Category				
	W1	WR	S1	SR	GR
Raise floor by 24 units	58	92	–	–	–
Raise floor by 512 units (lift speed)	–	–	140*	–	–
Raise floor to match next higher floor	119*	128*	18	69	–
Turbo version of above	130*	129*	131*	132*	–
Raise floor by shortest lower texture	30	96	–	–	–
Move floor up to lowest local ceiling	5	91	101	64	24
Move floor down to lowest adjacent floor	38	82	23	60	–
Move floor down to highest adjacent floor	19	83	102	45	–
Move floor down to 8 units above highest adjacent floor	36	98	71	70	–
Move floor to 8 below ceiling, crushing	56	94	55	65	–

Changing floors

Floor movement	Role-model type	Special transferred	W1	WR	S1	SR	G1
Up to next higher	Trigger	0	22	95	20	68	47
Up 24 units	Trigger	0	–	–	15	66	–
Up 24 units	Trigger	X	59	93	–	–	–
Up 32 units	Trigger	0	–	–	14	67	–
Down to lowest adjacent 1st Neighbor		X	37	84	–	–	–

Entraining actions

Action	W1	WR	S1	SR
Donut eater	–	–	9	–
Build 8-unit stairs, slow	8	–	7	–
Build 16-unit stairs, turbo	100*	–	127*	–

Moving ceilings

Action	W1	WR	S1	SR
Move ceiling up to highest adjacent ceiling	40	85	–	–
Lower ceiling to floor	–	–	41	43
Lower ceiling to 8 above floor	44	72	49	–

Crushing ceilings

Action	W1	WR
Start/resume slow perpetual crusher	25	73
Start/resume fast perpetual crusher	6	77
Start/resume slow, "silent" crusher	141*	–
Pause crusher	57	74

Teleports

	Activation Category	
Action	W1	WR
Player/monster teleport	39	97
Monster only teleport	125*	126*

Exits

	Activation Category	
Exit type	W1	S1
Standard exit	52	11
Secret exit	124*	51

Effects

Effect	Code
Sideways scrolling texture	48

Table B.2. Special attributes of lines, arranged by code.

Code	Activation	Sound	Speed	Effect
1	MR†	Door	Medium	Door: Open, pause, close
2	W1	Door	Medium	Door: Open & stay
3	W1	Door	Medium	Door: Close
4	W1†	Door	Medium	Door: Open, pause, close
5	W1	Mover	Slow	Floor: Raise to lowest local ceiling
6	W1	Crusher	Fast	Crusher: Start/resume (fast)
7	S1	Mover	Slow	Stairs: 8-unit
8	W1	Mover	Slow	Stairs: 8-unit
9	S1	Mover	Slow	Donut eater
10	W1	Lift	Fast	Lift: Down, pause, up

continues

Table B.2. continued

Code	Activation	Sound	Speed	Effect
11	S1			Exit: standard
12	W1			Lights: Match brightest adjacent
13	W1			Lights: On full
14	S1	Mover	Slow	Changer (Trigger): Raise floor 32, nullify special
15	S1	Mover	Slow	Changer (Trigger): Raise floor 24, nullify special
16	W1	Door	Medium	Door: Close for 30 seconds, then open
17	W1			Lights: Blink on every 1.0 second
18	S1	Mover	Slow	Floor: Raise to match next higher floor
19	W1	Mover	Slow	Floor: Lower to highest adjacent floor
20	S1	Mover	Slow	Changer (Trigger): Raise floor to match next higher floor, nullify special
21	S1	Lift	Fast	Lift: Down, pause, up
22	W1	Mover	Slow	Changer (Trigger): Raise to floor match next higher floor, nullify special
23	S1	Mover	Slow	Floor: Lower to lowest adjacent floor
24	G1	Mover	Slow	Floor: Raise to lowest local ceiling
25	W1	Crusher	Medium	Crusher: Start/resume (Slow)
26	MR	Door	Medium	Door: Open, pause, close: (Blue)
27	MR	Door	Medium	Door: Open, pause, close: (Yellow)
28	MR	Door	Medium	Door: Open, pause, close: (Red)
29	S1	Door	Medium	Door: Open, pause, close
30	W1	Mover	Slow	Floor: Raise by shortest lower texture
31	M1	Door	Medium	Door: Open and stay
32	M1	Door	Medium	Door: Open and stay: (Blue)
33	M1	Door	Medium	Door: Open and stay: (Red)
34	M1	Door	Medium	Door: Open and stay: (Yellow)
35	W1			Lights: Off
36	W1	Mover	Fast	Floor: Lower to 8 above highest adjacent

Code	Activation	Sound	Speed	Effect
37	W1	Mover	Slow	Changer (First Neighbor): down to lowest adjacent, special transferred
38	W1	Mover	Slow	Floor: Lower to lowest adjacent floor
39	W1[†]	Teleport		Teleport: Player/monster
40	W1	Mover	Slow	Ceiling: Raise to match highest adjacent, with crush
41	S1	Mover	Slow	Ceiling: Lower to floor
42	SR	Door	Medium	Door: Close
43	SR	Mover	Slow	Ceiling: Lower to floor
44	W1	Mover	Slow	Ceiling: Lower to 8 above floor
45	SR	Mover	Slow	Floor: Move down to highest adjacent floor
46	GR	Door	Medium	Door: Open and stay
47	G1	Mover	Slow	Changer (Trigger): Raise floor to match next higher, nullify special
48	—			Effect: Scroll texture sideways
49	S1	Mover	Slow	Ceiling: Lower to 8 above floor
50	S1	Door	Medium	Door: Close
51	S1			Exit: To secret level
52	W1			Exit: To next standard level
53	W1	Lift	Slow	Lift: Start/resume (perpetual)
54	W1			Lift: Pause
55	S1	Mover	Slow	Floor: Move to 8 below ceiling, crushing
56	W1	Mover	Slow	Floor: Move to 8 below ceiling, crushing
57	W1			Crusher: Pause
58	W1	Mover	Slow	Floor: Raise 24 units
59	W1	Mover	Slow	Changer (Trigger): Raise floor 24 units, special transferred
60	SR	Mover	Slow	Floor: Lower to lowest adjacent floor
61	SR	Door	Medium	Door: Open and stay
62	SR	Lift	Fast	Lift: Down, pause, up

continues

Table B.2. continued

Code	Activation	Sound	Speed	Effect
63	SR	Door	Medium	Door: Open, pause, close
64	SR	Mover	Slow	Floor: Raise to lowest local ceiling
65	SR	Mover	Slow	Floor: Raise to 8 below ceiling, crushing
66	SR	Mover	Slow	Changer (Trigger): Raise floor 24 units, nullify special
67	SR	Mover	Slow	Changer (Trigger): Raise floor 32 units, nullify special
68	SR	Mover	Slow	Changer (Trigger): Raise floor to match next higher floor, nullify special
69	SR	Mover	Slow	Floor: Raise to match next higher
70	SR	Mover	Fast	Floor: Lower to 8 above highest adjacent
71	S1	Mover	Fast	Floor: Lower to 8 above highest adjacent
72	WR	Mover	Slow	Ceiling: Lower to 8 above floor
73	WR	Crusher	Slow	Crusher: Start/resume (slow)
74	WR			Crusher: Pause
75	WR	Door	Medium	Door: Close
76	WR	Door	Medium	Door: Close for 30 seconds, then open
77	WR	Crusher	Fast	Crusher: Start/resume (fast)
78	WR			Lights: Match dimmest adjacent
79	WR			Lights: Off
80	WR			Lights: Match brightest adjacent
81	WR			Lights: On full
82	WR	Mover	Slow	Floor: Lower to lowest adjacent floor
83	WR	Mover	Slow	Floor: Lower to highest adjacent floor
84	WR	Mover	Slow	Changer (First Neighbor): lower floor to lowest adjacent, special transferred
85	WR	Mover	Slow	Ceiling: Raise to highest adjacent
86	WR	Door	Medium	Door: Open and stay
87	WR	Lift	Slow	Lift: Start/resume (perpetual)

Code	Activation	Sound	Speed	Effect
88	WR†	Lift	Fast	Lift: Down, pause, up
89	WR			Lift: Pause
90	WR	Door	Medium	Door: Open, pause, close
91	WR	Mover	Slow	Floor: Raise to lowest local ceiling
92	WR	Mover	Slow	Floor: Raise by 24 units
93	WR	Mover	Slow	Changer (Trigger): Raise floor 24 units, special transferred
94	WR	Mover	Slow	Floor: Raise to 8 below ceiling, crushing
95	WR	Mover	Slow	Changer (Trigger): Raise floor to match next higher, nullify special
96	WR	Mover	Slow	Floor: Raise by shortest lower texture
97	WR†	Teleport		Teleport: Player/monster
98	WR	Mover	Fast	Floor: Lower to 8 above highest adjacent
99*	SR	Blaze	Turbo	Door: Open & stay: (Blue)
100*	W1	Mover	Turbo	Stairs: 16-unit
101	S1	Mover	Slow	Floor: Raise to lowest local ceiling
102	S1	Mover	Slow	Floor: Lower to highest adjacent floor
103	S1	Door	Medium	Door: Open & stay
104	W1			Lights: Match dimmest adjacent
105*	WR	Blaze	Turbo	Door: Open, pause, close
106*	WR	Blaze	Turbo	Door: Open & stay
107*	WR	Blaze	Turbo	Door: Close
108*	W1	Blaze	Turbo	Door: Open, pause, close
109*	W1	Blaze	Turbo	Door: Open & stay
110*	W1	Blaze	Turbo	Door: Close
111*	S1	Blaze	Turbo	Door: Open, pause, close
112*	S1	Blaze	Turbo	Door: Open & stay
113*	S1	Blaze	Turbo	Door: Close
114*	SR	Blaze	Turbo	Door: Open, pause, close

continues

Table B.2. continued

Code	Activation	Sound	Speed	Effect
115*	SR	Blaze	Turbo	Door: Open & stay
116*	SR	Blaze	Turbo	Door: Close
*117**	MR	Blaze	Turbo	Door: Open, pause, close
*118**	M1	Blaze	Turbo	Door: Open & stay
119*	W1	Mover	Slow	Floor: Raise to match next higher
120*	WR	Lift	Turbo	Lift: Down, pause, up
121*	W1	Lift	Turbo	Lift: Down, pause, up
122*	S1	Lift	Turbo	Lift: Down, pause, up
123*	SR	Lift	Turbo	Lift: Down, pause, up
124*	W1			Exit: to secret level
125*	1†	Teleport		Teleport: Monster only
126*	R†	Teleport		Teleport: Monster only
127*	S1	Mover	Turbo	Stairs: 16-unit
128*	WR	Mover	Slow	Floor: Raise to match next higher
129*	WR	Mover	Turbo	Floor: Raise to match next higher
130*	W1	Mover	Turbo	Floor: Raise to match next higher
131*	S1	Mover	Turbo	Floor: Raise to match next higher
132*	SR	Mover	Turbo	Floor: Raise to match next higher
133*	S1	Blaze	Turbo	Door: Open and stay: (Blue)
134*	SR	Blaze	Turbo	Door: Open and stay: (Red)
135*	S1	Blaze	Turbo	Door: Open and stay: (Red)
136*	SR	Blaze	Turbo	Door: Open and stay: (Yellow)
137*	S1	Blaze	Turbo	Door: Open and stay: (Yellow)
138*	SR			Lights: On full
139*	SR			Lights: Off
140*	S1	Mover	Medium	Floor: Raise 512 units
141*	W1	Lift	Fast	Crusher: Start/resume ("Silent")

INDEX

Add to Your Sams Library Today with the Best Books for Programming, Operating Systems, and New Technologies

The easiest way to order is to pick up the phone and call

1-800-428-5331

between 9:00 a.m. and 5:00 p.m. EST.

For faster service please have your credit card available.

ISBN	Quantity	Description of Item	Unit Cost	Total Cost
0-672-30507-0		Tricks of the Game Programming Gurus (Book/CD-ROM)	$45.00	
0-672-30562-3		Teach Yourself Game Programming in 21 Days (Book/CD-ROM)	$39.99	
0-672-30448-1		Teach Yourself C in 21 Days, Bestseller Edition	$24.95	
0-672-30619-0		Real-World Programming with Visual Basic (Book/CD-ROM)	$45.00	
0-672-30471-6		Teach Yourself Advanced C in 21 Days (Book/Disk)	$34.95	
0-672-30715-4		Teach Yourself Visual Basic in 21 Days, Bestseller Edition	$35.00	
0-672-30599-2		Tricks of the Internet Gurus (Book/Disk)	$35.00	
0-672-30495-3		Teach Yourself More Visual Basic 3 in 21 Days (Book/Disk)	$35.00	
0-672-30546-1		Tom Swan's Mastering Borland C++ 4.5, Second Edition (Book/Disk)	$49.99	
0-672-30466-X		The Internet Unleashed (Book/Disk)	$44.95	
0-672-30667-0		Teach Yourself Web Publishing with HTML in a Week	$25.00	
0-672-30617-4		The World Wide Web Unleashed	$35.00	
❏ 3 ½" Disk		Shipping and Handling: See information below.		
❏ 5 ¼" Disk		TOTAL		

Shipping and Handling: $4.00 for the first book, and $1.75 for each additional book. Floppy disk: add $1.75 for shipping and handling. If you need to have it NOW, we can ship product to you in 24 hours for an additional charge of approximately $18.00, and you will receive your item overnight or in two days. Overseas shipping and handling adds $2.00 per book and $8.00 for up to three disks. Prices subject to change. Call for availability and pricing information on latest editions.

201 W. 103rd Street, Indianapolis, Indiana 46290

1-800-428-5331 — Orders   1-800-835-3202 — FAX   1-800-858-7674 — Customer Service